Introduction

Welcome to the *Columbus Tourist Attractions & Events of the World* combined with the *Columbus World Travel Dictionary*. The attractions and events sections have been fully revised and updated covering over 500 of the world's most important tourist attractions and includes detailed information on each. The book covers well-known landmarks such as Sydney Opera House alongside lesser-known attractions such as the ancient city of Bagan in Myanmar. The *Columbus World Travel Dictionary* is a specialist dictionary for the travel trade in the 21st century

The attractions and events sections are organised by country and individual listings are arranged alphabetically within each. The book covers a range of both natural and manmade attractions. Each entry contains a detailed description of the attraction including its history and highlights, transportation information and a contact address. Each attraction also includes easy to read symbols detailing the available facilities and other practical information.

It must be stressed that the attraction entries included in this book are only a selection of the thousands of tourist attractions around the world. Entries have been chosen to reflect a number of different criteria, and those that appear are not necessarily the most popular attractions in their respective countries.

Top cultural and sporting events in major cities around the world have also been revised and updated for this edition of the guide. We have listed over 200 top events and festivals from around the world, ranging from Edinburgh's Hogmanay to India's spectacular Pushkar Fair. The list is by no means inclusive of all annual events which take place around the world; it is nonetheless a comprehensive list of major events which take place on an annual basis in some of today's most important tourist destinations.

The aim of the *World Travel Dictionary* is to provide clear, accurate and concise definitions of over 4,000 words and phrases that are commonly used within the travel industry and in the materials it produces for its clients. This latter consideration has led to the inclusion of a number of terms in areas such as geography, history, cartography, religion and insurance which are widely used in guide books, brochures and websites but often without their meanings being clearly explained.

Columbus Travel Guides would like to thank the many tourist offices, embassies, high commissions, consulates, chambers of commerce and public relations departments that assisted in the preparation of the attractions and events sections of this guide.

Many individuals and organisations have provided specialist assistance in the preparation of the *Columbus World Travel Dicti* name on the credits page. Two particular debts of gr iyne, whose considerable knowledge and experience during the updating; and secondly to Richard ons of this title and on whose excellent work the subs

The Editors
Tourist Attractions & Events of the World combined with the Columbus World Travel Dictionary
Columbus Travel Guides, Media House, Azalea Drive, Swanley, Kent BR8 8HU
Tel: +44 (0) 1322 616344 Fax: +44 (0) 1322 616323
E-mail: travel.editor@nexusmedia.com

D1437910

E156735

ISBN: 1-902221-92-3

Columbus Travel Publishing Limited
Media House
Azalea Drive
Swanley, Kent BR8 8HU
Tel: (01322) 616344
Fax: (01322) 616323
E-mail: booksales@nexusmedia.com

Editor (Tourist Attractions):	Dominic Tombs
Editor (Travel Dictionary):	Brian Quinn
Editorial Consultant:	Graeme Payne
Research:	Graham Johnson, Gemma Palmer
Sales & Marketing:	Martin Newman
Production:	Mile Budimir, Micheal Popejoy, Nigel Tansley
Cartographer:	David Burles
Publisher:	Pete Korniczky
Printed & bound by	UP Group, Lithuania

The publishers would like to thank all the organisations and individuals who have assisted in the preparation of this publication. Whilst every effort is made by the publishers to ensure the accuracy of the information contained in this edition of Tourist Attractions & Events of the World, the publishers can accept no responsibility for any loss occasioned to any person acting or refraining from acting as a result of the material contained in this publication, nor liability for any financial or other agreements which may be entered into with any organisations or individuals listed in the text.

Contents

Key to symbols used in all entries:	£........Entry charged	........Parking
	&........Disabled access	✗........Restaurant
	........Man-made attraction	........Shop
	........Natural attraction	........UNESCO site

Contents

Contents

Contents

Contents

Contents

United Kingdom - Isle of Man

United Kingdom - Northern Ireland

United Kingdom - Scotland

Contents

Contents

The World Travel Dictionary

Andorra

FRANCE

• Arcalis
• El Serrat
△ Coma Pedrosa 2946m
Valls d'Andorra
Valira • Soldeu
Pal • Ordino • Canillo
ANDORRA
ANDORRA LA VELLA ■ • Engordany
• Encamp • Grau Roig
❶
• Les Escaldes
P Y R E N E E S
• Sant-Julià-de-Lòria
SPAIN

10km
5mls

1 Caldea

Tourist Information

Andorra Tourist Office
Tourist Office of Andorra la Vella, Plaça de la Rotonda, Andorra la Vella, CP: AD500
Tel: (376) 827 117
Website: www.andorra.ad

Andorra Tourist Delegation
63 Westover Road, London SW18 2RF
Tel: (020) 8874 4806
Website: www.andorra.ad

Caldea

Benefiting from its location nestled between Spain and France in the heart of the Pyrenees, Andorra has a world-renowned reputation for its clean mountain air and spa treatments. Built at an altitude of 1,100m (3,600ft) on a site measuring 25,000 sq m (269,100 sq ft), *Caldea* is the largest spa centre in Southern Europe. Treatments and facilities at the centre include spas, high pressure indoor and outdoor jacuzzis, saunas, hammam, UVA cabins, massages and a whole programme of facial and body treatments. There's also a water bar and a nighttime underwater music and light show. The site also boasts cafes, bars and a gastronomic restaurant. Caldea is open all year round and is a popular place to cool off in the summer and a welcome distraction from the ski slopes in the winter.

Transportation
Air: Barcelona International Airport in Spain and Toulouse-Blagnac Airport and Perpignan Airport in France. **Rail:** There are no direct rail services to Andorra. **Road:** Bus: Daily services from Spain and France to Andorra then public services to Caldea.

Contact Addresses
Caldea, Parc de la Mola, 10 Escaldes-Engordany, Andorra
Tel: (376) 800 995
Website: www.caldea.ad

P ✗ 🧺 ♿ £ 🏭

Caldea

Tourist Office of Andorra la Vella ©

Argentina

BOLIVIA
PARAGUAY
Tropic of Capricorn
Gran Chaco
Iguazú Falls
Tucumán
BRAZIL
Corrientes ❶
Paraná
Córdoba
Santa Fe
Aconcagua 6960m
URUGUAY
Mendoza Rosario
BUENOS AIRES
La Plata
Pampas
ARGENTINA
SOUTH ATLANTIC OCEAN
Bahía Blanca
Mar del Plata
San Carlos de Bariloche
Valdes Peninsula
❸
Patagonia
Sarmiento
Comodoro Rivadavia
❷ Los Glaciares National Park
Falkland Is./ Malvinas (UK)
Tierra del Fuego
Ushuaia
Cape Horn
PACIFIC OCEAN
CHILE
ANDES

1000km
500mi

✈ international airport

1 Iguazú Falls
  (Cataratas del Iguazú)

2 Los Glaciares National Park (Parque
  Nacional Los Glaciares)

3 Nahuel Huapi National Park
  (Parque Nacional Nahuel Huapi)

Tourist Information

National Tourist Board
(Secretaría de Turismo de la Nación)
Calle Suipacha 1111, 20º, 1368 Buenos Aires,
Argentina
Tel: (011) 4312 5621
Website: www.turismo.gov.ar

Embassy of the Argentine Republic
65 Brooke Street, London W1K 4AH, UK
Tel: (020) 7318 1300
Website: www.argentine-embassy-uk.org

Iguazú Falls
(Cataratas del Iguazú)

The *Iguazú Falls* fittingly receive their name from the Guarani Indian word meaning 'great waters'. Surrounded by the virgin jungle of *Iguazú National Park*, which is home to 2000 species of flora and 400 species of bird, the *Paraná River* divides into 275 separate falls. The highest, the *Garganta del Diabolo* (Devil's Throat) reaches 70m (230ft), which is one-and-a-half times the height of the Niagara Falls. Besides taking in the stunning view from a series of catwalks, visitors may enjoy kayaking, canoeing and other watersports. Historic Jesuit Mission ruins nearby, such as those at *San Ignacio Miní*, are also popular.

Transportation
Air: Ministro Pistarini Airport (Buenos Aires).
Road: Coach: Services to bus terminal from Buenos Aires.

Contact Addresses
Iguazú National Park, Victoria Aguirre 66, 3370 Puerto Iguazú, Misiones, Argentina
Tel: (037) 5742 0722 *or* 5742 0180 *or* 5742 0382
Website: www.parquesnacionales.gov.ar

Los Glaciares National Park
(Parque Nacional Los Glaciares)

Los Glaciares National Park is the second largest in Argentina and runs for 170km (106 miles) along the border with Chile; it is characterised by rugged mountains and clear lakes. Some 40 per cent of the Park's 6600 sq km (2548 sq miles) is covered by vast ice fields that hold 47 major glaciers. The largest glacier is *Upsala*, but the most popular is the mighty *Moreno* glacier, where massive chunks of ice shear off and fall into *Lago Argentino*, the largest lake in Argentina, to form icebergs. Visitors can view the advancing Moreno glacier from catwalks and platforms.

Transportation

Air: Ministro Pistarini Airport (Buenos Aires) or El Calafate International Airport. **Road:** Coach: Services to the bus terminal on Avenida Julia Roca (from El Calafate); services to El Calafate (from Río Gallegos). Car: Provincial Route 5, National Route 40 and Provincial Route 11 (from Río Gallegos).

Contact Addresses

Los Glaciares National Park, 1302, Libertador Avenue, Z94054AHG - Els Calafate, Santa Cruz, Argentina
Tel: (02) 491 005 *or* 491 755 *or* 491 026
Website: www.parquesnacionales.gov.ar *or* www.losglaciares.com

Nahuel Huapi National Park (Parque Nacional Nahuel Huapi)

In 1903 Dr Francisco P Moreno donated 710,000 hectares (1,754,386 acres) of land which became a state national park known as *Nacional del Sur* (Southern National Park). In 1934 it was renamed *Nahuel Huapi National Park* which comes from the Mapuche language, Nahuel meaning 'tiger' and Huapi meaning 'island'. The park offers trekkers and sightseers many areas of natural beauty, including an extinct volcano called *Tronador*, alpine meadows and amazing fauna. The sprawling glacial lake, Lake Nahuel Huapi, stretches over 100km (63 miles) to the border with Chile; the lake contains a nature reserve, the Isla Victoria, which can be reached by private or organised boat trips.

Transportation

Air: Ministro Pistarini Airport (Buenos Aires). **Road:** Coach: Services from San Carlos de Bariloche.

Contact Addresses

Nahuel Huapi National Park, 24 San Martin St, (8400) San Carlos de Bariloche, Rio Negro, Argentina
Tel/Fax: (029) 4442 3121/11 *or* 4442 2366
Website: www.parquesnacionale.gov.br

Argentinean National Secretariat of Tourism©

Australia

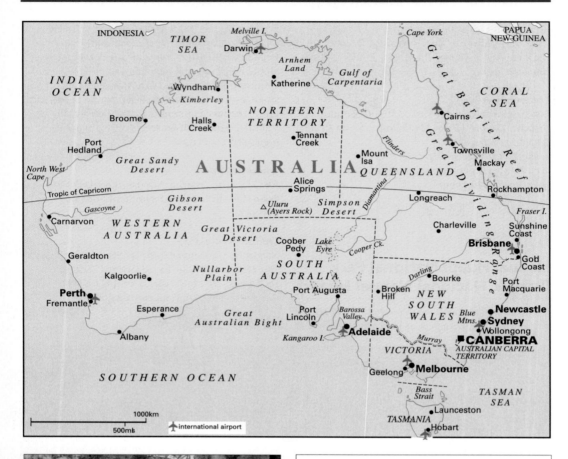

Northern Territory Rock Art

Tourist Information

Australian Tourist Commission
PO Box 2721, Sydney, NSW 2001, Australia
Tel: (02) 9360 1111
Website: www.australia.com

Tourism Australia
Australia Centre, Australia House, 6th Floor,
Melbourne Place, The Strand, London
WC2B 4LG, UK
Tel: (020) 7438 4601
Website: www.tourism.australia.com *or*
www.australia.com

Key to symbols: £ Entry charged & Disabled access
⚑ Man-made attraction ♥ Natural attraction
🅿 Parking ✘ Restaurant 🛍 Shop 🏛 UNESCO site

Australian Capital Territory

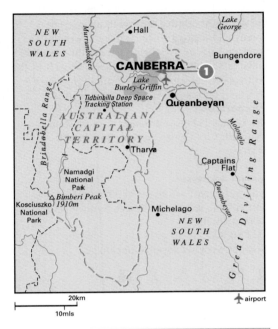

NEW SOUTH WALES

Murrumbidgee

Hall

Lake George

CANBERRA

Bungendore

Lake Burley-Griffin

Tidbinbilla Deep Space Tracking Station

Queanbeyan

Brindabella Range

AUSTRALIAN CAPITAL TERRITORY

Molonglo Range

Tharwa

Namadgi National Park

Captains Flat

Queanbeyan

Great Dividing Range

△ Bimberi Peak 1910m

Kosciuszko National Park

Michelago

NEW SOUTH WALES

20km
10mls

✈ airport

1 National Gallery of Australia

National Gallery of Australia

The *National Gallery of Australia* houses many of Australia's finest art collections, and boasts a selection of indigenous works. The gallery, which opened in 1982, has a permanent art collection which is home to more than 100,000 works and is also home to regular international art and photography exhibitions. There is also a beautiful landscaped garden located in the grounds between the gallery and the banks of Lake Burley Griffin, where many sculptures are on permanent display.

Transportation
Air: Canberra International Airport. **Rail:** Train: Canberra Station. **Road:** Car: The gallery is situated in central Canberra, on the banks of Lake Burley Griffin.

Contact Addresses
National Gallery of Australia, GPO Box 1150, Canberra, ACT 2601, Australia
Tel: (02) 6240 6502
Website: www.nga.gov.au

🅿 ✗ 🧺 ♿ ⛴

National Gallery of Australia

Tourism Australia©

New South Wales

1 AMP Centerpoint Tower
2 Sydney Harbour Bridge and The Rocks
3 Sydney Opera House

AMP Centerpoint Tower

Standing at 305m (1001ft) high, *Sydney Tower* is the tallest building in Sydney. Located in the Central Business District in the heart of the city, visitors can experience amazing views across *Sydney Harbour* and as far as the *Blue Mountains* from the *Observation Deck*. The tower, which was completed in 1981, also has a revolving restaurant offering 360° views. Visitors can also experience the *OzTrek* attraction, a simulated journey showcasing Australia's culture, history and geography. This experience includes a storytelling room; a room with a small stage with moving

models of Australian landscapes and holograms; and a fake Aboriginal cave with appropriate sounds and melodies. The Sydney Tower itself forms part of the Westfield Centrepoint complex which is home to around 140 shops, as well as the Centrepoint Convention and Exhibition Centre.

Transportation
Air: Sydney (Kingsford Smith) Airport. **Rail:** Monorail: City Centre Station. **Bus:** Public services.

Contact Addresses
Sydney Tower, Podium Level, Westfield Centrepoint, 100 Market Street, Sydney NSW 2000, Australia
Tel: (02) 9223 1341
Website: www.sydneyskytour.com.au

Sydney Harbour Bridge and The Rocks

Sydney Harbour Bridge is one of the most famous man-made structures in the world, and is undoubtedly one of Sydney's most recognisable icons. The bridge, affectionately known as 'the Coathanger', took 1400 workers (16 of whom were killed in the process) eight years to complete and was officially opened in 1932. Thrill-seekers can do the *BRIDGECLIMB* - a guided walk to the top of the 50-storey-high bridge, over the cars and trains rumbling across the deck below. The area at the foot of the bridge is known as *The Rocks* and is recognised as Sydney's historical birthplace. The area was the site of the first landing from

Sydney Harbour and Bridge

Tourism New South Wales©

Sydney Opera House

Tourism New South Wales®

Plymouth, England in 1788; today The Rocks is a busy area consisting of cafés, restaurants, galleries, museums and countless souvenir shops. Historic buildings in the district include the *Museum of Contemporary Art*, *Merchants' House*, *Garrison Church* and *Susannah Place.*

Transportation
Air: Sydney Airport. **Rail:** Train: Circular Quay Station. **Bus:** Public services.

Contact Addresses
BRIDGECLIMB: 5 Cumberland Street, The Rocks, Sydney NSW 2000, Australia
Tel: (02) 8274 7777
Website: www.bridgeclimb.com

Pylon Lookout: South East Pylon, Sydney Harbour Bridge, Sydney NSW 2000, Australia
Tel: (02) 9240 1100
Website: www.pylonlookout.com.au

The Rocks: Sydney Visitor Centre, 106 George Street, The Rocks, NSW 2000, Sydney, Australia
Tel: (02) 9240 8788
Website: www.rocksvillage.com *or* www.sydneyvisitorcentre.com *or* www.viewsydney.com

Sydney Opera House

Opened in 1973, the *Sydney Opera House* is the most recognisable symbol of both the city of Sydney and the country of Australia, and is also considered one of the 20th century's great buildings. Revolutionary in concept, the building's Danish architect, Jørn Utzon, designed the building to resemble a ship at sea with its roof appearing as a billowing white sail. It is one of the busiest performing arts centres in the world, housing a large complex of theatres and halls that play host to a wide range of performing arts. Located on Bennelong Point, the Opera House, which offers spectacular views of Sydney Harbour, is visited by more than 4.5 million tourists every year. Various tours – including the Front of House and Backstage areas – can be taken.

Transportation
Air: Sydney Airport. **Rail:** Train: Circular Quay Station. **Road:** Bus: Public services.

Contact Addresses
Sydney Opera House, Bennelong Point, GPO Box 4274, Sydney NSW 2001, Australia
Tel: (02) 9250 7111
Website: www.sydneyoperahouse.com

Northern Territory

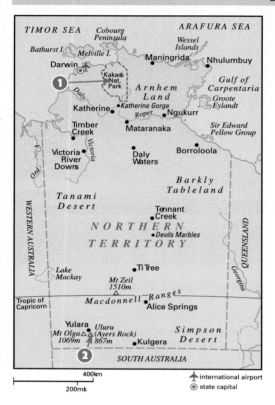

```
TIMOR SEA    Cobourg           ARAFURA SEA
             Peninsula
                               Wessel
Bathurst I.                    Islands
         Melville I.    Maningrida    Nhulumbuy
  Darwin
           Kakadu              Gulf of
           Nat.      Arnhem    Carpentaria
           Park      Land      Groote
                  Katherine Gorge  Eylandt
    Katherine    Roper  Ngukurr
      Timber                  Sir Edward
      Creek      Mataranaka   Pellow Group

    Victoria              Borroloola
    River         Daly
    Downs         Waters
                         Barkly
                         Tableland
    Tanami
    Desert
                  Tennant
                  Creek
       NORTHERN
                     Devils Marbles
       TERRITORY

    Lake          Ti Tree
    Mackay
              Mt Zeil
              1510m
    Macdonnell  Ranges
                  Alice Springs

    Yulara   Uluru
  Mt Olga  (Ayers Rock)   Simpson
  1069m    867m           Desert
                Kulgera
                    
        SOUTH AUSTRALIA
```

400km
200mls

✈ international airport
◉ state capital

1 Kakadu National Park
2 Uluru-Kata Tjuta National Park

Kakadu National Park

Located in Australia's tropical Northern Territory and stretching from Arnhem Land in the east to Katherine Gorge in the south, *Kakadu National Park* is one of the few UNESCO World Heritage Sites to be listed for both natural and cultural reasons. Many believe the park has been continuously inhabited for up to 40,000 years, and rock paintings and other archaeological sites testify to the Aboriginal history of the region. Kakadu is also home to many different species of plant and animals. Covering an area of 2 million hectares (4.9 million acres), the park is still home to around 300 Aboriginals today and encompasses river floodplains, savannah woodlands, rich tidal wetlands and sandstone escarpments.

Transportation
Air: Darwin International Airport. **Road:** Coach: Coach tours operate between Darwin, Jabiru and Cooinda. Car: Arnhem Highway off the Stuart Highway leads from Darwin to Jabiru. Kakadu Highway leads into the park (from Jabiru).

Contact Addresses
Kakadu National Park, PO Box 71, Jabiru, NT 0886, Australia
Tel: (08) 8938 1120
Website: www.deh.gov.au/parks/kakadu

Uluru-Kata Tjuta National Park

Uluru-Kata Tjuta National Park is home to one of Australia's most popular tourist attractions and best-known national symbols: *Uluru*, which means 'great pebble' in the Aboriginal language. Formerly known as *Ayers Rock*, Uluru is a 3.6km-long (2.2 mile-), 348m-high (1142ft-) smooth chunk of sandstone that rises abruptly out of the sandy scrubland. It is the world's largest rock monolith and the most famous natural landmark in Australia. The rock also holds deep significance for the local Aboriginal people who believe it was formed during the creation period. The nearby *Kata Tjuta*, meaning 'many heads' and formerly known as *The Olgas*, is a series of 36 massive rock domes and a system of gorges and valleys. Visitors can walk through the *Valley of the Winds* and the *Olga Gorge*, and also visit the *Uluru-Kata Tjuta Cultural Centre*.

Transportation
Air: Darwin International Airport, Connellan Airport. **Rail:** Train: Alice Springs Station. **Road:** Bus: Services from Uluru. Car: Stuart Highway from either Darwin (in the north) or Alice Springs (in the south), then signs to Uluru-Kata Tjuta.

Contact Addresses
Uluru-Kata Tjuta National Park, PO Box 119, Yulara, NT 0872, Australia
Tel: (08) 8956 2299
Website: www.deh.gov.au/parks/uluru

Queensland

Torres Strait
PAPUA NEW GUINEA
Bamaga
Cape York Peninsula
Gulf of Carpentaria
Cape Melville
Great Barrier Reef
CORAL SEA
Cooktown
Wellesley Is.
Cairns
△ Mt Bartle Frere 1612m
Normanton
Hinchinbrook I.
NORTHERN TERRITORY
Mount Isa
Townsville
Whitsunday Is.
Proserpine
Hughenden
Mackay
Boulia
QUEENSLAND
Rockhampton
Tropic of Capricorn
Longreach
Gladstone
Fraser Island
Birdsville
Channel Country
Charleville
Bundaberg
Gympie
Sunshine Coast
Balonne
SOUTH AUSTRALIA
Brisbane
Ipswich
Gold Coast
Lake Eyre
NEW SOUTH WALES

800km
400ml

✈ international airport
◉ state capital

1 Fraser Island
2 Great Barrier Reef

Fraser Island

Stretching over 120km (75 miles) from tip-to-tip and covering an area of 165,280 hectares (408,423 acres), *Fraser Island* is the largest sand island in the world. Located of Australia's East Coast in the state of *Queensland*, Fraser Island was listed as a UNESCO World Heritage site in 1992. Characterised by its stunning freshwater lakes, coloured sand cliffs, lush rainforests growing in the sand, secluded creeks and long, white sandy beaches, the idyllic island attracts thousands of visitors each year who come on 4x4-led camping trips or to stay in lodges including the new award-winning eco lodge, *Kingfisher Bay*, built on the island's west coast. The island is also famous for its resident populations of dingoes that are said to be Australia's purest breed. Aside from its swimming holes, creeks and stunning natural beauty, other attractions on the island include the rusting wreck of the *Maheno* ship which ran aground during a cyclone in 1935 and the former logging camp of *Central Station* that's now home to an exhibition about the island's unique environment. Day trips to the island are possible but many people choose to spend a few nights on this idyllic natural phenomenon.

Fraser Island

Transportation

Air: Brisbane Airport (international arrivals). Hervey Bay Airport (domestic services) **Water:** Ferry: Services from Hervey Bay. **Rail:** Maryborough Station then travel by bus or taxi on to Hervey Bay. **Road:** Bus: Public services to Hervey Bay then ferry to Fraser Island.

Contact Addresses

Maryborough Fraser Island Visitor Information Centre, Maryborough South Travel Shop, Bruce Highway, Maryborough, Queensland, 4650 Australia
Tel: (07) 4121 4111
Website: www.maryborough.qld.gov.au

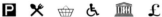

Great Barrier Reef

The *Great Barrier Reef* is the most famous marine-protected area in the world and the largest UNESCO World Heritage area. Covering a geographical area of 35 million hectares (86 million acres) and stretching approximately 2300km (1429 miles) along the coast of northeastern Australia from *Bundaberg* to *Cape York*, the Reef is bigger in size than the states of Victoria and Tasmania combined. The Great Barrier Reef is the largest coral reef system in the world and home to approximately 400 different types of coral. It is also an area of outstanding natural beauty and home to around 1500 different species of fish, 4000 types of mollusc and many endangered species. There are also more than 30 historic shipwrecks in the area and a number of archaeological sites which are of Aboriginal origin. In 2005, more coral reefs were discovered in the *Gulf of Carpentaria* off Australia's north coast.

Transportation

Air: Brisbane Airport, Cairns Airport; many domestic airlines fly to national airports located closer to the Reef on the Australian mainland. **Water:** The Great Barrier Reef can only be reached by boat; tour operators can arrange transfer from mainland Australia to resort islands.

Contact Addresses

Great Barrier Reef Marine Park Authority, 2-68 Flinders Street, PO Box 1379, Townsville, Queensland 4810, Australia
Tel: (07) 4750 0700
Website: www.gbrmpa.gov.au

The Great Barrier Reef

Tourism Queensland©

Tasmania

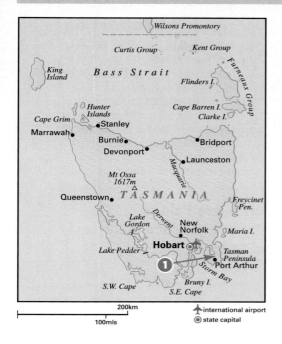

200km
100mls

✈ international airport
◉ state capital

---

1 Port Arthur

Port Arthur

Port Arthur is a former penal colony which originally opened as a timber station in 1830. It became a prison settlement for male convicts in 1833 and quickly gained a reputation for being 'hell-on-earth'. Convicts ranged from boys as young as nine through to hardened criminals. The prison closed in 1877 and was renamed *Carnarvon* in an attempt to lose its former associations; however, in 1927 it was reinstated as Port Arthur. Today, the prison is open to the public and visitors can take part in guided tours and harbour cruises. There is also an interpretation gallery where visitors can find out about some of the convicts that were sentenced there.

Transportation

Air: Hobart International Airport. **Road:** Coach: Tigerline and Experience Tasmania operate day tours (from Hobart). Car: Reached by scenic drive, which takes approximately 1.5 hours along the Tasman and Arthur highways.

Contact Addresses

Visitor Centre, Port Arthur Historic Site, Port Arthur, Tasmania 7182, Australia
Tel: (1800) 659 101
Website: www.portarthur.org.au

Port Arthur Penitentiary

Key to symbols
used in all entries:
£....Entry charged
&....Disabled access
⌐....Man-made attraction
⌄....Natural attraction
P....Parking
✗....Restaurant
⌂....Shop
🏛..UNESCO site

Austria

Tourist Information

Österreich Werbung (Austrian National Tourist Office - ANTO)
Margaretenstrasse 1, 1040 Vienna, Austria
Tel: (01) 588 660 (information)
Website: www.austria.info

Austrian National Tourist Office (ANTO)
9-11 Richmond Buildings, London W1D 3HE, UK
Tel: (0845) 101 1818
Website: www.austria-tourism.at

1 Belvedere Palace (Österreichishce Galerie Belvedere)

2 Giant Ferris Wheel (Riesenrad)

3 Hofburg Palace (Hofburg)

4 Mozart's Birthplace and Residence (Mozarts Geburtshaus und Mozarts Wohnhaus)

5 Museum of Fine Art (Kunsthistorisches Museum)

6 Schönbrunn Palace (Schloss Schonbrunn)

Belvedere Palace (Österreichishce Galerie Belvedere)

Belvedere Palace, situated right in the heart of Vienna, is Austria's most famous art gallery and home to *der Kuss* (The Kiss) which was painted by Gustav Klimt. There are two permanent collections – *Oberes Belvedere* (Upper Belvedere) and *Unteres Belvedere* (Lower Belvedere) – in the Palace. The palace was built by Lukas von Hildebrandt between 1714 and 1723 as a summer residence for Prince Eugene of Savoy. The two museums house an impressive collection of Austrian art from the Middle Ages through to the 20th century. Today, the Upper Belvedere is home to the Austrian Gallery and works by Renoir, Monet, Klimt,

Belvedere Palace

Österreichische Galerie Belvedere©

Kokoschka and Schiele, whilst the Lower Belvedere houses the Baroque Museum and the Museum of Medieval Austrian Art.

Transportation
Air: Vienna International Airport. **Rail:** Underground: Südtirolerplatz or Taubstummengasse. Tram: Public services. **Road:** Bus: Service to Südbahnhof.

Contact Addresses
Österreichische Galerie Belvedere, Prinz Engen-Strasse 27, 1030 Vienna, Austria
Tel: (01) 7955 7134
Website: www.belvedere.at

Giant Ferris Wheel (Riesenrad)

Located in the giant wooded park and fairground known as the *Prater*, Vienna's *Giant Ferris Wheel* is one of Austria's best-known and best-loved landmarks. The Ferris Wheel was completed in 1897 at a time when other such ferris wheels stood in cities like London, Paris and Blackpool, but it is the only one of its era still surviving. Constructed to celebrate the 50th jubilee of Emperor Franz Joseph I, several unusual events have taken place on the wheel, most notably the suicide of local resident Marie Kindl, who hanged herself from the window of a car in 1898 to draw attention to the economical plight of her family. After dark, the wheel lights up and acts as a giant clock for the city by flashing the correct number of times on the hour.

Transportation
Air: Vienna International Airport. **Rail:** Train: S-Bahn to Wien Nord (Praterstern) from Wien Mitte. Underground: Praterstern. Tram: Public services. **Road:** Bus: Wien Prater. Car: Signs for Vienna city centre, then take Praterstrasse.

Contact Addresses
Wiener Riesenrad, Prater 90, 1020, Vienna, Austria
Tel: (01) 729 5430
Website: www.wienerriesenrad.com

     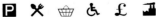

Hofburg Palace (Hofburg)

The *Hofburg Palace* was home to the Austrian Hapsburg emperors until 1918. The palace buildings have been constantly added to for over 800 years, with the first fortifications being erected by King Ottakar Premysl in the 13th century. Today, the palace serves as a repository of Austrian culture and history, embracing 22 separate museums, a 14th-century Augustinian church, the famous *Spanische Hofreitschule* (Spanish Riding School), the *Österreichische Nationalbibliothek* (National Library), as well as the president's offices. The most popular of the museums is the *Kaiserappartements*, which takes visitors on a tour of the Kaiser's Imperial apartments. The *Vienna Boys' Choir* sings Sunday mass at the Royal Chapel.

Transportation
Air: Vienna International Airport. **Rail:** Underground: Herrengasse. Tram: B-line to Burgtor. **Road:** Bus: Services to Michaelerplatz. Car: A1 Westautobahn or A2 Südautobahn to the city centre.

Contact Addresses
Hofburg, Michaelerkuppel, 1010 Vienna, Austria
Tel: (01) 533 7570
Website: www.schoenbrunn.at/en

Mozart's Birthplace and Residence (Mozarts Geburtshaus und Mozarts Wohnhaus)

Born Joannes Christosomos Wolfgang Theophulis Mozart to Leopold and Anna Maria Mozart on January 27 1756, Mozart is one of the most famous musicians of all times. The musical genius was born in *Getreidegasse 9* in Salzburg, known today as *Mozarts Geburtshaus* (Mozart's Birthplace), where the family lived from 1747 until 1773 when the family moved to a house in *Makartplatz* which is known today as *Mozart Wohnhaus* (Mozart's Residence), where they remained until 1787. Both houses are now popular museums. Most of Mozart's Residence was destroyed by a bomb in 1944; the building has however been restored to its original glory by the Mozarteum Foundation.

Kunsthistorisches Museum©

Museum of Fine Art

gallery) contains works by Rubens, Rembrandt, Vermeer, Dürer and Titian, and the largest collection of work by Brueghel in the world.

Transportation
Air: Vienna International Airport. **Rail:** Underground: Volkstheater. Tram: Tram D to Burging/ Kunsthistorisches Museum (from Südbahnof); U3 tram to Volkstheater (from Westbahnof). **Road:** Bus: Public services. Car: A1 Westautobahn or the A2 Sudautobahn to the city centre.

Contact Addresses
Kunsthistorisches Museum, Main Building, Maria-Theresien-Platz, 1010 Vienna, Austria
Tel: (01) 525 24-590
Website: www.khm.at

     £

Schonbrunn Palace (Schloss Schönbrunn)

One of the most renowned Baroque structures in Europe, *Schönbrunn Palace* began life as a hunting lodge during the 16th century, but was turned into a lavish palace by the Empress Maria Theresa in 1750. Home to the Hapsburg emperors from the 18th century to 1918, the palace was built by the architects Johann Bernhard Fischer von Erlach and Nicolaus Pacassi. A tour offers visitors the chance to admire the site's opulent elegance, including the famous ceiling frescoes of the *Great Gallery*, and the *Hall of Mirrors* where Mozart played. The Baroque grounds include a *Flower Garden*, *Tiergarten* (a zoo dating from 1752) and a reproduction of a maze created at the beginning of the 18th century.

Transportation
Air: Vienna International Airport. **Rail:** Train: Schönbrunn Station. Underground: Schönbrunn. **Road:** Bus: Public services to Schönbrunn. Car: Ostautobahn from the airport towards Vienna, then the A23 (Sudosttangente) towards Graz.

Contact Addresses
Schloss Schönbrunn Kultur und Betriebs GmbH, Schloss Schönbrunn, 1130 Vienna, Austria
Tel: (01) 8111 3239
Website: www.schoenbrunn.at

     £

Transportation
Air Salzburg Airport. **Rail:** Train: Salzburg Central Station.

Contact Addresses
Mozarts Geburtshaus, Getreidegasse 9, 5020 Salzburg, Austria
Tel: (06) 6284 4313

Mozart Wohnhaus, Makartplatz 8, 5020 Salzburg, Austria
Tel: (06) 62874 22740

  £

Museum of Fine Art (Kunsthistorisches Museum)

Opened in 1891 to house the imperial family's vast art collection, *Vienna's Museum of Fine Art* was designed by Gottfreid von Semper and Karl Hasenauer. It was built in the style of the Italian Renaissance to firmly establish the building's link with one of history's great artistic periods. Today, the museum, which is located in *Marie-Theresien-Platz*, holds one of the most important art collections in the world. The *Gemäldegalerie* (picture

Azerbaijan

Azerbaijan Republic, Ministry of Youth, Sport and Tourism©

Azerbaijan man with craft items

1 Walled City of Baku

Tourist Information

Azerbaijan Ministry of Foreign Affairs
4 Shykhali Qurbanov Street, 1009 Baku,
Azerbaijan
Tel: (12) 492 9692
Website: http://azerbaijan.tourism.az

Embassy of the Azerbaijan Republic
4 Kensington Court, London W8 5DL, UK
Tel: (020) 7938 3412
Website: http://azerbaijan.tourism.az

Azerbaijan Republic, Ministry of Youth, Sport and Tourism©

Walled City of Baku

Located on the western shore of the *Caspian Sea*, the ancient *Walled City of Baku* in the Azerbaijani capital of Baku was inscribed on the UNESCO World Heritage list along with the *Shirvanshah's* *Palace and Maiden Tower* in 2000. The walled fort is built on a site inhabited since the Palaeolithic Period (thought to be between 100,000BC and 30,000BC) and archaeologists have found evidence of Zoroastrian, Sassanian, Arabic, Persian, Shirvani, Ottoman and Russian influences. The Shirvanshah's Palace was built in the 12th century by the Shirvanshah Dynasty who moved their capital to Baku from *Shamakha* after an earthquake. Baku developed as an important trading port and was captured and conquered by many warring empires before finally becoming the capital of Azerbaijan in 1920. The Walled City is the old part of the Baku and its maze of alleyways and ancient buildings still thrive with life today with the modern city fanning out around it.

Transportation
Air: Baku International Airport. **Water:** Ferry: Passenger ferry. **Rail:** Baku City Train Station. Underground services. **Road:** Bus: Public services.

Contact Addresses
For more information on the Walled City of Baku, contact the Ministry of Foreign Affairs (see **Tourist Information** above).

Bahrain

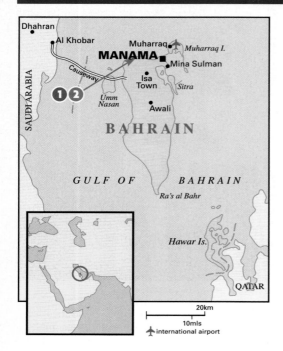

Dhahran
Al Khobar
MANAMA
Muharraq
Muharraq I.
Mina Sulman
Causeway
SAUDI ARABIA
❶ ❷
Isa Town
Umm Nasan
Sitra
Awali
BAHRAIN
GULF OF BAHRAIN
Ra's al Bahr
Hawar Is.
QATAR

20km
10mls
✈ international airport

1 Bahrain Fort   2 Barbar Temple

Tourist Information

Bahrain Tourism Company
PO Box 5831, Manama, Bahrain
Tel: (17) 530 530
Website: www.alseyaha.com

Embassy of the Kingdom of Bahrain
30 Belgrave Square, London SW1X 8QB
Tel: (020) 7201 9170
Website: www.bahraintourism.com

Bahrain Fort (Qal'at al-Bahrain)

Excavations at the *Bahrain Fort* began in 1950 and uncovered a tell – an artificial mound created by several layers of human occupation. Research at the site has shown that the earliest habitation dates back to approximately 2300BC with evidence of continuous habitation through until the 16th century when the fort was constructed by the Portuguese to protect their island possessions.

The site was once an important trading port and is now a UNESCO World Heritage site.

Transportation
Air: Bahrain International Airport. **Water:** Ferry: Public services. Rail: Currently no rail network but plans to build one are under way. **Road:** Bus: Public services.

Contact Addresses
For more information on the Bahrain Fort, contact the Bahrain Tourism Company (see **Tourist Information** above).

Barbar Temple

Located in the village of *Barbar*, the most recent of the three Barbar temples was rediscovered by a Danish archaeological team in 1954. A further two temples were discovered on the site with the oldest dating back to 3000BC. The three temples were built atop one another with the second built approximately 500 years later and the third added between 2100BC and 2000BC. It's thought that the temples were constructed to worship the God Enki, the god of wisdom and freshwater, and his wife Nankhur Sak. The temple contains two altars and a natural water spring that is thought to have held spiritual significance for the worshippers. During the excavation of the site many tools, weapons, pottery and small pieces of gold were found which are now on display in the *Bahrain National Museum* (www.bnmuseum.com).

Transportation
Air: Bahrain International Airport. **Water:** Ferry: Public services. **Rail:** Currently no rail network but plans to build one are under way. **Road:** Bus: Public services.

Contact Addresses
For more information on the Barbar Temple, contact the Bahrain Tourism Company (see **Tourist Information** above).

Bangladesh

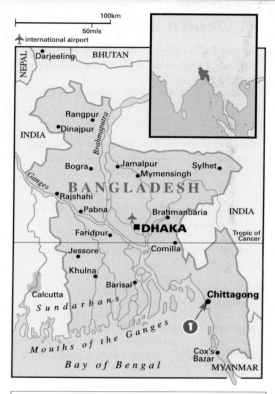

NEPAL
Darjeeling BHUTAN
INDIA
Rangpur
Dinajpur
Brahmaputra
Bogra Jamalpur Sylhet
Mymensingh
Ganges
B A N G L A D E S H
Rajshahi
Pabna
Brahmanbaria INDIA
Faridpur ■DHAKA Tropic of Cancer
Jessore Comilla
Khulna
Barisal
Calcutta Chittagong
S u n d a r b a n s
Mouths of the Ganges ①
Cox's Bazar
Bay of Bengal MYANMAR

1 Chittagong

Tourist Information

Bangladesh Parjatan Corporation (National Tourism Organisation)
233 Airport Road, Tejgaon, Dhaka-1215, Bangladesh
Tel: (02) 811 7855-9
Website: www.parjatan.org

High Commission for the People's Republic of Bangladesh
28 Queen's Gate, London SW7 5JA, UK
Tel: (020) 7584 0081

Chittagong

Chittagong, the second largest city in Bangladesh, is a port city, set against the blue waters of the

Bay of Bengal and surrounded by green forests, coconut groves and sandy beaches. Attractions include the *Ethnological Museum*, the 17th-century *Shahi Jama-e-Masjid Mosque*, the colourful multi-domed *Chandanpura Mosque* and the *Tomb of Sultan Bayazid Bostami*. *Foy's Lake*, an artificial lake named after the Englishman responsible for its design, is located 8km (5 miles) from Chittagong, and is a popular picnic site. Chittagong is also a good base from which to explore the *Rangamati Hill District*, famous for its beautiful flora and lakes and the predominantly Buddhist tribal culture. Entrance fees are charged for some of the attractions.

Transportation
Air: Chittagong MA Hannan International Airport.
Rail: Train: Chittagong Station.

Contact Addresses
Tourist Information Centre, Motel Shaikat, Station Road, Chittagong, Bangladesh
Tel: (031) 209 845

Bay of Bengal

Bangladesh Parjatan Corporation©

Belgium

Map of Belgium showing: NORTH SEA, NETHERLANDS, Maas, Zeebrugge, Ostend, Bruges, Antwerp, Ghent, Mechelen, FLANDERS, BRUSSELS, Liège, Tournai, BELGIUM, Namur, Mons, Charleroi, WALLONIA, Dinant, Ardennes, Arlon, LUX., FRANCE, GERMANY, Scheldt, Meuse, Moselle

100km
50mls
✈ international airport

1 Atomium
2 Cathedral of Our Lady (Onze Lieve Vrouwe-Kathedraal)
3 Central Square (Grand' Place)
4 Flanders Fields
5 Statue of the Pissing Boy (Manneken-Pis)

Tourist Information

Belgian Tourist Office – Brussels & Wallonia (Office de Promotion du Tourisme Wallonie-Bruxelles)
30 rue Saint Bernard, 1060 Brussels, Belgium
Tel: (02) 504 0390
Website: www.belgium-tourism.net

Tourism Flanders-Brussels (Toerisme Vlaanderen)
Grasmarkt 63, B-1000 Brussels, Belgium
Tel: (02) 504 0300 or 504 0390
Website: www.visitflanders.com

Belgium Tourist Office – Brussels & Ardennes
217 Marsh Wall, London E14 9FJ, UK
Tel: (0906) 302 0245 (calls cost 60p per minute) or (0800) 954 5245 (brochure request line; toll free UK only)
Tel: (020) 7531 0390
Website: www.belgium-tourism.org
Website: www.belgiumtheplaceto.be

Tourism Flanders-Brussels
1a Cavendish Square, London W1G 0LD, UK
Tel: (0906) 3020 245 (calls cost 60p per minute)
Website: www.visitflanders.co.uk

Atomium

The *Atomium* was designed by engineer André Waterkeyn as a celebration of scientific progress for the 1958 World Fair. The structure stands 102 m (334 ft) high, weighs 2400 metric tonnes (2439 tons), and represents an iron crystalline molecule enlarged 165 billion times. Inside the nine spheres, visitors can see an exhibition showing how the Atomium has been depicted in comic strips through the years and an audiovisual presentation on the construction of the Atomium. There are splendid views across Brussels and the surrounding countryside from the top of the structure.

Transportation
Air: Brussels Airport. **Rail:** Train: Bruxelles Centrale Station. Underground: Heysel. Tram: Public services. **Road:** Bus: Public services. Car: Ring road West (exit 8 Wemmel-Heizel).

Contact Addresses
ASBL Atomium, Atomium Square, 1020 Brussels, Belgium
Tel: (02) 475 47 77
Website: www.atomium.be

Cathedral of Our Lady (Onze Lieve Vrouwe-Kathedraal)

The *Cathedral of our Lady* is the largest Gothic church in the Low Countries and rises to a height of 123m (404ft), piercing the skyline of historic Antwerp. Although construction began on the cathedral in 1352, it was not completed until 1521; the roof and Gothic furniture were then destroyed by fire in 1533. The interior of the cathedral is Baroque in style, the original

Gothic features having been destroyed by religious idealists in the late 16th century. There are many fine works of art in the nave, the most famous being Ruben's 'Descent from the Cross' (1611-14).

Transportation
Air: Brussels Airport or Antwerp Airport. **Rail:** Train: Antwerp Central Station. Tram: Regular public services. **Road:** Car: N1. Bus: Regular public services.

Contact Addresses
Onze Lieve Vrouwe-Kathedraal, Groenplaats 21, 2000 Antwerp, Belgium
Tel: (02) 213 9951
Website: www.dekathedraal.be

Central Square (Grand' Place)

The *Grand' Place* has been at the heart of Brussels' life since the 11th century. Almost totally destroyed by the French bombardment ordered by Louis XIV in 1695, it was later rebuilt in its original architectural style by various workers' guilds. The splendid neo-Gothic and Baroque houses that surround the cobbled square once housed the headquarters of corporations of artists, merchants and tailors; the *City of Brussels Museum* in the former *Maison du Roi* (King's Residence) allows visitors to explore the city's illustrious trading history. Other buildings in the Grand' Place which provide insights into Brussels' traditions are the *Town Hall*, the *Museum of Cocoa and Chocolate* and the *Museum of Brewing*.

Transportation
Air: Brussels Airport. **Rail:** Train: Bruxelles Centrale Station. Underground: Bourse, De Brouckère, Gare Centrale.

Contact Addresses
Office de Tourisme et d'Information de Bruxelles, Hôtel de Ville, Grand-Place, 1000 Brussels, Belgium
Tel: (02) 513 8940
Website: www.belgium-tourism.org

Central Square, Brussels

Corel©

Statue of the Pissing Boy

Flanders Fields

Flanders Fields was the site of around half a million deaths in the horrific trenches of World War I. There are numerous military cemeteries and 'Missing Memorials' in the region commemorating those of all nationalities who fell in battle. Most of the soldiers who perished were the victims of poison gas attacks – the deadly gas *Yperite* was invented in the nearby city of Ypres, which was a renowned trading centre during the Middle Ages but was almost completely destroyed during World War I. At the *In Flanders Fields* museum in Ypres, visitors can discover what it was like to be a soldier in the trenches and learn about major events and aspects of the war such as the first gas attack, the Christmas Truces of 1914, and No Man's Land.

Transportation
Air: Brussels Airport. **Rail:** Train: Ieper/Ypres Station. **Road:** Car: N369 (from Ostend).

Contact Addresses
In Flanders Fields, Lakenhallen – Grote Markt 34, 8900 Ieper, Belgium
Tel: (057) 239 220
Website: www.inflandersfields.be

Statue of the Pissing Boy (Manneken-Pis)

The *Manneken-Pis*, situated in Rue de l'Etuve, is as funny as it is well known. Crowds of tourists patrol the meandering cobbled streets near Brussels' Grand' Place hoping to find this small statuette of a little boy in the midst of a never-ending pee. Sometimes known as 'Little Julian', the statue is, in its own way, a typically Belgian symbol of cultural self-mockery. Since its creation by J Duquesnoy in the 17th century, the Manneken-Pis has attracted a great deal of attention, having been stolen (by the English in 1745 and the French in 1747), vandalised and dressed in over 600 costumes, which are on display at the *City of Brussels Museum*.

Transportation
Air: Brussels Airport. **Rail:** Train: Bruxelles Centrale Station. Underground: Bourse. Tram: Regular services. **Road:** Public services.

Contact Addresses
Office de Tourisme et d'Information de Bruxelles, Hôtel de Ville, Grand-Place, 1000 Brussels, Belgium
Tel: (02) 513 8940
Website: www.belgium-tourism.org

Bolivia

Map scale: 500km / 250mls
✈ international airport

BRAZIL

Cobija • Riberalta

PERU

① Trinidad
ORIENTE
BRAZIL

Lake Titicaca 3812m
LA PAZ
BOLIVIA
Nev. Sajama 6542m △ • Cochabamba
• Oruro • Santa Cruz
• Arica L. Poopó • Roboré
• Sucre
Altiplano
• Potosí
CHILE • Tarija • Villa Montes
ARGENTINA PARAGUAY

1 Lake Titicaca (Lago Titicaca)

Tourist Information

Bolivian Tourist Board (Viceministerio de Turismo)
Avenida Mariscal Santa Cruz, Palacio de las Comunicaciones, Piso 16, La Paz, Bolivia
Tel: (591) 2 236 6474 or 1665
Website: www.embassyofbolivia.co.uk

Embassy and Consulate of the Republic of Bolivia
106 Eaton Square, London SW1W 9AD, UK
Tel: (020) 7235 4248 or 7235 2257
Website: www.embassyofbolivia.co.uk

Lake Titicaca (Lago Titicaca)

At an elevation of 3810m (12,492ft), *Lake Titicaca* is one of the world's highest navigable lakes. It is named after the native word for 'puma of stone'

and its shape bears a strong resemblance to this animal when viewed from above. Measuring 194km (121 miles) long and 65km (45 miles) wide, it has been revered in history, featuring prominently in Inca creation myths. There are daily tours to the *Uros* and *Taquile Islands*; the *Uros* people live on floating islands made out of reeds that grow in the lake, while the inhabitants of *Taquile Island* are renowned for maintaining ancient traditions and for their remarkable weaving skills.

Transportation
Air: El Alto Airport (La Paz). **Road:** Bus: Daily services leave La Paz every 30 minutes. Car: From La Paz (journey time: 2.5 hours).

Contact Addresses
For more information on Lake Titicaca, contact the Viceministerio de Turismo (see **Tourist Information** above).

P ✕ 🧺 ♿ ✤

Traditional Bolivian Boatman

Sky Bolivia©

Botswana

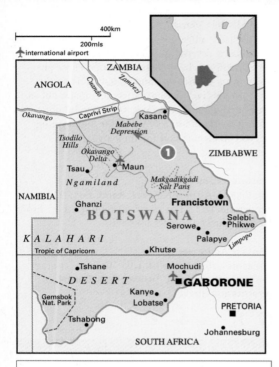

400km
200mls
⤉ international airport

ZAMBIA
ANGOLA
Chaundo
Zambezi
Okavango
Caprivi Strip
Kasane
Mabebe
Depression
Tsodilo
Hills
Okavango
Delta
Maun
ZIMBABWE
Tsau
Ngamiland
Makgadikgadi
Salt Pans
NAMIBIA
Ghanzi
Francistown
BOTSWANA
Serowe
Selebi-
Phikwe
KALAHARI
Palapye
Limpopo
Tropic of Capricorn
Khutse
Tshane
Mochudi
DESERT
GABORONE
Kanye
Gemsbok
Nat. Park
Lobatse
PRETORIA
Tshabong
Johannesburg
SOUTH AFRICA

1　Moremi Wildlife Reserve

Tourist Information

Department of Tourism
Ministry of Commerce and Industry, Private
Bag 0047, Gaborone, Botswana
Tel: 353 024
Website: www.gov.bw/tourism or
www.botswanatourism.org.uk

Department of Tourism UK
Representation Office/Botswana Tourism UK
c/o Southern Skies Marketing, Old Boundary
House, London Road, Sunningdale, Berkshire
SL5 0DJ, UK
Tel: (01344) 298 982

Moremi Wildlife Reserve

Botswana's *Moremi Wildlife Reserve* lies in the
centre of the Okavango Delta, the largest inland
delta in the world. Named after the chief of the
Batawana tribe who declared the reserve in 1963,
it is characterised by seasonal and permanent
swamped areas and covers an area of 3000 sq km
(1170 sq miles). The reserve encompasses a wide
range of habitats – from wetland, floodplain and
reed beds to forest and savannah woodland. The
fauna inhabiting the park is abundant and equally
diverse, ranging from exotic birds, zebras, buffalo,
wildebeest and giraffes to hippos and lions; the
only large African mammals not found here are
rhino. Boats take visitors to various lagoons, such
as Xakanaxa, Gcobega and Gcodikwe, to view
game and birdlife. There are many campsites and
lodges in the reserve, each with its own viewing
possibilities and activities.

Transportation
Air: Maun Airport (internal), Gaborone Sir Seretse
Khama International Airport. **Rail:** Train:
Francistown Station. **Road:** Car: Main road to
Maun, then road to Maqwee via Showobe; from
here there are various routes into the park (visitors
must have a 4x4 vehicle to enter the reserve and
most visitors are accompanied by a qualified
guide).

Contact Addresses
Moremi Wildlife Reserve, Department of Wildlife
and National Parks, Parks and Reserves
Reservation Office, PO Box 131, Gaborone,
Botswana
Tel: (267) 598 0774

Aerial view of the Okavango Delta

Botswana Tourism©

Brazil

1 Copacabana Beach (Praia de Copacabana)
2 Iguazu Falls (Foz do Iguaçú)
3 Statue of Christ the Redeemer (Cristo Redentor)
4 Sugar Loaf Mountain (Pâo de Açucar)

Tourist Information

Brazilian Tourist Board (EMBRATUR – Instituto Brasileiro do Turismo)
SCN, Quadra 2, Bloco 'G', CEP 70712-907
Brasília, DF, Brazil
Tel: (061) 429 7773
Website: www.embratur.gov.br

Brazilian Embassy and Tourist Office
32 Green Street, London W1K 7AT, UK
Tel: (020) 7629 6909
Website: www.brazil.org.uk

Copacabana Beach (Praia de Copacabana)

Copacabana Beach is one of the world's most famous beaches. Located right in the heart of Rio de Janeiro, it is also one of the most lively beaches in the world with thousands of visitors flocking to its 4km (2.5 mile) stretch of sand every year. Located in front of the black and white wavy mosaics on *Avenida Atlântica* which were designed by Burle Max, the area is busy both day and night and lined with shops, bars, restaurants and luxury hotels. There are also fine examples of *Art Deco* architecture in the area, such as the *Copacabana Palace Hotel* which was built in 1923. *Copacabana Fort*, which was built in 1914 to defend Guanabara Bay, is situated at the end of the beach and offers panoramic views of the surrounding area.

Transportation
Air: Rio de Janeiro Galeão Antonio Carlos Jobim International Airport. **Road:** Coach: Novo Rio Coach Station.

Contact Addresses
RIOTUR – City of Rio de Janeiro Tourism Authority, Rua da Assembléia, 10 / 9° Floor, Centro 20011-000, Rio de Janeiro, RJ, Brazil
Tel: (021) 2217 7575
Website: www.rio.rj.gov.br/riotur/en

Iguazú Falls (Foz do Iguaçú)

The *Iguazú Falls* fittingly receive their name from the Guarani Indian word meaning 'great waters'. Surrounded by the virgin jungle of *Iguazú National Park*, home to 2000 species of flora and 400 species of bird, the *Paraná River* divides into 275 separate falls. The highest, the *Garganta del Diabolo* (Devil's Throat) reaches 70m (230ft), which is one and a half times the height of the Niagara Falls. Besides taking in the stunning view from a series of catwalks, visitors may enjoy kayaking, canoeing and other watersports. Historic Jesuit Mission ruins nearby, such as those at *San Ignacio Miní*, are also popular.

Transportation
Air: Ministro Pistarini Airport (Buenos Aires).
Road: Coach: Services to bus terminal from Buenos Aires.

Iguazú Falls

Brazilian Tourist Board©

Transportation
Air: Rio de Janeiro Galeão Antonio Carlos Jobim International Airport. **Rail:** Train: Rua Cosme Velho Station. **Road:** Coach: Novo Rio Coach Station. Car: Routes to Corcovado.

Contact Addresses
RIOTUR – City of Rio de Janeiro Tourism Authority, Rua da Assembléia, 10 – 9° Floor, Centro 20011-000, Rio de Janeiro, RJ, Brazil
Tel: (021) 2217 7575
Website: www.rio.rj.gov.br/riotur

Contact Addresses
Iguazú National Park, Victoria Aguirre 66, 3370 Puerto Iguazú, Misiones, Argentina
Tel: (037) 5742 0722 *or* 5742 0180 *or* 5742 0382
Website: www.parquesnacionales.gov.ar

Sugar Loaf Mountain (Pâo de Açucar)

Shaped like a Victorian sugar loaf and 396m (1299ft) tall, *Sugar Loaf Mountain* stands high above the city of Rio de Janeiro and *Baía de Guanabara* (Guanabara Bay). The mountain is one of the most famous in the world and is a spectacular backdrop to Brazil's most lively city. Visitors can see excellent views of Rio de Janeiro from the top of the mountain and sunsets are particularly spectacular. Cable cars, which were introduced by the engineer Augusto Ferreira Ramos in 1912, take visitors to the top of the mountain, although more adventurous travellers may choose to make the steep climb on foot.

Statue of Christ the Redeemer (Cristo Redentor)

The *Statue of Christ the Redeemer*, standing 30m (98ft) tall and overlooking the city of Rio de Janeiro, is one of the tallest statues in the world. The statue represents Jesus standing with outstretched arms and is one of the most famous symbols of this lively city. Developed by the engineer Heitor da Silva Costa and originally conceived in 1921, construction started in mid-1926 and was completed in 1931. The statue sits on top of *Corcovado Mountain* (Hunchback Mountain) located in *Tijuca National Park*, a popular area for picnics and walking. From the statue there are superb views of Sugar Loaf Mountain, downtown Rio de Janeiro and Rio's beaches.

Transportation
Air: Rio de Janeiro Galeão Antonio Carlos Jobim International Airport. **Road:** Bus: Regular public bus services. Car: Road towards city centre, then coastal road past Ipanema and Copacabana beaches to 'Urca' (from the south); south towards Ipanema and Copacabana beaches, then the exit marked 'Urca' (from the city centre).

Contact Addresses
RIOTUR – City of Rio de Janeiro Tourism Authority, Rua da Assembléia, 10 – 9° Floor, Centro 20011-000, Rio de Janeiro, RJ, Brazil
Tel: (021) 2217 7575
Website: www.rio.rj.gov.br/riotur

Statue of Christ the Redeemer

Brazilian Tourist Board©

Brunei

high and can be seen from virtually anywhere in the city. The building was completed in 1958 and is an impressive example of Islamic architecture, with magnificent mosaic stained glass, as well as many arches, domes and columns. Marble from Italy, granite from Shanghai and chandeliers from England were all used in the construction of Brunei's most ornate building.

Transportation
Air: Bandar Seri Begawan International Airport.
Road: Taxi: Taxis can be hailed in the city centre to take visitors to the mosque. Bus: A number of bus routes run to the mosque.

Contact Addresses
For more information on Omar Ali Saifuddin Mosque, contact Brunei Tourism (see **Tourist Information** above).

1 Omar Ali Saifuddin Mosque (Masjid Omar Ali Saifuddin)

Tourist Information

Brunei Tourism
Ministry of Industry and Primary Resources, Jalan Menteri Besar, Bandar Seri Bagawan 1220, Brunei Darussalam
Tel: 6732 382 822
Website: www.industry.gov.bn

High Commission of Brunei Darussalam
19-20 Belgrave Square, London SW1X 8PG, UK
Tel: (020) 7581 0521

Omar Ali Saifuddin Mosque (Masjid Omar Ali Saifuddin)

Omar Ali Saifuddin Mosque is one of the most spectacular mosques in Asia Pacific and is a magnificent sight. Named after the 28th Sultan of Brunei, the mosque, which is seen as a symbol of the Islamic faith in Brunei, dominates the skyline in the capital city, Bandar Seri Begawan. The golden dome of the mosque stands at 52m (171ft)

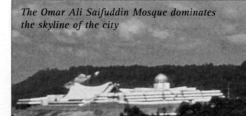

The Omar Ali Saifuddin Mosque dominates the skyline of the city

Royal Brunei Airways©

Bulgaria

200km
100mls
✈ international airport

ROMANIA

YUGOSLAVIA
SERBIA

①
③
Danube •Ruse   Dobrich
•Pleven   ✈•Varna
B U L G A R I A

SOFIA■   Kazanlūk•   Nessebŭr
Rila•   Stara Zagora•   Burgas•   BLACK
Maritsa   SEA

FYR OF   Pirin   **Plovdiv**
MACE- Mtns.   Rhodope Mo **④** ains
DONIA

② GREECE   TURKEY

Sea of
Marmara

AEGEAN
SEA

---

1 Baba Vida Castle
2 Rila Monastery (Rilski Manastir)
3 St Alexander Nevski Cathedral
   (Hram-pametnik Aleksander Nevski
4 Trigrad Gorge

Tourist Information

**National Information and Advertising Center
to the Ministry of Economy**
1 St Sophia Street, Sofia 1040, Bulgaria
Tel: (02) 987 9778 *or* 987 1152
Website: www.bulgariatravel.org

Embassy of the Republic of Bulgaria
186-188 Queen's Gate, London SW7 5HL, UK
Tel: (020) 75849 8402
Website: www.bulgarianembassy.org.uk

Baba Vida Castle

Built on the banks of the *River Danube* in the

town of *Vidin* in the northwestern tip of the country, *Baba Vida Castle* occupies a commanding position overlooking the town. The present castle is actually built upon the foundations of a Roman fortress known as *Bononia* which marked the Danubian Frontier of the Roman Empire from the first to the seventh centuries. Baba Vida Castle was actually built during the 10th century and is the only medieval fortress to have survived intact to the present day. The castle is protected by inner and outer walls and is ringed by a moat filled with water from the Danube. Today, the castle hosts numerous theatre productions during the summer months and is often used as a historical film set. There's also an onsite museum with exhibitions about the region's history.

Transportation
Air: Sofia International Airport. **Rail:** Vidin Station. **Road:** Bus: Public services to Vidin.

Contact Addresses
For more information on the Baba Vida Castle, contact the National Information and Advertising Center (see **Tourist Information** above).

Rila Monastery (Rilski Manastir)

Rila Monastery, the largest monastery in Bulgaria, is situated in the spectacular *Rhodope Mountains* in *Rila National Park* and is included on the UNESCO list of World Cultural Heritage Sites. Rila was the first Christian monastery to be built in Bulgaria and was founded by followers of John of Rila (the patron saint of Bulgaria) during the 10th century. Rila was damaged by fire several times over the years and was not fully restored to its current state until 1816. The monastery is ornately decorated with murals which were painted by famous artists, including Kosta Valyov and Zahari Zograph, between 1840 and 1848.

Transportation
Air: Sofia Airport. **Road:** Car: E79 south of Sofia

for 100km (62 miles), then a further 21km (13 miles) to arrive at Rila Monastery.

Contact Addresses
For more information on Rila Monastery, contact the National Information and Advertising Center to the Ministry of Economy (see **Tourist Information** above).

St Alexander Nevski Cathedral (Hram-pametnik Aleksander Nevski)

St Alexander Nevski Cathedral is one of Sofia's most famous monuments. This neo-Byzantine structure, which is surmounted by copper and golden domes, was built between 1882 and 1912 in honour of the Russian soldiers who died trying to liberate Bulgaria from Ottoman rule during the War of Liberation in 1878. The cathedral, which is also one of the finest buildings in the Balkan States, takes its name from Alexander Nevski, the patron saint of the family of the Russian Tsar at the time, Alexander II. Visitors can also see the *Icon Museum*, located in the Crypt, which houses around 300 exhibits following the development of Bulgarian icon-painting from the ninth to 19th centuries. Sofia also has many other attractions, including the *Rotunda of St George*, *St Sofia Church*, the *Church of St Nedely*, *Vassil Levski Monument* and the *Dragalevtsi* and *Boyana* churches.

Transportation
Air: Sofia Airport. **Rail:** Train: Sofia Station. **Road:** Public bus and minibus services. Car: Signs for Sofia city centre, then over Orlov Most (Eagle Bridge).

Contact Addresses
For more information on St Alexander Nevski Cathedral, contact the National Information and Advertising Center to the Ministry of Economy (see **Tourist Information** above).

Trigrad Gorge

The spectacular *Trigrad Gorge* is in the *Rhodope Mountains* close to the town of Trigrad in

Southern Bulgaria and is flanked by walls rising to 250m (820ft). One of the most popular sites at the gorge is *Devil's Throat Cave* which formed when layers of the mountain collapsed. From here, visitors can travel through a manmade tunnel to see the highest underground waterfalls in Europe which cascade 42m (138ft) into the abyss below. Nearby is the famous *Haramiiska Cave* where archaeologists discovered evidence of human habitation dating back over 4,000 years. There are over 150 other caves in the region and the area is popular with rock climbers; numerous companies provide guides and tuition. The region is also popular with birdwatchers who come to see Pallid Swifts, Crag Martins, Rock Partridges and the rare Wallcreeper.

Transportation
Air: Sofia International Airport. **Road:** Bus: Public services to Trigrad.

Contact Addresses
For more information on the Trigrad Gorge, contact the National Information and Advertising Centre (see **Tourist Information** above).

Rila Monastery

Cambodia

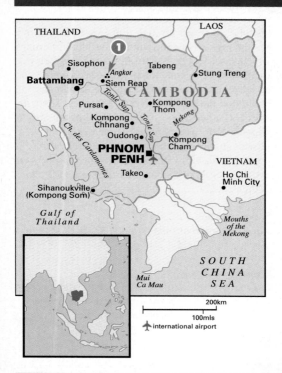

200km
100mls
✈ international airport

built in honour of the god Vishnu – began in AD 879 during the reign of King Suryavarman II and was completed in 1191. It lay concealed for many years, however, until the site was discovered by Frenchman Henri Mahout in 1860. The central complex, *Angkor Wat* (Angkor Temple), features an elaborate, unmortared 66m (215ft) central tower surrounded by four smaller towers. Stretching around the outside of the temple complex is an 800m-long (2625ft-) bas-relief, the longest in the world.

Transportation

Air: Siem Reap Airport. **Road:** Car: Route 6 (from Phnom Penh to Siem Reap). Taxi: Moto-taxi and tuk-tuk services are available (from Siem Reap).

Contact Addresses

Ministry of Tourism, Boulevard Monivong, Phnom Penh 12258, Cambodia
Tel: (023) 212 837 *or* 880 623 (Phnom Penh office)
Website: www.mot.gov.kh

🅿 ✗ 🧺 ♿ 🏛 £ 🏭

1 Angkor Temple Complex (Angkor)

Tourist Information

Ministry of Tourism (Krâsuong Teschor)
3 Boulevard Monivong, Phnom Penh, 12258 Cambodia
Tel: (023) 212 837
Website: www.mot.gov.kh

Royal Embassy of Cambodia
28-32 Wellington Road, St. John's Wood, London NW8 9SP UK
Tel: +44 (0) 20 7483 9063

Angkor Temple Complex

Angkor, the former capital of the ancient Khmer Empire, is one of the greatest and most spectacular Hindu religious sites in the world. Construction of this elaborate temple complex –

Angkor Temple

Cambodian Ministry of Tourism©

Canada

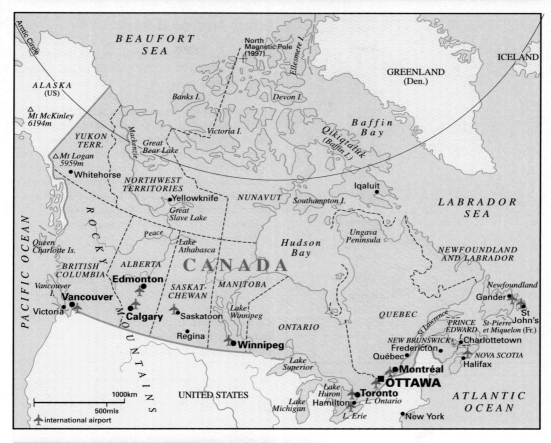

Travel Manitoba©

Tourist Information

Canadian Tourism Commission
55 Metcalfe Street, Suite 600,
Ottawa, Ontario K1P 6LS, Canada
Tel: (613) 946 1000
Website: www.canadatourism.com

Visit Canada Centre
PO Box 5396, Northampton NN1
2FA, UK
Tel: (0906) 871 5000 (24-hour
consumer and tourism enquiries
line; calls cost 60p per minute)
Website: www.travelcanada.ca

Alberta

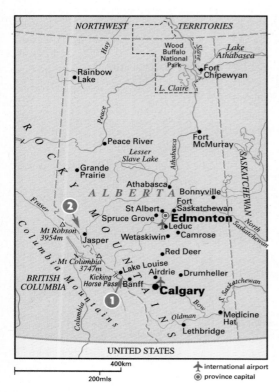

NORTHWEST TERRITORIES

Wood Buffalo National Park
Lake Athabasca
Rainbow Lake
Fort Chipewyan
L. Claire
Hay
Slave
Peace
Peace River
Fort McMurray
Lesser Slave Lake
Grande Prairie
Mt Robson 3954m
Jasper
BRITISH COLUMBIA
Mt Columbia 3747m
Kicking Horse Pass
Fraser
Columbia
Athabasca
A L B E R T A
St Albert
Spruce Grove
Leduc
Wetaskiwin
Camrose
Red Deer
Lake Louise
Airdrie
Drumheller
Banff
Calgary
Bonnyville
Fort Saskatchewan
Edmonton
North Saskatchewan
Athabasca
SASKATCHEWAN
Oldman
Bow
Lethbridge
Medicine Hat
S. Saskatchewan
②
①

UNITED STATES

400km
200mls

✈ international airport
◉ province capital

1 Banff National Park
2 Jasper National Park

Tourist Information

Travel Alberta
PO Box 2500, Edmonton, Alberta T5J 2Z4, Canada
Tel: (403) 297 2700 or (780) 427 4321 or (800) 661 8888 (toll free USA and Canada only)
Website: www.travelalberta.com

Travel Alberta UK
Travel Alberta UK, 11 Cornflour Way, West Sussex RH13 7WB, UK
Tel: (01403) 754 424

Key to symbols: £ Entry charged �& Disabled access
🔩 Man-made attraction ✔ Natural attraction
🅿 Parking ✗ Restaurant 🛒 Shop 🏛 UNESCO site

Banff National Park

Banff National Park was created by the Canadian government in 1885 as the country's first national park. The park, which includes the Rocky Mountains, has 6641 sq km (2564 sq miles) of mountains, rivers, forests, lakes, glaciers and hot springs, and is home to wolves, mountain goats, eagles, grizzly bears and elk. The most famous man-made addition to the area is the *Banff Springs Hotel*, completed in 1888. It was built to resemble a baronial Scottish castle and accommodates more than 800 guests. *Lake Louise*, named in honour of Queen Victoria's daughter, Princess Louise Caroline Alberta, is one of the most popular sites in the *Rocky Mountains*.

Transportation
Air: Calgary International Airport. **Road:** Coach: Services from Calgary. **Car:** Trans-Canada Hwy-1.

Contact Addresses
Banff Lake Louise Tourism Bureau, Box 1298, Banff, Alberta T1L 1B3, Canada
Tel: (403) 762 8421
Website: www.banfflakelouise.com

🅿 ✗ 🛒 �& 🏛 £ ✔

Travel Alberta©

Moraine Lake and the Valley of the Ten Peaks, Banff National Park

Travel Alberta©

Jasper National Park

Jasper National Park was established in 1907 and is the largest of Canada's *Rocky Mountains* parks, spanning 10,878 sq km (4200 sq miles). The spectacular scenery is characterised by glaciers, rugged mountains, forests and meadows carpeted with alpine flowers. The park protects a range of fragile mountain ecosystems – elk, moose, bear, bighorn sheep and mule deer are regular sights – and is home to the threatened woodland caribou. *Maligne Lake*, 48km (30 miles) southeast of Jasper is surrounded by snow-capped mountains and its crystal clear waters are popular for boating and fishing.

Transportation

Air: Calgary International Airport, Edmonton International Airport. **Rail:** Train: Jasper Station. **Road:** Bus: Jasper Bus Station. Car: Hwy-16 (from Edmonton); Hwy-1 (from Calgary); Hwy-93 (from Lake Louise).

Contact Addresses

Jasper National Park, Visitor Information Centre, PO Box 10, Jasper, Alberta T0E 1E0, Canada
Tel: (780) 852 6176 *or* (888) 773 8888
Website: www.pc.gc.ca/banff

Ontario

International airport
Province capital

1 Algonquin Provincial Park
2 CN Tower
3 National Gallery of Canada
4 Niagara Falls, Canada

Tourist Information

Ontario Tourism Marketing Partnership
Tenth Floor, Hearst Block, 900 Bay Street,
Toronto, Ontario M7A 2E1, Canada
Tel: (1) 800 668 2746 (toll free USA and
Canada only)
Website: www.ontariotravel.net

Ontario Tourism Marketing Partnership
c/o CIB, 1 Battersea Church Road,
London SW11 3LY, UK
Tel: (020) 7771 7004 (trade enquiries only) or
(01622) 832 288 (brochure request line)

Algonquin Provincial Park

Spanning 7725 sq km (4800 sq miles), *Algonquin Provincial Park* was established in 1893 to develop a wildlife sanctuary in a rugged, beautiful part of

Southern Ontario. It soon became popular with outdoor enthusiasts and canoeists because of its beautiful lakes, forests, bogs, rivers, cliffs and beaches. For campers and day visitors, *Highway 60* is the centre of the park, offering campgrounds, walking trails, conducted hikes and access to public wolf-howling sessions. In winter, cross country skiing trails are popular. Visitors can also soak up the history of the park in the *Logging Museum,* or in the *Algonquin Gallery,* which focuses on the Canadian artist Tom Thomson's (1877-1917) famous group of painters, the *Group of Seven.*

Transportation
Air: Lester B Pearson International Airport (Toronto). **Rail:** Train: Huntsville Station. Road: Coach: Services to Huntsville (from Toronto). **Car:** Hwy-11, Hwy-17 or Hwy-60.

Contact Addresses
Algonquin Provincial Park, PO Box 219, Whitney, Ontario K0J 2M0, Canada
Tel: (705) 633 5572 (information)
Website: www.algonquinpark.on.ca

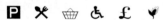

CN Tower

As the world's tallest free-standing structure on land, the *CN Tower* is the defining feature of Toronto's lakefront skyline. Completed in 1976, the 553m (1815ft) tower offers stunning views of Toronto and Lake Ontario. It takes only 58 seconds to reach the LookOut level in a glass-fronted lift which travels at 22km (15 miles) per hour. Once there, visitors can enjoy a meal at the revolving *360° Restaurant,* walk across a glass floor on the 113th storey or get an even better view from the *Sky Pod* that is 447m (1465ft) high. There is also a collection of entertainment attractions at the base of the tower, including two motion simulator rides, and a short documentary film describing the feat of engineering undertaken to build this colossal structure.

Transportation

Air: Lester B Pearson International Airport (Toronto). **Rail:** Train: Union Station. Underground: Union Station. **Road:** Car: Hwy-427 (from the north).

Contact Addresses

CN Tower, 301 Front Street West, Toronto, Ontario M5V 2T6, Canada
Tel: (416) 868 6937
Website: www.cntower.ca

National Gallery of Canada

The *National Gallery of Canada* was founded in 1880 by the Governor General, the Marquess of Lorne and since then has grown to become an internationally-renowned art museum. The permanent collections reflect Canada's diverse history, and includes works by European masters such as Monet, Turner and Di Cosimo, as well as avant-garde Canadian paintings from the 1960s and religious sculptures from Québec. The museum also contains a large collection of Inuit art, including prints, drawings and whale bone sculptures, many of which portray the cultural and social issues that have affected Canada's indigenous population since World War II.

Transportation

Air: Ottawa Macdonald-Cartier International Airport. **Rail:** Train: Ottawa VIA Rail Station. **Road:** Bus: 3. Car: Hwy-417 (Metcalfe exit). Then Metcalfe Street, right onto Wellington Street and left onto Sussex Drive.

Contact Addresses

National Gallery of Canada, 380 Sussex Drive, Box 427, Station A, Ottawa, Ontario K1N 9N4, Canada
Tel: (613) 990 1985
Website: www.national.gallery.ca

Niagara Falls, Canada

Niagara Falls is one of the most popular tourist destinations in North America. The falls are made up of two separate parts, *Horseshoe Falls* on the Canadian side and *American Falls* on the USA side. Although not the highest waterfall in the world they move a staggering 168,000 cubic metres (219,600 cubic yards) of water per minute over a drop of 51m (167ft), making them one of the natural wonders of the world. The surrounding town, a celebrated North American honeymoon destination, offers a wealth of visitor activities including a casino, as well as land and boat tours of the falls.

Transportation

Air: Buffalo Niagara Airport or Lester B Pearson International Airport (Toronto). **Rail:** Train: Niagara Falls VIA Rail Station. **Road:** Bus: Falls Shuttle to the Niagara Falls (from downtown). Coach: Niagara Falls Coach Station. Car: Queen Elizabeth Way (QEW) towards Niagara, then Hwy-420 to Niagara Falls (from Toronto).

Contact Addresses

Niagara Falls Tourism, 5515 Stanley Avenue, Niagara Falls, Ontario L2G 3X4, Canada
Tel: (905) 356 6061
Website: www.niagarafallstourism.com

Niagara Falls

Ontario Tourism©

Quebec

1 Old Port of Montréal (Vieux Port de Montreal)

2 Old Québec (Vieux Québec)

Old Port of Montréal (Vieux Port de Montréal)

The *Old Port* is located in the historic heart of the cosmopolitan, francophone city of Montréal. It was once the sea-trading hub of North America and in the first half of the 20th century was the second largest port in North America after New York. After port operations declined in the late 1950s, the Canadian government decided to redevelop the area, and it is now a thriving arts and entertainment venue, visited by five million people each year. The port is surrounded by the city's original 17th century walled fortifications and the activities on offer reflect both the area's illustrious past and its modern, forward-looking philosophy. The *Clock Tower* offers excellent views across the city and houses an exhibition tracing the city's history.

Caleche in de la Commune Street in Old Montréal

Tourisme Montréal, Stéphan Poulin©

Tourist Information

Tourisme Québec
Centre Infotouriste Montréal,
1001 Square Dorchester,
Bureau 100, Montréal, Québec
H3B 4V4, Canada
Tel: (514) 873 2015 or (800) 363 777 (toll free USA and Canada only)
Website: www.bonjourquebec.com

Destination Québec
Suite 116, Fourth Floor, 35-37 Grosvenor Gardens, London SW1W 0BS, UK
Tel: (020) 7233 8011
Website: www.quebec4u.co.uk

Transportation

Air: Montréal Dorval International Airport, Montréal Mirabel International Airport. **Rail:** Train: Montréal Station (Gare Centrale). Underground: Square-Victoria, Champ-de-Mars or Place d'armes. **Road:** Car: Ville-Marie Expressway (Hwy-720).

Contact Addresses

Old Port of Montréal Inc., 333 rue de la Commune Ouest, Montréal, Québec H2Y 2E2, Canada
Tel: (514) 496 7678
Website: www.oldportofmontreal.com

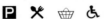

Old Québec (Vieux Québec)

The only walled city north of Mexico, *Québec* was settled in 1608 as a fur trading post. Its fortified exterior and strategic position high above the St Lawrence River is a testament to the historical territorial tensions between France and England that culminated in the Battle of the Plains of Abraham (1759). Divided into two sections, *Haute* and *Basse*, the old town seems more like an island of old Europe, with winding cobblestone streets, 17th- and 18th-century buildings and churches, squares, parks and numerous monuments. The *Château Frontenac*, a Canadian landmark, is its most prominent building – built in 1893, it is now a luxury hotel with views over the St Lawrence River and Old Québec.

Transportation

Air: Jean-Lesage International Airport. **Rail:** Train: Québec Station (Gare du Palais). **Road:** Bus: Gare du Palais. Car: Hwy-20 or Hwy-40.

Contact Addresses

Tourisme Québec, PO Box 979, Montréal, Québec H3C 2W3, Canada
Tel: (514) 873 2015
Website: www.bonjourquebec.com

Cannon and Château Frontenac, Québec

Corel©

Yukon Territory

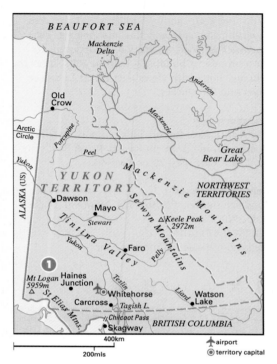

BEAUFORT SEA

Mackenzie Delta

Anderson

Old Crow

Arctic Circle

Porcupine

Mackenzie

Peel

Great Bear Lake

YUKON TERRITORY

Mackenzie Mountains

NORTHWEST TERRITORIES

Dawson

Mayo

Stewart

Selwyn Mountains

△Keele Peak 2972m

Tintina Valley

Yukon

Faro

Pelly

Mt Logan 5959m △

Haines Junction

St Elias Mtns.

Whitehorse

Teslin

Liard

Watson Lake

Carcross

Tagish L.

Chilcoot Pass

Skagway

BRITISH COLUMBIA

1

400km
200mls

✈ airport
◉ territory capital

1 Kluane National Park and Reserve

Tourist Information

Tourism Yukon
PO Box 2703, Whitehorse, Yukon Territory
Y1A 2C6, Canada
Tel: (867) 667 5340
Website: www.touryukon.com

Yukon First Nations Tourism Association
PO Box 4518, Whitehorse, Yukon Y1A 2R8,
Canada
Tel: (867) 667 7698
Website: www.yfnta.org

Key to symbols: £ Entry charged & Disabled access
⌐ Man-made attraction ♥ Natural attraction
P Parking ✗ Restaurant ⌂ Shop ⏛ UNESCO site

Kluane National Park and Reserve

Established in 1972, *Kluane National Park and Reserve* has been the home of the Southern Tutchone First Nations people for thousands of years. The park is a vast expanse of mountains and ice and encompasses the *Icefield Ranges*; the highest mountain in this range, *Mount Logan*, rises to 5959m (19,545ft) and is the highest peak in Canada. Other popular activities on offer in the park include cross country skiing, boating, fishing, snowmobiling, cycling, mountainbiking and horseriding. A rafting trip down the *Alsek River* allows visitors to view the wildlife (including grizzly bears, Dall sheep and golden eagles) and glaciers along the way; however, permits for rafting on this Canadian Heritage river are strictly limited to one departure per day and visitors are advised to arrange their trip well in advance.

Transportation
Air: Vancouver International Airport, then Whitehorse Airport (domestic flight). **Road:** Car: Alaska Highway (from Whitehorse) or Haines Highway (from Haines, Alaska) to Haines Junction.

Contact Addresses
Kluane National Park and Reserve, PO Box 5495, Haines Junction, Yukon Y0B 1L0, Canada
Tel: (867) 634 7250
Website: www.pc.gc.ca/kluane

Kluane Glacier

Tourism Yukon ©

Chile

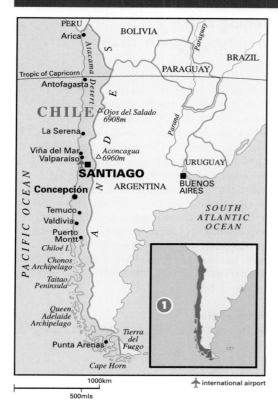

1000km
500mls

✈ international airport

1 Easter Island (Rapa Nui)

Tourist Information

Servicio Nacional de Turismo (SERNATUR)
Avenida Providencia 1550,
PO Box 14082, Santiago, Chile
Tel: (269) 67141
Website: www.visitchile.org

Embassy and Consulate of the Republic of Chile
12 Devonshire Street,
London W1G 7DS, UK
Tel: (020) 7580 6392 (embassy and tourist office) or 7580 1023 (visa section)
Website: www.echileuk.demon.co.uk

Easter Island (Rapa Nui)

A lonely volcanic island in the middle of the Pacific Ocean, as far away from Chile as from Tahiti, *Easter Island* is famous for its mysterious stone statues, or *moais*, that form an almost unbroken ring around the coast. Three hundred statues and related items of stonework, which were built during the 10th to 16th centuries, grace the island. Scientists are fascinated to learn how native inhabitants designed and forged the massive sculptures from hard volcanic rock, and how they transported them to the coast from inland quarries. Today, about 2000 people inhabit *Easter Island*, most of them living in the town of Hanga Roa.

Transportation
Air: Mataveri International Airport (Easter Island).

Contact Addresses
SERNATUR, Tourist Information, Tuu Maheke s/n, esquina Apina, Easter Island, Chile
Tel: (032) 100 255
Website: www.sernatur.cl

A stone moais on Easter island

Zena Turner©

People's Republic of China

1 Beijing Zoo (Beijing Dongwu Yuan)
2 Forbidden City (Zijin Cheng)
3 Great Wall of China (Wanli Changcheng)
4 Potala Palace (Kukhar Potrang)
5 Summer Palace (Yi He Yaun)
6 Terracotta Army (Bingma Yong)
7 Three Gorges of the Yangtze River (Sanxia)
8 Victoria Peak (Tai Ping Shan)

Tourist Information

China National Tourism Administration (CNTA)
Department of Marketing and Communications, 9A Jianguomennei Avenue, Beijing 100740, People's Republic of China
Tel: (010) 6520 1114
Website: www.cnta.com/lyen/index.asp

China National Tourist Office (CNTO)
71 Warwick Road, London SW5 9H8 UK
Tel: (020) 7373 0888

Tibet Tourism Administration
Yuanlin Road, Lhasa, Tibet 850001, People's Republic of China
Tel: (0891) 683 4313

Beijing Zoo (Beijing Dongwu Yuan)

Beijing Zoo is the oldest zoo in Asia Pacific and home of the world-famous giant pandas. Located in the northwest area of the city, it is home to more than 7000 animals, including golden monkeys from Sichuan, yaks from Tibet, sea turtles from the Chinese sea, Manchurian tigers and snow leopards. The zoo is also famous for being the home of zoological research and for housing many rare birds and animals. During the Qing Dynasty (1644–early 20th century), the zoo was a private garden, but later became an experimental farm and small menagerie. It was first opened to the public in 1908, but was destroyed during the Japanese occupation of Beijing (1937-1945), only to reopen in 1950.

Transportation
Air: Beijing Capital Airport. **Rail:** Train: Beijing Station.

Contact Addresses
Beijing Dongwu Yuan, 137 Xizhimenwai, Xicheng District, Beijing, People's Republic of China
Tel: (010) 6831 4411
Website: www.beijingzoo.com

Forbidden City (Zijin Cheng)

Built in the early 15th century during the Ming dynasty, the 74-hectare (183-acre) *Forbidden City* served as the home for 24 of China's Ming and Qing emperors. The palace drew its name from the fact that vast sections of it were off limits to virtually all save the emperor himself. Its 9000 rooms, filled with paintings, pottery and bronzes, are redolent of China's imperial past, an era of concubines, palace eunuchs and a rigid power structure. Among the Forbidden City's more notable landmarks are the *Meridian Gate*, the *Hall of Supreme Harmony* and the *Imperial Garden*.

Transportation

Air: Beijing Capital Airport. **Rail:** Train: Beijing Station. Underground: Qianmen. **Road:** Bus: Regular public services. Car: Towards Beijing city centre.

Contact Addresses

For more information on the Forbidden City, contact China National Tourism Administration (see **Tourist Information** above).

Great Wall of China (Wanli Changcheng)

One of the only man-made structures visible from space, the *Great Wall of China*, which stretches for some 6700km (4163 miles) through northern China, is the greatest symbol of the country's history and grandeur. Begun in the third century BC, the Great Wall connected a number of earlier walls to create a defence against nomads invading from the north. Although the wall ultimately failed in this regard, it was effective in bringing stability and continuity to Chinese culture. Much of the wall that exists today was rebuilt between the 14th and 18th centuries by the Ming dynasty. Many tourists choose to walk along a stretch of the wall, as it passes through some of China's most spectacular scenery.

Transportation

Air: Beijing Capital Airport. **Rail:** Train: Badaling Station. **Road:** Bus: Tourist bus (from Beijing city centre). Car: Motorway to Badaling (from Beijing).

Contact Addresses

For more information on the Great Wall of China, contact China National Tourism Administration (see **Tourist Information** above).

Potala Palace (Kukhar Potrang)

The *Potala Palace* is the largest monumental structure in Tibet, covering 41 hectares (101 acres). It stands high above the Lhasa Valley and was built in the seventh century AD as a retreat for the local lord, Songtsen Gampo, and his bride Princess Wen Cheng. Thirteen storeys high and

perched on a huge cliff face, it is the world's highest palace. The palace complex is made up of two sections, the *Red Palace* and the *White Palace*, which together consist of 1000 rooms. The palace is the headquarters of the Dalai Lama and is a treasure house of traditional Tibetan culture.

Transportation

Air: Gonggar International Airport, Bangda Airport. **Road:** Taxi: From various locations in Lhasa (the palace is located in the centre of Lhasa). Car: Chengdu-Lhasa Highway (from Chengdu); Lhasa-Zham Friendship Bridge-Kathmandu Highway (from Kathmandu, Nepal).

Contact Addresses

Tibet Tourism Bureau, Yuanlin Road, Lhasa, Tibet 85001, People's Republic of China
Tel: (0891) 633 5472 *or* 683 4315

Summer Palace (Yi He Yaun)

Considered to be one of the finest classical gardens in China, the *Summer Palace* was first built in 1153 and served as a retreat for the royal court to escape the heat in the city. The imperial residences are built on the shores of Kunming Lake, which contains small islands, ornamental bridges and a marble boat that was once a teahouse. The palace was rebuilt in 1888 by the Empress Dowager Ci Xi who spent large amounts of money, from a fund intended for building a Chinese navy, on bringing the garden to its present state of glory. Covering an area of 290 hectares (717 acres), the gardens consist of a large lake with halls, towers, galleries, pavilions and bridges dotting the surrounding hilly land.

Transportation

Air: Beijing Capital Airport. **Rail:** Train: Beijing Station. **Road:** Bus: Public services.

Contact Addresses

Summer Palace, Yiheyuan Road, Haidian District
Tel: (010) 6288 114
Website: www.summerpalace-china.com

Terracotta Army (Bingma Yong)

The *Terracotta Army* is an enormous collection of Chinese warriors made out of hardened clay, 40km (25 miles) east of the town of Xi'an. The army, which is set out in rigid columns, was created in the second century BC by the emperor Shih Huang-Ti, the first emperor of a unified China, and was entombed with him upon his death. It was discovered in 1974 during an attempt to dig a well, and since then three separate chambers have revealed over 10,000 figures. The clay figures are all individual, and are made to represent actual members of the imperial army, including both soldiers and officers. Some are armed with real weapons, standing in battle formation next to real wooden chariots. The collection also includes clay horses and is often referred to as 'the eighth wonder of the world'.

Transportation
Air: Xi'an Xianyang International Airport. **Rail:** Train: Xi'an Station. **Road:** Taxi: Services from Xi'an.

Contact Addresses
Terracotta Warriors and Horses Museum, Qinling town, Lintong District, Shanxi Province, Peoples Republic of China.
Tel: (029) 8139 9046
Website: www.bmy.com.cn

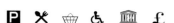

Three Gorges of the Yangtze River (Sanxia)

The *Three Gorges of the Yangtze River* are a system of breathtaking gorges on China's longest river, which is also the third longest river in the world (after the Amazon and the Nile), stretching for 6300km (3915 miles). The *Qutang Gorge* is best known for its steep precipices that form an enormous gateway over the river. The *Wu Gorge* is home to the famous 12 peaks of the Wushan Mountains. And the *Xiling Gorge* is known for its hidden reefs, perilous cliffs and tumbling rapids. The controversial Three Gorges Project involves the construction of a dam which will be the largest hydroelectric project in the world. The dam, estimated to have a total cost in excess of $25 billion, is sheduled for completion in 2009.

The first tourist tickets to enable visitors to take a closer look at the dam were sold in the summer of 2005.

Transportation
Air: Beijing Capital Airport, Shanghai Hong Qiao Airport, Shanghai Pudong Airport. **Water:** Ferry: Services from Yichang. **Rail:** Train: Yichang Station.

Contact Addresses
Chongqing Tourism Administration, 50 Jiuchikan, Cangibai Road, Yuzhong District, Chongqing, Peoples Republic of China
Tel: (023) 8903 3037
Website: www.cqta.gov.cn

Victoria Peak (Tai Ping Shan)

At 552m (1514ft) above sea level, *Victoria Peak* is the most conspicuous landmark in Hong Kong. The Peak was rarely visited until 1888, the year the *Peak Tramway* opened, and its popularity has risen steadily since. Today, it is home to Hong Kong's wealthiest executives and bankers who favour the rarefied, natural surroundings. The view from the top is breathtaking even offering views of Macau and mainland China on a clear day. There are many restaurants and attractions, including a *Madame Tussaud's Wax Museum* in the *Peak Galleria* at the summit. Walking trails allow visitors to explore The Peak's natural beauty, including forests of bamboo and fern, stunted Chinese pines and sightings of birds, such as magpies, goshawks and kites.

Transportation
Air: Hong Kong International Airport. **Rail:** Train: MTR Central Station. Tram: Peak Tram (from Garden Road). **Road:** Bus: Public services.

Contact Addresses
Hong Kong Tourism Board, 9-11th Floors, Citicorp Centre, 18 Whitefield Road, North Point, Hong Kong, People's Republic of China
Tel: (852) 2807 6543
Website: www.discoverhongkong.com

Costa Rica

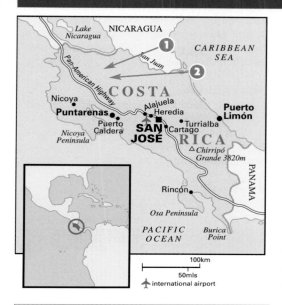

National Park offers trails around the slopes and views of the summit; there are also hot spring spas with views over the surrounding area. At night, the view is even more spectacular, as molten rocks and lava tumble down the slopes, creating a dramatic 'firework' display that is fortunately always at least 5km (3 miles) away.

Transportation

Air: Juan Santamaria International Airport (San José) or Daniel Oduber Airport. **Road:** Coach: Services to La Fortuna (from San José and Ciudad Quesada). Car: Pan-American Highway (from San José).

Contact Addresses

Arenal Observatory Lodge, PO Box 321-1007, Centro Colón, Costa Rica
Tel: (506) 290 7011
Website: www.arenalobservatorylodge.com

Tourist Information

Costa Rica Tourist Board (Instituto Costarricense de Turismo)
Apartado 777, 1000 San José, Costa Rica
Tel: (506) 299 5800
Website: www.visitcostarica.com

Embassy and Consulate of the Republic of Costa Rica
Flat 1, 14 Lancaster Gate, London W2 3LH, UK
Tel: (020) 7706 8844
Website: www.embrclon.demon.co.uk

Arenal Volcano (Volcán Arenal)

One of the world's most active volcanoes, *Arenal* can be seen for miles around. The volcano had lain dormant for over 400 years until 1968, when it erupted, forming a lava landscape around the base. Research centre *Arenal Observatory Lodge* provides excellent views and *Arenal Volcano*

Arenal Volcano

ICT – Instituto Costarricense de Turismo©

Monteverde Cloud Forest (Bosque Nuboso de Monteverde)

Straddling the Continental Divide and covering 170 sq km (66 sq miles), this vast forest has its head – and its feet – in the clouds. The ever-present drizzle and mist provide a home to an amazing array of flora and fauna. Trails, overnight shelters for camping and a 91m (300ft) suspension bridge enable visitors to experience the incredible biodiversity of the forest. There is also a *Visitor Centre*, *Butterfly Centre*, *Orchid Garden*, *Serpentarium* and *Hummingbird Gallery*, as well as the *Frog Pond of Monteverde Herpetarium*. Other highlights include the *Sky Trek* and the *Sky Walk*, a series of trails and platforms reaching high into the jungle canopy.

Transportation

Air: Juan Santamaria International Airport (San José). **Road:** Coach: Services to Santa Elena (from Puntarenas) services from Monteverde (from Tilarán); express service to Monteverde (from San José). Car: Pan-American Highway to Kilometre #149 (from San José).

Contact Addresses

Monteverde Cloud Forest Preserve, Apdo 55-5655, Monteverde, Puntarenas, Costa Rica
Tel: (506) 645 5122
Website: www.cct.or.cr or
www.cloudforestalive.org

Monteverde Cloud Forest

ICT – Instituto Costarricense de Turismo©

Croatia

1 Dubrovnik
2 Plitvice Lakes National Park (Nacionalni Park Plitvicka Jezera)
3 Split

Tourist Information

Hrvatska turisticka zajedni (Croatian National Tourist Board)
Iblerov jrg 10/IV, 10000 Zagreb, Croatia
Tel: (01) 455 6455
Website: www.croatia.hr

Croatian National Tourist Office
Croatia House, 162-164 Fulham Palace Road,
London W6 9ER, UK
Tel: (020) 8563 7979

Dubrovnik

This small fortified city with a population of about 43,000 lies on the Dalmatian coast in southern Croatia and is often referred to as the 'Pearl of the

Adriatic'. Founded in the seventh century, *Dubrovnik* reached its heyday as an important sea-trading port in the late Middle Ages, and the proliferation of Gothic, Renaissance and Baroque buildings are a legacy of its rich and glorious past. The most famous sights are the *Franjevaèkog Samostana Mala Braca* (Franciscan Friars Minor Monastery) in the west, which houses one of the three oldest pharmacies in Europe, the 15th-century *Dominikanskog Samostana* (Dominican monastery), located in the east of the city, and the 17th-century *Katedrale* (cathedral). The *Dubrovaèki Muzej* (Dubrovnik Museum) housed in the splendid *Kneažev Dvor* (Rector's Palace) is also worth a visit.

Transportation
Air: Dubrovnik International Airport or Zagreb International Airport. **Water:** Ferry: Services from Bari (Italy). **Road:** Bus: Public services. Coach: Services from Split. Car: Adriatic Coastal Road from Split, Trieste and Zagreb).

Contact Addresses
Dubrovnik Tourist Board, Cvijete Zuzoric 1/ 2, 20000 Dubrovnik, Croatia
Tel: (020) 324 999
Website: http://web.tzdubrovnik.hr

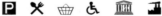

Plitvice Lakes National Park (Nacionalni Park Plitvicka Jezera)

Plitvice Lakes National Park in the heart of Croatia consists of 16 beautiful blue-green lakes, linked by a series of waterfalls and cascades to form a chain through a wooded valley. Over thousands of years, the waters that flow through this area have

Plitvice Lakes National Park

Croatian National Tourist Board©

passed over limestone and chalk, creating deposits which form natural barriers between the lakes. The lakes range in height from *Proscansko Jezero* at 636.6m (1746ft) above sea level, to the lowest, *Kaludjerovac*, at 505.2m (1386ft), and in surface area from 81 hectares (200 acres) to 1 hectare (2.5 acres).

Transportation
Air: Zagreb International Airport. **Road:** Coach: All coaches on the Zagreb-Zadar route stop at Plitvice; it is also possible to visit Plitvice as a day trip from most coastal resorts between the Kvarner Riviera and mid-Dalmatia.

Contact Addresses
Plitvice Lakes National Park, 53231 Plitvièka jezera, Croatia
Tel: (053) 751 015
Website: www.np-plitvicka-jezera.hr/

Split

Located on Croatia's stunning *Dalmatia Coast*, *Split* is the largest city in the area and cultural centre of the region. The city dates back nearly 2,000 years boasting a variety of architectural styles and historical landmarks. Most famous of these is the *Palace of Diocletian* which is inscribed on the UNESCO World Heritage List. The palace was built in the third century by the emperor Diocletian in the style of a Roman fort around a rectangular plot with turrets and huge palace gates. At the time, Split itself did not exist and the town sprang up around the palace. Other important attractions in Split include the *Museum of Croatian Archaeological Monuments*, the *Museum of Marine History*, the *Museum of Natural Science* and *Split Cathedral's Treasury* containing important sacral works of art dating back to the seventh century. A pleasant 15-minute stroll from the historic city centre is *Marjan Forest Park* which is home to *Split Zoo* and numerous walking trails that offer spectacular views of the peninsular and surrounding area.

Transportation
Air: Split Airport. **Water:** Ferry: Ferry services link Split with Rijeka and Dubrovnik as well as some of the bigger Dalmatia islands. **Rail:** Split Station. **Road:** Bus: Public services. Car: Adriatic Coastal Road.

Contact Addresses
Split Tourist Board, HR-21000 Split, Trg Republike 2
Tel: (021) 348 600
Website: www.visitsplit.com

 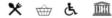

Split

Croatian National Tourist Board©

Cuba

1 Old Havana (Vieja Habana)

Tourist Information

Ministry of Tourism (Ministerio de Turismo)
Calle 19, No 710, Entre Paseo y A, Vedado,
Havana, Cuba
Tel: (07) 330 545
Website: cubatravel.cu

Cuba Tourist Board
154 Shaftesbury Avenue, London WC2H 8JT, UK
Tel: (020) 7240 6655 or (09001) 600 295 (24-hour brochure request line)

Old Havana (Vieja Habana)

Old Havana harks back to Cuba's days as a colonial outpost and its subsequent era as a glamorous, sophisticated Caribbean playground. Although some of the crumbling palaces look like they could do with a lick of paint, many of its colonial buildings, majestic boulevards, elegant plazas and side streets have been restored, attracting more and more visitors each year. The *Plaza de la Catedral* (Cathedral Square), dominated by the towers of the 18th-century Baroque *Catedral de San Cristobal de La Habana* (St Cristobal Cathedral), perhaps best captures Old Havana's spirit.

Transportation
Air: Havana Jose Marti International Airport. **Rail:** Train: Miramar Station. **Road:** Bus: Public services. Car: Carreterra Central (across Cuba via Havana); Autopista (from Pinar del Rio or Ciego de Avila to Havana).

Contact Addresses
Infotur, 5ta Avenida esq. 112, Miramar, La Habana, Cuba
Tel: (07) 247 036
Website: www.infotur.com

Havana Cathedral

Ministry of Tourism©

Cyprus

Kykkos Monastery

1 Kykkos Monastery (Panagia tou Kykkou)
2 Paphos (Pafos)

Tourist Information

Cyprus Tourism Organisation
PO Box 24535, Nicosia 1390, Cyprus
Tel: (02) 337 715
Website: www.visitcyprus.org.cy

Cyprus Tourism Organisation – UK
17 Hanover Street, London W1S 1YP, UK
Tel: (020) 7569 8800
Website: www.visitcyprus.org.cy

Kykkos Monastery (Panagia tou Kykkou)

Kykkos Monastery is the largest and most famous monastery in Cyprus. Founded in AD 1100 by the Byzantine emperor Alexios Komnenos, the monastery is dedicated to the Virgin Mary and is home to one of the three surviving icons painted by the Apostle Luke. Kykkos Monastery is ornately decorated and covered in a silver gilt, enclosed in a tortoiseshell shrine. It is also famous for its museum, located within the monastery grounds, which houses an impressive collection of icons, woodcarvings and manuscripts, and other Cypriot antiquities. The nearby *Troodos Mountains*, with magnificent hills and valleys, should also be explored as they are home to nine Byzantine churches, included on UNESCO's World Heritage List, and richly decorated with murals and Byzantine paintings.

Transportation
Air: Paphos International Airport. **Road:** Car: Road to Pedoulas which leads to Kykkos (from Troodos); road north towards Platres, past Pedoulas to Kykkos (from Limassol); towards Limassol, then northeast past Kedares to Platres (from Paphos). The monastery is well-signposted.

Contact Addresses
Kykkos Monastery, PO Box 24850, 1304 Nicosia, Cyprus
Tel: (02) 942 736 (museum) *or* 590 768 (office)
Website: www.kykkos-museum.cy.net

Paphos (Pafos)

The town of *Paphos* is famed for being the birthplace of Aphrodite (the Goddess of Love) and home to *Aphrodite's Rock* (Petra Toy Romiou), which was erected by the Myceneans in the 12th century BC. The town also boasts majestic landscapes, lovely coastline, as well as numerous historic sites including the beautiful *Mosaics of Paphos*, the *Tombs of the Kings*, the *Medieval Fort*, the *Paphos District Archaelogical Museum*, the *Byzantine Museum* and the *Ethnographical Museum*. The impressive second century *Odeon*, which was rediscovered in 1973, the 12th-century *Saranta Kolones Castle*, which was built by the Lusignans but virtually destroyed by an earthquake in 1222, and the fifth-century *Panagia Limeniotissa Basilica* are all also worth a visit for their architectural and historical importance.

Transportation

Air: Paphos International Airport. **Road:** Car: Coastal road east to Paphos (from Limassol); coastal road south to Paphos (from the Polis region); road southwest, past Platres and Kedares. Then join coast road east from Limassol (from Troodos).

Contact Addresses

Pafos Chamber of Commerce and Industry (PCCI), 7 Athinon Avenue and Alexandrou Papagou Corner, Tolmi Court, First Floor, Office 101-102, Pafos 8100, Cyprus
Tel: (00357) 269 35115
Website: www.ccci.org.cy

Paphos Odeon

Cyprus Tourism Organisation©

Czech Republic

1 Charles Bridge (Karluv Most)
2 Kutná Hora
3 Old Town Square (Staromestskee namesti)
4 Prague Castle and St Vitus Cathedral

Tourist Information

**Czech Tourist Authority
(Ceská centrála cestovního ruchu)**
Vinohradská 46, PO Box 32,
120 41 Prague 2, Czech Republic
Tel: (02) 2158 0611
Website: www.visitczechia.cz

Czech Tourist Authority
2nd floor, Morley House, 320 Regent Street,
London W1B 3BG
Tel: (020) 7631 0427
Website: www.visitczechia.cz

Charles Bridge (Karluv Most)

The *Charles Bridge* is Prague's most familiar
monument. Built in 1357, this 520m-long bridge
(1770ft) was the only connection between the
two halves of Prague for 400 years. Originally,

the bridge was bare of ornamentation except for
one solitary cross; however, as the Counter
Reformation took hold in Bohemia, the bridge
eventually gained over 30 Baroque statues. The
earliest, erected in 1683, is a bronze statue of
martyr St John of Nepomuk who was thrown off
the bridge. Craft stalls and buskers along the
bridge add to the atmosphere and make it a
popular meeting place.

Transportation
Air: Praha Ruzyně International Airport. **Rail:**
Train: Hlavní nádraží Station (Prague Station).
Underground: Staromestská. Tram: From Karlovy
Lazne. **Road:** Bus: From Staromestská. Coach:
Praha-Florenc Coach Station. Car: E48, E50, E55
or E67 towards Prague.

Contact Addresses
Prague Information Service, Betlémské námìstí 2,
116 98 Prague 1, Czech Republic
Tel: (02) 12444
Website: www.prague-info.cz

Kutná Hora

Kutná Hora once rivalled Prague and even
London in terms of size and importance. The
discovery of silver ore here in the 14th century
led to the creation of the Royal Mint and the
town became the political, cultural and
economic centre of Bohemia. The legacy of this
glorious epoch can be seen in the fine Gothic
and Italianate buildings that line the cobbled
streets. The most famous of all is the
magnificent *St Barbara's Cathedral*, built between
1388-1565 by the town's miners (St Barbara is
the patron saint of miners) to rival St Vitus'
Cathedral in Prague. Visitors with a taste for the
macabre should pay a visit to the monastic
church at nearby *Sedlec*, the interior of which is
made entirely of human bones.

Transportation
Air: Praha Ruzynì International Airport. **Rail:**
Train: Kutná Hora Mesto Station. (From Prague,

change at Kolin for Kutná Hora). **Road:** Coach: Kutná Hora Lorecka Bus Station (from Prague Florenc Coach Station). Car: Road to Kolin, then follow signposts for Kutná Hora (from Prague).

Contact Addresses
Information Center, Sankturinovsky dum, Falackého námestí 377 284 01, Kutna Hora, Czech Republic
Tel: (327) 512 378
Website: www.kutnahora.cz

Old Town Square (Staromestské námestí)

Prague's picture-book *Old Town Square*, with its colourful facades and cobbled surface, is perhaps one of the most familiar tourist scenes of Central Europe. Although many of the facades are Baroque in style, the houses actually date from Medieval times when the square was the centre of the Bohemian world, and a meeting place for merchants and traders from across Europe. The square is home to many of Prague's best-loved attractions but perhaps the most famous is the *Astronomical Clock* on the *Town Hall (Staroměstská radnice)* which dates from the 14th century. Much of the original structure was destroyed when the Nazis set fire to it in May 1945 during the Prague Uprising.

Transportation
Air: Prague Ruzyně International Airport. **Rail:** Train: Hlavní nádraží Station (Prague Station). Underground: Staromìstská or Mùstek. **Road:** Bus: Regular public services. Car: E55 (from Dresden/Berlin); E67 (from Warsaw/Wroclaw) or E50 (from Paris). Visitors should note that the historic centre of Prague is pedestrianised.

Contact Addresses
Prague Information Service,
Betlémské námestí 2,
116 98 Prague 1,
Czech Republic
Tel: (224) 371 111
Website: www.prague-info.cz

Charles Bridge

Czech Tourist Authority©

Prague Castle and St Vitus Cathedral (Prazsky Hrad and Katedrála sv Vita)

The reaching spires of *Prague Castle*, the seat of Bohemian government for a thousand years, can be seen from virtually anywhere in Prague. It is actually more of a complex than a castle, covering 45 hectares (110 acres) and comprising three courtyards, fortifications and gardens. Its most famous attraction is the Gothic *St Vitus Cathedral*, the country's largest church, which was begun in 1344 under Charles IV but not completed until 1929, and is much loved for its stained glass. *St Wenceslas' Chapel* contains the tomb of the country's most famous patron saint and a cycle of paintings depicting scenes from his life.

Transportation
Air: Praha Ruzyně International Airport. **Rail:** Train: Hlavní nádraží Station (Prague Station) or Praha-Holesovice Station (for some international express trains). Tram: To Prazsky Hrad. **Road:** Coach: Praha-Florenc Coach Station.

Contact Addresses
Prazsky Hrad, 11908 Prague 1, Czech Republic
Tel: (02) 2437 3368
Website: www.hrad.cz

Denmark

200km
100mls
✈ international airport

NORWAY

Skagerrak

Grenen

Frederikshavn

Laesø

Kattegat

Mors

Aalborg

① SWEDEN

Viborg

DENMARK

Århus

Elsinore • Helsingborg

Jutland Samsø

COPENHAGEN

Legoland ① Billund

Esbjerg

Roskilde

Zealand

Malmö

Odense •

Fyn

Nyborg

Rønne •
Bornholm

NORTH SEA

② Als

Møn

Lolland Falster

Rügen

Kiel •

③
④ • Rostock

GERMANY

1 Kronborg Castle (Kronborg Slot)
2 Legoland
3 Little Mermaid (Lille Havfrue)
4 Tivoli

Tourist Information

Danish Tourist Board (Danmarks Turistråd)
Vesterbrogade 6 D, DK-1620 Copenhagen V,
Denmark
Tel: 3311 1415
Website: www.dt.dk *or* www.visitdenmark.com

Danish Tourist Board
55 Sloane Street, London SW1X 9SY, UK
Tel: (020) 7259 5959

Kronborg Castle (Kronborg Slot)

Strategically located on a site overlooking the
Sound, the stretch of water between Denmark and
Sweden, *Kronborg Castle* at Helsingør (Elsinore) is of
great historical importance playing a key role in the
history of Northern Europe during the 16th to 18th
centuries. Work began on the castle in 1574, with its
defences being reinforced in the late 17th century.
Kronborg, which is one of the most important
Renaissance castles in Northern Europe, is also
famous for being the setting for William
Shakespeare's play *Hamlet* (the Prince of Denmark)
and has staged many performances of the play over
the centuries. Most of the rooms and fortifications in
and around the castle are open to the public, along
with the *Danish Maritime Museum*, which is home to
many temporary and permanent exhibitions.

Transportation
Air: Copenhagen Airport. **Rail:** Train: Elsinore
Station or Grønnehave Station. The castle is
approximately 15 minute's walk from Elsinore
Station. **Road:** Bus: Public services.

Contact Addresses
Kronborg Castle, Kronborg 2c, 3000 Elsinore,
Denmark
Tel: 4921 3078
Website: www.ses.dk/kronborgcastle

Legoland

The renowned 10-hectare (25-acre) amusement
park located north of Billund features attractions
and rides built from no less than 40 million
plastic LEGO blocks. Shows are performed daily
by the Children's Theatre, and there are also circus
acts in high season. Adults and children can
marvel at the detailed LEGO reconstructions of
famous sights from around the world in *Miniland*;
Duplo Land, with its chunkier bricks, is particularly
popular with younger children. Other popular
attractions include *Pirateland* and *Castleland*. The
sophisticated *Port of Copenhagen* exhibit, featuring
electronically controlled trains, cranes and ships,
is also popular. The *Falck Fire Brigade* was a new
attraction added in 2005.

Transportation
Air: Billund International Airport. **Rail:** Train:
Vejle, Kolding or Fredericia stations. **Road:** Bus:

Regular public services. Car: A7/E-45 (exit 63), then route 441 and route 28 (from the south); E-45 (exit 60), then route 28 (from the north); E-20 (exit 61), then route 18 and route 28 (from Copenhagen).

Contact Addresses
Legoland A/S, Nordmarksvej 9, DK-7190 Billund, Denmark
Tel: 7533 1333
Website: www.lego.com

Little Mermaid (Lille Havfrue)

Denmark's most famous cultural symbol comes from a tale told by its most renowned poet, Hans Christian Andersen. In his story the youngest daughter of the Sea King rescues a drowning prince and falls in love, but in the end gets turned into sea foam. The idea for the statue originated in 1909 when brewer Carl Jacobsen saw the ballet version of the *Little Mermaid* and was so impressed that he commissioned sculptor Edvard Eriksen to create a bronze statue on Copenhagen's waterfront. Eriksen modelled the mermaid on his wife and she is now Copenhagen's most famous symbol as she stares dreamily across the water from *Langelinie*.

Transportation
Air: Copenhagen Airport. **Rail:** Train: Copenhagen Central Station or S-Bahn to Østerport. **Road:** Bus: Public services. Car: Signs to København harbour and Langelinie waterfront, then Lille Havfrue.

Contact Addresses
Wonderful Copenhagen Tourist Information, Copenhagen Right Now, Vesterbrogade 4A, 1620 Kobenhavn V
Tel: 7022 2442
Website: www.visitcopenhagen.dk

Tivoli

Opened in 1843 as a theme park and public garden, *Tivoli Gardens* has outlasted the great parks of Europe that were its inspiration – the Tivoli in Paris and Vauxhall Gardens in London. Tivoli Gardens still retains a flavour of that era, seeming more like an open-air garden than it does a theme park. However, there are plenty of rides including the *Golden Tower*, *Valhalla Castle*, a *Ferris Wheel* and a roller coaster. The less daring can enjoy the many concerts, circus acts, and theatrical performances that also find a home at Tivoli. The famous *Copenhagen Christmas market* is held here in November and December, making this a particularly atmospheric time to visit.

Transportation
Air: Copenhagen Airport. **Rail:** Train: Copenhagen Central Station or S-Bahn to København H. **Road:** Bus: Services to Town Hall Square. Car: Signs to the city centre and the Town Hall.

Contact Addresses
Tivoli, Vesterbrogade 3, DK 1631 Copenhagen V, Denmark
Tel: 3315 1001
Website: www.tivolidk.com

The main entrance at Tivoli

Danish Tourist Board/Ireneusz Cyranek©

Dominica (Commonwealth of)

20km
10mls

✈ international airport

Cape Capucin

Cabrits
Peninsula
Prince
Rupert Bay ● **Portsmouth**

Melville Hall ✈
Marigot

Morne Diablotin
Colihaut ● △1447m

Carib
Reserve

DOMINICA

ATLANTIC OCEAN

St Joseph ● Layou

Morne
Trois Pitons
1387m △ Rosalie ●

Canefield

■ **ROSEAU**

CARIBBEAN
SEA

Soufrière ●
Soufrière Bay Grand
Bay
Scotts Head

---

1 Morne Trois Pitons National Park

Morne Trois Pitons National Park

The *Morne Trois Pitons National Park* encompasses 69 sq km (27 sq miles) of varied landscape – lush tropicana and rainforests contrast starkly with volcanic terrain characterised by deep valleys and bubbling pools. The park was created in 1975 and is centred around the *Morne Trois Pitons* (meaning 'mountain of three peaks'), a triple-spiked mountain formed from volcanic remains, which rises to 1342m (3681ft) above sea level. The *Valley of Desolation* is a barren area of volcanic rock which contains over 50 fumaroles (geysers) emitting sulphurous gases and steam. One of the most beautiful sites in the park is the *Emerald Pool*, a waterfall grotto located against a backdrop of tropical plants and flowers.

Transportation
Air: Melville Hall Airport.
Road: Bus: Regular public services. Car: Imperial Road to *Emerald Pool* (from Roseau); Trafalgar Road, then Laudat Road to *Trafalgar Falls* (from Roseau); Valley Road to *Freshwater Lake* or *Boiling Lake* (from Roseau).

Contact Addresses
Morne Trois Pitons National Park, Forestry, Wildlife and Parks Division, Botanical Gardens, Roseau, 10017 Commonwealth of Dominica
Tel: 448 2401

🅿 ✖ 👜 🏛 £ ❦

Morne Trois Pitons National Park

Dominica Division of Tourism, UK office©

Tourist Information

National Development Corporation (NDC) – Division of Tourism
PO Box 293, Valley Road, Roseau, Commonwealth of Dominica
Tel: 448 2045
Website: www.dominica.dm

Dominica Tourist Office
MKI Ltd, Mitre House, 66 Abbey Road, Bush Hill Park, Enfield, Middlesex EN1 2QE, UK
Tel: (020) 8350 1004

Key to symbols: £ Entry charged & Disabled access
🎦 Man-made attraction ❦ Natural attraction
🅿 Parking ✖ Restaurant 👜 Shop 🏛 UNESCO site

Ecuador

Tourist Information

Ministry of Tourism (Ministerio de Turismo)
Avenida Eloy Alfaro N32-300 and
Carlos Tobar, Quito, Ecuador
Tel: (02) 250 7555/9
Website: www.vivecuador.com

Embassy of the Republic of Ecuador
Flat 3B, 3 Hans Crescent,
London SW1X 0LS, UK
Tel: (020) 7584 2648

---

1 Galapagos Islands (Islas Galapagos)

Galapagos Islands (Islas Galapagos)

Straddling the Equator 1000km (622 miles) off the coast of Ecuador, the *Galapagos Islands* are famous for being the inspiration for Charles Darwin's theory of evolution. There are 13 large islands and six small, which were formed by oceanic volcanoes some three to five million years ago. Visitors come to the islands to see the unparalleled variety of wildlife that flourishes due to the remote location and temperate climate. The most famous residents are the giant tortoises after whom the islands are named, although other common species include iguana, dolphins, boobies and cormorants. The animals are so used to human company visitors can even swim with penguins and sea lions. Snorkelling and sailing are also popular.

Transportation
Air: Baltra Airport.

Contact Addresses
Galapagos National Park Service, Puerto Ayora,
Santa Cruz, Galapagos, Ecuador
Tel: (05) 526 189
or
CAPTURGAL, Galapagos Chamber of Tourism,
Puerto Ayora, Santa Cruz, Galapagos, Ecuador
Tel: (05) 526 206
Website: www.galapagostour.org

Galapagos Islands

Metropolitan Touring©

Egypt

400km
200mls
✈ international airport

Crete

MEDITERRANEAN SEA

2

Nile Delta PALESTINE
Mersa Matruh • **Alexandria** Port Said
El Alamein • ∴Abu Mena • Tanta | Suez Canal JORDAN ISRAEL
Qattara Depression -133m ▽ **Giza** ■**CAIRO**
• Siwa Giza Pyramids & Sphinx *Sinai*
5 El Ras Tur *Gulf of Aqaba* SAUDI ARABIA
Minia • Gharib •
E G Y P T Asyut • Hurghada • *Ras Muhammad*
Thebes & Valley of the Kings • Karnak *R E D S E A*
El Kharga • Luxor •
The Great Oasis Edfu • **4**
S A H A R A **3** • Aswan
dam • Philae
Tropic of Cancer **6** *Lake Nasser*
Abu Simbel • Admin. bndy.
1 Halaib •
SUDAN Political bndy.

LIBYA

1 Abu Simbel
2 Egyptian Antiquities Museum (El Mathas El Massry)
3 Hatshepsut's Temple (Deir el-Bahri)
4 Karnak Temple (Ipet-Isut)
5 Pyramids at Giza and the Sphinx (Ahramat Al-Jizah and Abu el-Hol)
6 Valley of the Kings and Valley of the Queens (Biban-el-Melouk and Biban-el-Harem)

Tourist Information

Ministry of Tourism (Wezarit El Suaha)
Misr Travel Tower, Abassiya Square, 11381
Cairo, Egypt
Tel: (202) 6845828/4870802

Egyptian State Tourist Office
Egyptian House, Third Floor, 170 Piccadilly,
London W1V 9DD, UK
Tel: (020) 7493 5283 or (09001) 600 299 (24-hour
brochure service: calls cost 60p per minute)
Website: www.egyptnow.com/english

Abu Simbel

One of the most famous ancient Egyptian sites, the two temples of *Abu Simbel* were carved out of sandstone cliffs high above the River Nile in 1257BC, under the orders of Pharaoh Ramses II (1304-1237BC). The most famous of the two features four colossal 20m-high (65ft) statues of Ramses II flanking the entrance, although they are actually dedicated to the sun god Re-Herakhte. The temples, which were rediscovered by the Swiss explorer Burckhardt in 1813, withstood the passage of time until the construction of the Nasser Dam in 1970, which caused the waters of Lake Nasser to rise significantly. With the support of UNESCO, an international appeal was launched and the temples were gradually relocated to a higher elevation over a four-year period between 1964 and 1968.

Transportation
Air: Luxor International Airport. Internal flights are available to Aswan International Airport and Abu Simbel Airport. **Water:** Boat: Cruise boats and feluccas take visitors to the site. **Road:** Bus: Public services leave from Aswan.

Contact Addresses
For more information on Abu Simbel, contact the Ministry of Tourism (see **Tourist Information** above).

Egyptian Antiquities Museum (El Mathas El Massry)

The 107 halls of the *Egyptian Antiquities Museum* in Cairo were built in 1900 by the French architect Marcel Dourgnon and opened in 1902. The collection itself dates back to 1835, however, when the *Service des Antiques de l'Egypte* (Egyptian Antiquities Service) was set up to protect government-owned artefacts and put a halt to the raiding of archaeological sites. Today, the museum houses a number of ancient Egypt's greatest artefacts, with by far the most popular being the treasures from Tutankhamun's tomb, which include the boy-king's famous golden facemask, as well as approximately 1700 other objects. The museum exhibits around 120,000 objects in total.

Transportation
Air: Cairo International Airport. **Train:** Rail: Ramses Station. Underground: Sadat (Tahrir) Station. **Road:** Bus: Abdel Mouneem Riyad Bus Terminal. Car: Delta Road or Alexandria Desert Road to Cairo (from Alexandria).

Contact Addresses
Tahrir Square, Cairo 11557, Egypt
Tel: (02) 579 6974
Website: www.egyptianmuseum.gov.eg

Hatshepsut's Temple (Deir el-Bahri)

Hatshepsut's Temple is the mortuary temple of Queen Hatshepsut. Located on the West Bank in Luxor, this spectacular temple was built by the Queen's architect, Senenmut, in honour of the only woman ever to reign over Egypt as Pharaoh. Set against towering cliffs in the *Theban Hills*, this unique temple attracts bus loads of tourists every day to see one of the most impressive sites in the *Necropolis*. The temple, with its many monumental ramps, fine terraces, elegant columns and hieroglyphic paintings, also tells the story of Hatshepsut's journey to the *Land of Punt* (which is believed to be modern-day Somalia) to bring back treasures such as ebony, ivory, gold, perfumes and myrrh trees.

Transportation
Air: Luxor International Airport. **Water:** Ferry: A tourist ferry leaves from the East Bank to take passengers across the River Nile. Motor boats can also be hired. **Road:** Coach: The majority of tourists visit the temple as part of an organised coach tour. Taxi: Taxis are available to take visitors to the temple and can be hired on arrival on the West Bank.

Contact Addresses
Luxor Tourist Office, Nile Sreet, Luxor, Egypt
Tel: (095) 382 215 *or* 373 294
Website: www.luxorguide.com

Karnak Temple (Ipet-Isut)

Karnak Temple is a vast complex consisting of three main temples, several smaller enclosed temples, and a number of outer temples. The most spectacular of these is the *Temple of Amun* (*Amun's Precinct*). This is entered via the *Avenue of the Sphinxes* that once connected Karnak and *Luxor Temples*, and led through the ancient city of Thebes, the capital of Egypt during the period of the Middle and New Kingdoms. The whole complex was built over a period of 1300 years and includes several of the finest examples of ancient Egyptian design and architecture. Among them are the *Hypostyle Hall*, considered one of the world's great architectural achievements with around 130 enormous carved columns covering an area of 6000 sq m (64,586 sq ft), and the *Obelisk of Thutmose I*, a 22m (71ft) monument, the only one of four original obelisks that is still standing.

Transportation
Air: Luxor International Airport. **Rail:** Train: Luxor Station. **Road:** Coach: The vast majority of tourists visit the temple as part of an organised coach tour. Bus: Luxor Bus Station. Taxis: Taxis can be hired from the centre of Luxor; alternatively visitors can travel by *caleche* (horse and cart).

Contact Addresses
Luxor Tourist Office, Nile St, Luxor, Egypt
Tel: (095) 382 215 *or* 373 294
Website: www.luxorguide.com

Pyramids at Giza & the Sphinx (Ahramat Al-Jizah & Abu el-Hol)

The *Pyramids* at Giza are among the best-known ancient monuments in the world and the only one of the Seven Wonders of the ancient world still standing. Of the three pyramids, the *Pyramid of Chephren*, which is sometimes known as the *Second Pyramid*, is the most famous due to its imposing size, with its base once covering an area of 216 sq m (2325 sq ft). The famous *Sphinx* stands in front of the Great Pyramid, with the body of a lion joined to the head of a man. There is a Sound and Light show every night at Giza which adds to the atmosphere surrounding these mysterious ancient sights.

Transportation
Air: Cairo International Airport. **Rail:** Train: Ramses Station. **Road:** Bus: From Midan Tahrir. Public buses also run from Ahmed Helmi Bus Station. Taxi: Many visitors take a taxi from Cairo city centre. Car: Sharia al-Ahram (Pyramids Road) (from Cairo city centre).

Contact Addresses
For more information on the Pyramids at Giza and the Sphinx, contact the Ministry of Tourism (see **Tourist Information** above).

Valley of the Kings and Valley of the Queens (Biban-el-Melouk and Biban-el-Harem)

The *Valley of the Kings* is a limestone valley situated in the Theban Hills where the mummified bodies of many Egyptian pharaohs were interred. The area marks a period in ancient Egyptian history in which the pharaohs abandoned the pyramid style and chose instead tombs dug within limestone in order to preserve the mummies for eternity and prevent grave robbing. The tombs, although stripped of many of their contents centuries ago, still display fantastic wall paintings depicting the lives of the pharaohs in ancient Egypt, down to the minutest detail. The most famous tomb is that of Tutankhamun, discovered in pristine condition by Howard Carter in 1922. The many treasures found in the tomb are now exhibited in the *Egyptian Antiquities Museum* in Cairo. Nearby, the wall paintings in the tombs of the *Valley of the Queens* and the *Valley of the Nobles* are equally fascinating. The most famous tomb in the Valley of the Queens is the *Tomb of Queen Nefertari*, the principal wife of Ramses II, which was only opened to the public in 1995.

Transportation
Air: Luxor International Airport. **Water:** Ferry: A tourist ferry leaves from the East Bank to take passengers across the River Nile. Motor boats can also be hired. **Road:** Coach: The majority of tourists visit the temple as part of an organised coach tour. Taxi: Taxis are available to take visitors to the temple and can be hired on arrival on the West Bank. Bicycle: Bicycles can be hired in Luxor.

Contact Addresses
Luxor Tourist Office, Nile St, Luxor, Egypt
Tel: (095) 382 215 *or* 373 294
Website: www.luxorguide.com

The famous Sphinx, with the body of a lion and the head of a man

Corel©

Estonia

1 Kadriorg Palace and Park
2 Tallinn Town Hall Square (Raekoja Plats)

Tourist Information

Eesti Turismiagentuur (Estonian Tourist Board)
Roosikrantsi 11, Tallinn 10119, Estonia
Tel: (06) 279 770
Website: www.visitestonia.com

Embassy of the Republic of Estonia
16 Hyde Park Gate, London SW7 5DG, UK
Tel: (020) 7589 3428
Website: www.estonia.gov.uk

Kadriorg Palace and Park

The Russian Tsar Peter I began building *Kadriorg Palace and Park* in 1718 in honour of the empress Catherine I. Designed by the Italian architect Niccolo Michetti, the building was inspired by Italian villas and stands as one of the finest examples of Baroque architecture in Northern Europe. By 1921 the palace had become home to the *Estonian Museum of Tallinn* which later became the *Art Museum of Estonia* in

1928. The *Kadriorg Park* was originally 100 hectares (247 acres) and consists of beautiful landscaped gardens, the *Flower Garden* and the popular *Swan Lake*.

Transportation
Air: Tallinn Airport. **Rail:** Tallinn Station. **Road:** Bus: Public services.

Contact Addresses
Kadriorg Palace, 37 Weizenbergi Street, 10127 Tallinn, Estonia
Tel: (06) 066 400
Website: www.ekm.ee/kadriorg

Tallinn Town Hall Square (Raekoja Plats)

With its colourful buildings, turreted walls and gabled roofs, Tallinn is one of the best-preserved historic centres in Europe. All the winding cobbled streets lead on to the *Raekoja plats* (Town Hall Square), which is dominated by the imposing façade of the *Raekoda*, or Town Hall. The building was constructed in the 14th and 15th centuries and is the only surviving late Gothic town hall in Northern Europe. Its soaring steeple bears a 16th-century weather vane portraying the medieval warrior, 'Old Thomas', guardian of the city. Open-air concerts are held here in summer and its many cafés, bars and restaurants make it a bustling meeting place for both tourists and Tallinners alike.

Transportation
Air: Tallinn Airport. **Water:** Ferry: Reisisadam Sea Port (Tallinn). **Rail:** Train: Balti jaam Station. **Road:** Coach: Autobussijaam (Tallinn Bus Station).

Contact Addresses
The Tallinn Tourist Information Centre, Niguliste 2/ Kullassepa 4, Tallin 10146, Estonia
Tel: (06) 457 777
Website: www.tourism.tallinn.ee

Finland

ARCTIC OCEAN
North Cape
BARENTS SEA
NORWAY
Lake Inari
LAPLAND
Sodankyla
Arctic Circle
Rovaniemi
Tornio
Oulu
Lake Oulu
FINLAND
SWEDEN
KARELIA
Vaasa
Kuopio
Joensuu
Jyväskylä
Lake Saimaa
Pori
Tampere
Lake Päijänne
Hämeenlinna
Lahti
Lake Ladoga
Turku
HELSINKI
Åland Is.
Gulf of Finland
St Petersburg
BALTIC SEA
ESTONIA
RUSSIAN FEDERATION
Gulf of Bothnia
Muonio

400km
200mls
international airport

1 Linnanmäki Amusement Park
2 Suomenlinna Sea Fortress (Suomenlinna Sveaborg)

Linnanmäki Amusement Park

Founded in 1950, *Linnanmäki* amusement park is one of the most popular tourist attractions in Finland. This giant theme park was opened by six Finnish child welfare organisations to promote children's events in the country. The *Children's Day Foundation* was set up by these six charities with responsibility for managing the park in 1956. This is still the case today and all profits are donated to charity. Rides include a *Wooden Roller Coaster* which was built in 1951, the *Space Express* roller coaster and the *Space Shot* adventure ride. A *Toy and Play Museum* opened in 1996.

Tourist Information

Finnish Tourist Board (Matkailun Edistämiskeskus)
Head Office: Töölönkatu 11, PO Box 625, 00101 Helsinki, Finland
Tel: (09) 417 6911
Website: www.mek.fi
Eteläesplanadi 4, PO Box 249, 00131 Helsinki, Finland
Tel (09) 4176 9300 *or* 4176 9211
Website: www.visitfinland.com

Finnish Tourist Board
PO Box 33213, London W6 8JX, UK
Tel: (020) 7365 2512 (information and brochures only) *or* (020) 8600 5680 (trade and press only)
Website: www.finland-tourism.com *or* www.mek.fi

The wooden rollercoaster at Linnanmäki Amusement Park

Linnanmäki Amusement Park©

Suomenlinna Sea Fortress

The maritime barracks at Suomenlinna

Transportation

Air: Helsinki-Vantaa Airport. **Rail:** Tram: 3T (from Mannerheimintie). **Road:** Bus: Public services from Helsinki city centre.

Contact Addresses

Linnanmäki, Tivolikuja 1, 00510 Helsinki, Finland
Tel: (09) 773 991
Website: www.linnanmaki.fi

Suomenlinna Sea Fortress (Suomenlinna Sveaborg)

Suomenlinna Sea Fortress was built over 250 years ago and once had a population of 4600, larger than the population of Helsinki at the time. Construction began off the coast of Helsinki in 1748, when Finland was part of the Swedish Empire and the Swedes built a fortress on the islands as a counter to the increasing Russian naval strength in Kronstadt. In 1808, the fortress surrendered to the Russians, with Finland becoming part of the Russian empire. The fortress was originally called *Sveaborg*

(literally, 'Sweden's Fortress'), but was renamed *Suomelinna* ('Finland's Fortress') in 1918, one year after Finland finally gained independence from Russia. Today, the fortress is an integral part of the city and home to around 900 inhabitants. There are a variety of attractions on the islands, including guided walks, the *Suomenlinna Museum* (with the *Suomenlinna Experience* multi-media show), the *Ehrensvärd Museum*, the *Doll and Toy Museum*, the *Manege Military Museum*, *Submarine Vesikko*, the *Coast Artillery Museum* and the *Customs Museum*.

Transportation

Air: Helsinki-Vantaa Airport. **Water:** Ferry: Ferries leave from the eastern edge of the main market square, Kauppatori. Waterbuses also operate in summer and leave from their own jetty at Market Square.

Contact Addresses

Suomenlinna Tourist Information, Visitor Centre, Suomenlinna C74, 00190 Helsinki, Finland
Tel: (09) 684 1880
Website: www.suomenlinna.fi

France

400km
200mls
↑ international airport

UNITED
KINGDOM
BELGIUM
Calais
Boulogne
Cherbourg
Dieppe **Lille**
Le Havre Amiens
St-Malo Chartres ■**PARIS**
Fontainebleau
Nantes Tours
Chartres
Nancy
LUX. GERMANY
Strasbourg
Dijon
SWITZ.
Limoges
Lyon
Grenoble
△*Mont Blanc*
4807m
ITALY
Bay of
Biscay
Bordeaux
Massif
Central
Avignon
Nice MONACO
Côte d'Azur
Cannes
Bayonne
Toulouse
Marseille
ANDORRA
P y r e n e e s
SPAIN
MEDITERRANEAN
SEA Ajaccio
Corsica
F R A N C E
Jura
Rhine
Seine
Loire
Garonne
Rhône
Nantes

1 Arc de Triomphe de l'Étoile
2 Bayeux Tapestry (Tapisserie de Bayeux)
3 Cave of Lascaux (Grotte de Lascaux)
4 Claude Monets House and Water Garden (Maison de Claude Monet et Le Jardin d'eau)
5 D-Day Beaches (Plages du Débarquement de la Bataille de Normandie)
6 Disneyland Resort Paris
7 Eiffel Tower (Tour Eiffel)
8 Louvre (Musée du Louvre)
9 Mont Saint-Michel Abbey (Abbaye du Mont Saint-Michel)
10 Orsay Musuem (Musée d'Orsay)
11 Palace of Versailles (Château de Versailles)
12 Parc Astérix
13 Paris Notre-Dame Cathedral (Cathédrale Notre-Dame de Paris)
14 Popes' Palace (Palais des Papes)
15 Regional Nature Park of the Volcanoes of Auvergne (Parc Naturel Régional des Volcans d'Auvergne)
16 Rocamadour
17 Roman Ampitheatre in Arles (Arénes d'Arles)
18 The Walled Town of Carcassonne (Cité de Carcassonne)

Tourist Information

Maison de la France (French Tourist Office)
20 avenue de l'Opéra, 75041 Paris, Cedex 01, France
Tel: (01) 4296 7000
Website: www.franceguide.com

French Tourist Office
178 Piccadilly, London W1V 0AL, UK
Tel: (09068) 244 123 (information line; calls cost 60p per minute)
Website: www.franceguide.com

Arc de Triomphe de l'Étoile

Commissioned by Napoleon to commemorate the victorious French Army, the *Arc de Triomphe* has been a defining symbol of Paris ever since completion in 1836. Engraved on the arch are numerous names of important and not so important victories and beneath it lies the *Tomb of the Unknown Soldier*. Visitors can reach the 50m-tall (164ft-) top of the arch for stunning views of Paris, including the *Louvre* and the *Champs-Elysées*, or tour the museum inside which charts the history and construction of the arch. The Champs-Elysées is considered to be one of the most elegant boulevards in the world and used to be a showground for Parisian high society. It still retains an air of exclusivity, with luxury boutiques and expensive cafés.

Transportation
Air: Paris Roissy-Charles de Gaulle Airport, Paris Orly Airport. **Rail:** Train: Paris Gare du Nord (Eurostar) Station. Underground: Charles-de-Gaulle-Étoile. RER: Charles-de-Gaulle-Étoile. **Road:** Bus: Regular public services.

Contact Addresses
Centre des monuments nationaux, Arc de
Triomphe de l'Étoile, 75008 Paris, France
Tel: (01) 5537 7377
Website: www.monum.fr

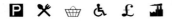

Bayeux Tapestry (Tapisserie de Bayeux)

The *Bayeux Tapestry*, which is one of the most
historically important, and unusual, chronicles of
its day, is now located in the town of Bayeux in
Normandy. The 70m-long (231ft-) tapestry offers
a splendidly vivid depiction of the events leading
up to the Norman Conquest of England in 1066.
It begins with Harold of Wessex's visit to
Normandy and his meeting with Duke William in
1064, and culminates with the flight of the
English army at Hastings. All the main
intervening events are covered in painstaking
detail. Although it was almost destroyed in 1792
when French revolutionaries used it as a wagon
cover, the whole tapestry (with the exception of
the final section, thought to have depicted
William's coronation in Westminster Abbey on
Christmas Day 1066) has survived to this day and
can still be viewed by visitors to the town of
Bayeux.

Transportation
Air: Caen-Carpiquet Airport. **Rail:** Train: Bayeux
Station. **Road:** Bus: Public services. Car: N13, A14,
A13, N413, N175, E46, N13 and D6 (from Paris).

Contact Addresses
Tapisserie de Bayeux, Centre Guillaume le
Conquérant, 13 bis rue de Nesmond, 14400
Bayeux, France
Tel: (02) 3151 2550
Website: www.normandy-tourism.org

Cave of Lascaux (Grotte de Lascaux)

Discovered by chance in 1940 by a group of
teenagers, the cave paintings at Lascaux are
considered to be among the world's best examples
of prehistoric art. The area around Périgueux
features many such cave paintings, although the
15,000-year-old images of bulls, horses and
reindeer are believed to be some of the best. After
the discovery of the cave, the increasing levels of
carbon dioxide emitted by visitors were found to
be damaging the paintings and, as a result, the
caves were sealed in 1963, following an order
from the French Ministry of Cultural Affairs. In
order to compensate for the closure, a precise
cement replica of the original caves, known as
Lascaux II, was opened to the public in 1983;
these caves feature the two most important parts
of the original caves, the *Great Hall of the Bulls*
and the *Painted Gallery*.

Transportation
Air: Périgueux-Basillac Airport. **Rail:** Train:
Condat-Le-Lardin Station. **Road:** Bus: Services to
Périgueux (from Montignac). Car: D901, D31 and
D86 (from Brive-La-Gaillarde) or N21, D705, D4,
D75, D7, D31 and D86 (from Périgueux).

Contact Addresses
Grotte de Lascaux, Semitour Périgord, 25 rue du
Président Wilson, BP 1024, 24001 Périgueux
Cedex, France
Tel: (05) 5335 5010
Website:
www.culture.gouv.fr/culture/arcnat/lascaux/en

Claude Monet's House and Water Garden (Maison de Claude Monet et Le Jardin d'eau)

The Impressionist painter Claude Monet, who was
born in Paris in 1840, spent the latter part of his
life in Giverny in Northern France. Monet
purchased a house in the village in 1883 and
remained there until his death in 1926. Today,
visitors can see the renovated house and wander
around the beautiful gardens at Giverny. Inside
the house, the walls are filled with a collection of
Monet's Japanese prints. Visitors can also see a
beautiful display of waterlilies in the gardens
which greatly inspired the painter and featured in
some of his most famous works.

Transportation
Air: Paris Roissy-Charles de Gaulle Airport. **Rail:** Train: Vernon Station (from St Lazare Station in Paris). **Road:** Bus: Buses from Vernon Station.

Contact Addresses
84 rue de Claude Monet et Le Jardin d'Eau, Fondation Claude Monet, 27620 Giverny, France
Tel: (02) 3251 2821
Website: www.fondation-monet.com

D-Day Beaches (Plages du Débarquement de la Bataille de Normandie)

The Allied Landings that took place at dawn on D-Day, June 6 1944, signalled the beginning of the end of World War II. Some 83,000 British and Canadian and 73,000 US troops landed by sea and air along a 64-km (40-mile) stretch of the Normandy coast in northern France. The horrific conditions, with many of the floating tanks sunk before they even reached the beaches, meant that thousands of soldiers never returned. The war cemeteries where many of the soldiers were laid to rest are open to the public, and some contain chapels and memorials. One of the most famous beaches is Omaha Beach, portrayed in Steven Spielberg's film 'Saving Private Ryan', where there is a large American cemetery overlooking the beach at *Colleville-sur-Mer*.

Transportation
Air: Caen-Carpiquet Airport, Paris Roissy-Charles de Gaulle Airport, Paris Orly Airport. **Water:** Ferry: Services to Cherbourg, Caen and Le Havre (from Ireland and the UK). **Rail:** Train: Caen Station or Bayeux Station (services from Paris St Lazare Station). **Road:** Car: D514 or D513, N158, N13 (to Caen).

Contact Addresses
Comité Régionale de Tourisme de Normandie, 14 rue Charles Corbeau, 27000 Evreux, France
Tel: (02) 3233 7900
Website: www.normandy-tourism.org

Disneyland Resort Paris

Opened in 1992, *Disneyland Paris*, located within the *Disneyland Resort Paris*, was the Walt Disney Company's first attempt to win the hearts of the Europeans. The park is very much like its American cousin, featuring sections like *Mainstreet USA*, *Discoveryland*, *Adventureland*, *Frontierland* and *Fantasyland*, however, enthusiasts rave that the more modern engineering of the French Parks make for a superior experience. Although locals took some time to warm to the park, the resort's success eventually led to Disney opening a second theme park, *Walt Disney Studios Park*, in 2002.

Transportation
Air: Paris Roissy-Charles de Gaulle Airport, Paris Orly Airport; shuttle services are available from both airports to the park. **Rail:** Train: Eurostar, SNCF, Thalys or RER to Marne-la-Vallée/Chessy Station. **Road:** Car: A4, 32km (20 miles) east of Paris (exit 14) (signposted Parcs Disney).

Contact Addresses
Disneyland Paris, Guest Relations, BP100, 77777, Marne la Vallée, Cedex 4, France
Tel: (01) 6030 6053 (in France)
Website: www.disneylandparis.com

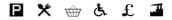

Eiffel Tower (Tour Eiffel)

Originally created as the centrepiece of Paris' *Exposition Universelle* in 1889, in commemoration of the centenary of the French Revolution, the *Eiffel Tower* went on to become the centrepiece of the city itself. The tower that has become symbolic of Paris the world over weighs 10,100 tonnes (990 tons) and contains 18,000 pieces of iron, held together by 2,500,000 rivets. At 324m (888ft) high, it was, until 1929, the tallest structure in the world; although that record was broken many years ago, there are still superb views over Paris from the first floor, which can be reached by a stairway, and even better views from the third floor, which is accessible by lift. The tower was designed by architect Stephen Sauvestre and took 2 years, 2 months and 5 days to build.

Transportation
Air: Paris Roissy-Charles de Gaulle Airport or Paris Orly Airport. **Rail:** Train: Paris Gare du Nord (Eurostar). Underground: Bir-Hakeim, Trocadéro or Ecole Militaire. RER: Champ de Mars-Tour Eiffel. **Road:** Bus: Public services.

Contact Addresses
Tour Eiffel, Champ de Mars, 75007 Paris, France
Tel: (01) 4411 2323
Website: www.tour-eiffel.fr

Louvre (Musée du Louvre)

Constructed as a fortress in the Middle Ages and rebuilt in the mid-16th century as a royal palace, it wasn't until 1793 that the *Louvre* became a museum. Today, it is the home of some of the world's most famous works of art, including the *Mona Lisa* and *Venus de Milo*. The rest of the permanent collection includes Greek, Etruscan, Roman, Egyptian and oriental antiquities, as well as sculptures, *objets d'art* and prints and drawings. Entrance to the museum is through the largest of the three glass pyramids that dominate the courtyard. The huge global success of Dan Brown's novel *The Da Vinci Code*, which opens with the murder of the museum's curator, has swelled visitor numbers as literary pilgrims flock to see the places featured in the novel.

Transportation
Air: Paris Roissy-Charles de Gaulle Airport, Paris Orly Airport. **Rail:** Train: Paris Gare du Nord (Eurostar). Underground: Palais Royal-Musée du Louvre. **Road:** Bus: Regular services. Car: A1 (from Lille); A16 (from Boulogne); E60 (from Brussels); A62, then A20, A71 and A10 (from Toulouse); A3 (from Paris Roissy-Charles de Gaulle Airport); A4 (from Strasbourg); A6 (from Lyon and Marseille) or A13 (from Caen).

Contact Addresses
Musée du Louvre, 75058 Paris Cedex 01, France
Tel: (01) 4020 5151 (recorded information)
Website: www.louvre.fr

Eiffel Tower at dusk

Maison de la France©

Mont Saint-Michel Abbey (Abbaye du Mont Saint-Michel)

Mont Saint-Michel (Saint Michael's Mount) is a rocky island surrounded by perilous waters 1km (0.6 miles) off the coast of Normandy. It was founded in 708 by the Bishop of Avranches who built a chapel there after the Archangel Michael appeared to him in a dream. Construction of the spectacular *Abbaye du Mont Saint-Michel* (Mont Saint-Michel Abbey) started in 1023 and finished some 400 years later. Fashioned from granite, its delicate contours are an extension of the shape of the island and encompass a range of architectural styles, from Norman to Gothic. For centuries, the Abbey was a place of pilgrimage but it has also variously served as a prison, a fortress against the English and a monastery.

Contact Addresses

Abbaye du Mont Saint-Michel, 50116 Le Mont Saint-Michel, France
Tel: (02) 3389 8000
Website: www.monum.fr/m_stmichel/indexa.dml

Transportation

Air: Caen-Carpiquet Airport, Paris Roissy-Charles de Gaulle Airport, Paris Orly Airport. **Water:** Sea: Ferry services from the UK and Ireland to Cherbourg, Caen, Le Havre and Dieppe. **Rail:** Train: Pontorson Railway Station; high-speed TGV services from Paris Gare Montparnasse via Rennes. **Road:** Car: N176 (from St Malo and Avranches) or N175 (from Rennes).

Orsay Museum (Musée d'Orsay)

This magnificently restored railway station houses the French national collection of art from 1848 to 1914. Since opening in 1986, the museum has attracted pilgrims from far and wide who come to take in the stunning collection of Impressionist and Post Impressionist art. Paintings include five Monet canvases of Rouen Cathedral, ballet scenes by Dégas, Courbet's shocking *L'Origine du Monde* (the Origins of the World), a hyperrealistic painting depicting a naked woman lying on her back, and works by Cézanne, Van Gogh, Renoir and Toulouse-Lautrec. The museum's collection also contains several fine sculptures as well as examples from the Art Nouveau movement. The museum works upwards in chronological order, and there is a café on the sky-lit upper level, where views of Paris can be enjoyed from behind the original station clock. The museum's restaurant is a finely decorated dining room, preserved in its original state, and popular with its many visitors.

Contact Addresses

Musée d'Orsay, 62 rue de Lille, 75343 Paris, France
Tel: (01) 4049 4872
Website: www.musee-orsay.fr

Transportation

Air: Paris Roissy-Charles de Gaulle Airport or Paris Orly Airport. **Rail:** Paris Gare du Nord (Eurostar) Station. RER: Musée d'Orsay. Underground: Solférino. **Road:** Bus: Public services. Car: A1 (from Lille); A16 (from Boulogne); E60 (from Brussels); A62, then A20, A71 and A10 (from Toulouse); A3 (from Roissy-Charles de Gaulle Airport); A4 (from Strasbourg); A6 (from Lyon and Marseille) or A13 (from Caen).

Palace of Versailles (Château de Versailles)

The *Palace of Versailles* is one of the most visited sites in France and famous for its immense size. The palace began as a 'modest' hunting lodge, built by Louis XIII in 1623, and was transformed by the architect Jules Hardouin Mansart under the guidance of Louis XIII's son, Louis XIV, into a grand palace complex surrounded by lavish gardens designed by André Le Nôtre. Louis XIV was so taken with the palace that by 1682 it had become the official residence of the court of France and a lavish statement of monarchical power. Today, visitors are still able to view much of the palace, including the renowned 75m (250ft) *Galerie des Glaces* (Hall of Mirrors), where the Treaty of Versailles was signed in 1919, signifying the end of World War I.

Transportation

Air: Paris Roissy-Charles de Gaulle Airport or Paris Orly Airport. **Rail:** Train: Versailles-Chantier Station or Versailles-Rive-Droite Station. RER:

Versailles-Rive-Gauche Station on line C. **Road:** Bus: Public services to Versailles-Place d'Armes. Car: A13 towards Rouen, first exit signposted Versailles-Château.

Contact Addresses
Château de Versailles, RP 834, 78008 Versailles, France
Tel: (01) 3083 7800
Website: www.chateauversailles.fr

Parc Astérix

Opened in 1989, *Parc Astérix* is a giant theme park based on the adventures of the popular cartoon character, Astérix. Located in the heart of protected forest, north of Paris, the park takes visitors on a humorous journey through ancient Gaul, the Roman Empire and the Middle Ages to the 21st century. Visitors can meet the Gauls of prehistoric times, step back in time to Le Moyen-Âge (the Middle Ages), travel through Rome and Ancient Greece, and shake hands with the Three Musketeers. There are around 30 permanent rides at the park, as well as regular shows to entertain visitors.

Transportation
Air: Paris Roissy-Charles de Gaulle Airport. **Rail:** Train: Roissy-Charles de Gaulle 2 TGV Station, then bus to Parc Astérix. Underground: Roissy-Charles de Gaulle 1, then bus to Parc Astérix. **Road:** Bus: Public services. Car: A1 Paris–Lille motorway, 35km (22 miles) north of Paris (exit 7-8) (signposted Parc Astérix).

Contact Addresses
Parc Astérix, BP8, 60128, Plailly, France
Tel: (03) 4462 3404 *or* 4462 3030
Website: www.parcasterix.com

Paris Notre-Dame Cathedral (Cathédrale Notre-Dame de Paris)

Begun in 1163 by the architect Maurice de Sully and completed in about 1345, *Notre Dame* ranks as one of France's finest examples of Gothic architecture. During its long life, besides being a resplendent medieval cathedral, Notre Dame was reportedly set on fire during the Commune of 1871, when the Communards rose against the French government in the wake of their defeat during the Franco-Prussian war and was also used to house livestock. It has also been the site of many historical events, including the crowning of Henry VI of England in 1430 and the marriage of the Catholic Marguerite de Valois to the Huguenot (Protestant) Henri of Navarre in 1572, which sparked the St Bartholomew's Day Massacre during the French Wars of Religion. Today, the cathedral still awes visitors with its massive rose windows, its 7800-pipe organ, towering spire and splayed flying buttresses.

Transportation
Air: Paris Roissy-Charles de Gaulle Airport or Paris Orly Airport. **Rail:** RER: Châtelet-Les Halles or St-Michel-Notre-Dame. Underground: Cité. **Road:** Bus: Public services. Car: A1 (from Lille); A4 (from Strasbourg); A16 (from Dunkirk); A13 (from Caen) or A6 (from Lyon). In Paris, from either bank of the River Seine, signs are marked to Ile de la Cité.

Contact Addresses
Cathédrale Notre-Dame de Paris, Ile de la Cité, 6 Place du Parvis, 75004 Paris, France
Tel: (01) 4234 5610
Website: www.cathedraledeparis.com

Paris Notre-Dame Cathedral

Corel©

Popes' Palace (Palais des Papes)

The imposing *Popes' Palace* towers over Avignon and dates back to the time when the Provençal city was the centre of the Christian world after the papacy was moved here from Rome in 1309. Although the papacy moved back to Rome in 1377, Avignon remained the property of the Holy See and was used to house members of the Papacy. Various popes added to the buildings during the Middle Ages, creating the largest Gothic palace in Europe, and today visitors can visit many of the rooms. The *Great Chapel*, also built by Clement VI, is spectacular and is more like a cathedral than a chapel in terms of size. The palace also gave its name to the famous *Châteauneuf-du-Pape* wine, and regular tastings are held in a new wine store located in the heart of the palace.

Transportation
Air: Marseille-Provence Airport. **Rail:** Train: High-speed TGV services to Avignon (from Paris Gare de Lyon, Montpellier, Barcelona and Lyon). **Road:** Car: A7 or A9 (from Lyon, Marseille and Nîmes).

Contact Addresses
Palais des Papes, RMG - 6 rue Pente Rapide Charles Ansidéi, BP 149, 84008 Avignon, Cedex 1, France
Tel: (04) 9027 5074
Website: www.palais-des-papes.com

Regional Nature Park of the Volcanoes of Auvergne (Parc Naturel Régional des Volcans d'Auvergne)

Covering an area of more than 395,000 hectares (976,085 acres), the *Parc Naturel Régional des Volcans d'Auvergne* was created in 1977 and is home to four volcanic massifs: the *Chaîne des Puys* (*Puy de Dôme*, 1465m/4792ft high), *Monts Dore* (*Puy de Sancy*, 1886m/6188ft high), *Monts du Cézalier* (*Signal du Luguet*, 1551m/5089ft high) and *Monts du Cantal* (*Plomb du Cantal*, 1855m/6086 ft high). There are glaciers, lakes and peatland throughout the park, as well as numerous exhibitions of flora, fauna and traditional architecture. Activities include hiking, riding, cycling, hand-gliding and hot-air ballooning. There are numerous other educational centres located within the park.

Transportation
Air: Clermont Ferrand Airport. **Rail:** Train: Clermont Ferrand Station. **Road:** Car: A71 (from Paris); A72 (from Lyon).

Contact Addresses
Regional Nature Park of the Volcanoes of Auvergne Information Centre, Montlosier 63970 Aydat, France
Tel: (04) 7365 6400
Website: www.parc-volcans-auvergne.com

Rocamadour

Built into limestone cliffs, with its medieval houses clinging precariously overlooking the gorge of the River Alzou, *Rocamadour* is a major pilgrimage site. The town is famed for being the site where the body of St Amadour was discovered near the town's chapel in 1166, an event which led to a succession of miracles in the town. Dedicated to the Virgin Mary, the town ranks behind Rome, Jerusalem and Santiago de Compostela as a pilgrimage site. Visitors to the town can climb the *Grand Escalier* (Great Ladder) to the 12th-century *Cité Religeuse* (Religious City) at the top, which consists of seven chapels. Visitors can also climb the *Chemin de Croix* (Way of the Cross) for exceptional views of the Dordogne from the ramparts of the 14th-century château. Other attractions nearby include the *Rocher des Aigles* birds of prey conservation centre, the *Forêt des Singes* monkey sanctuary and the *Grottes de Lacave* underground caves.

Transportation
Air: Bordeaux Airport, Toulouse International Airport. **Rail:** Train: The four levels of the city are connected by a small train and a lift. **Road:** Bus: Public services. Taxis: Available to take visitors from Rocamadour-Padirac Station. Car: Well signposted from all directions. A winding road leads from the village at the base of the hill to the top.

Contact Addresses
Office de Tourisme de Rocamadour, 46500
Rocamadour, France
Tel: (05) 6533 2200
Website: www.rocamadour.com

Roman Amphitheatre in Arles (Arénes d'Arles)

The two-tiered *Roman Amphitheatre* is probably the most prominent tourist attraction in the charming city of Arles, which thrived in Roman times. Measuring 136m (446ft) in length and 109m (358ft) wide, the 120 Romanesque arches date back to the first century BC. The amphitheatre was capable of seating over 20,000 spectators, and was built to provide entertainment in the form of chariot races and bloody hand-to-hand battles. Today, it draws large crowds for a sport only slightly less brutal – bullfighting – as well as plays and concerts in summer.

Transportation
Air: Marseille-Provence Airport. **Rail:** Train: Arles Station. **Road:** Bus: Public services. Car: A54 (exit Arles-Centre).

Contact Addresses
Arènes d'Arles, Rond-Point des
Arènes, 13200 Arles, France
Tel: (04) 9049 3686

The Walled Town of Carcassonne (Cité de Carcassonne)

Set on a hillside allowing extensive views over the *Pyrénées* mountains and the surrounding countryside, the medieval town of *Carcassonne*, which is the largest former fortress in Europe, dates back to the Roman Empire. The ramparts were built during the fourth

century, whilst the château was built during the 12th century by Vicomte Trencavel. Because of its strategic importance, the town was attacked and invaded many times over its history. The town was renovated and restored during the 19th century giving it back some of its former glory and importance. Today, the town, which is beautifully lit up at night, remains an impressive site. The main attractions within the city's walls are the *Château Domtal*, the *Cour du Midi* and the torture chamber at the *Exposition Internationale*.

Transportation
Air: Carcassonne Salvaza Airport. **Water:** Boat: Cruise and leisure boats have moorings along the Canal du Midi just after Carcassonne lock. **Rail:** Train: Carcassonne Station. **Road:** Car: N9, D213, A9, A61 and N113 (from Narbonne) or A620, A61, N161, D118 and N113 (from Toulouse).

Contact Addresses
Cité de Carcassonne, Château Vicomtal, Monument National, 11000 Carcassonne, France
Tel: (04) 6811 7077
Website: www.carcassonne.culture.fr

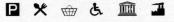

Rocamadour

Corel©

Germany

NORTH SEA · DENMARK · BALTIC SEA · Rügen · Helgoland · Kiel · Rostock · Greifswald · Frisian Islands · Lübeck · Hamburg · Elbe · POLAND · Oder · Bremen · BERLIN · NETHS. · Hanover · Magdeburg · Münster · Harz · Halle · SAXONY · Duisburg · Dortmund · Weser · Essen · Düsseldorf · Kassel · Erfurt · Leipzig · Cologne · Chemnitz · Dresden · Aachen · Bonn · GERMANY · BELG. · Frankfurt-am-Main · Rhine · CZECH REPUBLIC · LUX. · Trier · Main · Saarbrücken · Nuremberg · Stuttgart · FRANCE · Black Forest · Danube · BAVARIA · Munich · L. Constance (Bodensee) · AUSTRIA · SWITZ.

200km
100mls
✈ international airport

1 Brandenburg Gate (Brandenburger Tor)
2 Checkpoint Charlie Museum (Haus am Checkpoint Charlie)
3 Cologne Cathedral (Kölner Dom)
4 English Garden (Englischer Garten)
5 Freiburg Cathedral (Freiburger Kathedrale)
6 German Parliament (Reichstag)
7 Heidelberg Castle (Schloss Heidelberg)
8 Jewish Museum Berlin
9 Munich Residence (Residenz München)
10 Neuschwanstein Castle (Schloss Neuschwanstein)
11 Pergamon Museum
12 Sanssouci Palace (Schloss Sanssouci)

Tourist Information

German National Tourist Office (Deutsche Zentrale für Tourismus)
Beethovenstrasse 69,
60325 Frankfurt/M, Germany
Tel: (069) 974 640
Website: www.germany-tourism.de

German National Tourist Office
PO Box 2695, London W1A 3TN, UK
Tel: (09001) 600 100 (recorded information and brochure request line; calls cost 60p per minute) or (020) 7317 0908 (general enquiries)
Website: www.germany-tourism.de

Brandenburg Gate (Brandenburger Tor)

Built in 1791 as a triumphal arch, the *Brandenburg Gate*, the only remaining town gate in the country, is an enduring symbol of Berlin. The design, by architect Carl Gotthard Langhans, is modelled on the entrance to the Acropolis in Athens, and is crowned by a statue of a horse-drawn chariot, which symbolises Victory. The overall effect was intended to testify to the might and power of the Prussian Empire. It has survived multiple wars, including the long Cold War, during which it was sealed off in no-man's land by the *Berlin Wall*, and became a symbol of division between east and west. In 1989 it was reopened to the public following the destruction of the Berlin Wall.

Transportation
Air: Berlin Tegel Airport. **Rail:** Train: S-Bahn to Unter den Linden. Underground: Friedrichstrasse, Französische Strasse or Mohrenstrasse. **Road:** Bus: Public services (to Pariser Platz).

Contact Addresses
Berlin Tourism Marketing, Am Karlsbad 11, 10785 Berlin, Germany
Tel: (0)30 2500 2424
Website: www.btm.de

Checkpoint Charlie Museum (Haus am Checkpoint Charlie)

Checkpoint Charlie was the monitoring tower used to control the area around the *Berlin Wall* that divided the city during the Cold War. It was demolished soon after the 1989 revolution, but the *Haus am Checkpoint Charlie* museum that stands in its place is well worth a visit to discover the historic significance of this apparently unremarkable site. A cinema shows films on the Third Reich and the Cold War era, and the museum also details the history of the Berlin Wall, a piece of which still stands a short distance from the museum, complete with decorations on the western side.

Transportation
Air: Berlin Tegel Airport, Berlin Schönefeld Airport. **Rail:** Train: Bahnhof Berlin Zoologischer Garten Station or Lehrter Bahnhof Station. Underground: U6 Kochstrasse or U1 Stadtmitte. **Road:** Bus: Public services. Coach: Zentraler Omnibusbahnhof (ZOB) am Funkturm.

Contact Addresses
Haus am Checkpoint Charlie, Friedrichstrasse 43-45, 10969 Berlin–Kreuzberg, Germany
Tel: (030) 253 7250
Website: www.mauer-museum.com

Brandenburg Gate

German National Tourist Board©

Cologne Cathedral (Kölner Dom)

Begun in 1248 and completed in 1880, *Cologne Cathedral* is a celebration of the finest aspects of Gothic architecture with intricate detail and elaborate decoration. Its twin towers stand 157m (515ft) above the city, on the left bank of the Rhine, and made the cathedral the tallest structure in the world until the *Eiffel Tower* was built in 1889. The interior is equally impressive, with 14th-century stained glass, a resplendent choir, and a large gold shrine, considered a masterpiece of medieval goldwork. Remarkably the cathedral survived a total of 14 bomb raids during World War II and today visitors can climb the tower for superb views over Cologne and the *Rhineland*.

Transportation
Air: Cologne/Bonn Airport. **Rail:** Train: Cologne Station. Tram: Dom or Hbf (Hauptbahnhof). **Road:** Car: A1, A3, A4, A57 or A555; signs are marked either 'Hauptbahnhof' or 'Dom'.

Contact Addresses
Dompfarramt Domkloster 3, 50667 Köln, Germany
Tel: (0221) 17940 200
Website: www.koelner-dom.de

English Garden (Englischer Garten)

The *Englischer Garten*, measuring 3.7 sq km (1.4 sq miles), is one of Europe's oldest urban landscaped parks, originally laid out in 1789 by American Benjamin Thomson as a garden for the military. It was soon opened to the public, however, and has been popular with locals and visitors ever since due to the natural landscapes and wide open spaces which make it an oasis in the centre of the city. Popular activities include boating on the *Kleinhesselhoher Lake* and sunbathing (there is even a special area for naturists). In winter, the garden hosts a Christmas market and in summer there are open-air concerts and plays performed in the amphitheatre.

Transportation
Air: Munich International Airport. **Rail:** Tram: 17 (Tivolistrasse). Underground: U 3/6 to

Universität, Giselastrasse or Münchener Freiheit. **Road:** Bus: Public services. Car: A9 to Schwabing, signs then marked Englischer Garten.

Contact Addresses
Verwaltung des Englischen Gartens München, Englischer Garten 2, 80538 Munich, Germany
Tel: (089) 3866 639-0

Freiburg Cathedral (Freiburger Kathedrale)

Consecrated in 1513 and taking over 300 years to build, *Freiburg Cathedral* is a masterpiece of Gothic architecture. The 116-m (318-ft) high west tower, which soars above the jumbled rooftops of the Black Forest city, was described by Swiss historian Jacob Burckhardt as 'the most beautiful spire in Christendom' and contains the 'Hosanna' bell which dates from 1258. Visitors can climb the tower for excellent views over Freiburg and the picturesque *Black Forest*. The interior of the cathedral is just as beautiful, the highlight being Hans Baldung Grien's Renaissance *High Altar*, depicting the life of the Virgin Mary. *Münsterplatz*, the cathedral square, is a lively venue all year round, but is particularly atmospheric on long summer evenings, when people sit outside cafés enjoying the wine that is produced in local vineyards.

Contact Addresses
Freiburg Wirtschaft und Touristik GmbH & Co KG, Rotteckring 14, 79098 Freiburg, Germany
Tel: (0761) 388 1880
Website: www.freiburg.de

Transportation
Air: Euro-Airport Basel-Mulhouse-Freiburg. **Rail:** Train: ICE (InterCity Express) trains to Freiburg Hauptbahnhof (from Hamburg, Frankfurt and Basel) and IC/EC (InterCity and regional) trains to Freiburg Hauptbahnhof (from Hamburg, Frankfurt and Cologne). Tram: Bertoldsbrunnen, Oberlinden. **Road:** Car: A5 Frankfurt-Basel (exit Freiburg-Mitte).

German Parliament (Reichstag)

The imposing neo-Renaissance *Reichstag*, located in the heart of Berlin's city centre near the River Spree and the *Brandenburg Gate*, was completed in 1894. It was home to the *Deutscher Bundestag* (German Parliament) until 1933, when a huge fire destroyed the building – an event that coincided with Adolph Hitler assuming dictatorial control of the country. In 1999, following the fall of the *Berlin Wall* in 1989 and German re-unification, the parliament moved permanently to a renovated and renewed Reichstag. A new glass dome symbolises the transparency of the democratic process, and visitors can walk along the different levels of the dome to watch the government in session below.

Transportation
Air: Berlin Tegel Airport. **Rail:** Train: S-Bahn 1, 2 or 25 to Unter den Linden. **Road:** Bus: Public services to Reichstag/Bundestag. Car: Signs are marked for the Reichstag in Berlin city centre.

Contact Addresses
Deutscher Bundestag, Besucherdienst (Visitor Services), Platz der Republik 1, 11011 Berlin, Germany
Tel: (030) 227 73834
Website: www.bundestag.de

Heidelberg Castle (Schloss Heidelberg)

Situated high above the *River Neckar*, *Heidelberg Castle* is one of Germany's most romantic locations. It has had a long and turbulent history since it was first constructed in the early 15th century as a residence for the Palatine princes, the powerful secular rulers who presided over this part of southern Germany during the Holy Roman Empire. Having been totally destroyed during the Thirty Years War, and later by the French in 1689 and 1693, the red sandstone building was struck by lightning in 1764 and even its stones were taken for use in other building projects. All this rebuilding has led to a variety of architectural styles and yet the castle's delapidated air adds to its charm. The best way to reach the site is by cable car. There are excellent views over the university city of Heidelberg and the *Neckar Valley* from the summit.

Transportation

Air: Frankfurt Airport (a coach service runs directly from the airport to Heidelberg). **Rail:** Train: Direct services from across Europe or via Mannheim to Heidelberg Hauptbahnhof. Funicular: Services up to the castle. **Road:** Coach: Heidelberg Busbahnhof. Bus: Public services.

Contact Addresses

Convention and Visitors Bureau, Ziegelhäuser Landstraße 3, 69120 Heidelberge
Tel: (06221) 14220
Website: www.cvb-heidelberg.de

Jewish Museum Berlin

Designed by the Polish-born architect David Libeskind, the *Jewish Museum Berlin* opened in 2001 to worldwide acclaim. Famed for its innovative use of space and challenging designs, the museum site is in the shape disrupted Star of David representing the dislocation and exile of Jews within Europe. The museum explores Jewish history tracing it back from Roman times through to the present day with particular emphasis on the holocaust. One of the most moving areas of the museum is the *Holocaust Tower* in which visitors enter a cold, concrete void where the only source of light, air and sound comes from small shafts at the top representing the isolation and fear of the Nazi extermination camps. The museum is the first Jewish museum in Berlin since the last one was destroyed by the Nazis in 1938.

Transportation

Air: Berlin Tegel Airport and Berlin Schoenefeld Airport. **Rail:** Bahnhof and underground stations. **Road:** Bus: Public services.

German Parliament (Reichstag)

Image supplied by Wikipedia

Contact Addresses

Jewish Museum Berlin Lindenstraße 9-14, 10969 Berlin
Tel: (030) 2599 3300
Website: www.jmberlin.de

Munich Residence (Residenz München)

The *Munich Residence*, located in the centre of the city, is a magnificent complex of buildings constructed by the powerful Wittelsbach family who ruled Bavaria for 800 years. Although originally dating from the 14th century, subsequent additions and alterations gave the Residence a variety of architectural styles, right up until the fall of the Wittelsbach dynasty in 1918. Renaissance features predominate and one of the most impressive rooms in the complex is the *Imperial Hall*. The *Antiquarium*, built in 1571, is the oldest part of the palace and houses the family's collection of antiquities, whilst the *Schatzkammer* (treasury) holds an exquisite array of diamonds, rubies and other precious stones.

Transportation

Air: Munich International Airport. **Rail:** Train: München Hauptbahnhof (Munich Station). Underground: Odeonsplatz or Marienplatz. Tram: 19 (Nationaltheater).

Contact Addresses

Residenz München, Residenzstrasse 1, 80333 Munich, Germany
Tel: (089) 290 671
Website: www.schloesser.bayern.de

Neuschwanstein Castle (Schloss Neuschwanstein)

Neuschwanstein Castle is one of three castles built by 'mad' Ludwig II of Bavaria, who was born in 1845 and died in 1886. This fairytale castle sits perched among the natural splendour of the Alps. Its Neo-Romanesque architecture imitates that of a medieval castle and, in turn, Neuschwanstein was the inspiration for Disney's Magic Kingdom. Built between 1869 and 1886, only about a third of the castle was actually completed as Ludwig II was found to be mentally unfit by a government commission. Nearby *Marienbruecke* (Mary's Bridge), which spans a deep gorge, provides magnificent views of the castle.

Transportation

Air: Munich International Airport. **Rail:** Füssen Station. **Road:** Coach: Services from Füssen to Hohenschwangau. Car: A9 (from Berlin and Nuremberg); A92 (from Passau); A95 (from the Alps); A8 (from Salzburg); B17 (from Munich).

Contact Addresses

Schlossverwaltung Neuschwanstein, Neuschwansteinstrasse 20, 87645 Schwangau, Germany
Tel: (08362) 939880 (admin) 930830 (tickets)
Website: www.schloesser.bayern.de

Pergamon Museum

One of the world's great museums, the *Pergamon Museum* lies on Berlin's *Museumsinsel* (Museum Island) complex, which is situated between the River Spree and Kupfergraben. Five museums were built here between 1824 and 1930 to house archaeological treasures and art collections. The last of the five to be built was the Pergamon Museum which was designed by Alfred Messel and houses spectacular works of architectural antiquities, including collections of Greek, Assyrian, Islamic and Far Eastern art.

Transportation

Air: Berlin Tegel Airport.
Rail: Train: S-Bahn to Friedrichstrasse or Hackescher Markt. Tram: Regular services. Underground: Friedrichstrasse. **Road:** Bus: Regular services.

Contact Addresses

Pergamon Museum, Bodestrasse 1-3, 10178 Berlin, Germany
Tel: (030) 2090 5577
Website: www.germany-tourism.co.uk

Sanssouci Palace (Schloss Sanssouci)

Sanssouci Palace was built for the Prussian emperor Frederick II as his summer retreat. Its name, which literally means 'no worries' in French, reflects the fact that he intended it as an escape from the pressures of Berlin and married life. The real showpiece of Sanssouci, however, is the park. Visitors can wander through a series of beautifully landscaped gardens, including the *Sizilianischer Garten* (Sicilian Garden), which is filled with subtropical plants. A series of fountains and terraces leads to other structures within the park, such as the *Neue Orangerie* (New Orangery) and the *Bildergalerie* (Picture Gallery), which holds paintings by Renaissance artists, including Caravaggio, Rubens and Van Dyck.

Transportation

Air: Berlin Tegel Airport or Berlin Schönefeld Airport. **Rail:** Train: S-Bahn to Potsdam-Hauptbahnhof Bahn (from Berlin Zoo).

Contact Addresses

Stiftung Preussische Schlösser und Gärten, Berlin-Brandenburg, Postfach 60 14 62, 14414 Potsdam, Germany
Tel: (0331) 969 4202
Website: www.spsg.de

Sanssouci Palace

German National Tourist Board©

Gibraltar

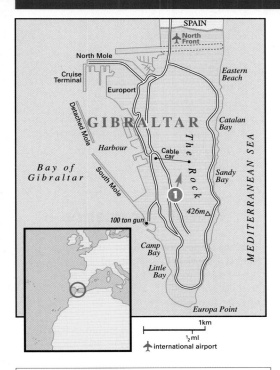

SPAIN

North Front

North Mole

Cruise Terminal

Europort

Eastern Beach

GIBRALTAR

Detached Mole

Harbour

Catalan Bay

Cable car

The Rock

Bay of Gibraltar

South Mole

Sandy Bay

100 ton gun

426m△

MEDITERRANEAN SEA

Camp Bay

Little Bay

Europa Point

1km

½ ml

✈ international airport

1 Upper Rock Nature Reserve

Tourist Information

Gibraltar Tourist Board
Duke of Kent House, Cathedral Square,
Gibraltar
Tel: 74950
Website: www.gibraltar.gi

Gibraltar Tourist Board
Arundel Great Court, 178/9 The Strand,
London WC2R 1EL, UK
Tel: (020) 7836 0777
Website: www.gibraltar.gov.uk

Upper Rock Nature Reserve

The *Upper Rock Nature Reserve* is a protected area
of great natural beauty perched about 421m
(1380ft) above sea level on the limestone
peninsular of Gibraltar. Its most famous residents
are the *Barbary Apes*, which have lived on the
Rock for hundreds of years as Europe's only free-
roaming apes. According to legend, when the apes
leave, Gibraltar will cease to be British. The
Reserve is also home to many species of bird, such
as buzzards and Barbary partridges. Visitors also
come to see *St Michael's Cave*, one of a vast
warren of caves containing stalagmites and
stalactites, and the *Siege Tunnels*, which were used
as a defence system by the British in the Great
Siege (1779-1783) against the French and Spanish.
Another popular site in the Reserve is the 14th-
century *Moorish Castle*, which testifies to the
diverse history of the peninsular.

Transportation
Air: Gibraltar Airport. **Rail:** Cable Car: From Grand
Parade. **Road:** Bus: Public services. Car: Access
from the border with Spain at La Linea.

Contact Addresses
For more information on the Upper Rock Nature
Reserve, contact the Gibraltar Tourist Board (see
Tourist Information above).

The famous Rock of Gibraltar

Gibraltar Tourist Board©

Greece

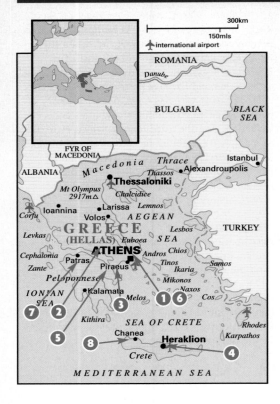

300km
150mls
✈ international airport

ROMANIA

Danube

BULGARIA

BLACK SEA

FYR OF MACEDONIA

ALBANIA

Macedonia *Thrace*

Istanbul

Thessaloniki

Thassos •Alexandroupolis

Mt Olympus 2917m△ *Chalcidice*

Ioannina •Larissa *Lemnos*

Corfu Volos• *A E G E A N*

GREECE (HELLAS)

Levkas *Euboea* *Lesbos* *SEA* TURKEY

Cephalonia ATHENS *Andros* *Chios*

Patras *Tinos*

Zante Piraeus *Ikaria* *Samos*

Peloponnese *Mikonos*

IONIAN SEA •Kalamata *Melos* *Naxos* *Cos*

⑦ ② ③ ① ⑥

Kithira *SEA OF CRETE* *Rhodes*

⑤ ⑧ Chanea *Karpathos*

Heraklion

Crete ④

M E D I T E R R A N E A N   S E A

1 Acropolis (Akrópoli)
2 Delphi (Delfí)
3 Epidaurus (Epídavros)
4 Knossos
5 Mycenae (Mikines)
6 National Archaeological Museum of Athens (Ethnikó Archaiologiko Mouseio)
7 Olympia (Olimbía)
8 Samarian Gorge (Samaria)

Tourist Information

Ellinikos Organismos Tourismou (Greek National Tourism Organization)
No 7 Tsoha Street, 11521, Athens, Greece
Tel: (210) 870 7000
Website: www.gnto.gr

Greek National Tourism Organization (GNTO)
4 Conduit Street, London W15 2DJ, UK
Tel: (020) 7495 9300 or 7499 8161
Website: www.gnto.co.uk

Acropolis (Akrópoli)

The *Acropolis* is one of the most famous sites of the ancient world and a symbol of Greek civilization. It is the site of three different temples dedicated to Athena Parthenos, the patron goddess of Athens, the most famous of which is the internationally-renowned *Parthenon*. Completed in 438BC, its broad flank of Doric columns is synonymous with ancient culture throughout the world. Built entirely of marble that glows at sunset, the Parthenon once housed a statue of Athena. Visitors can also see the *Propylaea* constructed in 437-432BC, the *Temple of Athena Nike* (the Goddess of Victory), the *Erechtheion Temple*, and the *Acropolis Museum*, which houses many treasures from the Acropolis.

Transportation
Air: Athens International Airport. **Rail:** Underground: Acropolis Station. **Road:** Bus: Plaka

Station. **Car:** B8A towards Athens and signs for the Acropolis.

Contact Addresses
Acropolis Museum, First Ephorate of Prehistoric and Classical Antiquities, 2-4 Makrygianni Street, 11742 Athens, Greece.
Tel: (010) 321 0219 (Acropolis) *or* 323 6665
Website: www.culture.gr

Delphi (Delfí)

According to Greek mythology, *Delphi* stands at the point where two eagles, released to the east and west by the god Zeus, met, thus marking the centre of the world. Soaring high above the Gulf of Corinth, on Mount Parnassos, it has long been home to the sanctuary of Apollo and the seat of his oracle. Perhaps the best known of Delphi's ancient inhabitants, dating from the second millennium BC, the oracle's predictions affected matters as grand as those of warfare. Today, the ancient site lies in ruins, although visitors still come in their thousands to see the remains. The *Delphi Museum*, which was built in 1903, exhibits various statues and offerings from the sanctuary of Delphi.

Transportation
Air: Athens International Airport. **Road:** Bus: Arahova Bus Stop. Car: Road to Galaxidi, then road to Arahova Acropolis (from Athens).

Contact Addresses
Delphi Museum, 33054 Delphi, Greece
Tel: (026) 5082 313
Website: www.culture.gr

Epidaurus (Epídavros)

The *Sanctuary of Asclepius* at *Epidaurus* was once an important healing centre as well as a religious centre and spa. Built in the fourth century BC, the sanctuary was dedicated to the healer god, Asclepius, and boasts a well-preserved 1400-seat theatre, which was designed by Polycleitus, who built similar buildings at Olympia and Delphi. The theatre is the most famous of all the ancient theatres in Greece and comes alive every summer with theatrical performances. There is also a small excavation museum near Epidaurus, which was built between 1902 and 1909, and contains many remains from the sanctuary.

Transportation
Air: Athens International Airport. **Rail:** Train: Náfplion Station (services from Athens). **Road:** Bus: Public services.

Contact Addresses
Epídavros, Lygourio 21052, Argolis, Peloponnesos, Greece
Tel: (075) 3022 009
Website: www.culture.gr

Knossos

Located on the island of Crete, *Knossos* is the site of the most important palace of the ancient Minoans, the earliest of the Aegean civilisations. It was home to King Minos and, as legend has it, the Minotaur, a giant bull who inhabited the perilous Labyrinth. The Minoan civilisation spread to mainland Greece to form the Mycenaean civilisation, a precursor to the Ancient Greeks. The site was first discovered by Minos Kalokairinos in 1878 and was excavated further by Arthur Evans between 1900 and 1931. Today, Knossos offers the modern-day visitor an abundance of ancient sites, including the *Palace of Knossos*, the *Little Palace*, the *Royal Villa*, the *House of Frescoes* and the *Temple Tomb*.

Transportation
Air: Heraklion Airport. **Road:** Bus: Services to Knossos (from Heraklion Airport). Car: E-75 to Knossos (from Heraklion).

Contact Addresses
Knossos Palace, Heraklion, Crete, Greece
Tel: (081) 231 940
Website: www.culture.gr

Mycenae (Mikines)

Mycenae was first inhabited during Neolithic times and is located between Corinth and Argos, on top of a hill halfway up the Euboea Mountain. It was a citadel palace that included extensive fortifications, shrines and private dwellings. The site continued to be inhabited until the end of the third century AD. Mycenae was first discovered in 1874 by the German archaeologist Heinrich Schliemann, who began excavation in search of gold and believed the site he had found to be the home of Agamemnon, the leader of the Greek assault on Troy. Highlights at Mycenae, which is one of the most popular attractions in Greece, include the *Citadel*, the *Treasury of Atreus*, the *Lion Gate* and the *Royal Cemetery*.

Transportation
Air: Athens International Airport. **Road:** Bus: Public services. Car: E-94 to Corinth, then N-7 (from Athens); N-70 to Árgos, then N-7 (from Náfplion).

Contact Addresses

Mycenae 21200, Argolis, Peloponnesos, Greece
Tel: (075) 1076 585
Website: www.culture.gr

National Archaeological Museum of Athens (Ethnikó Archaiologiko Mouseio)

The most important museum in Athens, the *National Archaeological Museum* houses one of the richest collections of Ancient Greek art in the world. Completed in 1899, the collection includes artefacts from all periods of Ancient Greek civilisation. It is particularly well known for objects found at the ancient city of *Mycenae*, including the *Mask of Agamemnon*, gold vases and elaborate weapons. The museum also has a large collection of Cycladic art on display, as well as the *Statue of Poseidon*, the *Helène Stathatos Collection* of gold jewellery which dates from the ancient and Byzantine worlds.

Transportation

Air: Athens International Airport. **Rail:** Underground: Victoria. **Road:** Bus: Museum Bus Stop. Car: B8A towards Athens, then signs for the city centre.

Contact Addresses

Ethnikó Archaiologikó Mouseio, Patission 44, Athens 10682, Greece
Tel: (010) 821 7717
Website: www.culture.gr

Olympia (Olimbía)

Dedicated to the father of the gods, Olympian Zeus, *Olympia* is the birthplace of the Olympic Games, which were first held here in 776BC. Situated in a Peloponnesus Valley in Southern Greece, the site has been inhabited since prehistoric times and boasts many ancient buildings, including the *Heraeum*, the *Stadium* and the *Hippodrome* where ancient horse races were held. There was also a *Palaestra*, or wrestling school, and a *Gymnasium* where competitors were obliged to train for at least a month. Today, visitors to Olympia come to see the *Temple of Zeus*, which once contained a gold and ivory statue of

Zeus, and the nearby *Archaelogical Museum*, which contains many artefacts from Olympia, including a collection of terracottas, statues and bronzes.

Transportation

Air: Athens International Airport. **Rail:** Train: Train to Pirgos, then change for Olympia (from Athens). **Road:** Bus: Services to Olympia or services via Pirgos. Car: E-65, then E-55 (from Athens).

Contact Addresses

Olimbía, Seventh Ephorate of Prehistoric and Classical Antiquities, 27065, Ancient Olympia, Greece
Tel: (062) 4022 517
Website: www.culture.gr

Samarian Gorge (Samaria)

Regarded as one of Europe's greatest natural wonders, the *Samarian Gorge* is a beautiful 18km- (11 mile-) hike through the *Samaria National Park* in Crete's *White Mountains*. The gorge is believed to be the longest in Europe and is home to beautiful flora and fauna and dramatic rock formations. There are several churches and chapels, including the church dedicated to Saint Maria of Egypt, found in the village of Samaria and dating back to 1379, where the name Sa(int)maria comes from. After a long day's hike, visitors can relax on beaches at the end of the gorge before taking a boat back along the coast to embark on their return journey to Chania.

Transportation

Air: Chania International Airport. **Water:** Boat: Services to Soúyia or Hóra Sfakíon (from Ayía Roúmeli), then bus service back to Chania. **Road:** Coach: Many visitors book trips through tour operators. Bus: Public services. Car: It is not advisable to travel by car to the entrance of the gorge, as visitors must return to their starting point to pick up their car.

Contact Addresses

Samaria, Forest Directorate of Chania, Chania GR 73100, Greece
Tel: (082) 1092 287

Guatemala

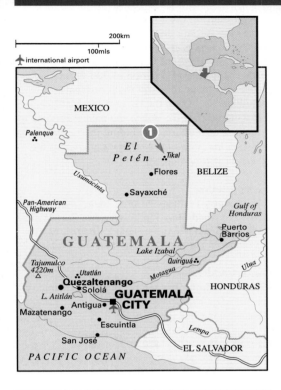

200km
100mls

✈ international airport

MEXICO

Palenque

El
Petén   ∴Tikal

●Flores   BELIZE

Usumacinta

●Sayaxché

Pan-American
Highway

Gulf of
Honduras

GUATEMALA
Lake Izabal

Puerto
Barrios

Quiriguá ∴

Tajumulco
4220m
△   Utatlán

Ulua

Quezaltenango
Sololá

Motagua

HONDURAS

L. Atitlán
Antigua●   GUATEMALA
Mazatenango   CITY

Escuintla

Lempa

San José

EL SALVADOR

PACIFIC OCEAN

---

1 Tikal

Tourist Information

**Instituto Guatemalteco de Turismo (INGUAT)
(Guatemala Tourist Commission)**
7a Avenida 1-17, zona 4, Centro Cívico,
Guatemala City, Guatemala
Tel: 331 1333 or (888) 464 8281 (24-hour toll
free USA only) or (801) 464 8281 (24-hour
toll free Guatemala only)
Website: www.guatemala.travel.com.gt

Embassy of the Republic of Guatemala
13 Fawcett Street, London SW10 9HN, UK
Tel: (020) 7349 0346 (tourism section)

Key to symbols: £ Entry charged & Disabled access
⚒ Man-made attraction ♥ Natural attraction
P Parking ✗ Restaurant ⚗ Shop 🏛 UNESCO site

Tikal

Located 548km (341 miles) north of Guatemala
City, the ancient site of *Tikal* was once home to an
estimated 100,000 Maya. Unlike many other
ancient Mayan sites, the wonders of Tikal are
hidden deep within the rainforest. Every year,
visitors come to gaze at its towering 70m- (230ft)
high pyramid and ancient plazas to the
accompaniment of jungle sounds. The site has
more than 3000 structures including temples and
palaces and is located in *Tikal National Park*, which
is listed as a UNESCO World Heritage Site and is
home to many species of wildlife. There is also an
on-site museum, which contains a collection of
objects found during excavations at the site.

Transportation
Air: Guatemala City La Aurora International
Airport. **Road:** Coach: Services to Flores and Santa
Elena, then on to Tikal (from Guatemala city). Car:
CA9 to junction Ruidosa, then the main CA11
road from Flores (from Guatemala city).

Contact Addresses
For more information on Tikal, contact Guatemala
Tourist Commission (see **Tourist Information**
above).

P ✗ ⚗ 🏛 £ ⚒

Tikal

Inguat©

Hungary

1 Buda Castle Palace (Budavári Palota)
2 Budapest Central Synagogue (Nagy Zsinagóga)
3 Fisherman's Bastion (Halászbástya)
4 Gellért Bath

Tourist Information

Magyar Turizmus Rt. (Hungarian National Tourist Office – HNTO)
1052 Budapest, Sütö Utcha 2, Hungary
Tel: 800 3600 0000 (call centre info line)
Website: www.hungarytourism.hu

Hungarian National Tourist Office (HNTO)
46 Eaton Place, London SW1X 8AL, UK
Tel: (020) 7823 1032 or 7823 1055
Website: www.hungary.com

Buda Castle Palace (Budavári Palota)

Located in Budapest's picturesque Old Town, *Buda Castle Palace* was first inhabited by King Béla of

Hungary during the 13th century. The king, who fled to the Adriatic Sea in 1241 following the Mongol invasion, returned to live in the palace, building a stronghold to protect the palace from further attack. Over a period of 700 years, the palace was home to many royal residents, including King Lajos the Great, King Matthias I and King Charles III. Today, the palace is home to a number of museums, including the *Ludwig Museum*, the *Hungarian National Gallery* and the *Budapest History Museum*.

Transportation
Air: Budapest Ferihegy Airport. **Rail:** Tram: 18 to Dózsa tér. **Road:** Bus: Public services. Car: M1 to Budapest (from Vienna or Graz). Road signs are then marked for the 'centrum' and the 'citadella'.

Contact Addresses
I Budvári Palota, Dísz tér 17, Budapest, Hungary
Tel: (01) 375 7533
Website: www.budapestinfo.hu

Budapest Central Synagogue (Nagy Zsinagóga)

Budapest Central Synagogue is the largest synagogue in Europe and the second largest in the world after the *Emanuel Synagogue* in New York. Completed in 1859, it was built in a Moorish-Byzantine style by the Austrian architect Ludwig Förster. The building was partly destroyed by bombing campaigns during World War II, but has been the subject of much renovation to restore its two shining Moorish domes to their former brilliance. The *Jewish Museum* next door recounts the horrors of the Holocaust and displays exhibits dating as far back as the Middle Ages. The museum, which was built between 1931 and 1936, stands on the former home of Theodor Herzl, who was the founding father of Zionism and responsible for developing the idea of a modern Jewish state.

Transportation
Air: Budapest Ferighegy Airport. **Rail:** Train: Keleti

Station (East). Underground: Astoria. Tram: Astoria. **Road:** Bus: Public services. Car: M1, M5, M7 or main roads 5, 6, 7, 51 to M0 (circular road around Budapest) or M3 towards Budapest. Follow signs to Astoria (city centre).

Contact Addresses
Nagy Zsinagóga, VII. Dohány utca 2, Budapest, Hungary
Tel: (01) 342 1335
Website: www.budapestinfo.hu

Fisherman's Bastion (Halászbástya)

The *Fisherman's Bastion* was built in 1905 and named after the guild of fishermen responsible for defending this stretch of wall from enemy attack during the Middle Ages. An almost Disney-like tower dominates this stone wall with seven turrets representing the Magyar tribes who once populated the country. Excellent views can be had from the top of the tower across the River Danube to *Margaret Island*, *Parliament*, *St Stephen's Basilica* and the *Chain Bridge*. Visitors can also see the nearby *Nagyboldogasszony Templom* (Church of Our Lady), which was built at the beginning of the 14th century and is more commonly called *Matthias Church* (AD1443-1490) after King Matthias who held both his wedding ceremonies here.

Transportation
Air: Budapest Ferihegy Airport. **Rail:** Underground: Moszka tér. **Tram:** 18. **Road:** Bus: Public services. Car: No access.

Contact Addresses
1052 Budapest, Sütö Utcha 2, Hungary
Tel: 800 3600 0000 (call centre info line)
Website: www.hungary.com

Gellért Bath

Located next door to the *Danubius Hotel Gellért* in the heart of Budapest, the *Gellért Bath* is a world-famous thermal bath and spa complex that first opened its doors in 1918. Based around the natural hot springs of *Gellért Hill* on the banks of the Danube, Gellért Bath is a traditional thermal bath house that's renowned for its healing properties and consists of 13 indoor and outdoor pools. It's the most famous of Budapest's thermal spas and is admired for its opulent style and baths adorned with tiles, statues and marble pillars. The natural remedies use water that's naturally rich in calcium, magnesium, hydrocarbonate, alkalis, chloride, sulphide and fluoride. It's reputation is international and visitors travel from all over the world for treatments which include physiotherapy, hydrotherapy, balneotherapy and electrotherapy.

Transportation
Air: Budapest Ferihegy Airport. **Rail:** Budapest Station. **Tramway:** Public services. **Road:** Bus: Public services.

Contact Addresses
Gellért Thermal Bath, Kelenhegyi út 4, H-1118 Budapest, Hungary
Tel: (01) 466 6166
Website: www.spasbudapest.com

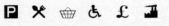

Buda Castle Palace and Chain Bridge by Night

Hungarian National Tourist Office©

Iceland

Strokkur in the Geyser area

1 Geyser (Geysir)
2 Golden Waterfall (Gullfoss)
3 The Pearl (Perlan)

Tourist Information

Icelandic Tourist Board (Islenska Tourist Board)
Laekjargata 3, 101 Reykjavik, Iceland
Tel: 535 5500
Website: www.icetourist.is

Geyser (Geysir)

Until 1916, *Geyser*, located 125km (78 miles) northeast of Reykjavik, was one of the world's great geysers, spouting boiling water and steam 60-80m (165-220ft) into the air at three-hourly intervals. Mysteriously, it fell dormant (some say due to hundreds of tourists filling its chamber with objects) and has come to life only once since then, in 1935. The smaller *Strokkur* geyser nearby makes up for its big brother's silence by erupting every five to ten minutes. The entire area is a geothermal park, with belching mud pits, hissing steam vents, hot and cold springs, warm streams and primitive plants. The *Geysir Center* offers visitors year-round exhibitions on geothermal activity, and also contains a folk museum with displays on the history of the area and Icelandic flora and fauna.

Transportation
Air: Reykjavik Keflavik Airport. **Road:** Bus: Public services. Car: Ring road 1, then left near Selfoss to Road 35.

Contact Addresses
Gesyir Center, 801 Selfoss, Iceland
Tel: (354) 480 6800
Website: www.geysircenter.is

Golden Waterfall (Gullfoss)

Located just a few kilometres from Geyser, *Golden Waterfall* (Gullfoss) is the most dramatic section of the *Hvita River* (White River) in southern Iceland. In the midst of lush vegetation, white water thunders down a 32-m (105-ft) drop into a narrow canyon 70m (192ft) deep and 2.5km (1.5 miles) long. The site was bought by the Icelandic government to prevent foreign investors from turning it into a commercial site, and the footpath is opened each morning by a local farmer to allow visitors to see the waterfall from a viewing platform.

Transportation
Air: Reykjavik Keflavik Airport. **Road:** Bus: Public services. Car: Hwy-1, then Road 35 (from Reykjavik).

Contact Addresses
For more information on Gullfoss, contact the Icelandic Tourist Board (see **Tourist Information** above).

The Pearl (Perlan)

The Pearl (Perlan) is as much an architectural masterpiece as it is a feat of engineering. Designed by architect Ingimundur Sveinsson, this awesome 10-storey building opened to the public in 1991. It's geothermally heated by water forced through steel supports and provides a means of water storage and power for the greater Reykjavik region. Excellent views of Reykjavik can be had from the *Viewing Deck* on level four. There is a revolving restaurant in the glass dome at the top of the building. Cocktails are the speciality in the Perlan bar, and art exhibitions and concerts are held regularly.

Transportation
Air: Reykjavik Keflavik Airport. **Road:** Bus: Public services to Perlan. Car: Bustrdrvegur Road towards Perlan (from Reykjavik).

Contact Addresses
Perlan, Post 5252, 125 Reykjavik, Iceland
Tel: 562 0200
Website: www.perlan.is

Restaurant at the Pearl, Reykjavik

Icelandic Tourist Board/Randall Hyman©

India

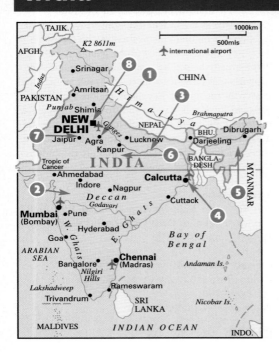

TAJIK.
1000km
500mls
✈ international airport
K2 8611m
AFGH.
Srinagar
CHINA
Amritsar
PAKISTAN
Punjab Shimla
NEW DELHI
NEPAL
Brahmaputra
Jaipur Agra Lucknow
BHU. Dibrugarh
Darjeeling
Kanpur
Tropic of Cancer
INDIA
BANGLA-DESH
Ahmedabad
Calcutta
Indore Nagpur
Deccan
Cuttack
Godavari
MYANMAR
Mumbai Pune
(Bombay)
Hyderabad
Goa
Bay of Bengal
ARABIAN SEA
Bangalore Chennai
Nilgiri (Madras)
Hills
Andaman Is.
Lakshadweep
Rameswaram
Trivandrum
SRI LANKA
Nicobar Is.
MALDIVES
INDIAN OCEAN
INDO.

1 Crown Palace (Taj Mahal)

2 Ellora Temple Caves

3 Ghats at Varanasi (Banaras Ghats)

4 Indian Museum, Calcutta

5 Kaziranga National Park

6 Khajuraho

7 Palace of the Winds (Hawa Mahal)

8 Red Fort (Lal Quila)

Tourist Information

India Tourism
88 Janpath, New Delhi 110 001, India
Tel: (011) 332 0342 *or* 332 0005 *or* 332 0008
Website: www.incredibleindia.org

India Tourism
7 Cork Street, London W15 3LH, UK
Tel: (020) 7437 3677 *or* (0870) 010 2183
(brochure request line)
Website: www.incredibleindia.org

Crown Palace (Taj Mahal)

The *Taj Mahal* has been described as the most extravagant monument ever built for love. It is also India's most emblematic and famous tourist attraction. Renowned for its tree-lined reflective pond leading up to the fabulous domed roof, few know that the Taj Mahal is, in fact, a mausoleum not a mosque. Completed in 1653, it was built by the Emperor Shah Jahan in memory of his second wife, Mumtaz Mahal, who died in childbirth. The elaborate marble designs are inlaid with semi-precious stones such as jade, crystal, turquoise and coral. Many people choose to spend at least several hours here as the changing light and shadows affect the colour and patterns of the Taj Mahal, and it is also possible to picnic in the tranquil gardens.

Transportation
Air: Indira Gandhi International Airport, Agra Airport (domestic flights). **Rail:** Train: Agra Cantt Station. **Road:** Bus: Services to Indian Tourist Office bus stop. Car: NH24, then NH2 (from Delhi); NH11 (from Jaipur); NH25, then NH2 (from Lucknow).

Contact Addresses
India Tourism, 191 The Mali, Agra 282001 Uttar Pradesh, India
Tel: (0562) 363 959
Website: www.incredibleindia.org

Ellora Temple Caves

The *Ellora Temple Caves* consist of 34 separate religious shrines carved into the actual rock of a basaltic hill and containing a wealth of sculptural and architectural treasures. Carved between the fourth and ninth centuries AD, the caves represent three separate faiths: Buddhism, Jainism and Hinduism. The 16 *Buddhist Caves* are the oldest in the group. The *Jain Caves* illustrate the non-violent, ascetic beliefs of this religion, depicting scenes of pastoral beauty and images such as lotus flowers. In terms of stylistic ambition, the *Hindu Caves* outdo their neighbours – one cave alone, the *Temple of Kailasa*, covers twice the area of the *Parthenon* in Athens and took 100 years to complete. Dedicated to Lord Shiva, this temple is the largest monolith in the world and is undoubtedly the most visited site at Ellora.

Transportation
Air: Mumbai Chhaprati Shivaji International Airport, Aurangabad Airport (domestic flights). **Rail:** Train: Aurangabad Station. **Road:** Bus: MSRTC Services to Ellora Temple Caves (from Aurangabad). Car: NH50 towards Nashik and major roads to Ellora (from Pune).

Contact Addresses
India Tourism Aurangabad, Krishna Vilas, Station Road, Aurangabad, 431005, Maharastra, India
Tel: (0240) 331 217
Website: www.incredibleindia.org

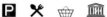

many temples lining the riverbank. Huge crowds of pilgrims gather to take part in this ancient ritual which involves making offerings (*puja*) to the rising sun and is often watched by tourists who come to photograph this incredible sight.

Transportation
Air: Indira Gandhi International Airport, Babatpur Airport. **Rail:** Train: Varanasi Station. **Road:** Bus: Main bus stop in Varanasi City Centre. Car: NH2 to Delhi, then NH7 to Kanya and NH29 to Gorakhpur (from Calcutta).

Contact Addresses
India Tourism, 15B The Mall, Cantt, Varanasi 221002, Uttar Pradesh, India
Tel: (0542) 2501784
Website: www.incredibleindia.org

Ghats at Varanasi (Banaras Ghats)

Varanasi, which was created by Lord Shiva, is one of the oldest and holiest cities in India and home to the most famous *ghats* (steps leading down to the river) in the country. Worshippers flock to these *ghats* every day to bathe in the holy River Ganges and then worship at the

Indian Museum, Calcutta

Originally established in 1814, and moved to its present site in 1878, Calcutta's *Indian Museum* is the largest and best museum in the country. Founded by Dr Nathaniel Wallich and housed in a magnificent Italian-style building, the museum has over 60 galleries and is divided into six

Ghats at Varanasi

Ministry of Tourism, India©

different sections: archaeology, art, anthropology, geology, zoology and industry. The art section contains a picture gallery, with Persian- and Indian-style drawings and paintings, and also contains other artefacts and textiles, including silk-woven Tibetan temple banners. Other sections of the museum contain diverse treasures, such as an Egyptian mummy, the skeleton of a whale, rare statues and a collection of meteorites.

Transportation

Air: Calcutta International Airport. **Rail:** Train: Howrah Station or Sealdah Station. Underground: Park Street Station. **Road:** Bus: Jawaharlal Nehru Road. Car: NH2 (from Delhi); NH28A, NH28, NH31 and NH34 (from Kathmandu); NH5 and NH6 (from Bhubaneswar).

Contact Addresses

Indian Museum, 27 Jawaharlal Nehru Road, Calcutta 700016, West Bengal, India
Tel: (033) 22 49 56 99
Website: www.indianmuseum-calcutta.org

Kaziranga National Park

Kaziranga National Park was set aside as a game sanctuary in 1926 and became a national park in 1974. It's made up of 688 sq km (266 sq miles) of breathtaking land containing rainforests, rivers, sprawling grasslands and herds of wild elephant. It is best known for its thriving population of one-horned Indian rhino, which is the largest in the world. The rhino's natural enemy, the tiger, also lives in the park along with many other typical species of Indian wildlife. Visitors can use jeeps or cars to travel around the park; alternatively, opt for a more traditional experience on the back of an elephant. The park has been on the UNESCO World Heritage List since 1985.

Transportation

Air: Indira Gandhi International Airport, Kolkhata International Airport, Gopinath Bordoloi Airport (Guwahati), Jorhat Airport. **Rail:** Train: Furkating Station. **Road:** Bus: Services to Kohara. Car: NH37 to Kohora (from Guwahati). Visitors are advised to travel by air from Guwahati to Jorhat airport and then by bus.

Contact Addresses

Kaziranga National Park, PO Bokakhat 785612, District Golaghat, Assam, India
Tel: (0376) 266 8321

Khajuraho

The famous erotic temples of *Khajuraho* are one of the most popular tourist attractions in India. Built between AD 950 and 1050 by the kings of the Chandela, the site originally possessed 85 temples, of which 20 are still reasonably preserved. Lost for centuries after the decline of the Chandela, the small village of Khajuraho was rediscovered in 1838 by a British army captain. The temples are best known for the erotic friezes on their walls. The name Khajuraho is derived from Khajur, the local word for the date trees which grow in abundance in the region. A *son et lumière* show every evening tells the story of the Chandela Kings and the history of the temples.

Transportation

Air: Indira Gandhi International Airport, Khajuraho Airport (domestic flights). **Rail:** Train: Harpalpur or Jhansi stations. **Road:** Coach: Services from Satna, Harpalpur and Jhansi.

Contact Addresses

Regional Office, Madhya Pradesh State Tourism Development Corporation Ltd, Chandela Cultural Centre, Khajuraho, India
Tel: (0768) 644 051
Website: www.incredibleindia.org

Palace of the Winds (Hawa Mahal)

Built in 1799, *Hawa Mahal* is the most stunning sight in the city of Jaipur. The palace, part of a huge complex, overlooks one of Jaipur's main streets and was originally constructed to offer women of the court a vantage point, behind stone-carved screens, from which to watch the activities taking place in the bazaar and the surrounding streets. For this purpose, it was designed with over 900 niches, and the entire building is shaped like a crown adorning Lord Krishna's head. The site offers superb views of the city, including the many old palaces and houses which were painted ochre-pink, the colour of hospitality, by the Rajputs, for the 1853 visit of Prince Albert.

Transportation

Air: Indira Gandhi International Airport, Sanganer Airport (domestic flights). **Rail:** Train: Jaipur Station. **Road:** Bus: Public services. Car: NH8 (from Delhi); NH11 (from Agra); NH12 (from Bhopal).

Contact Addresses

India Tourism, Khasa-Kothi, Jaipur 302001, India
Tel: (0141) 372 200
Website: www.incredibleindia.org

Red Fort (Lal Quila)

Completed in 1648, the *Red Fort* is the largest of Old Delhi's monuments. Its red sandstone walls dominate Old Delhi's Muslim district, rising above a wide dry moat to a height of up to 33m (108ft), and are lined with turrets and bastions. Today, rather than repel enemy invaders, they keep out the noise of the surrounding city, and the serene gardens and pavilions within the fort hark back to the power and majesty of the Mughal emperors. The main entrance of the Red Fort opens onto a bazaar that was at one time home to the city's most skilled goldsmiths, carpet makers and jewellers. Farther within lies the *Hall of Public Audiences*, where the emperor would listen to the complaints of the common people, and the spectacular *Royal Baths*

Transportation

Air: Indira Gandhi International Airport. **Rail:** Train: Main Delhi Station (Old Delhi). **Road:** Bus: Services to Lal Quila entrance. Car: Grand Trunk Road NH1 (from Amritsar and north); Mathura Road (from Agra and south); NH2 (from Calcutta and east); Gurgaon Road (from Jaipur and west).

Contact Addresses

Government of India Tourist Office (GITO), 88 Janpath, New Delhi 110 001, India
Tel: (011) 332 0005 *or* 332 0342
Website: www.incredinleindia.org

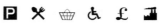

Khajuraho

Indonesia

Prambanan Temple Compounds

1 Prambanan Temple Compounds
(Loro Jonggrang)

Tourist Information

Indonesian Tourism Promotion Board (ITPB)
Wisma Nugra Santana Building, 9th Floor,
Jalan Jend Sudirman Kav 7-8, Jakarta 10220,
Indonesia
Tel: (21) 570 4879
Website: www.tourismindonesia.com

Indonesian Embassy
38 Grosvenor Square, London W1K 2HW
Tel: (020) 7499 7661
Website: www.indonesianembassy.org.uk

Prambanan Temple Compounds (Loro Jonggrang)

The *Prambanan Temples* form the largest temple
complex on the Indonesian island of Java.
Constructed around AD 900, the compound was
deserted soon after it was completed, possibly
due to the eruption of nearby Mount Merapi.
The temples were restored in 1953 and now

form one of the world's great Hindu shrines.
There are 224 temples in total, but the site is
dominated by the imposing figures of the three
main temples: the *Brahma Temple*, the *Vishnu
Temple* and the *Shiva Temple*. From May to
October, the *Ramayana Ballet*, a traditional
Indonesian dance based on the Hindu epic, is
performed at the
open-air theatre.

Transportation
Air: Adi Sucipto
Airport
(Yogyakarta),
Jakarta
Soekarno-Hatta
Airport. **Road:**
Coach: Services
from Yogyakarta.
Car: Signposted
Central Java,
Yogyakarta, then
Prambanan (from
Jakarta).

Contact Addresses
The Ministry of Culture and Tourism of the
Republic of Indonesia,
Jl. Merdeka Barat No.17,
Jakarta 10110, Indonesia
Tel: (21) 3838 436
Website: www.indonesiatourism.go.id

Islamic Republic of Iran

800km
400mls

✈ international airport

RUSSIAN FEDERATION
UZBEK-ISTAN
GEORGIA
AZERBAIJAN
ARMENIA
TURKEY
CASPIAN SEA
Tabriz
Lake Urmia
Rasht
Damavand 5681m
Elburz △ Mtns.
Kopet Dag
TURKMENISTAN
Karaj
IRAQ
Hamadan
TEHRAN
Mashhad
Kermanshah
Qom
Dasht-e Kavir
Tigris
Zagros Mtns.
IRAN
Birjand
AFGHAN-ISTAN
Euphrates
① Esfahan
Karun
② Dasht-e Lut
Ahvaz
Abadan
KUWAIT
Persepolis
Kerman
Shiraz
Bushehr
Bandar-e Abbas
Iranshahr
The Gulf
Qeshm I.
Strait of Hormuz
Makran
PAKISTAN
BAHRAIN
QATAR
SAUDI ARABIA
U.A.E.
OMAN
Gulf of Oman

1 Imam Square (Naghsh-é Jahan)
2 Persepolis (Takht-é Jamshid)

Tourist Information

Iran Touring and Tourism Organisation (ITTO)
238 Sindhokht Street, Fatemi Avenue, Tehran, Iran
Tel: (021) 643 5650
Website: www.irantourism.org

Embassy of the Islamic Republic of Iran
16 Prince's Gate, London SW7 1PT, UK
Tel: (020) 7225 3000
Website: www.iran-embassy.org.uk

Imam Square (Naghsh-é Jahan)

With its tiled mosques and exotic palaces, the city of Isfahan is considered by many to be the jewel in the Iranian crown. The central square, *Naghsh-é Jahan*, is framed by a series of elegant archways and contains several of the city's most important

monuments. *Masjid-é Imam*, the Imam Mosque, was built by Shah Abbas the Great during the city's Golden Age in the early 17th century. The women's mosque, the *Sheikh Lotfollah*, is decorated with exquisite Persian tilework and is the highlight of the square for many visitors. The magnificent *Ali Qapu Palace* stands opposite. The central area consists of a formal park and a lake with a fountain and covered bazaar which leads out of the square to the enormous *Masjid-é Jamé* (Friday Mosque).

Transportation

Air: Tehran Mehrabad International Airport, Isfahan Airport (domestic flights). **Road:** Coach: Services from Tehran.

Contact Addresses

Isfahan Tourist Office, Naghsh-é Jahan, Isfahan, Iran
Tel: (0311) 663 5231

Persepolis (Takht-é Jamshid)

Persepolis is thought to have been founded by Darius I in 518BC as the capital city of the vast and powerful Achaemenid Empire. The name Persepolis translates from Greek as 'Persian City' and it was built over a period of 120 years. Set on fire and looted by Alexander the Great in 330BC, it is nevertheless still astounding in its size and splendour; constructed on a large terrace 10m (27ft) high, access is up a wide staircase, and the huge pillars of the *Audience Hall* dwarf the visitors who come to see the impressive ruins.

Transportation

Air: Tehran Mehrabad International Airport, Shiraz Airport (domestic flights). **Road:** Taxi: Services from Shiraz.

Contact Addresses

For more information on Persepolis, contact Iran Touring and Tourism Organisation (see **Tourist Information** above).

Ireland

100km
50mls
✈ international airport

1 Aran Islands
2 Bantry House
3 Blarney Castle
4 Bunratty Castle and Folk Park
5 Cliffs of Moher
6 Croach Patrick
7 Dingle Peninsula
8 Dublin Castle
9 Dublin Zoo
10 Fota Wildlife Park
11 Glendalough
12 Guinness Storehouse
13 Killarney National Park
14 Kinsale
15 National Gallery of Ireland
16 National Shrine of Our Lady of Knock
17 Phoenix Park
18 RDS Arena
19 Ring of Kerry
20 Rock of Cashel
21 Trinity College Dublin
22 Waterford Crystal Visitor Centre

Tourist Information

Irish Tourist Board (Bord Fáilte Eireann)
Baggot Street Bridge, Dublin 2,
Republic of Ireland
Tel: (01) 525 525
Website: www.failteireland.ie

Irish Tourist Board
150 New Bond Street, London W1S 2AQ, UK
Tel: (020) 7518 0800 *or* (0800) 039 7000
(travel enquiries)
Website: www.irelandtravel.co.uk

Aran Islands

The *Aran Islands* are located approximately 48km (30 miles) out from the mouth of *Galway Bay* in the *Atlantic Ocean*. The largest of the three islands is *Inishmore* (or *Inis Mór*) which measures just 14km (9 miles) from tip to tip and 4.8km (3 miles) at its widest point. The islands are famous for

their prehistoric and Christian monuments including the spectacular *Dún Aengus* fort that is one of best examples of this type of fort in all of Europe. The fortified inner citadel is protected by huge semicircular ringed defences and the *chevaux-de-frise*, a cliff face peppered with sharp shards of rock jutting out intended to impede the advance of an attacking army. Other ancient stone forts worth visiting include *Dún Eoghanachta* and the crumbling *Dún Dúcathair*. The stunning islands are criss-crossed with thousands of miles of stone walls and visitors flock to the islands to enjoy the cliff-top walks and spectacular coastal scenery. The islands are also home to more than 430 different varieties of wild flowers and plants making them popular with botanists. Inishmore can get quite busy during the summer months but the other islands, *Inishmaan* (or *Inis Meáin*) and the smallest, *Inisheer* (*Inis Thiar*, or *Inis Oírr*), are less busy and can offer visitors a more authentic experience. But all three islands have held on to their ancient traditions including the use of Gaelic language (although English is also widely spoken).

Transportation
Air: Knock International Airport and Shannon International Airport. Inverin Airport (domestic flights). **Water:** Ferry: Services from Rossaveal and Doolin on the mainland to Kilronan. **Rail:** Galway Station. **Road:** Bus: Public services.

Contact Addresses
Aran Heritage Centre, Cill Ronain, Inis Mor, Arainn, Co na Gaillimhe
Tel: (099) 61355
Website: www.visitaranislands.com

Bantry House

Overlooking *Bantry Bay* in the south west of *Ireland*, *Bantry House* is a spectacular stately home that's been open to the public since 1946. Originally called *Blackrock*, the house was built in the 17th century as the ancestral home of the Earls of Bantry and is still lived in today by their descendants. The house was extended several times during the 18th century and gradually acquired an extensive collection of tapestries, paintings, furniture and artefacts that had been collected during their travels all over the world. Today, Bantry House consists of approximately 40 hectares (100 acres) of land of which approximately half is landscaped gardens and accessible woodland. Parts of the house can be rented out for weddings and private functions.

Transportation
Air: Cork International Airport. **Water:** Ferry: Services to Ringaskiddy Ferry Port. **Rail:** Killarney Station or Cork Station. **Road:** Bus: Public services. Car: N71.

Contact Addresses
Bantry House, Bantry, Cork, Ireland
Tel: (027) 50047
Website: www.bantryhouse.com

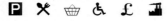

Blarney Castle

Set in idyllic Irish countryside, *Blarney Castle* is home to the famous *Blarney Stone*. Situated high in the battlements of the castle, the stone is thought to be half of the Stone of Scone, an ancient Scottish stone believed to have special powers. Those that kiss the stone are said to inherit the gift of eloquent speech. The castle itself began life as a 10th-century hunting lodge and was rebuilt in stone in 1210, only to be demolished and reconstructed in its original form by Dermot McCarthy, King of Munster, in 1446. Today, much of it lies in ruins.

Transportation
Air: Cork Airport. **Rail:** Train: Cork Station. **Road:** Bus: Regular bus services to Blarney (from Cork Station). Car: N20 (from Cork).

Contact Addresses
Blarney Castle, Blarney, County Cork, Ireland
Tel: (021) 438 5252
Website: www.blarneycastle.ie

Bunratty Castle and Folk Park

Built in 1425 by the McNamara family on the site of an earlier Viking settlement, and later acquired by the Anglo-Irish Studdart family, the spectacular *Bunratty Castle* is one of the finest examples of an Irish tower house still existing today. Inside is a beautifully preserved collection of Medieval furniture which serves as a reminder of Ireland's rich Celtic heritage. A Medieval banquet is served every night on demand to enable guests to experience what it was like to be entertained in the castle's heyday. The adjacent *Folk Park* recreates daily life as it was in 19th-century rural Ireland – farmhouses, shops and cottages have all been reconstructed in detail to provide visitors with an authentic experience.

Transportation
Air: Shannon Airport. **Rail:** Train: Limerick Station. **Road:** Bus: Services from Limerick or Ennis. Car: N18 (from Limerick, Ennis or Galway City).

Contact Addresses

Central Reservations, Bunratty Castle and Folk
Park, Bunratty, County Clare, Ireland
Tel: (061) 360 788
Website: www.shannonheritage.com

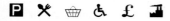

Cliffs of Moher

The majestic *Cliffs of Moher* are one of Ireland's
most spectacular and most visited tourist
attractions and tower 213m (700 ft) above the
Atlantic Ocean. The best vantage point from
which to see the Cliffs is *O'Briens Tower*,
constructed in 1835 by Cornelius O' Brien, a local
Member of Parliament who was responsible for
many other local landmarks, and restored in 1970.
The locals know each of the cliffs by name from
north to south: *Aillenasharragh*, *Carrickatreel*,
Knockardachuan, *Branawnmore*, *Stookeen* and *Hag's
Head*. Visitors also go to the cliffs to see the rich
birdlife of the area, including puffins, shags,
kittiwakes and razorbills. Nearby is an area
known as the *Burren* consisting of rolling hills and
cliff faces covered in limestone rock. The area
supports a diverse range of flora and fauna and is
also famous for its megalithic tombs and
monuments that pre-date the Egyptian pyramids.

Transportation
Air: Shannon Airport. **Rail:** Train: Ennis Station or
Galway Station. **Road:** Car: N-85 (from Ennis);
N-67 (from Galway).

Contact Addresses
Cliffs of Moher Centre, Shannon Heritage Visitor
Centre, Liscannor, County Clare, Ireland
Tel: (065) 708 1171 *or* 708 1565
Website: www.shannonheritage.com

Croach Patrick

Situated close to the town of *Westport* in *County
Mayo*, the peak of *Croach Patrick* rises 765m
(2,510ft) and was a sacred pagan site of spiritual
significance for hundreds of years before the
arrival of Christianity. Saint Patrick travelled across

Ireland spreading the word of God and, according
to religious stories, arrived at what is now known
as Croach Patrick in AD 441 where he spent forty
days and forty nights fasting on the summit of the
mountain. By the seventh century, Croach Patrick
had become one of the most important Christian
pilgrimage sites in Ireland. And still today, each
summer millions of pilgrims, many walking
barefoot as a penance for wrongdoings, ascend
Croach Patrick to visit the small church at the
summit. The last Sunday in July is the main
pilgrimage day attracting thousands of pilgrims.
The climb is also popular throughout the year with
walkers who ascend the mountain for the
spectacular views across *Clew Bay* below.

Transportation
Air: Knock International Airport and Shannon
International Airport. **Rail:** Westport Station.
Road: Bus: Public services.

Contact Addresses
Ireland West Tourism, Aras Failte, Forster Street,
County Galway, Ireland
Tel: (091) 537700
Website: www.irelandwest.ie

Dingle Peninsula

Located on the very south-western most tip of
Ireland in *County Kerry*, the dramatic *Dingle
Peninsula* is a popular diversion off the *Ring of
Kerry* tourist trail (see separate entry). The
spectacular peninsula is made up the
Macgillicuddy's Reeks mountain range, a series of
granite peaks that rise out of the *Atlantic*. Also in
and around the town of Dingle are approximately
2,000 archaeological sites. One of the most
famous Christian sites is the *St Gallarus Oratory*
which was thought to have been built between the
seventh and ninth century. Paid-entry attractions
in the region include the ever-popular *Oceanworld
Aquarium* (www.dingle-oceanworld.ie), and the
Blasket Centre, an exhibition celebrating Irish
culture, language and heritage. A popular resident
is *Fungie* the *Dingle Dolphin*. First spotted in *Dingle
Harbour* in 1984, the wild dolphin has returned
from feeding grounds further afield each summer
and can frequently be seen playing in the surf as

boats pass in and out of the harbour. With miles of secluded sandy beaches, rocky outcrops and stunning coastal paths, the Dingle Peninsula is popular with walkers.

Transportation
Air: Kerry Airport (domestic connections). **Water:** Ferry: Services from Europe to Cork. **Rail:** Killarney Station. **Road:** Bus: Public services.

Contact Addresses
Dingle Peninsula Tourism, Dingle, Count Kerry, Ireland
Website: www.dingle-peninsula.ie

Dublin Castle

Located in the heart of historic *Dublin*, *Dublin Castle* was built on the orders of King John, the first Lord of Ireland, in 1210 on the site of a former Danish Viking Fortress. Much of the castle has been rebuilt several times over its history with most of the modern day structure built at points during the 18th century. Of the original structure, only the *Record Tower* still stands today and is now more like a palace than a castle with lavish architecture and opulent rooms. Over the years the castle has been used as a royal residence, court house and prison and the *Irish Crown Jewels* were kept here until they were stolen in 1907. And it was here that on December 6 1921 the Anglo-Irish Treaty was signed effectively ending 700 years of colonial rule and forming what is now the *Republic of Ireland*. Nowadays, the castle is used for ceremonial procedures and to entertain visiting heads of state. It remains one of the most lavish places in all of Dublin.

Transportation
Air: Dublin International Airport. **Water:** Ferry: Services to Dun Laoghaire Port and Dublin Port. **Rail:** Dublin Station. **Road:** Bus: Public services.

Contact Addresses
Dublin Castle, Dublin 2, Ireland
Tel: (01) 677 7129
Website: www.dublincastle.ie

    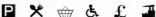

Dublin Zoo

First opened in 1830 with animals supplied by London Zoo, *Dublin Zoo* is one of the city's most popular attractions. It covers a 173-hectare (70-acre) site at *Phoenix Park* in the west of Dublin and houses a wide variety of animals, including red panda, South American birds, arctic fox, otter, elephants, and even a pack of grey wolves. Another popular attraction within the zoo is *City Farm*, which has a special children's corner and a flock of Galway sheep, and the Californian sea lion pool where audiences watch the animals train at regular intervals throughout the day.

Transportation
Air: Dublin Airport. **Water:** Ferry: Services from Holyhead (Wales) and Stranraer (Scotland) to Dun Laoghaire Port and Dublin Port. **Rail:** Train: Heuston Station. **Road:** Bus: Public services. Car: N1 (from Dublin Airport); M11, then N11 (from Wicklow); N7 (from Kildare); N11 (from Dun Laoghaire port), then signs to Dublin city centre and to Dublin Zoo.

Contact Addresses
Dublin Zoo, Phoenix Park, Dublin 8, Ireland
Tel: (01) 474 8900
Website: www.dublinzoo.ie

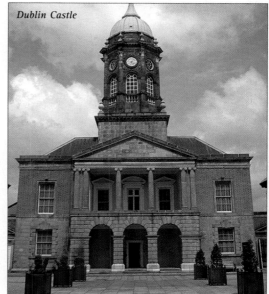
Dublin Castle

Fota Wildlife Park

Located just a few miles outside *Cork*, *Fota Wildlife Park* opened in 1983 as a joint project between the Zoological Society of Ireland and the University of Cork. It's primary objective was the conservation of wildlife and today the zoo is home to over 70 species of exotic wildlife including giraffes, zebra, antelope and ostrich which are all free to roam together within the park as they would in their natural habitats in the wild. Of all the animals in the zoo, only the resident cheetahs are in conventional enclosures. The entrance ticket to Fota Wildlife Park also includes entrance to the *Fota Aboretum* containing a fine collection of plants and trees from around the world.

Transportation
Air: Cork International Airport. **Water:** Ferry: Services to Ringaskiddy Ferry Port. **Rail:** Cork Station then connection to Fota Wildlife Park's own station. **Road:** Bus: Public services.

Contact Addresses
Fota Wildlife Park, Carrigtwohill, County Cork, Ireland
Tel: (021) 481 2678
Website: www.fotawildlife.ie

Glendalough

Known in Irish as 'glenn of the two lakes', *Glendalough* is a glacially sculpted beautiful green valley. During Ireland's 'Golden Age' (AD 500-900) the country flourished as the poetry, music and writing of its missionaries and teachers influenced scholars across Europe. During this time, Glendalough was home to a monastic settlement established by St Kevin, a reclusive monk, who for seven years enjoyed a simple and solitary existence, with animals and birds as his only companions. St Kevin came to the area during the sixth century and founded his monastery in AD 498, remaining there until his death at the grand old age of 120

Transportation
Air: Dublin Airport. **Rail:** Train: Rathdrum Station. **Road:** Bus: Public services. Car: N11 (exit Kilmacanogue), then R755 and R756 to Glendalough (from Dublin).

Contact Addresses
Glendalough Visitor Centre, Glendalough, Co Wicklow, Ireland
Tel: (0404) 45325 *or* 45352
Website: www.heritageireland.com

Guinness Storehouse

Opened in December 2000, the *Guinness Storehouse* is a whole museum dedicated to Ireland's most famous export, Guinness stout. Arthur Guinness first began brewing the 'black gold' on the site in 1759, with the present-day building being designed by the architect A H Hignett in 1904. Used for fermenting and storing Guinness until the 1980s, the Storehouse is a listed building with exhibitions spanning over six floors. Entry to the Guinness Storehouse is through a pint glass-shaped atrium capable of holding 10,000 pints of stout, and there is a free pint of the magic brew for every visitor in the *Gravity Bar* which offers spectacular views across the city.

Transportation
Air: Dublin Airport. **Water:** Ferry: Services from Holyhead (Wales) and Stranraer (Scotland) to Dun Laoghaire Port and Dublin Port. **Rail:** Train: Connolly Station or Heuston Station.

Contact Addresses
Guinness Storehouse, St James's Gate, Dublin 8, Ireland

The Guinness Storehouse

The Guinness Storehouse©

Tel: 353 1 453 8364 (recorded information) *or*
353 1 408 4800 (customer services)
Website: www.guinness-storehouse.com

Killarney National Park

Killarney National Park covers over 10,000
hectares (25,000 acres) of woodland, lakes,
mountains, parks and gardens in the far
southwest of Ireland. It was Ireland's first
national park and was founded in 1932 when the
Muckross estate was given to the Irish people by
Senator Arthur Vincent. Popular sports include
trout fishing in the three lakes, boating at *Ross
Castle*, walking and cycling. *Muckross House*, a
Victorian mansion completed in 1843, is open to
the public as is its working farm and the
beautiful landscaped gardens. Other attractions
within the grounds of the park include the 15th-
century *Muckross Abbey* and the ruined seventh-
century monastery at *Inisfallen Island* on *Lough
Leane*, where the 'Annals of Inisfallen', detailing
Ireland's early history, were written by the
monks.

Transportation
Air: Cork Airport. **Road:** Car: Killarney National
Park is located 6.5km (4 miles) from Killarney on
the N71 (Kenmare Road).

Contact Addresses
Muckross House, Muckross, Killarney, Ireland
Tel: (064) 31440
Website: http://homepage.tinet.ie/~knp

Kinsale

The coastal town of *Kinsale* in the county of
Cork in the southwest of the country is one of
the most picturesque regions in *Ireland*. Two
17th-century forts guard the entrance to the
harbour and guided tours are available of the
star-shaped *Charles Fort* that was built in 1677.
The 15th-century *Desmond Castle* had originally
been used as a customs house before being
converted to a prison in the 17th century.

Nowadays, it's home to the *International Museum
of Wine* that details Kinsale's role in the early
international wine trade. Other attractions
include an interesting museum housed within
the old *Courthouse* and the 13th-century *St
Multose Church* that's still in use today. Away
from the harbour, visitors can explore the
winding cobbled streets through a maze of bars
and fine seafood restaurants. A walk away from
the town up to the *Old Head of Kinsale* offers
stunning coastal views.

Transportation
Air: Cork International Airport. **Water:** Ferry:
Services to Ringaskiddy Ferry Port. **Rail:** Cork
Station. **Road:** Bus: Public services.

Contact Addresses
Kinsale Tourist Office, Pier Road, Kinsale, Cork,
Ireland
Tel: (021) 477 2234
Website: www.kinsale.ie

National Gallery of Ireland

The *National Gallery of Ireland* was founded in
1854 and houses the national collection of Irish
art, the national collection of European Old
Masters including works by Caravaggio and
Rubens, the *National Portrait Collection* and the
Yeats Collection. The latter features many works
by Jack B Yeats, Ireland's most important 20th-
century artist. The grand National Gallery
building stands in the south of the city and
dominates Merrion Square, one of Dublin's finest
Georgian squares. The *Millennium Wing* features
temporary exhibitions and themed collections.
Visitors to the Gallery can take advantage of the
free public tours every Saturday and Sunday.

Transportation
Air: Dublin Airport. **Water:** Ferry: Services from
Holyhead (Wales) and Stranraer (Scotland) to Dun
Laoghaire Port and Dublin Port. **Rail:** Train:
Heuston Station, Connolly Station or Tara Street
Station. DART (electric rail): Pearse Station. **Road:**
Bus: Public services. Car: N1 (from Dublin
Airport); M11, then N11 (from Wicklow); N7 (from
Kildare); N11 (from Dun Laoghaire port), then
signs to Dublin city centre.

Contact Addresses
National Gallery of Ireland, Merrion Square West,
Dublin 2, Ireland
Tel: (01) 661 5133
Website: www.nationalgallery.ie

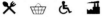

National Shrine of Our Lady of Knock

Located in *County Mayo* on the *West Coast* of
Ireland, the *National Shrine of Our Lady of Knock*
marks the site where, on August 21 1879, it is
said Our Lady the Virgin Mary appeared in an
apparition. Our Lady is said to have appeared with
St. Joseph and St. John the Evangelist at the
church's south gable on a wet and windswept
evening in August and was witnessed by 15
people. The shrine attracts many visitors
throughout the year but the main pilgrimage
season is from the last Sunday in April until the
second Sunday in October.

Transportation
Air: Knock International Airport. **Water:** Ferry:
Services to Ringaskiddy Ferry Port. **Rail:** Cork
Station then bus services to Knock. **Road:** Bus:
Public services.

Contact Addresses
Shrine Office, County Mayo, Ireland
Tel: (94) 9388 100
Website: www.knock-shrine.ie

Phoenix Park

Dublin's *Phoenix Park* located to the west of the
city centre is one of the largest city parks in
Europe. With a circumference of 11km (7 miles)
and a total area of 712 hectares (1,760 acres),
Phoenix Park is made up of open grasslands,
tree-lined avenues, ornamental gardens, lakes
and nature trails. The park is also home to a
herd of wild deer. *Dublin Zoo* (see separate entry)
is located within the park. Also within the park
grounds is a 63-m (206-ft) obelisk in memory of
the Duke of Wellington who was born in Dublin
in 1769 and the *Phoenix Monument* located in
the very centre of the park. The *Phoenix Park
Visitor Centre* is at Ashtown Castle, a medieval
tower house that is thought to date back to the
17th century, and now houses an excellent
exhibition about the history and wildlife of the
park and surounding region. Access to the park
is free but entry is charged for the Phoenix Park
Visitor Centre.

Rock of Cashel

Corel©

Transportation

Air: Dublin International Airport. **Water:** Ferry: Services to Dun Laoghaire Port and Dublin Port. **Rail:** Dublin Station. **Road:** Bus: Public services.

Contact Addresses

Phoenix Park Visitor Centre, Phoenix Park, Dublin 8, Ireland
Tel: (01) 677 0095
Website: www.heritageireland.ie

RDS Arena

Dublin's RDS (Royal Dublin Society) Irish International Convention and Exhibition Centre is the country's premier venue for meetings, conferences, exhibitions, trade shows, entertainment and sporting events. The Society itself was founded in 1731 to promote the development of agriculture, arts, science and industry in Ireland. The arena measures over 20,000 sq m (215,280 sq ft) and regularly hosts the city's major events and exhibitions.

Transportation

Air: Dublin International Airport. **Water:** Ferry: Services to Dun Laoghaire Port and Dublin Port. **Rail:** Dublin Station. DART connections to the venue. **Road:** Bus: Public services.

Contact Addresses

Merrion Road, Ballsbridge, Dublin 4, Ireland
Tel: (01) 668 0866
Website: www.rds.ie

Ring of Kerry

The famous *Ring of Kerry* is a 170km (106 miles) tourist trail that takes in some of the southwest of Ireland's most spectacular sights along the *Iveragh Peninsula*. Beginning at *Killarney*, visitors can travel in either direction (although tour buses should travel anti-clockwise) on the circular route which passes through *Kenamare*, *Sneem*, *Waterville*, *Cahersiveen*, *Kells*, *Glenbeigh* and *Killorglin* with specific sights of interest in each location.

Highlights of the trail include the *Bog Village*, *Derrynane House* – former home of Daniel O'Connel, the 15th-century *Muckross Abbey*, *Staigue Fort* and *Ross Castle*. Natural attractions along the route include the picturesque *Rossbeigh* beach, the thundering waters of *Torc Waterfall*, and the spectacular *Blue Pool Nature Reserve*. There are also established Ring of Kerry walking and cycling routes that use, where possible, quieter roads and tracks with the cycling route taking in the additional sights of *St Finian's Bay* and the island of *Valentia*. The scenic drive can be comfortably completed in one day but accommodation is available in each location (although this may need to be booked in advance) for visitors who want to spend longer exploring specific attractions.

Transportation

Air: Kerry Airport (domestic connections). **Rail:** Killarney Station. **Road:** Bus: Public services.

Contact Addresses

Killarney Tourist Information Office, Beech Road, Killarney, Country Kerry, Ireland
Tel: (064) 31633
Website: www.corkkerry.ie

Rock of Cashel

Located on a limestone base on the outskirts of the town, the *Rock of Cashel* (also known as the *Cashel of the Kings*) is one of *Ireland*'s most spectacular archaeological sites. The origins of the site date back to the fourth century and the Welsh Eoghachta clan who conquered and became kings of the region building a hilltop stronghold on the site. King Aengus was baptised here by St Patrick, Ireland's patron saint, in the fifth century. A *Cathedral* and *Romanesque Chapel* were added to the compound and the site was eventually given to the church in the 12th century. Visitors also come to the Rock of Cashel to see the *Hall of the Vicars Choral* and the 28-metre (92-foot) *Round Tower*. The Rock sits high on a hill offering good views of the surrounding area and there's also a museum at the site.

Transportation

Air: Shannon Airport, Dublin Airport or Cork Airport. **Water:** Ferry: Accessible from Rosslare Port, Cork Port, Dublin Port and Dun Laoghaire.

Rail: Thurles Station and Limerick Junction Station. **Road:** Bus: Public services.

Contact Addresses
Rock of Cashel, Cashel, Tipperary, Ireland
Tel: (062) 61437
Website: www.heritageireland.ie

Trinity College Dublin

Founded in 1592 by a small group of Dublin citizens who obtained a royal charter from Queen Elizabeth I of England, *Trinity College* is Ireland's most prominent university. It's famous scholars through the years include Samuel Beckett, Jonathan Swift and Oscar Wilde. It has played a somewhat controversial role in Irish politics and religion, since, until 1873, only Anglicans could enrol as full members of the university to obtain degrees and scholarships; Catholics were not even permitted to use the library. Today, as well as strolling through the campus' lush grounds, visitors flock to the *Old Library*. Built in 1732, the Old Library is the largest in Ireland and holds four million volumes and an extensive collection of manuscripts. The most famous work in the collection is the *Book of Kells*, one of the finest examples of medieval decorated manuscripts, which was written in about AD 800. The *Dublin Experience* is a multimedia presentation of Dublin, featuring photographs and music, and provides an excellent introduction to the city.

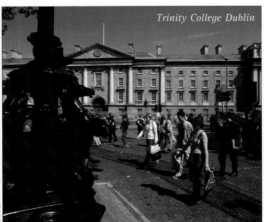

Trinity College Dublin

Corel©

Transportation
Air: Dublin Airport. **Water:** Ferry: Services from Holyhead (Wales) and Stranraer (Scotland) to Dun Laoghaire Port and Dublin Port. **Rail:** Train: Heuston Station, Connolly Station or Tara Street Station. DART (electric rail): Pearse Station. **Road:** Bus: Public services. Car: N1 (from Dublin Airport); M11, then N11 (from Wicklow); N7 (from Kildare); N11 (from Dun Laoghaire port), then signs to Dublin city centre.

Contact Addresses
Trinity College Library, College Street, Dublin 2, Ireland
Tel: (01) 608 2320
Website: www.tcd.ie

Waterford Crystal Visitor Centre

Waterford is famous the world over as the home of beautiful crystal designs. The *Waterford Factory* was opened in 1783 by George and William Penrose, and bowls, vases and ornaments continue to be made on the site. The crystal mix is transformed into glass in a 1200°C (2192°F) furnace before being blown and decorated with deep engravings by skilled workers. Visitors to the centre can watch the glass being formed into decanters, bowls and wine glasses and learn about the unique production techniques used at Waterford, through audiovisual displays and chatting to the craftsmen in their workshops. Many of the most prestigious pieces of Waterford Crystal, which have been presented to celebrities and politicians, are on display in the *Gallery*.

Transportation
Air: Shannon Airport, Dublin Airport, Waterford Airport (domestic flights). **Rail:** Train: Plunkett Station (Waterford). **Road:** Bus: Public services. Car: N25 (from Cork).

Contact Addresses
Waterford Crystal Visitor Centre, Kilbarry, Cork Road, Waterford, Ireland
Tel: (051) 332 500
Website: www.waterfordvisitorcentre.com

Israel

Tourist Information

Ministry of Tourism (Misrad Hatayarut)
PO Box 1018, King George Street 24,
Jerusalem, Israel
Tel: (02) 675 4811
Website: www.infotour.co.il

Israel Government Tourist Office
UK House, 180 Oxford Street, London W1D
1NN, UK
Tel: (020) 7299 1111
Website: www.goisrael.com

Dead Sea (Yam Ha-melah)

Lying 400m (1320ft) below sea level and
spanning the border between Israel and Jordan,
the *Dead Sea* is a natural wonder. It contains more
minerals and salt than any other stretch of water
in the world, and thus it is possible to float on
top of the water. Its natural properties make it a
prime centre for spa treatments and relaxation
therapies and there are a number of resorts in the
area. The Dead Sea has strong Biblical
connections: the salt mountain range of *Mount
Sodom* is, according to the Bible, the site of the
sinful city that perished alongside Gomorra. In
turn, the *Dead Sea Scrolls*, the oldest Biblical
documents known to be in existence, were
discovered at *Qumran*, a restored archaeological
site in the north. *Masada* is also located on the
Israeli shores of the Dead Sea. The *Ein Gedi Nature
Reserve and Kibbutz* provides opportunities for
spotting desert wildlife and offers trails to
waterfalls, canyons, caves and shallow pools.
Metzoke Dragot, located in a deep crater, is a
popular site for more adventurous sports such as
abseiling, climbing (with amazing desert views)
and mountain biking.

Transportation
Air: Ben-Gurion International Airport. **Road:**
Coach: Public services. Taxi: Sheshir taxis (from
Ben-Gurion International Airport).

Contact Addresses
Dead Sea Regional Tourist Organization, NP Dead
Sea 86910, Israel
Tel: (07) 668 8808
Website: www.deadsea.co.il

Masada (Horvot Mezada)

Perched high on a sheer-sided plateau, *Masada* is
famous for being the site of a mass suicide by a
group of Jewish people who put their religous
beliefs and cultural pride before their own lives.
Located in the Negev desert on the southern coast
of Israel, the fortress was originally built in

around 35BC as a luxurious refuge for King Herod. But it was seized by the Jewish people following a Jewish revolt in AD 66. In AD 72, the Roman army lay siege to Masada and seeing that the Romans would soon breach their defences, the Jewish people chose to take their own lives rather than being captured alive and becoming slaves. The site was excavated between 1963-65 and today many visitors climb the steep, winding 'snake path' to the fortress to enjoy the beautiful views. A gentler climb from the other side is possible or visitors can opt to take a cable car to the summit. Sunrise ascents are particularly popular.

Transportation
Air: Ovda Airport (Eilat) or Ben-Gurion International Airport. **Rail:** Cable Car: A cable car runs from the Masada Cable Car Station at the bottom of the mountain to the summit. **Road:** Bus: Services run from Jerusalem, Tel Aviv and Bersheva. **Car:** Route 3199 (from Arad).

Contact Addresses
Horvot Mezada, M P Yam Hamelach, Negev, Israel
Tel: (08) 658 4207
www.goisrael.com

Temple Mount (Al-Haram al-Sharif)

Temple Mount, a walled section of the Old City of Jerusalem, is a site of tremendous religious significance to Jews, Muslims and Christians. The area, which is one of Jerusalem's most famous landmarks, is believed to be the site of the holy rock where Abraham offered his son Isaac for sacrifice. It is also reputedly the site where Solomon erected the First Temple to house the Ark of the Covenant, which had been brought to Jerusalem by his father David, and also the area from where Mohammed ascended to heaven. The Babylonians captured Jerusalem in 587BC and burned down the temple, exiling many of the people to Babylonia. A Second Temple was subsequently constructed in 515BC, only to be destroyed by the Roman Emperor Titus in AD 70. Today, the site is dominated by the Dome of the Rock and is also home to the silver-domed Al Aqsa

Mosque, which is a Muslim place of worship, as well as the Islamic Museum, which houses a collection of Korans, as well as Islamic artefacts and relics.

Transportation
Air: Ben-Gurion International Airport. **Road:** Bus: Public services to the Dung Gate. **Car:** Hwy-1 (from Tel Aviv).

Contact Addresses
For more information on Temple Mount, contact the Ministry of Tourism (see **Tourist Information** above).

 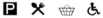

Western Wall (HaKotel HaMaaravi)

The Western Wall, known to non-Jews as the 'Wailing Wall', is a 488-m (1601-ft) stretch of wall which is all that remains of the Second Temple of Jerusalem. The most sacred Jewish place in the world, it attracts thousands of devout Jews every year who come to pray, and push prayer notes and messages of goodwill into the cracks of the wall. The wall was built more than two thousand years ago under King Herod, and has been under Israeli control since 1967. It is also sacred to Muslims who believe that the wall marks the place where the prophet Mohammed tied up his winged horse, al-Burak, before ascending to heaven. It has been divided into two sections of prayer, the left for men and the right for women, and forms part of a larger wall surrounding the Dome of the Rock and Al Aqsa Mosque. Visitors are able to watch the religious ceremonies.

Transportation
Air: Ben-Gurion International Airport. **Road:** Bus: Public services. **Car:** Hwy-1 to central Jerusalem (from Tel Aviv).

Contact Addresses
Western Wall Heritage Foundation, 2 HaOmer Street, Old City, Jerusalem 97500, Israel
Tel: (02) 627 1333
Website: www.hakotel.org.il

Italy

Tourist Information

**Italian State Tourist Office – ENIT
(Ente Nazionale Italiano per il Turismo)**
Via Marghera 2, 00185 Rome, Italy
Tel: (06) 49711
Website: www.enit.it

Italian State Tourist Office (ENIT)
1 Princes Street, London W1R 8AY, UK
Tel: (020) 7408 1254 or 7355 1557 (trade enquiries only) or (09001) 600 280 (brochure line; calls are charged at 60p per minute)
Website: www.enit.it

Colosseum (Colosseo)

The *Colosseum* is arguably ancient Rome's most famous building. This massive structure, with arch upon arch reaching 48m (157ft) into the air and measuring 190m by 155m (620ft by 513ft), used to hold up to 50,000 boisterous Roman citizens. Opened in AD 80 by Emperor Titus in a ceremony that included 100 days of games, the Colosseum played host to Rome's favourite spectator sports – gladiatorial contests, combats between men and wild animals and even mock naval battles. Today, only the shell remains along with a view down to the passages through which slaves and animals were led before entering into battle. Unlike other Roman amphitheatres that are dug into hillsides, the Colosseum is a free-standing structure of stone and concrete and has long served as a model for stadia around the world.

Transportation
Air: Rome Leonardo da Vinci Airport (Fiumicino), Rome Ciampino Airport. **Water:** Ferry: Civitavecchia port, from where there are services to central Rome. **Rail:** Train: Roma Termini Station, Roma Tiburtina Station, Roma Ostiense Station or Roma Trastevere Station. Underground: Colosseo. Tram: Piazza del Colosseo. **Road:** Bus: Regular public services. Car: A12 (from the west); A24 (from the east); SS7 (from Rome Ciampino Airport).

Contact Addresses

Piazza Del Colosseo, Rome, Italy
Tel: (06) 39 96 7700
Website: www.enit.it

Doges' Palace (Palazzo Ducale)

Located in Venice's renowned *Piazza San Marco*, adjacent to the *Basilica di San Marco*, the *Doges' Palace* was home to the government of the former Venetian Republic from AD 697 to 1797. Although the palace was originally built in AD 814, the present structure was completed in the early 15th century. The palace was a showplace for artistry, craftsmanship and architecture, and still exemplifies the splendour of Venetian Gothic style. As well as ruling the city state, the doges (a Venetian word from the Latin *dux*, meaning leader) were great patrons of the arts and the palace is filled with works by Venetian Renaissance masters such as Veronese and Tintoretto. The *Ponte dei Sospiri*, or Bridge of Sighs, is an integral part of the palace and forms the link between the courts and the prisons across the canal. It is named after the noise prisoners used to make as they were led to confinement in the damp and gloomy cells, which can still be visited on a tour of the palace.

Transportation

Air: Venice Marco Polo Airport. **Water:** Ferry: Public services. **Rail:** Train: Venezia Santa Lucia Station (Venice Station). **Road:** Bus: Public services. Car: A4 (from Turin); A13 (from Bologna); A1 (from Rome or Florence); A1, then A13, then A4 (from Naples); SS11 (from Padua).

Contact Addresses

Palazzo Ducale, San Marco 1, 30124 Venice, Italy
Tel: (041) 522 4951

Florence Duomo (Duomo Santa Maria del Fiore)

Florence's *Duomo*, or cathedral, completed in 1466 after 170 years of work and its domed roof is symbolic of the meeting of Renaissance craft and culture. Engineered by the architect and sculptor Filippo Brunelleschi (1377-1446), using specially invented machines, the *cupola* (dome) was one of the greatest achievements of the Italian Renaissance. Its octagonal form has a diameter of 46.5m (153ft) at the base, and was completed in 1434; it is possible to climb to the top of the dome for magnificent views over the city. The vast interior boasts frescoes by Renaissance masters such as Paolo Uccello and Andrea del Castagno, as well as a monument to the poet Dante and his *Divina Commedia* (Divine Comedy). The nearby *campanile* (bell tower) is decorated inside with frescoes and statues by Giotto and Donatello, amongst others.

Transportation

Air: Amerigo Vespucci Airport (Florence), Galileo Galilei Airport (Pisa). **Rail:** Train: Firenze Santa Maria Novella Station (Florence). **Road:** Bus: Public services. Car: A1 (from Milan, Bologna, Rome or Naples); A11 (from Pisa, Lucca, Prato or Siena).

Contact Addresses

Opera di Santa Maria del Fiore, Via della Canonica 1, 50122 Florence, Italy
Tel: (055) 230 2885
Website: www.operaduomo.firenze.it

Leaning Tower of Pisa (Torre Pendente di Pisa)

Constructed in 1174, at a time when the Pisans were enjoying an era of military success, the *Leaning Tower of Pisa*, located in Pisa's *Campo dei Miracoli* (Field of Miracles) is famous not only because of its striking beauty but also because of its awkward geometry. It served as the bell tower of the equally impressive *Cattedrale* (Cathedral) and *Battistero* (Baptistry), and, as a result of the poor swampy soil beneath, has leaned almost since construction first started. Today, one side is 5m (16ft) closer to the ground than the other. Galileo used the tower for experiments to prove his theory of motion whilst he was chair of mathematics at the *Università di Pisa* (Pisa University) in 1589.

Transportation
Air: Pisa Galileo Galilei Airport. **Rail:** Train: Pisa Centrale Station. **Road:** Car: A12 (from Genoa and the north); A11 (from Florence).

Contact Addresses
Opera della Primaziale Pisana, Via B Croce 26, 56125 Pisa, Italy
Tel: (050) 560 547
Website: http://torre.duomo.pisa.it or www.pisae.it

Mount Etna

Mount Etna is one of the most active volcanoes in Europe and is Sicily's best-known natural attraction. It is also the highest mountain on the island currently measuring 3,350m (10,990ft); the height varies each time the volcano erupts. Its mythical importance dates back to the Ancient Greeks who believed it was here that Cyclops helped forge lightning bolts for Zeus, deep within the volcano's core. Mount Etna is situated within the *Etna Regional Park* (Parco Regionale dell'Etna), Sicily's first national park that was established in 1987. The park offers skiing opportunities in the winter and some great hiking trails with mountain refuges during the summer. The park is popular with volcanologists all year round and drew particular attention in 2001, the year of the volcano's last major eruption. The fertile volcanic terrain supports an array of flora and fauna including vineyards and magnificent forests.

Doges' Palace

Archivo Fotografico A.P.T di Venezia©

Transportation
Air: Catania Airport (Fontanarossa Airport) and Palermo Airport. **Rail:** Services from Catania to Riposto. **Road:** Bus: Public services from Catania.

Contact Addresses
Etna Regional Park, Via Etnea 107, Nicolosi, Sicily
Tel: (095) 914 588
Website: www.agriturismosicilia.com

Old Bridge (Ponte Vecchio)

This famous 14th-century bridge, built by Taddeo Gaddi and home to medieval Florence's gold and silversmiths, is still paved with jewellers' shops today. The *Ponte Vecchio*'s genteel atmosphere dates back to the days of Cosimo de' Medici, a member of the city's ruling dynasty in Renaissance times, who threw out a group of butchers who set up shop on the bridge. Above the shops that line the bridge is a secret passageway known as the *Corridoio Vasariano*, linking the *Palazzo Vecchio*, *Uffizi Gallery* and the *Pitti Palace*, and originally built as a private passage for the Medici family. The Ponte Vecchio was the only bridge across the River Arno to be spared German bombing during World War II.

Transportation
Air: Amerigo Vespucci Airport (Florence), Pisa Galileo Galilei Airport. **Rail:** Train: Santa Maria Novella Station.

Contact Addresses
Opera Della Primaziale, Pisa, Piazza Duomo 17, CAP S6126, Pisa, Italy
Tel: (055) 23320
Website: www.firenze.turismo.toscana.it

Pantheon (Panteone)

Considered by many to be the best preserved of all the great classical monuments, the *Pantheon* was dedicated in 27BC by Agrippa, the admiral who defeated Anthony and Cleopatra, and rebuilt by Hadrian in AD 125 after it had been struck by lightning and burnt down sometime between AD 98-117. The Pantheon possesses a dome with a span of 43.2m (142ft), the largest of its kind until the *Duomo* in Florence was built in the 15th century. The bronze and gold décor was stripped away to be used in other Roman monuments, such as *St Peter's Basilica*, but the sheer size and age of the building cannot fail to impress. Inside visitors can see the tomb of the Renaissance master Raphael.

Transportation

Air: Rome Leonardo da Vinci Airport (Fiumicino), Rome Ciampino Airport. **Water:** Ferry: Civitavecchia port, from where there are services to central Rome. **Rail:** Train: Roma Termini Station, Roma Tiburtina Station, Roma Ostiense Station or Roma Trastevere Station. **Road:** Bus: Public services. Car: A12 (from the west); A24 (from the east); SS7 (from Rome Ciampino Airport).

Contact Addresses

Piazza della Rotunda, Panteone 00186, Rome, Italy
Tel: (06) 6830 0230
Website: www.romeguide.it

Pompeii

Once a lavish resort town for wealthy Romans, *Pompeii*, situated 25km (16 miles) south of Naples, was literally buried alive under hot volcanic ash and mud during an eruption of nearby *Mount Vesuvius* in AD 79. The city was eventually forgotten, and it was not until the 16th century that it was rediscovered. Now excavated, it provides an enthralling insight into the everyday lives of the ancient Romans. Visitors can view restored villas complete with erotic and religious wall paintings, temples and the forum, as well as actual brothels and plaster casts of fallen volcano victims. Nearby *Ercolano* (Herculaneum) was also destroyed by Vesuvius, and is a smaller but better-preserved site consisting of villas and shops. From Ercolano, the modern town, it is possible to take a bus to the top of Mount Vesuvius.

Transportation

Air: Naples International Airport. **Rail:** Train: Pompeii FS Station, Pompeii Santuario, Pompeii–Villa dei Misteri Station or Ercolano

Station. Circumvesuviana (Bay of Naples rail system): Pompeii-Scavi-Villa dei Misteri Station. **Road:** Car: A3 to Pompeii (from Naples); S18 to Ercolano (from Naples).

Contact Addresses

Azienda di Cura, Soggiorno e Turismo Pompeii (Pompeii Visitors Centre), Via Satra 1, CAP 80045, Pompeii (NA), Italy
Tel: (081) 850 7255

Rialto Bridge

The foundations for the famous *Rialto Bridge* that crosses the *Grand Canal* were laid in 1588 and today lies at the cultural heart of *Venice*. Completed in 1591, the bridge was built to replace earlier wooden versions that frequently collapsed into the canal. Until the building of the *Accademia Bridge* in 1854, the Rialto Bridge was the only means of crossing the Grand Canal on foot. The bridge was built by Antonio da Ponte who competed for the contract against other acclaimed designers of his day such as Michelangelo and Palladio. Antonio's bridge has a 7.3-metre (24-ft) arch to allow boats to pass beneath it and is wide enough to accommodate shops that predominantly cater to the tourists who flock here each day to see this Venetian landmark.

Transportation

Air: Venice Marco Polo Airport. **Water:** Ferry: Public services. **Rail:** Train: Venice Station (Venezia Santa Lucia Station). **Road:** Bus: Public services. Foot: Follow signs for Rialto.

Contact Addresses

For more information on the Rialto Bridge, contact the Italian State Tourist Office (see **Tourist Information** above).

Roman Forum (Foro Romano)

The *Roman Forum*, located between the Capitoline and Palatine hills in the centre of Rome, was the main focus of the Roman Republic and later the symbolic heart of an empire that stretched from England to Carthage. The religious and political institutions, law courts, shops and markets would have bustled with life, and the temples and imperial monuments were architectural triumphs. Fire, invasions and general decay have all detracted from its former glories and in 1932 the Italian fascist dictator Mussolini ordered a main road to be built straight through the site. Among the best-preserved monuments are the triumphal *Arch of Septimius*, eight columns of the *Temple of Saturn* and the rectangular *House of the Vestal Virgins*.

Pompeii

Archivio Fotografico A.P.T di Venezia©

Transportation
Air: Rome Leonardo da Vinci Airport (Fiumicino), Rome Ciampino Airport. **Water:** Ferry: Civitavecchia port, from where there are services to central Rome. **Rail:** Train: Roma Termini Station or Roma Tiburtina Station. Underground: Colosseo. **Road:** Bus: Public services to Piazza del Colosseo or Via dei Fori Imperiali. Car: A12 (from the west); A24 (from the east); SS7 (from Rome Ciampino Airport).

Contact Addresses
Foro Romano, Piazza Santa Maria Nova 53, 00186 Rome, Italy
Tel: (06) 699 0110
Website: www.archeorm.arti.beniculturali.it

San Siro Stadium

The world-famous *San Siro Stadium* (also known as the 'Stadio Giuseppe Meazza') is jointly home to Milan's two main football teams and two of the best teams in Italy's Serie A football league, *AC Milan* (www.acmilan.com) and *Internazionale* (www.inter.it). Both clubs have proud footballing traditions and the *San Siro Museum* tells the histories of both clubs with memorabilia including cups, medals and shirts as well as life-size replicas of some of the clubs' great players including Franco Baresi, Paolo Maldini, Marco Van Basten, Ruud Gullit and Nereo Rocco. Guided tours of this incredible 86,000 capacity ground are available. Both sets of fans are fiercely proud of their clubs and derby games between the two teams often have an electric atmosphere. The San Siro also hosts rock concerts during the closed season.

Transportation
Air: Linate Airport and Malpensa Airport. **Rail:** Milan Centrale Station, Milan Porta Garibaldi Station and Milan Lambrate Station. Metro: Molino Dorino Station. Tram: Line 24. **Road:** Bus: Public services.

Contact Addresses
San Siro Stadium, Via Piccolomini 5, 20151 Milan, Italy
Tel: (02) 4042 432
Website: www.sansirotour.com

Siena Main Square (Piazza del Campo)

The shell-shaped *Piazza del Campo* lies at the heart of Siena and has served as a focus for life in the city for centuries. The *Palazzo Pubblico* (Town Hall), which stands proudly at the top of the piazza, was constructed between 1297 and 1310 as the seat of the *Governo dei Nove*, or Government of Nine, who ruled Siena from 1287-1355. The interior of the building, which is now the *Museo Civico* (Civic Museum), contains many paintings by Sienese masters such as Simone Martini and Ambrogio Lorenzetti, as well as the remains of the *Gaia Fountain*. Next to the Palazzo Pubblico stands the *Torre del Mangia* (Mangia Tower), a belltower which rises to 102m (334ft); visitors can climb to the top for views of the winding cobbled streets which fan out from the piazza, and timeless vistas of the Tuscan countryside.

Italy

Transportation
Air: Pisa Galileo Galilei Airport. **Rail:** Train: Siena Station. **Road:** Bus: Public services. Car: A1 (from Rome, exit Valdichiana); Superstrada del Palio (from Florence); A12 (from Genoa). The historic centre of Siena is pedestrianised.

Contact Addresses
Museo Civico, Palazzo Comunale, Piazza del Camponoz, 53100 Siena, Italy
Tel: (057) 7292 263
Website: www.enit.it

Spanish Steps and Keats Shelley Memorial House

Although they have been known as the *Spanish Steps*, after the nearby Spanish Embassy, ever since their construction between 1721-25, the steps that lead up to the rose-coloured *Trinità dei Monti* church were in fact constructed and funded by the French King, Charles VIII. At the bottom of the steps is the *Piazza di Spagna* (Spanish Square), and Pietro Bernini's *Fontana della Barcaccia* (Barcaccia Fountain). The steps have served as a meeting point for generations of travellers, from the English Grand Tourists of the 18th century, to the young people of all nationalities who flock here today. The English Romantic poet, John Keats, spent the last few months of his life in the *Casina Rossa*, or Little Red House, nearby before he tragically died of tuberculosis in 1821. The house was left to go to ruin until it was bought by a group of British and Americans in 1903 and turned into a museum where visitors can learn about the lives of Keats, Shelley, Byron and other English poets who were inspired by Italy.

Transportation
Air: Rome Leonardo da Vinci Airport (Fiumicino), Rome Ciampino Airport. **Water:** Ferry: Civitavecchia port, from where there are services to central Rome. **Rail:** Train: Roma Termini Station, Roma Tiburtina Station, Roma Ostiense Station or Roma Trastevere Station. Underground: Spagna. **Road:** Bus: Publics services. Car: A12 (from the west); A24 (from the east); SS7 (from Rome Ciampino Airport).

Contact Addresses
Keats-Shelley Memorial House, Piazza di Spagna 26, 00187 Rome, Italy
Tel: (06) 678 4235
Website: www.Keats-Shelley-House.org

St Mark's Basilica (Basilica di San Marco)

The glittering facade of *St Mark's Basilica* dominates the vast expanse of *St Mark's Square* and stands as a potent symbol of Venice's status as city state and maritime power in the late Medieval period. The basilica, which was consecrated in 1094, is the third church to be built on the site since the body of St Mark, the city's patron saint, was reputedly brought here to be buried in AD 828. The exotic Byzantine architecture of the basilica reflects the Venetian lagoon's strong trading links with the Orient and the exterior is decorated with marble brought back after the Venetian conquest of Constantinople in 1204; the five vaulted domes which form the roof are set in the shape of a Greek cross There are further displays of riches brought back from foreign crusades in the *Tesoro* (treasury), whilst the *Pala D'Oro* (Golden Altarpiece) is an ornate altar screen in a gilded frame with enamel panels made in Byzantium. Visitors can enter the *Gallerie* to see the four magnificent Horses of St Mark that were brought from the hippodrome in Constantinople in the 13th century, symbolising Venice's links with Byzantium. It is also possible to climb up to the *Loggia* (veranda) on the front of the basilica for views over the lagoon and the surrounding islands, or to ascend the nearby *Campanile* (bell tower) which, at 99m (272ft), is the tallest building in Venice.

Transportation
Air: Venice Marco Polo Airport. **Water:** Ferry: Line 1, 51 or 82. Waterbus (Vaporetto): San Marco or San Zaccaria. **Rail:** Train: Venezia Santa Lucia Station (Venice Station). **Road:** Bus: Public services

Contact Addresses
Basilica di San Marco, Piazza San Marco, 30124 Venice, Italy
Tel: (041) 522 5205 *or* 522 5697

St Peter's Basilica (Basilica di San Pietro)

St Peter's Basilica stands in the Vatican City above the supposed resting place of the remains of St Peter. A church was first built on the site in the fourth century by Constantine but the 16th-century popes decided to build a monument and place of worship that would better reflect the power of the Catholic church. Construction began in 1506 under Pope Julius II, but it was not completed until 120 years later, and the result is awe-inspiring. Michelangelo designed its graceful *cupola* (dome) and the interior is an unbridled display of Renaissance and Baroque grandeur and features Bernini's *Throne of St Peter* made from bronze taken from the *Pantheon*.

Transportation

Air: Rome Leonardo da Vinci Airport (Fiumicino), Rome Ciampino Airport. **Water:** Ferry: Civitavecchia port, from where there are services to central Rome. **Rail:** Train: Roma Termini Station, Roma Tiburtina Station, Roma Ostiense Station or Roma Trastevere Station. Underground: Ottaviano. **Road:** Bus: Public services. Car: A12 (from the west); A24 (from the east); SS7 (from Rome Ciampino Airport).

Contact Addresses

Tourist Information, Vatican City, St. Peter's Square
Tel: (06) 6988 1662
Website: www.roma2000.it

Trevi Fountain (Fontana di Trevi)

Located in the heart of Rome's *centro storico* (historic centre), the *Trevi Fountain* derives its name from its position at the intersection of three roads (*tre vie*). According to legend, anyone who throws a coin into the water is guaranteed to return to the Eternal City. There has been a source of water at this site for over a thousand years, although it was not until 1485 that Pope Nicholas V commissioned Gianlorenzo Bernini to create the actual fountain – and even then the project was abandoned after the death of Pope Urban VIII in 1644. In 1732, Pope Clement XII employed Niccolò Salvi to continue the work, and the result is a Baroque masterpiece that dominates the square. Although the water is no longer safe to drink, the fountain is still a popular place to enjoy an icecream from one of the *gelaterie* in the square.

Transportation

Air: Rome Leonardo da Vinci Airport (Fiumicino), Rome Ciampino Airport. **Water:** Ferry: Civitavecchia port, from where there are services to central Rome. **Rail:** Train: Roma Termini Station, Roma Tiburtina Station, Roma Ostiense Station or Roma Trastevere Station. Underground: Barberini. **Road:** Car: A12 (from the west); A24 (from the east); SS7 (from Rome Ciampino Airport).

St Mark's Basilica

Contact Addresses

For more information on the Trevi Fountain, contact Ente Nazionale Italiano per il Turismo (see **Tourist Information** above).

Uffizi Gallery (Galleria degli Uffizi)

The *Uffizi Gallery* in Florence houses one of richest and most important art collections in the world. The building, located in the *Piazza della Signoria* close to the banks of the River Arno, was designed in the 16th century by the painter and architect Giorgio Vasari to house Florence's government offices (*uffizi*), and was bequeathed to the gallery as the Medici art collection in 1737, on the condition that it should never leave the city. The museum is a showcase for the Renaissance movement, one of the greatest periods in the history of art, and focuses more specifically on the Florentine School.

Transportation

Air: Amerigo Vespucci Airport (Florence), Pisa Galileo Galilei Airport. **Rail:** Train: Santa Maria Novella Station. **Road:** Bus: Services to Galleria degli Uffizi Castellani. Car: A1 (from Milan, Bologna, Rome or Naples); A11 (from Pisa, Lucca, Prato or Siena), then signs to Centro Storico.

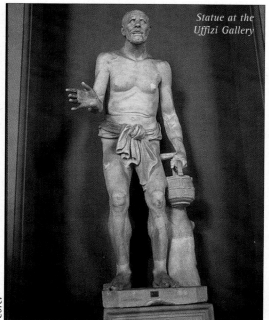

Statue at the Uffizi Gallery

Corel©

Contact Addresses

Loggiato Degli Uffizi, 6-Florence, Italy
Tel: (055) 238 8651 *or* 238 8652
Website: www.arca.net/uffizi

Vatican Museums and Sistine Chapel (Musei Vaticani e Capella Sistina)

The *Vatican Museums* constitute the largest museum complex in the world. Founded in 1506 by Pope Julius II, the collections are staggeringly diverse and are essentially the legacy of the Popes who were not only fabulously rich, but also great patrons of the Arts. Egyptian antiquities, classical statues, Etruscan relics and Byzantine paintings all have their place, but two areas that should not be missed are the *Stanze di Raffaello* (Raphael Rooms) and the *Cappella Sistina* (Sistine Chapel). Renowned equally for the crowds that line up to see it as it is for its breathtaking beauty, the Sistine Chapel was constructed between 1475 and 1480 as the chapel of the papal palace. The painting of its ceiling was charged to a reluctant Michelangelo, whose subsequent depiction of the *Creation of Adam* ranks among the most famous painted images of all time and is considered to be one of the finest achievements of the Renaissance. The *Last Judgement*, also by Michelangelo, hangs behind the altar, while other famous Renaissance works by artists such as Botticelli and Ghirlandaio adorn the rest of the interior.

Transportation

Air: Rome Leonardo da Vinci Airport (Fiumicino), Rome Ciampino Airport. **Water:** Ferry: Civitavecchia port, from where there are services to central Rome. **Rail:** Underground: Ottaviano. **Road:** Bus: Public services.

Contact Addresses

Musei Vaticani, Viale Vaticano, 00120
Vatican City
Tel: (06) 6988 3860 *or* 6988 3332
Website: www.vatican.va

Jamaica

1 Dunn's River Falls

Tourist Information

Jamaica Tourist Board (JTB)
64 Knutsford Boulevard, Kingston 5, Jamaica
Tel: 929 9200
Website: www.jamaicatravel.com

Jamaica Tourist Board
1-2 Prince Consort Road, London SW7 2BZ, UK
Tel: (020) 7224 0505 *or* (0800) 445 533
(brochure request line)

Dunn's River Falls

Located in a dense tropical forest, *Dunn's River Falls* is Jamaica's most famous attraction. This Caribbean paradise consists of a number of waterfalls, which cascade over rock terraces down to the Caribbean Sea below, and beautiful natural pools that have formed in the rockface. The falls are shallow enough to enable visitors to climb the 183m (600ft) limestone tiers to reach a tropical shower, from where they can enjoy panoramic views of the surrounding area. There are beautiful beaches at the bottom of these magnificent falls that are also famous for featuring in the first James Bond film, 'Dr No'.

Dunn's River Falls.

Transportation
Air: Norman Manley International Airport. **Road: Car:** A3 North Coast Highway (from Kingston).

Contact Addresses
Dunn's River Falls and Park, Ocho Rios, St Ann, Jamaica
Tel: 974 2857 *or* 974 4767
Website: www.dunnsriverja.com

Japan

800km
400mls
✈ international airport

RUSSIAN FED.   Sea of Okhotsk

CHINA

Hokkaido
• Sapporo
Hakodate •
Aomori • ② ⑥
DPR OF KOREA   Akita •   Honshu
Sea of Japan   Sendai
Sado I.
Niigata
REP. OF KOREA   ④ ⑤   JAPAN
Oki Is.   Mt. Fuji   TOKYO
Osaka   3776m   • Yokohama
Kobe •   Na goya
Hiroshima •   Osaka
Kitakyūshu •   Takamatsu
Fukuoka •   Shikoku
Nagasaki •
Kyus…u   ③
East China Sea   ①
Southwest Islands   PACIFIC OCEAN
Amami Is.
Naha • Okinawa
Iwo Jima
Ryukyu Is.
Southern Islands

1 Hiroshima Peace Memorial Museum
  (Heiwa Kinen Shiryôkan)

2 Meiji Shrine (Meiji Jingu)

3 Mount Fuji (Fuji-san)

4 Nijo Castle (Nijo-jo)

5 Sanjusangen-do Temple

6 Senso-ji Temple

Tourist Information

Kokusai Kanko Shinkokai
(Japan National Tourist Organisation – JNTO)
10th Floor, Tokyo Kotsu Kaikan Bldg, 2-10-1,
Yurakucho, Chiyoda-ku, Tokyo, Japan
Tel: (0) 3210 3331
Website: www.jnto.go.jp

Japan National Tourist Organisation (JNTO)
Heathcoat House, 20 Savile Row, London
W1S 3PR, UK
Tel: (020) 7734 9638
Website: www.seejapan.co.uk

Hiroshima Peace Memorial Museum (Heiwa Kinen Shiryôkan)

Hiroshima in Western Honshu is known around
the world as the city which was destroyed by the
world's first atomic bomb on August 6, 1945.
Every year, millions of visitors come to the city to
pay their respects in the *Hiroshima Peace Memorial
Park* and the *Peace Memorial Museum*. The park,
which was reconstructed in 1949, is home to
many famous monuments and buildings,
including the *Children's Peace Monument* and the
A-Bomb Dome, which was built in 1915 and
designed by the Czech architect Jan Letzel. The
ruins of the dome, which are included on the
UNESCO World Heritage List, have become the
symbol of an international desire for peace.

Transportation
Air: Hiroshima Airport. **Road:** Bus: Public services.
Streetcar: Direction Ujina via Kamiya-cho, stop
marked Chuden-mae. Alternatively direction
Koi/Eba/Miyajima, stop marked Genbaku-Dome-mae.

Contact Addresses
Hiroshima Peace Memorial Museum, 1-2
Nakajimamachi, Naka-ku, Hiroshima City, Japan
Tel: (0) 82 242 7798
Website: www.hiroshima-navi.or.jp

Meiji Shrine (Meiji Jingu)

Tokyo's *Meiji Shrine* is one of the holiest and most
visited temples in the country. This Shinto shrine is
dedicated to the Emperor Meiji, who was credited
with opening Japan up to the outside world, and to
his wife Empress Shoken. Built in 1920 following
their deaths in 1912 and 1914 respectively, the
original shrine burnt down during World War II,
only to be rebuilt by 1958. Today, as well as the
Naihaiden (Inner Shrine), which is home to the
main shrine, visitors can also see the *Gehaiden*
(Outer Shrine), which was completed in 1926. Other
highlights are the *Homotsuden* (Treasure Museum),
which was built in 1921 and houses photos and
personal belongings of the emperor and empress.

Japan National Tourist Organization©

Mount Fuji in Spring

Transportation
Air: New Tokyo International Narita Airport, Haneda Airport (domestic flights). **Rail:** Train: Harajku Station. Underground: Meiji-jingu-mae. **Road:** Bus: Public services. Car: Tomei-Meishin expressway from Kobe (via Nagoya, Kyoto and Osaka); Tohoku expressway (from northern Japan); Chuo expressway (from Nagano and Nagoya).

Contact Addresses
Meiji Jingu, 1-1 Kamizonomachi, Yoyogi, Shibuya-ku, Tokyo, Japan
Tel: (03) 3379 5511
Website: www.meijijingu.or.jp

Mount Fuji (Fuji-san)

This 3776m (12,389ft) volcanic cone is one of the most famous volcanoes in the world and the highest peak in Japan. Of extreme historical and religious importance to the Japanese, *Mount Fuji* is also one of the nation's most significant emblems. Although it has erupted 16 times since AD 781, the mountain is safe and popular for climbing, last erupting in 1707 when it covered the streets of Tokyo in volcanic lava. The summit offers overnight huts, a volcanic crater and unparalleled views of Japan. Although the mountain can be climbed at any time of year, the official climbing season is July-August; outside these months, facilities – including lodging huts – are closed. The *Fuji Five Lakes* located on the northern side of the mountain were created by volcanic eruptions and are fantastic sites from which to see Mount Fuji itself.

Transportation
Air: New Tokyo Narita International Airport, Haneda Airport (domestic flights). **Rail:** Train: Shinjuku (Tokyo) Station to Kawaguchi-ko Station. **Road:** Bus: Public services.

Contact Addresses
Fuji Visitor Center, 663-1 Funatsu Kawaguchi-ko Town, Yamanashi, 401-301, Japan
Tel: (0555) 720 259
Website: www.mt-fuji.com

Nijo Castle (Nijo-jo)

Nijo Castle was built in 1603 by Tokugawa Ieyasu, one of Japan's most powerful shoguns and founder of the Tokugawa Shogunate. The shoguns ruled Japan for a total of 700 years between the 13th and 19th centuries, with Tokugawa Ieyasu founding his dynasty in 1600. Built as a symbol of his power, the castle is filled with many fine works of art, including beautiful paintings of trees and animals by some of Japan's most famous artists of the period. The castle, set in stunning gardens in the old capital of Japan, Kyoto, was built almost entirely of Hinoki wood (Japanese Cypress).

Transportation
Air: Kansai International Airport, Osaka Itami Airport (domestic flights). **Rail:** Underground: Nijo-jo-mae Station. Train: Kyoto Station. **Road:** Bus: Services from Kyoto Station.

Contact Addresses

Nijo Castle Office, Nijojo-cho, Nakagyo-ku, Kyoto, Japan

Tel: (075) 841 0096

Sanjusangen-do Temple

Completed in 1266, the *Sanjusangen-do Temple* which is officially called Rengeo-in Temple, is a faithful copy of an original that was built in 1164, but burned down in 1249. Originally built by Taira no Kiyomori for the emperor Go-Shirakawa, the temple is today a national treasure. It is best known for its wooden image of the *Thousand-Armed Kannon* (the Buddhist Goddess of Mercy), a masterpiece of the Kamakura period, which stands surrounded by 1000 smaller statues of the same goddess. The *hondo* (main building) is split into 33 *sanjusan* (bays) that exist between its many pillars to symbolise the 33 incarnations of Kannon, hence the name Sanjusangen-do Temple, which literally means '33 bay hall'.

Senso-ji Temple

Japan National Tourist Organization©

Transportation

Air: Kansai International Airport. **Rail:** Train: Keihan Railway to Shichijo Station. **Road:** Bus: Public services. Car: Hiezan Driveway (from Imazu-cho); Meishin Expressway (from Osaka); Tomei Expressway or Meishin Expressway (from Nagoya).

Contact Addresses

Department of Industry and Tourism, Tourist Section, Kyoto City Government, Kyoto Kaikan, Okazaki, Sayo-ku, Kyoto, Japan

Tel: (075) 752 0215 (administration) *or* 525 0033 (Temple)

Website: http://raku.city.kyoto.jp/sight_e.phtml

Senso-ji Temple

Tokyo's most revered temple, the *Senso-ji Temple*, was founded in AD 628 to enshrine a gold statuette of the *Kannon Bodhisattva* (the Goddess of Mercy) which, according to legend, was found by two local fishermen. Also known as *Asakusa Kannon* in Japan, the temple and its five-storey pagoda may today be a post-war concrete reconstruction, but nonetheless its precincts are always bustling with worshippers. A huge incense burner at the front of the temple is said to have healing powers. The *Kaminarimon* (Thunder Gate) is one of Tokyo's most recognised sites and is famous for its enormous red paper lantern and guardian statues. There are also many Shinto shrines within the temple's grounds.

Transportation

Air: New Tokyo Narita International Airport, Haneda Airport (domestic flights). **Rail:** Train: Tokyo Station. Underground: Asakusa. **Road:** Bus: Public services. Car: Tomei-Meishin Expressway (from Kobe); Chuo Expressway (from Nagano and Nagoya).

Contact Addresses

Kinryuzan Senso-ji, 2-3-1 Asakusa, Taito-ku, Tokyo 111-0032, Japan

Tel: (03) 3842 0181

Jordan

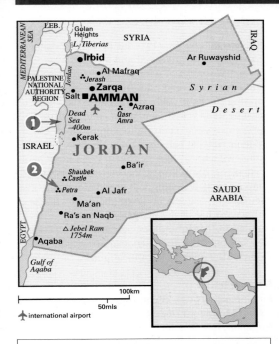

1 Dead Sea (Al-bahr Al-mayyit)

2 Petra

Tourist Information

Jordan Tourism Board
PO Box 830688, Amman 11183, Jordan
Tel: (06) 567 8294 *or* 2314
Website: www.see-jordan.com

Jordan Tourism Board
Kennedy House, 115 Hammersmith Road,
London W14 0QH, UK
Tel: (020) 7371 6496
Website: www.see-jordan.com

Dead Sea (Al-bahr Al-mayyit)

Lying 400m (1320ft) below sea level and spanning
the border between Israel and Jordan, the *Dead Sea*
contains more minerals and salt than any other
stretch of water in the world. Its natural properties
make it a prime centre for spa treatments and
relaxation therapies with three resorts in the area:

the *Movenpick Dead Sea*, the *Dead Sea Spa Hotel* and
the *Dead Sea Rest House*. There are also several
interesting sites around the Dead Sea, including
Bethany, where it is believed Jesus was baptized,
and *Lot's Cave*, where the prophet Lot lived. The
Wadi Mujib Nature Reserve on the eastern shores is a
beautifully preserved area of mountains and rivers,
providing a natural habitat for eagles, vultures,
wolves and the endangered Nubian ibex. There are
many hiking trails within the reserve.

Transportation
Air: Queen Alia International Airport. **Road:** Car:
Desert Highway (from Amman).

Contact Addresses
For more information on the Dead Sea, contact the
Jordan Tourism Board (see **Tourist Information** above).

Petra

Jordan's best-known tourist attraction, *Petra*, is one of
the great wonders of the Middle Eastern world – a
city carved straight into solid rock. It unfolds grandly
after a 2km (1.2 mile) walk through a very narrow
chasm. Built during the fifth and sixth centuries BC,
Petra is the ruined capital of the Nabatean Arabs. Its
immense facades were lost for almost 1000 years
until they were rediscovered by the Swiss traveller
Johann Ludwig Burckhardt in 1812. Today, there are
still many sites to see including the *el Khazneh* (The
Treasury) monument, a giant tomb carved out of
rock, the *Temple of the Winged Lions*, the *al-Deir*
(Monastery) and the *Archaeological Museum*, which
displays artefacts found at Petra during the 19th and
20th centuries.

Transportation
Air: Queen Alia International Airport. **Road:** Coach:
Abdali Bus Station or Wahdat Bus Station. Car:
Desert Highway or King's Highway (from Amman).

Contact Addresses
For more information on Petra, contact the Jordan
Tourism Board (see **Tourist Information** above).

Kenya

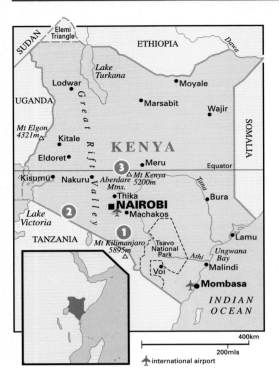

Tourist Information

Kenya Tourist Board
RE Towers, Ragati Road,
PO Box 30630-00100,
Nairobi, Kenya
Tel: (02) 724 044
Website: www.magicalkenya.com

Kenya Tourist Board
Nottcut House,
36 Southwark Bridge Road,
London SE1 9EU, UK
Tel: +44 (0) 0207 202 6376
Website: www.magicalkenya.com

Amboseli National Park

Amboseli National Park extends across 392 sq km (151 sq miles) of grassland and swamps at the foot of *Mount Kilimanjaro*, Africa's highest peak. It was designated a national park in 1948 and, despite suffering floods in 1993 which caused many of the animals to retreat, it remains one of Africa's best-known game spotting locations. Park residents include baboons, lions, cheetah, black rhinos, wildebeest, hippos, gazelles and large herds of elephant. As well as game-viewing, hiking and camping, bird-watching and camel safaris are also popular and visitors can learn about the culture and way of life of the indigenous Maasai population through homestead visits and lectures. More adventurous travellers can arrange to climb Mount Kilimanjaro with a local guide.

Transportation
Air: Jomo Kenyatta International Airport. **Road:** Coach: Many tour operators provide transport to Amboseli. Car: Via the towns of Namanga and Emali (from Nairobi); via Tsavo West, then through Kimana (Olkelunyiet) Gate (from Mombasa).

Contact Addresses
Senior Warden, Amboseli National Park, PO Box 18 Namanga, Amboseli, Kenya
Tel: (045) 22251
Website: www.kws.org/amboseli.html

Maasai Mara National Reserve

Opened in 1974, the *Maasai Mara National Reserve* is the most popular game park in Kenya. Managed by the Maasai tribe, the area is named after this group of people who first migrated to South Kenya from the Nile Valley in the mid-17th century. The Maasai herdsmen are nomadic people who do not believe in the concept of land ownership and choose instead to live in harmony with the wildlife grazing in the area. The reserve, which occupies a 320 sq km (124 sq miles) chunk of the famous Serengeti plains, is inhabited by many of Africa's most popular wild animals, including lions, cheetahs, elephants, leopards, black rhinos and hippos. There are also over 500 resident birds in the park including ostrich, lark, sunbird and 57 species of birds of prey. The area is famous for rolling grassland and for the Mara River, which runs through the reserve from north to south. It is also the place for one of nature's best spectacles – the annual migration from the dry plains of Tanzania of thousands of wildebeest crossing crocodile-infested waters in order to reach more fertile grazing.

Transportation
Air: Jomo Kenyatta International Airport, Wilson Airport (domestic flights). **Rail:** Train: Naivasha Station (services from Nairobi); visitors must then travel by road into the Maasai Mara. **Road:** Bus: Private tour operators run safaris into the Maasai Mara National Reserve (from Nairobi and Lake Nakura). Car: Nairobi–Naivasha Road to Maai-Mahiu, then B3 to Ewaso Nyiro, then C12 to Aitong, then E177 (from Nairobi); A1 (from Migori).

Contact Addresses
Maasai Mara National Reserve, PO Box 44595, Nairobi, Kenya
Tel: (02) 311 054 *or* 343 968
Website: www.go2africa.com

Mount Kenya National Reserve

Mount Kenya, which is an extinct volcano sitting on the Equator, is Africa's second-highest mountain and stands at a height of 5199m (17,058ft). Opened as the *Mount Kenya National Park* in 1949, the mountain has been revered by local inhabitants for generations and is the official home of 'Ngai', the Kikuyu tribe's Supreme Being. The snowy peak of the volcano was first sighted by an outsider in 1849 – the missionary Johann Ludwig Krapf – although the idea that there could be snow on the Equator was not believed until the British geographer Halford John Mackinder reached the summit in 1899. The park itself, which covers an area of 600 sq km (232 sq miles), offers exotic mountain scenery, starting with upland forest near the bottom and progressing to mountain forest, bamboo forests and glacier peaks. A wide variety of wildlife inhabits the park, some unique to it, including Sykes and Colobus monkeys, buffalo, elephants, black rhinos, leopards, the elusive Bongo antelopes and giant forest hogs. It is also home to many species of birds such as the giant kingfisher, olive pigeons and red-fronted parrots.

Transportation
Air: Jomo Kenyatta International Airport, Wilson Airport. **Rail:** Train: Thika Station. **Road:** Bus: Services to Nanyuki (from Nairobi). Car: A2 heads northwest from Nairobi, by-passing Murunga, before heading west around the base of Mount Kenya to Nanyuki.

Contact Addresses
Senior Warden, Mount Kenya National Park, PO Box 69, Naru Moru, Kenya
Tel: (0171) 2383
Website: www.kws.org/mountkenya.html

Maasai Mara National Reserve

Republic of Korea

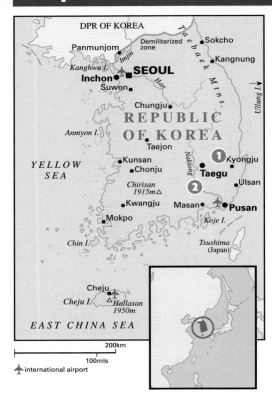

DPR OF KOREA
Panmunjom • Sokcho
Demilitarized zone
• Kangnung
Kanghwa I. **SEOUL**
Inchon •
• Suwon
• Chungju
R E P U B L I C
Anmyon I. O F K O R E A
• Taejon
• Kunsan
• Chonju ❶ • Kyongju
Taegu
Chirisan • Ulsan
1915m△
• Kwangju ❷
• Mokpo • Masan ■ **Pusan**
Koje I.
Chin I. Tsushima (Japan)
YELLOW SEA
Naktong
Taebaek Mtns.
Imjin
Han
Ullung I.

Cheju ✈
Cheju I. △Hallasan
1950m
EAST CHINA SEA

200km
100mls
✈ international airport

1 Gyeongju
2 Haeinsa Temple

Tourist Information

Korea National Tourism Organization – KNTO (Hangook Kwankwong Kongsa)
40, Cheonggyecheonno, Jung-gu, Seoul, 100-180, Republic of Korea
Tel: (02) 729 9600
Website: www.tour2korea.com

Korea National Tourism Organization (KNTO)
Third Floor, New Zealand House, Haymarket, London SW1Y 4TE, UK
Tel: (020) 7321 2535
Website: www.tour2korea.com

Gyeongju

The city of *Kyongju* was once one of the six largest cities in the world and the capital of the Silla Kingdom, which existed between 57BC and AD 935. Known today as the 'museum without walls' and now spelt *Gyeongju*, the city houses numerous historical sites and relics, and is one of the most important ancient cities in the world, attracting around eight million visitors every year. The city has many royal tombs, museums, temples and monuments and houses an impressive collection of relics from the Silla period in the *Gyeongju National Museum*. Highlights include artefacts found in the *Geumgwanchiong* and *Cheonmachong* tombs, as well

KNTO Korea National Tourist Office®

KNTO Korea National Tourist Office©

as the *Seokguram Grotto* and *Bulguska Temple*, which both feature on the UNESCO World Heritage List.

Transportation
Air: Seoul Gimpo Domestic Airport. Internal flights are available to Busan, Ulsan and Daegu airports. Shuttle buses operate from these airports to Gyeongju. **Rail:** Train: Gyeongju Station. **Road:** Bus: Public services. Taxis: Taxis can be hailed in the street.

Contact Addresses
For more information on Gyeongju, contact the Korea National Tourism Organization (see **Tourist Information** above).

Haeinsa Temple

Haeinsa Temple was originally built in AD 802 by two monks, Sunung and Ijong, during King Aejang of the Silla Kingdom's reign. Despite many fires and subsequent reconstructions, the temple remains one of the most beautiful in Korea set in an idyllic location deep in *Gayasan National Park*.

It eventually reached its present-day size during the mid-10th century. The temple is famous for housing the *Tripitaka Koreana* – 80,000 wooden printing blocks carved during the Goryo Dynasty (AD 918-1392), which, together, make up the oldest and best-preserved collection of Buddhist scriptures in the world. The temple also houses a great number of artefacts that have been designated national treasures including the *Seated Stone Buddha*, found at *Cheongyangsa Temple*, and the *Stone Pagoda* at *Wolgwang Temple*.

Transportation
Air: Seoul Gimpo Domestic Airport. **Road:** Bus: Local buses to Haeinsa Temple (from Daego Seobu Bus Terminal) (journey time: 70 minutes); (from Hapcheon Bus Terminal) (journey time: 60 minutes); (from Jinju Bus Terminal) (journey time: two hours 30 minutes). Car: 88 Expressway to Haeinsa Temple (from Seoul).

Contact Addresses
Haeinsa Temple, Information Office, Daegu, Seoul, Republic of Korea
Tel: (055) 931 1001

Latvia

200km
100mls
✈ international airport

BALTIC
SEA

ESTONIA

Gulf
of
Riga

•Ventspils

Valmiera
•
VIDZEME

Sigulda
Jurmala •LATVIA
KURZEME •RIGA ①

•Liepaja ② Jelgava
ZEMGALE

Rezekne
•

RUSSIAN FED.

LATGALE

Daugavpils

LITHUANIA

BELARUS

---

1 Riga's Historic Town Centre
2 Rundale Palace

Tourist Information

Latvia Tourism Development Agency
Pils Lauqums 4, LV-1050 Riga, Latvia
Tel: 722 9945
Website: www.latviatourism.lv

Embassy of Latvia
45 Nottingham Place, London W1U 5LY, UK
Tel: (020) 7312 0040
Website: www.london.am.gov.lv

Riga's Historic Town Centre

Situated on the *Daugava River* on the shores of the *Riga Gulf* of the *Baltic Sea*, *Riga* benefits from pleasant coastal air and is the gateway into the Baltic region. Riga came to prominence during the 13th-15th centuries, benefiting from its geographic location as a trade port between Central and Eastern Europe. Riga is particularly renowned for its Art Nouveau structures which many believe is the finest collection of this style of architecture anywhere in Europe. Riga's attractions are numerous and include

Riga Castle, the *Jewish Museum*, *Gauja National Park*, *Riga Zoo* and *St Mary's Dome Cathedral* completed in 1270 with one of the largest organs in the world.

Transportation
Air: Riga International Airport. **Water:** Ferry: Free Port of Riga. **Rail:** Train: Public services to Riga's Central Station. Public Trolley and Tram services. **Road:** Bus: Public services to Riga International Bus Station.

Contact Addresses
For more information about Riga, contact the Latvia Tourism Development Agency (see **Tourist Information** above).

Rundale Palace

Located 79km (49 miles) south of the Latvian capital of *Riga*, *Rundale Palace and Museum* lie just outside the town of *Bauska*. Built as the summer residence of the Duke of Courland Ernst Johann Biron, the opulent palace was completed in two stages from 1736 to 1740 and 1763 to 1768. After many years of neglect, the palace was given to the Republic of Latvia in 1920. Visitors are able to tour the museum that was opened in 1972 and several of the grand rooms are open to the public as well as many in the eastern block, including the *Room of Roses* and the *Duke's Bedroom*. The palace is ringed by a canal, gardens and a hunting park. Some of the palace rooms are also available for hire for wedding ceremonies and private functions.

Transportation
Air: Riga International Airport. **Water:** Ferry: Free Port of Riga. **Rail:** Train: Public services to Bauska (then travel on to Rundale Palace by bus or taxi). **Road:** Bus: Public services.

Contact Addresses
The Rundale Palace Museum, Bauska, 3921 Latvia
Tel: (+371) 3962 274
Website: www.rpm.apollo.lv/engl/

Lebanon

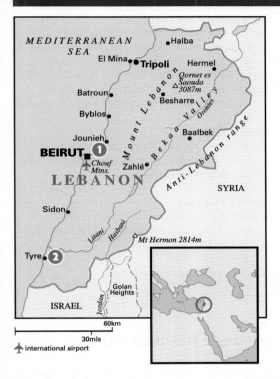

MEDITERRANEAN SEA

Halba

El Mina • Tripoli · Hermel

Qornet es Saouda △3087m

Batroun •

Besharre •

Byblos •

Jounieh •

BEIRUT ❶

Chouf Mtns. Zahlé •

Baalbek •

LEBANON

Anti-Lebanon range

SYRIA

Sidon •

Mt Hermon 2814m

Tyre ❷

Golan Heights

ISRAEL

60km
30mls
✈ international airport

Tourist Information

Ministry of Tourism (Wzart al Siaha)
PO Box 11-5344, Beirut, Lebanon
Tel: (01) 340 940-4
Website: www.lebanon-tourism.gov.lb

Embassy of the Republic of Lebanon
15-21 Palace Gardens Mews, London W8 4RB, UK
Tel: (020) 7727 6696 *or* 7229 7265 (consular section)

Jeita Grotto

Situated under Mount Lebanon in the *Nahr el Kalb (Dog River) Valley*, these caves, which have been known to man since Paleolithic times, consist of a lower and upper gallery. The caves were rediscovered by the American missionary Reverend William Thomson in 1836, who ventured 50m (164ft) underground. In 1873 engineers working for the Beirut Water Company explored a further 1000m (3281ft) into the caves. Today, visitors can explore the 6200-metre deep (20,341ft) lower gallery by boat, whilst the upper gallery, which was not discovered until 1958, can be visited on foot by travelling down a 120m (394ft) tunnel.

Transportation
Air: Beirut International Airport. **Road:** Coach: Many tourists visit the sites as part of an organised tour. Taxi: Taxis can be hired in Beirut to take visitors to the site.

Contact Addresses
For more information on Jeita Grotto, contact the Ministry of Tourism (see **Tourist Information** above). Website: www.jeitagrotto.com

Tyre

The city experienced a golden age during the first millennium BC under Hiram, King of Tyre, but later suffered at the hands of its jealous enemies, including the King of Babylon in the sixth century BC, and Alexander the Great in 332BC. *Tyre* eventually fell under Roman rule in 64BC when, an aqueduct, triumphal arch and hippodrome were built. The impressive 480m (131ft) hippodrome, which once seated up to 20,000 spectators, is one of the main attractions.

Transportation
Air: Beirut International Airport. **Road:** Coach: Many tourists visit the sites as part of an organised tour. Taxi: Taxis can be hired in Beirut to take visitors to the site.

Contact Addresses
For more information on Tyre, contact the Ministry of Tourism (see **Tourist Information** above).

Malawi

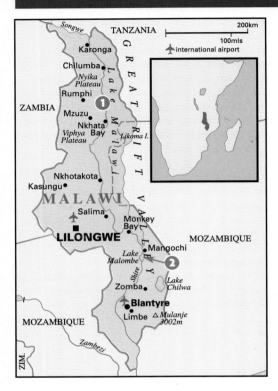

1 Lake Malawi National Park
2 Liwonde National Park

Tourist Information

Ministry of Tourism, Parks and Wildlife
Ex-French Embassy, Private Bag 326,
Lilongwe, Malawi
Tel: (0) 771 295 or 772 702

Malawi Tourist Office
33 Grosvenor Street, London W1X 0DE, UK
Tel: (020) 7491 4172

Lake Malawi National Park

Lake Malawi National Park was created in 1980 as the world's first freshwater national park on the southern shore of *Lake Malawi*, Africa's third-largest lake, which stretches for 600km (373 miles) and forms a natural border between Malawi, Tanzania and Mozambique. The lush vegetation is home to a range of wildlife, including many species of bird and fish. The clear blue waters of the lake are popular for snorkelling and scuba diving, as well as sailing, kayaking and swimming.

Transportation
Air: Lilongwe Airport. **Road:** Car: Direct from Lilongwe. Many tour operators provide transport to Lake Malawi National Park.

Contact Addresses
Malawi Tourism Information Service, c/o Geo Group & Associates, 4 Christian Fields, London SW16 3JZ, UK
Tel: (0115) 982 1903
Website: www.malawitourism.com

Liwonde National Park

Due to its unspoilt environment and prolific game, *Liwonde National Park* is generally regarded as the best game reserve in Malawi. It covers 550 sq km (212 sq miles) of mopane and savanna woodland on the floodplains of the *River Shire* and *Lake Malombe* in the south of the country. The river plains are home to many species of bird. Plants and trees found in Liwonde National Park include the baobab, a large native African tree bearing a gourd-like fruit. Despite the incredible sights, the park is still relatively peaceful and uncommercialised.

Transportation
Air: Lilongwe Airport. **Road:** Car: Direct from Lilongwe. Many tour operators provide transport to Liwonde National Park.

Contact Addresses
Central African Wilderness Safaris, PO Box 489, Lilongwe, Malawi
Tel: (0) 771 153
Website: www.wilderness-safarismalawi.com

Malaysia

Tourist Information

Tourism Malaysia
Menara Dato' Onn, 17th, 24-27th, 30th floors,
Putra World Trade Centre, 45 Jalan Tun
Ismail, 50480 Kuala Lumpur, Malaysia
Tel: (03) 2615 8188
Website: www.tourism.gov.my

Tourism Malaysia
Malaysia House, 57 Trafalgar Square, London
WC2N 5DU, UK
Tel: (020) 7930 7932
Website: www.malaysiatrulyasia.co.uk

Batu Caves (Gua Batu)

The *Batu Caves* were discovered over 100 years ago and are now one of Kuala Lumpur's most visited sites. Located in an area of outstanding beauty, the caves contain stalactites and stalagmites, and impressive fauna and flora. There are three main caves and numerous smaller ones. The most famous is the *Temple Cave* and is only accessible by a 272-step climb. Below it is the *Dark Cave*, a vast network of caverns inhabited by several indigenous species of animals. Discovered

Monkeys are a famous feature of the Batu Caves

Zena Turner©

Petronas Twin Towers

by the American explorer William Hornaby in 1878, the Batu Caves are also an important Hindu shrine, attracting as many as 80,000 devotees during the holy festival of Thaipusam, which takes place in January or February every year.

Transportation
Air: Kuala Lumpur International Airport, then Sultan Abdul Aziz Shah Airport (domestic flights). **Rail:** Train: Kuala Lumpur Station. **Road:** Bus: Public services.

Contact Addresses
For more information on Batu Caves, contact Tourism Malaysia (see **Tourist Information** above).

Petronas Twin Towers

Standing 452m (1483ft) tall, the 88-storey *Petronas Twin Towers* in Kuala Lumpur was the tallest building in the world until Taipei's 101 was built measuring 508m (1666ft). Other projects for even taller buildings are currently underway and are likely to push Petronas further down the list in coming years. Nevertheless, the development also includes a 50 acre (20 hectare) park designed by the late Brazilian landscape artist Roberto Burle Marx, a retail complex and an entertainment centre. Completed in 1997 and designed by Cesar Pelli & Associates, the building consists of two similarly shaped towers joined by a 58m (192ft) *Skybridge* on the 41st and 42nd floors. Entrance is free but visitors do a need a ticket, of which a limited number are issued each day.

Transportation
Air: Kuala Lumpur International Airport, Sultan Abdul Aziz Shah Airport (domestic flights). **Rail:** Train: PUTRA light rail transit to KLCC. **Road:** Bus: Public services.

Contact Addresses
Petronas Twin Towers, Kuala Lumpur City Centre, 50088 Kuala Lumpur, Malaysia
Tel: (603) 2051 5000
Website: www.petronas.com.my *or* www.klcc.com.my

Mali

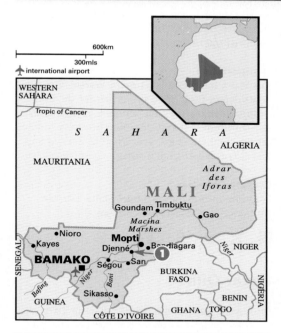

1 Djenne Mosque

Tourist Information

Tourist Office of Mali (Office Malien du Tourisme et de l'Hôtellerie)
Rue Mohamed V., Bamako, Mali
Tel: 222 5673
Website: www.malitourisme.com
There is no active Tourist Office for Mali in the UK.

Djenne Mosque

Situated 354 km (220 miles) southwest of *Timbuktu* on the floodplains of the *Bani* and *Niger* rivers, *Old Djenne* is thought to be the oldest known city in Sub-Saharan Africa. Situated along the ancient trans-Sahara trading routes, Djenne had developed into an important settlement in the region and a centre for Islamic learning by the 16th century. Completed in 1907 to replace an earlier mosque, the famous *Djenne Mosque* (also known as the *Grand Mosque*) dominates the old town. Built in the Sudanic style and constructed from sun-baked mud-bricks, each year after the rainy season the entire town turn out to repair the structure at the Spring Festival. Wooden posts that adorn the structure enable workers to scale the walls during the restoration process. A traditional African market is located around the mosque's perimeter. In 1988, Old Djenne and the Grand Mosque were added to the UNESCO list of World Heritage sites.

Transportation
Air: Bamako International Airport. **Water:** River taxis along the Niger River. **Rail:** Train: Bamako Station. **Road:** Bus: Public services or shared bush taxis to Djenne.

Contact Addresses
For more information on the Djenne Mosque, contact the Tourist Office of Mali (see **Tourist Information** above).

Djenne Mosque

Key to symbols: £ Entry charged ♿ Disabled access ⛏ Man-made attraction ⚘ Natural attraction 🅿 Parking ✕ Restaurant 🛍 Shop 🏛 UNESCO site

Malta

1 Blue Grotto (Il-Hnejja)

2 Hagar Qim

Tourist Information

Malta Tourism Authority
Auberge Ditalie, 229 Merchants Street,
Valletta CMR 02, Malta
Tel: 21 22 4444
Website: www.visitmalta.com

Malta Tourism Authority – UK & Eire
Malta House, 36-38 Piccadilly,
London W1J 0LD, UK
Tel: (020) 7292 4900

Blue Grotto (Il-Hnejja)

The *Blue Grotto* is the most famous cave in Malta,
with its deep waters displaying magnificent
dazzling colours, ranging from turquoise to deep
blue. Situated near the village of Zurrieq in
southwestern Malta, the cave, which is known as
Il-Hnejja, meaning 'The Arch', in Maltese, was
given its English name by British soldiers who
thought that its blue waters resembled the *Grotta
Azzurra* (Blue Grotto) in Capri. To get to the grotto,
visitors travel by boat, passing under a massive
arch, deep into the 43m (140ft) high cave which is
hollowed out of the cliff rockface.

Transportation
Air: Malta International Airport. **Water:** Boat:
Boats depart from Wied iz-Zurrieq for the Blue
Grotto. **Road:** Bus: Public services. Car: Road to
Zurrieq (from Valletta). The Blue Grotto is situated
off the southern coast, near Wied iz-Zurrieq and
2.5km (1.6 miles) from Zurrieq.

Contact Addresses
For more information, contact Malta Tourism
Authority (see **Tourist Information** above).

Hagar Qim

Discovered under a mound of rubble in 1839, the
Neolithic temples of *Hagar Qim*, which date from
300BC, are some of the oldest manmade structures
in the world. Reminiscent of England's
Stonehenge, the temples are built of limestone
rock, some towering 6m (20ft) high, and weighing
several tonnes. The complex is an impressive maze
of corridors, chambers, niches and altars, carved
out of stone using flint. On the morning of the
summer solstice, sunlight passes through a hole
known as the 'oracle hole' and fills the apse of the
temple. The nearby *Mnajdra* temples are included,
along with the Hagar Qim, *Tarxien*, *Ta'Hagrat*,
Skorba and *Ggantija* temple complexes, on the
UNESCO World Heritage List.

Transportation
Air: Malta International Airport. **Road:** Bus: Public
services. Car: Road towards Wied Zurrieq (from
Valletta).

Contact Addresses
Museum of Archaeology, Auberge de Provence,
Republic Street, Valetta, Malta
Tel: 2122 1623 *or* 2123 9545
Website: www.heritagemalta.org

Mexico

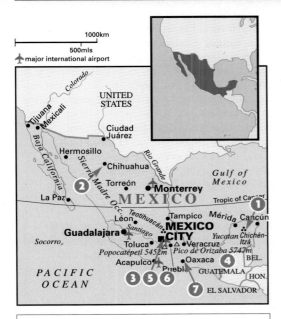

1000km
500mls
✈ major international airport

1 Chichén Itzá

2 Copper Canyon (Barrancas del Cobre)

3 National Museum of Anthropology
(Museo Nacional de Antropología)

4 Palenque

5 Parroquia (San Miguel de Allende
Parish Church)

6 Teotihuacán

7 White Mountain (Monte Alban)

Tourist Information

**Ministry of Tourism
(Secretaria de Turismo – SECTUR)**
Mariano Escobedo SSO Piso 6 Col. Anzures
C.P. 11590 Mexico Df Delagacion Cuauhtemoc
Tel: (055) 278 4200
Website: www.mexico-travel.com

Mexican Tourism Promotion Board
Wakefield House, 41 Trinity Square, London
EC3N 4DJ, UK
Tel: (020) 7488 9392
Website: www.visitmexico.com

Chichén Itzá

Located deep within the jungles of *Yucatán,* 193km (120 miles) west of *Cancún,* lies *Chichén Itzá*, one of the most impressive sites of the mysterious Mayan civilisation. Chichén Itzá was the site of countless human sacrifices and flourished until about the year 1200, when it was suddenly abandoned. Today, the old road between Cancún and *Mérida* cuts through the middle of the site, creating two separate ruins, *Chichén Viejo* and *Chichén Nuevo*, which together form the most intact ruins from the Mayan period. Highlights at the complex, which covers an area of approximately 15 sq km (6 sq miles), include the *Kukulcán Pyramid* (also known as the Castle), the *Ball Court* (the largest Mayan ball court ever discovered), the *Thousand Columns* and the *Tzompantli.*

Transportation
Air: Mexico City International Airport, Mérida Airport (domestic flights). **Road:** Coach: Public services. Car: Highway (Autopista) from Cancún or Mérida.

Contact Addresses
Secretária de Turismo de Mérida, Calle 59 #514 entre 62 y 64, Col. Centro, CP 97000 Mérida, Yucatán, Mexico
Tel: (999) 924 9389

Copper Canyon (Barrancas del Cobre)

One of the largest canyon systems in the world, *Copper Canyon* is a land of mountains, rivers, waterfalls, desert and forest. Four of the canyons are deeper than Arizona's famous *Grand Canyon*, although none of them are as wide. Perhaps the most famous attraction for visitors is the *Chihuahua al Pacífico Railway*, a scenic journey that crosses 36 major bridges, travels through 87 tunnels and climbs to a height of 2438m (8000ft) before descending back down to sea level. The *Sierra Tarahumara* mountains are inhabited by

Tarahumara Indians, who live in isolated communities along the railway line.

Transportation
Air: Mexico City International Airport, then Los Mochis Airport or Chihuahua Airport. **Rail:** Train: Copper Canyon Railway to Creel (from Los Mochis or Chihuahua City). **Road:** Coach: Public services. Car: Hwy-16 to Creel (from Chihuahua City).

Contact Addresses
For more information on the Copper Canyon, contact the Secretaria de Turismo (see **Tourist Information** above).

National Museum of Anthropology (Museo Nacional de Antropología)

Mexico's *National Museum of Anthropology* is one of the world's great museums. Opened in 1964, the exhibition halls house Mexico's greatest archaeological collection, celebrating the country's pre-Columbian inhabitants and its existing indigenous peoples. As it is impossible to cover the whole museum at once, it is more rewarding to limit a visit to a few areas of particular interest. Some of the most fascinating rooms are the *Mexica*, which showcases Aztec culture, the *Maya* hall, and the *Teotihuacán* hall. The *Sala de Orientación* provides an overall view of the main Mexican cultures through an audiovisual presentation, and there are also rooms devoted to recent archaeological discoveries.

Transportation
Air: Mexico City International Airport. **Rail:** Underground: Auditorio. **Road:** Car: 57/57D (from the north); 95D (from the south); 150D (from the east); 45D (from the west).

Contact Addresses
Museo Nacional de Antropologia, Paseo de la Reforma, Chapultepec Park, Mexico City, Mexico
Tel: (05) 553 6266
Website: www.mna.inah.gob.mx

Palenque

Located in *Palenque National Park* in the northern *Chiapas* highlands, *Palenque* is one of the grandest of all classical Mayan sites. Situated on a ledge picturesquely overlooking swampy plains to the north, and set against a backdrop of lush, green mountains, Palenque was in its prime between AD 500-700. Visitors can wander from one structure to another amongst waterfalls and jungle, taking in the marvels of this ancient settlement, which is all the more remarkable for having been constructed without the aid of metal tools, the wheel or pack animals. The most notable structures are the *Palace* and the *Temple of Inscriptions* pyramid crypt.

Transportation
Air: Mexico City International Airport, Villa Hermosa Airport (domestic flights). **Road:** Coach: Public services. Car: Main road (from Villa Hermosa or Tuxtla Gutierriz).

Contact Addresses
Chiapas Tourist Board, Blvd. Belisario Dominguez 950 PB, 29060 Tuxtla Gutierrez, Mexico
Tel: (961) 602 5298
Website: www.chiapas.gob.mx

Parroquia (San Miguel de Allende Parish Church)

La Parroquia, a pink, Gothic parish church, is one of *San Miguel de Allende's* most famous landmarks, as well as one of the finest examples of colonial architecture in Mexico. Standing in the city's main square *(El Jardin)*, the church was originally built in 1683 but was given a facelift in 1880. The crypt underneath the main altar contains the remains of Felipe Gonzalez and General Anastasio Bustamante, both of whom were heroes of the Mexican War of Independence (1810-1821) against Spain. There is also a sculpture of Ignacio Allende, who is the city's namesake, displayed on the main altar; he was born in San Miguel in 1779 and became a leader during the Mexican independence movement, with execution in 1811 resulting in his status as a martyr.

Transportation

Air: Mexico City International Airport, Leon/Guanajuato International Airport. **Road:** Bus: Public services. Car: Federal Hwy-57 (from Querétaro); Hwy-49 and Hwy-45D (from Irapuato). San Miguel de Allende is 274km (171 miles) northwest of Mexico City.

Contact Addresses

Secretaria de Turismo (SECTUR), San Miguel de Allende, Guanajuato, Mexico
Tel: (415) 152 0900
Website: www.sanmiguelguide.com

Teotihuacán

Located 50km (31 miles) northeast of *Mexico City*, *Teotihuacán* grew to be the largest of Mexico's pre-Hispanic cities, with an estimated population of 200,000 during its prime in the sixth century AD. Its greatest building is the *Pyramid of the Sun*, standing at a height of 63m (207ft). It is joined on the *Avenue of the Dead*, Teotihuacán's main street, by another enormous building, the *Moon Pyramid*, which was originally part of a 'Moon Plaza'. The site was first excavated in 1884. Visitors can also see the various palaces once inhabited by the priests who ruled the city; research has brought to light many of the rituals of this ancient civilisation, including ceremonial human sacrifice and elaborate festivals.

Transportation

Air: Mexico City International Airport. **Road:** Coach: Public services. Car: Main road to Hidalgo (from Mexico City).

Contact Addresses

Zona Arqueológica de Teotihuacán, Km 22+600 Autopista Ecatapec–Pirámides, CP 55800, Estado de México, Mexico
Tel/Fax: (594) 956 0276

White Mountain (Monte Alban)

Monte Alban was at one time home to 50,000 Zapotec people. The builders of Monte Alban artificially levelled the top of the mountain, which overshadows the three surrounding valleys of *Oaxaca*. The site emerged as a political centre in around 400BC, and later developed as an important cultural centre between 500BC to AD 700. The site was abandoned by the Zapotecs when they began to lose political power, which resulted in conflict between them and the Mixtecs, who moved into the Valley and used it as a burial ground. It was later invaded by the Aztecs and then by the Spanish who gave the site the name Monte Alban, meaning White Mountain, due to the white flowering trees that grow in the area.

Transportation

Air: Mexico City International Airport. **Road:** Coach: Public services. Car: Access from Oaxaca.

Contact Addresses

Monte Alban, Office of Administration, Archaeological Site, Pino Suarez 715, Centro, CP 68000, Mexico
Tel: (0951) 516 1215

Chichén Itzá

Zena Turner©

Moldova

100km
50mls
✈ international airport

UKRAINE

Dniester

② .et.
Soroca•

Bălți   Răbnița•

MOLDOVA
Orhei•   Dubăsari

CHIŞINĂU
①✈
Tighina   •Tiraspol

Basarabeasca•

ROMANIA   UKRAINE

•Cahul

Lake
Yalpuh
BLACK
SEA

Danube
Delta

Danube

Prut

1 Alexandr Pushkin House and Museum

2 Emil Racovita

Tourist Information

Moldova National Tourism Agency
180 Stefan cel Mare Street, Office 901,
Chisinau MD 2004, Moldova
Tel: (22) 210 774
Website: www.turism.md
Embassy of the Republic of Moldova
5 Dolphin Square, Edensor Road, London
W4 2ST, UK
Tel: (020) 8995 6818
Website: www.turism.md

Alexandr Pushkin House and Museum

The famous Russian poet A.S. Pushkin was sent in
to exile in Moldova in 1820 for writing subversive

poetry and arrived in the Moldovan capital of
Chisinau in September of that year. He took up
residence in the house of General Iznov in the city
which today stands as a popular museum
recounting the events of his life. During his time
in Moldova, Pushkin wrote many famous poems
including 'The Gypsies', 'The Black Shawl' and
part of 'Eugene Onegin', one his most celebrated
works.

Transportation
Air: Chisinau International Airport. Rail: Train:
Chisinau Station. Road: Bus: Public services.

Contact Addresses
A.S. Pushkin House and Museum, 19 Anton Pann
Street, Chisinau, Moldova
Tel: (22) 292 685 *or* 242 653

🅿 ♿ £ 🏛

Emil Racovita

Named after the eminent 19th-century Romanian
biologist, Emil Racovita, the cave complex in the
village of *Criva* in Moldova is one of the biggest
in the world. A network of underground galleries
stretches over 89,000m (291,991ft) and is split
across several levels. Discovered in 1959, the cave
is the third-largest gypsum cave in the world and
parts of the complex are only accessible via large
wells. The huge caves have been given names
such as *Cinderella's Hall* and *Dacia's Hall,* reflecting
their size and grandeur, and there are also several
underground lakes, including the *Blue Lake* and the
Dinosaur Lake. There are no trail markers but
visitors are able to explore the caves in small
groups with an experienced guide.

Transportation
Air: Chisinau International Airport. **Rail:** Train:
Public services. **Road:** Bus: Public services.

Contact Addresses
For more information on the Emil Racovita Cave,
contact the National Tourism Agency (see **Tourist
Information** above).

🅿 ✕ 🧺 £ 🌿

Morocco

1 Fès Medina (Fès el Bali)

2 Hassan Tower (Tour Hassan)

3 Place of the Dead (Djemaa el Fna)

4 Saadian Tombs

Tourist Information

Office National Marocain de Tourisme
22 Avenue d'alger, Rabat, Morocco
Tel: (037) 73 0562
Website: www.tourism-in-morocco.com

Moroccan National Tourist Office
Second Floor, 205 Regent Street,
London W1B 4HB, UK
Tel: (020) 7437 0073
Website: www.visitmorocco.org

Fès Medina (Fès el Bali)

Founded shortly after the Arabs first entered North
Africa in the eighth century AD, *Fès* is the oldest of
Morocco's imperial cities. Its *medina*, the ancient

quarter or the old city, is also the largest medina in
Morocco, an enchanting, winding, medieval maze of
mosques, food markets and covered bazaars filled
with crafts, such as metalwork objects and rugs. The
Souk Dabbaghin houses the tanneries where leather
has been dyed for hundreds of years. Today, this
traditional craft is still practised and visitors can see
the huge vats of dye and the coloured leather that is
laid out to dry in the sun. The medina is also home
to the *Al-Qarawiyin Theological University*, founded in
AD 857, which is the oldest university in the western
world. The *Medersa Bou Inania* was founded in 1350
as a rival to the Al-Qarawiyin University and is a
splendid example of Andalusian architecture.

Transportation
Air: Marrakech Ménara Airport. **Rail:** Train:
Marrakech Station. **Road:** Coach: Public services.

Contact Addresses
For more information on Fès Medina, contact the
Moroccan National Tourist Office in London (see
Tourist Information above).

Hassan Tower (Tour Hassan)

The *Hassan Tower*, the grandiose minaret of a vast
yet incomplete mosque, is Rabat's most famous
landmark. Begun in AD 1195, the minaret was
intended to be the largest in the Muslim world,
soaring 86m (260ft) into the sky. Construction was
abandoned, however, upon the death of the sultan,
Yacoub al-Mansour, in AD 1199 and the tower
instead rises to just 44m (140ft). Two hundred
columns mark out the area where the mosque was
to stand. Today, the site also houses the *Mosque
and Mausoleum of Mohammed V*, the grandfather
of the present king of Morocco, which is one of
the few sacred sites in the country that non-
Muslims are allowed to enter.

Transportation
Air: Casablanca Mohammed V Airport or Rabat
Salé Airport. **Rail:** Train: Rabat Agdal Station or
Rabat-Ville Station. **Road:** Car: Casablanca-Rabat
Highway.

Contact Adresses

For more information on the Hassan Tower, contact the Moroccan National Tourist Office in London (see **Tourist Information** above).

Place of the Dead (Djemaa el Fna)

Djemaa el Fna is the hub of daily life in *Marrakech*, and this town square is as much a focus for the local people as it is for the tourists who flock here to find their bearings and watch the daily spectacle unfold. During the day the square serves more as a thoroughfare for traffic with just a few fresh fruit and juice stalls. The square leads in to the *medina*, or old quarter, where the famous *souks*, or bazaars, can be found. At night, the square really comes alive and turns into an open-air stage filled with acrobats, storytellers, snakecharmers and musicians. There are literally hundreds of food stalls to choose from, selling anything from hearty *harira* soup and couscous to grilled meats and french fries. All this is not merely a show for the tourists either – the entertainers who perform here do so to earn a living, and are carrying on a centuries-old tradition that remains a fundamental part of Marrakech life.

Transportation

Air: Marrakech Ménara Airport. **Rail:** Train: Marrakech Station. **Road:** Coach: Public services.

Contact Addresses

Marrakech Tourist Office, Place Abdelmoumen Ben Ali, Marrakech, Morocco
Tel: (04) 443 6231
Website: www.visitmorocco.com

Saadian Tombs

Situated in the old *Kasbah Quarter* of *Marrakech*, the *Saadian Tombs* were built in the late-16thcentury by the Saadian Sultan Ahmed el Mansour as the final resting place for himself, three other Sultans and 62 of their family members. The series of 66 elaborately decorated indoor tombs were only accessible via the mosque next door but were rediscovered and made accessible to visitors in 1917 and have become one of the city's most visited sites. Famed for their ornate decoration, the central mausoleum known as the *Hall of Twelve Columns* is the most stunning chamber of the complex with high vaulted ceilings, marble columns and intricate mosaics.

Transportation

Air: Marrakech Ménara Airport. **Rail:** Marrakech Station. **Road:** Bus: Public services.

Contact Addresses

For more information on the Saadian Tombs, contact the Moroccan National Tourist Board (see **Tourist Information** above).

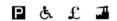

Visit Morocco©

Myanmar

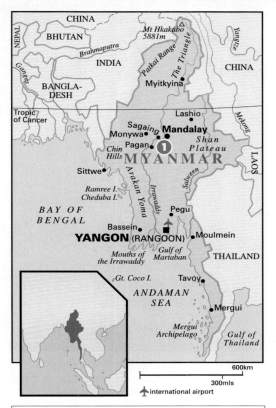

1 Bagan

Tourist Information

Myanmar Ministry of Hotels & Tourism
77-91 Sule Pagoda Road, Yagon, Myanmar
Tel: (01) 25 44 17 *or* 25 28 59
Website: www.myanmar-tourism.com

Embassy of the Union of Myanmar
19a Charles Street, London W1J 5DX, UK
Tel: (020) 7499 43401

plaster carvings and other artefacts from the empire. Many visitors take a river excursion to take in large stretches of the site, which is particularly beautiful at sunset.

Transportation
Air: Yangon International Airport, then Nyaung-u Airport (located 11km (7 miles) from Bagan and next to the archaeological site). **Rail:** Train: Bagan Station. **Road:** Bus: Nyaung-u Bus Station is located 6.5km (4 miles) from Bagan; there are regular buses to/from Yangon and Mandalay. Car: There are road connections to Bagan.

Contact Addresses
Myanmar Travel and Tours, c/o Ministry of Hotels and Tourism, 77-91 Sule Pagoda Road, Yangon, Myanmar
Tel: (01) 283 997 *or* 252 859

Bagan

The ancient city of *Bagan* (also known as Pagan) was founded in AD 849 by the Myanmar, or Burmans, as the capital of their empire. It is one of the most amazing archaeological sites in the world – 5000 temples, *stupas* (Buddhist dome-shaped monuments believed to contain relics of the Buddha himself) and pagodas lie scattered across an area of 42 sq km (16.2 sq miles) on the eastern bank of the Ayeyarwaddy River, testifying to the power and status of Bagan in bygone times. The most significant pagoda is the golden *Shwezigon Pagoda*, constructed in 1057 by King Anawrahta, the founder of the Myanmar dynasty, as a place of prayer and meditation. The informative *Archaeological Museum* displays murals,

Bagan

Myanmar Ministry of Hotels & Tourism©

Namibia

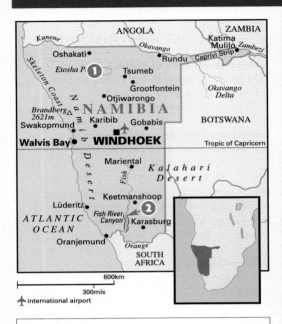

Namibia Tourism Board©

1 Etosha National Park

2 Fish River Canyon

Tourist Information

Namibia Tourism
Ground Floor Sanlam Center, Private Bag
13244, Windhoek, Namibia
Tel: (061) 290 6000
Website: www.met.gov.na

Namibia Tourism
6 Chandos Street, London W1G 9LU, UK
Tel: (0870) 330 9333
Website: www.namibiatourism.co.uk

Etosha National Park

Etosha National Park is located 500km (311 miles) north of Namibia's capital city, Windhoek. It is one of the largest game reserves in the world and famous for its many species of wildlife. Until the 1960s, it was the largest game reserve in the world, when its surface area was reduced due to political reasons. Today, Etosha has three main restcamps – *Okaukejo*, *Namutoni* and *Halali*. Okaukejo is famed for floodlit waterholes that are home to elephants, giraffes, black rhino and lions; Namutoni is centred around a historic fort and Halali is situated halfway between the two and is the quietest. The park has an estimated 300 lions, 2000 giraffes and 1500 elephants and owes its unique landscape to the *Etosha Pan*, a giant clay salt pan forming a shallow depression which allows amazing views of the game.

Transportation
Air: Windhoek International Airport. **Road:**
Car: C38 road (from Outjo); C39 road (from Khorixas).

Contact Addresses
Namibia Wildlife Resorts Ltd, Erkrath Building,
Independence Avenue, Private Bag 13267,
Windhoek, Nambia
Tel: (061) 256 446
Website: www.namibiawildliferesorts.com

www.fotoseeker.com©

Fish River Canyon

Fish River Canyon

Fish River Canyon is the largest canyon in the Southern Hemisphere, second only in the world to the *Grand Canyon*. The whole gorge measures 160km (99 miles) in length and is 127km (79 miles) wide, whilst its impressive inner canyon is an amazing 550m (1804ft) deep. The gorge which has formed over hundreds of millions of years, winds through the arid desert landscape, cutting through the great plateau and surrounded by imposing cliffs and large boulders. The site is the main tourist attraction in the far south of Namibia, popular with hikers who set out on the testing trail through the canyon. At the southern end of the canyon, after a long hike through the desert terrain, weary walkers arrive at *Ai-Ais* (meaning Burning Water in the local Nama language), a hot water spring which wells from the earth and is believed to cure rheumatism.

Transportation
Air: Windhoek International Airport. **Road:** Car: B4 southwest for around 44km (27 miles), then left onto the C12 (from Keetmanshoop). After 77km (48 miles) a right turn is signposted for Fish River Canyon.

Contact Addresses
Namibia Wildlife Resorts Ltd, Erkrath Building, Independence Avenue, Private Bag 13267, Windhoek, Namibia
Tel: (061) 236 975
Website: www.namibiawildliferesorts.com

  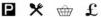

Nepal

1 Kathmandu Durbar Square

Durbar Square

Nepal Tourism Board©

Tourist Information

Nepal Tourism Board
Bhrikuti Mandap, PO Box 11018, Kathmandu,
Nepal
Tel: (01) 256 909 or 256 229Website:
www.welcomenepal.com

Royal Nepalese Embassy
12a Kensington Palace Gardens, London W8
4QU, UK
Tel: (020) 7229 1594 or 7229 5352
Website: www.nepembassy.org.uk

Kathmandu Durbar Square

Kathmandu's *Durbar Square* is one of three *durbar*
(royal palace) squares in the Kathmandu Valley. It
is the site of the *Hanuman Dhoka Palace Complex*,
which was the royal Nepalese residence until the
19th century and where important ceremonies,
such as the coronation of the Nepalese monarch,
still take place today. The palace is decorated with
elaborately-carved wooden windows and panels
and houses the *King Tribhuwan Memorial Museum*

and the *Mahendra Museum*. It is also possible to
visit the *State Rooms* inside the palace. At the
southern end of Durbar Square is one of the most
curious attractions in Nepal, the *Kumari Chowk*.
This gilded cage contains the Raj Kumari, a young
girl chosen through an ancient and mystical
selection process to become the human
incarnation of the Hindu mother goddess, Durba.
She is worshipped during religious festivals and
makes public appearances at other times for a fee
paid to her guards.

Transportation
Air: Kathmandu International Airport. **Road:**
Coach: Services from Darjeeling, Calcutta and
Varanasi (India). Car: Prithvi Highway (from
Pokhara).

Contact Addresses
Department of Archaeology, Hanumandhoka
Section, Ramshah Path, Kathmandu, Nepal
Tel: (01) 250 683 *or* 250 685

Netherlands

1 Anne Frank House (Anne Frank Huis)
2 Keukenhof Gardens (Keukenhof)
3 Royal Palace (Koninklijk Paleis)
4 State Museum (Rijksmuseum)
5 Van Gogh Museum

Tourist Information

**Netherlands Board of Tourism
(Nederlands Bureau voor Toerisme)**
PO Box 458, 2260 MG Leidschendam,
The Netherlands
Tel: (070) 370 5705
Website: www.holland.com

Netherlands Board of Tourism
PO Box 30783, London WC2B 6DH, UK
Tel: (020) 7539 7950 *or* (09068) 717 777
(recorded information; calls cost 60p per minute)
Website: www.holland.com/uk

Anne Frank House (Anne Frank Huis)

Anne Frank House is the historic house where Jewish teenager Anne Frank, her family and four other Jews hid from the Nazis during World War II. Anne herself shared a tiny room with family friend Fritz Pfeffer (known to Anne as Albert Dussel). In August 1944, after more than two years living in a cramped secret annex of the canalside townhouse on Prinsengracht in the centre of Amsterdam, they were betrayed to the Germans. Anne died at the Bergen-Belsen concentration camp; however, her father survived and published her diary, which became world famous as testament to one person's courage in the face of persecution. Today, the house is a permanent exhibition dedicated to the memory of Anne Frank, and the place where the original diary is on display. Visitors can see the room where Anne wrote most of her diary and, although the house was stripped by the Nazis after the Franks' arrest, audiovisual presentations document how the rooms would have looked.

Transportation
Air: Amsterdam Airport Schiphol. **Rail:** Train: Amsterdam Centraal Station. Tram: Public services. **Road:** Bus: Public services to Westermarkt. Car: Hwy-A10 (exit Centrum S105).

Contact Addresses
Anne Frankhuis, PO Box 730, 1000 AS Amsterdam, The Netherlands
Tel: (020) 556 7100
Website: www.annefrank.nl

Keukenhof Gardens (Keukenhof)

Located in the town of Lisse, *Keukenhof Gardens* are named after the kitchen gardens where Countess Jacoba of Bavaria grew fruit, vegetables and herbs in the grounds of her estate between 1401-1436 (hence the name Keukenhof, which literally means kitchen garden). Keukenhof was

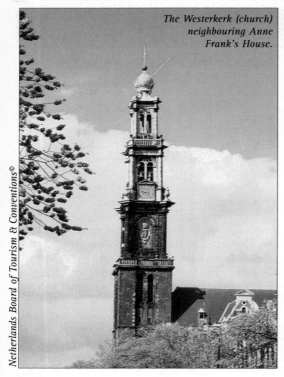

The Westerkerk (church) neighbouring Anne Frank's House.

Netherlands Board of Tourism & Conventions©

designed as a park by two horticultural architects called Zochter in 1840, with the flower garden opening in 1949 when a bulb-growing consortium acquired the site and decided to develop an open-air flower exhibition. Today, Keukenhof Gardens, which is the largest flower attraction in the Netherlands and the largest display of bulbs in the world, is an impressive and flamboyant example of the Dutch population's love of tulips. Although open daily, the best time of year to visit is between the last week in March and the last week in May when the beautiful bulb flowers are in full bloom.

Transportation
Air: Amsterdam Airport Schiphol. **Rail:** Train: Leiden Central Station or Haarlem Station. **Road:** Bus: Public services.

Contact Addresses
Keukenhof, Stationsweg 166 A, 2160 AB Lisse, The Netherlands
Tel: (0252) 465 564
Website: www.keukenhof.nl

Royal Palace (Koninklijk Paleis)

The *Royal Palace*, which dates from 1648 and was designed by Jacob van Campen, was originally Amsterdam's town hall and is regarded today as the most important cultural and historical building from 17th-century Amsterdam. The building's exterior was originally made of white stone, although none of the white is actually visible today, whilst famous painters including Rembrandt and Ferdinand Bol were brought in to contribute to the interior. Today, the palace, which has been state property since 1936, houses an impressive collection of furniture left behind by Napoleon who made it his home in 1808, as well as chandeliers and clocks from this period. The palace is the official residence of the Dutch Royal Family and the present Queen, Beatrix, still uses the Royal Palace to host official functions such as the Queen's New Year reception and various state visits.

Transportation
Air: Amsterdam Airport Schiphol. **Rail:** Train: Amsterdam Centraal Station. Tram: Public services. **Road:** Signs are marked for Dam Square (from Amsterdam Centraal Station).

Contact Addresses
Ministry of General Affairs (RVD), Binnenhof 19, Postbus 20009, 2500 ea den haag, The Netherlands.
Tel: (0) 70 356 or 4166
Website: www.koninklijkhuis.nl

State Museum (Rijksmuseum)

The largest and most popular museum in the Netherlands, the *Rijksmuseum* was first opened as the *Nationale Konstgallerij* (National Art Gallery) in 1800 in *Huis ten Bosch* in The Hague. The museum houses an impressive collection of 15th- to 19th-century paintings, including work by the Dutch masters Rembrandt, Frans Hals, Jan Steen and Vermeer, and a fine collection of sculpture, furniture and historical items from the Low Countries. Highlights include the museum's most famous piece, Rembrandt's *The Night Watch*, painted in 1642, and *The Kitchen Maid* by Vermeer, dating from 1658. The *Print*

Corel©   *Keukenhof Gardens*

Room is also worth visiting and regularly exhibits famous prints, drawings and photos.

Transportation
Air: Amsterdam Airport Schiphol. **Rail:** Train: Amsterdam Centraal Station. Tram: Public services. **Road:** Car: A10 towards Amsterdam (RAI exit). Signs are marked for the Rijksmuseum (from the city centre).

Contact Addresses
Rijksmuseum, PO Box 74888, 1070 DN Amsterdam, The Netherlands
Tel: (020) 674 7047
Website: www.rijksmuseum.nl

Van Gogh Museum

Opened in 1973, the *Van Gogh Museum* houses some of the painter's most celebrated works. Located in the Museumplein in the centre of Amsterdam, between the Rijksmuseum and the Stedelijk Museum, the modern glass building was designed by the Dutch architect Gerrit Rietveld. It contains the world's largest collection of works by Van Gogh, including some 200 paintings, 500 drawings, 700 letters and the artist's own collection of Japanese prints. Highlights of the Van Gogh collection include his first large-scale painting, *The Potato Eaters* and *The Sunflowers*, one of his most famous pieces, painted in 1889. The museum also houses a large collection of work by Van Gogh's contemporaries, including paintings by Claude Monet and Paul Gauguin.

Transportation
Air: Amsterdam Airport Schiphol. **Rail:** Train: Amsterdam Centraal Station. Tram: Public services to Museum Square. **Road:** Bus: Public services to Museum Square. Car: A10 towards Amsterdam (exit S106). Signs are marked for Museum Square (from the city centre).

Contact Addresses
Van Gogh Museum, PO Box 75366, 1070 AJ Amsterdam, The Netherlands
Tel: (020) 570 5200 *or* 570 5252
Website: www.vangoghmuseum.nl

New Zealand

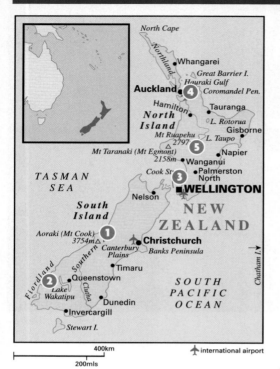

North Cape
Northland
Whangarei
Great Barrier I.
Hauraki Gulf
Auckland ④ Coromandel Pen.
Hamilton
North Tauranga
Island L. Rotorua
Gisborne
Mt Ruapehu L. Taupo
△2797
Mt Taranaki (Mt Egmont) ⑤ Napier
2158m Wanganui
Cook St. Palmerston
③ North
TASMAN ■**WELLINGTON**
SEA Nelson
South **N E W**
Island **Z E A L A N D**
Aoraki (Mt Cook) ①
3754m△ Christchurch
Canterbury Banks Peninsula
Plains
Timaru
② Queenstown *S O U T H*
Lake *P A C I F I C*
Wakatipu Dunedin *O C E A N*
Invercargill
Stewart I.

400km
200mls
✈ international airport

1 Aoraki Mount Cook

2 Fiordland National Park

3 Museum of New Zealand Te Papa Tongarewa

4 Sky City Tower

5 Tongariro National Park

Aoraki Mount Cook

Standing 3754m (12,316ft) high, *Aoraki Mount Cook* is the highest mountain in New Zealand. The mountain, which attracts climbers from all over the world to its snow-covered peaks, stands in *Aoraki/Mount Cook National Park*, on New Zealand's South Island. Aoraki means 'Cloud Piercer' in Maori and the mountain is so called due to its breathtaking peaks which tower high above the clouds. The national park was formally declared in 1953 and covers an area of 70,111 hectares (173,251 acres). There are regular guided tours from Mount Cook to the *Tasman Glacier*,

which, at 27km (17 miles) long, 3km (1.9 miles) wide and 600m (1968ft) deep, is New Zealand's largest glacier. Other highlights include the smaller *Hooker Glacier, Murchison Glacier Mount Tasman* and *Mount Dampier*. Outdoor activities include helicopter rides, alpine flights, horse trekking, hunting and fishing, mountain biking and hiking through the mountains.

Transportation
Air: Christchurch International Airport, Aoraki/Mount Cook Airport (domestic flights); there are regular shuttle buses from Aoraki/Mount Cook Airport throughout the Mackenzie region.
Road: Bus: Public services.

Contact Addresses
Mackenzie Tourism and Development Board, Lake Pukaki Visitor Centre, State Highway 8, PO Box 68, Twizel, New Zealand
Tel: (03) 435 3280
Website: www.mtcook.org.nz

Fiordland National Park

At nearly 1.2 million hectares (3 million acres), *Fiordland National Park* is New Zealand's largest national park – a breathtaking stretch of coastal landscape that typifies the country's natural splendour. Created in 1952, it is a land of ice, beech forests, mountains and waterfalls that tumble into the ocean below. One of the park's most famous sights is *Milford Sound*, which is the largest glacier-carved fiord on New Zealand's coastline and attracts large numbers of sightseers and cruise ships every year. Popular activities in the park include hiking, sea kayaking, diving, cycling, golf, fishing and sailing. The *Milford Track*, which stretches some 53.5km (33 miles) from Glade Wharf to Sandfly Point, has been described as the finest walk in the world, taking visitors on a rugged, alpine journey through the park's most breathtaking scenery. Visitors should, however, note that a permit is required for the track and these must be booked through the Visitor Centre in Te Anau.

Transportation
Air: Christchurch International Airport, Te Anau Airstrip (domestic flights). **Road:** Bus: Public services to Milford Sound and Queenstown.

Contact Addresses
Fiordland National Park Visitor Centre, c/o Department of Conservation, Lakefront Drive, PO Box 29, Te Anau, New Zealand
Tel: (03) 249 7924
Website: www.doc.govt.nz

 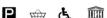

Museum of New Zealand Te Papa Tongarewa

Te Papa (meaning 'Our Place' in Maori), the national museum of New Zealand, is located on Wellington's waterfront, from where it enjoys magnificent views across the harbour. The museum was opened to enable the people of New Zealand to learn more about their cultural identity and their country's geography and has attracted international acclaim for its ultra-modern and interactive displays. It occupies a floor space measuring 36,000 sq m (387,513 sq ft)

and houses many national artefacts, enabling visitors to learn about the art, history and natural environment of New Zealand. It also has several permanent exhibitions, including the *Time Warp* display, which allows visitors to travel back in time to New Zealand's prehistoric age.

Transportation
Air: Wellington International Airport. **Road:** Bus: Public services. Car: Wellington motorway (Aotea Quay exit), then along Waterloo, Customhouse and Jervois Quay, which leads directly to Cable Street.

Contact Addresses
Museum of New Zealand Te Papa Tongarewa, PO Box 467, Cable Street, Wellington, New Zealand
Tel: (04) 381 7000
Website: www.tepapa.govt.nz

Sky City Tower

The *Sky City Tower* stands at 328m (1076ft) high and is situated in the *Sky City* entertainment complex, which also houses *Sky City Casino*, *Sky City Theatre*, *Sky City Hotel and Conference Centre* and *Sky City Restaurants*. The postmodern Sky City Tower was designed by the architect *Craig Moller* and completed in 1997. The tower has three circular observation levels, the highest of which is the *Sky Deck*, which gives a 360-degree view across Auckland and Waitemata Harbour, over the top of Rangitoto Island to the other islands in the Hauraki Gulf, allowing visitors to see up to 82km (51 miles) on a clear day. Visitors can also eat in the *Orbit* rotating restaurant and travel to the top of the tower in one of six high-tech glass-fronted lifts.

Transportation
Air: Auckland International Airport. **Road:** Bus: Public services.

Contact Addresses
Sky Tower, Sky City, PO Box 90643, Auckland, New Zealand
Tel: (09) 363 6400
Website: www.skycity.co.nz

Auckland with the Sky City Tower

New Zealand Tourist Board©

Tongariro National Park

Originally a gift to Queen Victoria from the Tuwharetoa Maori chief Te Heuheu Tukino IV in 1887, *Tongariro National Park* was the first national park in New Zealand and the fourth oldest in the world. Since its inception, the park has grown to a size of nearly 80,000 hectares (197,688 acres). The area is of religious and cultural importance to the Maoris who first occupied the area in the ninth century when they arrived from Polynesia. In particular, they believed the region's mountains had god-like ancestors, and the core of the park centres around three active volcanoes, *Tongariro*, *Ngauruhoe* and the largest, *Ruapehu*, which erupted in a spectacular fashion in 1995 and again in 1996. Some areas resemble a lunar landscape, which has been created by flowing lava, alongside forests and tussock lands. The *Tongariro Crossing*, completed by about 70,000 hikers every summer, is considered to be one of the best one-day walks in the country, offering magnificent volcanic scenery and fine views of *Lake Taupo* and *Mount Taranaki*.

Transportation
Air: Wellington International Airport, then Taupo Airport. **Rail:** Train: National Park and Ohakune stations (from Auckland and Wellington). **Road:** Bus: Public services. Car: State Hwy-1 (from Auckland in the north or from Wellington in the south).

Contact Addresses
Tongariro National Park, Private Bag, Mt Ruapehu 2650, New Zealand
Tel: (07) 892 3814
or
Tongariro/Taupo Conservancy, Private Bag, Turangi, New Zealand
Tel: (07) 386 8607
Website: www.doc.govt.nz

Norway

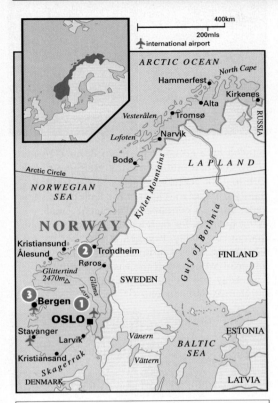

400km
200mls
✈ international airport

ARCTIC OCEAN
North Cape
Hammerfest
Kirkenes
Alta
Vesterålen • Tromsø
Lofoten • Narvik
Bodø
Arctic Circle
LAPLAND
NORWEGIAN
SEA
Kjølen Mountains
NORWAY
Kristiansund
Ålesund ②Trondheim
FINLAND
Røros
Glittertind
2470m
SWEDEN
Gulf of Bothnia
③
Bergen ①
OSLO
Stavanger
Larvik
Vänern
ESTONIA
BALTIC
SEA
Kristiansand
Vättern
Skagerrak
DENMARK
LATVIA
RUSSIA

1 Hardanger Fjord
2 Nidaros Cathedral (Nidarosdomen)
3 Wharfside (Bryggen)

Tourist Information

Norweigan Tourist Board (Norges Turistrad)
PO Box 722, Santrum 0105, Oslo, Norway
Tel: 2414 4600
Website: www.ntr.no or www.visitnorway.com

Norwegian Tourist Board
Charles House, 5 Lower Regent Street, London
SW1Y 4LR, UK
Tel: (09063) 022 033 (brochure request line)
or (020) 7839 2650 (trade)
Website: www.visitnorway.com

Hardanger Fjord

Hardanger Fjord, which is located 75km (47 miles) east of Bergen, is one of the most popular tourist destinations in Norway. This scenic area offers virtually every kind of natural landscape available in the country, from scenic waterways, apple and cherry orchards, and hiking trails, to mountain plateaux. The area also contains *Hardangervidda*, Norway's largest national park, two of Norway's largest glaciers, *Folgefonna* and *Hardangerjøkulen*, and some of Norway's most popular waterfalls, including *Vøringfossen, Steinsdalsfossen* and *Låtefossen*. There are also various museums in the area, including *Hardanger folkemuseum* (Hardanger Folk Museum) and *Hardanger Fartøyvernsenter* (Hardanger Ships Preservation Centre) treeboat museum.

Transportation
Air: Bergen Flesland Airport. **Rail:** Train: Voss Station. **Road:** Bus: Public services to Norheimsund. Car: Route 7 towards Norheimsund (from Bergen); E-16 and Route 7 (from Oslo).

Contact Addresses
Destination Hardanger Fjord, PO Box 66, 5601 Norheimsund, Norway
Tel: 5655 3870
Website: www.hardangerfjord.com

🅿 ✕ 🛍 ♿ ❦

Nidaros Cathedral (Nidarosdomen)

According to Norwegian history, King Olav Haraldsson, who was killed in the battle of Stiklestad in 1030 and who subsequently became Norway's patron saint several days later, was buried on the exact spot where *Nidaros Cathedral* in Trondheim now stands. Construction of the church began in 1070 after pilgrims began to flock to St Olav's grave, but it was not completed until 1300, when it was widely reputed to be the most beautiful church in Norway. Now restored after fire damage and years of decay and pillage endured during the Reformation, it is particularly renowned for its fine stone statues on the exterior

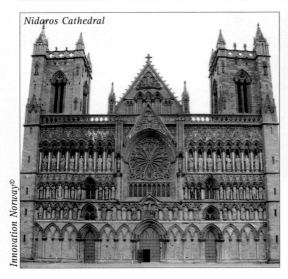

Nidaros Cathedral

Innovation Norway©

Wharfside, Bergen

and the quality and quantity of stained glass in the Gothic interior. Norway's monarchs are still crowned and buried in the cathedral and there are regular music recitals under the high-vaulted arches. Visitors can admire the *Crown Jewels* on display and also climb the tower for fine views over Trondheim.

Transportation
Air: Bergen Flesland Airport, Oslo Gardermoen International Airport, Trondheim Værnes Airport.
Water: Ferry: Hurtigruten coastal steamer (from Bergen). **Rail:** Train: Trondheim Station. **Road:** Bus: Public services. Car: E6 (from Oslo, Gothenburg or Copenhagen).

Contact Addresses
Nidarosdomen, Nidaros Domkirkes Restaureringsarbeider, Postboks 4447, Hospitalsløkkan, 7418 Trondheim, Norway
Tel: 7353 9160
Website: www.nidarosdomen.no

Wharfside (Bryggen)

Considered by UNESCO to be one of the world's foremost showcases of the Middle Ages, *Bryggen* consists of a series of gabled buildings situated on the old wharf of Bergen. It stands as a reminder of Bergen's prominent role in the days of the Hanseatic League, an organisation founded by a group of northern German towns to protect their mutual trading interests in the 13th to 15th centuries. The buildings were mainly used as warehouses for the dried fish trade, but also contained offices and simple living quarters for merchants, journeymen and apprentices. Today, Bryggen is alive with restaurants, cafés and artists' workshops, and a colourful attraction at the eastern end is *Torget*, a weekday market selling fruit and vegetables, handicrafts and souvenirs.

Wharfside, Bergen

Transportation
Air: Bergen Flesland Airport. **Rail:** Train: Bergen Central Station. Road: Bus: Public services. **Car:** E16 (from Oslo); E39 (from Stavanger, Ålesund or Kristiansand, then signs are marked for the city centre).

Contact Addresses
Bergen Tourist Board, PO Box 4055, Dreggen, 5835 Bergen, Norway
Tel: 5531 3860 *or* 5532 1480
Website: www.visitbergen.com

Panama

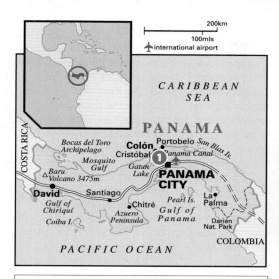

200km
100mls
✈ international airport

CARIBBEAN SEA

PANAMA

COSTA RICA

Bocas del Toro Archipelago
Mosquito Gulf
Baru Volcano 3475m
David
Santiago
Gulf of Chiriquí
Coiba I.
Azuero Peninsula
Chitré
Colón
Cristóbal
Portobelo *San Blas Is.*
Panama Canal
Gatun Lake
PANAMA CITY
Pearl Is.
Gulf of Panama
La Palma
Darién Nat. Park
COLOMBIA

PACIFIC OCEAN

1 Panama Canal (Canal de Panamá)

Locks on the Panama Canal

Tourist Information

Instituto Panameño de Turismo (IPAT) (Institute of Tourism)
Apartado 4421, Centro de Convenciones ATLAPA, Vía Israel, Panamá 5, Republic of Panamá
Tel: 226 7000 *or* 226 4614/3164
Website: www.ipat.gob.pa

Embassy of Panama
40 Hertford Street, London W1J 7SH, UK
Tel: (020) 7493 4646

Panama Canal (Canal de Panamá)

The idea of building a canal across the Isthmus of Panama dates back to the 16th century when people first recognised the advantage of building a canal which would avoid having to sail around Cape Horn in South America. It was not until 1880, however, that the French made an attempt to build a canal across this stretch of water. Unfortunately the attempt failed miserably due to high costs, with over 22,000 workers dying from malaria and yellow fever. The United States began construction work in 1904, employing nearly 75,000 men and women to build the canal, which opened to traffic ten years later in 1915. Today, the 80km (50 mile) canal still stands as one of the most important engineering feats in the world, providing passage for over 12,000 ships every year. An open-air balcony at *Miraflores Locks* offers visitors good views of the electrical locomotives or 'mules' pulling giant ships through as the water levels are balanced.

Transportation
Air: Tocument International Airport. **Road:** Coach: Many private companies operate coach tours to the canal (from Panama City). Car: Corredor Sur Highway to central Panama City, then through the Albrook Residential and Commercial Area, and right to Miraflores Locks (from Tocument International Airport).

Contact Addresses
Panama Canal Authority, PO Box 5413, Miami, FL 33102, USA
Tel: 272 3165 *or* 272 3202 (in Panama)
Website: www.pancanal.com

Peru

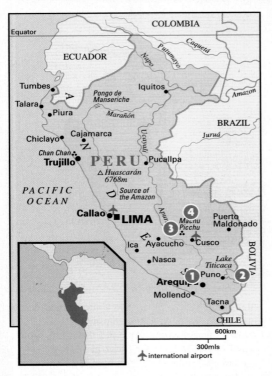

COLOMBIA

Equator

ECUADOR

Tumbes
Talara
Piura
Iquitos
Amazon
Pongo de
Manseriche
Marañón

BRAZIL

Chiclayo
Cajamarca
Jiruá

Chan Chan
Trujillo
PERU
Pucallpa
Huascarán
6768m
Source of
the Amazon

PACIFIC
OCEAN

Callao
LIMA
Machu
Picchu
Puerto
Maldonado
Ica
Ayacucho
Cusco
Nasca
Lake
Titicaca
Puno
BOLIVIA
Arequipa
Mollendo
Tacna
CHILE

600km
300mls
international airport

1 Arequipa-Colca Canyon (Cañon del Colca-Arequipa)

2 Lake Titicaca (Lago Titicaca)

3 Machu Picchu

4 Manu National Park (Parque Nacional del Manu)

Tourist Information

PromPerú (Commission for the Promotion of Peru)
Calle 1 Oeste 50, Edificio Mitinci, 13th Floor, Urb. Córpac, San Isidro, Lima 27, Peru
Tel: (01) 224 3271
Website: www.peru.org.pe

Embassy of the Republic of Peru
52 Sloane Street, London SW1X 9SP, UK
Tel: (020) 7235 1917 *or* 7235 2545
Website: www.peruembassy-uk.com

Arequipa-Colca Canyon (Cañon del Colca-Arequipa)

At a depth of more than 3400m (11,333ft), the *Arequipa-Colca Canyon* is one of the deepest in the world and almost twice the depth of the Grand Canyon (1829m/6000ft). The Rio Colca winds its way through the gorge, with the impressive Sabancaya and Ampato volcanoes looming high in the background. The canyon, which is named after the *Colcas* (warehouses) where the Incas used to store grain in sealed vaults in the canyon walls, is dotted with flora and fauna. A highlight of any trip to the region is a chance to see the giant Andean Condor that inhabits the canyon; visitors can view these great birds soaring into the wind from the *Cruz del Condor* observation point. The valley towns, such as Yanque and Chivay, which have maintained their original appearance for almost 400 years, and the many pre-Inca tombs and ruins in the area, are also of interest.

Transportation
Air: Lima Jorge Chavez International Airport, Cusco Airport (domestic flights). **Rail:** Train: Services to Arequipa. **Road:** Car: Arequipa-Lima road then road from Arequipa to the canyon.

Contact Addresses
Dirección Regional de Industria y Turismo, Jacinto Ibanez 456, Parque Industrial, Arequipa, Peru
Tel: (054) 213 044 *or* 235 660
Website: www.promperu.gob.pe

Lake Titicaca (Lago Titicaca)

At an elevation of 3810m (12,492ft), *Lake Titicaca* is one of the world's highest navigable lakes. It is named after the native word for 'puma of stone' and its shape bears a strong resemblance to this animal when viewed from above. Measuring 194km (121 miles) long and 65km (45 miles) wide, it has been revered in history, featuring prominently in Inca creation myths. There are daily tours to the *Uros* and *Taquile Islands*; the *Uros* people live on floating islands made out of reeds that grow in the lake, while the inhabitants of

Machu Picchu

Brian Wilkinson©

Taquile Island are renowned for maintaining ancient traditions and for their remarkable weaving skills.

Transportation
Air: El Alto Airport (La Paz). **Road:** Bus: Daily services leave La Paz every 30 minutes. Car: From La Paz (journey time: 2.5 hours).

Contact Addresses
For more information on Lake Titicaca, contact PromPeru (Commission for the Promotion of Tourism) (see **Tourist Information** above).

  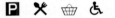

Machu Picchu

Located 112km (70 miles) northwest of Cusco and constructed as a refuge against the Spanish in the 16th century, *Machu Picchu* is the most spectacular and best known Inca site in South America. Although it is now of great spiritual and cultural significance to millions of Peruvians, its existence was known only to a few locals until American explorer Hiram Bingham happened upon it on July 24 1911. Machu Picchu also possesses the last *Inihuatana* (sundial) remaining in South America. Located within an incredible cloud forest, the site marks a fitting and dramatic conclusion to the end of the Inca Trail. Due to the high number of visitors, trekking permits are limited and are issued each day and must be applied for in advance.

Transportation
Air: Lima Jorge Chavez International Airport, Cusco Airport (domestic flights). **Rail:** Train: Aguas Calientes Station (from Cusco). **Road:** Coach: Services from Aguas Calientes Station. Car: Hwy-101 (from Lima) then road to Cusco.

Contact Addresses
Dirección Regional de Industria y Turismo Cusco, Avenida de la Cultura 734-3er, Piso, Cusco, Peru
Tel: (084) 223 701
Website: www.promperu.gob.pe

Manu National Park (Parque Nacional del Manu)

Manu National Park covers a staggering 1.5 million hectares (3.7 million acres) of terrain, consisting of successive tiers of vegetation. It is protected by UNESCO as a World Biosphere Reserve, can only be entered as part of a licensed tour, and is so remote that some of the indigenous tribes that live there have had no contact with the outside world. Its unspoiled atmosphere means that it is home to species that are unknown elsewhere in the world; the tropical Amazon jungle in the lower section is home to literally thousands of species of plants, butterfly and bird, and countless reptiles and insects. Further up, the *Andean High Plateau* rises to 4300m (14,100ft) and the *Tres Cruces* lookout on the road from Manu to Cusco offers far-reaching views across the Amazon.

Transportation
Air: Lima Jorge Chavez International Airport, Boca Manu Airstrip (domestic flights). **Water:** Motorised launch: Services from Atalaya to Boca Manu, then down the Madre de Dios river. **Road:** Coach: Services from Cusco to Atalaya; access is then by river.

Contact Addresses
Instituto Nacional de Recursos Naturales (INRENA), Calle Diecisiete 355, Urb, El Palomar, San Isidro, Peru
Tel: (01) 224 3298
Website: www.inrena.gob.pe

Philippines

500km
250mls
✈ international airport

SOUTH CHINA SEA

Batan Is.

Luzon Strait

Babuyan Is.

Laoag

① Baguio

Luzon

Mt Pinatubo△ • Angeles
MANILA • **Quezon City**
Manila Bay
San Pablo • Laguna de Bay

PHILIPPINE SEA

PHILIPPINES

Catanduanes

Calapan •
Mindoro

Legaspi

Busuanga •
Culion

Masbate

Roxas • **Visayas** Samar
Panay
Iloilo • Cebu • Tacloban
Bacolod • Leyte
Negros • Bohol Dinagat
Palawan Siargao

Puerto Princesa

SULU SEA

Bohol Sea • Butuan
Iligan • Cagayan de Oro
L. Lanao **Mindanao**

Mapin Zamboanga
Moro Gulf △ Mt Apo 2954m • **Davao**
Basilan
Jolo • General Santos

MALAYSIA Sulu Archipelago
Tawitawi CELEBES SEA INDONESIA

1 Banaue Rice Terraces

Tourist Information

Philippines Department of Tourism
Department of Tourism Building,
T M Kalaw Street, Rizal Park,
Manila 1000, Philippines
Tel: (02) 523 8411/30
Website: www.wowphilippines.com

Philippine Cultural and Tourism Office
146 Cromwell Road, London
SW7 4EF, UK
Tel: (020) 7835 1100
Website: www.wowphilippines.com

Banaue Rice Terraces

Banaue Rice Terraces

Nestled deep in the heartlands of the *Cordilleras* mountains and rising to an altitude of 1525m (5000ft) are the *Banaue Rice Terraces*. The terraces were carved out of the mountain range over 3000 years ago by the *Ifugaos*, the oldest mountain tribe in the area, using only the most primitive tools. The irrigation system uses gravity to harness water from the forests 1800m (2185ft) above thus ensuring a continuous supply of crops. Measured from end to end, the terraces would stretch a total length of 22,400km (13,919 miles), enough to encircle half the globe. They are often dubbed the eighth wonder of the ancient world as their age and scale is comparable to that of the official seven wonders, of which only the Pyramids of Giza remain.

Transportation
Air: Manila Ninoy Aquino International Airport, Baguio Airport (domestic flights), Bagabag Airport (domestic flights). **Rail:** Train: Manila Station. **Road:** Bus: Publice services.

Contact Addresses
Tourism Office, Cordillera Administrative Region, Department of Tourism, DOT Complex, Government Pack Road, 2600 Baguio City, Philippines
Tel: (074) 442 6708 *or* 442 7014
Website: www.tourism.gov.ph

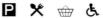

Poland

300km
150mls
✈ international airport

LATVIA

BALTIC SEA

LITHUANIA

Bornholm (Den.)

Nemunas

Gdynia•
Koszalin•
Gdansk• •Elblag
Pomerania

RUSSIAN FEDERATION

Mazuria

Szczecin•
Bydgoszcz• •Torun

Bialystok•

Poznan•

Vistula

Warta

BELARUS

WARSAW ✈ **3**

POLAND

Oder

Wroclaw• **Lodz** Radom•

Lublin•

Bug

Sudety Mtns.

Katowice•
1 ✈ **Cracow**
2 4

Silesia

Elbe

CZECH REPUBLIC

Tatra Mtns.

Zakopane△Rysys
2499m

SLOVAK REP.

UKRAINE

San

GERMANY

1 Auschwitz-Birkenau

2 Main Market Square, Krakow (Rynek Glowny, Krakow)

3 Warsaw Royal Castle (Zamek Królewski w Warsawie)

4 Wawel Royal Castle (Zamek Królewski na Wawelu)

Auschwitz-Birkenau

Auschwitz-Birkenau, situated 70km (46 miles) west of Krakow, is the most infamous and the largest of the Nazi death camps. It saw the cruel death of an estimated one million European Jews. Today, the camp is a museum dedicated to the memory of those who suffered and perished there. The forbidding entrance gate, surrounded by barbed wire, still bears the words *Arbeit Macht Frei* (Work Brings Freedom) and the railway and gas chambers remain as they were when the camp

was liberated by Soviet troops in May 1945. The *Museum of Martyrdom* shows a film depicting the nature of the atrocities, and there are further displays of photos and personal articles, such as children's shoes, women's hair and toothbrushes, that were taken from the victims.

Transportation
Air: Krakow-Balice John Paul II International Airport. **Rail:** Train: Oswiecim Station. **Road:** Bus: Services to the museum (from Oswiecim). A shuttle bus runs between the two sites, Auschwitz I and Birkenau.

Contact Addresses
Auschwitz-Birkenau State Museum, ulica Wiêzniów Oœwiêcimia 20, 32-620 Oœwiêcim, Poland
Tel: (033) 843 2022
Website: www.auschwitz.org.pl

Main Market Square, Krakow (Rynek Glowny, Krakow)

Krakow's magnificent *Rynek Glowny* is one of the largest Medieval squares in Europe and dates from 1257. It is dominated by the *Sukiennice*, the arcaded Renaissance cloth hall that stands in the centre, crowned by an elaborate attic construction known as a Polish parapet, and decorated with carved masks. The lower part of the building still serves as a market, selling traditional Polish crafts and food, and the upper floor is devoted to an exhibition of 19th-century Polish painting. On the southern side is the copper-domed *Kosciol sw Wojchiecha* (St Adalbert's Church), Krakow's first church, which dates from the 10th century and is the oldest building in the square. The *Ratusz* tower, with its Baroque spire, is all that remains of the 14th-century town hall after it was demolished in 1820 as part of a city development project. There are fine views over Krakow from the top.

Transportation
Air: Krakow-Balice John Paul II International Airport. **Rail:** Train: Krakow Station. Road: Coach: Services from Lviv (Ukraine), Prague (Czech Republic) and Vienna (Austria) to Dworzec PKS (Central Bus Station).

Contact Addresses
Krakowskie Centrum Informacji Turystycznej i Zakwaterowania (Krakow Tourist Information and Accommodation Centre), ulica Pawia 8, Krakow, Poland
Tel: (012) 422 6091
Website: www.krakow.pl

Warsaw Royal Castle (Zamek Królewski w Warsawie)

Set on a plateau overlooking the River Vistula, Warsaw's *Royal Castle* was built in the 14th century as a wooden fortress for the Dukes of Mazovia. It became a royal residence when King Zygmunt III made plans to move the Polish capital to Warsaw from Krakow in 1569 (although the final move to Warsaw was not made until the early 17th century). The castle then remained the seat of the monarchy and the *Sejm* (Polish parliament) for almost 250 years. In 1918, the castle became the official residence of the Polish president but was completely destroyed by the Nazis during World War II. The building that visitors enter today is thus a remarkable reconstruction, carried out in the 1970s, with only a few parts of the interior salvaged from the ruins. Neo-Baroque rooms are filled with museum pieces, including period furniture, porcelain, tapestries, and Oriental rugs.

Transportation
Air: Warsaw-Okecie Airport. **Rail:** Train: Warszawa Centralna (Warsaw Central Station). Tram: Public services. **Road:** Bus: Public services. Car: E30 (from Berlin and Lodz); E67 (from Wroclaw); E77 (from Gdansk and Krakow).

Contact Addresses
Zamek Królewski, Plac Zamkowy 4, 00277 Warsaw, Poland
Tel: (022) 657 2170
Website: www.zamek-krolewski.art.pl

Wawel Royal Castle (Zamek Królewski na Wawelu)

Wawel Royal Castle was the seat of Polish royalty from the 11th century until the early 17th century when King Zygmunt III moved the Polish capital to Warsaw. Today, it functions as a museum, with some of the original Renaissance decoration, including Flemish tapestries, Italian furniture and various Italian and Dutch paintings, still existing. Among its many treasures are the *Crown Treasury and Armoury*, where visitors can see the *Szczerbiec*, a weapon once used to crown Polish monarchs. The *Lost Wawel* exhibition is centred around excavations of Wawel hill's oldest ruins, including the oldest church known to exist in Poland, the Rotunda of St Felix and St Adauctus, which dates from the 11th century. Visitors can also enter the *Dragon's Den*, a cave with karstic limestone features, where, according to Polish legend, a child-eating creature called the Wawel Dragon once lived.

Transportation
Air: Krakow-Balice John Paul II International Airport. **Rail:** Train: Krakow Glowny Station. **Road:** Bus: Public services. Car: A77 (from Warsaw), then signs to the city centre.

Contact Addresses
Zamek Krolewski, Wawel 5, 31-001 Krakow, Poland
Tel: (012) 422 5155
Website: www.cyf-kr.edu.pl/wawel

Portugal

Tourist Information

ITP Instituto do Turismo de Portugal (National Tourist Office)
Rua Ivone Silva, Lote 6 1050-124, Lisbon, Portugal
Tel: 217 810 000
Website: www.vsitportugal.com

ICEP/Portuguese Trade and Tourism Office
Portuguese Embassy, 11 Belgrave Square, London SW1X 8PP UK
Tel: (0845) 355 1212 (Brochure request line).
Website: www.visitportugal.com or www.icep.pt

Castle of St George (Castelo de São Jorge)

Perched on the highest of Lisbon's seven hills, above the old Moorish quarter, the *Castle of St George* was the royal residence until the late 15th century. Originally built by the Visigoths and later named after King Joao I, the castle, along with much of Lisbon, was severely damaged by a devastating earthquake in 1755. The castle was declared a National Monument in 1910, with rebuilding work starting in 1940 restoring the site to its former state of luxury. Today the castle offers spectacular views of Lisbon from the well-preserved ramparts, as well as beautiful gardens. There is also a giant periscope in the *Torre de Ulisses* (Tower of Ulysses-Camera Obscura), from where visitors can see spectacular, live images of Lisbon below, reflected onto a large screen.

Transportation
Air: Lisbon International Airport. **Rail:** Tram: Public services. **Road:** Bus: Public services. Car: A1 to Lisbon (from Porto); A2 (from the Algarve via Almada); A8 (from Caldas da Rainha in the north).

Contact Addresses
Castelo de São Jorge, Porta de São Jorge, Rua do Chão da Feira, Lisbon, Portugal
Tel: 218 877 244 *or* 218 882 831
Website: www.visitlisboa.com

Jeronimos Monastery (Mosteiro dos Jerónimos)

This 16th-century monastery is one of the few surviving examples of medieval, Manueline architecture. Commissioned by Manuel I (after whom the style of architecture is named), work

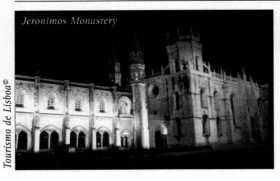

Jeronimos Monastery

Turismo de Lisboa©

Portuguese discovery and colonisation, and examines the impact this had on the formation of the modern world. Other interesting exhibits include the *Deep Sea Fishing Room* which details the history of 15th century Portuguese fleets that went on fishing expeditions in the Atlantic waters off the coast of Newfoundland in Canada.

Transportation
Air: Lisbon International Airport. **Rail:** Belem Station. Tram: Public services. **Road:** Bus: Public services.

Contact Addresses
Maritime Museum, Praça do Império, 1400-206 Lisbon, Portugal
Tel: 213 620 010
Website: www.museumarinha.pt/museu /ENG/Homepage/index.aspx

Tower of Belém (Torre de Belém)

Completed in 1515, the *Tower of Belém* is one of Lisbon's most famous sights. Built under the instruction of the architect Francisco de Arruda, who was greatly influenced by the style of fortifications in Morocco, the tower was intended to provide strategic defence to the River Tagus during Portugal's naval ascendancy in the 16th century. Symbolically, it was also the last sight seen by seafarers leaving the city. The tower has a famous 18th-century statue of Virgin and Child, Our Lady of Safe Homecoming, built into the terrace of the bastion, as well as sentry posts on each corner. Access to the the interesting museum is over a gangway; there is also a drawbridge and bulwark, as well as a terrace that offers superb views across the river and of the western part of Lisbon.

began on the monastery in 1502. It is listed (along with the *Torre de Belém*) as a UNESCO World Heritage Site and is a spectacular building with high arches, impressive columns and ornate spires. It is also the resting place of Vasco da Gama who set sail from Bélem in 1497 to discover India, and of Luís de Camões, Portugal's most famous poet who wrote *Os Lusiadas* (the Lusiads). Other places of interest are the chapels, which house the tombs of royal descendants of Manuel I, and the cloister, which has many impressive galleries.

Transportation
Air: Lisbon International Airport. **Water:** Boat: Bélem River Station (from Trafaria and Porto Brandão). **Rail:** Train: Bélem Station. Tram: Public services. **Road:** Bus: Public services.

Contact Addresses
Mosteiro dos Jerónimos, Praca do Império, 1400-206 Lisbon, Portugal
Tel: 213 620 034/8
Website: www.mosteirojeronimos.pt

Maritime Museum

Originally founded by King Luis in 1863 in the city's *Naval School*, Lisbon's *Maritime Museum* had to be moved in 1916 after the building was gutted by a fire that destroyed many of the exhibits. After resurrection at the *Palace of Count Farrobo*, in 1962, the museum was relocated once more to its present home in the *Jerónimos Monastery*. Today the museum's collection includes over 17,000 items, 30,000 photographs as well as original plans and archives of approximately 1,500 ships. The first of the museum's halls looks at the early days of

Transportation
Air: Lisbon International Airport. **Rail:** Train: Belém Station. Tram: Public services. **Road:** Bus: Public services.

Contact Addresses
Torre de Belém, Avenida Brasília, 1400 Lisbon, Portugal
Tel: 213 600 34
Website: www.mosteirojeronimos.pt

Romania

300km

150mls

✈ international airport

POLAND

SLOVAK
REPUBLIC

Carpathian Mountains

Tisza

HUNGARY · Baia Mare · Cluj-Napoca · Oradea

· Arad

Mureş

Timişoara · Moldoveanu 2544m△ · Sibiu

ROMANIA

Transylvanian Alps

WALACHIA

SERBIA · Craiova · Danube · Giurgiu

BULGARIA

UKRAINE

· Moldovita MOLDOVA

· Iaşi Prut

MOLDAVIA

· Bacău

① Braşov
· Galaţi
· Brăila
· Ploieşti · Tulcea Danube Delta

BUCHAREST

· Constanţa
· Mangalia

BLACK SEA

Dniester

1 Bran Castle (Castelul Bran)

Tourist Information

Ministry of Tourism (Ministerul Turismului)
Bd. Dinicu Golescu 38, Mezanin 38, 010867
Bucharest, Romania
Tel: (01) 410 0491
Website: www.mturism.ro *or*
www.MTRomania.ro

Romanian National Tourist Office
22 New Cavendish Street, London W1H 8TT,
UK
Tel: (021) 314 9957

Bran Castle (Castelul Bran)

Perched high on a rock in the midst of
Transylvanian forest, *Bran Castle*, named after the
Romanian word for gate or fortified place, is one
of Romania's most famous attractions, thanks to
its connections with Bram Stoker's novel,
'Dracula'. In fact, Stoker cites his further north

than Bran Castle, but its Gothic towers, winding
corridors and labyrinth of secret passages fit the
image of the vampire's home so perfectly that it
has been dubbed *Dracula's Castle*. Built between
1377 and 1382 as a palace and military fortress, it
was once the residence of Queen Maria of
Romania, the granddaughter of Queen Victoria,
whose heart is reputed to have been found hidden
in the castle in a silver box. Nowadays, visitors
who dare enter the eerie chambers can see
collections of furniture, weaponry and armour,
and admire the well-preserved Gothic architecture.

Transportation

Air: Bucharest Otopeni Airport. **Rail:** Brasov
Station. **Road: Coach:** Services to Bran (from
Brasov). **Car:** Drum National Road 1, then
National Road 73A and National Road 73 (from
Bucharest); National Road 71, then National Road
72A and National Road 73 (from Bucuresti).

Contact Addresses

Castelul Bran, 498 Traian Mosoiu Street, Bran,
Romania
Tel: (068) 238 332

P ✗ 🛒 £ 🏰

Bran Castle

Romanian National Tourist Office©

Russian Federation

3000km
1500mls

✈ international airport

1 Hermitage Museum

2 Kremlin (Moskovksy Kreml)

3 Lake Baikal

4 Red Square (Krasnaya Ploshchad)

5 St Basil's Cathedral (Pokrovsky Sobor)

Tourist Information

Ministry of Tourism (Ministerstvo Turisma)
18 ul. Kazakova, 103064 Moscow, Russian
Federation
Tel: (095) 202 7117 *or* 202 3891

Russian National Tourist Office
70 Piccadilly, London W1J 8HP, UK
Tel: (020) 7495 7555

Key to symbols: £ Entry charged & Disabled
access ◪ Man-made attraction ♥ Natural
attraction ₽ Parking ✖ Restaurant ☞ Shop
🏛 UNESCO site

Hermitage Museum

Situated in an impressive location on the
banks of the *River Neva* in *St Petersburg*, the
State Hermitage Museum consists of six
magnificent buildings housing one of the most
important art collections in the world. The
origins of the collection date back to 1764 and
Catherine the Great who began her own
personal collection. The centre point of the
Hermitage is the *Winter Palace* that began
construction in 1754 as a royal residence.
Built by the famous Italian architect Francesco
Bartolomeo Rastrelli, visitors will be amazed at
the grandeur and extravagance of the three-
storey Baroque palace. Other impressive
buildings include the *Small Hermitage*, the
Great Hermitage, the *New Hermitage*, the
Theatre and the *Menshikov Palace*. Aside from
the incredible architecture, the museum houses
one of the best displays of art and artefacts in
the world, some of which is thought to date
back over 500,000 years to Palaeolithic times.
Works of art in the collection include
masterpieces by such celebrated artists as
Michelangelo, Rembrandt, Monet, Renoir, Van
Gogh, Matisse and Picasso.

Transportation
Air: Pulvoko Airport, St Petersburg. **Rail:**
Metro: Kanal Griboyedova, Nevsky Prospekt
and Gostiny Dvor stations. Trolley: Public
services. **Road:** Bus: Public services.

Contact Addresses
Hermitage Museum, 2 Dvortsovaya Square,
190000, St Petersburg, Russia
Tel: (812) 710 9625
Website: www.hermitagemuseum.org

Kremlin (Moskovksy Kreml)

The *Kremlin* (literally 'fortified town') is a
walled fortress dating back to the founding of
Moscow in 1147, when it was erected above
the Neglina and Moskva rivers. From 1276 to
1712, it was the seat of government for the
grand princes and tsars of Russia, and from
1917 onwards it has been the seat of power for
the Communist government. The heart of the
Kremlin centres around *Cathedral Square*,
which is surrounded by several important
churches, including the *Cathedral of the
Assumption*, the *Cathedral of the Archangel* and
the *Cathedral of the Annunciation*. The redbrick
walls and towers house many other historic
sights, including the *Armoury Museum*, the
State Diamond Fund, the *Patriarch's Palace*, the
Tsar Cannon and the *Tsar Bell*.

Transportation
Air: Moscow Sheremetyevo International
Airport. **Rail:** Train: Kiev Station.
Underground: Biblioteka imeni Lenina or
Aleksandrovski Sad. **Road:** Trolleybus: Public
services. Car: M1 (from Minsk); M2 (from
Kiev); M7 (from Nizhny Novgorod); M9 (from
Riga); M10 (from St Petersburg). Then,
Moskovskaya Koltsevaya Avtomobilnaya
Doroga (Moscow ring road surrounding the
city).

Contact Addresses
The State Historical-cultural Museum-preserve,
Moscow Kremlin, Moscow 103073, Russian
Federation
Tel: (095) 202 6649 *or* 202 3832
Website: www.kremlin.museum.ru

Lake Baikal

Situated in south-east *Siberia* in southern *Russia*,
Lake Baikal is the oldest freshwater lake in the
world dating back an estimated 25 million years.
It's also the deepest freshwater lake in the world
with a recorded depth of 1,700m (5,577ft) that
contains approximately 20 per cent of the total
unfrozen freshwater in the world. Lake Baikal is
so big, it's estimated that if it was drained it
would take a year for all the world's rivers to
refill it. This incredible natural habitat supports an
array of flora and fauna including the Nerpa – the
only freshwater seal in the world that's unique to
Lake Baikal. During the winter the temperature
plummets and the lake completely freezes over for
approximately two months each year. During the
summer, many visitors choose to take boat tours
out on the lake. Lake Baikal is ringed by stunning
mountain scenery and forests that are home to
bears, elk, lynx, and sables. Lake Baikal has been
protected as a natural park since 1992 and is a
popular trekking destination famed for its natural
beauty.

Transportation
Air: Irkutzk International Airport. **Water:** Ferry
services and boat excursions on Lake Baikal. **Rail:**
Train: Irkutzk Station. **Road:** Bus: Public services.

Contact Addresses
For more information about Lake Baikal, contact
the Russian National Tourist Office (see **Tourist
Information** above).

Red Square (Krasnaya Ploshchad)

Moscow's *Red Square* has seen centuries of
Russian history played out across its vast 700-
metre (2,300-foot) expanse. Laid out during the
reign of Ivan III in the 15th century and
originally serving as a market place, it has borne
the name *Krasnaya*, from the old Russian for
'beautiful', since the late 17th century. Nowadays,
it is framed by three structures of world renown –
the *Kremlin, St Basil's Cathedral* and the *Lenin
Mausoleum*, which contains the embalmed body of
the founder of the Russian Communist Party and
leader of the 1917 Russian Revolution. It has been

Kremlin and St Basil's Cathedral at night

Corel©

the scene of numerous executions, riots, parades and demonstrations. The square also contains various monuments commemorating Bolsheviks who fell during the 1917 Revolution and past Soviet leaders such as Stalin and Brezhnev.

Tranportation

Air: Moscow Sheremetyevo International Airport. **Rail:** Train: Kiev Station. Underground: Kitay-Gorod. **Road:** Bus: Public services. Car: M1 (from Minsk); M2 (from Kiev); M7 (from Nizhny Novgorod); M9 (from Riga); M10 (from St Petersburg). Then, Moskovskaya Koltsevaya Avtomobilnaya Doroga (Moscow ring road) to the city centre.

Contact Addresses

For more information on Red Square, contact the Ministry of Tourism (see **Tourist Information** above).

St Basil's Cathedral (Pokrovsky Sobor)

The wildly coloured, onion-shaped domes of *St Basil's Cathedral* are one of Russia's most famous images. Situated in Moscow's Red Square, each dome has a distinctive patterning and colour

scheme, creating a stunning effect. The cathedral was commissioned by Ivan the Terrible and built during the 1550s to commemorate Russia's military victory over the Khanates of Kazan in 1552. Designed by the architects Postnik and Barma, it has been a branch of the State Historical Museum since 1929. A chapel was added in 1588 to house the tomb of the holy fool Basil (Vasily) the Blessed, after whom the cathedral is now known. Basil, who died in 1552, was a well-known prophet who wandered the streets of Moscow and predicted, correctly, that there would be a fire in the city in 1547.

Transportation

Air: Moscow Sheremetyevo International Airport. **Rail:** Train: Kiev Station. Underground: Kitay-Gorod. **Road:** Trolleybus: Public services to Okhotny ryad. Car: M1 (from Minsk); M2 (from Kiev); M7 (from Nizhny Novgorod); M9 (from Riga, Latvia); M10 (from St Petersburg). Then, Moskovskaya Koltsevaya Avtomobilnaya Doroga (Moscow ring road surrounding the city).

Contact Addresses

Pokrovsky Sobor, Krasnaya ploshchad 4, Moscow, Russian Federation
Tel: (095) 298 3304

Serbia and Montenegro

160km
80mls

✈ international airport

1 Visoki Decani Monastery

Visoki Decani Monastery

Located at the foot of the *Prokletje Mountains* in the western province of *Kosovo*, the *Visoki Decani Monastery* was built in the 14th century for the Serbian King Stefan Decanski. In a picturesque location in a valley surrounded by mountains and the *Bistrica River*, the Decani Monastery is the biggest and best preserved medieval monastery in Serbia. The monastery contains exceptional Byzantine frescoes, Gothic sculptures and the original marble floor is still intact. The monastery is particularly well-known for its *Narthex Room* with its incredible ceiling paintings. Today, the monastery is home to a brotherhood of 30 monks who continue to live according to ancient traditions. The monastery was declared a UNESCO World Heritage site in 2004.

Visoki Decani Monastery

NTOS©

Tourist Information

National Tourist Office of Serbia (NTOS)
Tourist Organization of Belgrade Information Centre, Knez Mihajlova Street 18, 11000 Belgrade, Serbia
Tel: (+381) 11 629 992
Website: www.serbia-tourism.org

National Tourist Office of Serbia (NTOS)
7 Dering Street, London W1R 9AB, UK
Tel: 0207 629 2007
Website: www.serbia-tourism.org

Transportation
Air: Belgrade International Airport or Pristina Airport in Kosovo. **Road:** Bus: Public services to Decani District.

Contact Addresses
For more information about the Visoki Decani Monastery, contact the National Tourist Office of Serbia (see **Tourist Information** above).

Key to symbols:
£ Entry charged & Disabled access ⛫ Man-made attraction
♥ Natural attraction 🅿 Parking ✖ Restaurant 🛒 Shop 🏛 UNESCO site

Singapore

Johor
Bahru
Woodlands
Johor Strait
MALAYSIA
Mandai
Seletar
Reservoir
Pulau
Ubin
Pulau
Tekong
SINGAPORE
Bukit Timah△
163m
Paya Lebar
Tampines
Changi
Tuas
Jurong
Tanglin
Queenstown
Katong
Jurong
Island
SINGAPORE
Brani
Bukum
Sentosa
Kusu
Sudong
Semakau
St John's
Pawai
Senang
Strait of
Singapore
20km
10mls
✈ international airport

1 Raffles Hotel
2 Sentosa

Tourist Information

Singapore Tourism Board
Tourism Court, 1 Orchard Spring Lane,
Singapore 247729
Tel: 736 6622
Website: www.stb.com.sg *or* www.newasia-singapore.com

Singapore Tourism Board
First Floor, Carrington House, 126-130 Regent
Street, London W1B 5JX, UK
Tel: (020) 7437 0033 or (08080) 656 565 (toll
free UK only)

Raffles Hotel

Opened in 1887 by four Armenian brothers, the
Raffles Hotel is one of the few remaining original
grand hotels of the East. This world-famous hotel,
which was named after Sir Stamford Raffles, the
founder of modern Singapore, began life as a
modest bungalow. Over the years, it has welcomed
many famous guests, including Rudyard Kipling,
Joseph Conrad and Charlie Chaplin, attracted by

the hotel's luxury and elegance. Today, the hotel
continues to attract the rich and famous, and a
recent S$160-million facelift has ensured that it
has the trappings of modern luxury yet retains the
unique charm of the colonial era. Tourists regularly
flock to drink afternoon tea in the *Tiffin Room* and
enjoy a Singapore Sling in the *Long Bar*. The hotel
was declared a National Monument in 1987.

Transportation
Air: Singapore Changi Airport. **Rail:** Train: City Hall
MRT Station. **Road:** Bus: Public services.

Contact Addresses
Raffles Hotel, 1 Beach Road, Singapore 189673
Tel: 6337 1886
Website: www.raffleshotel.com

Sentosa

A purpose-built island theme park, *Sentosa* (which
means 'peace and tranquility' in Malay) offers history,
golf and gastronomy, as well as a host of themed
attractions, including *VolcanoLand* and *Underwater
World*, one of Asia's largest tropical fish aquariums.
Owned and managed by Sentosa Development
Corporation, Sentosa is Singapore's largest offshore
island and home to beautiful beaches and gardens.
The island's highlights include the *Butterfly Park*,
which houses more than 2500 butterflies, *Fort Siloso*
preserved fortification, which was built in the 1880s,
and the *Images of Singapore Museum*, which exhibits
artefacts from the history of Singapore.

Transportation
Air: Singapore Changi Airport. **Sea:** Ferry: Services
depart from the World Trade Centre in Singapore
City. **Rail:** Cable Car: Services to Sentosa (from
Mount Faber). **Road:** Bus: Public services.

Contact Addresses
Sentosa Development Corporation, 33 Allanbrooke
Road, Sentosa, Singapore 099981
Tel: 275 0388
Website: www.sentosa.com.sg

Slovak Republic

international airport

1 Caves of Aggtelek
2 Spiš Castle (Spissky Hrad)
3 Tatrus National Park
(Tatransky Národny Park)

Tourist Information

Slovak Tourist Board (Slovenskej agentúry pre cestovný ruch)
Nám. L Stura 1, PO Box 35, 974 05 Banská Bystrica, Slovak Republic
Tel: (048) 413 6146-8
Website: www.slovakiatourism.sk

Embassy of the Slovak Republic
25 Kensington Palace Gardens, London W8 4QY, UK
Tel: (020) 7313 6470 *or* (09065) 508 956 (recorded visa information; calls cost £1 per minute).
Website: www.slovakembassy.co.uk

Caves of Aggtelek

The *Caves of Aggtelek* are located in the *Aggtelek National Park* in southeastern Slovak Republic bordering Hungary. Aggtelek was the country's first national park that was set up to protect its geological formations. Formed in shallow seas during the Triassic Period over 200 million years ago, the park lies on limestone bedrock that is prone to karstification – the natural creation of caverns and sinkholes. There are over 260 caves that have been formed in this way in the park. The Aggtelek National Park, which crosses the border into Hungary, also contains the ruins of the *Háromhegyi Pálos* church and monastery near *Martonyi* village. The Pálos were the only religious order to be founded in Hungary whose origins date back to 1308. The Caves were declared a UNESCO World Heritage site in 1995.

Transportation
Air: Kosice International Airport. **Rail:** Train: Kosice Railway Station. **Road:** Coach: Public services to Aggtelek.

Contact Addresses:
For more information about the Caves of Aggtelek, contact the Slovak Tourist Board (see **Tourist Information** above).

Spiš Castle (Spissky Hrad)

Spiš Castle is one of the largest Medieval castles in central Europe. Dating back to the early 13th century, this imposing fortification stands 634 metres (2080ft) above sea level on cliffs dominating the Spišské region in eastern Slovak Republic. It was once one of the most important Gothic castles in Europe and was owned by the Royal Family. It was declared a national monument in 1961 and attempts were made to restore it in order to make it accessible to the public. The castle has a small museum which is open to the public and documents the history of the castle during its prime in the late Middle Ages. Although many parts of the castle's Gothic tower, chapel ramparts and dungeons still stand in ruins, there are fine views of the surrounding countryside from the summit of the hill.

Transportation
Air: Bratislava Airport. **Road:** Car: The castle can be reached from the Šibenik Pass (from the east and from Levoča). Foot: Visitors should approach the castle from the town of Spišské Podhradie.

Tatrus National Park

Slovak Tourist Board©

Contact Addresses

Spissky Hrad, 05304 Spišské Podhradie, Slovak
Republic
Tel: (053) 454 1336
Website: www.spisskyhrad.sk

Tatrus National Park (Tatranský Národný Park)

Tatras National Park is the oldest national park in the
Slovak Republic and home to the famous *High Tatras
Mountains*. Founded in 1949 and covering an area of
741 sq km (286 sq miles), Tatras National Park is a
hiker's paradise. The landscape incorporates dense
forest on the mountains' lower slopes, as well as
glacial lakes and mountain streams. The High Tatras
is the only alpine mountain range in Eastern Europe
and one of the smallest in the world. The mountains
are also famous for their plant and wildlife, with
chamois (mountain goat), bear and marmot roaming
free on the slopes. Also of interest are the *TANAP
Museum*, which describes the natural history and
ethnography of the region through geology, flora
and fauna displays and exhibits.

Transportation

Air: Bratislava Airport. Special charter flights and
private airplanes land at Poprad-Tary Airport.
Rail: Cable car: Peaks reached by aerial tram
include Skalnate Pleso, Lomnicky Stit, Solisko and
col Lomnicke sedlo. **Road:** Bus: Buses Public
services.

Contact Addresses

Tatranský národný park, Tatranska Lomnica,
Slovak Republic
Tel: (052) 446 7195
Website: www.tanap.sk

Slovenia

1 Lipica Stud Farm (Kobilarna Lipica)
2 Postojana Cave (Postojnska Jama)

Tourist Information

**Slovenian Tourist Organisation
(Slovenska Turisticna Organizacija)**
WTC, Dunajska 156, 1000 Ljubljana, Slovenia
Tel: (01) 589 1840
Website: www.slovenia-tourism.si

Slovenian Tourist Office
49 Conduit Street, London W1R 9FB, UK
Tel: (020) 7287 713
Website: www.slovenia-tourism.si

Lipica Stud Farm (Kobilarna Lipica)

Lipica Stud Farm is the home of one of the world's
most famous breed of horses, the Lippizaner.
Founded by Archduke Charles of Austria in 1580,
the farm has continuously bred the sturdy white
horses for over four centuries and some of the best
perform at the *Spanish Riding School* in Vienna. As
well as watching the horses perform at the
Classical Riding School at Lipica, visitors can take
the reins of a thoroughbred Lippizaner themselves
and there are pony rides for children. With its own
hotels, swimming pools, fitness centre as well as a
wide range of other activities on offer, it is
possible to spend an entire holiday on and around
the stud farm.

Transportation
Air: Ljubljana Brnik Airport. **Rail:** Train: Divaca
Station or Sezana Station. **Road:** Car: A10 (from
Ljubljana); A1 (from Klagenfurt, Austria); S14
(from Trieste, Italy).

Contact Addresses
Kobilarna Lipica, Lipica 5, 6210 Sezana, Slovenia
Tel: (05) 739 1580
Website: www.lipica.org

Postojana Cave (Postojnska Jama)

Postojna Cave in western Slovenia is a 20-km (12-
mile) labyrinth of subterranean passages, filled with
fantastical stalagmites, stalactites and other rock
formations. It is considered by experts to be one of
the finest examples of karst landscape, where
limestone rock has been heavily eroded to form
underground streams, a phenomenon that has
created several other caves in the area. Postojna
Cave is also home to the Proteus Anguinus, a
unique creature with no eyes, which can grow up
to 30cm (1ft) in length and feeds on snails and
worms. Speleological equipment can be provided at
the cave for caving enthusiasts.

Transportation
Air: Ljubljana Brnik Airport. **Rail:** Train: Postojna
Station. **Road:** Car: E61 or E70 (from Ljubljana);
E751 (from Trieste, Italy).

Contact Addresses
Postojna jama – turizem, Jamska c. 30, 6230
Postojna, Slovenia
Tel: (05) 700 0100
Website: www.postojnska-jama.si

South Africa

1 Anglo-Boer War Battlefields

2 Blyde River Canyon Nature Reserve

3 Cape Point

4 Kruger National Park

5 Robben Island

6 Table Mountain

Tourist Information

South African Tourism Board (SATOUR)
Private Bag X10012, Sandton 2146,
South Africa
Tel: (011) 778 8000.
Website: www.southafrica.net

South African Tourism Board (SATOUR)
5-6 Alt Grove, London SW19 4DZ, UK
Tel: (0870) 155 0044 (tourism enquiry
and brochure request line)
Website: www.south-african-tourism.org

Key to symbols: £ Entry charged ⅙ Disabled access ⚒ Man-made attraction
⚓ Natural attraction ⓟ Parking ✕ Restaurant ⊜ Shop ⛪ UNESCO site

Anglo-Boer War Battlefields

The Anglo-Boer War began in 1899 with the British retaliation against President Paul Kruger's refusal to grant political rights to the mainly English outsiders in the gold- and diamond-rich Transvaal. In 1902, after three years of bitter fighting, the British claimed victory, having destroyed Boer farms and sent their occupants to concentration camps where 20,000 people perished. Today, various museums and memorial sites remember those bloody events. The main museum is the *Anglo-Boer War Museum* in Bloemfontein (website: www.anglo-boer.co.za), which displays artwork and artefacts and provides an insight into the horrors of the concentration camps. *Talana Museum* (website: www.talana.ca.za), is located at Talana Hill, near Dundee, the site of the first battle of the Anglo-Boer War on October 20 1899; it is now an eight-hectare (20-acre) heritage park with a cemetery dedicated to those who fought and lost their lives there, and also features displays on local bush traditions.

Transportation
Air: Johannesburg International Airport, Durban International Airport, Cape Town International Airport, Pretoria Airport. **Rail:** Train: Johannesburg Park Station, Durban Station, Cape Town Station, Dundee Station or Pretoria Station.

Contact Addresses
KwaZulu Natal Tourism Authority, PO Box 2516, Durban 400, South Africa
Tel: (031) 304 7144
Website: www.zulu.org.za/kzn

Blyde River Canyon Nature Reserve

Blyde River Canyon provides some of South Africa's most breathtaking scenery and is the third largest gorge in the world, after the Grand Canyon (USA) and Fish River Canyon (Namibia). The 29,000-hectare (71,662-acre) reserve is

Cape Town

South African Tourist Board©

home to a rich variety of wildlife including rare birds and lichens. At the heart of the nature reserve is the *Blyde Dam*, which provides a natural habitat for hippo and crocodile, whilst further afield, in the Lowveld plain at the entrance to the canyon, blue wildebeest, waterbuck and zebra can be seen. Popular activities in the reserve include fishing and hiking to beauty spots such as *God's Window*, which offers unparalleled views across the canyon and the Lowveld. The town of *Pilgrim's Rest* is of particular interest as a former gold-mining town between 1873 and 1972.

Transportation
Air: Johannesburg International Airport. **Rail:** Train: Johannesburg Park Station or Pretoria Station. **Road:** Car: N4 (from Pretoria); N12, then R36, then R532 (from Johannesburg).

Contact Addresses
For more information on Blyde River Canyon, contact the South African Tourism Board (see **Tourist Information** above).

Cape Point

Part of the *Cape Peninsula National Park*, *Cape Point* is an 8000-hectare (19,770-acre) narrow promontory of land jutting into a stretch of open sea popularly believed to be the meeting point of the Atlantic and Indian oceans. The peninsula, situated 60km (37 miles) southwest of Cape Town, is characterised by towering sea cliffs, the highest in South Africa, which reach a height of 249m (817ft). Criss-crossed by spectacular walks and trails, the area also features whale and penguin watching, tidal pools, over a thousand species of indigenous plants and a variety of mammals, such as baboon and buck. Popular activities around Cape Point also include abseiling, parasailing, horseriding and surfing.

Transportation
Air: Cape Town International Airport. **Rail:** Train: Simon's Town Station. **Road:** Bus: Public services. Car: M3 towards Muizenberg (from Cape Town); M4 towards Cape Point (via Simon's Town).

Contact Addresses
Cape Peninsula National Park, PO Box 37,

Constantia, 7848 Western Cape, South Africa
Tel: (021) 701 8692
Website: www.cpnp.co.za

Kruger National Park

At 20,000 sq km (7722 sq miles), *Kruger National Park* is the largest game reserve in South Africa and boasts the world's highest concentration of species. Created in 1898 to protect the flora and fauna of the *South African Lowveld*, the park is named after its original proponent, President Paul Kruger. Today, it is home to a wealth of wildlife, including cheetahs, leopards, lions, rhinos, wildebeest, buffalo, elephants, giraffes, antelope and impala. The park is also renowned for its cultural heritage sites, including many native rock art sites. At *Thulamela Hill*, visitors can see the excavated remains of a late Iron Age settlement, whilst the village of *Masorini* provides an excellent example of the way of life of the Stone Age hunter-gatherers who inhabited South Africa long before the first white settlers arrived.

Transportation
Air: Johannesburg International Airport, Skukuza Airport (domestic flights). **Road:** Coach: Services from Mpumalanga. Car: Mpumalanga Highway.

Contact Addresses
South African National Parks, PO Box 787, Pretoria 0001, South Africa
Tel: (012) 248 9111
Website: www.sanparks.org

Robben Island

Situated 11km (7 miles) north of Cape Town harbour, *Robben Island* is the notorious island prison where thousands of political prisoners were incarcerated between 1961 and 1991 for campaigning against apartheid. Its most famous resident was Nelson Mandela, who referred to it as a 'harsh, iron-fisted outpost'. Used as a prison as far back as 1525, it has also housed the mentally ill and lepers; its long history as a place of cruelty and isolation has turned it into a worldwide symbol of the triumph of the human spirit over oppression. Since 1996, there has been a *National Museum* and cultural centre on Robben Island, where visitors can see, among other things, the cell where Nelson Mandela was imprisoned. Some of the tour guides are former political prisoners, able to provide a personal testimony of the terrible conditions suffered by the inmates.

Transportation
Air: Cape Town International Airport. **Water:** Ferry: From Jetty 1 at the V&A Waterfront (Cape Town) to Autfhumato, Makana.

Contact Addresses
Robben Island Museum, Robben Island 7400, South Africa
Tel: (021) 411 1006
Website: www.robben-island.org.za

Table Mountain

Like Cape Point, *Table Mountain* is part of the strip of land forming *Cape Peninsula National Park*. Table Mountain, however, stands in the middle of Cape Town and defines the downtown area, with the forested ravines of its eastern buttresses flanking the southern suburbs. So named for its flat top, the mountain rises to a height of 1086m (3562ft). Since 1929, a cable car has carried visitors up to the summit, which offers spectacular views of the city and its beaches. The mountain is also home to an indigenous rodent-like creature called the Rock Hyrax or 'dassie', the closest living relative to modern elephants.

Transportation
Air: Cape Town International Airport. **Rail:** Train: Cape Town Station. **Road:** Bus: Public services. Car: N1 (from Johannesburg); N2 (from Overberg and Garden Route); N7 (from West Coast or Namibia).

Contact Addresses
Table Mountain Cableway, PO Box 730, Cape Town 8001, South Africa
Tel: (021) 424 8181 (24-hour information line) *or* 424 0015 (administration)
Website: www.tablemountain.net

Spain

400km
200mls
✈ international airport

1 Alhambra

2 Cathedral of Santiago de Compostela
(Santiago de Compostela Cathedral)

3 Caves of Drach (Cuevas del Drach)

4 Expiatory Temple of the Sagrada Familia
(Temple Expiatori de la Sagrada Familia)

5 Güell Park (Park Güell)

6 Guggenheim Museum Bilbao (Museo
Guggenheim Bilbao)

7 Monastery of San Lorenzo de El Escorial
(Monasterio de San Lorenzo de El Escorial)

8 Nou Camp

9 Pilgrim's Way

10 Prado Museum (Museo del Prado)

11 Roman Aqueduct at Segovia (Acueducto
de Segovia)

12 Seville Cathedral (Cathedral de Sevilla)

13 Terra Mítica

14 Universal Mediterranea

Key to symbols: £ Entry charged & Disabled access
⚒ Man-made attraction ♥ Natural attraction
🅿 Parking ✖ Restaurant 🛍 Shop 🏛 UNESCO site

Tourist Information

Spanish National Tourist Office (Dirección General de Turespaña)
Jose Lázaro Galdiano 6, 28036 Madrid, Spain
Tel: (091) 343 3500 or 343 3689
Website: www.tourspain.es

Spanish National Tourist Office
22-23 Manchester Square, London W1U 3PX, UK
Tel: (020) 7486 8077 or (0906) 364 0630
(brochure request line; calls cost 60p per minute)
Website: www.tourspain.es

Alhambra

Overlooking the city of Granada, the *Alhambra* is the most important and most spectacular piece of Moorish architecture in Spain. The name means 'the red' in Arabic, and the building is so called because of the colour of the bricks forming the outer walls. It was begun in 1238 as both a palace and a fortress by Ibn Ahmar, founder of the Nasrid dynasty (who made Granada the capital of his Moorish kingdom), and it was subsequently elaborated upon by his successors until its completion in 1358. Visitors can explore the *Alcazaba*, or citadel, which is the oldest remaining part of the complex, as well as the *Alhambra Palace*, containing the fabled *Patio de los Leones* (Court of the Lions), an alabaster basin supported by 12 white marble lions. The *Generalife* gardens, dotted with pools and fountains, are located on the neighbouring hill and were laid out in the 14th century.

Transportation
Air: Malaga Airport. **Rail:** Train: Granada Station.
Road: **Bus:** Public services. Car: N-IV, then E5, then N323 (from Madrid); N334, then N342 (from Seville).

Contact Addresses
Patronato de la Alhambra y Generalife, Real de la Alhambra s/n, 18009 Granada, Spain
Tel (0958) 220 912 *or* (091) 346 5936 (ticket sales)
Website: www.alhambra-patronato.es

Cathedral of Santiago de Compostela (Santiago de Compostela Cathedral)

According to legend, the *Catedral de Santiago de Compostela* holds the remains of one of Christ's apostles, St James (Santiago in Spanish), who was martyred in Jerusalem around AD 44. King Alfonso II of Asturias built a church over the tomb in the ninth century and this was expanded in later years, making the town the most important place of Christian pilgrimage after Jerusalem and Rome. One of the best, but also most crowded, times to visit the cathedral is during one of the special masses, where priests swing a huge incense-burner on a rope-and-pulley system from one end of the transept ceiling to the other.

Transportation
Air: Madrid Barajas Airport, Santiago de Compostela Lavacolla International Airport. **Rail:** Train: Hórreo Station, Santiago de Compostela. **Road:** Coach: Public services. Car: A52 (from Madrid); A9 (from La Coruña or Ferrol); N-VI, then A9 (from Madrid).

Contact Addresses
Comisión de Cultura, Praza das Praterías s/n, 15704 Santiago de Compostela, Spain
Tel: (0981) 583 548
Website: www.archicompostela.org

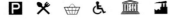

Caves of Drach (Cuevas del Drach)

The *Caves of Drach* are the most famous tourist attraction on the island of Mallorca. There are three chambers inside the caves, *Cueva Negra* (Black Cave), *Cueva Blanca* (White Cave) and *Cueva Luis Salvator* (Luis Salvator Cave). The latter is named after the Archduke Ludwig Salvator of Austria who invited Édouard-Alfred Martel to explore the caves in 1896; the caves are also home to *Lago Martel* (Lake Martel), one of the largest subterranean lakes in the world. Visitors can take a boat ride on the lake and see the beautiful limestone formations, including stalagmites protuding from the rockface and stalactites hanging

down from the roof of the cave. As part of their journey underground, they are accompanied by the sound of musicians performing classical music, including compositions by Chopin on a boat.

Transportation
Air: Palma de Mallorca Airport. **Water:** Boat: Services from Cala Ratjada, Canyamel, Cala Millor, Sa Coma and Sillot. **Road:** Car: The caves are located 1.5km (0.9 miles) south of Porto Cristo. Bus: Many hotels and resorts on the island offer a bus service to the caves.

Contact Addresses
Cuevas del Drach, Ctra Cuevas s/n 07680, Porto Cristo, Baleares, Spain
Tel: (0971) 820 753 or 821 617
Website: www.cuevasdeldrach.com

Expiatory Temple of the Sagrada Familia (Temple Expiatiori de la Sagrada Familia)

The *Expiatory Temple of the Sagrada Familia* is the unfinished masterpiece of Barcelona's most celebrated architect, Antonio Gaudí, who began work on it in 1882. Known around the world simply as *La Sagrada Familia*, Gaudí worked on this towering example of Barcelona's modernist architecture for more than 40 years, right up until his death in 1926. Its eerie, snaking lines and omnipresent detail make it unique among Europe's many cathedrals, and its eight spires, which stand 100m (328ft) high, were intended, with the addition of another four, to represent Christ's Twelve Apostles. Despite the fact that work still continues on the cathedral to this day, it lies in a perpetual state of incompleteness, with only one of its three façades actually finished. There is a small Gaudí museum inside the temple, which details Gaudí's life and provides information on the history of the building.

Transportation
Air: Barcelona International Airport. **Rail:** Train: Passeig de Gràcia Station. Underground: Sagrada Familia. **Road:** Bus: Public services. Car: A7 (from France in the north); A2 from (Zaragoza in the south).

Expiatory Temple of the Sagrada Familia

Corel©

has fantastic pavilions, stairways and columned halls. Highlights include the giant lizard that divides the grand stairway, reputedly the most photographed symbol of the park. Gaudi's former residence in the park, *Casa-Museu Gaudí* houses a collection of Gaudi's furnishings and other memorabilia.

Transportation
Air: Barcelona International Airport. **Rail:** Underground: Vallcarca or Lesseps. **Road:** Bus: Public services.

Contact Addresses
Casa-Museu Gaudí, Park Güell, Carrer del Carmel, s/n 08024, Barcelona, Spain
Tel: (093) 219 3811
Website: www.bcn.es/parcsijardins

Guggenheim Museum Bilbao (Museo Guggenheim Bilbao)

The *Guggenheim Museum Bilbao*, which opened in 1997, has quickly become one of the most famous museums in the world. The museum's collection focuses primarily on American and European art from the 20th century, featuring styles such as Pop Art, Minimalism, Arte Povera, Conceptual Art and Abstract Expressionism, as well as artwork that contemporary European and American artists created specifically for the museum. The building itself was designed by renowned American architect Frank O Gehry and is as well known for its striking architecture as for its collection. Other Guggenheim museums around the world include the *Solomon R Guggenheim* in New York, the *Guggenheim Las Vegas* and the *Guggenheim Hermitage Museum* in Las Vegas, the *Peggy Guggenheim Collection* in Venice and the *Deutsche Guggenheim Berlin* in Germany.

Transportation
Air: Bilbao Airport. **Rail:** Train: Bilbao-Abando Station, Atxuri Station or Santander Station. Underground: Moyua Station. **Road:** Bus: Public services. Car: A8 (from San Sebastian or Santander).

Contact Addresses
Museo Guggenheim Bilbao, Avenida Abandoibarra 2, 48001 Bilbao, Spain

Contact Addresses
Temple Expiatiori de la Sagrada Familia, Calle Mallorca 401, 08013 Barcelona, Spain
Tel: (093) 207 3031
Website: www.sagradafamilia.org

Güell Park (Park Güell)

Created by the renowned Spanish architect, Antonio Gaudí between 1900 and 1914, *Parc Güell* is a fantasy land that combines the natural and the man-made. The park was originally conceived as a residential garden city and built for Gaudí's patron, Eusebi Güell Bacigalupi, a textile manufacturer who had a keen interest in the arts and helped develop the architect's career. The project was not a great commercial success, however, and the park became municipal property in 1923. Covering a hill to the north of Barcelona and offering excellent views of the city, the park

Tel: (094) 435 9080 (information) *or* 435 9023 (group admission)
Website: www.guggenheim-bilbao.es

Monastery of San Lorenzo de El Escorial (Monasterio de San Lorenzo de El Escorial)

The *Monastery of San Lorenzo de El Escorial* was built in the latter half of the 16th century by King Philip II of Spain, to commemorate his victory over the French at the battle of San Quentin. Housing a monastery, two palaces and a library, the complex was intended to serve all the functions of church and state. The magnificent interior houses numerous works of art as well as 40,000 volumes in the library that was founded by Philip II himself. The monastery is famous for its symmetrical design, with four towers marking each of the monastery's four corners, and for being the resting place of the remains of many Spanish kings and queens in the *Baroque Royal Pantheon*.

Transportation
Air: Madrid Barajas Airport. **Rail:** Train: El Escorial Station. **Road:** Bus: Public services. Car: M505 (from Las Rozas); N-VI Highway (from Madrid).

Contact Addresses
Monasterio de San Lorenzo de El Escorial, c/Juan de Borbón y Battemberg s/n, 28200 San Lorenzo de El Escorial (Madrid), Spain
Tel: (091) 890 5902 or 890 5903

Nou Camp

Opened for the start of the new season in 1957, the *Nou Camp* (*Camp Nou* in Spanish) is home to *Barcelona Football Club* and is renowned as one of the greatest football stadiums in Europe. Barcelona is one of the most popular teams in Spain's La Liga and the atmosphere at home matches is usually electric. In 1984 the *Nou Camp Museum* was added to the complex which has been extended several times since that date

to accommodate new exhibits and now attracts over a million visitors each year. Guided tours of the ground are available from the museum. The stadium is also used to host other events such as music concerts.

Transportation
Air: Barcelona International Airport. **Rail:** Underground: Public services. **Road:** Bus: Public services.

Contact Addresses
Nou Camp Museum Avenida Arístides Maillol, Barcelona 08028, Spain
Tel. (093) 496 3608
Website: www.fcbarcelona.com

Pilgrim's Way

The *Pilgrim's Way* (also known as *St James' Way*) is in fact a number of different walking trails that all lead to the cathedral of St James in *Santiago de Compostela* in *Galicia* in northwest Spain. It's here where the body of the fisherman and apostle Saint James the Great is said to have been laid to rest in the eighth century. The origins of the trail date back to this time when Christian pilgrims would set off on the annual journey to the saint's final resting place. It is one of the most important Christian pilgrimages alongside those to *Rome* and *Jerusalem*. The Pilgrim's Way still attracts thousands of pilgrims each year in addition to recreational walkers who come to enjoy this popular walking trail. The route is marked with a scallop shell, the symbol of St James. The trail was declared a European Cultural Route in 1987 and a UNESCO World Heritage site in 1993.

Transportation
Air: Vigo Airport or Santiago Airport, Galicia. **Rail:** Train: Vigo Station. **Road:** Bus: Public services.

Contact Addresses
For more information about the Pilgrim's Way, contact the Spanish National Tourist Office (see **Tourist Information** above).

Prado Museum
(Museo del Prado)

The *Prado Museum,* which opened to the public in 1819 to house the Royal art collection, is one of Europe's great museums. It houses a collection of over 4000 paintings, emphasising Spanish, Flemish and Italian art from the 15th to 19th century including masterpieces by Titian, Bosch, Botticelli, Rembrandt and Fra Angelico. The museum also possesses a renowned collection of paintings by Francisco de Goya. The museum was originally designed by the architect Juan de Villanueva, with work starting on it in 1785. Today, there are two buildings at the museum, the *Villanueva* and the *Casón del Buen Retiro*, which also house many coins, drawings, etchings and medals.

Transportation
Air: Madrid Barajas Airport. **Rail:** Train: Atocha Station. Underground: Atocha or Banco de España. **Road:** Bus: Public services. Car: N-1 (from Santander); N-2 (from Zaragoza); N-3 (from Valencia); N-4 (from Seville); N-5 (from Badajoz); A6 (from Tordesilos).

Contact Addresses
Museo del Prado, Villanueva Building, Paseo del Prado s/n, 28014 Madrid, Spain
Tel: (091) 330 2800 *or* 330 2900 (information)
Website: http://museoprado.mcu.es

Roman Aqueduct at Segovia
(Acueducto de Segovia)

One of the best preserved Roman constructions, the *Roman Aqueduct at Segovia* was still in use as recently as 50 years ago. Constructed around AD 50 during the reign of the Roman Emperor Trajan out of some 200,400 granite blocks, the aqueduct was made without concrete and stands due to the equal balance of forces. When in use, it carried water from the River Frio to the city of Segovia over a distance of 16km (10 miles). The portion of the aqueduct that is above ground is 728m (2388ft) in length and consists of 165 arches, each over 9m (30ft) high, which are spectacularly illuminated at night. It is possible to climb a staircase next to the aqueduct to get views over the structure itself as well as the city.

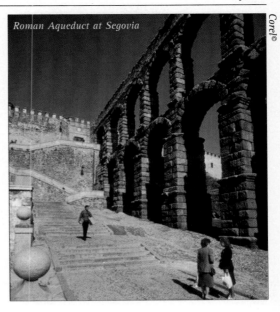

Roman Aqueduct at Segovia

Corel©

Transportation
Air: Madrid Barajas Airport. **Rail:** Train: Segovia Station. **Road:** Bus: Public services. Car: A6, then N603 (from Madrid).

Contact Addresses
Spanish National Tourist Office, Plaza Mayor 10, 40001 Segovia, Spain
Tel: (0921) 460 334
Website: www.turismocastillayleon.com

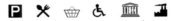

Seville Cathedral
(Cathedral de Sevilla)

Seville Cathedral, which dates from the 15th century, is located in the city's *Plaza Virgen de los Reyes*, on the site of the *Gran Mezquita* (Great Mosque) originally used by the retreating Moors, who had invaded Spain from North Africa in the eighth century AD. Originally, the mosque was simply converted into a cathedral, but in 1402 the chapter, or ruling body of the cathedral, began plans to construct 'a church so large that everyone who sees it will think we are mad'. Builders retained the minaret and patio from the former mosque, and the cathedral they constructed remains the largest Gothic structure in the world. The main altarpiece, *Retablo Mayor*, is the largest altar in the world and features 45

Seville Cathedral

Corel©

scenes from the life of Christ, carved from wood by Pierre Dancart. The cathedral also houses the remains of the world-famous explorer, Christopher Columbus.

Transportation
Air: Seville Airport. **Rail:** Train: Santa Justa Station. **Road:** Bus: 32 to Plaza de la Incarnación, then on foot. Car: N-IV (from Madrid).

Contact Addresses
Cabildo Catedral de Sevilla, Avenida de la Consitución s/n, 41001 Seville, Spain
Tel: (0954) 563 150 *or* 563 321

Terra Mítica

Opened in 2000, Terra Mítica is a giant amusement park located just outside the popular Spanish resort of Benidorm. As well as regular live shows, there are five different areas at the park, all of which are associated with the Mediterranean Sea: *Egypt, Iberia, Greece, Rome* and *The Islands*. At the park, visitors can travel through ancient civilisations and go on the many themed rides. En route, visitors will encounter characters and creatures from many myths and legends, including coming face-to-face with the Minotaur on *El Laberinto del Minotauro* (Minotaur's

Labyrinth) and attempting to rescue Ulysses on the *El Rescate de Ulises* (Ulysses' Rescue) ride.

Transportation
Air: Alicante Airport. **Rail:** Train: Terra Mítica Station. **Road:** Car: A-7 to Terra Mítica's exit which is signposted between Benidorm and Villajoyosa (from Valencia or Alicante).

Contact Addresses
Terra Mitica, Ctra: Benidorm a Finestrat, Camino de Moralet s/n, 3500 Benidorm, Alicante, Spain
Tel: (0902) 020 220
Website: www.terramiticapark.com

Universal Mediterranea

This giant theme park, which opened in 1994, attracts thousands of holidaymakers every year who journey through its five worlds (*Mediterránia, Far West, Mexico, Polynesia* and *China*) on its many rides and attractions. Enjoying an enviable coastal location, between Salou and Vila-seca on Spain's Costa Dorada, this 117-hectare site (289 acre) boasts entertainment aimed at all age groups. There are nightly shows, including *Fiestaventura* in the Mediterranean world, as well as many other attractions, including the *Sea Odyssey* underwater adventure, the *Stampida* roller coaster ride, and the *Grand Canyon Rapids* and *Tutuki Splash* water rides. Visitors who wish to spend a few days in the park can stay in one of the many hotels on site.

Transportation
Air: Barcelona International Airport, Reus Airport. **Rail:** Train: Port Aventura Station. **Road:** Car: Hwy-A7 or Hwy-N340 (from Valencia or Barcelona); Hwy-N240 or Hwy-N420 (from Tarragona).

Contact Addresses
Universal Studios Port Aventura, Avenue Alcalde Pere Molas, Km 2, 43480 Vila-seca, Tarragona, Spain
Tel: (0977) 779 090
Website: www.portaventura.es

Sri Lanka

160km
80mls

✈ international airport

INDIA
Palk Strait
Jaffna
Jaffna Peninsula
Palk Bay
Mullaittivu
Adam's Bridge
Mannar I.
Mannar
Aruvi
Trincomalee
Koddiyar Bay
Anuradhapura
Puttalam Lagoon
Puttalam
Sigiriya ①
Mahaweli
INDIAN OCEAN
Gulf of Mannar
Dambulla
Polonnaruwa
Kalkudah
Batticaloa
SRI LANKA
Kurunegala
Kandy ②
Negombo
Adam's Peak 2243m △
Pidurutalagala 2524m
Badulla
Colombo
Nuwara Eliya
Pottuvil
SRI JAYEWARDENEPURA KOTTE
Kalutara
Walawe
Hambantota
Galle
Matara
Dondra Head

1 Sigiriya
2 Temple of the Sacred Tooth (Dalada Maligawa)

Tourist Information

Sri Lanka Tourist Board
PO Box 80, Galle Road, Colombo 3, Sri Lanka
Tel: (01) 437 059 *or* 437 060 *or* 427 055
Website: www.srilankatourism.org

Sri Lanka Tourist Board
Clareville House, 26-27 Oxendon Street,
London SW1Y 4EL, UK
Tel: (020) 7930 2627
Website: www.srilankatourism.org

Sigiriya

Taking its name from *giriya* ('jaws and throat') and
sinha ('lion'), *Sigiriya* is a palace in central Sri Lanka.

It contains the ruins of an ancient royal fortress and
city founded in the fifth century AD by King Kasyapa.
Three kilometres (1.8 miles) wide and one kilometre
(0.6 miles) long, it stands on a steep, large rock,
known as *Lion Mountain*, that rises 180m (600ft)
above the surrounding plain. The magnificent site
also features a series of water gardens, trees and
pathways. It is considered one of the best preserved,
first-millennium city centres in Asia and is also
renowned for its fifth-century rock paintings.

Transportation
Air: Colombo Bandaranayake International Airport.
Rail: Train: Habarane Station. **Road:** Coach: Services
from Dambulla. Car: Main road from Colombo.

Contact Addresses
For more information on Sigiriya, contact the Sri
Lanka Tourist Board (see **Tourist Information** above).

Temple of the Sacred Tooth (Dalada Maligawa)

Located in Kandy, an ancient religious centre for
Buddhism, the octagonal, golden-roofed *Temple of
the Sacred Tooth*, built between 1687 and 1707, is
a stunning sacred temple, which is believed to
house the left upper canine of the Lord Buddha
himself. According to legend, the tooth was taken
from the Buddha as he lay on his funeral pyre
and smuggled to Sri Lanka hidden in Princess
Hemamali's hair, where it survived numerous
attempts to capture and destroy it. Today, this
famous religious relic attracts white-clad pilgrims,
bearing lotus blossoms and frangipani, every day.

Transportation
Air: Colombo Bandaranayake International Airport. **Rail:**
Train: Kandy Station (from Colombo). **Road:** Bus: Public
services. Car: Colombo–Kandy road (from Colombo).

Contact Addresses
For more information on the Temple of the Sacred
Tooth, contact Sri Lanka Tourist Board (see
Tourist Information above).

Sweden

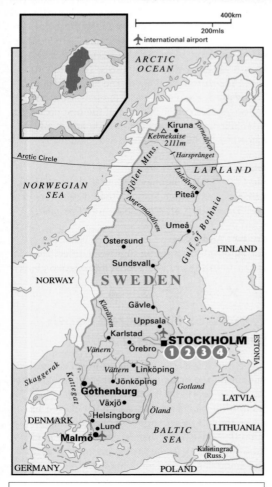

1 Drottningholm Palace
(Drottningholms Slott)

2 Museum of National Antiquities
(Statens Historiska Museum)

3 Royal Palace (Kungliga Slottet)

4 Vasa Museum (Vasamuseet)

Drottningholm Palace (Drottningholms Slott)

Home to the Swedish Royal Family since 1981, when they moved from the *Kungliga Slottet* (Royal Palace) in Stockholm, *Drottningholm Palace* is one of the most magnificent legacies of Sweden's imperial age. King Johan III first built a palace on the site during the late-16th century; this building was destroyed, however, by fire in 1661 and work began on building a new palace in 1662. Over the years, the interior has been improved upon by successive residents and it is now renowned for its Rococo decorations. The palace was handed over to Princess Lovisa Ulrika of Prussia in 1744 on her marriage to Adolf Fredrik of Sweden. Drottningholm is surrounded by splendid Baroque gardens, including the great English Park and the French formal garden, and is home to many fine buildings such as the *Chinese Pavilion*, the *Court Theatre* and the *Castle Church*.

Transportation
Air: Stockholm Arlanda Airport. **Water:** Boat: Services to Drottningholm (from Stadshuskajen). **Rail:** Underground: Brommaplan. **Road:** Bus: Public services. Car: The palace is located in central Stockholm.

Contact Addresses
Drottningholms Slott, 17802 Drottningholm, Sweden
Tel: (08) 402 6280
Website: www.royalcourt.se

Tourist Information

Swedish Travel & Tourism Council (Sveriges Rese – och Turistråd AB)
PO Box 90, 88122 Solleftea, Sweden
Tel: (08) 725 5500
Website: www.swetourism.se (travel trade) or www.visit-sweden.com (public)

Swedish Travel & Tourism Council
Sweden House, 5 Upper Montagu Street, London W1H 2AG, UK
Tel: (020) 7870 5600 (trade enquiries) *or* (00800) 3080 3080 (consumer enquiries)
Website: www.visit-sweden.com

Museum of National Antiquities (Statens Historiska Museum)

Sweden's *Museum of National Antiquities* traces more than 12,000 years of the nation's history from the Stone Age to the 16th century. Its most famous attraction is the Gold Room, which houses magnificent silver and gold treasures found in Swedish soil from prehistoric times to the Middle Ages. The Viking exhibit features a unique collection of artefacts from the Viking period, whilst the museum also houses one of the world's finest and best preserved collections of Medieval religious art.

Transportation
Air: Stockholm Arlanda Airport. **Rail:** Underground: Karlaplan or Östermalmstorg. **Road:** Bus: Public services.

Contact Addresses
Statens Historiska Museum, Box 5428, 114 84 Stockholm, Sweden
Tel: (08) 5195 5600
Website: www.historiska.se

Royal Palace (Kungliga Slottet)

The *Royal Palace* is the official residence of Sweden's monarch, currently King Carl XVI Gustaf, and houses the offices of the King and Queen and the Duchess of Halland; the latter is the most senior member of the royal family after the King and Queen and their children. A fortress was first built on the site in the 13th century and, as Sweden increased in status, so did the castle, finally becoming the official royal residence in 1521 under Gustav Vasa. The Vasa family developed the palace on a grand scale, adding Renaissance and Baroque features. After fire struck in 1697, much of the interior of the palace was reconstructed over the next 60 years, resulting in a variety of architectural styles. Visitors can view some of the magnificent rooms within the palace, such as the *Royal Apartments*, the *Treasury* and the *Apartments of the Orders of Chivalry* and watch the changing of the guard, which takes place every day.

Transportation
Air: Stockholm Arlanda Airport. **Rail:** Train: Stockholm Central Station. Underground: Gamla Stan. **Road:** Bus: Public services. Car: E4 (from Malmö); E18 (from Oslo, Norway); E20 or E6 (from Gothenburg).

Contact Addresses
Kungliga Slottet, 111 30 Stockholm, Sweden
Tel: (08) 402 6130
Website: www.royalcourt.se

Vasa Museum (Vasamuseet)

The mighty Swedish warship, the *Vasa*, was the most powerful vessel of her day. Commissioned by King Gustavus Adolphus in 1625 as one of a fleet of battleships in the war against Poland, she was constructed by experienced Dutch shipbuilder Henrik Hybertsson who died one year before her completion. The *Vasa* was capable of holding 445 crew and weighed 1210 tonnes (1191 tons). Tragically, due to problems with her stability, the ship keeled over on her maiden voyage on August 10 1628 and sank killing around 40 of the 150 people on board. It was not until 1961 that the remarkably intact wreckage was salvaged by the Swedish Navy and preserved in a temporary museum until the opening of the *Vasa Museum* in 1990. Exhibitions, interactive displays and audiovisual presentations tell of the salvage operation, life on board ship and sea battles of the period.

Transportation
Air: Stockholm Arlanda Airport. **Water:** Ferry: Services from Slussen (all year) and Nybroplan (summer) to Djurgården Island. **Rail:** Train: Stockholm Central Station. **Road:** Bus: Public services. Car: E18 (from Oslo); E20 or E6 (from Gothenburg); E4 (from Malmö).

Contact Addresses
Vasamuseet, Box 27131, 10252 Stockholm, Sweden
Tel: (08) 5195 4800
Website: www.vasamuseet.se

Switzerland

150km
100mls

✈ international airport

FRANCE

Rhine

S W I T Z E R L A N D

GERMANY

Lake Constance
(Bodensee)

Winterthur

Basle
Zurich
St Gall

Jura Mtns.

Aare

LIECH.

Neuchâtel
Lucerne
Lake
Lucerne

AUSTRIA

Lake
Neuchâtel

■BERNE

Rhine

Davos

Lausanne
Interlaken

Lake Thun

Andermatt

St
Moritz
S

Inn

Lake
Geneva

③

Montreux

②

Rhône

Geneva

④

①

P

Matterhorn
4478m

L

Lugano

Adda

Lake Como

Mont Blanc
4807m△

Dufour-
spitze
4634m

A

Lake
Maggiore

FRANCE

ITALY

1 Chillon Castle
   (Château de Chillion)

2 Jungfraujoch

3 Olympic Museum Lausanne
   (Musée Olympique Lausanne)

4 Water Fountain
   (Jet d'Eau)

Tourist Information

Switzerland Tourism (Schweiz Tourismus)
Tödistrasse 7, 8027 Zürich, Switzerland
Tel: (01) 288 1111
Website: www.myswitzerland.com

Switzerland Tourism
Tenth Floor, Swiss Centre, 10 Wardour Street,
London W1D 6QF, UK
Tel: (00800) 1002 0030 (toll-free Europe only)
or (020) 7292 1550
Website: www.myswitzerland.com

Chillon Castle (Château de Chillon)

Chillon Castle is the most famous castle in Switzerland. It enjoys a spectacular location on the eastern edge of Lake Geneva, near Montreux, with the *Dents du Midi* (literally meaning the Teeth of the South) mountains in the background. Built in the 13th century on Roman foundations, Lord Byron visited the chateau and later wrote the poem 'Prisoner of Chillon' (1816) about the fate of François de Bonivard (1493-1570). Bonivard was the castle's most famous prisoner, incarcerated between 1530 and 1536 for trying to bring protestantism to Switzerland. The castle was once an important medieval fort, strategically located on an island to guard against invasion. Today, visitors can see the castle's famous prison, and also tour the the *Grand Hall*, the *Hall of Justice*, the *Armouries*, the *Grand Hall of the Count*, the *Duke's Chamber* and *Saint George's Chapel*.

Transportation
Air: Geneva International Airport. **Water:** Boat: Boats dock at the CGN jetty next to the castle. **Rail:** Train: Veytaux-Chillon Station. **Road:** Bus: Daily trolley bus service to the castle. Car: A1 and A9 towards Montreux (from Geneva); the castle is within walking distance of Montreux.

Contact Addresses
Association du Château de Chillon, 1820 Veytaux, Switzerland
Tel: (021) 966 8910
Website: www.chillon.ch

Jungfraujoch

The stereotypically Swiss hiking trails and snow-covered Alps of the *Jungfraujoch* have been attracting visitors for hundreds of years. The peak of the Jungfrau is 4158m (13,642ft) high, with the ridge or 'joch' lying below it, where visitors can see the longest glacier in Europe, the 24km (15 miles) long *Aletsch Glacier*. Skiing and alpine activities are immensely popular but one of the best ways to take in the region is by train.

Completed in 1912, the *Jungfraujoch Railway* takes passengers to the mountain's summit where they can get off at the highest railway station in Europe, which reaches an altitude of 3454m (11,333ft).

Transportation
Air: Geneva International Airport, Berne-Belp Airport. **Rail:** Train: Jungfrau Station. **Road:** Car: Via Bern to Interlaken, then Interlaken-Grindelwald Grund exit (from Zurich). Visitors must then take a train (from Grindelwald Grund).

Contact Addresses
Interlaken Tourism, PO Box 369, Hoehweg 37, 3800 Interlaken, Switzerland
Tel: (033) 826 5300
Website: www.interlakentourism.ch
or
Jungfrau Railways, Harderstrasse 14, 3800 Interlaken
Tel: 9033) 828 7111
Website: www.jungfraubahn.ch

Olympic Museum Lausanne (Musée Olympique Lausanne)

Inaugurated in June 1993, the *Olympic Museum* in Lausanne sits on the shores of Lake Geneva. Set in the beautiful *Olympic Park* gardens, the museum displays sport, art and cultural collections from ancient Greece through to modern times. It is the centre of information on the Olympic Movement and preserves the heritage of the Olympic Games. The museum was totally renovated in 2000-2001 and now includes permanent collections, such as The Olympic Adventure, dedicated to the history and origins of the Olympic Movement, and *The Athletes and the Games*, which is fully devoted to the Olympics and athletes' exploits.

Transportation
Air: Geneva International Airport, Zurich International Airport. **Water:** Boat: Steamboats depart from Geneva, Vévey and Montreux and stop in Ouchy. **Rail:** Train: Lausanne Station. Cable Car: Cable train 'La Ficelle' to Ouchy (from Lausanne Station). **Road:** Car: Motorway signs for Lausanne Sud, then the road to Ouchy.

Hiking in the Alps

Interlaken Tourismus©

Contact Addresses
Musée Olympique Lausanne, 1 Quai d'Ouchy, 1001 Lausanne, Switzerland
Tel: (021) 621 6511
Website: www.museum.olympic.org

Water Fountain (Jet d'Eau)

Geneva's *Jet d'Eau* has been breaking the calm of this peaceful city for over a hundred years. The idea that a water fountain might be a tourist attraction came about purely by chance in 1886, when a solution was needed to relieve pressure at the *Forces Motrices* pumping and power station. The water initially reached a height of 30m (98ft), and quickly began to draw large crowds. This led to a more impressive fountain being introduced on Eaux-Vives jetty in 1891 to coincide with the 600th anniversary of the Swiss Confederation and the opening of the Federal Gymnastics Festival. The fountain, which reached a height of 90m (295ft) in 1891, has been technologically improved to spurt water 140m (460ft) into the air. At three times the height of the *Statue of Liberty*, it is now Europe's tallest fountain and today, two electric pumps are used to blast an estimated seven tonnes of water aloft at a speed of 200kmph (124mph).

Transportation
Air: Geneva International Airport. **Rail:** Train: Cornavin Station. Tram: Cours de Rive Station. **Road:** Bus: Eaux-Vives Bus Stop. Car: A1 (from Lausanne).

Contact Addresses
Jet d'Eau, Services Industriéls de Genève, PO Box 2777, 1211 Geneva, Switzerland
Tel: (022) 420 7250
Website: www.sig-ge.ch

Syrian Arab Republic

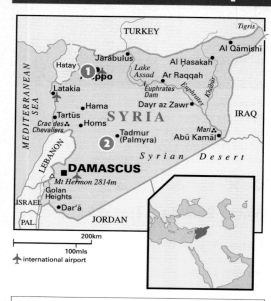

200km
100mls
✈ international airport

| 1 Aleppo (Halab) |
| 2 Palmyra (Tadmor) |

Tourist Information

Ministry of Tourism (Wazaretal Siyaha)
Barada Street 14, Damascus, Syrian
Arab Republic
Tel: (011) 221 0122 or 224 6096
Website: www.syriatourism.org

Embassy of the Syrian Arab Republic
8 Belgrave Square, London SW1X 8PH, UK
Tel: (020) 7245 9012 or (09065) 508 935 (recorded
visa information; calls cost 60p per minute)

Aleppo (Halab)

Aleppo vies with Syria's capital Damascus for the
record of the world's oldest continuously inhabited
city. The city's name was first mentioned in texts
as far back as the third millennium BC and has had
a long and extremely rich history under Hittite,
Egyptian, Mitannian, Assyrian, Hellenic, Roman
and Ottoman rule. The legacies that these empires
left behind have provided Aleppo with numerous

attractions, most famously the 12th-century which
served first as a Greek acropolis and later as an
Islamic fortress. Another draw for visitors is the 12
kilometres (8 miles) of covered bazaars, or *souks*.
The *Great Mosque*, or *Ommayad Mosque*, was built
in AD 715 and is one of the best examples of
Islamic architecture in Syria.

Transportation
Air: Aleppo International Airport. **Rail:** Train:
Aleppo Station. **Road:** Coach: Services from
Damascus. Car: Route 5 (from Damascus).

Contact Addresses
For more information on Aleppo, contact the
Ministry of Tourism (see **Tourist Information**
above).

Palmyra (Tadmor)

The ancient city of *Palmyra* rises out of the Syrian
desert 210km (130 miles) northeast of Damascus.
It was originally known as *Tadmor*, meaning 'city
of dates' and its existence was recorded on stone
tablets dating from the 19th century BC. In the
first century AD, Tadmor came under Roman rule
and was renamed Palmyra, meaning 'city of palm
trees'. After a succession of rulers, Palmyra was
captured by the Muslim leader Khalid ibn al-
Walid in AD 634, and its status as a great trading
city and cultural centre declined. Today visitors
can explore the ruins, which include the *Temple of
Bel* and the *Valley of the Tombs*. In the first week
of May, the *Palmyra Festival* is held, featuring
camel races, folk dancing, music, traditional
costume and handicrafts.

Transportation
Air: Damascus International Airport, Aleppo
International Airport. **Road:** Car: Damascus –
Palmyra Highway.

Contact Addresses
For more information on Palmyra, contact the
Ministry of Tourism (see **Tourist Information** above).

Tanzania

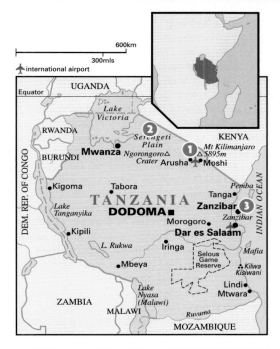

Tourist Information

Tanzania Tourist Board
PO Box 2485, Dar es Salaam, Tanzania
Tel: (022) 211 1244 *or* 213 6105
Website: www.tanzania-web.com

Tanzanian Trade Centre
80 Borough High Street, London SE1 1LL, UK
Tel: (020) 7407 0566
Website: www.tanzania-online.gov.uk

Kilimanjaro National Park

Kilimanjaro National Park is the home of *Mount Kilimanjaro*'s equatorial snow-capped peaks, which form some of the most famous images of Africa. At 5896m (19,340ft), Mount Kilimanjaro, situated in northeast Tanzania, is the highest mountain in Africa and one of the largest free-standing mountains in the world. It is actually an active volcano and possesses the highest walkable summit in the world, Uhuru Peak, one of six glaciers and volcanic peaks at the top. The scenery is varied and visitors climbing to the summit pass through hot savannah, alpine tropics and finally an arctic moonscape and may even spot elephant wandering the higher slopes. A game reserve since 1921, the area was designated a national park in 1973.

Transportation
Air: Kilimanjaro International Airport, Dar-es-Salaam International Airport. **Rail:** Train: Moshi Station. **Road:** Bus: Services to Moshi Bus Station. Car: North–south route through Chalinze to Moshi (from Dar-es-Salaam).

Contact Addresses
Kilimanjaro National Park, PO Box 96, Marangu, Tanzania
Tel: (027) 275 3195
Website: www.tanzaniaparks.com

P ✕ 🧺 🏛 £ ✔

Kilimanjaro National Park Corel©

Serengeti National Park

Made a game reserve in 1921 and a national park since 1951, *Serengeti National Park* is the largest park in Tanzania and one of the most famous in the world. Serengeti fittingly means 'endless plain' in the local Maasai tongue and at 14,763 sq km (5700 sq miles), it features a diversity of environments, ranging from savannah and grass

Corel©

plains to woodland and black clay plains. The glory of the Serengeti, however, is its wildlife, and the park is most famous for the annual migration of wildebeest, zebra and Thomson's gazelle. It also teems with lions, elephants and ostriches, and is home to around 500 different species of birds. The *Seronera Valley* is popular amongst visitors who come to see the resident prides of lions and photograph the many leopards that can be found in the branches of the acacia and sausage trees. The two saline lakes in the park, the *Lagaja* and the *Magadi*, are famous for attracting flamingos that feed on the lakes' animal and plant life.

Transportation
Air: Kilimanjaro International Airport. Charter flights are available from Arusha, Lake Manyara and Mwanza. **Rail:** Train: Moshi Station. **Road:** Bus: Arusha Bus Station.

Corel©

Contact Addresses
Serengeti National Park, Tanzania National Parks Authority, PO Box 3134, Arusha, Tanzania
Tel: (028) 262 1569 *or* 262 1510 *or* 262 1504
Website: www.tanzaniaparks.com

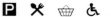

Stone Town, Zanzibar

Zanzibar is situated about 40km (25 miles) off the coast of Tanzania, and is 97km (60 miles) long and 32km (20 miles) wide. *Stone Town* is the old city and cultural centre of Zanzibar, which rose to prominence in the 17th century. The town is made up of narrow streets and winding alleys, bazaars and mosques. It is also home to many grand Arab houses, which were built in the 19th century when Zanzibar was one of the most important trading centres in the Indian Ocean. Key attractions in Stone Town include the *Old Dispensary*, *Livingstone's House*, the *Peace Memorial Museum*, the *Palace Museum*, the *Arab Fort* and the *House of Wonders* (which translates from its local name, *Beit el Jaib*). Zanzibar itself has many breathtaking beaches and is also famed for the rare Kirk's Red Colobus monkey, which can be found in the *Jozani Forest*. As well as Zanzibar, Tanzania boasts many smaller islands which are just a short trip from Stone Town, including *Prison* (*Changu Island*), *Chapwani*, *Chumbe* and *Bawe Islands*.

Transportation
Air: Zanzibar Airport. **Water:** Ferry: Ferries operate to Zanzibar (from Dar-es-Salaam). **Road:** Car: Stone Town is located on the Western side of Zanzibar and can be reached via the main road (from the airport).

Contact Addresses
Zanzibar Commission for Tourism, PO Box 1410, Zanzibar, Tanzania
Tel: (024) 223 3485/6
Website: www.zanzibartourism.net

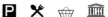

Key to symbols:
£ Entry charged
& Disabled access
⚓ Man-made attraction
✦ Natural attraction
P Parking
✗ Restaurant
🏺 Shop
🏛 UNESCO site

Thailand

400km

200mls

✈ international airport

1 Bridge Over The River Kwai (Menam Kwai)

2 Damnoen Saduak Floating Market (Talat Naam Damnoen Saduak)

3 Phang Nga Bay (Ao Phang-Nga)

4 Royal Barges National Museum (Piphit Thapan Sathan Hang Chart Ruer Pra Raj Pithee)

5 Royal Grand Palace (Phra Barom Maha Rajcha Wang)

6 Temple of the Reclining Buddha (Wat Pho)

Bridge Over The River Kwai (Menam Kwai)

Internationally famous due to the 1957 film the *Bridge Over the River Kwai*, it was constructed as part of the *Japanese Siam-Burma 'Death' Railway* during World War II. An estimated 16,000 Allied prisoners of war died, forced to endure back-

Tourist Information

Tourism Authority of Thailand (Kan Tong Teow Hang Prated Thai)
Le Concorde Building, 202 Ratchadapisek Road, Bangkok 10310, Thailand
Tel: (02) 694 1222
Website: www.tat.or.th *or* www.tourismthailand.org

Tourism Authority of Thailand (UK & Ireland)
49 Albemarle Street, London W1S 4JR, UK
Tel: (09063) 640 666 (consumer enquiries; calls cost 60p per minute) *or* (0870) 900 2007 (brochure request line) *or* (020) 7499 7679 (trade only).
Website: www.thaismile.co.uk

breaking work under terrible conditions to complete the railway, and large numbers of troops perished during bombing raids on the iron structure by the Allies in 1945. The moving *JEATH War Museum* (JEATH representing the first letter of Japan, England, America, Australia, Thailand and Holland, the countries who lost soldiers in the region) is located in the provincial capital, Kanchanaburi and features photographs and various other memorabilia from World War II.

Transportation
Air: Bangkok International Airport. **Rail:** Train: Services to Kanchanaburi Station (from Bangkok Noi Station). **Road:** Bus: Public services. Car: Hwy-4 (from Bangkok), then Hwy-323.

Contact Addresses
Kanchanaburi Tourist Office: Tourism Authority of Thailand, Region 1, Saeng Chuto Road, Amphoe Mueang, Kanchanaburi 71000, Thailand
Tel: (03) 451 1200 *or* 451 2500

JEATH War Museum: Wat Chaichumpol, Ban Tai, Mueang, Kanchanaburi, Thailand
Tel: (034) 515 203

Damnoen Saduak Floating Market (Talat Naam Damnoen Saduak)

Located 80km (50 miles) southwest of Bangkok, *Damnoen Saduak Floating Market* is a daily riot of colour and noise. Farmers and smallholders from the surrounding hills turn up each morning to sell and exchange fruit and vegetables from their heavily-laden barges, as they sail up and down the canals amongst the orchards and vineyards. Trading starts early, at around 0600 and lasts only until 1100, with the main clients being other farmers and the residents of the stilt-houses that line the canals. Visitors can also take boat trips to see the way of life in the many villages up river.

Transportation
Air: Bangkok International Airport. **Road:** Bus: Public services to Damnoen Saduak Bus Terminal. Car: Hwy-4 (from Bangkok), then Bangpae–Damnoen Saduak Road.

Contact Addresses
For more information on Damnoen Saduak Floating Market, contact the Tourism Authority of Thailand (see **Tourist Information** above).

Phang Nga Bay (Ao Phang-Nga)

Phang Nga Bay is one of the world's great scenic wonders. It covers an area of 400 sq km (154 sq miles) and consists of verdant limestone islands, some of which reach 300m (984ft) high. The area is famous for its caves and aquatic grottoes. Apart from the occasional village, few of the islands are densely populated. The most famous of the islands in the bay are *Ko Ping Kan* (more commonly known as *James Bond Island*) and *Koh Pannyi*. The former featured in the James Bond movie 'The Man with the Golden Gun', whilst the latter, which literally means 'Sea Gypsy Island', is a village built out over the water on stilts, guarded by a giant rock monolith. The area suffered badly during the Boxing Day tsunami in 2004 but has recovered well.

Transportation
Air: Phuket International Airport. **Water:** Boat: Many tourists visit Phang Nga Bay by boat; local companies operate day trips to the islands. **Rail:** Train: Surathani Station. **Road:** Bus: Phuket Bus Terminal in Phuket Town. Car: Hwy-402 (Tepkassatri Road, from Phuket), then Route 4.

Contact Addresses
Tourism Authority of Thailand Southern Office, Region 4, 73-75 Phuket Road, Amphoe Mueang, Phuket 83000, Thailand
Tel: (07) 621 1036 *or* 7138 *or* 2213
Website: www.phukettourism.org

Royal Barges National Museum (Piphit Thapan Sathan Hang Chart Ruer Pra Raj Pithee)

The *Royal Barges National Museum* houses several royal barges, which formerly served as war vessels and were subsequently used on royal and state occasions along the Chao Phraya River. The earliest evidence of the use of these decorative barges during royal processions dates back to 1357. The barges are incredibly intricate in design, reflecting Thai religious beliefs and local history. The figure on the bow of each boat signifies whether it carries the King and Queen or other members of the royal family. Today, the royal barges, being so old, are rarely used by the royal family; they were last used at the end of 1999 to celebrate the king's 72nd birthday.

Transportation
Air: Bangkok International Airport. **Rail:** Train: Thonburi Station. **Road:** Bus: Public services from central Bangkok. Car: Hwy-4 (from Hua Hin); Hwy-3 (from Pattaya); Hwy-117 (from Phitsanulok), then Hwy-32. Taxi: Taxis can be hailed in the street to go to the museum.

Contact Addresses
Royal Barges National Museum, Arun Amarin Road, Bangkok Noi, Bangkok 10700, Thailand
Tel/Fax: (02) 424 0004

Damnoen Saduak Floating Market

Tourism Authority of Thailand©

Royal Grand Palace (Phra Barom Maha Rajcha Wang)

The *Royal Grand Palace* is made up of a vast complex of intricate buildings, including *Wat Mahathat* (Palace Temple) and *Wat Phra Keow* (Royal Chapel). Construction of the palace began in 1782 and was completed in time for the coronation of King Rama I, opening in 1785 to signify the end of the Burmese invasion of Thailand. The palace lies in the heart of the old town and covers an area of 218,400 sq m (2,350,857 sq ft). The compound is surrounded by a moat and contains two sections, the former royal residence and the Buddhist temple. The Royal Chapel houses the famous *Emerald Buddha*, which is carved from a single piece of jade, and is the holiest and most revered religious object in Thailand.

Transportation
Air: Bangkok International Airport. **Rail:** Train: Hualamphong Station. **Road:** Bus: Public services. Car: The entrance to the palace is on Na Phra Lan Road, near Sanam Luang in the centre of Bangkok.

Contact Addresses
Phra Barom Maha Rajcha Wang, Bureau of Royal Household, Na Phra Lan Road, Phra Nakhon, Bangkok 10200, Thailand
Tel: (02) 623 5500 *or* 623 5499
Website: www.palaces.thai.net

Temple of the Reclining Buddha (Wat Pho)

Occupying a 20-hectare (50-acre) site next to the *Royal Grand Palace*, *Wat Pho* is the oldest and largest temple in Bangkok. It was built in 1688 during the reign of King Petraja of Ayutthaya and contains one of Thailand's most spectacular sights, a 46m- (150ft) long and 15m- (72ft-) high statue of a reclining Buddha. The statue itself, which is gold-plated and inlaid with mother-of-pearl on the soles of the feet, was not added until 1832 during the reign of King Rama III, and serves to illustrate the passing of Buddha into nirvana (the state of absolute blessedness). Visitors can wander amongst the peaceful rock gardens, chapels and stupas. King Rama III also established Wat Pho as an important centre for Thai medicine and massage and thus founded Thailand's oldest seat of learning. It is still possible to have a massage or learn about the art of Thai massage and medicine at Wat Pho today.

Transportation
Air: Bangkok International Airport. **Rail:** Train: Hualamphong Station. **Road:** Bus: Public services. Car: Hwy-4 (from Hua Hin); Hwy-3 (from Pattaya); Hwy-117 (from Phitsanulok), then Hwy-32.

Contact Addresses
Wat Pho, Thai Wang Rd, Bangkok, Thailand
Tel: (02) 222 0933
Website: www.watpho.com

Tunisia

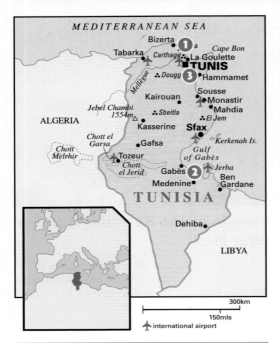

MEDITERRANEAN SEA

Bizerta
Tabarka • Carthage ① a Cape Bon
La Goulette
TUNIS
•• Dougg ③ • Hammamet
Sousse
Kairouan • Monastir
Jebel Chambi •• Sbeitla • Mahdia
ALGERIA 1554m△ •• El Jem
Kasserine **Sfax**
Chott el Gafsa • Kerkenah Is.
Garsa Gulf
Chott ⚔ Tozeur of Gabès
Melrhir Chott • Gabès ② Jerba
el Jerid Medenine • Ben
Gardane

T U N I S I A

Dehiba •

LIBYA

300km
150mls
✈ international airport

---

1 Carthage
2 Matmata
3 Medina in Tunis (al-Madinah)

Tourist Information

Tunisian National Tourist Office (Office National du Tourisme Tunisien/ONTT)
1 avenue Mohamed V, 1000 Tunis, Tunisia
Tel: (071) 341 077.
Website: www.tourismtunisia.com

Tunisian National Tourist Office
77a Wigmore Street, London W1U 1QF, UK
Tel: (020) 7224 5561 (enquiries)
Website: www.cometotunisia.co.uk

Carthage

The city of *Carthage*, which is located on the outskirts of Tunisia's capital city, Tunis, was, for many years, the arch-enemy of the ancient

Roman empire. Between 264 and 146 BC, the two great cities were embroiled in a series of wars that saw Hannibal's famous attack on Rome, and Rome's subsequent sacking of Carthage in 146 BC. The Romans eventually settled in the conquered city, which went on to become the administrative capital of Roman Africa. Today, it is mainly Roman sites, including theatres, temples, villas and baths, which can be seen by visiting tourists. Many of the sites now stand in ruins, including the *Roman Amphitheatre* and the thermal *Antoine Baths*, which were once the largest baths built by the Romans. Visitors can gain a superb view of Carthage by climbing the nearby *Byrsa Hill*.

Transportation
Air: Tunis–Carthage International Airport.
Water: Ferry: Services from Sardinia, Sicily, Genoa, Naples, Marseille and Malta. **Rail:** Train: TGM (light rail) to Carthage Byrsa Station.
Road: Bus: Public services. Car: Avenue Habib Bourguiba towards Sidi Bou Said (from Tunis city centre).

Contact Addresses
Site de Carthage, Carthage, Tunisia
Tel: (071) 730 036

Matmata

Matmata is one of the most famous villages in Tunisia as it was the setting for the opening scenes of the film 'Star Wars'. The village's lunar-like landscape and subterranean cave dwellings attract hundreds of visitors every day. They come to see the home of the Star Wars characters Uncle Owen and Aunt Beru, which was located in the fictional town of Sidi Driss. The Berber people first dug homes out of the ground over 1000 years ago in order to escape the midday heat. These Troglodyte communities formed craters beneath the earth and constructed tunnels between some of the courtyards to build an underground labyrinth. Today, *Hotel Sidi Driss*, which was the cantina in Star Wars, still stands, and visitors can spend the night in Berber-style accommodation as part of the whole experience.

Matmata

Transportation
Air: Tunis-Carthage International Airport. **Road:**
Coach: The majority of tourists visit Matmata as
part of an organised coach tour. Bus: Public
services. Car: Road southwest out of Gabes, which
leads to New Matmata. Camel: Many tourists
prefer to hire camels.

Contact Addresses
For more information on Matmata, contact the
Office National du Tourisme Tunisien (see **Tourist
Information** above).

Medina in Tunis (al-Madinah)

The *medina*, or old quarter, of Tunis was built
during the seventh century AD. From the 12th to
the 16th centuries, Tunis was considered to be one
of the greatest and wealthiest cities of the Islamic
world and its medina is testimony to its former
grandeur. Today, visitors can step back in time
through the maze of narrow, winding streets and
barter for souvenirs with the locals; goods on sale

include colourful hand-made carpets, hand-
crafted jewellery, copper and brassware, pottery
and exotic spices. Among the more frequented
attractions found within the walls of the medina
are: the ninth-century *Ez-Zitouna Mosqu* (*Mosque
of the Olive Tree*), the perfume makers' *Souk el
Attarine,* the *Bardo Museum*, home to a fine
collection of mosaics and Tunis's first Ottoman-
style mosque, *Sidi Yousef*, built in the 17th century.

Transportation
Air: Tunis-Carthage International Airport.
Water: Ferry: Services from Sardinia, Sicily,
Genoa, Naples, Marseille and Malta. **Rail:** Train:
Tunis Ville Station. Underground: Medina.
Road: Car: Avenue Habib Bourguiba, Place de
l'Independence and Avenue de France (from
Carthage).

Contact Addresses
For more information on the Medina in Tunis,
contact the Office National du Tourisme Tunisien
(see **Tourist Information** above).

Turkey

Divine Wisdom, in the year AD 537, it was the most impressive building in the world and remained the crowning achievement of the Byzantine Empire for over a millennium. In the 15th century, Mehmet the Conqueror converted it from a Christian church to a mosque, adding the minarets, tombs and fountains. Turkey became a secular republic in 1923 and Hagia Sophia was established as a museum 12 years later, with many of its Byzantine mosaics revealed from underneath layers of Ottoman plaster. Designed to represent the heavens, visitors marvel at the huge 56m (183ft) high dome.

Transportation
Air: Istanbul Atatürk Airport, Istanbul Sabiha Gökçen International Airport. **Rail:** Train: Sirkeci Station. Tram: Sultanahmet. **Road:** Bus: Public services. Car: E80 or D100 (from Ankara, Izmit and Greece).

Contact Addresses
Museum of Hagia Sophia, Sultanahmet, Istanbul, Turkey
Tel: (0212) 522 0989 *or* 522 1750

1 Ayasofya (Hagia Sophia)

2 Blue Mosque (Sultanahmet Camii)

3 Ephesus (Efes)

4 Göreme National Park (Göreme Milli Parklar)

5 Topkapi Palace (Topkapi Sarayi)

6 Troy (Truva)

Blue Mosque (Sultanahmet Camii)

With its cascade of opulent domes and slender, balconied minarets soaring towards the sky, Istanbul's *Blue Mosque* is one of the city's most striking images. Construction was begun in 1609 under the Ottoman Sultan Ahmet Khan I, who wished to create a place of Islamic worship to rival the *Aya Sofya*, or Hagia Sophia, constructed under the Roman ruler Justinian II in AD 532 and located across the *Hippodrome*, the old city's central plaza. Completed in 1619, the interior of the mosque features a massive dome supported by four grand columns, 5m (16ft) in diameter, as well as characteristic Ottoman tile patterns and brightly-coloured windows. Hundreds of Muslims still use the mosque for daily prayer and worship. Visitors of all faiths who are modestly dressed may enter the Blue Mosque; special slippers and head and shoulder coverings are distributed at the entrance.

Tourist Information

Ministry of Tourism (Turizm Bakanligi)
Ismet Inönü Bulvar 5, Bahçelievler, Ankara, Turkey
Tel: (0312) 212 8300
Website: www.turizm.gov.tr

Turkish Tourist Office
First Floor, 170-173 Piccadilly, London W1J 9EJ, UK
Tel: (020) 7629 7771 *or* (09001) 887 755 (brochure request line; calls are charged at the rate of 60p per minute).

Ayasofya (Hagia Sophia)

When the Christian Emperor Justinian inaugurated *Hagia Sophia*, meaning Church of

Transportation

Air: Istanbul Atatürk Airport, Istanbul Sabiha Gökçen International Airport. **Rail:** Train: Sirkeci Station. Tram: Sultanahmet. **Road:** Bus: Public services. Car: E-80 or D-100 (from Edirne).

Contact Addresses

Sultanahmet Camii, Sultanahmet Meydani, Istanbul, Turkey
Tel: (0212) 518 1319

Ephesus (Efes)

Ephesus, located 600km (373 miles) southwest of Istanbul, is one of the grandest and best-preserved ruins of the ancient world. According to evidence dating from around 1400BC, the Hittites were the first to settle the site, which they named Apasas. Ephesus first attained importance in the first century BC, due to its position as a sheltered harbour and the starting point of the royal road leading to Susa, the capital of the Persian Empire. The temple was originally founded in the seventh century BC as a shrine to the Anatolian goddess, Cybele. It was destroyed and subsequently rebuilt seven times; the classical marble structure with Ionic columns built around 550BC was one of the seven wonders of the ancient world. The Romans captured the city in 189BC and it continued to flourish, with fountains, pools and the second largest library outside of Alexandria. One of Ephesus' attractions is the fact that so much of it remains intact and little imagination is required to see what the Roman city would have looked like.

Transportation

Air: Istanbul Atatürk Airport, Istanbul Sabiha Gökçen International Airport, Dalaman Airport, Adnanmenderes Airport, Izmir (domestic flights). **Rail:** Train: Selçuk Station. **Road:** Bus: Public services. Car: Selçuk–Kusadasi Road (from Selçuk or Kusadasi).

Contact Addresses

Tourist Information Office, Selçuk, Izmir 35920, Turkey
Tel: (0232) 892 6945
Website: www.ephesusguide.com

Göreme National Park (Göreme Milli Parklar)

Göreme National Park in *Cappadocia*, central Turkey, is home to one of nature's most intriguing phenomena. Commonly referred to as the *Valley of the Fairy Chimneys*, after the strange rock formations that proliferate in the region, this weird and wonderful landscape of 9572 hectares (23,653 acres) was formed when three volcanoes, *Erciyes*, *Hasan* and *Melendiz Dağlari* erupted around 30 million years ago. The deposits they created make up a material called tuff, a soft rock that is easily eroded to form extraordinary table mountains, fairy chimneys and undulating, sand-dune like cliff faces. For hundreds of years, the indigenous population had carved homes out of the rocks, many of which have been turned into comfortable *pansiyon* (guesthouses). St Paul introduced Christianity to the region in the first century AD, and one of Cappadocia's chief attractions is the array of rock churches and monasteries that were hewn out of the landscape, thus being hidden from the pursuing Arab invaders. The town of *Göreme* has an open-air museum where many of these preserved houses and churches, adorned with frescoes, can be seen.

Transportation

Air: Ankara Esenboga Airport, Istanbul Atatürk Airport, Istanbul Sabiha Gökçen International Airport, Nevsehir Airport (domestic flights), Kayseri Airport (domestic flights). **Road:** Coach: Public services.

Contact Addresses

Nevsehir Directorate of Tourism, Atatürk Bulvari 14, Nevsehir, Turkey
Tel: (0384) 213 3659

Topkapi Palace (Topkapi Sarayi)

Topkapi Palace was created on the orders of Mehmed II, the 23-year-old sultan who captured the Roman city of Constantinople in 1453 and made it the capital of his mighty Ottoman empire, under the new name of Istanbul. The palace was constructed between 1459 and 1478 and rapidly grew to become a jumbled complex of elaborate living quarters and administrative offices. The

Blue Mosque

Ruth Blakeborough©

Sultanahmet, Istanbul, Turkey
Tel: (0212) 512 0480 *or* 512 0484
Website: www.kultur.gov.tr

P ✖ 🧺 ♿ 🏛 £ 🏭

Troy (Truva)

Until 1871, classical scholars the world over had thought the city of *Troy* the stuff of legend. That changed when Austrian millionaire-cum-archaeologist, Heinrich Schliemann, discovered the city that was the site of the famous war between the Greeks and the Trojans in the 12th century BC. According to Homer, war broke out when Paris, the son of King Priam of Troy, eloped with Helen, the beautiful wife of Menelaus of Sparta. An army led by Menelaus' brother, Agamemnon, set out in revenge to attack the Trojans. The ensuing war lasted 10 years, until the Greeks made a pretence of retreating. Instead they hid inside a specially-constructed horse, which the Trojans foolishly believed to be a peace offering and took inside their walls,

layout of the palace features a series of interconnected courtyards which progress inwards, from the first, which was open to all citizens, through to the fourth, where the sultans had their gardens and *harem* and private living area. Today visitors can enter the gardens and courtyards, and take a guided tour of the harem to gain an impression of the extravagant lifestyle of the rulers of one of the world's greatest empires.

Transportation
Air: Istanbul Atatürk Airport, Istanbul Sabiha Gökçen International Airport. **Rail:** Train: Sirkeci Station. Tram: Sultanahmet. **Road:** Bus: Public services. Car: E80 or D100 (from Ankara, Izmit or Greece).

Contact Addresses
Topkapi Palace Museum, 34400 Sarayii,

whereupon the cunning Greeks emerged and ransacked the city. The story was made into a successful Hollywood movie called 'Troy' starring Brad Pitt in 2004.

Transportation
Air: Istanbul Atatürk Airport, Istanbul Sabiha Gökçen International Airport, Izmir Adnan Menderes International Airport. **Rail:** Train: Balekesir Station or Bandirma Station. **Road:** Bus: Local Dolmus (minibus) services (from Çanakkale).

Contact Addresses
Canakkale Tourist Informaton Office, Regional Directorate, Valilik Binasi, Kat 1, Canakkale, Turkey
Tel: (0286) 217 5012

P ✖ 🧺 🏛 £ 🏭

Uganda

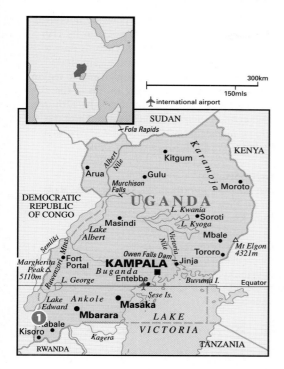

300km
150mls

✈ international airport

SUDAN
~Fola Rapids

Karamoja

KENYA

•Kitgum

•Arua
Albert Nile
Murchison
Falls
•Gulu
•Moroto

DEMOCRATIC
REPUBLIC
OF CONGO

U G A N D A

L. Kwania
•Masindi
L. Kyoga
•Soroti

Lake
Albert

Victoria Nile

Mbale

△ Mt Elgon
4321m

Semliki
Owen Falls Dam
Tororo•

Margherita
Peak △
5110m
•Fort
Portal
KAMPALA
B u g a n d a
•Jinja

Rwenzori Mtns
L. George
Entebbe
Buvuma I.
Equator

Lake
Edward
Ankole
Masaka
•Sese Is.

•Mbarara
L A K E

①Kabale
V I C T O R I A

Kisoro•
Kagera

RWANDA
TANZANIA

---

1 Bwindi Impenetrable National Park

Bwindi Impenetrable National Park

Bwindi Impenetrable National Park, located in southwestern Uganda, on the edge of the western Rift Valley, covers an area of 331 sq km (128 sq miles). The forest, which was designated a UNESCO World Heritage Site in 1994, is a sanctuary for around half the world's mountain gorillas, including the Mubare and the Habinyanja groups. It is also famed for being the home of the Colobus monkey, various species of chimpanzee, hundreds of species of birds and many other animals, including forest birds, snakes, lizards, chameleons and butterflies. As well as animals, the park is home to huge trees covered in creepers, a bamboo zone and rare plants, including mistletoe and orchids. Trekking

Tourist Information

Uganda Tourist Board
PO Box 7211, Impala House, Ground Floor, Kimathi Avenue, Kampala, Uganda
Tel: (041) 342 196/7
Website: www.visituganda.com

High Commission for the Republic of Uganda
Uganda House, 58-59 Trafalgar Square, London WC2N 5DX, UK
Tel: (020) 7839 5783

permits for visitors wishing to see the gorillas are strictly limited and must always be booked in advance.

Transportation
Air: Entebbe International Airport. **Road:** Car: Kabale–Buhoma Road to the park headquarters at Buhoma (from Kabale). Four-wheel drive vehicles are advised.

Contact Addresses
Uganda Wildlife Authority, Plot 3, Kintu Road, Nakasero, PO Box 3530, Kampala, Uganda
Tel: (041) 346 287/8
Website: www.uwa.or.ug

Bwindi Impenetrable National Park

UWA – Uganda Wildlife Authority©

Ukraine

600km
300mls

✈ international airport

BELARUS
RUSSIAN
FEDERATION

POLAND
Rivne● Chornobyl●
●Lviv **KYIV**■ ✈ **Kharkiv**●
U K R A I N E ●Poltava
SLOVAK *Dniester* Kremenchuk● *Dnieper* D O N E T S
HUN● Mt Hoverla **Dnipropetrovsk**● **Donetsk**
2061m Kryvyy Rih●
●Zaporizhzhya
MOLDOVA Mykolayiv *Kakhovska* ●Mariupol
Resvr.
ROMANIA **Odesa**● *Sea*
of Azov
●Izmayil *Crimea*
Simferopol●
Danube Sevastopol●●Yalta
BULGARIA *BLACK SEA*

1 Saint Sophia Cathedral

Tourist Information

Ministry of Foreign Affairs
Mykhailovska Square 1, 01018 Kyiv, Ukraine
Tel: (44) 238 1777
Website: www.mfa.gov.ua

Intourist Travel Ltd
9 Princedale Road, Holland Park, London W11
4NW, UK
Tel: (020) 7792 5240
Website: www.intouristuk.com

Saint Sophia Cathedral

The outstanding *Saint Sophia Cathedral* in *Kiev*
dates back to 1037 when the foundations were
laid under the orders of Prince Yaroslav the Wise.
The impressive cathedral is characterised by its 13
domes (*cupolas*) that dominate the skyline and the
ornate, gold-topped dome of the *Saint Sophia Bell*

Tower. Inside, much of the Byzantine interior is
intact and the cathedral is famous for its 11th
century mosaics and frescoes. There is now a
museum on the site detailing the cathedral's
spiritual and intellectual influence in the region
and how it contributed to the spread of the
Orthodox faith across Russia from the 17th to the
19th century. Saint Sophia Cathedral and the
related monastic buildings were declared as a
UNESCO World Heritage site in 1990.

Transportation
Air: Boryspil International Airport, Kiev. **Rail:**
Train: Kiev Station. **Road:** Bus: Public services
from Kiev Central Station.

Contact Addresses
Kiev-Pechersk Lavra Monastery, 25 Sichnevogo
Povstannya st., 01015 Kiev, Ukraine
Tel. + 380 (44) 254 2257
Website: www.lavra.kiev.ua

P ✗ 🧺 ♿ 🏛 £ 🏭

Saint Sophia Cathedral Bell Tower

Ministry of Foreign Affairs©

United Arab Emirates

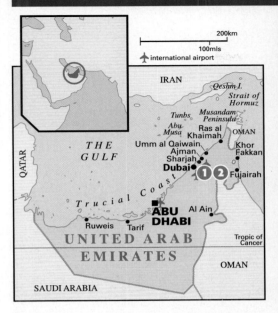

Dubai Spice Souk

1 Dubai Creek
2 Jumeirah Archaeological Site

Tourist Information

Government of Dubai Department of Tourism & Commerce Marketing
National Bank of Dubai Building, 10th–12th Floors, Baniyas Road, Deira, Dubai, UAE
Tel: (4) 223 0000
Website: www.dubaitourism.ae

Government of Dubai Department of Tourism & Commerce Marketing
1st Floor, 125 Pall Mall, London SW1Y 5EA, UK
Tel: (020) 7839 0580
Website: www.dubaitourism.ae

Key to symbols: £ Entry charged & Disabled access ⏚ Man-made attraction ❤ Natural attraction ℗ Parking ✘ Restaurant ⛺ Shop ⛫ UNESCO site

Dubai Creek

The 14km (8.7 mile) *Dubai Creek* is a natural seawater inlet that divides the city of Dubai into two parts – *Deira Dubai* and *Bur Dubai* – and has been the heart and soul of the city ever since it was a center for pearl fishing and the pearl trade. Long established for its ancient sea routes that reached as far as India and the East African coast, the Creek was originally only deep enough to accommodate smaller vessels and goods had to be transferred to traditional Arab sailing dhows at the entrance to the Creek. Recognising the Creek's strategic importance to the region, it was deepened in the 1960s and today functions as a vibrant port and vital part of the city with eight wharfages, each capable of catering to 31 ships of up to 800 tonnes in capacity. Around 720,000 tonnes of cargo pass through the port each year but only wooden ships are allowed to enter the creek in order to maintain its traditional appearance. Abras (small wooden boats) serve as taxis for those who want to cross from the Deira side to the Bur Dubai side. A wildlife sanctuary that's home to over 27,000 birds has been set up at the inland end of

Dubai Creek at night

Images provided by The Government of Dubai, Department of Tourism and Commerce Marketing©

the Creek. Reflecting the wealth of one of the fastest growing economies in the world, boutique hotels, golf courses and yachting clubs have sprung up along the Creek's banks.

Transportation

Air: Dubai International Airport. **Water:** Water taxis operate between Dubai and Deira. **Rail:** Currently no rail network but construction of a rail and underground network is underway. **Road:** Bus: Public services.

Contact Addresses

For more information on the Dubai Creek, contact the Department of Tourism (see **Tourist Information** above).

Jumeirah Archaeological Site

The archaeological site at *Jumeirah* is thought to date back to the sixth century AD and was the site of a caravan station along an ancient trade route through the desert that linked Iraq to Oman. It's one of the most significant archaeological sites in the United Arab Emirates with sections of walling, a souq and houses – one of which is thought to have been the governor's palace all having been found at the site. Other finds, such as pottery, tools and coins, are on display at the *Heritage Village* in Diera.

Transportation

Air: Dubai International Airport. **Water:** Water taxis operate between Dubai and Deira. **Rail:** Currently no rail network but construction of a rail and underground network are underway. **Road:** Bus: Public services.

Contact Addresses

For more information on the Jumeirah Archaeological site, contact the Department of Tourism (see **Tourist Information** above).

United Kingdom

Channel Islands, Guernsey

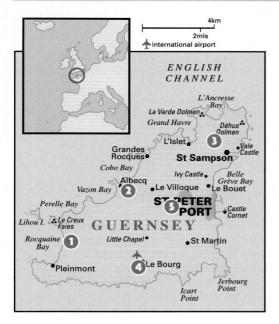

4km
2mls
✈ international airport

1 Fort Grey Shipwreck Museum
2 German Underground Hospital
3 Oatlands Craft Centre
4 Occupation Museum
5 Victor Hugo's House

Tourist Information

Visit Guernsey
PO Box 23, St Peter Port, Guernsey, Channel
Islands GY1 3AN, UK
Tel: (01481) 723 552
Website: www.visitguernsey.com

Jersey Tourism
Liberation Square, St Helier, Jersey JE1 1BB,
Channel Islands
Tel: (01534) 500 700 or 500 777 (general
visitor enquiries) or 500 800 (brochure line)
or 500 888 (accommodation reservations)
Website: www.jersey.com

Fort Grey Shipwreck Museum

Located on the island's rocky west coast, *Fort Grey
Shipwreck Museum* was built in 1804 as part of the
island's defences against French attacks. It was
restored in 1976 and turned into a popular visitor
attraction. Overlooking the *Hanois Reefs,* many
ships have sunk off its shores and a small
museum housed within the small *Martello Tower*
tells the maritime history of the region. The
museum is closed during the winter months.

Transportation
Air: Guernsey International Airport. **Water:** Ferry:
Services to St Peter Port. **Road:** Bus: Public
services.

Contact Addresses
Rocquaine Coast Road, St. Peters, Guernsey
Tel: (0)1481 265 036
Website: www.museum.guernsey.net

P ✗ 🛒 ♿ £ 🛥

German Underground Hospital

The incredible complex of tunnels at the *German
Underground Hospital* is the largest construction in
the *Channel Islands* and was hewn out of solid
rock by forced labourers of many nationalities
during the German occupation of the island
during the Second World War. Measuring 7,000 sq
m (75,348 sq ft), the complex consists of two sets
of nine parallel tunnels which were originally
built as shelters for the German forces. It was later
used as an underground hospital and could house
up to 1,000 patients in times of emergency.
Visitors enter the complex through an entrance
that is barely visible from above ground. The
Underground Hospital is only open during the
summer months.

Transportation
Air: Guernsey International Airport. **Water:** Ferry:
Services to St Peter Port. **Road:** Bus: Public
services.

Fort Grey maritime museum, also known as 'the cup and saucer'

Visit Guernsey©

Contact Addresses
Les Eperons, La Vassalerie, Guernsey, GY6 8XR
Tel: (01481) 239100

P £ 🎢

Oatlands Craft Centre

The *Oatlands Craft Centre* in the north of the
island provides visitors with the opportunity to
watch local craftspeople at work at a number of
different traditional industries. *Guernsey* is famed
for its dairy herds and visitors are able to see
traditional cheese makers at work and sample
some of the famous products. There are also some
traditional brick kilns that were built in 1892 and
visitors can see how these craftspeople once
worked. Other craftspeople exhibiting their work
at the centre include glass blowers, potters and
silversmiths. There's also a small farm at the
centre where visitors can see how a traditional
farm was managed and run. There's a children's
play area too that's staffed by professional carers.

Transportation
Air: Guernsey International Airport. **Water:** Ferry:
Services to St Peter Port. **Road:** Bus: Public services.

Contact Addresses
Les Gigands, Braye Road, St Sampson's, Guernsey
Tel: (01481) 244282

P ✗ 🧺 ♿ 🎢

Occupation Museum

Opened in 1966 by Richard Heaume, a founder
member of the *Occupation Society*, the *German*

Occupation Museum has one of the most extensive
collections of war memorabilia on the island. The
museum has many artefacts and exhibits covering
the five years of German occupation during WWII
from 1940 to 1945. There are also two fortification
sites that are the property of the museum that have
been faithfully restored and are open to visitors.

Transportation
Air: Guernsey International Airport. **Water:** Ferry:
Services to St Peter Port. **Road:** Bus: Public services.

Contact Addresses
German Occupation Museum, Les Houards, Forest,
Guernsey GY8 0BG
Tel: (01481) 238205

P ✗ 🧺 ♿ £ 🎢

Victor Hugo's House

Born in France in 1802, the island's most famous
resident was the poet and writer Victor Hugo whose
celebrated works include 'Notre Dame de Paris' and
'Les Miérables', the latter which he actually
completed in Guernsey. Hugo's outspoken political
views led to his expulsion from France and his
arrival in Guernsey in 1855. The following year he
published a collection of his poetry called Les
Contemplations which was a big success. With the
money it earned he bought *Hauteville House* which
is now a popular visitor attraction on the island.
Although legally entitled to return to France in
1859, he chose to reside on the island he adored
until 1870 when Louis Bonaparte fell from power.
Hauteville House is a large distinctive white
building with a commanding position that overlooks
the sea. Hugo was an avid collector of eccentric
furniture and bric-a-brac and today visitors are able
to wander through the house and grounds which
has been preserved as it was when Hugo lived there.

Transportation
Air: Guernsey International Airport. **Water:** Ferry:
Services to St Peter Port. **Road:** Bus: Public services.

Contact Addresses
For more information about Victor Hugo's House,
contact the Visit Guernsey (see **Tourist
Information** above).

P ✗ 🧺 ♿ £ 🎢

Channel Islands, Jersey

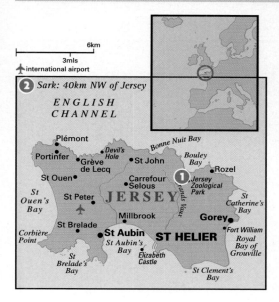

6km
3mls
✈ international airport

② Sark: 40km NW of Jersey

ENGLISH CHANNEL

Plémont
Portinfer • Devil's Hole
Grève de Lecq • St John
Bonne Nuit Bay
Bouley Bay
St Ouen • Rozel
Carrefour Selous
① Jersey Zoological Park
St Ouen's Bay
St Peter
JERSEY
St Catherine's Bay
Millbrook
Gorey
Corbière Point
St Brelade
St Aubin • Fort William
ST HELIER
Royal Bay of Grouville
St Aubin's Bay
St Brelade's Bay
Elizabeth Castle
St Clement's Bay

1 Jersey Zoo
2 Sark

Jersey Zoo

Jersey Zoo was established in 1959 by Gerald Durrell (1925-1995) and is located around his home, *Les Augrès Manor*, where Durrell's widow, Dr Lee Durrell, still lives. The manor is also the headquarters of the *Durrell Wildlife Conservation Trust*. At just 12.55 hectares (31 acres), Jersey Zoo is relatively small but it is still one of the island's most popular attractions focussing as it does on providing safe habitats for some of the world's most endangered species. There's a strong emphasis on education and there are many interactive displays aimed at promoting awareness about animal conservation. Two of the most popular enclosures at the zoo include the orang-utan and gorilla parks. In addition to providing an attraction for visitors, the zoo also manages many research and breeding programmes and is committed to animal conservation. The zoo also has its own organic farm to ensure its animals get chemical-free produce.

Transportation
Air: St Peters International Airport. **Water:** Ferry: Services to Jersey Port. **Road:** Bus: Public services.

Contact Addresses
Durrell Wildlife Conservation Trust, Les Augrés Manor, La Profonde Rue, Trinity, Jersey JE3 5BP
Tel: (01534) 860000
Website: www.durrellwildlife.org

Sark

Located approximately 128.75km (80 miles) south of the English Coast, the island of *Sark* is the smallest of the four *Channel Islands*. Sark stands as the smallest independent feudal state in Europe and has belonged to the British Crown since the time of William the Conqueror when it, along with the other *Channel Islands*, formed part of the *Duchy of Normandy*. King John retained the islands when the Duchy of Normandy was returned to the French in the 13th century. Aside from the island's unique history, Sark is a car-free zone so offers visitors a unique and tranquil experience. Its 65km (40 miles) of dramatic coastline is peppered with caves, bays and picturesque inlets, many of which can be accessed via a network of paths and walkways. The island supports a wide variety of flora and fauna and its spectacular coastal paths are popular with ramblers and bird watchers. Manmade attractions include the *Sark Lighthouse* built in 1912, the *Harbour* and the island *Prison* which was built in 1856 and is still in use today.

Transportation
Air: Guernsey International Airport or St Peters Airport on Jersey then ferry services to Sark.
Water: Ferry: Services to Sark Harbour. **Road:** Motorised vehicles are banned from the island but bicycles are available for hire.

Contact Addresses
Isle of Sark Tourism
Tel: (01481) 832345
Website: www.sark-tourism.com

England

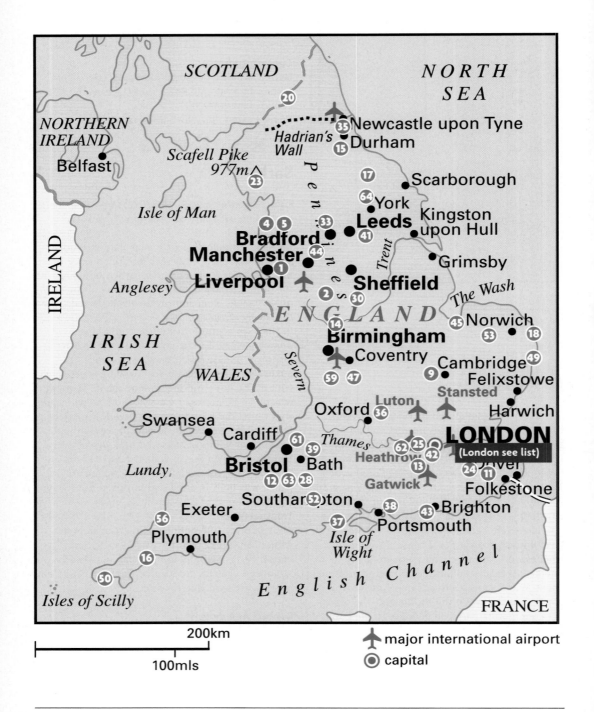

SCOTLAND

NORTH SEA

NORTHERN IRELAND

Belfast

Scafell Pike 977m△

Hadrian's Wall

20

35 Newcastle upon Tyne

15 Durham

23

17

64 York

33

Leeds

41

Isle of Man

Scarborough

Kingston upon Hull

Bradford

4 5

Manchester

44

1

Liverpool

2

Anglesey

Grimsby

Sheffield

30

The Wash

ENGLAND

45 Norwich

53

18

14

Birmingham

Coventry

Cambridge

49

9

Felixstowe

59 47

Stansted

Severn

Oxford

Luton

36

Harwich

WALES

LONDON
(London see list)

Swansea

Cardiff

61

39

Thames

62 25

42

Dover

Heathrow

13

24 11

Bristol

Bath

12 63 28

Gatwick

Folkestone

Lundy

Southampton

52

38

43 Brighton

37

Portsmouth

Exeter

56

Plymouth

16

Isle of Wight

English Channel

50

FRANCE

Isles of Scilly

Pennines

Trent

IRELAND

IRISH SEA

200km

100mls

✈ major international airport

◉ capital

Tourist Information

British Tourist Authority
Thames Tower, Black's Road, Hammersmith, London W6 9EL, UK
Tel: (020) 8846 9000
Website: www.visitbritain.com

1 Albert Dock
2 Alton Towers
3 Big Ben and the Houses of Parliament (London)
4 Blackpool Pleasure Beach
5 Blackpool Tower
6 British Airways London Eye (London)
7 British Museum (London)
8 Buckingham Palace (London)
9 Cambridge University
10 Camden Market (London)
11 Canterbury Cathedral
12 Cheddar Caves and Gorge
13 Chessington World of Adventures
14 Drayton Manor Theme Park
15 Durham Castle and Cathedral
16 Eden Project
17 Flamingo Land Theme Park and Zoo
18 Yarmouth Pleasure Beach
19 Greenwich (London)
20 Hadrians Wall
21 Hampton Court Palace
22 Harrods (London)
23 Lake Windermere
24 Leeds Castle
25 Legoland Windsor
26 London Dungeon (London)
27 London Zoo (London)
28 Longleat
29 Madame Tussaud's and Tussaud's London Planetarium (London)
30 Matlock Bath
31 National Gallery (London)
32 National Museum of Photography, Film and Television
33 Natural History Museum (London)
34 Neasden Temple (London)
35 New Metroland
36 Oxford University
37 Poole Harbour
38 Portsmouth Historic Dockyard
39 Roman Baths and Pump Room
40 Royal Academy of Arts (London)
41 Royal Armouries Leeds
42 Royal Botanic Gardens, Kew
43 Royal Pavilion
44 Salford Quays
45 Sandringham Estate
46 Science Museum (London)
47 Shakespeare Houses
48 Somerset House (London)
49 Southwold
50 St Michael's Mount
51 St Paul's Cathedral (London)
52 Stonehenge
53 Swaffam I Ecotech Centre
54 Tate Britain (London)
55 Tate Modern (London)
56 Tintagel Castle
57 Tower of London (London)
58 Victoria and Albert Museum (London)
59 Warwick Castle
60 Westminster Abbey (London)
61 Westonbirt Arboretum
62 Windsor Castle
63 Wookey Hole Caves
64 York Minster

Albert Dock

Recognised for its historic importance, Liverpool's *Maritime Mercantile City* was inscribed onto UNESCO's World Heritage List in 2004 to help preserve one of the world's most recognisable ports as a historic site. In the 19th century, the city of Liverpool was a flourishing export and passenger port that employed thousands of workers from around Britain and Ireland, and it was from here that many set sail for new lives in America. With the decline of the British Empire, the area fell into disrepair until the city council embarked upon a major renewal project in the 1980s. The centrepiece of this project is the *Albert Dock*, 3 hectares (7 acres) of water surrounded by renovated warehouses with iron colonnades. The warehouses have been converted into lively spaces for restaurants, shops and cafés, interspersed with museums chronicling the city's contribution to British history and culture. *The Beatles Story*, dedicated to the famous Fab Four, is one of Liverpool's top attractions, featuring a replica of the Cavern Club where the group performed in the early days alongside posters, personal memorabilia, and other displays. The area is also home to the *Tate Gallery Liverpool*, Britain's largest gallery of contemporary art outside London, featuring displays of art from the Tate museums in London.

Transportation
Air: Liverpool Airport, Manchester Airport. **Rail:** Train: Liverpool Lime Street Station. **Road:** Bus: Public services.

Contact Addresses
22 Edward Pavilion, Albert Dock, Liverpool
L3 4AF, UK
Tel: (0151) 708 7334
Website: www.albertdock.com

Alton Towers

Alton Towers is the most popular theme park in the UK. Set on an estate owned by the Earl of Shrewsbury, this amusement park has a wide range of rides and attractions aimed at young and old alike. The park, which opened in 1980, also includes 200 acres (81 hectares) of landscaped gardens, live entertainment and the historic towers building which was the residence of the Talbot family (the Earls of Shrewsbury) until 1923. Today, visitors can explore different kingdoms in the grounds of the estate, such as *Ugland*, the *Forbidden Valley*, *Towers Street* and *Cred Street*. Popular rides include the *Black Hole*, the famous *Corkscrew* and *Nemesis* rollercoasters and the *Log Flume* water slide. New for 2005 is *Rita - Queen of Speed* rollercoaster.

Transportation
Air: Manchester Airport. **Rail:** Train: Alton Towers Station. Buses are available to take visitors to the park. **Road:** Coach: Public services.

Contact Addresses
Alton Towers, Staffordshire, ST10 4DB, UK
Tel: (08705) 204 060
Website: www.altontowers.com

Big Ben and the Houses of Parliament

The elaborate neo-Gothic *Palace of Westminster*, gracefully located beside the River Thames, is one of London's most iconic images. The adjoining clock tower, *St Stephen's*, is often mistakenly assumed to be called *Big Ben*, although this is actually the name of the bell inside. Big Ben rings every hour on the hour and is shown on British television at midnight on December 31 to count in the New Year. The original Palace of Westminster, constructed in the 12th century by Edward the Confessor and enlarged by William the Conqueror, was used as a royal palace until 1512 when it was damaged by fire. It only became the seat of the British government in the mid-16th century, and was rebuilt in its current style, to designs by architect Sir Charles Barry, after it was completely ravaged by fire in 1834. There are special guided tours of the building through August to October but foreign visitors are no longer able to tour the Houses of Parliament during session.

Transportation
Air: London Heathrow Airport, London Gatwick Airport, London Stansted Airport, London Luton Airport. **Rail:** Train: London Victoria Station or London Waterloo Station. Underground:

Westminster (Circle, District or Jubilee lines).
Road: Bus: Public services.

Contact Addresses
House of Commons Information Office,
Westminster, London SW1A 0AA, UK
Tel: (020) 7219 4272
Website: www.parliament.uk

Blackpool Pleasure Beach

Blackpool Tower

The city of Blackpool has been attracting holiday
visitors ever since 1735, when the first guest
house opened. In the 19th century, it became a
popular working-class destination among the
British and, in 1896, *Blackpool Pleasure Beach* was
opened. Today, this American-style amusement
park with a distinctly British feel has a variety of
rides to suit all tastes and ages. Rides suitable for
children include the parks' oldest attraction, a
centrifugal rocket ride called *Flying Machines*.
Valhalla, which opened in 2000, is the world's
biggest ride in the dark. There are also several
shows to entertain visitors, such as *Eclipse at the
Globe*, featuring acrobats, aerialists and dancers,
and a separate *Beaver Creek* theme park with rides
aimed specifically at children. Entrance to the
park is free but rides are paid for.

Transportation
Air: Manchester Airport, Blackpool Airport
(domestic flights). **Rail:** Train: Blackpool North
Station or Blackpool Pleasure Beach Station.
Road: Bus: Public services.

Contact Addresses
Blackpool Pleasure Beach, 525 Ocean Boulevard,
South Shore, Blackpool, Lancashire FY4 1EZ, UK
Tel: (0870) 444 5566
Website: www.blackpoolpleasurebeach.com

Blackpool Tower

The 156-m (518-ft) *Blackpool Tower* houses a
ballroom, an aquarium and play area and
dominates the skyline along Blackpool's lively
promenade. Most visitors head to the top of the
tower for views back across the city or out across

the Irish Sea. The viewing deck includes the *Walk
of Faith*, a clear glass platform enabling visitors to
see the world passing by beneath their feet.
Attractions at the tower include the *Tower Circus*
featuring traditional acts. In 2004, the circus
introduced workshops where children can learn
skills such as plate spinning, juggling and
acrobatics. Also for the younger visitors, *Jungle
Jims* is one of Europe's biggest indoor adventure
playgrounds featuring ball pools, slides and
climbing nets. The famous *Blackpool Tower
Ballroom* hosts dances and concerts in its ornate
halls.

Transportation
Air: Blackpool Airport. **Rail:** Blackpool Station.
Road: Bus: Public services. Car: M55 links
Blackpool with the M6.

Contact Addresses
Blackpool Tower, Promenade, Blackpool,
Lancashire FY1 4BJ, UK
Tel: (01253) 292029
Website: www.blackpooltower.co.uk

British Airways
London Eye

The Flat Earth Collection©

British Airways London Eye

At 135m (443ft) tall, the *British Airways London Eye* is the world's largest observation wheel and the fourth tallest structure in London. Designed by Marks Barfield Architects and managed by the Tussaud's Group, the wheel was erected in 1999. It differs from a ferris wheel in that it has an A-frame support structure on only one side, while the pods are located on the exterior. These are stabilised by internal motors that keep them horizontal as the wheel slowly moves around. The structure has 32 separate capsules that rotate and can carry up to 25 people at any one time, taking passengers on a 30-minute trip high above London's skyline. Designed to be visually appealing from the exterior, the wheel provides staggering views of central London to a distance as far away as 40km (25 miles) on clear days. The London Eye continues to be one of the UK's most visited paid for attractions.

Transportation
Air: London Heathrow Airport or London Gatwick Airport. **Water:** The Tate Boat runs along the Thames between Tate Britain, the London Eye and Tate Modern. **Rail:** Train: London Waterloo Station or London Charing Cross Station. Underground: Westminster (Circle and District lines), Waterloo (Bakerloo, Jubilee or Northern lines), Embankment (Bakerloo, Circle, District or Northern lines). **Road:** Bus: Public services for the South Bank.

Contact Addresses
British Airways London Eye, Customer Services, Riverside Building, County Hall, Westminster Bridge Road, London SE1 7PB, UK
Tel: (0870) 500 0600 *or* (0870) 990 8883
Website: www.ba-londoneye.com

P ✕ 🧺 ♿ £ 🏔

British Museum

The British Museum was founded in 1753 to promote a better public understanding of the arts, natural history and science. It contains one of the world's greatest displays of antiquities, documenting the rise and fall of civilisations from all over the world. The museum opened to the public in 1759, with the famous Rosetta Stone being presented to the museum in 1802, along with many other Egyptian antiquities. As well as the Rosetta Stone, the museum also houses many other famous objects including the Elgin Marbles, currently at the centre of debate as to whether they should be returned to Greece. Today, the museum's collection, which is in excess of six million objects, comprises art and antiquities from Egypt, Western Asia, Greece, Rome and Europe, amongst others. The spectacular Great Court, with its impressive glass roof, was opened in 2000, following the relocation of the British Library to St Pancras, and is the largest covered public square in Europe. Entry is free but there is a charge for some temporary exhibitions.

Transportation
Air: London Heathrow Airport. **Rail:** Train: London Kings Cross Station. Underground: Holborn (Central and Piccadilly lines), Tottenham Court Road (Central and Northern lines) or Russell Square (Piccadilly Line). **Road:** Bus: Public services.

Contact Addresses
British Museum, Great Russell Street, London WC1B 3DG, UK
Tel: (020) 7323 8000
Website: www.thebritishmuseum.ac.uk

✕ 🧺 ♿ 🏔

Buckingham Palace

Work began on *Buckingham Palace* in 1702 and has been the official London residence of the British Royal Family since 1837. After several expansions, the palace now has a total of 52 bedrooms, 78 bathrooms and 92 offices. The palace enjoys an imposing location in the centre of London, opposite *St James's Park*. Every year, millions of visitors come to see the *Changing of the Guard* ceremony, which takes place outside the palace at 1130 daily from April to July and on alternate days at other times of the year. Visitors can also tour the inside of the palace during the summer months. The *Ball Room*, which is the largest room in the palace, opened to the public for the first time in 2000. The 19 *State Rooms* at the palace, which include the *Throne Room* and the *Picture Gallery*, house treasures including English and French furniture, paintings by Rembrandt and Rubens and sculpture by Canaletto. Visitors can also see inside the *Royal Mews*, which is one of the grandest working stables in the world.

Transportation
Air: London Heathrow Airport. **Rail:** Train: London Victoria Station. Underground: St James's Park (District or Circle lines); Victoria (Victoria, District or Circle lines); Green Park (Piccadilly, Jubilee or Victoria lines). **Road:** Bus: Public services.

Contact Addresses
Buckingham Palace, Buckingham Palace Road, London SW1A 1AA, UK
Tel: (020) 7839 1377
Website: www.royal.gov.uk

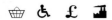

Cambridge University

Cambridge University is the second oldest university in England, and shares with Oxford University an unrivalled reputation for excellence and tradition. Founded in the 13th century by scholars from universities in Oxford and Paris, its distinguished alumni include Sir Isaac Newton, John Milton and Stephen Hawking. The university's various colleges, many of them architectural masterpieces, are scattered throughout the city. *St John's College* was founded by Lady Margaret Beaufort, mother of King Henry VII, in 1511 and contains the *New Bridge*, often referred to as Cambridge's *Bridge of Sighs*. *Kings College* is perhaps the most famous of all the colleges due to its magnificent *chapel*, built between 1446 and 1515; the choir's Christmas Eve service of nine lessons and carols is internationally renowned, and constitutes an integral part of the festive season in Britain. *Trinity College*, founded in 1546 by King Henry VIII, who hoped it would produce the future leaders of the reformed Church of England, is the largest college.

Transportation
Air: London Heathrow Airport, London Gatwick Airport, London Stansted Airport, London Luton Airport. **Rail:** Train: Cambridge Station. **Road:** Bus: Public services including Park and Ride.

Contact Addresses
Tourist Information Centre and Shop, The Old Library, Wheeler Street, Cambridge CB2 3QB, UK
Tel: (01223) 322 640
Website: www.tourismcambridge.com

Camden Market

Camden Market is the largest street market in the UK that attracts around 100,000 visitors every weekend. There are various markets located in *Camden Town*, which are collectively known as *Camden Market*; these are *Camden Lock Market*, *Camden Canal Market*, *Inverness Street Market*, *Camden (Bute Street) Market* and *Camden Stables Market*. The area around *Camden Lock* was first developed in around 1791 by the Earl of Camden, with the famous Regent's Canal opening in 1820. The first market to appear in Camden was *Camden Lock Market*, which opened in 1972. Today, there are hundreds of stalls selling a wide array of goods, including arts and crafts, vintage clothes, second-hand household items, records and CDs, jewellery and exotic food.

Transportation
Air: London Heathrow Airport. **Rail:** Train: Camden Road Station and Kentish Town Station. Underground: Camden Town, Chalk Farm or Mornington Crescent (Northern Line). **Road:** Bus: Public services.

Contact Addresses

Camden Lock Limited, 56 Camden Lock Place,
Chalk Farm Road, London NW1 8AF, UK
Tel: (020) 7284 2084
Website: www.camdenlockmarket.com

Canterbury Cathedral

Canterbury Cathedral's history as a religious site
dates back to AD 597 when Pope Gregory's
missionary, St Augustine, was given a church in
the town by King Ethelbert. The cathedral is a
masterpiece of Romanesque and Gothic
architecture. Inside, visitors can see stained glass
windows dating from the 12th century and the
medieval tombs of King Henry IV and Edward the
Black Prince, as well as those of numerous
archbishops. The cathedral is also the former site
of the shrine to the Archbishop Thomas Becket,
who was murdered in the northwest transept in
1170. His shrine, which was desecrated in 1538
during the Reformation, became one of the most
visited by pilgrims during the Middle Ages, many
of whom travelled the famous Pilgrims' Way from
Winchester to see it.

Transportation

Air: London Gatwick Airport. **Rail:** Train:
Canterbury East Station or Canterbury West
Station. **Road:** Bus: Canterbury Bus Station.
Coach: Public services. Car: M26, M20 and A28 or
A2 and M2 (from the M25). There are tourist signs
to the Cathedral.

Contact Addresses

Canterbury Cathedral, Cathedral House, 11 The
Precincts, Canterbury CT1 2EH, UK
Tel: (01227) 762 862
Website: www.canterbury-cathedral.org

Cheddar Caves and Gorge

Parts of the spectacular *Cheddar Caves and Gorge*
complex have been attracting visitors for over
200 years. The largest and most famous cave is
Gough's Cave, so named because it was
discovered by a Sea Captain named Richard
Gough in 1890. It stretches 0.4km (0.25 miles)

underground and is often referred to as a
cathedral because of the vast caverns – such as
the magnificent *Diamond Chamber* and *Solomon's
Temple* – that were carved out by Ice Age melt
waters over a million years ago. When Gough's
Cave was blasted with dynamite to open it up
for further exploration, archaeologists
discovered what's now known as *Cheddar Man*,
the oldest complete skeleton found in Britain
that's thought to date back over 9,000 years.
Other archaeological finds date human
habitation in and around the site back over
40,000 years. The smaller *Cox's Cave* was
discovered by local mill owner George Cox in
1837 when one of his workers fell through a
hole in the roof of the cave whilst collecting
rocks for a new building. Above ground, a series
of 274 steps known as *Jacob's Ladder* take
visitors from the foot of Britain's biggest gorge
to the very top where the *Lookout Tower* and the
cliff top *Gorge Walk* are located. Caving,
climbing and abseiling courses can also be
arranged at the site.

Transportation

Air: Bristol International Airport. **Rail:** Bristol
Station or Weston-Super-Mare Station. **Road:** Bus:
Public services. Car: B3135.

Contact Addresses

Cheddar Caves and Gorge, Cheddar, Somerset
BS27 3QF, UK
Tel: 01934 742343
Website: www.cheddarcaves.co.uk

Chessington World of Adventures

Chessington World of Adventures is the biggest
theme park and zoo in the South of England. The
park began life as a zoo, but was transformed into
a theme park during the late 1980s, with the first
rollercoaster ride opening in 1991. The park
attracts thousands of visitors each day who come
to enjoy the rides and zoo. The latter, which has
been combined with the park, is home to one of
the biggest families of gorillas in Europe and some
of the world's rarest large cats. The *Trail of the
Kings* animal enclosure allows visitors to see
animals safely from behind viewing screens.

VisitBritain©

Transportation

Air: London Heathrow Airport, London Gatwick Airport. **Rail:** Train: Chessington South Station. **Road:** Bus: Public services. Car: M25, junction 9 and then the A243 towards central London (from the south); A3 to Hook, then A243 to Chessington (from Central London).

Contact Addresses

Chessington World of Adventures, Chessington, Surrey KT9 2NE, UK
Tel: (0870) 999 0045
Website: www.chessington.com

Drayton Manor Theme Park

Drayton Manor Theme Park is set in 280 acres (113 hectares) of lakes and parkland and offers a fun day out for young and old alike. Thrill seekers will enjoy rides such as *Cyclone*, *Shockwave*, *Pandemonium*, *G-Force* and *Apocalypse* – the world's first stand-up drop tower. There's also a zoo that's home to over 100 species from all over the world including big cats, monkeys, reptiles and an exotic creature reserve. In addition to the theme park and zoo, Drayton Manor also hosts wedding receptions and corporate events in its function rooms.

Chessington World of Adventures

Transportation

Air: Birmingham International Airport. **Rail:** Tamworth Station. **Road:** Bus: Public services. Car: A4091.

Contact Addresses

Drayton Manor Park, near Tamworth, Staffordshire B78 3TW, UK
Tel: 08708 725252
Website: www.draytonmanor.co.uk

Durham Castle and Cathedral

Durham Castle and *Cathedral*, seated high on a peninsula overlooking the River Wear, have been the first sight to greet visitors to this historic city for hundreds of years and were jointly designated a UNESCO World Heritage Site in 1986. Construction on the castle began in 1072, just after the Norman Conquest, under the orders of William the Conqueror. From the 11th century onwards it was used as the seat of power of the Prince Bishops appointed by the British Crown to rule the Palatinate of Durham, the remote area of northern England vulnerable to attack from the Scots. In 1837, the last Prince Bishop, Bishop Van Mildert, helped found the *University of Durham* and donated the castle as its first home. It still houses students of *University College*, the oldest of the 14 university colleges, who live in the keep and dine in the wood-panelled Great Hall, containing portraits of the Prince Bishops. Across the lawned area, known as Palace Green, stands the *Cathedral Church of Christ and Blessed Mary the Virgin*, the best example of Norman-style architecture in England.

Transportation

Air: Newcastle Airport. **Rail:** Train: Durham Station. **Road:** Coach: Durham Bus Station. Car: A1 (to Junction 62), then A690 (from London, the Midlands, Scotland or Newcastle). Visitors should avoid driving in the city centre where possible, as the streets are very narrow. The site is a short walk from the bus and train stations.

Contact Addresses

Castle: Durham Castle, Palace Green, Durham DH1 3RW, UK
Tel: (0191) 374 3863
Website: www.durhamcastle.com

Cathedral: The Dean and Chapter of Durham Cathedral, The Chapter Office, The College, Durham DH1 3EH, UK
Tel: (0191) 386 4266
Website: www.durhamcathedral.co.uk

Eden Project

Opened in March 2001, the *Eden Project* consists of two enormous greenhouses built into a 50m- (164ft-) deep claypit overlooking St Austell Bay in Cornwall. Through plants, the dome promotes environmental awareness enabling visitors to understand 'the vital relationship between plants, people and resources'. The most impressive of the two giant domes is the *Humid Tropics Biome* that's filled with towering plants from the tropics, including balsa teak and mahogany, and there is also a Malaysian stilt house and garden as an example of how one culture uses its natural resources to survive. The second dome, the *Warm Temperate Biome*, contains plants from California, the Mediterranean and South Africa, such as lemon groves and olive trees. Visitors follow a path around the biomes, stopping to hear talks and sketches on the plants and learn about their uses from interactive displays; for those with a particular interest, there are themed trails, such as plants and medicine and plants and sport. Outside, 10 hectares (25 acres) of landscaped rockeries and gardens provide the setting for various events, including puppet shows and storytelling for children; visitors of all ages can discover more about natural products through chocolate days, tea-tasting and dyeing workshops.

Transportation
Air: Exeter International Airport, Southampton International Airport, Bristol International Airport, Plymouth City Airport or Newquay Airport. **Rail:** Train: St Austell Station. **Road:** Bus: Public services.

Contact Addresses
Eden Project, Bodelva, St Austell, Cornwall PL24 2SG, UK
Tel: (01726) 811 911
Website: www.edenproject.com

Flamingo Land Theme Park and Zoo

Flamingo Land in north Yorkshire is one of the region's biggest theme parks and zoos and receives over one million visitors each year. The zoo is home to over 1,000 animals including White Rhinos, Siberian Tigers, Bactrian Camels, Humboldt Penguins and meerkats. There is also a Children's Farm aimed at teaching younger visitors about the realities of a traditional working farm. The Theme Park has a wide range of rides and attractions and a new rollercoaster, Velocity, opened in July 2005.

Transportation
Air: Leeds Bradford International Airport. **Rail:** York Railway Station. **Road:** Bus: Publis services.

Contact Addresses
Flamingo Land Holiday Village, Kirby Misperton, Malton, North Yorkshire YO17 6UX, UK
Tel: 0870 752 8000
Website: www.flamingoland.co.uk

Great Yarmouth Pleasure Beach

Great Yarmouth's *Pleasure Beach* is set along a 3.6 hectare (9 acre) seafront site on the picturesque East Anglian coastline. The Pleasure Beach is a traditional seaside resort built around a lively promenade and is a popular attraction for families. The Pleasure Beach's attractions include traditional fairground rides, arcades, flower gardens, mini golf and candy floss and ice cream stalls. It may have lost some of its grandeur but it nevertheless remains one of the most popular attractions in East Anglia and attracts close to 1.5 million visitors each year.

Transportation
Air: Norwich Airport and Stansted Airport. **Rail:** Norwich Railway Station with links to Great Yarmouth Station. **Road:** Bus: Public services.

VisitBritain©

Greenwich Park and the Observatory

Contact Addresses
Great Yarmouth Pleasure Beach, Pleasure and
Corporation Plc, South Beach Parade, Great
Yarmouth, Norfolk NR30 3EH
Tel: 01493 844 585
Website: www.pleasure-beach.co.uk

P ✗ 🧺 ♿ £ ⛴

Greenwich

The *London Borough of Greenwich*, which is
situated on south of the River Thames, is home to
a host of attractions, and recognised
internationally for its military and naval
connections and as the home of Greenwich Mean
Time. Famous sites in Greenwich include the
Cutty Sark Clipper Ship (www.cuttysark.org.uk),
built in 1869, *Greenwich Market* (www.greenwich-
market.co.uk), and the *Royal Observatory
Greenwich*. The latter was designed by the
famous architect, Sir Christopher Wren in the
17th century and is home to the *Greenwich
Meridian*, the prime meridian of the world,
responsible for setting the world clock on zero
degrees longitude. The *National Maritime Museum*
(www.nmm.ac.uk), the largest maritime museum
in the world, and the *Old Royal Naval College*

(www.greenwichfoundation.org.uk), which
began life as Greenwich Hospital in 1694 to
treat seamen, are also located in Greenwich.
The borough has an historic past and was the
birthplace of King Henry VIII and Queen Elizabeth
I. The area also boasts many open
green spaces, including *Greenwich Park*
(www.royalparks.gov.uk/parks/greenwich_park),
which forms one of eight royal parks in the
capital and is the only royal park in East London;
it is actually home to the Royal Observatory
Greenwich, the National Maritime Museum and
the Old Royal Naval College. The *Millennium Dome*
(www.millennium-dome.com) is also situated in
Greenwich and is visible across London's skyline.
Greenwich town centre and park was inscribed as
a UNESCO World Heritage Site in 1997, under the
name 'Maritime Greenwich'. The whole area boasts
a wide selection of restaurants and shops, and is a
magnet for shoppers in search of interesting or
unusual gifts or souvenirs.

Transportation
Air: London City Airport, London Gatwick
Airport, London Heathrow Airport. **Rail:** Train:
Greenwich Station or Maze Hill Station.
Docklands Light Railway: Cutty Sark Station or
Greenwich Station. **Road:** Bus: Public services.

Contact Addresses

Greenwich Tourist Information Centre, Pepys
House, 2 Cutty Sark Gardens, Greenwich,
London SE10 9LW, UK
Tel: (0870) 608 2000
Website: www.greenwich.gov.uk

Hadrian's Wall

Built by order of the Emperor Hadrian in AD
122, *Hadrian's Wall* is the best known and most
important Roman monument in Britain,
stretching 117km (73 miles) across the north of
England, from Wallsend-on-Tyne to Bowness-
on-Solway. The wall was built to mark the
northern boundary of the Roman Empire in the
British Isles and to keep out the barbarians to
the north. After the Empire receded in the fifth
century AD, the wall was left to decay, and
many of its stones were used in the
construction of nearby buildings. Vast sections
of the wall still remain and there are many
different sites to be visited. *Housesteads Roman
Fort and Museum* is an excavated fort located
amidst spectacular scenery, and contains the
only visible example of a Roman hospital in
Britain. *Vindolanda Fort and Museum* is an open-
air museum containing reconstructions of the
wall, as well as a Roman temple, house and
shop. The *Roman Army Museum* at Carvoran
provides an insight into the life of a Roman
soldier, through models, reconstructions and
artefacts. *Chesters Roman Fort and Museum* is an
extensively excavated cavalry fort with
impressive Roman bathhouse remains.

Transportation
Air: London City Airport, London Gatwick
Airport, London Heathrow Airport. **Rail:** Train:
Greenwich Station or Maze Hill Station.
Docklands Light Railway: Cutty Sark Station or
Greenwich Station. **Road:** Bus: Public services.

Contact Addresses
Hadrian's Wall Tourism Partnership, 14b Gilesgate,
Hexham, Northumberland NE46 3NJ, UK
Tel: (01434) 602 505 *or* 322 002
Website: www.hadrians-wall.org

Hampton Court Palace

Built by Cardinal Wolsey in the early 16th
century and later owned by King Henry VIII
(1491-1547), *Hampton Court Palace* occupies a
beautiful riverside site 23km (14 miles)
southwest of London. The palace was once the
centre of royal and political life in England,
with many famous monarchs residing there
between 1525 and 1737, including King Henry
VIII, King William III and Queen Mary during
the 17th century, and King George II and
Queen Caroline in the 18th century. The palace
has been associated with many important
events in history: King Henry VIII spent his
honeymoon in the palace with Anne Boleyn in
1533 and married his sixth wife Catherine Parr
there in 1543, whilst King Charles I was held
prisoner in the palace in 1647 by Oliver
Cromwell, who came to live there in 1653. The
palace was opened to the public in 1838 by
Queen Victoria and today, visitors can still see
much of the grandeur of this impressive Tudor
palace. In the *Palace Gardens*, visitors can
happily lose their way in the famous maze
which was planted in the North Gardens in
1702.

Transportation
Air: London Heathrow Airport. **Water:** Boat:
Services run along the River Thames in the
summer (from Westminster, Richmond-upon-
Thames and Kingston-upon-Thames). **Rail:** Train:
Hampton Court Station. Underground: Wimbledon
or Vauxhall, then overland train services to
Hampton Court Station. **Road:** Bus: Public
services.

Contact Addresses
Hampton Court Palace, Surrey KT8 9AU, UK
Tel: (020) 8781 9500
Website: www.hrp.org.uk

Harrods

Harrods, perhaps London's most famous
department store, is named after Charles Henry
Harrod, who opened a family grocers shop on the
site in 1849. The shop has grown to become a
byword for expensive and glamourous shopping,

Corel©

Hampton Court Palace

priding itself on its motto *Omnia Omnibus Ubique*, meaning 'All things, for all people, everywhere'. Bought by Egyptian businessman Mohamed Al Fayed in 1985, the eye-catching seven-storey building, which is illuminated by 11,500 lightbulbs each night, contains over 300 departments selling luxury items, from furniture and ladies fashion to polo mallets and wax coats for dogs. For those on a tighter budget, there is a Harrods gift shop, selling assorted souvenirs such as pencils and teddybears. One department not to be missed is the world-famous *Food Halls*. Harrods also provides banking and real estate services, currency exchange facilities and, for those who want to see the British capital in style, a luxury coach tour of London complete with tea and biscuits.

Transportation
Air: London Heathrow Airport, London Gatwick Airport, London Stansted Airport, London Luton Airport. **Rail:** Train: London's Victoria, Euston, Kings Cross, Liverpool Street or Waterloo Stations. Underground: Knightsbridge (Piccadilly Line). **Road:** Bus: Public services.

Contact Addresses
Harrods Ltd, 87-135 Brompton Road, Knightbridge, London SW1X 7XL, UK
Tel: (020) 7730 1234
Website: www.harrods.com

Lake Windermere

At 17kms (10.5 miles) long and plunging to 61m (200ft) deep in places, *Lake Windermere* is the largest lake in England. It forms part of the *Lake District National Park* and is in an area of outstanding natural beauty with numerous stunning walking trails. Many visitors prefer to explore the lake from the water itself and *Windermere Lake Cruises* (www.windermere-lakecruises.co.uk) operate an extensive network of steamers and launches; a popular trip is the Islands Cruise from Bowness, which passes wooded islands and secluded bays. Other attractions in the area include the *Aquarium of the Lakes*, the *Beatrix Potter Attraction*, the *Lakeside and Haverthwaite Railway*, *Fell Foot Park* and the *South Lakes Wild Animal Park*.

Legoland Windsor

VisitBritain©

Transportation
Air: Manchester Airport, Blackpool Airport and Newcastle Airport. **Rail:** Oxenholme Station (then bus or taxi). **Road:** Bus: Public services. Car: A591.

Contact Addresses
Windermere Tourist Information Centre, Victoria Street, Windermere, UK
Tel: 015394 46499
Website: www.golakes.co.uk

Leeds Castle

Leeds Castle in Kent is built on two islands in a lake. It was originally built as a royal manor in AD 857, but from 1278 onwards was used as a royal palace by King Edward I. Over the centuries, the castle has been home to six Medieval Queens of England. It was also home to Henry VIII and is full of many fine arts, furnishings and tapestries from its illustrious past. The castle was sold to Lady Baillie in 1926 who transformed the interior, filling it with fine furniture, tapestries and paintings. The castle is also famous for its *Aviary*, which is home to many birds including black swans and was built as a memorial to Lady Baillie, opening in 1988. The castle's grounds are also spectacular and include the *Maze*, *Wood Garden*, *Vineyard* and *Culpeper Garden*.

Transportation
Air: London Heathrow Airport, London Gatwick Airport. **Rail:** Train: Bearsted Station (from London Victoria Station) and then connect with a coach service. **Road:** Coach: Public services.

Contact Addresses
Leeds Castle Enterprises Limited, Leeds Castle, Leeds, Maidstone, Kent ME17 1PL, UK
Tel: (01622) 765 400
Website: www.leeds-castle.com

Legoland Windsor

Following on from the success of the original *LEGOLAND* park in Billund, Denmark, *LEGOLAND Windsor* welcomed its first visitors in 1996 and since then has become one of England's most popular theme parks. The park is split into nine different areas, each with its own theme. *Miniland* was the Danish counterpart's founding feature and remains one of the biggest attractions for visitors of all ages, consisting of miniature models of European towns and cities, all created from a total of 35 million LEGO bricks. There are attractions for old and young alike and children can create their own inventions from the thousands of bricks in the *Imagination Centre* workshops, and visitors as young as three can learn to drive around a special LEGO driving track, complete with traffic lights. There are shows every day, including the spectacular live action stunt show at *The Harbour* which is packed with stunning special effects, thrilling gymnastics and hilarious comic routines.

Transportation
Air: London Heathrow Airport, London Gatwick Airport, London Stansted Airport, London Luton Airport. **Rail:** Train: Windsor, Eton Central Station and Eton Riverside Station. **Road:** Bus: Public services.

Contact Addresses
LEGOLAND Windsor, Winkfield Road, Windsor, Berkshire SL4 4AY, UK
Tel: (08705) 040 404
Website: www.lego.com/legoland/windsor

London Dungeon

This horror theme park situated on London's *South Bank* gives visitors the opportunity to explore the darker side of British and European history. The *London Dungeon*, which opened in 1975, is a creepy recreation of many of history's most gruesome events. Visitors can go on various themed rides, which are based around historical murders and executions; they can explore the streets of Victorian London that were home to the serial killer Jack the Ripper, relive the Great Fire of London and take a barge down the *River Thames* to *Traitors Gate*, where they are sentenced to death by an 18th-century judge. The London Dungeons are patrolled by scary characters, dressed in gruesome costumes, who wait in dark corners and jump out at unsuspecting tourists.

Transportation
Air: London Heathrow Airport, London Gatwick Airport. **Rail:** Train: London Bridge Station. Underground: London Bridge or Monument/Bank. **Road:** Bus: Public services.

Contact Addresses
London Dungeon, 28-34 Tooley Street, London SE1 2SZ, UK
Tel: (0870) 846 0666 *or* (020) 7403 7221
Website: www.thedungeons.com

London Zoo

London Zoo, which opened in 1828, is situated on the north side of Regent's Park. The zoo was the site of the world's first children's zoo, which opened in 1838, followed by the first reptile house in 1849, the first public aquarium in 1853 and the first insect house in 1881. Today, the Zoo is home to around 12,000 animals, including Asian lions, Sumatran tigers, Sloth bears, Leadbeater's possums and Death adders. The famous spiral-shaped *Penguin Pool*, which is Grade I listed, is the home of Black-footed penguins, whilst the *Aquarium* houses sharks, piranhas and other sea creatures. The zoo also has beautiful gardens, as well as innovative zoo buildings, designed by architects such as Decimus Burton who designed the *Giraffe House*, Berthold Lubetkin who was responsible for the Penguin Pool and Sir Hugh Casson, responsible for the *Elephant and Rhino Pavilion*.

Transportation
Air: London Heathrow Airport, London Luton Airport. **Rail:** Train: London Euston or London Kings Cross stations. Underground: Camden Town or Regent's Park. **Road:** Bus: Public services.

Contact Addresses
London Zoo, Outer Circle, Regent's Park, London NW1 4RY, UK
Tel: (020) 7722 3333
Website: www.zsl.org/london-zoo/

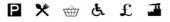

Longleat

Set in over 3,520 hectares (8,700 acres) of landscaped parkland, woodlands, lakes and farmland, *Longleat* stately home first opened its doors as a safari park nearly 40 years ago. Home to the 7th Marquess of Bath, *Longleat House* dates back to 1580 and is regarded as one of Britain's most beautiful stately homes and a fine example of high Elizabethan architecture. In 1966, Longleat opened the first *Safari Park* outside Africa and provided the concept for many of Britain's successful safari parks that exist today. Visitors to the park drive through a series of separate enclosures including the *East Africa Reserve*, *Monkey Jungle*, *Big Game Park*, *Deer Park*, *Pelican Pond*, *Tiger Territory*, *Lion Country* and *Wolf Wood*. The *Safari Boat* takes visitors on a leisurely cruise to see the *Gorilla Park* and *Hippo Pools*. Attractions specifically for children include an *Adventure Castle* with turrets and rope bridges, the *Blue Peter Maze* and a *Postman Pat Village*. Set amidst beautiful gardens, the *Orangery* is licensed to conduct civil wedding ceremonies. *Longleat House* also hosts corporate functions and wedding receptions.

Transportation
Air: Bristol Airport. **Rail:** Warminster Station or Westbury Station and then taxi to Longleat.

Contact Addresses
The Estate Office, Longleat, Warminster, Wiltshire BA12 7NW, UK
Tel: (01985) 844400
Website: www.longleat.co.uk

Madame Tussaud's and Tussaud's London Planetarium

Over 400 lifesize wax models of the rich and famous are exhibited in *Madame Tussauds*. Lifesize replicas of stars of the stage and screen, musicians and monarchs are displayed alongside footballers and politicians. Madame Tussaud was born in Strasbourg in 1761 and after inheriting a wax museum from Philippe Curtius in 1794, moved to London to set up an exhibition on London's Baker Street. Following her death in 1850, her grandsons moved the display to its present location on Marylebone Road. Today, visitors can have their photo taken with the likes of filmstar Marilyn Monroe, Australian popstar Kylie Minogue, footballer David Beckham and even members of the British Royal Family. They can also descend into the *Chamber of Horrors* to see some of history's most notorious criminals and various torture instruments. *Tussaud's London Planetarium*, which is adjacent to Madame Tussaud's and opened in 1958, enables budding astronomers to see the stars and is one of the largest planetariums in the world.

Transportation
Air: London Heathrow Airport. **Rail:** Underground: Baker Street. **Road:** Bus: Public services.

Contact Addresses
Madame Tussaud's and Tussaud's London Planetarium, Marylebone Road, London NW1 5LR, UK
Tel: (0870) 999 0046
Website: www.madame-tussauds.com *or* www.london-planetarium.com

Matlock Bath

Matlock Bath in the heart of Derbyshire has been attracting tourists since the turn of the 18th century when the wealthy aristocrats of the day would travel to bathe in the warm springs and enjoy its fine climate. A railway line established in the 1840s opened up the area to ordinary tourists and Matlock Bath lost some of its upper-class haughtiness. And nowadays, situated on the A6 that runs through the *Peak District National Park*, visitors still flock here in their thousands each year and is a popular stop-off for cyclists and bikers who come to enjoy the dramatic scenery and wide open spaces. However, Matlock Bath still holds on to some of its gentile charm and there are a number of fine buildings dating back to the 18th century that sit alongside modern day souvenir shops and arcades. Matlock Bath lies at the bottom of *High Tor*, a 137m (450ft) limestone cliff that rises from the *River Derwent*'s eastern bank and is popular with climbers. There are plenty of walking tracks in the area or there's a cable car that takes visitors up to an area known as the *Heights of Abraham* where the *Whistlestop Countryside Centre* is also located. Visitors can also access two old mining caverns, the *Grand Masson Cavern* and the *Great Rutland Cavern*. Other attractions in Matlock Bath include the *Peak District Mining Museum* which tells the story of lead mining in the area that dates back to Roman times. Close by is *Gulliver's* amusement park, a popular day trip for families.

Transportation
Air: Birmingham International Airport and East Midlands Airport. **Rail:** Matlock Bath train station. **Road:** Bus: Public services. Car: A6.

Contact Addresses
Matlock Bath Tourist Information Centre, Pavilion, Matlock Bath, Derbyshire DE4 3NR, UK
Tel: 01629 55082
Website: www.derbyshireuk.net

National Gallery

With its Classical façade gracing the northern side of London's Trafalgar Square, the UK's *National Gallery* possesses one of the world's greatest collections of Western paintings. On display are around 2300 pictures covering every European school of painting from the 13th to the 19th century. Paintings by English masters include Constable's 'The Haywain' and Gainsborough's 'The Watering Place'. There are regular exhibitions at the National Gallery, ranging from displays of schoolchildren's artwork inspired by Hogarth's painting 'The Graham Children', to an exhibition of 19th-century German painting.

Transportation
Air: London Heathrow Airport, London Gatwick Airport, London Stansted Airport or London Luton Airport. **Rail:** Train: London Charing Cross Station.

Underground: Charing Cross, Leicester Square, Embankment or Piccadilly Circus. Road: Bus: Public services.

Contact Addresses
National Gallery, Trafalgar Square, London WC2N 5DN, UK
Tel: (020) 7747 2885
Website: www.nationalgallery.org.uk

National Museum of Photography, Film and Television

Founded in 1983 as part of the *National Museum of Science and Industry*, the decision to locate the *National Museum of Photography*, *Film and Television* outside the capital was based on Bradford's contribution to the development of UK cinema and the city's accessible location. This is an interactive museum and visitors have the opportunity to discover the media world through a variety of hands-on experiences, including reading the news to camera, discovering the workings of a television camera and creating their own animations. The museum reflects ever changing developments within the industry, and contains a gallery devoted to digital media, as well as Europe's first *IMAX* cinema showing 3-D films and two cinemas showing new releases.

Transportation
Air: Leeds/Bradford International Airport or Manchester Airport. **Rail:** Train: Bradford Forster Square Station or Bradford Interchange Station. **Road:** Bus: Public services.

Contact Addresses
National Museum of Photography, Film and Television, Bradford, West Yorkshire BD1 1NQ, UK
Tel: 0870 7010200
Website: www.nmpft.org.uk

Natural History Museum

The *Natural History Museum* in South Kensington began its life as the natural history section of the British Museum, featuring the collections of

The Flat Earth Collection©

Victorian Doorway to Natural History Museum London

London physician and collector Sir Hans Sloane, who wished his collection to remain together to benefit as many people as possible after his death. Following a competition to choose the architect of the new building, Captain Robert Fowke drew up the original designs, seeing the museum as a cathedral of science, hence its church-like appearance. When he died in 1865, his work was continued by Alfred Waterhouse, who was responsible for the elaborate Romanesque carvings of animals and plants throughout the building. The Natural History Museum moved into its new home in 1883, since which time it has considerably increased the size of its collections, perhaps most famously to include the dinosaur gallery, where visitors can see huge dinosaur skeletons and even an animated T-Rex. The *Earth Galleries* explore the effects human life has on the planet around us and how scientists harness the resources we use in our everyday lives, as well as featuring displays of minerals and gemstones and an earthquake simulator. The *Life Galleries* allow visitors to explore human biology, Darwin's theory

The Gateshead Tyne and Wear MetroCentre shopping complex

VisitBritain©

of natural selection and to see an enormous life-size model of a blue whale. There are also regular exhibitions, and outside the building, the wildlife garden provides an opportunity to discover British wildlife in the heart of London.

Transportation
Air: London Heathrow Airport, London Gatwick Airport, London Stansted Airport, London Luton Airport. **Rail:** Train: London Paddington Station, London Victoria Station or London Waterloo Station. Underground: South Kensington.

Contact Addresses
Natural History Museum, Cromwell Road, London SW7 5BD, UK
Tel: (020) 7942 5000 (Mon-Fri only) *or* 7942 5011 (Sat-Sun)
Website: www.nhm.ac.uk

Neasden Temple

The exotic sight of the Neasden *Shri Swaminarayan Temple* sits alongside suburban houses in Neasden in northwest London. The limestone Hindu temple was inspired by Lord Swaminarayan, an 18th century Indian guru who walked barefoot across the length of India raising awareness about the plight of the country's poor and downtrodden

people. It was built using an estimated 2,000 tons of Italian marble and 3,000 tonnes of Bulgarian limestone which had first been shipped to India where 1,000 local craftsmen volunteered their skills to sculpt the elaborate structure that now stands in West London.

Transportation
Air: Gatwick Airport, Heathrow Airport and London City Airport. **Rail:** Neasden Station. **Road:** Bus: Public services. Car: B453.

Contact Addresses
105 Brentfield Road, Neasden, London NW10 8JP, UK
Tel: (020) 8965 2651

New Metroland

The *New MetroLand* is part of the Gateshead Tyne and Wear *MetroCentre* shopping complex and is Europe's largest indoor funfair, with 12 major attractions on the site. MetroLand first opened its doors to the public in 1988 and has gone on to become one of the region's most popular paying attractions with over 800,000 visitors each year. MetroLand was conceived as a marketing tool that would attract more visitors to the MetroCentre shopping complex and the strategy has been a resounding success; the MetroCentre receives close to 20 million visitors each year. As part of the MetroCentre, visitors are free to walk around the MetroLand complex and rides are paid for on an individual basis or with a wristband giving access to all the rides and attractions. Those travelleing to Tyneside will be greeted by the open arms of Antony Gormley's iconic sculpture, the *Angel of the North*. Situated high on a hill top along the A1, the sculpture towers 20m (65 ft) into the sky and is seen by over 90,000 drivers each day as well as by all rail passengers arriving in the region. Erected in 1998, the Angel of the North has become the quintessential symbol of the region and is now said to be more recognisable than the *Tyne Bridge*.

Transportation
Air: Newcastle International Airport. **Rail:** Metroland has its own station, Newcastle Metro. **Road:** Bus: Public services. Car: Well signposted and large car parks.

Contact Addresses
The New MetroLand, 39 Garden Walk, MetroCentre, Gateshead, NE11 9XY, UK
Tel: (0191) 493 2048
Website: www.metroland.uk.com

Oxford University

As a centre of education dating back to the early 12th century, *Oxford University* ranks as the oldest university in England and one of the most famous in the world. Its extensive list of important past students includes John Locke, Christopher Wren, Lewis Carroll, Jonathan Swift, Oscar Wilde and, more recently, Tony Blair and Bill Clinton. The university itself is made up of a number of colleges, most displaying stunning architecture and trim lawns, situated throughout the city. Of particular interest to visitors are *Christ Church College*, founded in 1524 by Cardinal Wolsey, whose college chapel also serves as Oxford's cathedral; *Merton College*, one of the smaller colleges with only 250 undergraduates and with particularly beautiful gardens and courtyards; and the *Bodleian Library*, the central library of Oxford University, which is the oldest library in Europe and was originally founded in 1320 by Thomas Cobham, Bishop of Worcester.

Transportation
Air: London's Heathrow, Gatwick, Stansted and Luton Airports. **Rail:** Train: Oxford City Station. **Road:** Bus: Public services.

Contact Addresses
Oxford Tourist Information Centre, 15/16 Broad Street, Oxford OX1 3AS, UK
Tel: (01865) 726 871
Website: www.oxford.gov.uk/tourism

Poole Harbour

Poole Harbour is a vibrant quay on England's southern coast that bustles with an array of bars, cafes and restaurants. Visitors wanting to learn more about the history of the region can follow the newly developed *Cockle Trail* discovering myths and legends about Poole's smugglers and ghosts of yesteryear. A series of brass plaques mark the way charting 750 years of Poole's history culminating at the *Waterfront Museum*. Popular sports in and around the harbour include windsurfing, kitesurfing, water-skiing, wakeboarding, surfing, snorkelling and kayaking. Of course, boat trips are popular and visitors can sail out to the National Trust's *Brownsea Island*, protected for its wildlife and peaceful woodland walks. Away from the harbour, nearby *Poole Pottery* (www.poolepottery.co.uk) produces one-off handmade pottery and is famed for its traditional craft that stretches back 130 years. In 2005, it opened its doors for a week for the first time enabling visitors to tour the factory to see how the prize-winning pieces are made.

Transportation
Air: Bournemouth International Airport. **Water:** Ferry: Daily crossings to France and summer sailings to the Channel Islands. **Rail:** Poole Station. **Road:** Bus: Public services.

Contact Addresses
Poole Tourism, Enefco House, Poole Quay, Poole, Dorset BH15 1HJ, UK
Tel: (01202) 253253
Website: www.pooletourism.com

City of Bath, the Roman Baths

VisitBritain©

Portsmouth Historic Dockyard

Portsmouth Historic Dockyard is home to three famous ships: the *Mary Rose, HMS Victory* and *HMS Warrior 1860*. The Mary Rose, which was Henry VIII's favourite warship, sank in 1545, but was raised from the sea in 1982. Today, visitors can enter the *Mary Rose Museum* and *Ship Hall*, where more than 1000 artefacts are on display. They can also see *HMS Victory*, which is the world's oldest commissioned warship, used by Nelson in the Battle of Trafalgar (1805) to defeat the Franco-Spanish fleet. Also on display is the *HMS Warrior 1860*, the world's first iron battleship, one of the largest and fastest warships at the time. The *Royal Naval Museum* is closeby and houses an interactive *Dockyard Apprentice Exhibition*. In 2005 *Flagship Portsmouth* opened a special Trafalgar exhibition commerating the 200th anniversary of the famous battle.

Transportation
Air: Southampton International Airport. **Rail:** Train: Portsmouth Harbour Station. **Road:** Bus: Public services.

Contact Addresses
Flagship Portsmouth Trust, Building 1/7, Porter's Lodge, College Road, HM Naval Base, Portsmouth, PO1 3LJ, UK
Tel: (023) 9286 1512 (24-hour information line) *or* 9286 1533
Website: www.flagship.org.uk

Roman Baths and Pump Room

The ancient Romans were the first to capitalise on the only natural hot spring in Britain, building a temple and bathing complex more than 2000 years ago in the city of Bath. The healing spring, which is located within the bathing complex, produces approximately 2,273,050 litres (500,000 gallons) of water per day at a temperature of 46.5°C (116°F). The baths were once one of the finest in the Roman world, although the Roman structure gradually fell into disrepair. It was not until a visit by the ailing Prince George in 1702 that the baths once again became a popular healing destination. Over the course of the town's redevelopment, the Roman ruins were rediscovered (in 1879) and restored. Visitors can now view the Georgian grandeur of the Pump House and see the remains of the ancient Roman baths and temple.

Transportation
Air: London Heathrow Airport, Bristol International Airport. **Rail:** Train: Bath Spa Station. **Road:** Bus: Public services.

Contact Addresses
Roman Baths and Pumproom, Museum Enquiries, Stall Street, Bath BA1 1LZ, UK
Tel: (01225) 477 785
Website: www.romanbaths.co.uk

Royal Academy of Arts

Located in the historic *Piccadilly* area in the heart of London, the *Royal Academy of Arts* is an independent fine arts institution which supports contemporary artists and promotes interest in the arts through a comprehensive exhibition programme. The Academy is completely independent and as such is a self-funded organisation which is governed by the Royal Academicians – eminent practising painters, printmakers, sculptors and architects who are elected to the position. The Academy has a long history and was founded in 1768 with Sir Joshua Reynolds as its first President. The Academy is located in Burlington House which itself has a long a colourful history with parts of the original structure estimated as dating back to 1664. Today, the Academy attracts well over one million visitors each year making it one of London's top 10 attractions for paying visitors.

Transportation
Air: London's City Airport, Gatwick Airport, Heathrow Airport, Luton Airport and Stansted Airport. **Rail:** Underground: Piccadilly and Green Park or a short walk from Oxford Circus and Bond Street. **Road:** Bus: Public services.

Contact Addresses
Royal Academy of Arts, Burlington House, Piccadilly, London W1J 0BD, UK
Telephone (020) 7300 8000
Website: www.royalacademy.org.uk

Royal Armouries Leeds

The *Royal Armouries* is Britain's national collection of arms and armour, and was moved from its former home in the Tower of London to a specially-created building in Leeds in 1996. Visitors can enter five galleries, each with its own theme covering self-defence, war, armour of the Orient, hunting and tournament. There is a wealth of different objects on display, including over 7500 swords, King Henry VIII's equestrian equipment, several longbows excavated from the sunken British battleship the *Mary Rose*, 50 instruments of torture, and arms and armour from as far afield as central Asia, India, Africa and Japan. The Armouries also hold a variety of events and exhibitions, many of them aimed at children including the popular Easter-egg trails and Hallowe'en stories.

Transportation
Air: Leeds/Bradford International Airport. **Rail:** Train: Leeds Station. **Road:** Coach: Leeds Bus Station.

Contact Addresses
Royal Armouries Museum, Armouries Drive, Leeds LS10 1LT, UK
Tel: 08700 344344 (24-hour information line) or (0113) 220 1916
Website: www.armouries.org.uk/leeds

Royal Botanic Gardens, Kew

Kew Gardens comprise 132 hectares (326 acres) of herbaceous bedding, water features, botanical glasshouses, a large arboretum and historic buildings located on the banks of the River Thames in southwest London. Founded in 1759, this vast oasis on the outskirts of the metropolis has become a favourite with visitors wishing to escape the pressures of the city, and has been extensively developed. Its attractions include an aquatic garden, a bamboo garden, a woodland glade, a conservation area and a Japanese landscape. There are several glasshouses to explore, one of which, *Evolution House*, showcases 3500 million years of plant evolution. *Queen Charlotte's Cottage*, located within the grounds of *Richmond Lodge*, was a wedding gift to Queen Charlotte in 1861 and was also used by Queen Victoria until she presented it to the public upon her Diamond Jubilee in 1897; the building has now been restored to its original state. Visitors to Kew can either join in a guided tour, follow one of several themed trails, or wander around the attractions at their own pace.

Transportation
Air: London Heathrow Airport, London Gatwick Airport, London Stansted Airport, London Luton Airport. **Rail:** Train: Kew Gardens Station (from north and south London); Kew Bridge Station (from London Waterloo Station). Underground: Kew Gardens (District Line). **Road:** Bus: Public services.

Contact Addresses
Royal Botanic Gardens, Kew, Richmond, Surrey TW9 3AB, UK
Tel: (020) 8332 5000 *or* 8332 5655 (24-hour recorded information line)
Website: www.rbgkew.org.uk

Royal Pavilion

The Royal Pavilion Libraries & Museum©

Royal Pavilion

The *Royal Pavilion*, which is the former seaside home of King George IV, is one of the most exotic-looking buildings in the UK. It was originally a farmhouse, but was transformed into a neo-classical villa in 1787 by the architect Henry Holland. The building was further re-modelled by John Nash in 1820 in the style of an Indian palace. It was also used by George IV's brother, William IV and his niece Queen Victoria, but was sold to the town of Brighton by Victoria in 1850. Today, the exterior of this Regency building still has many domes and minarets, whilst the interior features a huge banqueting room with an impressive chandelier as its centrepiece, as well as a music room with lanterns hanging from a high-domed ceiling. The palace is ornately decorated with an array of Chinese and English furnishing and is set in lavish surrounding gardens.

Transportation
Air: London Gatwick Airport. **Rail:** Train: Brighton Station. **Road:** Bus: Public services.

Contact Addresses
Royal Pavilion, Pavilion Buildings, Brighton BN1 1EE, UK
Tel: (01273) 292 822
Website: www.royalpavilion.org.uk

Salford Quays

Salford Quays is a joint tourism initiative between Salford City Council and Trafford Borough Council and is supported by *The Lowry*, *Imperial War Museum North*, *Manchester United Football Club*, *Lancashire County Cricket Club*, the *Lowry Outlet Mall* and the *Copthorne Hotel* which are private sector partners in the area. The Lowry is one of Manchester's most renowned centres for arts and performance and is the architectural flagship of the redeveloped Salford Quays waterside location. Incorporating two theatres, a range of galleries, as well as restaurants, bars and cafés, the Lowry's eyecatching architecture won it the 2001 building of the year award. The building takes its name from the celebrated painter LS Lowry (who died in 1976) and houses a permanent Lowry exhibition alongside displays of more contemporary artists. In line with regeneration projects throughout the city, Salford Quays has been built around the regenerated docklands and today is a vibrant hub of the city's arts, leisure and sports scenes.

Transportation
Air: Manchester Airport. **Rail:** Services to Manchester Piccadilly or Victoria train stations then services on from there. Tram: Regualar tram services to the Quays. **Water:** During the summer, ferries run between the Quays down the Mersey to Liverpool. **Road:** Bus: Public services and park and ride service from the city.

Contact Addresses
Salford Tourist Information Centre, The Lowry, Pier 8, Salford Quays M50 3AZ, UK
Tel: (0161) 848 8601 or 0870 420 4145
Website: www.thequays.org.uk

Sandringham Estate

Set within beautiful grounds, *Sandringham* was built in 1870 by the Prince and Princess of Wales who later became King Edward VII and Queen Alexandra. Passed down through four generations of British Monarchs, the estate is now the country residence of the Queen and the Duke of Edinburgh. Over the years the estate has acquired many objets d'art and each room is lavishly decorated with fine furniture and paintings. The *Estate Museum* was created by King George V as early as 1928 and visitors can see, amongst other things, the fine collection of Royal Vehicles and Carriages. Visitors are able to enjoy 243 hectares (600 acres) of *Country Park* that lies within the *Norfolk Coast Area of Outstanding Natural Beauty*. Also on the estate are a working sawmill and fruit farm. There's a *Visitor Centre* set within the Country Park with a restaurant, shop and further information about the history of the estate.

Transportation
Air: Norwich Airport and Stansted Airport. **Rail:** Kings Lynn Station. **Road:** Bus: Public services. Car: A148.

Contact Addresses
Estate Office, Sandringham, Norfolk PE35 6EN, UK
Tel: (01553) 772675
Website: www.sandringhamestate.co.uk

Science Museum

Together with the *National Railway Museum* and the *National Museum of Photography, Film & Television*, the *Science Museum* is part of the *National Museum of Science & Industry*. Located in central London, the museum owns an impressive collection of science exhibits, including the Apollo 10 Command Module, the V-2 rocket, which was the world's first long-range missile, and Stephensons' Rocket locomotive. The Science Museum, which originally opened along with the *Victoria and Albert Museum* in 1857 as the *South Kensington Museum*, now houses one of the largest collections of scientific, medical, industrial and technological exhibits in the world. There are numerous interactive displays and permanent exhibitions. Entry to the museum is free but there are charges for some exhibitions.

Transportation
Air: London Heathrow Airport. **Rail:** Train: London Victoria Station. Underground: South Kensington. **Road:** Bus: Public services.

Contact Addresses
Science Museum, Exhibition Road, South Kensington, London SW7 2DD, UK
Tel: (0870) 870 4771
Website: www.sciencemuseum.org.uk

Shakespeare Houses

William Shakespeare, considered by many to be the greatest dramatist and poet the world has ever known, was born in the market town of Stratford-upon-Avon in 1564 and maintained strong links with the town until his death in 1616. His legacy has turned Stratford into a major tourist destination crammed with historic houses relating to the writer's life and that of his family. *Shakespeare's Birthplace* is a half-timbered house in the centre of Stratford, which remained the property of his descendants until 1806, when it was bought by a board of trustees and restored as a museum. The adjacent *Shakespeare's World Museum* guides visitors through the life and times of Shakespeare using drawings, maps, illustrations and audiovisual displays. In 1582, Shakespeare married Anne Hathaway, the daughter of a local farmer, and *Anne Hathaway's Cottage*, is closeby in the hamlet of Shottery, 1.6km (1 mile) from Stratford-upon-Avon. Shakespeare returned from London in 1597 as a successful playwright and bought *New Place*, the second largest house in the town, where he spent the last years of his life. Visitors can also tour the home of Shakespeare's mother, *Mary Arden's House* at *Glebe Farm*, which was fortunately rescued from demolition by the Shakespeare Trust in 1960.

Transportation
Air: Birmingham International Airport. **Rail:** Train: Stratford-upon-Avon Station. **Road:** Bus: Public services.

Contact Addresses
The Shakespeare Centre, Henley Street, Stratford-upon-Avon CV37 6QW, UK
Tel: (01789) 204 016
Website: www.shakespeare.org.uk

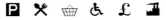

Somerset House

Established in 1997 in the heart of London, the *Somerset House Trust* was set up to conserve and develop *Somerset House* and the surrounding areas for public use. The stunning 18th century building has now been renovated and houses celebrated art collections in three exhibition areas: the *Courtauld Institute of Art*, the *Gilbert Collection* and the

Hermitage Rooms. Outside, the redeveloped *Courtyard* is the venue for a summer schedule of concerts and events; during the Christmas and New Year period, the Courtyard is transformed into a popular ice skating rink that provides a welcome distraction for Christmas shoppers. When not holding events, the Courtyard's acclaimed *Safra Fountain Court* bursts into life with daily displays during the summer months.

Transportation
Air: Heathrow Airport, Gatwick Airport and London City Airport. **Rail:** Charing Cross, Waterloo and Blackfriars. Underground: Temple, Covent Garden, Charing Cross and Embankment. **Road:** Bus: Public services.

Contact Addresses
Somerset House Trust, Somerset House, Strand, London WC2R 1LA, UK
Tel: (020) 7845 4600
Website: www.someset-house.org.uk

Southwold

Situated on the north Suffolk coastline, *Southwold* is a traditional seaside town that forms part of the Suffolk Heritage Coast. With its brightly painted beach huts, working lighthouse, harbour and bustling fish markets, Southwold is a quintessential English resort town of yesteryear with none of the razzmatazz of a pleasure beach. Walking south along the pier towards the harbour, visitors can watch sailors navigate their vessels up and down the River Blythe where it joins with the North Sea. A fire destroyed much of the old town in 1659, but some notable buildings survived and are still standing today; St Edmund's Church, which dates back to the 15th century, is well worth a visit. With just one road leading in and out, Southwold retains much of its old charm. However, the area is becoming increasingly popular with visitors and can get quite crowded at weekends during the summer. Nevertheless, its stunning scenery, coastal walks and excellent fish and chip restaurants make Southwold a great place to visit at any time of the year.

Transportation
Air: Norwich Airport or London Stansted Airport. **Rail:** Lowestoft Station then bus or taxi to Southwold. **Road:** Bus: Public services.

Contact Addresses
Tourist Information Centre, 69 High Street, Southwold, Suffolk IP18 6DS, UK
Tel: (01502) 724 729
Website: www.visit-suffolk.org.uk

St Michael's Mount

Perched proudly on a rocky island, *St Michael's Mount* rises 70m (230 ft) from sea level and is one of Cornwall's best-known attractions that dates back to the 12th century. According to legend, it was built by a giant called Cormoran who terrorised local farmers by wading ashore and raiding their flocks for food. A bounty was placed on his head and a local boy named Jack devised a plan to kill the giant. Jack made his way to the island in the dead of night and dug a deep pit, then, waking the giant from his slumber with a blast on his horn, the giant hastily gave chase falling into the pit. Jack became known as Jack the Giant Killer and was the toast of the town. But history tells us that the Abbot of Mont St Michel in Normandy, Bernard of Le Bec, built the Benedictine Priory of St Michael's Mount in 1135 as a dependency of the Norman Abbey. By the early 15th century, Henry V had declared war on France and in 1424 seized St Michael's Mount for the crown. Over the years, the Mount has been a priory, a fort, a site of pilgrimage and eventually became a private residence of the St Aubyn family 1659. In 1954, the St Aubyn's went into partnership with the National Trust opening up the castle and grounds to the public. At low tide it's possible to walk out across the causeway to St Michael's Mount (it's important to check local tide times (tel: 01736 710265 (for tide information only))). During the summer, a ferry service carries people to and from the Mount at high tide.

Transportation
Air: Newquay Airport, Exeter Airport and Plymouth Airport (domestic services). **Rail:** Penzance Station. **Road:** Bus: Public services.

Contact Addresses
St Michael's Mount, Manor Office, Marazion, Cornwall TR17 0EF, UK
Tel: (01736) 710507
Website: www.stmichaelsmount.co.uk

Stonehenge

Corel©

St Paul's Cathedral

Built in 1673, *St Paul's Cathedral* is Sir Christopher Wren's most famous work. Its dome, one of the largest in Europe, stands out as one of the most distinctive features of London's skyline. There has been a cathedral dedicated to St Paul on the site for more than 1400 years, and the present Cathedral stands on the site of an even older medieval cathedral that burned down during the Great Fire of 1666. Decorating the interior of the dome is the *Whispering Gallery*, so named for its incredible acoustics. Contained beneath the main cathedral floor is the *Crypt*, which is the largest in Europe, housing more than 200 tombs, including those of Admiral Nelson and the Duke of Wellington, and the tomb of Sir Christopher Wren himself. Over the years, the cathedral has been the setting for many historic events, including Sir Winston Churchill's funeral in 1965, and the wedding of Prince Charles and the late Princess of Wales in 1981.

Transportation
Air: London Heathrow Airport, London Gatwick Airport, London City Airport. **Rail:** Train: City

Thameslink Station or Blackfriars Station. Underground: St Paul's, Mansion House, Canon Street or Blackfriars. **Road:** Bus: Public services.

Contact Addresses
St Paul's Cathedral, The Chapter House, St Paul's Churchyard, London EC4M 8AD, UK
Tel: (020) 7236 4128
Website: www.stpauls.co.uk

✗ 🧺 ♿ £ 🏭

Stonehenge

Erected between 3000 and 1600 BC, *Stonehenge* is a giant stone circle that stands on Salisbury Plain and is considered today to be one of the most famous surviving sites from the ancient world. The stones, which are up to 6.7m (22ft) high, attract hundreds of visitors every day, who come to marvel at the ingenuity of those who engineered the construction of the site and the techniques used to move and position the stones. The first prehistoric structures appeared at the site in approximately 3000BC. However, it was not until 2550BC that the 3.9-ton (4-tonne) bluestones

Beefeater at the Tower of London

The Flat Earth Collection©

were brought to Stonehenge from the Preseli Mountains in Pembrokeshire, southwest Wales, using manpower alone. The 30 sarsen stones, which form the Sarsen Circle with raised lintels around the edge, were brought 150 years later from the Marlborough Downs, 32km (20 miles) away, the largest weighing an astonishing 49.2 tons (50 tonnes). *Avebury*, which is located 37km (24 miles) from Stonehenge, is another ancient mystery to modern-day man, and one of the biggest stone circles ever built. There are also many burial mounds nearby, as well as long barrows from the Neolithic Age, the most famous of which is *West Kennet Long Barrow*.

Transportation
Air: London Heathrow Airport. **Rail:** Train: Salisbury Station (from London Waterloo Station). **Road:** Bus: Public services.

Contact Addresses
Stonehenge, English Heritage, First Floor, Abbey Buildings, Abbey Square, Amesbury, Wiltshire SP4 7ES, UK
Tel: (01980) 624 715 (information line)
Website: www.english-heritage.org.uk

Swaffam I Ecotech Centre

Owned and operated by Ecotricity, *Swaffham I* is the first multi-megawatt wind turbine in the UK and is one of a new generation of direct drive, variable speed wind turbines. Located in Swaffham in rural Norfolk, the turbine was installed at the *Ecotech Centre* in 1999 and represents what the future could be like for power generation. A second turbine was built in 2003 and together the two turbines produce enough electricity for approximately 7,000 people – about 75 per cent of the town. The Ecotech Centre is an environmental education centre and Swaffham I includes a viewing platform which is accessed via a 300-step spiral staircase. Since opening, over 50,000 people have visited the site.

Transportation
Air: Norwich Airport. **Rail:** Norwich train station. **Road:** Bus: Public services. Car: A47.

Contact Addresses
Ecotech Centre, Swaffham, Norfolk, UK
Tel: (01760) 726100
Website: www.ecotricity.co.uk

 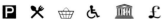

Tate Britain

Tate Britain, which was known as the *Tate Gallery* until *Tate Modern* was opened in 2000, houses the national collection of British art from 1500 to the present day, the largest and most comprehensive collection of British art in the world. Situated on the banks of the River Thames, it houses the art collection of the sugar tycoon Sir Henry Tate and first opened to the public in 1897. Unusually, works from different periods are arranged together according to theme to provide more thought-provoking displays and to enable visitors to see well-known paintings in a new light. The collection includes works by Blake, Constable, Gainsborough, Hogarth, Rosetti and Hockney. The *Clore Gallery*, opened in 1987, houses a magnificent collection of paintings by British Romantic landscape artist JMW Turner. Tate Britain also hosts special events such as themed talks, artists' talks, lectures and films.

Transportation

Air: London Heathrow Airport, London Gatwick Airport, London Stansted Airport, London Luton Airport. **Water:** The Tate Boat runs along the Thames between Tate Britain, the London Eye and Tate Modern. **Rail:** Train: London Victoria Station or London Vauxhall Station. Underground: Pimlico, Vauxhall or Westminster. **Road:** Bus: Public services.

Contact Addresses

Tate Britain, Millbank, London SW1P 4RG, UK
Tel: (020) 7887 8000 *or* 7887 8008 (recorded information)
Website: www.tate.org.uk

Tate Modern

Tate Modern, housed in the former Bankside Power Station on the south bank of the River Thames, opened in 2000. It showcases international modern art from 1900 to the present day and, like its sister museum, *Tate Britain*, it presents visitors with a themed, rather than a chronological, tour of art. Each theme is set in its own set of galleries where a variety of media, including photography, film, sculpture and painting are displayed. The themes are *Nude/ Action/Body*, *History/Memory/Society*, *Still Life/ Object/Real Life* and *Landscape/Matter/Environment*, and feature works by artists such as Dalí, Picasso, Matisse, Warhol, Rothko and Gilbert & George.

Transportation

Air: London Heathrow Airport, London Gatwick Airport, London Stansted Airport, London Luton Airport. **Water:** The Tate Boat runs along the Thames between Tate Britain, the London Eye and Tate Modern. **Rail:** Train: London Blackfriars Station or London Bridge Station. Underground: Southwark or Blackfriars. **Road:** Bus: Public services.

Contact Addresses

Tate Modern, Bankside, London SE1 9TG, UK
Tel: (020) 7887 8000 *or* 7887 8008 (recorded information
Website: www.tate.org.uk

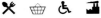

Tintagel Castle

The ruins of the legendary 12th-century *Tintagel Castle* stand on windswept cliffs in North Cornwall on one of England's most dramatic coastlines. The medieval castle was built in around 1250 by Richard, Earl of Cornwall and is believed to be the birthplace of King Arthur who, as legend has it, was protected from the evil magician Merlin by his magical sword, Excaliber. The castle is shrouded in mystery and little is actually known about its history. Today, the remains of the castle stand on rugged cliffs high above the sea. Over the years, the mainland has been eroded by the elements and the castle is now only accessible via a narrow bridge and steep steps. Many claim that Tintagel is one of the most romantic places in the UK, with beautiful walks along the Cornish Coastal Path.

Transportation

Air: Exeter International Airport. **Road:** Bus: Public services. Car: Tintagel Castle is situated on Tintagel Head, 0.8km (0.5 miles) from the main road; it cannot be reached by car. A Land Rover service is however in operation between April and October.

Contact Addresses

Tintagel Castle, Tintagel, Cornwall PL34 0HE, UK
Tel/Fax: (01840) 770 328
Website: www.english-heritage.org.uk

Tower of London

Work began on the infamous *Tower of London* in 1078 on the orders of William the Conqueror, 12 years after his Norman invasion of England. The tower, which is situated on the north bank of the River Thames and once dominated the city of London, is also known as the *White Tower*, after the Central Keep which is made of white Caen limestone. It remained a royal residence until the 16th century and was also a notorious prison where key historical figures, such as Catherine Howard, Sir Walter Raleigh, the two Royal Princes (Edward V and Richard Duke of York) and King Henry VI, lost their lives. Today, it houses the *Crown Jewels* and the *Royal Armouries*, and is also an important museum. The site is guarded by

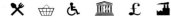

Statue of King Charles, Windsor Castle

Corel©

Yeoman Warders (or *Beefeaters*, so-called because they used to have to taste the king's food to see if it had been poisoned) and is apparently protected by ravens; according to legend if the ravens ever leave the tower a great disaster will take place in England.

Transportation
Air: London Heathrow Airport. **Rail:** Train: Fenchurch Street or London Bridge stations. Underground: Tower Hill. Docklands Light Railway: Tower Gateway. **Road:** Bus: Public services.

Contact Addresses
HM Tower of London, London EC3N 4AB, UK
Tel: (020) 7709 0765
Website: www.hrp.org.uk

✗ 🗑 ♿ 🏛 £ 🏭

Victoria and Albert Museum

The *Victoria and Albert Museum* is Britain's National Museum of Art and Design. It was first opened in 1852 at *Marlborough House* in central London as a *Museum of Manufacturers*, following the success of the *Great Exhibition* which had been held in London the previous year. In 1857 it was moved to Brompton in west London, where it was renamed the Victoria and South Kensington Museum. It acquired its current name in 1899 in honour of Queen Victoria (and her beloved husband, Albert) who had laid the foundation stone as her last public appearance. The V&A is the largest museum of decorative arts in the world and highlights include Italian Renaissance sculpture, paintings and drawings by Constable, the *Glass Gallery*, the *Dress Gallery* and the *Canon Photography Gallery*.

Transportation
Air: London Heathrow Airport, London Gatwick Airport, London Stansted Airport, London Luton Airport. **Rail:** Train: London Paddington Station, London Victoria Station or London Waterloo Station. Underground: South Kensington. **Road:** Bus: Public services.

Contact Addresses
Victoria and Albert Museum, Cromwell Road, South Kensington, London SW7 2RL, UK
Tel: (020) 7942 2000
Website: www.vam.ac.uk

🅿 ✗ 🗑 ♿ 🏭

Warwick Castle

Warwick Castle ranks amongst the most popular of all Britain's many historic attractions due to its size, picturesque location and turbulent history. The castle was created as a fortification in AD 914, to protect the small hilltop settlement from Danish invaders who posed a threat to the Anglo-Saxon kingdom of Mercia, and was later enlarged by William the Conqueror who turned it into a motte and bailey fort in 1068. Fortifications were added by King Richard III up until his death at the Battle of Bosworth in 1485. Today, visitors can explore the varied history of the castle's dungeons, fortifications and living quarters, as well as the *Rose Garden* and the formal gardens. The *Private Apartments* contain a display of waxwork figures, showing how the rooms would have looked in the late 19th century. Across the River Avon is the *Island*, where jesters, archers and craftsmen show off their skills in the summer months alongside re-enactments of battles and tournaments.

Transportation
Air: Birmingham International Airport. **Rail:** Train: Warwick Station. **Road:** Car: M40 (from London, Birmingham, Manchester, Leeds, Bristol or Stratford-upon-Avon).

Contact Addresses
Warwick Castle, Warwick CV34 4QU, UK
Tel: (0870) 442 2000 (recorded information line)
Website: www.warwick-castle.co.uk

Westminster Abbey

England's most visited religious site, *Westminster Abbey* is a living monument to British history. Inside there are buried kings, statesmen, warriors, scientists, musicians and poets, including Charles Darwin, Geoffrey Chaucer, Charles Dickens, Mary I, James I and Charles II. Initially the site of a Norman abbey, Henry III built the present building in the 13th century to compete with the great European cathedrals of the time. The abbey has seen the coronation of every English monarch since William the Conqueror, with the exception of Edward V and Edward VIII. The abbey continues to play a crucial role in royal state occasions and was the setting for the coronation of the present monarch, Queen Elizabeth II, on June 2 1953, as well as the funerals of the late Princess of Wales on September 6 1997 and Queen Elizabeth the Queen Mother on April 9 2002.

Transportation
Air: London Heathrow Airport. **Rail:** Train: Waterloo Station or Victoria Station. Underground: Westminster or St James Park. **Road:** Bus: Public services.

Contact Addresses
The Chapter Office, 20 Dean's Yard, Westminster Abbey, London SW1P 3PA, UK
Tel: (020) 7222 5152 *or* 7222 7110 (information desk)
Website: www.westminster-abbey.org

Westonbirt Arboretum

Westonbirt - The National Arboretum in Gloucestershire contains some of the country's oldest and rarest shrubs and is famous for its plants, trees and incredible landscaped gardens. Managed by the Forestry Commission, the collection contains over 18,000 specimens across 243 hectares (600 acres) of Grade 1 Listed Landscape. In 2001, Westonbirt was coupled with *Bedgebury* in Kent to form the *National Arboreta*. Visitors are able to enjoy guided walks or they can explore the grounds on their own along marked paths such as the new *Native Tree Time Trail*. Westonbirt also hosts open-air music events throughout the year.

Transportation
Air: Bristol Airport. **Rail:** Stroud Station and then bus or taxi. **Road:** Bus: Public services to Tetbury then taxi. Car: A433

Contact Addresses
Westonbirt, The National Arboretum, Tetbury, Gloucestershire GL8 8QS, UK
Tel: (01666) 880220
Website: www.forestry.gov.uk

Windsor Castle

Windsor Castle, overlooking the Berkshire town of Windsor, is one of the official homes of Queen Elizabeth II and is the largest and oldest occupied castle in the world. It was constructed under William the Conqueror (c. 1028-1087) as a means of guarding the western approaches to London, due to its position high above the River Thames on the edge of a Saxon hunting ground. Since then, it has been continuously inhabited by Britain's monarchs who have created both an impressive fortress and a regal residence. The castle was painstakingly restored after fire swept through more than 100 rooms and *St George's Chapel* in 1992. Visitors can now once again enter many parts of the castle. One of the highlights is St George's Chapel which was founded in 1475 by King Edward IV and completed by King Henry VIII. It is one of the best examples of Perpendicular Gothic architecture in Britain, and contains the remains of numerous British

Wookey Hole Caves

VisitBritain©

sovereigns, including King Henry VIII, Jane Seymour, Charles I and George V. 200 hectares (500 acres) of *Home Park* surround the castle. A popular place to go walking is in the sweeping 700-hectare (1800-acre) expanse of *Windsor Great Park*, which can be accessed by the *Long Walk*, a broad path lined with elm trees planted under the instructions of King Charles II in 1685.

Transportation
Air: London Heathrow Airport, London Gatwick Airport, London Stansted Airport, London Luton Airport. **Rail:** Train: Windsor Central Station (from London Paddington); Windsor & Eton Riverside Station (from London Waterloo). **Road:** Bus: Public services.

Contact Addresses
The Visitor Office, Windsor Castle, Windsor, Berkshire SL4 1NJ, UK
Tel: (01753) 869 898
Website: www.royalresidences.com

Wookey Hole Caves

Situated in the heart of Somerset, evidence of early man inhabiting the site around *Wookey Hole* can be traced back over 50,000 years. As well as human artifacts, the many archaeological finds include the bones of tropical and Ice Age animals such as rhinoceros, bear, mammoth and lion. It's thought that the caves were inhabited alternately by both man and hyenas between 35,000 and 25,000 BC. More recently, the Celts settled and farmed in the area before the Romans arrived approximately 2000 years ago and took over the region for its rich mineral mines. There are other attractions at the site including the *Dinosaur Valley* with life-size models of dinosaurs, a *Victorian Penny Arcade*, a *Mirror Maze* and the *River Axe Pirates* children's play area. There's also a *Victorian Papermill* and *Caves Museum* which are popular with school visits.

Transportation
Air: Exeter Airport and Plymouth Airport. **Rail:** Bristol Station (then bus or taxi). **Road:** Bus: Public services to Wells then taxi. Car: A39 and A371.

Contact Addresses
Wookey Hole Caves, Wookey Hole, Wells,
Somerset BA5 1BB, UK
Tel: 01749 672243
Website: www.wookey.co.uk

York Minster

The largest Gothic cathedral in Northern Europe, the present *York Minster* was constructed in 1220. For hundreds of years before this, however, the site had been of religious and political significance, witnessing numerous battles between the English and the Vikings. Today, half of the surviving medieval stained glass in England is in the minster, with the *Great East Window* displaying over 100 Biblical scenes. The elaborate astronomical clock in the *North Transept* was designed and constructed at the Royal Greenwich Observatory to commemorate 18,000 airmen from Yorkshire and northeast England who lost their lives in World War II. A fire in the South Transept in 1984 led to a £2 million-pound restoration project, and the ceiling now features 62 new bosses decorated with natural and local scenes designed by schoolchildren. There are views of the winding cobbled streets of York and the surrounding Yorkshire countryside from the *Central Tower*.

Transportation
Air: Manchester Airport, Leeds/Bradford International Airport, Newcastle Airport. **Rail:** Train: York Station. **Road:** Bus: Public services.

Contact Addresses
York Minster Visitors Department, St Williams College, 4-5 College Street, York YO1 7JF, UK
Tel: (01904) 557 216
Website: www.yorkminster.org

York Minster

VisitBritain©

Isle of Man

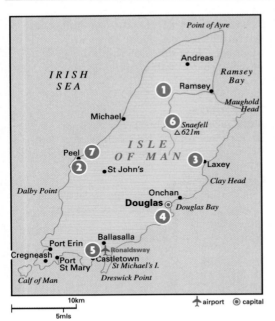

Point of Ayre

IRISH SEA

Andreas

Ramsey Bay

❶ Ramsey

Maughold Head

Michael

❻ *Snaefell △621m*

ISLE OF MAN

Peel ❼

❷ •St John's

❸ •Laxey

Clay Head

Dalby Point

Onchan

Douglas ◎ *Douglas Bay*

❹

Cregneash

Port Erin

Ballasalla

❺ ✈Ronaldsway

Port St Mary

Castletown

St Michael's I.

Calf of Man

Dreswick Point

10km
5mls

✈ airport   ◎ capital

1 Curraghs Wildlife Park
2 House of Manannan
3 Laxey
4 Manx Museum
5 Rushen Abbey and Castle Rushen
6 Snaefell Mountain Railway
7 St Patrick's Isle

Tourist Information

Isle of Man Government Tourism Department
Sea Terminal Building
Douglas IM1 2RG, Isle of Man
Tel: (01624) 686801
Website: www.gov.im/tourism

Curraghs Wildlife Park

Located at the edge of the *Ballaugh Curraghs*, *Curraghs Wildlife Park* is a wetland wildlife park ('curraghs' being a Manx word for wet) that's made up of boggy woodland and natural enclosures. Visitors are able to walk along designated paths through most of the enclosures with the emphasis being on trying to create environments as close as possible to the animals' natural habitats. Enclosures are based on geographical boundaries and represent the different countries of the world. *Close Beg* is a children's farm area aimed at teaching younger visitors about domestic animals and there are also indoor and outdoor play areas. *The Ark* is another educational attraction where visitors can learn about the problems facing many animals and the need to protect wild habitats. Visitors can also ride a miniature railway line.

Transportation

Air: Isle of Man Airport (Ballasalla). **Water:** Ferry: Douglas Ferry Port. **Rail:** Scenic steam railway travels south from Douglas. The Manx Electric Railway travels north from Douglas. **Road:** Bus: Public services.

Contact Addresses

For more information about Curraghs Wildlife Park, contact the Isle of Man Tourism Department (see **Tourist Information** above).

House of Manannan

Located by the harbour in the city of *Peel*, the award-winning *House of Manannan* is a museum that explores the island's Celtic, Viking and maritime traditions using a series of exhibitions and interactive displays. Manannan is a mythological sea god who was said to be able to blanket the island in a thick fog to protect it from its enemies. The island's history begins with pagan Celts who built wooden roundhouses, many of which have been excavated near the site and a reconstructed version is on display in the museum. Christianity arrived on the island around AD 500 and Viking settlers arrived soon after marrying into the local communities. The *Isle of Man*'s identity, past and present, is intimately linked to the sea and there's a permanent exhibition that explores these links with state-of-the-art displays and interactive exhibits.

Transportation

Air: Isle of Man Airport (Ballasalla). **Water:** Ferry: Douglas Ferry Port. **Rail:** Scenic steam railway travels south from Douglas. The Manx Electric Railway travels north from Douglas. **Road:** Bus: Public services.

Contact Addresses

Manx National Heritage Office, Douglas, Isle of Man, IM1 3LY
Tel: (01624) 648000
Website: www.gov.im/imh

Laxey

Built around a small harbour, the tranquil village of *Laxey* is located along the sides of a glen and dates back to the Viking era. Laxey is famous for the *Great Laxey Mines* which flourished between 1876 and 1882. Close to the hamlet of *Agneash* overlooking Laxey is the *Great Laxey Wheel*. Designed by Robert Casement and built in 1854, the wheel was used to pump water needed for the Great Laxey Mining Company. The wheel, named Lady Isabella after the Governor's wife, was acquired by the Manx Heritage Trust in 1989 and has been restored and still attracts thousands of visitors each year.

Transportation

Air: Isle of Man Airport (Ballasalla). **Water:** Ferry: Douglas Ferry Port. **Rail:** Scenic steam railway travels south from Douglas. The Manx Electric Railway travels north from Douglas. **Road:** Bus: Public services.

Contact Addresses

Manx National Heritage Office, Douglas, Isle of Man, IM1 3LY
Tel: (01624) 648000
Website: www.gov.im/imh

Manx Museum

The origins of the *Manx Museum* date back to 1886 but it was not until 1922 that the museum acquired its first permanent home in what was formerly known as *Noble's Old Hospital*. The

museum set about gathering various historical artefacts from around the island and it quickly became apparent that the museum needed bigger premises. In 1986 the museum underwent extensive development opening a new *Prehistoric Archaeology Gallery* and a film and lecture theatre. The museum is now the biggest museum on the island with award-winning exhibitions. A popular film, *The Story of Mann*, detailing the colourful history of the island is on permanent display at the museum. Other attractions at the museum include exhibitions on maps, geology, the Vikings as well as the renowned *National Art Gallery*.

Transportation

Air: Isle of Man Airport (Ballasalla). **Water:** Ferry: Douglas Ferry Port. **Rail:** Scenic steam railway travels south from Douglas. The Manx Electric Railway travels north from Douglas. **Road:** Bus: Public services.

Contact Addresses

Manx National Heritage Office, Douglas, Isle of Man, IM1 3LY
Tel: (01624) 648000
Website: www.gov.im/imh

Rushen Abbey and Castle Rushen

Situated in the *Silverdale Burn* in what is now known as *Ballasalla*, *Rushen Abbey* is one of the most important medieval structures on the *Isle of Man*. Originally built as a home for monks of the Sauvignac order, the abbey developed into the main religious seat of power on the island and a centre for religious study. The abbey was surrounded by a large estate and the abbey had control of other land holdings making it one of the largest estates on the island at the time. Visitors to the abbey can learn about the archaeological finds in the area and the ongoing excavation projects. Nearby at *Castletown* is *Castle Rushen*, one of Europe's finest medieval castles. The origins of the castle date back to Norse times and it was substantially developed between the 13th and 16th centuries. The oldest part of the structure is thought to be the central Keep and inner courtyard which was probably built by the last Viking King of Mann, Magnus. The imposing

Snaefell Mountain Railway

VisitBritain©

limestone walls would have been visible for miles around as a symbol of the power of the Kings and Lords of Mann.

Transportation
Air: Isle of Man Airport (Ballasalla). **Water:** Ferry: Douglas Ferry Port. **Rail:** Scenic steam railway travels south from Douglas. The Manx Electric Railway travels north from Douglas. **Road:** Bus: Public services.

Contact Addresses
Manx National Heritage Office, Douglas,
Isle of Man, IM1 3LY
Tel: (01624) 648000
Website: www.gov.im/imh

Snaefell Mountain Railway

The *Snaefell Mountain Railway* is an electric railway that first began service in 1895 and today still operates the 6.4-km (4-mile) stretch of track running from the village of *Laxey* (see separate entry) to the top of *Snaefell*, the island's highest peak. The train's only stop en route is known as the *Bungalow* and is midway up the mountain on the *Mountain Road*. The 30-minute journey takes in spectacular views of the surrounding countryside including *Laxey Glen*. A cafe, pub, and small museum are located at the summit stop. On a clear day, it's said that visitors can see across to *Ireland*, *Wales*, *Scotland* and *England*. There is no road access to the summit of Snaefell but there are walking paths.

Transportation
Air: Isle of Man Airport (Ballasalla). **Water:** Ferry: Douglas Ferry Port. **Rail:** Scenic steam railway travels south from Douglas. The Manx Electric Railway travels north from Douglas. **Road:** Bus: Public services.

Contact Addresses
Banks Circus, Douglas, Isle of Man, IM1 5PT
Tel: (01624) 675222 *or* 662525
Website: www.iombusandrail.info

St Patrick's Isle

Dominating *St Patrick's Isle*, *Peel Castle* is one of the *Isle of Man*'s most important historic sites with its origins dating back to the sixth century. Human habitation on the isle goes back much further to the hunter gatherers who were probably attracted by its relative safety and by the abundant fish stocks. But it was St Patrick who is said to have bought Christianity to the isle and established a church. *St Patrick's Church* and the *Round Tower* – one of the oldest surviving parts of the castle – were later ringed by a defensive *Curtain Wall*. The isle was an important site in Manx Christianity and the *Cathedral of St German* was added to the complex during the 13th century. Archaeological finds include the grave of a noble Norse lady who was buried with extravagant jewellery. By the 18th century, Peel Castle's importance was in decline and the buildings were abandoned and left to ruin. Today, the castle ruins are a picturesque attraction on an abandoned rocky outcrop that overlooks the *Irish Sea*.

Transportation
Air: Isle of Man Airport (Ballasalla). **Water:** Ferry: Douglas Ferry Port. **Rail:** Scenic steam railway travels south from Douglas. The Manx Electric Railway travels north from Douglas. **Road:** Bus: Public services.

Contact Addresses
St. Patrick's Isle, Peel Harbour, Peel,
Isle of Man IM5
Tel: (01624) 648000
Website: www.gov.im/imh

Northern Ireland

ATLANTIC OCEAN
Malin Head
SCOTLAND
Giant's Causeway
Rathlin I.
North Channel
④
Coleraine
L. Foyle
Bann
Londonderry
Strabane
Ballymena
Larne
NORTHERN
Mourne
Belfast L.
Omagh
Lough Neagh
Belfast
① ② ⑥ N D
Strangford Lough
L. h Erne
⑤
Portadown
③
Enniskillen
Dundalk
Upper Lough Erne
Newry
Shannon
Erne
IRELAND
IRISH SEA
Carlingford Lough

80km
40mls
✈ international airport
◉ capital

1 Belfast Zoo (Zoological Gardens)
2 Crawfordsburn Country Park
3 Exploris Aquarium
4 Giant's Causeway
5 Oxford Island National Nature Reserve
6 W5 , Belfast

Tourist Information

Northern Ireland Tourist Board
St Anne's Court, 59 North Street, Belfast BT1 1NB, UK
Tel: (0280) 9023 1221
Website: www.discovernorthernireland.com

Northern Ireland Tourist Board
24 Haymarket, London SW1Y 4DG, UK
Tel: (08701) 555 250 (information) *or* (020) 7766 9920 (trade and marketing)

Belfast Zoo (Zoological Gardens)

The origins of *Belfast Zoo* date back to 1911 with the creation of the *Bellevue Gardens* that were designed to provide the city of Belfast with a recreational area with gardens and a playground for children. In 1934, Bellevue Zoo was added to the site. After some years in decline, in 1974 the area underwent a massive redevelopment project to create the popular zoo that exists today. The zoo has a strong emphasis on conservation and education and zoo works closely with schools and youth groups. Popular sections of the zoo include the *Monkey Island*, the *African* and *Elephant Enclosures*, the *Penguin* and *Sea Lion Pools*, the *Gorilla Enclosure* and the *Children's Farm* where younger visitors can get close to traditional farm animals. The site is located at *Cavehill* which offers stunning views back across the city.

Transportation
Air: Belfast International Airport. **Rail:** Belfast Central Station. **Road:** Bus: Public services. Car: Signposted from the M1 and M2.

Contact Addresses
City of Belfast Zoological Gardens, Antrim Road, Belfast BT 36 7PN, Northern Ireland
Tel: (028) 9077 6277
Website: www.belfastzoo.co.uk

Crawfordsburn Country Park

Located on the southern shores of *Belfast Lough*, *Crawfordsburn Country Park* boasts stunning views along 3.5km (2.2 miles) of rugged coastline. The park includes two great beaches, woodland, ponds and meadows and visitors are able to enjoy three marked trails – the *Coastal Path*, the *Glen Walk* and the *Meadows Walk*. The Glen Walk is the shortest of the three but passes through some spectacular scenery including a five-arched railway viaduct and a beautiful waterfall. The *Coastal Path* is suitable for wheelchair users. Other attractions in the park include the *Grey Point Fort*, a coastal battery and gun emplacement dating from the 1900s. The park offers a series of informative guided walks during the summer months.

Transportation
Air: Belfast International Airport. **Rail:** Bangor Station then taxi or bus services to the park. **Road:** Bus: Public services. Car: Signposted from the A2.

Giants Causeway

Transportation
Air: Belfast International Airport. **Water:** Ferry:
Portaferry. **Rail:** Belfast Central Station then taxi
or bus. **Road:** Bus: Public services. Car: A20 from
Belfast.

Contact Addresses
Exploris, The Ropewalk, Castle Street, Portaferry,
County Down, Northern Ireland
Tel: (028) 4272 8062
Website: www.exploris.org.uk

Giant's Causeway

Situated on the northern coast of Ireland, the
Giant's Causeway is a unique geological feature
consisting of a protrusion of basalt hexagonal
columns jutting into the sea. The Causeway was
formed an estimated 62-65 million years ago by
the cooling of volcanic rock. According to local
legend, the Causeway was built by two feuding
giants, Finn MacCool in Ireland and
Benandonner in Scotland, who needed to travel
across the sea in order to do battle. The site was
discovered in 1692 by the Bishop of Derry and
attracts many visitors every year to see the
estimated 40,000 columns. Antrim's coastline
and the local scenery are both spectacular,
including *Lacada Point* and *Bengore Head*. As well
as being an area of outstanding natural beauty,
Lacada Point is also famed for being the place
where the *Girona*, a Neapolitan galleass which
was part of the Spanish Armada, sank in 1588
killing all 1200 men onboard. The Giant's
Causeway was declared a UNESCO World
Heritage Site in 1986.

Contact Addresses
Crawfordsburn Country Park, Bridge Road South,
Helen's Bay, County Down BT19 1LD, Northern
Ireland
Tel: (028) 9185 3621
Website: www.ehsni.gov.uk/places/parks/
crawfordsburn.shtml

Exploris Aquarium

Situated on the shores of the *Strangford Lough
Marine Nature Reserve*, *Exploris* began as the
Northern Ireland Aquarium which opened in 1987
to enable the public to view and learn more about
the diverse marine life that exists in the *Irish Seas*.
It underwent significant expansion and reopened
in 1994 as Exploris. A new, purpose-built *Seal
Sanctuary* was added in 2000 and is now one of
the most popular attractions at the site. Holding
250 tonnes of water, the *Open Sea Tank* is the
largest tank at Exploris and can be viewed from
the bridge that runs over it or from the cave
beneath. Species in this tank include shark, conger
eels as well as smaller fish such as cod, halibut
and bass.

Transportation
Air: Belfast International Airport or Belfast City
Airport. **Rail:** Train: Portrush Station. **Road:** Bus:
Public services.

Contact Addresses
Giant's Causeway Visitor Centre, 44 Causeway
Road, Bushmills, County Antrim BT57 8SU, UK
Tel: (028) 2073 1855
Website: www.northantrim.com/
giantscauseway.htm

Oxford Island National Nature Reserve

Situated on the southern shores of the large freshwater lake, *Lough Neagh*, the *Oxford Island National Nature Reserve* is a protected area of outstanding natural beauty. The area is made up of a variety of different habitats including reedbeds, woodland, meadows full of wild flowers and ponds that teem with life and is one of the most picturesque regions in *County Armagh*. The reserve includes a number of bird-watching hides, viewing areas, paddling pool and several marked walking trails – some of which are suitable for wheelchair users. The *Lough Neagh Discovery Centre* opened on the shores of the lake in 1993 and provides visitors with information and history about the area.

Oxford Island Lough Neagh Centre

Northern Ireland Tourist Board©

Transportation
Air: Belfast International Airport. **Rail:** Belfast Central Station then taxi or bus. **Road:** Bus: Public services. Car: Signposted from the M1.

Contact Addresses
Lough Neagh Discovery Centre, Oxford Island National Nature Reserve, Craigavon, County Armagh BT66 6NJ, Northern Ireland
Tel: (028) 3832 2205
Website: www.oxfordisland.com

W5, Belfast

W5 is a science and information attraction where visitors can learn more about science and the world around them through the many interactive exhibits. Popular permanent exhibits include the *Fire Tornado*, *Bubble Tubes*, *Cloud Rings*, *Musical Stairs*, the *Sound Wall* and *Tennis Ball Launchers*. Visitors can also learn more about animation with interactive exhibits. W5 also presents a varied programme of temporary exhibitions and events and there is a daily programme of live science demonstrations and shows throughout the day.

Transportation
Air: Belfast International Airport. **Rail:** Belfast Central Station (10-minute walk to W5). **Road:** Bus: Public services.

Contact Addresses
W5, Odyssey, 2 Queen's Quay, Belfast BT3 9QQ, Northern Ireland
Tel: (028) 9046 7700
Website: www.w5online.co.uk

Scotland

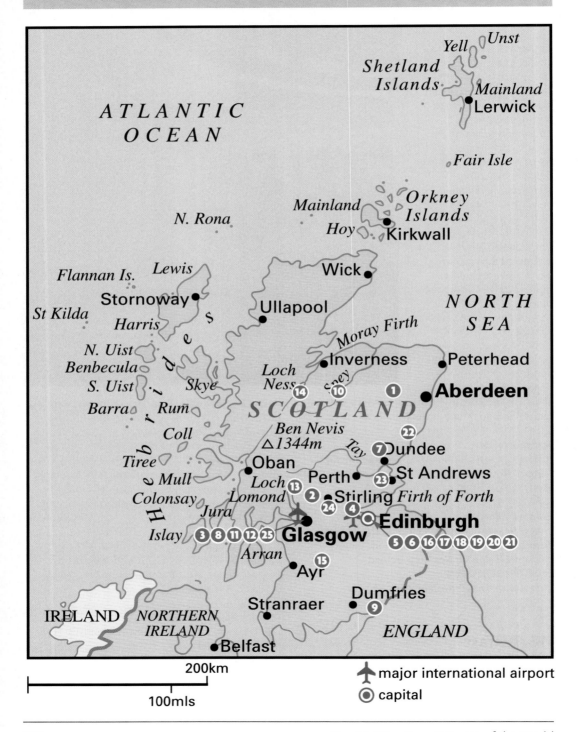

ATLANTIC
OCEAN

Yell *Unst*

*Shetland
Islands·*

Mainland
Lerwick

· Fair Isle

N. Rona

Mainland

Hoy

*Orkney
Islands*

Kirkwall

Wick

Flannan Is. *Lewis*

St Kilda

Stornoway

Harris

Ullapool

NORTH
SEA

N. Uist
Benbecula
S. Uist   *Skye*

Moray Firth

Inverness   Peterhead

Loch
Ness

Aberdeen

Barra   *Rum*

S C O T L A N D

(14)   (10)   (1)

Coll

(22)

Tiree

Ben Nevis
△1344m

Oban

(7) Dundee

Mull

Loch
Lomond

(13) Perth

St Andrews

Colonsay

Jura

(2) Stirling *Firth of Forth*

(23)

Islay

(3)(8)(11)(12)(25) **Glasgow**

(24) (4)

◉ **Edinburgh**

(5)(6)(16)(17)(18)(19)(20)(21)

Arran

(15)

Ayr

Dumfries

Stranraer

(9)

IRELAND *NORTHERN
IRELAND*

ENGLAND

Belfast

200km

100mls

✈ major international airport

◉ capital

Tourist Information

Visit Scotland
23 Ravelston Terrace, Edinburgh
EH4 3TP, UK
Tel: (0131) 332 2433
Website: www.visitscotland.com

Key to symbols: £ Entry charged & Disabled access ▟ Man-made attraction ♥ Natural attraction **P** Parking ✕ Restaurant ⛲ Shop ▥ UNESCO site

Balmoral Estate

Balmoral Estate is owned personally by the Queen (rather than as a Sovereign possession) and is a working estate that is closely integrated with the local community. *Balmoral Castle* was first rented by Queen Victoria and Prince Albert in 1948. They loved it so much they bought it four years later and it has been a favourite Royal Residence ever since. Visitors can tour parts of the castle including the famous *Ballroom* which houses several exhibitions including china and silverware from the estate. Visitors can also enjoy guided or marked walks through the gardens and surrounding grounds and there are also opportunities for pony trekking, fishing and Land Rover safaris. The estate rents out holiday cottages and some of the state rooms are available for hire for private functions. The estate is usually closed from August through until the end of March.

Transportation
Air: Aberdeen International Airport. **Rail:** Aberdeen Station then taxi or bus service to the estate. **Road:** Bus: Public services. Car: Located off the A93.

Contact Addresses
The Estates Office, Balmoral Estates, Ballater, Aberdeenshire AB35 5TB, UK
Tel: (01339) 742 534
Website: www.balmoralcastle.com

Blair Drummond Wildlife & Safari Park

Blair Drummond Wildlife and Safari Park opened in 1970 in the grounds of *Blair Drummond House*. The land had been purchased in 1916 by a wealthy Glasgow tea merchant named Sir John Kay. As he himself had no sons, his nephew Sir John Muir inherited the park who was the father of the present owner, Jamie Muir. Today, the safari park attracts thousands of visitors who come to drive through the park enclosures (park buses take visitors that arrived on public transport) to visit crowd-favourites such as elephants, lions, tigers, bears and bison. Visitors can also travel to *Chimp Island* on pleasure boats. In addition to the wildlife, there are also other attractions such as a wooden play castle, adventure play area, boating lake and fairground.

Transportation

Air: Glasgow International Airport or Edinburgh International Airport. **Rail:** Stirling Station. **Road:** Bus: Public services.

Contact Addresses

Blair Drummond Safari Park and Adventure Park, Blair Drummond FK9 4UR, UK
Tel: (01786) 841 456
Website: www.safari-park.co.uk

Celtic Park

Celtic Football Club is one of *Glasgow*'s two top teams, the other being Glasgow Rangers. Celtic moved to its present ground at *Celtic Park* in 1892. The all-seater ground, also known as *Parkhead* and *Paradise* to its fans, has a capacity of 60,500. A double tier rings most of the ground with the single tiered section housing the *Club Museum*. Celtic and Rangers have dominated Scottish football for years and the atmosphere on derby days is passionate and can be quite firey. The ground has good conference and hospitality facilities and is available for private hire.

Transportation

Air: Glasgow International Airport. **Rail:** Train: Glasgow Station then connection to Dalmarnock Station (five minutes walk to ground). **Road:** Bus: Public services. Car: Celtic Park is signposted off the M8.

Contact Addresses

Celtic Football Club, Celtic Park, Glasgow G40 3RE, UK
Tel: (0845) 671 1888
Website: www.celticfc.co.uk

Deep Sea World

Located beneath the famous *Forth Rail Bridge* at *North Queensferry* in *Fife*, *Deep Sea World* is a vast aquarium that's home to thousands of weird and wonderful creatures. Visitors can explore the aquatic world on the *Underwater Safari* via one of the longest underwater tunnels in the world as the impressive marine life – including tiger sharks

and conger eels – swim overhead. There are separate zones such as the *Amazonian Experience* and there's also amphibian and reptile displays. Open to visitors with no previous diving experience, those that want to get closer to the fish are able to take a diving induction course ending with a swim with the ever-popular resident sharks. Deep Sea World has also recently launched its *Shark Awareness* course for qualified divers. The *Seal Sanctuary* is another popular addition which is dedicated to the rehabilitation of orphaned or injured seals. The centre also has conference facilities which are available for private hire.

Transportation

Air: Edinburgh International Airport or Glasgow International Airport. **Rail:** Train: North Queensferry Station (a signposted 10-minute walk from the station). **Road:** Bus: Free shuttle bus operates during July and August with pick ups at the Waverley Bridge. Car: Junction 1 off M90.

Contact Addresses

Deep Sea World, Battery Quarry, North Queensferry, Fife, KY11 1JR, UK
Tel: (01383) 411 880
Website: www.deepseaworld.com

Edinburgh Castle

Edinburgh Castle looks over the city of Edinburgh from its perch on top of an extinct volcano. The oldest building in Edinburgh and its most popular tourist attraction, the castle has served both as fortress and royal residence. Today, it houses the *Scottish Crown Jewels*, the *Stone of Destiny* and *Mons Meg* (a massive 15th-century bombard), as well as the headquarters of the British Army's Scottish Division and a permanent exhibition which depicts the history of Scotland. The castle has had a rich and colourful history, withstanding numerous attacks from Oliver Cromwell's Roundheads in 1650, and William and Mary's army in 1689. It was also the birthplace of James VI of Scotland (who became James I of England in 1603), who was born to Mary Queen of Scots in a tiny room in the *Royal Residence* in 1566. Every day, except Sunday and Bank Holidays, the one o'clock gun is fired from the castle, and for three weeks in August, the annual *Military Tattoo* takes place in the *Castle Esplanade*.

Transportation
Air: Edinburgh Airport. **Rail:** Train: Waverley Station. **Road:** Bus: Public services.

Contact Addresses
Edinburgh Castle, Castle Hill, Edinburgh EH1 2NG, UK
Tel: (0131) 225 9846
Website: www.historic-scotland.gov.uk

Edinburgh Zoo

Founded in 1913 by the Royal Zoological Society of Scotland, *Edinburgh Zoo* is one of the most significant zoos in Europe. It is Scotland's most popular wildlife attraction, with over 1000 animals, including meerkats, pygmy hippos, snow leopards and blue poison arrow frogs. Set in 32 hectares (80 acres) of beautiful parkland on the slopes of Corstorphine Hill, with stunning views of the surrounding countryside, the zoo is famous for having the world's biggest penguin pool, which is home to the largest colony of penguins in Europe. As well as animals, there are many other attractions, such as the *African Plains Experience*, the *Maze*, the *Magic Forest* and the *Hilltop Safari Tour*.

Transportation
Air: Edinburgh Airport. **Rail:** Train: Waverley Station. **Road:** Bus: Public services.

Contact Addresses
Edinburgh Zoo, Murrayfield, Edinburgh EH12 6TS, UK
Tel: (0131) 334 9171
Website: www.edinburghzoo.org.uk

Glamis Castle

Set in the heart of the *Angus Glens*, *Glamis Castle* has been the family home of the Earls of Strathmore and Kinghorne for hundreds of years and has been a royal residence since 1372. It is also famous for being the childhood home of Elizabeth Bowes-Lyon, better known as the Queen

Edinburgh Castle

Mother, and her daughter, Princess Margaret, both of whom passed away in 2002 aged 101 and 71 respectively. The castle is now home to the 18th Earl of Strathmore and Kinghorne. Visitors are able to take a guided tour of the castle and grounds viewing the spectacular *Royal Apartments*. Outside, the *Italian Garden*, *Pinetum* and *Nature Trail* are particularly popular with visitors. Parts of Glamis Castle are available for hire for wedding receptions and private functions. The castle is usually closed from mid-December to mid-March.

Transportation
Air: Dundee Airport. **Rail:** Dundee Station then taxi or bus service to Glamis Castle. **Road:** Bus: Public services. Car: Off the A94.

Contact Addresses
The Castle Administrator, Estates Office, Glamis by Forfar, Angus DD8 1RJ, UK
Tel: (01307) 840 393
Website: www.glamis-castle.co.uk

GOMA (Gallery of Modern Art)

The *Gallery of Modern Art*, which is situated near George Square and Buchanan Street in the centre of Glasgow, is home to the city's principal modern art collection. Glasgow's most recent major art gallery, which opened in 1996, houses an impressive selection of Glasgow's post-war art and design, including work by international artists, such as Andy Warhol and David Hockney, and by Scottish artists, such as Ken Curry and John Bellany. The collection is housed in the Stirling Library in the historic Royal Exchange Square and spread over four floors, encompassing work themed around the four elements: earth, fire, air and water. Highlights include the artist Beryl Cook's paintings 'By the Clyde' and 'Karaoke', and the Scottish artist Avril Paton's painting 'Windows in the West'.

Transportation
Air: Glasgow Airport. **Rail:** Train: Queen Street Station. Underground: St Enoch or Buchanan Street stations. **Road:** Bus: Public services.

Contact Addresses
Gallery of Modern Art, Queen Street, Glasgow G1 3AZ, UK
Tel: (0141) 229 1996
Website: www.glasgowmuseums.com

Gretna Green

Situated on the old coach route that linked London and Edinburgh, *Gretna Green* gained notoriety as the first village across the border from *England* where young lovers would flee to get married due to Scotland's marriage laws. Marriages became a lucrative business and one of the most famous marriage venues was the *Old Blacksmith's Shop*. Owned by a family business called the Gretna Green Group Ltd that was founded in 1886, the site has now been developed into a popular tourist attraction with a museum, restaurant and heritage shops and still retains the feel and values of a small, family business. The centre now attracts thousands of visitors each year and is one of Scotland's most-visited tourist attractions.

Transportation
Air: Newcastle International Airport or Glasgow International Airport. **Rail:** Gretna Green Station. **Road:** Bus: Public services. Car: M4 or A75.

Contact Addresses
Gretna Green Group Ltd, Gretna Green, Dumfries & Galloway DG16 5EA, UK
Tel: (01461) 338441
Website: www.gretnagreen.com

Highland Wildlife Park

The *Highland Wildlife Park* in *Inverness-shire* in the very centre of *Scotland* opened in 1972 and is run by the *Royal Zoological Society* of Scotland. Visitors to this stunning park are able to drive through a series of enclosures and natural habitats of the *Main Reserve*. There are also several walking tracks which visitors can explore. One of the most popular parts of the park is the 2 hectare (5 acre) *Wolf Territory* which is viewable both from cars in the Main Reserve and also from a raised boardwalk *View Point* on one of the walking trails. Other animals at the park include European bison, elk, Highland cattle, red deer and wild sheep. There's also an informative *Visitor Centre*.

Transportation
Air: Aberdeen International Airport and Inverness Airport (domestic services). **Rail:** Kingussie Station then taxi to the park. **Road:** Bus: Public Services. Car: A9 and B9152 to the park.

Contact Addresses
Highland Wildlife Park, Kincraig, Kingussie, Inverness-shire PH21 1NL, UK
Tel: (01540) 651270
Website: www.highlandwildlifepark.org

Ibrox Football Stadium

Inaugurated in 1899, *Ibrox Stadium* is the home of Glasgow Rangers football club, one of the city's two top teams, the other being Celtic. The magnificent all-seater stadium has a capacity of 50,400 and is one of only 12 football grounds in Europe to have been awarded the highest 5-star

Loch Lomond

rating by UEFA, footballs' governing body. Visitors can take a tour of the ground as well as viewing the museum and the coveted *Trophy Room* that opened to the public in 1959. The ground itself is a great mix of old and new with visitors being greeted by the famous original red-brick entrance to Ibrox. Inside, the ground boasts executive boxes, conference rooms and hospitality suites and can be hired for corporate functions and wedding ceremonies.

Transportation
Air: Glasgow International Airport. **Rail:** Train: Glasgow Station. Underground: Ibrox Station (Copland Road). **Road:** Bus: Public services. Car: Ibrox is signposted off the M8.

Contact Addresses
The Rangers Football Club plc, Ibrox Stadium, Glasgow G51 2XD, UK
Tel: (0141) 580 8500
Website: www.rangers.premiumtv.co.uk

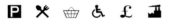

Kelvingrove Art Gallery and Museum

Kelvingrove Art Gallery and Museum, which is the principal art gallery and museum in the city of Glasgow, is one of Scotland's most popular free attractions. The imposing late-Victorian, red sandstone building, which opened in 1901, houses an impressive display of archaeology, natural history and ethnography, including European armour, prehistoric relics and military weapons. It also houses a wide range of European paintings by Botticelli, Rembrandt, Millet, Monet, Van Gogh, Derain and Picasso. On permanent show is the Glasgow 1900 exhibition which exhibits paintings, furniture and decorative art objects dating from Glasgow at the turn of the 20th century. The main attraction at Kelvingrove is a room dedicated to the works of the 19th-century architect Charles Rennie Mackintosh who studied at the famous Glasgow School of Art.

Transportation
Air: Glasgow Airport. **Rail:** Underground: Kelvinhall Station. **Road:** Bus: Public services.

Contact Addresses
Kelvingrove Art Gallery and Museum, Kelvingrove, Glasgow G3 8AG, UK
Tel: (0141) 287 2699
Website: www.glasgowmuseums.com

Loch Lomond

Loch Lomond Shores is an innovative visitor centre that acts as a gateway to the *Loch Lomond and the Trossachs National Park* (www.lochlomond-trossachs.org) on Scotland's west coast. At the heart of the centre is *Drumkinnon Tower* which was designed by one of Scotland's leading architects, David Page. The building is built in the style of an ancient castle and contains a mix of attractions aimed at offering visitors a greater understanding of the natural and cultural heritage of the Loch Lomond area. The *Legend of Loch Lomond* film tells the story behind the song 'The Bonnie, Bonnie Banks of Loch Lomond' which originated at the time of the 1745 Jacobite rebellion. There's also a family-orientated theatre show narrated by a young otter. The National Park was the first in Scotland and contains the deep waters of Loch Lomond, the glens of the Trossachs, the *Argyll Forest* and the spectacular mountains of *Breadalbane*.

Transportation
Air: Glasgow International Airport. **Rail:** Balloch Station (then bus or taxi to Loch Lomond Shores). **Road:** Bus: Public services.

Contact Addresses
Loch Lomond Shores, Balloch, UK
Tel: (01389) 722406
Website: www.lochlomondshores.com

Loch Ness seen from Fort Augustus

VisitBritain©

Loch Ness

Loch Ness in the heart of Inveness is the largest body of freshwater in the British Isles and has a greater volume than all the lakes and reservoirs in England and Wales. But it is not its size that has gained the loch its worldwide notoriety; Loch Ness is famed for the stories of the *Loch Ness Monster* that is said to live in its murky depths. The first sighting dates back to AD 565 when St Columba is said to have seen a strange 'water beast' on the *River Ness*. The legend of the Loch Ness Monster has endured ever since with images of 'Nessie' apparently caught in now famous photos in 1951 and again in 1955. There are plenty of viewing points around the loch and there's an official *Loch Ness Circular Car Tour* that visitors can take. There's an exhibition dedicated to the myths and legends of the loch at the *Loch Ness Visitor Centre*. The loch is surrounded by some of the finest *Highland* scenery in Scotland that's peppered with castles, forts, waterfalls and stunning valleys.

Transportation
Air: Aberdeen International Airport and Inverness Airport (domestic services). **Rail:** Inverness Station then taxi to the park. **Road:** Bus: Public services. Car: A82 and A321 to the centre.

Contact Addresses
The Original Loch Ness Visitor Centre,
Drumnadrochit, Inverness IV63 6TU, UK
Tel: (01456) 450342
Website: www.lochness-centre.com

New Lanark World Heritage Centre

The *New Lanark World Heritage Site* in Southern Scotland is a restored 18th-century cotton mill village. At the award-winning visitor centre visitors can explore what life would have been like for the 18th-century inhabitants of New Lanark which rose to fame in the early 1800s when Robert Owen was manager of the mill. Two of the most popular attractions at the centre are the *Millennium Experience* ride and an audio-visual theatre show called *Annie McLeod's Story* which tells the history of the region through the ghost of a mill-girl. From the centre, visitors can follow the trail to the spectacular *Falls of Clyde* close by where there's also a *Wildlife Centre* that's home to nesting peregrine falcons. The site is one of Scotland's top attractions attracting over 400,000 visitors each year. The visitor centre is closed during December and January.

Transportation
Air: Edinburgh International Airport or Glasgow International Airport. **Rail:** Lanark Station (then bus or taxi to the Visitor Centre). **Road:** Bus: Public services.

Contact Addresses
New Lanark, World Heritage Site, South Lanarkshire ML11 9DB, UK
Tel: (01555) 661345
Website: www.newlanark.org

Palace of Holyroodhouse

The splendid *Palace of Holyroodhouse* in Edinburgh is The Queen's official residence in Scotland in and was originally founded as an Augustinian monastery in 1128 by David I. As the Abbey prospered and Edinburgh became recognised as the Scottish capital, a succession of Royals chose to live here at Holyroodhouse rather than at *Edinburgh*

Castle in the city. James IV added the palace to the abbey during his stay from 1488 to 1513 and his successor, James V, added two massive towers during the early part of the 16th century. The residence has a rich history and was also the home of Mary, Queen of Scots who spent a turbulent time there from 1561 to 1567. After a brief period out of favour with the royals, life at Holyroodhouse was reinvigorated with the arrival of Queen Victoria who initiated an extensive renovation process. Today, the palace is the Queen's official residence in Scotland (with the Queen's official *Holyrood Week* traditionally spanning the end of June and the start of July during which she hosts the annual *Holyrood Garden Party*) that attracts thousands of tourists each year. The largest room in the palace is the spectacular *Great Gallery* used for banquets and official occasions. Other attractions include the *State Apartments*, *Mary, Queen of Scots' Chambers* and the *Queen's Gallery*.

Transportation
Air: Edinburgh International Airport. **Rail:** Edinburgh (Waverley) Station (the palace is a 15-minute walk from the station). **Road:** Bus: Public services from Waverley Bridge.

Contact Addresses
Ticket Sales and Information Office, The Official Residences of The Queen, London SW1A 1AA
Tel: (0131) 556 5100
Website: www.royal.gov.uk

Royal Botanic Garden Edinburgh

Regarded as Scotland's premier garden, the *Royal Botanic Garden Edinburgh* is one of the city's most popular tourist attractions. The garden, which was first opened in 1670 as a small physic (medicinal) garden near Holyrood House, was designed by two doctors, Andrew Balfour and Robert Sibbald. It was moved to its present location during the 1820s and expanded to cover an area of 31 hectares (78 acres). Today, the garden contains a unique collection of plants from around the world, housed in the world-famous *Rock Garden*, the *Chinese Hillside* and the *Glasshouse Experience*. Visitors can also see the *Woodland Gardens & Arboretum* and the *Winter Garden*, as well as enjoy spectacular views across the city of Edinburgh.

Transportation
Air: Edinburgh Airport. **Rail:** Train: Waverley Station. **Road:** Bus: Public services. The Garden lies 1.6km (one mile) north of Edinburgh city centre, off the A902.

Contact Addresses
Royal Botanic Garden Edinburgh, 20A Inverleith Row, Edinburgh EH3 5LR, UK
Tel: (0131) 552 7171
Website: www.rbge.org.uk

Royal Museum and Museum of Scotland

The *Royal Museum* and the *Museum of Scotland* are located on the same site in Edinburgh city centre. The Royal Museum, which has 36 galleries and is well known for its impressive Main Hall, houses an international collection of artistic, archaeological, scientific and industrial exhibits, ranging from Japanese art to natural history. The Museum of Scotland, which opened in 1998, has over 10,000 artefacts detailing the country's history from its geological formation and earliest inhabitants up to the 20th century. Many of Scotland's finest regional treasures are on display, including a communal drinking cup (the *Bute Mazer*), made after the Scots beat the English during the Battle of Bannockburn in 1314. There are also fine views of Edinburgh Castle from the museum's rooftop.

Transportation
Air: Edinburgh Airport. **Rail:** Train: Waverley Station. **Road:** Bus: Public services. Chambers Street is located just off the A7 South Bridge in central Edinburgh.

Contact Addresses
Royal Museum, Chambers Street, Edinburgh EH1 1JF, UK
Tel: (0131) 247 4219
Website: www.nms.ac.uk

Museum of Scotland, Chambers Street, Edinburgh, EH1 1JF, UK
Tel: (0131) 247 4422
Website: www.nms.ac.uk

Royal Yacht Britannia

Launched from *John Brown's Shipyard* in Clydebank in 1953, the *Royal Yacht Britannia* was in the service of the Queen and the Royal Family for over forty years travelling on 968 official voyages as far afield as the South Seas and Antarctica Decommissioned in 1997, the Britannia now resides in the port of *Leith* in *Edinburgh* and is a popular tourist attraction. Visitors to the Britannia are able to board the yacht and view exhibits and displays from the Royal voyages. A multilingual audio headset is also available. Highlights of the Britannia tour include *The Royal Apartments*, *The Sun Lounge*, *The Royal Bedrooms* and *The Drawing Room* – all lavishly furnished with prints, paintings and fine furniture. The *State Dining Room* has hosted many eminent guests over the years including Sir Winston Churchill, Rajiv Ghandi, Nelson Mandela, Bill Clinton, Boris Yeltsin, Ronald Reagan and Margaret Thatcher. Today, it can be hired for corporate functions. Other interesting exhibits onboard include the *Queen's Rolls-Royce Phantom V* worth over £1 million.

Transportation
Air: Edinburgh International Airport. **Rail:** Edinburgh (Waverley) Station. **Road:** Bus: Public services from Waverley Bridge.

Contact Addresses
The Royal Yacht Britannia, Ocean Terminal, Leith, Edinburgh EH6 6JJ, UK
Tel: (0131) 555 5566
Website: www.royalyachtbritannia.co.uk

Scotch Whisky Heritage Centre and Royal Mile

The historic *Royal Mile* in Edinburgh's Old Town leads from *Edinburgh Castle* to the *Palace of Holyrood House* and is actually one mile and 107 yards long. Visitors can tour the *Scotch Whisky Heritage Centre*, situated at the top of the Royal Mile, which allows them to see how whisky is made and is believed to have a resident ghost. The *Camera Obscura* at the top end of the Royal Mile, is also one of Edinburgh's top attractions, where visitors can see a panoramic view of the city reflected onto a white table. *Tron Kirk* is located at the junction of North Bridge and the Royal Mile and is a traditional place for partygoers to gather and hear the bells toll, ringing in the new year at midnight on Hogmanay (December 31). The long list of other attractions on the Royal Mile include: *Highland Tolbooth Kirk*, *Ramsay Garden*, *Writers' Museum*, *Brodie's Close*, *Parliament Square*, *John Knox's House*, *Museum of Childhood*, *Netherbow Port*, *Huntly House*, *Canongate Kirk*, *Abbey Lairds*, *Gladstone's Land*, *Queen Mary's Bath House* and *St Giles' Cathedral*.

Transportation
Air: Edinburgh Airport. **Rail:** Train: Waverley Station. **Road:** Bus: Public services. The Royal Mile is located in Edinburgh city centre, just off the A7 North Bridge.

Contact Addresses
Edinburgh and Lothians Tourist Board, 3 Princes Street, Edinburgh EH2 2QP, UK
Tel: (0131) 473 3800
Website: www.edinburgh.org

Scotch Whisky Heritage Centre, 354 Castlehill, The Royal Mile, Edinburgh EH1 2NE, UK
Tel: (0131) 220 0441
Website: www.whisky-heritage.co.uk

Scottish Parliament

The original *Scottish Parliament* was abolished in 1707 under the Act of Union to form the Parliament of Great Britain. The Scottish Parliament was reestablished in 1998 under the Scotland Act with the first session of the new Parliament held in 1999 at its brand new *Parliament Building* which lies at the end of Edinburgh's famous *Royal Mile* by *Holyrood Park*. Designed by Enric Miralles who was inspired by the dramatic landscape that surrounds the site, the striking building is made from a mix of steel, oak and granite. Sustainability and minimal impact were key factors in the design, and the building is famed as one of the most progressive and innovative buildings in *Britain* today. Access to the building is free but there is a charge for a guided tour.

Transportation
Air: Edinburgh International Airport. **Rail:** Edinburgh Waverley Station (15-minute walk to

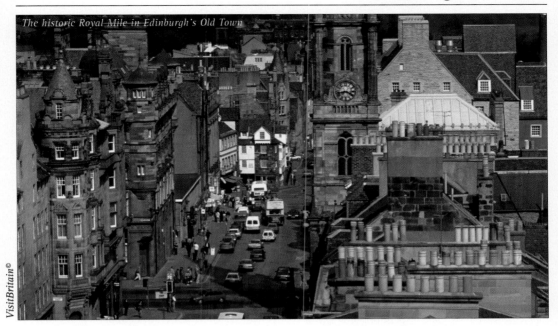

The historic Royal Mile in Edinburgh's Old Town

VisitBritain®

Scottish Parliament). **Road:** Bus: Public services from Waverley Bridge.

Contact Addresses
Public Information Services, The Scottish Parliament, Edinburgh EH99 1SP, UK
Tel: (0131) 348 5000
Website: www.scottish.parliament.uk

Speyside Whisky Trails

Originally celebrated for its apparent medicinal qualities, whisky grew to become an integral part of daily Scottish life, drank for its reviving properties and to warm the body during the long, cold Scottish winters. As its popularity grew, extortionate taxes were imposed on whisky production in the latter stages of the 16th century which drove many distilleries underground, with several establishing themselves in the hills of the *Grampian Highlands* away from the eyes of the excise men. Smuggling became common practice and distilleries would signal from one hilltop to the next when excise men entered the area. In 1823, a new tax system was introduced that made it possible for distilleries to make a profit and pay taxes, and the illegal production of whisky gradually phased out. But many of the old

distilleries remain in their dramatic locations in the hills and today form a popular whisky trail where visitors can tour distilleries and sample a wee dram or two of their favourite malt or scotch whisky. The distilleries on the *Speyside Trail* include *Benromach*, *Cardhu*, *Dallas Dhu*, *Glenfiddich*, *Glen Grant*, *Glenlivet*, *Glen Moray* and *Strathisla*. The award-winning *Speyside Cooperage* and visitor centre is also on the trail where visitors can see how the traditional oak casks used for maturing the whiskies are made. Other popular trails in the Grampian Highlands include the *Castle Trail*, the *Coastal Trail* and the *Victorian Heritage Trail* and the whole area is renowned for its stunning scenery.

Transportation
Air: Aberdeen International Airport. **Rail:** Aberdeen Station. **Road:** Bus: Public Services to Aberdeen. Coach: Many coach tours include the Whisky Trails as part of the their trips. Car: A9 then A95 through Speyside.

Contact Addresses
For more information on the Speyside Whisky Trails, contact Visit Scotland (see **Tourist Information** above) or visit the Speyside Whisky Trails website: www.maltwhiskeytrail.com.

St Andrews Golf Course

St Andrews Golf Course is one of Scotland's finest golf courses and plays host to the prestigious Open tournament every five years in which the world's best golfers compete. The origins of the game are hotly disputed but many believe Scotland and St Andrews to be the true home of the sport. But one thing that cannot be contested is St Andrews' long history and connection with the game; it's thought that golf was first played here in the 1400s before being banned in 1457 allegedly because the men were neglecting archery practice in favour of the sport. James IV acquired a taste for the game and the ban was lifted in 1502 allowing the game to flourish and develop into the international sport it has become today. St Andrews is a 'links' course – the name given to courses in coastal areas which is how the original game is thought to have been played – and is characterised by deep sand bunkers and strong winds. There are now six courses at St Andrews with a seventh due to be added in 2007. Other popular attractions close by include the prestigious *St Andrews University*, *St Andrews Museum*, *St Andrews Botanic Garden* and *Craigtoun Country Park*.

Transportation
Air: Glasgow International Airport or Edinburgh International Airport. **Rail:** Leuchars Station then taxi or bus service to St Andrews. **Road:** Bus: Public Services. Car: M90 then the A91 to St Andrews.

Contact Addresses
St Andrews Links Trust, Pilmour House,
St Andrews, Fife KY16 9SF, UK
Tel: (01334) 466666
Website: www.standrews.org.uk

Stirling Castle

The medieval *Stirling Castle*, which is perhaps the finest in Scotland, sits on a rocky outcrop, looking down upon some of the most famous battlefields in Scotland's history. These include *Stirling Bridge*, where William Wallace defeated the English in 1297 during the War of Independence, and *Bannockburn*, where Robert the Bruce was triumphant over King Edward II's troops in 1314. Historians are unclear as to the castle's exact date of construction, although it is believed to have been built between 1370 and 1750. Stirling also has famous associations with Mary Queen of Scots, who lived here during her childhood and was crowned in the *Chapel Royal* in 1543. There are many other attractions in or near Stirling, which include *Argyll's Lodging*, the *Wallace Monument*, the *Smith Art Gallery & Museum*, *Alloa Tower* and *Bannockburn*.

Transportation
Air: Glasgow International Airport. **Rail:** Stirling Station. **Road:** Car: M9 (from Edinburgh); A80 and M9 (from Glasgow).

Contact Addresses
Stirling Castle, Castle Wynd, Stirling FK8 1EJ, UK
Tel: (01786) 450 000
Website: www.historic-scotland.net

Waverley Historic Paddle Steamer

The *Waverley* is the last sea-going paddle steamer in the world and provides visitors with the opportunity to sail on scenic cruise journeys throughout the UK. Built on the Clyde in 1945, the Waverley originally sailed the waters between *Craigendorran* and *Arrochar* in West Scotland before falling into disrepair. After a lengthy repair project, the Waverley was fully restored in 2003 and is now docked in Glasgow from where it offers passengers the opportunity to sail on the Clyde as well as on longer voyages throughout the UK. The Waverley is also available for private hire.

Transportation
Air: Glasgow International Airport. **Rail:** Glasgow Station. **Road:** Bus: Public services.

Contact Addresses
Waverley Terminal, Anderston Quay, Glasgow G3 8HA, UK
Tel: (0141) 221 8152
Website: www.waverleyexcursions.co.uk

Wales

Tourist Information

Wales Tourist Board (Bwrdd Croeso Cymru)
First and tenth floors,
Brunel House,
2 Fitzalan Road,
Cardiff CF24 0UY, UK
Tel: (02920) 499 909
Website:
www.visitwales.com

1 Aberystwyth Arts Centre	12 Millennium Stadium
2 Anglesey	13 Museum of Welsh Life
3 Big Pit National Mining Museum of Wales	14 National Museum & Gallery Cardiff
4 Bodnant Garden	15 Oakwood Theme Park
5 Brecon Beacons National Park	16 Penrhyn Castle
6 Caernarfon Castle	17 Portmeirion
7 Cardiff Castle	18 Rhyl Suncentre
8 Chepstow Castle	19 Ruthin Craft Centre Gallery
9 Conwy Castle	20 Snowdonia National Park
10 Great Orme Tramway	21 St David's Cathedral
11 Manor House Wildlife Park	22 Welsh Slate Museum

Aberystwyth Arts Centre

The award-winning *Aberystwyth Arts Centre* is part of the *University of Wales Aberystwyth* and is the largest and busiest arts centre in the whole of Wales *Wales*. It underwent a massive redevelopment project in 2000 and today welcomes over 500,000 visitors each year. The centre hosts a wide-ranging programme of events, activities and workshops from across a variety of art forms. The venue includes the 900-seater *Great Hall* which opened in 1970 and the *Exhibition Gallery* and *Theatre* that was completed two years later. The refurbishment added or updated a number of facilities including a pottery studio, print room, darkroom, video suite, dance studios, studio theatre, recording studio and a new 120-seater cinema.

Transportation
Air: Cardiff International Airport. **Rail:** Aberystwyth Station. **Road:** Bus: Public services.

Contact Addresses
Aberystwyth Arts Centre, The University of Wales, Aberystwyth, Penglais Campus, Ceredigion SY23 3DE, UK
Tel: (01970) 622882
Website: www.aberystwythartscentre.co.uk

Anglesey

Located on the west coast of *Wales*, human habitation on the island of *Anglesey* dates back to 7000BC and the Mesolithic Period. Anglesey was one of the last Celtic strongholds to fall to the Romans during their invasion of Wales in the first century, and many historic sites from this period still exist today. Religious sites on Anglesey include *St Cybi's Monastery* at Holyhead, and *St Seiriol's Monastery* at Penmon that date back to the medieval period and suffered badly at the hands of Viking invaders. As testament to the island's rich history, Anglesey is home to many other historic structures including the *Marquess of Anglesey's Column*, *Plas Newydd* and the splendid *Beaumaris Castle* that was built – although never fully completed – by King Edward I as a sign of his power over the Welsh.

Archaeologists have uncoverd many sites over the years including burial chambers, standing stones and hill forts, and many are in good condition and are open to visitors. Anglesey is also renowned for its natural beauty and is characterised by cliffs, estuaries, dunes, heaths, wetlands, lakes, parks and stunning sandy beaches. The island also lays claim to the first Women's Institute in Britain which was founded in *Llanfairpwllgwyngyllgogerchwyrndrobwllllandysilliog ogogoch,* the Isle of Anglesey village with the longest name in the world.

Transportation
Air: Manchester International Airport. **Rail:** Holyhead Station. **Road:** Bus: Public services.

Contact Addresses
Holyhead Tourist Information, Stenna Line, Terminal 1, Holyhead, Anglesey LL65 1DQ, UK
Tel: (01407) 762622
Website: www.visitwales.co.uk

Big Pit National Mining Museum of Wales

The *Big Pit National Mining Museum* is located on the edge of the town of *Blaenafon* which played a vital role in the industrial revolution and has been awarded World Heritage Status. The Big Pit Museum is at the site of what was one of Britain's biggest coal mines until it closed in 1980. In 1983 it reopened as a museum where visitors can now tour the colliery buildings and venture 91m (300ft) underground with a former miner to see what life would have been like for those that worked in the mines.

Transportation
Air: Cardiff International Airport. **Rail:** Merthyr Tydfil, Newport or Abergavenny Stations. **Road:** Bus: Public services.

Contact Addresses
Big Pit National Mining Museum of Wales, Blaenafon, Torfaen NP4 9XP, UK
Tel: (01495) 790 311
Website: www.nmgw.ac.uk

Bodnant Garden

Situated above the *River Conwy* close to *Colwyn Bay*, *Bodnant Garden* contains plants and trees from all over the world and is regarded as one of the most beautiful gardens in the UK. Measuring 32.4 hectares (80 acres), the garden is made up of two sections. The first is set around Bodnant Hall and is made up of terraced gardens fringed by trees. The second part is lower down and known as the 'Dell' and contains a spectacularly wild garden in the valley of the *River Hiraethlyn*. Visitors are able to explore the grounds at their leisure or guided tours are available. The gardens close from early November to early March each year.

Transportation
Air: Manchester International Airport. **Rail:** Conwy Station. **Road:** Bus: Public services.

Contact Addresses
Bodnant Garden, Tal-y-Cafn, Nr Colwyn Bay, Conwy LL28 5RE, UK
Tel: (01492) 650460
Website: www.bodnantgarden.co.uk

Brecon Beacons National Park

The *Brecon Beacons National Park* is one of Wales's most beautiful outdoor areas. Situated amongst hills and mountains, the park covers an area of 1344 sq km (520 sq miles) and stretches from the Welsh/English border to Llandeilo. The park includes the *Black Mountains*, the *Brecon Beacons* and *Fforest Fawr*, as well as moorland, forests, valleys, waterfalls, lakes, caves and gorges. *Brecon Cathedral*, in the town of Brecon, and *Hay-on-Wye*, with its annual book fair and many bookshops, are also popular tourist attractions. There are also numerous castles in the park, including *Trecastle*, *Tretower*, *Bronllys* and *Morlais*. The *Brecon Beacons Mountain Centre*, which is located 9km (5.5 miles) southwest of Brecon, provides visitors with information on the park and offers a fine view of the surrounding area, including *Pen y Fan* and *Corn Du* peaks. Visitors can also take the *Brecon Mountain Railway*, which runs from near Merthyr Tydfil up into the park, and gives spectacular views across Wales.

Bodnant Garden

VisitBritain©

Transportation
Air: Cardiff International Airport. **Rail:** Train: Merthyr Tydfil Station or Abergavenny Station. **Road:** Bus: Public services.

Contact Addresses
Brecon Beacons National Park, 7 Glamorgan Street, Brecon, Powys LD3 7DP, UK
Tel: (01874) 624 437
Website: www.breconbeacons.org

Caernarfon Castle

Begun in 1283 by King Edward I, *Caernarfon Castle* is set on a peninsula overlooking the Menai Straits that divide North Wales from the island of Anglesey. The design of the castle, with its high walls marked with arrow slits and its angular towers, is said to have been inspired by the great city of Constantinople (now Istanbul), the former imperial power base of Rome. The castle was built when Edward conquered Wales in 1284 and was intended not only as a military fortress, but also as a royal palace and the English administrative centre of the area. The dual purpose of the castle was demonstrated by the fact that he also founded a town and market within its walls. The future Edward II, son of Edward I, was the first English Prince of Wales, and to this day the ruling British monarch may confer the title of Prince of Wales upon their eldest son. Prince Charles' investiture as the 21st Prince of Wales took place at the castle in 1969. Today, visitors can enjoy informative exhibitions and displays at the castle and walk around the ramparts for fine views over the town and the Menai Straits.

Transportation
Air: Manchester Airport. **Rail:** Train: Bangor Station. **Road:** Bus: Public services.

Contact Addresses
Caernarfon Castle, Castle Ditch, Caernarfon, Gwynedd LL55 2AY, UK
Tel: (01286) 677 617
Website: www.caernarfon.com

Cardiff Castle

Located within easy walking distance of the city centre, the origins of *Cardiff Castle* date back to between AD 55 and AD 400 when the Romans established a fort and trading post in the area. When the Normans invaded in the 11th century, they constructed a typical motte and bailey fortification largely covering up most of the original Roman structure. Robert the Consol, the natural son of King Henry I, became Lord of the Castle in the 12th century replacing the wooden keep with a 12-sided stone one that survives intact to this day. Over the next 500 years,

various medieval lords ruled the region, adding to and modifying the site with each successive reign. It was also a period of great turbulence that saw many civilian revolts and attacks on the castle itself. The Butes were the last of the great families to occupy the castle in the 19th century and employed master architect William Burges to restore the castle with mock-medieval features creating the different styles still apparent to visitors today. One of the most striking features of the castle is the bright clock face of the *Clock Tower* built seven stories high during 1869-1873. Wheelchair users are unable to access the *Castle Apartments* but can access most other parts of the castle.

Transportation
Air: Cardiff International Airport. **Rail:** Cardiff Station. **Road:** Bus: Public services.

Contact Addresses
Cardiff Castle, Castle Street, Cardiff CF10 3RB, UK
Tel: (029) 2087 8100
Website: www.cardiffcastle.com

Chepstow Castle

Located in the *Wye Valley* in picturesque *South Wales*, the *Chepstow Castle* occupies a commanding position on the banks of the *River Wye* guarding what was once a strategically important crossing point on the river. Construction of the castle began in 1066 just after the Battle of Hastings for William the Conqueror, and was the first castle in Britain to be built entirely of stone. The two towers were later added by the Earl of Pembroke around 1200 and his sons added a gatehouse and barbican. During the 16th century, Richard Bigod III added more comfortable living quarters and the place became more like a palace than a castle. It was to later serve as a prison for Henry Marten, a signatory to the death warrant of King Charles I, following the Restoration of Charles II in 1660. The castle opened its doors to tourists for the first time in 1953 and today welcomes guests with life-size models of its former inhabitants and rulers. The award-winning *Chepstow Museum* is in the 18th-century *Town House* located opposite the castle car park and tells the long history of the region.

Great Orme Tramway

Transportation

Air: Cardiff International Airport. **Rail:** Chepstow
Station. **Road:** Bus: Public services.

Contact Addresses

Chepstow Castle, Bridge Street, Chepstow NP16
5EZ, UK
Tel: (01291) 624065
Website: www.chepstow.co.uk

Conwy Castle

Constructed by the English monarch Edward I
between 1283 and 1289, the fortress of *Conwy
Castle* was one of a number of castles built in
North Wales to subdue the Welsh Princes after a
hard fought campaign lasting years and costing
thousands of pounds. The castle dominates the
town sitting high on a rocky plateau above the
Conwy Estuary surrounded by the dramatic scenery
of *Snowdonia National Park*. It was designed by the
master mason of Savoy, James of St George, who
was regarded as one of the greatest military
architects of his time. It took five years to
complete and is remarkable in that it only
required a garrison of just 30 men to defend it. It
proved to be an indomitable fortress. Visitors can
ascend the battlements which offer stunning views
of the surrounding area. The town itself is
protected by a circuit of walls and 22 towers that
add to the medieval feel of this incredible castle.

Transportation

Air: Manchester International Airport. **Rail:** Conwy
Station. **Road:** Bus: Public services.

Contact Addresses

Conwy Castle Visitor Centre, Conwy
LL32 8LD, UK
Tel: (01492) 592248 *or* 592358

Great Orme Tramway

The *Great Orme Tramway* is a funicular railway
consisting of two tramcars which use a system of
counterbalanced weights on cables so that as one
train descends the hill, it helps to pull the other
one up. The cable tramway is over 100 years old
and is one of only a few still in operation in the
world that today continues to take tourists up
Great Orme. From the top there are spectacular
views across the traditional Victorian seaside town
of *Llandudno* with its sandy beaches and
promenade. A half way station was added in 2001
where visitors can break their journey with a visit
to the nearby *Bronze Age Copper Mine*. At the
summit there's a *Visitor Centre* with children's play
area. The trams run every 20 minutes, seven days
a week from March through to October.

Transportation

Air: Manchester International Airport. **Rail:**
Llandudno Station. **Road:** Bus: Public services.

Contact Addresses

Great Orme Tramway, Victoria Station, Church
Walks, Llandudno LL30 1AZ, UK
Tel: (01492) 879306
Website: www.greatormetramway.com

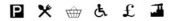

Manor House Wildlife Park

Located a few miles outside the coastal town of *Tenby* in the county of *Pembrokeshire*, the *Manor House Wildlife Park* is in beautiful grounds that surround an 18th-century *Manor House*. Paths through the 14-hectare (35-acre) park lead to animal enclosures that are home to animals such as zebras, camels, bison, llamas, antelope and reindeer. Visitors can opt for a tractor and trailer ride through the park that's accompanied by an informative commentary. There's also a picnic site and children's play area.

Transportation
Air: Cardiff International Airport. **Rail:** Tenby Station (then taxi or bus to the park). **Road:** Bus: Public services. Car: B4318.

Contact Addresses
Manor House Wildlife Park, St Florence Parade, Tenby, Pembrokeshire SA70 8RJ, UK
Tel: (01646) 651201
Website: www.safaripark.co.uk

Millennium Stadium

Cardiff's state-of-the-art *Millennium Stadium* opened in 1999 as the premiere sporting arena in the *UK* hosting many major sporting events whilst London's *Wembley Stadium* was being redeveloped (scheduled for completion in 2006). It has been built on the site of the old *National Stadium* at *Cardiff Arms Park* and was the first stadium in the UK with a retractable roof making it suitable for use throughout the year. Part funded by the Welsh Rugby Union, the stadium has a capacity of 74,500 and regularly hosts major football, rugby, athletics and speedway events as well as large music concerts.

Transportation
Air: Cardiff International Airport. **Rail:** Cardiff Central Station. **Road:** Bus: Public services.

Contact Addresses
Millennium Stadium plc, First Floor, Golate House, 101 St Mary Street, Cardiff CF10 1GE, UK
Tel: (0870) 013 8600
Website: www.millenniumstadium.com

Museum of Welsh Life

The *Museum of Welsh Life*, which is located on the outskirts of Cardiff, offers visitors an insight into how life in Wales used to be. Opened in July 1948, this open-air museum explains Welsh history over the past 500 years and allows visitors to imagine how rural life would have been over the centuries. The museum is set in 40 hectares (100 acres) of parkland, on the estate of the Elizabethan mansion, St Fagans Castle, a 16th-century manor house, which was donated to the people of Wales in 1947 by the Earl of Plymouth. Today, St Fagans, which has been refurbished in the style of a late-Victorian Welsh mansion, houses an exhibition on Welsh life through the ages. Other impressive buildings at the site include a chapel, a village store, several 19th-century farmhouses and a Victorian schoolhouse.

Transportation
Air: Cardiff International Airport. **Rail:** Train: Cardiff Central Station. **Road:** Bus: Public services. Car: The museum is signposted from junction 33 of the M4 motorway and can be accessed from the A4232.

Contact Addresses
Museum of Welsh Life, St Fagans, Cardiff CF5 6XB, UK
Tel: (029) 2057 3500
Website: www.nmgw.ac.uk

National Museum & Gallery Cardiff

Cardiff's *National Museum and Gallery* brings together collections and exhibits from the fields of art, science and history. The museum's art collection dates back over 500 years and is one of the finest exhibitions in *Europe* which includes one to the best Impressionist collections outside Paris. The *Natural History – Man and the Environment* display includes the skeleton of a blue whale and the largest leatherback turtle in the world. The popular *Evolution of Wales* display brings visitors face to face with dinosaurs and woolly mammoths in an exploration of evolution in the region. The *Glanely Gallery* is the museum's interactive area that encourages visitors to get closer to the museum's collections with the help of the specialist staff who are able to help with specific questions and research. Visitors are able to wear a headset for an audio tour which gives greater details on 45 of the museum's most popular exhibits.

Transportation
Air: Cardiff International Airport. **Rail:** Cardiff Station (20 minutes walk from station). **Road:** Bus: Public services.

Contact Addresses
National Museum & Gallery, Cathays Park, Cardiff CF10 3NP, UK
Tel: (029) 2039 7951
Website: www.nmgw.ac.uk

Oakwood Theme Park

Located east of *Haverfordwest*, *Oakwood Theme Park* is one of the top paid-entry attractions in *Wales* that receives close to the 400,000 visitors each year. Oakwood is a traditional theme park with rides aimed at all ages. A *Family Zone* includes small scale versions of traditional rides such as the *Pirate Ship* and the *Rollercoaster* as well as more relaxed activities such as *Mini Golf* and the *Boating Lake*. The white knuckle rides include *Megaphobia*, *The Bounce*, *Hydro* and *Vertigo* – a ride in which visitors are harnessed in to a huge 49m (160ft) swing. Indoor attractions include 10-pin bowling and the *Crystal Maze* puzzle area based on the popular television series of the same name.

Transportation
Air: Cardiff International Airport. **Rail:** Narberth Station then taxi. **Road:** Bus: There are no public services directly to Oakwood (except for a summer only service from Swansea). Car: Signposted from the A40 or A48 to Carmarthen.

Contact Addresses
Oakwood Theme Park, Canaston Bridge, Narberth, Pembrokeshire SA67 8DE, UK
Tel: (01834) 891376
Website: www.oakwood-leisure.com

Penrhyn Castle

VisitBritain©

Penrhyn Castle

Built in a dramatic location between *Snowdonia* and the *Menai Strait* by Thomas Hopper from 1820-37, *Penrhyn Castle* was the home of the Pennant family who made a fortune from a local slate quarry. The architecture and much of the interior of the castle has been designed in a mock Norman style and the main entrance to the house opens to a grand staircase adorned with carved stone. The restored Victorian kitchen and domestic rooms are open to the public and an *Industrial Railway Museum* and a *Dolls Museum* are housed in the old stable block. The castle is surrounded by parkland, semi-wooded walks and formal gardens including the famous *Victorian Walled Garden* which contains many exotic plant species.

Transportation
Air: Manchester International Airport. **Rail:** Bangor Station. **Road:** Bus: Public services.

Contact Addresses
Penrhyn Castle, Bangor, Gwynedd LL57 4HN, UK
Tel: (01248) 353084
Website: www.nationaltrust.org.uk

Portmeirion

Located close to the boundary of *Snowdonia National Park*, *Portmeirion* is a quaint holiday village on the Welsh coast. The abandoned site, formerly called *Glacial Estuary*, was bought by the architect Clough Williams-Ellis in 1925 for less than £5,000 and he immediately renamed it Portmeirion. It was to become his personal pride and joy and over the next 50 years he set about redeveloping the peninsula in a way that was sympathetic to the natural surroundings with a strong emphasis on subtle architecture and beautiful landscaping. Today, Portmeirion is owned by *The Second Portmeirion Foundation*, a registered charity that lets out some of the quaint cottages and buildings that characterise the village. Other famous buildings include the *Town Hall*, *Castell Deudraeth*, and the *Bristol Collonade*. A number of traditional industries thrive in the village including *Portmeirion Potteries*, *Pot Jam* selling a range of jams and preserves, and the *Dome Gallery* selling works of art by the local-born artist, Rob Piercy. The area is renowned for its landscaped gardens, woodland walks and long, sandy beaches. Portmeirion also gained notoriety as the location for the filming of the cult 1960s television series, 'Prisoner', which still attracts many fans today.

Transportation
Air: Manchester International Airport. **Rail:** Bangor Station then bus or taxi. **Road:** Bus: Public services. Car: Signposted from the A487 or B4573.

Contact Addresses
Portmeirion, Gwnedd LL46 6ET, UK
Tel: (01766) 770000
Website: www.portmeirion-village.com

Rhyl Suncentre

The *Rhyl Suncentre* is located on the coastal road and has the first indoor surfing pool in Britain. It's one of the most popular paid-entry attractions in Wales and includes the *Buzz* where visitors can ride a 91m- (300ft-) rapid chute on tubes, the 61m- (200ft-) *Black Hole* drop slide, and the *Lagoon Pool* with wave and weather simulators. There's also a rooftop *Monorail* and outdoor decking area with views over the nearby beach and coastline.

Transportation
Air: Manchester International Airport. **Rail:** Rhyl Station. **Road:** Bus: Public services.

Contact Addresses
Rhyl Sun Centre, East Parade, Rhyl LL18 3AQ, UK
Tel: (0)1745 344433
Website: www.rhylsuncentre.co.uk

Ruthin Craft Centre Gallery

The *Ruthin Craft Centre Gallery* is a modern gallery showcasing exhibitions of contemporary artists, many of which have studios on the premises. The centre is dedicated to promoting the local arts scene and has developed a strong programme of workshops aimed at introducing visitors of all ages to the arts through a series of classes and tuition.

Transportation
Air: Manchester International Airport. **Rail:** Chester, Rhyl and Wrexham Stations. **Road:** Bus: Public services.

Contact Addresses
Ruthin Craft Centre Gallery, Park Road, Ruthin, Denbighshire LL15 1BB, UK
Tel: (01824) 703992

Snowdonia National Park

Founded in 1951, *Snowdonia National Park* covers 2180 sq km (840 sq miles) of wild and unspoilt countryside in the western corner of North Wales. Mountain peaks, river valleys and lakes contrast with the 37km (23 miles) of craggy coastline and provide a natural habitat for many species of wildlife, some of which, such as the Snowdon Lily and Rainbow Beetle, are unique to Snowdonia. Much of the dramatic mountainous landscape is the result of millions of years of erosion, with the hanging valleys, moraines and glacial lakes having been formed over 10,000 years ago, during the Great Ice Age. The highest peak is *Mount Snowdon*, which at 1085m (3559ft) is also the highest mountain in Wales. The park's natural attractions have made it a popular place with outdoor enthusiasts, who come to the lakes, mountains and beaches to walk, climb and enjoy watersports. Another way to take in the park's scenery is to ride the *Ffestiniog Narrow Gauge Railway* which runs from *Porthmadog* to *Blaenau Ffestiniog*, stopping off at various beauty spots along the way. There are also many cultural events in the park, focusing on Welsh language and traditions which are very much kept alive in this part of Wales. Visitors to the park should look out for *Eisteddfodau*, which are Welsh cultural festivals featuring choral music, Celtic dancing and readings of poetry and folk tales, and are held in many towns and villages.

Transportation
Air: Manchester Airport. **Rail:** Train: Llandudno Junction Station, Blaenau Ffestiniog Station or Penrhyndeudraeth Station. **Road:** Bus: Public services.

Contact Addresses
Snowdonia National Park Authority, National Park Office, Penrhyndeudraeth, Gwynedd LL48 6LF, UK
Tel: (01766) 770 274
Website: www.eryri-npa.co.uk

St David's Cathedral

The tiny city of St David's, Britain's smallest city with a population of just 1500, is dominated by its cathedral. St David, the patron saint of Wales, was one of the earliest Celtic missionaries who sought to convert the barbaric tribes of western Europe to Christianity. He founded a monastery on the site where the cathedral now stands in AD 589. After Pope Calixtus canonised David (or Dewi as he is known in Welsh) in 1120, the site became a major place of pilgrimage. Bishop Bernard dedicated the cathedral in 1131 and construction work began in 1181. In the south transept there are some fine Celtic carvings on the Abraham Stone, the gravestone of the sons of Bishop Abraham who was killed by Vikings in 1080. Every May and June, the cathedral hosts the St David's Cathedral Festival, featuring nine days of classical music performances.

Transportation
Air: Cardiff International Airport. **Rail:** Train: Haverfordwest Station or Fishguard Station. **Road**: Bus: Public services.

Portmeirion VisitBritain©

Contact Addresses
St David's Cathedral, St David's, Pembrokeshire SA62 6RH, UK
Tel: (01437) 720 691
Website: www.stdavidscathedral.org.uk

Welsh Slate Museum

The *Welsh Slate Museum* in the *Padarn Country Park* at Llanberis details the history of the slate industry in Wales which was vitally important to the local economy. The mines were at their peak during the industrial revolution when vast quantities of slate was needed to roof the new buildings that were springing up around the country. The museum itself is located in Victorian workshops at the site of the vast *Dinorwig Quarry* with the impressive *Elidir Mountain* in the background. Four quarrymen's houses were saved from demolition in *Blaenau Ffestiniog* and faithfully re-erected at the site and furnished to show four different periods in Welsh history. There's also the largest working water wheel in mainland Britain and visitors can tour the old workshops and foundry. The museum is set in beautiful surroundings on the shores of *Llyn Padarn* at the terminus of the *Llanberis Lake Railway*.

Transportation
Air: Manchester International Airport. **Rail:** Bangor Station. Llanberis Lake Railway Station (scenic railway). **Road:** Bus: Public services.

Contact Addresses
Welsh Slate Museum, Llanberis, Gwynedd LL55 4TY, UK
Tel: (01286) 870630
Website: www.nmgw.ac.uk

USA

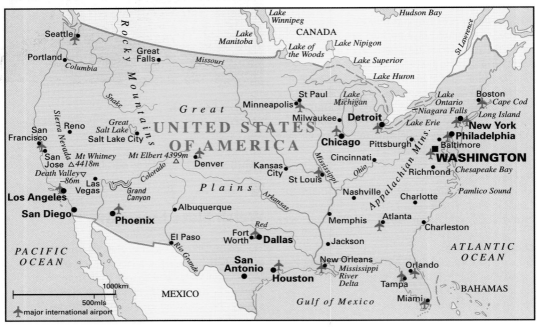

Seattle
Portland
Columbia
Great
Falls
Rocky Mountains
Snake
Missouri
Lake
Winnipeg
CANADA
Lake
Manitoba
Lake of
the Woods
Lake Nipigon
Lake Superior
Lake Huron
Hudson Bay
St Lawrence
San
Francisco
Reno
Sierra Nevada
*Great
Salt Lake*
Salt Lake City
San
Jose △4418m
Mt Whitney
Death Valley▽
–86m
Las
Vegas
Los Angeles
San Diego
*Grand
Canyon*
Phoenix
Mt Elbert 4399m
△
Colorado
Denver
Albuquerque
Great
UNITED STATES
OF AMERICA
Minneapolis
Milwaukee
St Paul
Lake
Michigan
Detroit
Chicago Pittsburgh
Cincinnati
Mississippi
Ohio
Kansas
City
St Louis
Plains
Arkansas
Nashville
Memphis
Lake
Ontario
Niagara Falls
Lake Erie
Appalachian Mtns.
Richmond
Boston
Cape Cod
Long Island
New York
Philadelphia
Baltimore
WASHINGTON
Chesapeake Bay
Charlotte
Atlanta
Charleston
Pamlico Sound
El Paso
Fort
Worth
Rio Grande
Red
Dallas
**San
Antonio**
Houston
Jackson
New Orleans
*Mississippi
River
Delta*
Orlando
Tampa
Miami
*ATLANTIC
OCEAN*
BAHAMAS
*PACIFIC
OCEAN*
1000km
500mls
MEXICO
Gulf of Mexico
✈ major international airport

Middleton Evans/Maryland Tourism©

Peter J. Schulz©

Kentucky Department of Travel©

Clockwise from above: the diversity of America shown in the natural splendour of the Great Falls (Maryland), the bustle of Chicago (Illinois) and the mountains of Kentucky

Arizona

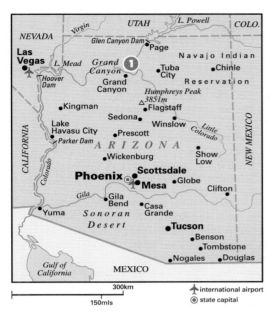

1 Grand Canyon National Park

Grand Canyon National Park

Located in the heart of the American West, the *Grand Canyon* is one of the seven natural wonders of the world. The canyon flows (in terms of river miles) for 365km (227 miles), and reaches a vertical depth of 1829m (6000ft) and a width of 29km (18 miles). Activities within the park include hiking, biking, whitewater rafting, cross-country skiing, snowshoeing and fishing. The Grand Canyon is divided into three geographically separated areas: the *South Rim*, the *North Rim* and the *Inner Canyon*. There are three visitor centres in the Grand Canyon National Park providing orientation guides and literature on the park's history and facilities. All three visitor centres offer restroom facilities; those who wish to stay overnight in the park can choose from a variety of lodges, log cabins and campsites (reservations are highly recommended).

Tourist Information

Arizona Office of Tourism
2702 North Third Street, Suite 4015, Phoenix, AZ 85004, USA
Tel: (602) 230 7733 *or* (888) 520 3434 (toll free USA and Canada only)
Website: www.arizonaguide.com

Arizona Office of Tourism
Ringway House, Bell Road, Basingstoke, Hants RG24 8FB, UK
Tel: (01256) 316 555

Transportation
Air: Las Vegas McCarran International Airport, Phoenix Sky Harbor International Airport or Grand Canyon Airport (domestic flights). **Rail:** Train: Services from Williams. **Road:** Coach: Services from Phoenix. Bus: Services from Williams and Flagstaff.

Contact Addresses
Grand Canyon National Park, PO Box 129, Grand Canyon, Arizona, AZ 86023, USA
Tel: (928) 638 7888
Website: www.nps.gov/grca

Grand Canyon National Park

Arizona Office of Tourism©

California

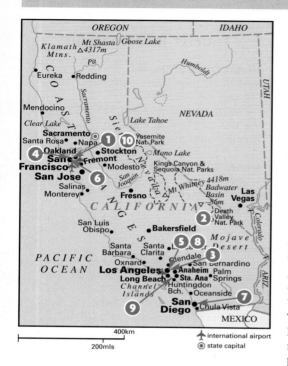

OREGON · IDAHO · NEVADA · UTAH · ARIZ. · MEXICO · CALIFORNIA · PACIFIC OCEAN

Klamath Mtns. · Mt Shasta △4317m · Goose Lake · Pit · Humboldt
Eureka · Redding · Sacramento
Mendocino · Lake Tahoe · NEVADA
Clear Lake · Sierra
Santa Rosa • Napa · Sacramento · Yosemite Nat. Park · Stockton · Mono Lake
Oakland · Fremont · Modesto · Kings Canyon & Sequoia Nat. Parks
San Francisco · San Jose · San Joaquin
Salinas · Fresno · Mt Whitney △4418m · Badwater Basin −86m · Las Vegas
Monterey · CALIFORNIA · Death Valley Nat. Park
San Luis Obispo · Bakersfield · Colorado
Santa Barbara · Santa Clarita · Mojave Desert
Oxnard · Glendale · San Bernardino
PACIFIC OCEAN · Los Angeles · Anaheim · Palm Springs
Long Beach · Sta. Ana · Huntingdon Bch. · Oceanside
Channel Islands · San Diego · Chula Vista
MEXICO

400km / 200mls

✈ international airport
◎ state capital

1 Alcatraz
2 Death Valley National Park
3 Disneyland Resort
4 Golden Gate Bridge
5 Hollywood Walk of Fame
6 Pier 39, Fisherman's Wharf
7 San Diego Zoo
8 Universal Studios Hollywood
9 Venice Beach
10 Yosemite National Park

Alcatraz

Alcatraz, which is also known as '*the Rock*', is the notorious American super-prison located on *Alcatraz Island*, a remote rocky outcrop in San Francisco Bay. It was home to the first lighthouse (1854) and the first US Fort on the West Coast (1859), before being used as a prison between 1934 and 1963. It was home to some famous

Tourist Information

California Tourism
1102 Q Street, Suite 6000, Sacramento, CA 95814, USA
Tel: (916) 322 2881 *or* (800) 862 2543 (toll free USA and Canada only)
Website: www.visitcalifornia.com

California Tourism
Molasses House, Plantation Wharf, Clove Hitch Quay, London SW11 3TN, UK
Tel: (020) 7978 5233

criminals including Al Capone, George 'Machine Gun' Kelly and Robert 'The Birdman' Stroud. Between 1969 and 1971, the island was taken over by Native Americans, when, under the leadership of Richard Oakes, they tried to lay claim to it for themselves. This led to the establishment of the US policy of self-determination for Indian tribes. Today, the whole island is preserved as part of the National Park system and is a venue for tourists rather than criminals, although a few former prisoners and guards can be heard on the prison's audio tour of the famous *Cell House*.

Transportation
Air: San Francisco International Airport. **Water:** Ferry: The only access to Alcatraz Island is by Blue and Gold Fleet Ferry from Pier 41, Fisherman's Wharf.

Contact Addresses
National Park Service, Alcatraz Island, Golden Gate National Recreation Area, Fort Mason, Building 201, San Francisco, CA 94123, USA
Tel: (415) 561 4900 *or* (415) 705 5555 (reservations only)
Website: www.nps.gov/alcatraz

Death Valley National Park

Although only a national park since 1994, *Death Valley* was established as a national monument in 1933 and has long been prized for its unique wildlife and desert beauty. Today, the park covers

13,500 sq km (5212 sq miles), the majority of
which is wilderness. Although there are occasional
winter storms, Death Valley's summers are
notorious for temperatures in excess of 48°C
(120°F). Despite this, the park attracts many
visitors who come to see rugged canyons, craggy
peaks, sand dunes and abandoned mines. One of
the most famous sites in Death Valley is *Badwater*,
a salty spring which lies 86m (282ft) below sea
level and said to be the lowest point in the
western hemisphere. From the pool, there are
spectacular views of Death Valley's mountains,
including *Telescope Peak*, which reaches to 3368m
(11,049ft), as well as the surrounding desert

Transportation
Air: Las Vegas McCarran International Airport,
Furnace Creek Airport (domestic flights). **Road:**
Car: California Hwy-190 (runs through the park
from east to west); US Hwy-95 (from Las Vegas);
I-15 (from California, Nevada or Utah).

Contact Addresses
Death Valley National Park, PO Box 579, Death
Valley, CA 92328, USA
Tel: (760) 786 3200
Website: www.nps.gov/deva

Disneyland Resort

Walt Disney first conceived the idea for the park in
1948 and had originally intended to call it 'Mickey
Mouse Park'. *Disneyland* welcomed its first guests in
1955 and celebrated its 50th anniversary in 2005.
Today, the park is one of America's most famous
attractions and undoubtedly California's most visited
theme park. There are eight 'lands' in total: *Main
Street USA*, *Tomorrowland*, *Frontierland*, *Fantasyland*,
Adventureland, *Critter Country*, *Mickey's Toontown* and
New Orleans Square. Some of the most popular rides
include the *Haunted Mansion*, *Space Mountain* and
Buzz Lightyear Astro Blasters. There are also regular
shows featuring such favourites as Mickey Mouse,
Donald Duck and Goofy.

Transportation
Air: John Wayne Airport, Los Angeles International
Airport, Burbank Airport. **Rail:** Metro Bus: Public
services. **Road:** Bus: There are shuttle buses from
the majority of hotels in the vicinity of the park.

Contact Addresses
Disneyland Resort, PO Box 3232, 1
313 South Harbor Boulevard, Anaheim,
CA 92803, USA
Tel: (714) 781 4565 (recorded information)
or 781 7290 (operator)
Website: www.disney.go.com

Golden Gate Bridge

Completed in 1937, San Francisco's best-known
landmark, the *Golden Gate Bridge*, stretches
2737m (8981ft) across San Francisco Bay,
connecting the city with Oakland Bay and the
Northern Counties. The elegant suspension
towers reach a height of 227m (746ft) and the
clearance over the channel below is 67m
(220ft). For those who wish to walk the 2.7km
(1.7 miles) across the bridge, access is from the
Joseph B Strauss statue (on the southeast side),
although the bridge can also be accessed from
the northeast side. Other viewing areas are
located at the north and south ends of the
pedestrians' east sidewalk. *Fort Point*, located
south of the bridge, is a military defence,
constructed between 1853 and 1861 to protect
San Francisco Bay from hostile attack. It was
also occupied by US federal troops during the
American Civil War (1861-65), but the last
troops were withdrawn in 1886. Nowadays,
visitors can explore the fort itself, as well as
learn about the history of the American Civil
War and the construction of the Golden Gate
Bridge through displays and video
presentations in the *Fort Point Bookstore Visitor
Center*.

Transportation
Air: San Francisco International Airport. **Rail:**
Train: Caltrain Station. **Road:** Bus: Golden Gate
Transit bus stop or Muni bus stop.

Contact Addresses
Golden Gate Bridge, PO Box 9000,
Presidio Station, San Francisco,
CA 94112, USA
Tel: (415) 921 5858
Website: www.goldengatebridge.org

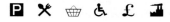

Hollywood Walk of Fame

In 1958, the *Hollywood Walk of Fame* was envisioned as a means of enshrining the memory of the Hollywood greats, with the first star being laid for the actress Joanne Woodward on February 9 1960. Today, it is the defining emblem of Los Angeles and one of its most popular tourist attractions. Two hectares (five acres) of bronze stars, embedded in pink and charcoal terrazzo squares, honour famous luminaries from the world of cinema, including Elvis Presley, John Travolta, Elizabeth Taylor and Frank Sinatra. The Walk of Fame takes visitors on a tour of Hollywood's entertainment industry, passing in front of the famous *Mann's Chinese Theatre*, where stars have literally made their mark, with their hand- and footprints. Visitors to Hollywood will undoubtedly also want to see the famous *Hollywood Sign*. Standing some 15m (50ft) tall and 137m (450ft) wide, this internationally renowned sign, which is located in the Hollywood Hills, was erected in 1923 by a property developer who wanted to advertise new homes in the area. It is one of the most photographed structures in the world, symbolising for many people all the glitz of the Hollywood film industry.

Transportation
Air: Los Angeles International Airport. **Rail:** Redline Station. **Road:** Bus: Public services.

Contact Addresses
Hollywood Chamber of Commerce, 7018 Hollywood Boulevard, Hollywood, CA 90028, USA
Tel: (323) 469 8311
Website: www.hollywoodchamber.net

Pier 39, Fisherman's Wharf

Claiming to be the most visited tourist attraction in the USA, *Fisherman's Wharf* is a bustling area located on San Francisco's waterfront. Developed solely to attract tourists, the area was once a working fishing port. Today, visitors throng the piers along Fisherman's Wharf, to buy souvenirs, eat in bay-side restaurants and visit the numerous attractions located along Embarcadero. *Pier 39*, which opened in 1978, is one of 29 piers located on the waterfront, and is San Francisco's number one attraction. It hosts daily street performances

and is home to many attractions, including *Turbo Ride* and *The Great San Francisco Adventure*. There are also the world-famous resident sea lions, which crowd onto pontoons and bask in the midday sun. Visitors can take sightseeing boats from Pier 39 and from neighbouring *Pier 41*, and enjoy fabulous views of the bay area and *Alcatraz* island.

Transportation
Air: San Francisco International Airport. **Rail:** Muni: Streetcar on the F-line to Beach Street. Cable Car: Bay Street on the Powell–Mason line. **Road:** Bus: Public services.

Contact Addresses
Fisherman's Wharf Merchants Association, 1873 Market Street, #3, San Francisco, CA 94103, USA
Tel: (415) 626 7070
Website: www.fishermanswharf.org

Pier 39, PO Box 193730, San Francisco, CA 94119, USA
Tel: (415) 705 5500
Website: www.pier39.com

San Diego Zoo

San Diego Zoo is undoubtedly the city of San Diego's most famous attraction. Located in the beautiful *Balboa Park*, just northeast of the city centre, the zoo is considered to be one of the most impressive in the world with the largest collection of animals, birds and reptiles in North America. Today, the San Diego Zoo houses more than 4000 animals from 800 different species and also has a large collection of more than 6500 species of plants. Balboa Park itself is home to one of the largest groups of museums in the United States, including the *Museum of Man*, *San Diego Museum of Art*, the *Museum of San Diego History*, the *National History Museum* and the *Aerospace Museum*. There are around 15,000 trees in the park, including palms, pines and eucalyptus, the most famous tree in the park is the Moreton Bay fig, located near the National History Museum and planted in around 1915.

Transportation
Air: San Diego International Airport. **Road:** Bus: Public services. Car: The zoo entrance is located off Park Boulevard at Zoo Place.

Golden Gate Bridge

Corel©

Contact Addresses

San Diego Zoo, PO Box 120551, San Diego, CA
92112, USA
Tel: (619) 234 3153 *or* 231 1515
Website: www.sandiegozoo.org

Universal Studios Hollywood

Universal Studios Hollywood is reputedly the
world's largest film studio and theme park, and
one of the most popular tourist attractions in Los
Angeles. The park opened to the public in 1964,
allowing the public to see behind the scenes of the
film world. Today, a visit to the park, which
attracts around 35,000 visitors per day, begins
with an exciting behind-the-scenes tram tour of
famous film sets, with a simulated earthquake, a
collapsing bridge, and several surprise attacks
from key Hollywood film characters, such as the
shark 'Jaws' and the famous giant gorilla 'King
Kong'. The park features the latest in state-of-the-
art video and audio technology, and uses
impressive special effects and stunt shows to
entertain visitors. It also provides musical
entertainment and a variety of thrill rides, such as
Back to the Future, *Jurassic Park* and *Revenge of the*

Mummy - The Ride. Guests can also see TV shows
being filmed for free by obtaining tickets from the
Audiences Unlimited Ticket Booth, which is
located next to the *Wild, Wild, Wild West Stunt
Show*. Universal Studios has other theme parks
around the world, including *Universal
Mediterránea*, *Universal Studios Japan* and *Universal
Orlando*.

Transportation
Air: Los Angeles International Airport, Burbank
Airport. Airport buses operate from Los Angeles
International Airport to Universal Studios
Hollywood. **Rail:** Metro: Universal City (Red Line).
Road: Bus: Public services. There is also a free
shuttle bus from hotels in Anaheim on
presentation of a Universal Studios Hollywood
ticket.

Contact Addresses
Universal Studios Hollywood, 100 Universal City
Plaza, Universal City, CA 91608, USA
Tel: (818) 622 3735 *or* (800) 8648 37725 (24-hour
recorded information line; toll free USA and
Canada only)
Website: www.universalstudios.com

Mirror Lake, Yosemite National Park

Corel©

Venice Beach

Originally developed in 1905 by Abbot Kinney, an ex-cigarette manufacturer who relocated to Los Angeles, the area around *Ballona Creek* was intended to attract Los Angeles's urban populace to live by the ocean. Based on the canals in Venice, the developers hoped to create a European/Bohemian atmosphere by the sea. It's now incredibly popular and the area around *Venice Boardwalk*, which is locally-known as *Venice Beach*, attracts thousands of Angelenos and tourists every week who come to soak up the party atmosphere. Venice Boardwalk is also known as the *Ocean Front Walk*, and is home to hundreds of street performers, including jugglers, palm readers, buskers, snake charmers, fire-eaters, cyclists and roller skaters. *Muscle Beach*, which is situated close by, is just as famous for its legendary weightlifters who work out daily in the sun.

Transportation
Air: Los Angeles International Airport. **Road:** Bus: Public services.

Contact Addresses
Los Angeles Convention & Visitors Bureau, 633 West Fifth Street, Suite 6000, Los Angeles, CA 90071, USA
Tel: (213) 624 7300
Website: www.lacvb.com

P ✗ 🧺 ♿ 🏔

Yosemite National Park

Designated a national park in 1890, *Yosemite National Park* stretches along California's eastern flank and covers almost 3108 sq km (1200 sq miles) of alpine meadows, rivers, lakes, cliffs and waterfalls in the central Sierra Nevada mountain range. The park is well known for its giant sequoia trees, particularly in *Mariposa Grove* where some of the trees are over 3000 years old and reach 80m (219ft) in height. Until 1969, when the tree fell during a heavy storm, it was possible to drive through the 3.4m (11.2ft) tunnel carved through the trunk of the famous Wawona Tunnel Tree. Other scenic highlights include *Yosemite Falls*, which cascade 739m (2425ft) into the valley below and *Glacier Point*, which offers spectacular views of the park. The area is also home to abundant wildlife and provides a natural habitat for approximately 250 species of bird, 80 species of mammal – including black bears, squirrels and chipmunks – and 24 species of amphibian and reptile. Visitors can stay at lodges and campsites situated around the park and enjoy activities such as hiking, fishing, climbing, horseriding and cross-country skiing.

Transportation
Air: Fresno Yosemite International Airport, Merced Air Terminal, Modesto City-County Airport. **Rail:** Train: Merced Amtrak Station. **Road:** Bus: Public services.

Contact Addresses
Yosemite National Park, PO Box 577, Yosemite, CA 95389, USA
Tel: (209) 372 0200
Website: www.nps.gov/yose

P ✗ 🧺 ♿ £ ✦

Florida

ALABAMA
GEORGIA
ATLANTIC OCEAN
△105m
Pensacola
Fernandina Beach
Panama City
Tallahassee
Jacksonville
St Augustine
Gainesville
Daytona Beach
FLORIDA
Orlando
Kennedy Space Center Visitor Complex
Walt Disney World
Tampa
Melbourne
Clearwater
Lakeland
St Petersburg
Bradenton
Fort Pierce
Sarasota
Lake Okeechobee
West Palm Beach
GULF OF MEXICO
Fort Myers
Cape Coral
Coral Springs
Fort Lauderdale
Naples
Hialeah
Hollywood
Everglades
Miami
Coral Gables
Key West
Florida Keys

300km
150mls

✈ international airport
◉ state capital

1 Everglades National Park
2 Kennedy Space Center Visitor Complex
3 SeaWorld Orlando
4 Universal Orlando
5 Walt Disney World Resort

Tourist Information

Visit Florida
PO Box 1100, Tallahassee, FL 32302-1100, USA
Tel: (850) 488 5607
Website: www.flausa.com

Visit Florida (UK)
Roebuck House, First Floor Mezzanine, Palace Street, London SW1E 5BA, UK
Tel: (020) 7630 6602 or (09001) 600 555 (24-hour information hotline; calls cost 60p per minute)

Everglades National Park

Florida's *Everglades* make up the largest sub-tropical wilderness on the United States mainland and were designated a national park in 1947. Both temperate and tropical plant communities are represented in the park's 610,684 hectares (1,509,000 acres), including cypress swamps,

pinelands and sawgrass prairies. *Florida Bay* is the largest body of water within the park, covering 2072 sq km (800 sq miles). The park is particularly well known for its abundant birdlife. Other endangered species protected in the park are the Green turtle, the Key Largo Cotton mouse, the American crocodile and the Schaus swallowtail butterfly. The park's five visitor centres provide information on the flora and fauna in the Everglades, as well as details of various park trails. Hiking and canoeing trails start at *Flamingo Visitor Center*, *Gulf Coast Visitor Center* and *Shark Valley Visitor Center*. Shark Valley Center also hires out bicycles and offers narrated tram and boat tours.

Transportation
Air: Miami International Airport or Southwest Florida International Airport (Fort Myers). **Rail:** Train: Miami Amtrak Station.

Contact Addresses
Everglades National Park, 40001 State Road 9336, Homestead, FL 33034, USA
Tel: (305) 242 7700
Website: www.nps.gov/ever

P ✗ 🧺 ♿ 🏛 £ ✿

Kennedy Space Center Visitor Complex

Visitors to the *Kennedy Space Center Visitor Complex* at Cape Canaveral in Florida find a mix of space-age technology and nature. The attraction is primarily known as the home of the *Space Shuttle*, where spectacular launches can be viewed from a safe distance. The centre has been pioneering space exploration since the success of the Apollo lunar programme in the late 1960s. Visitors can also tour the *Apollo/Saturn Visitor Center* to see an actual Saturn V moon rocket, which stands a staggering 111m (363ft) high, and experience *Astronout Encounter*, an interactive show hosted by real astronauts. Other facilities include a *Rocket Garden* and an *IMAX* cinema. The Kennedy Space Center's location on *Merritt Island National Wildlife Refuge*, home to bald eagles, alligators, otters and sea turtles, means that visitors can also enjoy wildlife walks or drives and learn about the animals that inhabit the area.

Kennedy Space Center Visitor Complex

Kennedy Space Centre Visitor Complex©

Transportation
Air: Melbourne International Airport, Orlando International Airport, Orlando Sanford Airport, Miami International Airport, Fort Lauderdale Hollywood International Airport. **Road:** Coach: Services from Orlando.

Contact Addresses
Kennedy Space Center Visitor Complex, Delaware North Park Services, Mail Code DNPS, Kennedy Space Center, FL 32899, USA
Tel: (321) 449 4444
Website: www.kennedyspacecenter.com

P ✕ 🧺 ♿ £ 🏭

SeaWorld Orlando

SeaWorld Orlando is the most popular marine theme park in the world. It has attracted over 80 million visitors since opening in 1978 and offers rides, shows and various other ocean-themed attractions. The site covers an area of 494 hectares (200 acres) and aims to educate visitors as well as entertain. *Terrors of the Deep* is an underwater ride past live sharks, eels, pufferfish and lionfish from the safe environment of an acrylic tunnel, whilst braver visitors can experience *Journey to Atlantis*, an 18m (60 ft) high roller coaster ride through a large-scale version of the mythical underwater city. Shows include the *Cirque de la Mer* (Circus of the Sea), featuring athletes, acrobats, singers and dancers together with comedy based on South American folklore. Children will particularly enjoy games such as *Shamu's Happy Harbor*, where they can explore a tropical paradise incorporating ball pools, slides, water mazes, tunnels and other exciting attractions.

Transportation
Air: Orlando International Airport. **Rail:** Train: Orlando Amtrak Station. **Road:** Car: I-4 (from Orlando or Tampa).

Contact Addresses
SeaWorld Orlando, 7007 SeaWorld Drive, Orlando, FL 32821, USA
Tel: (800) 327 2424 (toll free USA and Canada only)
Website: www.seaworld.com

P ✕ 🧺 ♿ £ 🏭

Universal Orlando

Universal Orlando is a 364 hectare (900 acre) entertainment complex, encompassing two theme parks, a dining and entertainment complex, and on-site hotels. *Universal Studios Florida*, the original theme park which opened in 1990, includes modern TV- and movie-making facilities alongside its ever-popular rides and attractions based on films and television, such as 'Men in Black', 'Back to the Future' and 'Shrek'. *Universal's Islands of Adventure* is one of the world's most technologically advanced theme parks with many themed rides. *Universal CityWalk*, a dining and entertainment complex, features restaurants, nightclubs, cinemas, street entertainers, shopping, live concerts and festivals. Both Universal Studios and Islands of Adventure also have many rides suitable for younger children, such as the interactive *ET Adventure*, part-designed by Steven Spielberg himself who is actually creative consultant for the entire complex.

Transportation
Air: Orlando International Airport. **Rail:** Train: Orlando Amtrak Station. **Road:** Bus: Public services. Car: Hollywood Way.

Contact Addresses
Universal Orlando, 1000 Universal Studios Plaza, Orlando, FL 32819, USA
Tel: (407) 363 8000
Website: www.universalorlando.com

P ✕ 🧺 ♿ £ 🏭

Walt Disney World

Disney Enterprises, Inc.

Walt Disney World Resort

The world's largest theme park, *Walt Disney World Resort*, covers a space twice the size of Manhattan, delivering the Disney promise of magical escapism and thrilling rides. It is divided into four theme parks, alongside water parks, restaurants, theatres and hotels. The best-known of the theme parks is the *Magic Kingdom*, which provides traditional Disney rides and attractions and allows visitors to meet their favourite Disney characters. *Disney's Animal Kingdom* is an animal park, where visitors can learn about the animal kingdom, enjoy shows such as the 'Festival of the Lion King', and go on an animated jungle trek or African-style safari. *Disney-MGM Studios* is a Hollywood-inspired theme park featuring rides, shows and tours of Hollywood sets, both real sets and reconstructions, including a children's playground adventure based on the film 'Honey, I Shrunk the Kids'. *Epcot* is a science-based park which explores the earth's natural phenomena and the human anatomy, as well as taking visitors on virtual trips around countries such as China and France (in *World Showcase*) and offering a glimpse into the technology of the future (in *Future World*).

Transportation
Air: Orlando International Airport. **Road:** Car: I-95, then I-4 (from New York, Jacksonville, Miami, Fort Lauderdale, Richmond, Baltimore or Washington, DC); I-4 to Osceola Parkway West (exit 3) (from Orlando International Airport).

Contact Addresses
Walt Disney World Resort, PO Box 10040, Lake Buena Vista, FL 32830, USA
Tel: (407) 824 2222 *or* 934 7639 (tickets)
Website: www.disneyworld.com

Hawaii

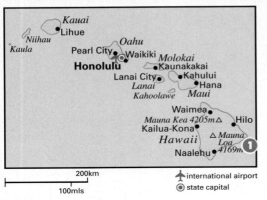

1 Hawaii Volcanoes National Park

years of volcanic activity is on display, encompassing the creation of Hawaii out of the ocean to the evolution of its complex and unique ecosystems. Many rare species of plant have flourished in the volcanic landscape, of which 90 per cent of the park's flora and fauna, including 10,000 species of insects and spiders, is unique to Hawaii. Hiking trails are a popular way of seeing the wildlife and also the dramatic lava fields and steam vents surrounding *Kilauea*, the world's most active volcano.

Transportation
Air: Honolulu International Airport, Hilo Airport, Kino Airport (domestic flights). **Road:** Bus: Services from Hilo. Car: Hwy-11 (from Hilo and Kailua-Kona); Hwy-11 or Hwy-19 (from Waimea).

Contact Addresses Hawaii Volcanoes National Park, PO Box 52, Hawaii National Park, HI 96718, USA
Tel: (808) 985 6000
Website: www.nps.gov/havo

Tourist Information

Hawaii Tourism Authority
Hawaii Convention Centre, 1801 Kalakaua Avenue, Honolulu, HI 96815, USA
Tel: (808) 973 2255

Hawaii Visitors & Convention Bureau
2270 Kalakaua Avenue, Eighth Floor, Honolulu, HI 96815, USA
Tel: (808) 923 1811 *or* (800) 464 2924 (brochure line; toll free Canada and USA only)
Website: www.gohawaii.com

Hawaii Visitors & Convention Bureau (UK Office)
PO Box 208, Sunbury-on-Thames, Middlesex TW16 5RJ, UK
Tel: (020) 8941 8166 (trade enquiries)
or (8941) 4009 (consumer enquiries)
Website: www.gohawaii.com

Hawaii Volcanoes National Park

Hawaii Volcanoes National Park is located on the *Big Island of Hawaii*, which is 800,000 years old. Established in 1916, the park spans 878 sq km (339 sq miles) and ranges from sea level to the top of *Mauna Loa*, the world's tallest volcano at 4169m (13,677ft) high. The result of 70 million

Hawaii Volcanoes National Park

Illinois

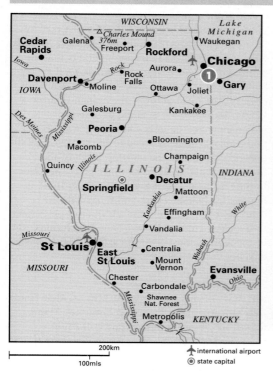

WISCONSIN

Lake Michigan

Cedar Rapids
Galena
△ Charles Mound 376m
Freeport
Rockford
Waukegan

Iowa
Aurora
Chicago
Rock Falls
Davenport
Moline
Ottawa
Joliet
Gary
IOWA
Galesburg
Kankakee

Peoria
Bloomington
Macomb
Champaign
Quincy
Illinois
I L L I N O I S
Decatur
INDIANA
Springfield
Mattoon
Kaskaskia
Effingham
White
Vandalia
Missouri
St Louis
East St Louis
Centralia
Wabash
MISSOURI
Mount Vernon
Chester
Carbondale
Evansville
Ohio
Shawnee Nat. Forest
Mississippi
Metropolis
KENTUCKY

200km
100mls

✈ international airport
◉ state capital

1 Sears Tower

Tourist Information

Illinois Bureau of Tourism
James R Thompson Center, Suite 3-400,
100 West Randolph Street, Chicago, IL
60601, USA
Tel: (312) 814 4732 *or* (800) 226 6632
(toll free USA and Canada only)
Website: www.enjoyillinois.com

Chicago and Illinois Tourism Office
c/o Global Enterprise Marketing,
15 Nonsuch Estate, Kiln Lane, Epsom,
Surrey KT17 1DH, UK
Tel: (01372) 729 140 (trade enquiries)
or 726 928 (consumer enquiries)
Website: www.chicago-illinois.co.uk

Sears Tower

Sears Tower

Image supplied by Wikipedia

Soaring 443m (1454ft) into the air above the 'Windy City' of Chicago, *Sears Tower*, opened in 1973 after a three-year building project. It was the world's tallest building until it was overtaken by Kuala Lumpur's *Petronas Towers* in 1996 (which itself has since been overtaken). It consists of 110 floors of black aluminium and bronze-tinted glass. The lift takes visitors up to the Skydeck on the 103rd floor in just seven seconds for spectacular views that can stretch as far as 80km (50 miles) to the surrounding states of Michigan, Illinois, Wisconsin and Indiana on a clear day. Although the tower is a working office building – it is owned by real estate and property management company TrizecHahn – there are various visitor attractions and entertainment facilities on the Skydeck. Attractions include interactive multimedia displays showcasing Chicago's history, music, literature and sport, with special knee-high versions for children, and several restaurants.

Transportation
Air: Chicago O'Hare International Airport, Midway Airport (domestic flights). **Rail:** Train: Chicago Union Station. Underground: Quincy Station. **Road:** Entrance to the car park is on Jackson Boulevard in central Chicago.

Contact Addresses
Sears Tower Skydeck, Sears Tower, 233 South Wacker Drive, Suite 3530, Chicago, IL 60606, USA
Tel: (312) 875 9696
Website: www.sears-tower.com *or* www.the-skydeck.com

Louisiana

Shreveport • Monroe
Driskill Mtn. 163m
Natchitoches
Toledo Bend Reservoir
Alexandria
TEXAS
LOUISIANA
Lake Charles • Lafayette
Intracoastal Waterway
Beaumont • New Iberia
Marsh I. • Houma
Gulf of Mexico

ARKANSAS
Yazoo
MISSISSIPPI
• Jackson
Ouachita
Mississippi
Red
Pearl
Baton Rouge • Hammond
• Bogalusa
Atchafalaya
Lake Pontchartrain
• New Orleans
Breton Sound
Mississippi River Delta

200km
100mls

✈ international airport
◎ state capital

1 New Orleans' French Quarter

Tourist Information

Louisiana Office of Tourism
Department of Culture, Recreation & Tourism,
PO Box 94291, Capitol Station, Baton Rouge,
LA 70804, USA
Tel: (225) 342 8100 *or* (800) 227 4386 (toll
free USA and Canada only)
Website: www.crt.state.la.us/crt/tourism.htm
or www.louisianatravel.com

Louisiana Office of Tourism
33 Market Place, Hitchin, Hertfordshire
SG5 1DY, UK
Tel: (01462) 458 696

New Orleans' French Quarter

New Orleans' French Quarter covers a grid of 98
square blocks stretching back from the *Mississippi
River* in downtown New Orleans. It was known to
the French, who colonised the state of Louisiana
in 1718, as *Vieux Carré*, or Old Square, and

contains some superb examples of 18th- and
19th-century architecture. It was in fact the
Spanish, who gained control of Louisiana in 1762,
who constructed many of the buildings that are
still there today after most of the original French
buildings were destroyed by fire in the late 18th
century. The focal point of the French Quarter is
Jackson Square which is home to several
monuments and churches including *St Louis
Cathedral*, the oldest cathedral in the USA, and the
Cabildo, which was the meeting place of the
Spanish council in colonial times and now home
to the *Louisiana State Museum*. *Bourbon Street* is
famous for its many jazz clubs and bars. In
February each year, the French Quarter plays host
to the city's colourful *Mardi Gras* celebrations, one
of the world's most famous carnivals, with music,
dancing, food, floats and parades.

Transportation
Air: New Orleans International Airport. **Rail:** Train:
New Orleans Union Passenger Terminal. Tram:
Riverfront Streetcar. **Road:** Car: I-10 (from
Houston, Los Angeles or Jacksonville); I-55 (from
Memphis, Chicago or St Louis); I-59 (from
Birmingham or Chattanooga).

Contact Addresses
New Orleans Metropolitan Convention and
Visitors Bureau Inc, 1520 Sugar Bowl Drive, New
Orleans, LA 70112, USA
Tel: (504) 566 5011
Website: www.neworleanscvb.com

New Orleans' French Quarter

Louisiana Travel & Tourism Marketing©

Massachusetts

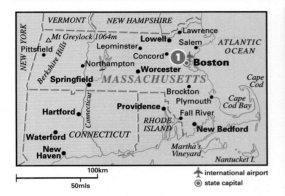

international airport
state capital

---

1 Freedom Trail

Tourist Information

Massachusetts Office of Travel & Tourism
State Transportation Building, 10 Park Plaza,
Suite 4510, Boston, MA 02116, USA
Tel: (617) 973 8500 *or* (800) 227 6277 (toll
free USA and Canada only)
Website: www.massvacation.com

**Massachusetts Office of Travel & Tourism
(UK Office)**
c/o First Public Relations, Molasses House,
Clove Hitch Quay, Plantation Wharf, York
Place, London SW11 3TN, UK
Tel: (020) 7978 7429

Freedom Trail

The *Freedom Trail* consists of a 4km- (2.5 mile-)
walking tour of historic Boston and Charlestown,
encompassing 16 sites and structures of historical
significance. Highlights include the *USS
Constitution* (website:
www.ussconstitution.navy.mil), the world's oldest
commissioned warship still afloat, which was used
in battle against France and Britain. Visitors can
tour *Paul Revere House* (website:
www.paulreverehouse.org), the one-time home of
the quintessential 'American Patriot', who was a
key figure in the Boston Tea Party and fought for

*The Old State
House, Freedom
Trail*

MOTT©

American independence. Also open to the
public is the *Old State House* (website:
www.bostonhistory.org), built in 1713, which was
once the seat of the British government in Boston.
Nearby is the 18th-century *Old South Meeting
House* where protesters gathered to challenge
British rulers in the years leading up to the
American Revolution. The trail begins at *Boston
Common* in the centre of the city.

Transportation
Air: Boston Logan International Airport. **Rail:**
Train: South Station. Underground: Park Street.
Road: Bus: Public services to South Station.

Contact Addresses
Freedom Trail Foundation, 3 School Street,
Boston, MA 02108, USA
Tel: (617) 227 8800
Website: www.thefreedomtrail.org

Minnesota

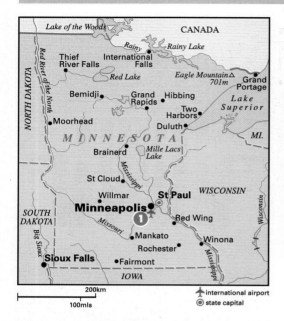

Lake of the Woods

CANADA

Rainy — Rainy Lake

Thief River Falls — International Falls

Red Lake

Eagle Mountain △ 701m — Grand Portage

Bemidji — Grand Rapids — Hibbing

Lake Superior

Two Harbors

Moorhead — Duluth

MINNESOTA

MI.

Brainerd — Mille Lacs Lake

St Cloud

Willmar — St Paul — WISCONSIN

Minneapolis ① — Red Wing

SOUTH DAKOTA — Mankato — Winona

Rochester

Sioux Falls • Fairmont

IOWA

NORTH DAKOTA

Red River of the North

Mississippi

Missouri

Big Sioux

Mississippi

200km
100mls

✈ international airport
◉ state capital

1 Mall of America

Tourist Information

Minnesota Office of Tourism
Suite 100, 121 Seventh Place East, St Paul,
MN 55101-2146, USA
Tel: (651) 296 5029 *or* (800) 657 3700
(toll free USA and Canada only)
Website: www.exploreminnesota.com

Mall of America

The *Mall of America*, opened in 1992, is the
world's largest undercover shopping centre,
covering 32 hectares (78 acres) of land just
outside Bloomington. It houses over 520 shops,
including American giants such as *Macy's*,
Bloomingdale's, *Nordstrom* and *Sears*, and attracts
more visitors each year than *Disney World Resort*,
the *Grand Canyon* and *Graceland* combined. In
addition to the shops, there are 14 cinema screens,
eight nightclubs, and over 50 restaurants,
including the *Rainforest Café*, complete with all the

Image supplied by Wikipedia / BjarteSorensen

Minnesota Office of Tourism©

Camp Snoopy, Mall of America

sights and sounds of the
Amazon, as well as a host of
other attractions. *Camp
Snoopy* is a three-hectare (seven-acre) indoor
theme park, featuring roller coasters, a ferris
wheel and 26 other rides. At *Underwater
Adventures*, a huge aquarium, visitors come face to
face with 300,000 sea creatures, whilst the *LEGO
Imagination Center* contains LEGO models and
thousands of LEGO bricks for children to play
with. Entrance to the Mall is free but some rides
and attractions charge on an individual basis.

Transportation
Air: Minneapolis-St Paul International Airport.
Rail: Train: Merced Amtrak Station. **Road:** Bus:
Public services. Car: I-94, then I-494 (from the
east); I-35, then I-35W, then I-94 (from the north
or south); I-94, then I-494, then Hwy-77 (from the
west).

Contact Addresses
Mall of America Management, 60 East Broadway,
Bloomington, MN 55425, USA
Tel: (952) 883 8800
Website: www.mallofamerica.com

🅿 ✕ 🧺 ♿ 🏭

Nevada

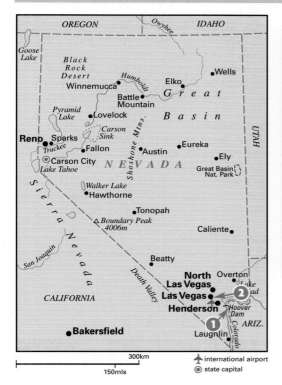

OREGON
IDAHO
Owyhee
Goose Lake
Black Rock Desert
Humboldt
Wells
Winnemucca
Elko
Great
Battle Mountain
Pyramid Lake
Lovelock
Basin
Reno
Sparks
Carson Sink
Truckee
Fallon
Austin
Eureka
Carson City
N E V A D A
Ely
Lake Tahoe
Great Basin Nat. Park
UTAH
Walker Lake
Hawthorne
Tonopah
Boundary Peak 4006m
Caliente
Beatty
North Las Vegas
Overton
Las Vegas
Lake Mead
CALIFORNIA
Henderson
Hoover Dam
Bakersfield
ARIZ.
Laughlin
Colorado

300km
150mls

✈ international airport
◎ state capital

1 Hoover Dam
2 Las Vegas Strip

Hoover Dam

Nevada Commission on Tourism©

Hoover Dam

Completed in 1935, after five years of intensive construction, the *Hoover Dam* is a modern engineering marvel. It stretches 380m (1247ft) across the Colorado River, holding in *Lake Mead* the equivalent volume of two years' worth of the river's flow. Thousands of workers were involved in the project, which provided much needed employment during the Great Depression, although tragically 96 men died in industrial accidents during its construction. The dam contains 2,486,250 cubic metres (3,250,000 cubic yards) of concrete. It provides flood control and functions primarily as a storage reservoir, supplying water to southern Nevada, southern California and Arizona. A natural by-product is power generation, with electricity transmitted to Nevada, as well as nearby California and Arizona. Visitor tours examine the construction of the dam and explore its hydroelectric generating facilities, whilst the *Hoover Dam Visitor Center* features displays on the engineering process and the operation of the dam.

Transportation
Air: Las Vegas McCarran International Airport.
Road: Coach: Chartered services from Las Vegas.
Car: US Hwy-93 (from Las Vegas).

Tourist Information

Nevada Commission on Tourism
401 North Carson Street, Carson City, NV 89701, USA
Tel: (775) 687 4322 *or* (800) 237 0774 (toll free USA and Canada only)
Website: www.travelnevada.com

Nevada Commission on Tourism (UK Office)
c/o Cellet Travel Services Ltd, Brook House, 47 High Street, Henley-in-Arden, Warickshire B95 5AA, UK
Tel: (01564) 794 999

Las Vegas Strip

Contact Addresses

DOI Bureau of Reclamation, Visitor Services, PO Box 60400, Boulder City, NV 89006, USA
Tel: (702) 294 3524
Website: www.usbr.gov/lc/hooverdam/

Las Vegas Strip

The *Strip* in Las Vegas (officially known as *Las Vegas Boulevard*) is, perhaps, the defining symbol of American excess. Every year, millions of people descend upon the city, the vast majority of whom come with the sole intention of gambling. In 2004, nearly 38 million visitors came to Las Vegas and brought in US$6.8 billion in gaming revenue to the city. Nevada is the only state in the USA where gambling is legal, and nowhere is this more evident than on the Las Vegas Strip, where there are more slot machines and roulette wheels than anywhere else in the world. Here, massive neon casino-hotel complexes vie for supremacy in an ongoing competition to be the biggest and the best. In order to attract trade, many of them have turned into brightly-lit mini-theme parks, open 24 hours a day. World-famous hotel-casinos include the *Luxor*, *Paris Las Vegas* and the legendary *Caesar's Palaces*. The whole place is a non-stop cabaret of glitz and extravagance, with nightly performances in all the big hotels, featuring dancing girls, stand-up comedians and live music to keep the punters entertained. The city is also

famous as a place to get hitched, with around 200,000 couples visiting Las Vegas every year to get married. Ceremonies range from the kitsch, complete with Elvis impersonator in the *Graceland Wedding Chapel* to ultra-quick drive-in weddings at the *Little White Chapel*, open 24 hours a day. If all this is not enough, there are also numerous museums in the area including *Madame Tussaud's Wax Museum*, *Guinness World of Records Museum*, the *Elvis-A-Rama Museum* and the *Liberace Museum*.

Transportation

Air: Las Vegas McCarran International Airport.
Road: Bus: Public services; Las Vegas Strip Trolley runs along the Strip. Car: I-15 into the centre of Las Vegas, then Spring Mountain Road, Desert Inn Road or Flamingo Road to join Las Vegas Boulevard (from the north or south).

Contact Addresses

Las Vegas Convention and Visitors Authority, 3150 Paradise Road, Las Vegas, NV 89109, USA
Tel: (702) 892 0711
Website: www.lvcva.com

Freemont Street, Las Vegas

Key to symbols used in all entries:	£........Entry charged	🅿........Parking
	♿........Disabled access	✗........Restaurant
	◪........Man-made attraction	🛍........Shop
	♥........Natural attraction	🏛......UNESCO site

New York

CANADA
Ogdensburg
Lake Champlain
VERMONT
St Lawrence Mtns.
Mt Marcy 1629m
N.H.
Watertown
Adirondack Mtns.
Lake Ontario
Niagara Falls
Niagara Falls
Rochester
Rome
Seneca Falls
Utica
Saratoga Springs
Syracuse
Mohawk
Schenectady
Lake Erie
Buffalo
Finger Lakes
Troy
Albany
MASS.
Jamestown
Watkins Glen
Ithaca
Woodstock
Springfield
Elmira
Catskill Mtns.
Binghampton
CONN.
Poughkeepsie
Newburgh
White Plains
PENNSYLVANIA
Tarrytown
New York
Yonkers
Hempstead
Long Island
Philadelphia
N.J.
ATLANTIC OCEAN

300km
150mls

✈ international airport
◉ state capital

1 Central Park
2 Empire State Building
3 Greenwich Village
4 Metropolitan Museum of Art
5 Niagara Falls, USA
6 Statue of Liberty
7 Times Square

Tourist Information

New York State Division of Tourism
PO Box 2603, Albany, NY 12220-0603, USA
Tel: (518) 474 4116 or (800) 225 5697 (toll
free USA, Canada and US External Territories)
Website: www.iloveny.com

**New York State Department of Economic
Development (Tourism Division)**
Media House, 4 Stratford Place, London
W1C 18T, UK
Tel: (020) 7629 2720
Website: www.empire.state.ny.us

Key to symbols: £ Entry charged ⅃ Disabled access
⅃ Man-made attraction ♥ Natural attraction
🅿 Parking ✗ Restaurant ⬢ Shop ⅏ UNESCO site

Central Park

Completed in 1873, *Central Park* was designed to provide New York with 341 hectares (843 acres) of rural paradise in what was, at the time, the out-of-the-way northern reaches of Manhattan. Now, located almost in the dead centre of New York due to urban expansion between 59th and 110th streets, Central Park is very much an integral part of the city's landscape. Apart from being a refreshing area of greenery in the middle of a very dense and busy city, Central Park has a cultural side, with public programmes offered by the Central Park Conservancy, as well as a small zoo, a dairy, fountains and an ice-skating rink. The park has featured in many films over the years and is also home to statues of famous people (real and fictional), including Ludwig Van Beethoven, Alice in Wonderland, Hans Christian Anderson and Robert Burns. It is also home to the Strawberry Fields Memorial, dedicated to the late John Lennon who was shot dead in the city on December 8 1980. The park attracts joggers, rollerbladers and buskers every day, as well as thousands of tourists who come to see the most famous urban park in the USA.

Transportation
Air: New York La Guardia International Airport, New York John F Kennedy International Airport.
Rail: Train: Grand Central Station. Underground: A, B, C, D, N, R, 4, 5 or 6 trains to Fifth Avenue or 59th Street/Columbus Circle. **Road:** Bus: Public services.

Contact Addresses
Central Park Conservancy, 14 East 60th Street, New York, NY 10022, USA
Tel: (212) 310 6600
Website: www.centralparknyc.org

Empire State Building

Completed in 1931 during the Great Depression at a cost of over US$40 million, the *Empire State Building* is an enduring symbol of New York City and the USA. It was built during an era of skyscraper wars, and at 443.2m (1454ft) tall, the Empire State Building defeated the world's then tallest building and fellow Art Deco gem, the nearby *Chrysler Building*. The developers, Empire State Inc, initially struggled to find any tenants for the gigantic office block, due to its size, although it was eventually leased to various companies. Visitors can access the observatory on the 86th floor for spectacular views over the Big Apple. In addition, there is a virtual-reality movie theatre with *NYSkyride* attraction (www.skyride.com) located on the second floor. The tower has also featured in numerous films, such as 'An Affair to Remember', 'When Harry Met Sally', 'King Kong', 'Independence Day', 'Taxi Driver' and 'Sleepless in Seattle'.

Transportation
Air: New York La Guardia International Airport, New York John F Kennedy International Airport. **Rail:** Train: Grand Central or Penn stations. Underground: 34th Street/Penn or Path to 34th Street/Avenue of the Americas. **Road:** Bus: Public services. Coach: Port Authority Bus Terminal.

Contact Addresses
Empire State Building, 350 Fifth Avenue, New York, NY 10118, USA
Tel: (212) 736 3100 *or* (888) 759 7433 (*Skyride*) (toll free USA and Canada only)
Website: www.esbnyc.com

Greenwich Village

Greenwich Village is one of the liveliest and trendiest districts of New York City. Originally a tobacco plantation located towards the tip of *Manhattan Island*, it was given its name by British naval commander, Sir Peter Warren who purchased a farm there in the early 18th century. It was not until New York's yellow fever outbreak in 1822 that people began to move here to escape the disease-ridden conditions of the city, and Greenwich quickly flourished, as banks and businesses sprang up alongside the elegant houses of their wealthy owners. By the turn of the last century, New York's richest residents had begun to move to more fashionable areas of town, such as *Fifth Avenue*. This exodus meant that the

houses were populated by struggling artists and writers, who spent their time in the Village's many bars and coffee houses, discussing political ideals. Greenwich thus gained its reputation as New York's Bohemian, anti-establishment quarter, as well as a centre for women's liberation. The Village also gained a reputation as the focus of the gay rights movement after the infamous Stonewall Riots that followed the police raid on the Stonewall Inn, a gay bar in Greenwich Village, in 1969. The area's reputation as a Bohemian melting pot has stuck, despite the fact that it has once again become home to the city's well-heeled professionals since the sharp rise in property prices during the 1980s economic boom forced writers and artists out. *Christopher Street*, which runs through the centre of the district, is the hub of New York's gay scene, whilst *Greenwich Avenue* is a good place to shop, with plenty of bookstores and second-hand clothes shops. Greenwich Village also has a thriving nightlife, with many of its lively cafés and bars staying open later than those elsewhere in Manhattan.

Transportation
Air: New York La Guardia International Airport or New York John F Kennedy International Airport. **Rail:** Train: Grand Central Station. Underground: Christopher Street or West 4 Street–Washington Square. **Road:** Bus: Public services. Coach: Port Authority Bus Terminal.

Contact Addresses
NYC & Company, 810 Seventh Avenue, Third Floor, New York, NY 10019, USA
Tel: (212) 484 1200
Website: www.nycvisit.com

Metropolitan Museum of Art

With a diverse collection embracing over two million works of art, the *Metropolitan Museum of Art* ranks as one of the world's great museums. The museum houses particularly impressive collections of work by Monet, Cézanne, Vermeer and Giovanni Battista Tiepolo. The modern art section comprises paintings by a wide variety of artists including Modigliani, Picasso, Braque and Charles Rennie Mackintosh. As would be expected,

New York State Division of Tourism©

Niagara Falls

there are also fine displays of American art, from colonial times to the present day; these include pieces of decorative art, such as ceramics and Tiffany glass. *The Cloisters* is a separate branch of the museum, located in Ford Tryon Park in north Manhattan overlooking the Hudson River, and is considered to be one of the greatest collections of Medieval art in the world.

Transportation
Air: New York La Guardia International Airport, New York John F Kennedy International Airport. **Rail:** Train: Grand Central Station. Underground: 77th Street, 86th Street or Fifth Avenue. **Road:** Bus: Public services.

Contact Addresses
Metropolitan Museum of Art, 1000 Fifth Avenue, New York, NY 10028, USA
Tel: (212) 535 7710
Website: www.metmuseum.org

Niagara Falls, USA

Niagara Falls is one of the most popular tourist destinations in North America, made up of two separate parts, *Horseshoe Falls*, on the Canadian side and *American Falls* on the US side. Although not the highest waterfall in the world (that record goes to the *Angel Falls* in Venezuela), they move a staggering volume of 168,000 cubic metres (219,600 cubic yards) of water per minute over a drop of 51m (167ft), making them one of the natural wonders of the world. In the past, people have attempted numerous daring stunts here, including dropping over the edge in a barrel. The most famous daredevil was the Frenchman Jean Francois Gravelot (known as The Great Blondin) who crossed the Niagara Falls on a tightrope in 1859 and lived to tell the tale. The town surrounding Niagara Falls, a celebrated North American honeymoon destination, offers a wealth of visitor activities including a casino, as well as land and boat tours of the falls.

Transportation
Air: Buffalo Niagara Airport or Pearson International Airport (Toronto). **Rail:** Train: Amtrak Station. **Road:** Bus: Public services. Car: Queen Elizabeth Way (QEW) towards Niagara, then Hwy-420 to Niagara Falls (from Toronto); I-190 (from Buffalo); I-81, I-90, I-290 and I-190 (exit 22) (from Syracuse).

Contact Addresses
Niagara Falls Convention and Visitors Bureau, 310 Fourth Street, Niagara Falls, NY 14303, USA
Tel: (716) 285 2400
Website: www.buffalocvb.org

Times Square

NYS DED©

Statue of Liberty

A gift to the USA from France in 1886 to celebrate the 100th anniversary of American independence, the *Statue of Liberty* greeted millions of immigrants during the 19th century who came to America to seek a better life. Enjoying a fine position in New York Harbour, this world-famous statue, which was originally called *Liberty Enlightening the World*, has become a defining American symbol of freedom and democracy. This 45m (151ft) statue of a woman holding a torch aloft, was designed by the French sculptor Frédéric-Auguste Bartholdi, and was modelled on the Colossus of Rhodes. A limited number of time passes are issued on the day allowing people to enter the monument. The grounds are still open to the public without a ticket and offer visitors the opportunity to see the statue up close. Nearby Ellis Island, part of the Statue of Liberty National Monument, houses a museum devoted to the history of immigration.

Transportation
Air: New York La Guardia International Airport, New York John F Kennedy International Airport

or Newark International Airport. **Rail:** Underground: Bowling Green. **Water:** Ferry: The Statue of Liberty/Ellis Island Ferry departs from Battery Park (New York City) and Liberty State Park (Jersey City, New Jersey). **Road:** Bus: Public services to ferry terminal.

Contact Addresses
Statue of Liberty National Monument and Ellis Island, Liberty Island, New York, NY 10004, USA
Tel: (212) 363 3200
Website: www.nps.gov/stli

Times Square

Located just north of 42nd Street, *Times Square* has long been associated with theatre and nightlife and all the excitement and glitz of New York City. There is no better way to discover the Big Apple than by going to see a show in a Broadway theatre, located just off Times Square; the area is home to over 50 theatres, around 30 hotels, cinemas, shops, restaurants and bars. Often referred to as the 'Crossroads of the World', the city's theatre district is alight with neon signs and giant TV screens. Always buzzing with energy, it is an ideal place to experience the atmosphere of life on New York's busy streets. Attracting over 30 million tourists every year, Times Square can be a daunting experience to first time visitors due to the constant stream of traffic and huge crowds. The square is a popular place to spend New Year's Eve when over half a million people gather to join in the festivities.

Transportation
Air: New York John F Kennedy International Airport, New York LaGuardia Airport or Newark International Airport. **Rail:** Underground: 15 subway lines go to Times Square; Amtrak and the Long Island Rail Road companies have services to Penn Station. **Road:** Bus: Public services.

Contact Addresses
Times Square Business Improvement District, 1560 Broadway, Suite 800, NY 10036, USA
Tel: (212) 768 1560
Website: www.timessquarenyc.org

Ohio

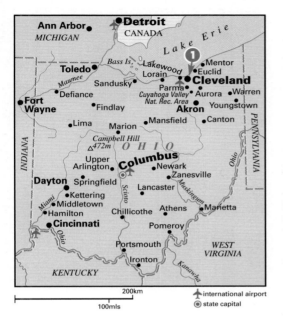

Ohio Division of Travel & Tourism
77 South High Street, 29th Floor, PO Box 1001, Columbus, OH 43216-1001, USA
Tel: (614) 466 8844 *or* (800) 848 1300 (toll free USA and Canada only)
Website: www.ohiotourism.com

Rock and Roll Hall of Fame

The *Rock and Roll Hall of Fame* celebrates the American rock music by honouring its most popular and influential performers, producers, songwriters and djs. The phrase 'rock and roll' was coined by the Cleveland dj Alan Freed in 1951, so it somehow seems fitting that Cleveland should have been chosen as the home of this attraction. Opened in 1995 and designed by the renowned Chinese architect I M Pei, the building is a 13,935 sq m (150,000 sq ft) modern structure with bold designs and a dramatic location on the shores of Lake Erie. The museum features a *Hall of Fame* exhibit, which includes a computerised juke-box containing nearly every song by performers featured, their signatures etched in glass, film exhibits and displays of artefacts. Exhibitions cover different musical genres focusing on icons from the world of rock and pop, including the Beatles, Elvis Presley and the Rolling Stones.

Transportation
Air: Cleveland Hopkins International Airport. **Rail:** Rapid: Downtown to Public Square. Waterfront Rapid: North Coast Harbour Station. **Road:** Bus: Public services.

Contact Addresses
Rock and Roll Hall of Fame, 1 Key Plaza, Cleveland, OH 44114, USA
Tel: (888) 764 7625
Website: www.rockhall.com

1 Rock and Roll Hall of Fame

Rock and Roll Hall of Fame

Ohio Division of Travel and Tourism©

South Dakota

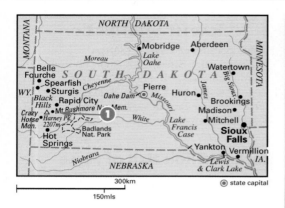

Mount Rushmore National Memorial

Corel©

---

1 Mount Rushmore National Memorial

Tourist Information

South Dakota Department of Tourism
711 East Wells Avenue, Pierre, SD 57501-3369, USA
Tel: (605) 773 3301 *or* (800) 732 5682 (toll free USA and Canada only)
Website: www.travelsd.com

Rocky Mountain International
PO Box 214, Fareham, Hampshire PO14 2TD, UK
Tel: (01329) 665 111 (trade enquiries only) *or* (09063) 640 655 (customer request line; 60p per minute)
Website: www.rmi-realamerica.com

Mount Rushmore National Memorial

Mount Rushmore National Memorial is one of the USA's most renowned national monuments. The site in South Dakota is home to 18m-tall (60ft) faces of four US presidents – George Washington, Thomas Jefferson, Theodore Roosevelt and Abraham Lincoln – perched 152m (465ft) in the air. These giant faces are carved into solid rock and stand as a gateway to America's majestic west. Originally called *The Shrine of Democracy*,

the idea to build a monument of this size was conceived by the historian Duane Robinson and the sculptor Gutzon Borglum in 1923. Work began on the monument, which is surrounded by the *Black Hills National Forest*, in 1927, and took over 14 years to complete the fundraising and carving. Today, the memorial is an internationally recognised symbol of the first 150 years of America's history and the part the four presidents played in founding it. The memorial hosts many exhibits, walks and lectures during the summer months.

Transportation
Air: Rapid City Regional Airport. **Road:** Car: Hwy-16 and Hwy-244 (from Rapid City).

Contact Addresses
Mount Rushmore National Memorial, PO Box 268, Keystone, SD 57751, USA
Tel: (605) 574 2523 *or* 574 3171 (recorded information)
Website: www.nps.gov/moru

Tennessee

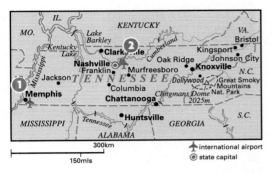

300km
150mls

✈ international airport
◉ state capital

1 Graceland
2 Grand Ole Opry

Tourist Information

Tennessee Department of Tourism Development
Rachel Jackson Building, 320 Sixth Avenue
North, Fifth Floor, Nashville, TN 37243, USA
Tel: (615) 741 2159 *or* (800) 836 6200 (toll
free USA and Canada only)
Website: www.tnvacation.com

Tennessee Tourism (UK)
Lofthouse Enterprises, Woodland Park Street,
Hitchin, Herts SG4 9AH, UK
Tel: (01462) 440 784
Website: www.deep-south-usa.com/tenn.html

Graceland

Graceland is America's monument to one of its
favourite musicians and icons, Elvis Presley. The
'King' bought the colonial-style mansion in 1957
and lived there until his death in 1977. The
house has been open to the public since 1982,
becoming a shrine to his music and his legacy.
At the site, which is located 16km (10 miles)
from Memphis, visitors can enter the rooms
where the star and his family lived, tour Elvis' jet
planes, shop at *Graceland Plaza* or stay at the
Heartbreak Hotel. Highlights include the *Trophy
Building* and the *Meditation Garden* where Elvis
was buried.

Transportation
Air: Memphis International Airport. **Rail:** Train:
Memphis Central Station. **Road:** Bus: Public
services. Car: I-55 (exit 5-B) (from St Louis,
Chicago or New Orleans); I-240 (from Memphis
International Airport).

Contact Addresses
Graceland, Elvis Presley Enterprises Inc, PO Box
16508, 3734 Elvis Presley Boulevard, Memphis, TN
38186-0508, USA
Tel: (901) 332 3322
Website: www.elvis.com

Grand Ole Opry

Grand Ole Opry is the world's longest running live
radio show. It was first broadcast as a weekly barn
dance show on November 28 1925, at a time
when the radio was fast growing in popularity. In
the early days, the show followed a classical music
program, and radio announcer George D Hay joked
that the Grand Opera that listeners had just heard
would be followed by performances of the 'Grand
Ole Opry' – Hay adopted this impromptu name
and it stuck. Within a few years the show became
so popular that thousands of fans flocked to see it
performed live. After a succession of venues, it
finally settled in the specially designed 4400 seat
Grand Ole Opry House in Nashville in 1974, from
where it has been broadcast ever since.

Transportation
Air: Nashville Airport. **Rail:** Train: Memphis
Amtrak Station. **Road:** Car: Hwy-40 (from
Knoxville or Memphis); Hwy-65 (from Louisville
or Birmingham); Hwy-24 (from Chattanooga or
Paducah).

Contact Addresses
Grand Ole Opry, 2802 Opryland Drive, Nashville,
TN 37214, USA
Tel: (615) 871 6779
Website: www.opry.com

Texas

Sixth Floor Museum, Dallas

Photo courtesy J. Griffis Smith

---

1 Sixth Floor Museum

Tourist Information

Texas Economic Development, Tourism Division

1700 North Congress, Suite 200, PO Box 12728, Austin, TX 78711-2728, USA
Tel: (512) 462 9191 *or* (800) 888 8839 (toll free USA and Canada only)
Website: www.traveltex.com

State of Texas Tourism Office

c/o First Public Relations, Molasses House, Clove Hitch Quay, Plantation Wharf, London SW11 3TN, UK
Tel: (020) 7978 5233

Sixth Floor Museum

The *Texas School Book Depository* was a rather ordinary building in downtown Dallas until the infamous assassination of US President John F Kennedy on November 22 1963 as he travelled in an open limousine through Dallas on a pre-election visit. Lee Harvey Oswald, the 24-year-old Dallas citizen who was accused of the crime, and was himself shot dead by nightclub owner Jack Ruby just two days later, had a filing job at the depository. The deadly shot was fired from the sixth floor of the building, which is now the *Sixth Floor Museum at Dealey Plaza* documenting both the assassination itself and the life and times of JFK. Visitors can immerse themselves in the events of the fateful day, with a minute-by-minute account of the action as well as recordings of news broadcasts and even material showing mourning vigils in India and Germany. Other exhibitions focus on the four investigations into the crime, the legacy of Kennedy's administration, and the various theories on who carried out the assassination. The corner staircase where the rifle was found, and down which the assassin is thought to have escaped, has been reconstructed according to official police photographs. Background information to the shooting is provided through displays on the 1960s political, cultural and social movements, and visitors can add their own comments to memorial books which are kept as part of the museum archives.

Transportation

Air: Dallas-Fort Worth International Airport, Dallas Love Field Airport (domestic flights). **Rail:** Train: Union Station. DART (Light Rail System): West End Station or Union Station. **Road:** DART Trolleybus: Route 706 to Union Station or West End Station. Bus: Public services.

Contact Addresses

Sixth Floor Museum at Dealey Plaza, 411 Elm Street, Dallas, TX 75202, USA
Tel: (214) 747 6660
Website: www.jfk.org

Washington, DC

Map showing Washington, DC area with numbered locations:

1 Lincoln Memorial
2 Smithsonian Institution
3 White House

20km / 10mls

✈ international airport

Tourist Information

Washington, DC Convention & Tourism Corporation
1212 New York Avenue, Suite 600, NW,
Washington, DC 20005, USA
Tel: (202) 789 7000
Website: www.washington.org

Washington, DC Convention & Tourism Corporation
c/o Representation Plus, 11 Blades Court, 121
Deodar Road, London SW15 2NU, UK
Tel: (020) 8877 4521

Lincoln Memorial

Modelled upon a Doric temple, the *Lincoln Memorial* is a tribute to President Abraham Lincoln and the nation he fought to preserve during the Civil War (1861-1865), the nation's bloodiest conflict. Enclosed by a colonnade and complemented by a reflecting pool in front, a large statue of President Lincoln, sculpted by Daniel Chester French, sits in solemn thought, grasping the arms of his throne-like chair. The monument has the Gettysburg Address inscribed on its southern wall and a mural painted by Jules Guerin above it, showing the angel of truth liberating a slave. As a symbol of freedom and racial harmony, the Lincoln Memorial was the site of Martin Luther King's 'I Have a Dream' speech in August 1963.

Transportation
Air: Washington Dulles International Airport, Washington Ronald Reagan National Airport, Baltimore-Washington Airport. **Rail:** Train: Union Station. Underground: Foggy Bottom. **Road:** Bus: Public services.

Contact Addresses
Lincoln Memorial, 900 Ohio Drive South West, Washington, DC 20024, USA
Tel: (202) 426 6841
Website: www.nps.gov/linc

Smithsonian Institution

The *Smithsonian Institution*, established in 1846 with money left to the United States by the English scientist James Smithson, is the largest museum complex in the world. It is composed of 16 museums and the National Zoo in Washington DC, as well as two museums in New York City. One of the most famous is the *National Air and Space Museum*. Opened in 1976, the National Air and Space Museum celebrates the history and evolution of air and space technology. Exhibits include the Wright Brothers' 1903 *Flyer*, Charles Lindbergh's *Spirit of St Louis*, and moon rock collected by the Apollo astronauts (Neil Armstrong and Buzz Aldrin) from the lunar surface, when they touched down on July 20 1969. Other museums in Washington include the *Anacostia Museum and Center for African American History and Culture*, *Arthur M Sackler Gallery*, *Art and Industries Building*, *Freer Gallery of Art*, *Hirshhorn Museum and Sculpture Garden*, *National Museum of African Art*, *National Museum of American History*, *National*

White House

Museum of Natural History, *National Portrait Gallery*, *National Postal Museum*, *Renwick Gallery*, *Smithsonian American Art Museum* and *Smithsonian Institution Building*. The New York museums include the *Cooper-Hewitt*, *National Design Museum* and the *National Museum of the American Indian*.

Transportation
Air: Washington Dulles International Airport, Washington Ronald Reagan National Airport. **Rail:** Train: Union Station. Metrorail: Smithsonian. **Road:** Bus: Public services.

Contact Addresses
Smithsonian Information Center, SI Building, Room 153, Washington, DC 20560, USA
Tel: (202) 357 2020
Website: www.si.edu

White House

The *White House* is where the President of the United States of America lives and carries out official duties as Head of State. It is the most famous building in Washington, DC and was built between 1792 and 1800 by the Irish-born architect James Hoban. Although commissioned during President George Washington's lifetime, the first residents of the White House were President

John Adams and his wife who moved into the house in 1800. The building has had a colourful past. It burned down during the War of 1812 (which is often called America's second War of Independence) between America and Great Britain which lasted until the end of 1814, and was rebuilt in 1815, only to endure (and survive) another fire in the West Wing in 1929. Self-guided tours of certain areas of the White House are possible but must be arranged in advance.

Transportation
Air: Washington Dulles International Airport, Washington Ronald Reagan National Airport. **Rail:** Train: Union Station. Metrorail: Federal Triangle (blue or orange lines), Metro Center (blue, orange or red lines) or McPherson Square (blue or orange lines). **Road:** Bus: Public services.

Contact Addresses
President's Park, White House Liaison, 1100 Ohio Drive, SW, Washington, DC 20242, USA *or* White House Visitor Center, National Park Service, 1450 Pennsylvania Avenue, NW, Washington, DC 20230, USA
Tel: (202) 208 1631 *or* 456 7041 (24-hour information line)
Website: www.nps.gov/whho *or* www.whitehouse.gov

Washington State

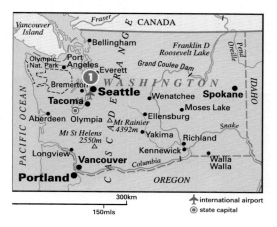

300km
150mls

✈ international airport
◎ state capital

1 Space Needle

Tourist Information

Seattle's Convention & Visitors Bureau
520 Pike Street, Suite 1300, Seattle, WA 98101, USA
Tel: (206) 461 5800 (administration) or 461 5840 (visitor information)
Website: www.seeseattle.org

Washington State Tourism Office
PO Box 42500, Olympia, WA 98504-2500, USA
Tel: (360) 725 5051 or (800) 544 1800 (toll free USA and Canada only)
Website: www.experiencewashington.com

Washington State Information Office
c/o First Public Relations, Molasses House, Clove Hitch Quay, Plantation Wharf, London SW11 3TN, UK
Tel: (020) 7978 5233

Space Needle

Standing at 185m (605ft) high, Seattle's most famous building is a great place from which to enjoy outstanding 360-degree views across the city and Washington State, including the *Cascade* and *Olympic* mountain ranges, Puget Sound and Mount Rainier. The *Space Needle* is the most recognised landmark in Seattle, and visitors can also eat in its famous revolving restaurant. Designed by Edward E Carlson and completed in 1961 for US$4.5 million, the top of this Space Age tower can be reached in just 43 seconds by a futuristic glass lift. The tower is located at the *Seattle Center*, a 30-hectare (74-acre) site built for the 1962 World Fair, which is also home to the *Pacific Science Center*, offering laser and hologram exhibits, the *Boeing IMAX Theater* and the *Children's Museum*.

Transportation
Air: Seattle-Tacoma International Airport. **Road:** Monorail: A monorail service operates from Westlake Center and stops near the Space Needle. **Road:** Coach: Coaches set down on Broad Street, west of Fifth Avenue. Bus: Public services.

Contact Addresses
Space Needle, 400 Broad Street, Seattle, WA 98109, USA
Tel: (206) 905 2100
Website: www.spaceneedle.com

Space Needle

Wyoming

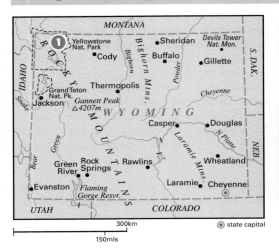

Yellowstone National Park at dusk — Corel©

300km
150mls
◉ state capital

1 Yellowstone National Park

Tourist Information

Wyoming Business Council – Tourism Office
I-25 at College Drive, Cheyenne, WY 82002, USA
Tel: (307) 777 7777 *or* (800) 225 5996 (toll free USA and Canada only)
Website: www.wyomingtourism.org

Rocky Mountain International
PO Box 214, Fareham, Hampshire PO14 2TD, UK
Tel: (01329) 665 111 (trade enquiries only) *or* (09063) 640 655 (customer request line; calls cost 60p per minute)
Website: www.rmi-realamerica.com

Yellowstone National Park

Established in 1872, *Yellowstone National Park* is the first and oldest national park in the world. Renowned for its geothermal phenomena, the park has more geysers and hot springs than the rest of the world combined. The mineral waters of *Mammoth Hot Springs* in the northwest of the park, have long been attracting visitors seeking a natural cure for various ailments. Other natural attractions include the *Grand Canyon of the Yellowstone River* (not to be confused with the *Grand Canyon* in Arizona), fossil forests and *Yellowstone Lake*. Natural wildlife, such as bears, wolves, elk, bison and trout, abound and can often be seen from the road. Evidence of human activity in the park, dating back as far as 12,000 years, has also been found and visitors can learn more about the area's history at the *Albright Visitor Center Museum*. The *Canyon Visitor Center* also features displays on the culture and wildlife of Yellowstone. Visitors who wish to stay overnight in the park can take advantage of the many inns, lodges and campsites located within the park boundaries.

Transportation
Air: Denver International Airport, Cody Airport (domestic flights), Jackson Airport (domestic flights), Bozeman Airport (domestic flights), Billings Airport (domestic flights), Idaho Falls Airport (domestic flights), West Yellowstone Airport (open Jun-early Sep) (domestic flights).
Road: Bus: Services to West Yellowstone (from Bozeman); summer services to West Yellowstone (from Idaho).

Contact Addresses
Yellowstone National Park, Visitor Services Office, PO Box 168, Yellowstone National Park, WY 82190, USA
Tel: (307) 344 7381
Website: www.nps.gov/yell

Venezuela

1 Angel Falls (Salto Ángel)

Tourist Information

**Venezuela Tourism Board
(Corporación de Turismo de Venezuela)**
Avenida v. Lecuna, Parque Central, Torre
Oeste, Piso 37, Caracas, Venezuela
Tel: (02) 574 1968

Embassy of the Republic of Venezuela
1 Cromwell Road, London SW7 2HW, UK
Tel: (020) 7584 4206 *or* 7581 2776
Website: www.venezlon.demon.co.uk

Angel Falls (Salto Ángel)

At 988m (3212ft), *Angel Falls* is the tallest waterfall
in the world. To many it is also the most stunning,
with water spilling into a freefall of nearly 1km
(0.6 miles) before crashing into a pool. Double
rainbows can often be seen in the spray-drenched
air above. Located in *Canaima National Park*,

600km (373 miles) south of Ciudad Bolívar and
50km (30 miles) southeast of Canaima village, the
waterfall was made public to the wider world in
1937 by American pilot Jimmie Angel, who was
searching for gold in the area. Angel Falls used to
be a holy site for the Incas, and is still sacred to
the local Venezuelan tribes today. Tours to the
falls can be arranged from the nearest town,
Ciudad Bolívar, by boat or plane.

Transportation
Air: Caracas Simon Bolivar International Airport
or Ciudad Bolívar Airport to Canaima Airport;
then private tour operator's plane or boat. **Water:**
Boat: Motorised canoe services from Ciudad
Bolívar (Jun-Dec). **Road:** Bus: Services from
Caracas or Ciudad Bolívar.

Contact Addresses
For more information on Angel Falls, contact
Corporación de Turismo de Venezuela (see **Tourist
Information** above).

Angel Falls

INATUR©

Vietnam

400km
200mls

↑ international airport

Tourist Information

Vietnam Tourism
30a Ly Thuong Kiet Street, Hanoi, Vietnam
Tel: (04) 825 7532 *or* 826 4154
Website: www.vn-tourism.com

Embassy of the Socialist Republic of Vietnam
12 Victoria Road, London W8 5RD, UK
Tel: (020) 7937 1912 *or* 7937 3222 (visa section)

Cu Chi Tunnels (Cu Chi Diadao)

The *Cu Chi Tunnels* is an underground network
excavated by the Vietnamese and used by the Viet

Cong during both the French-Indochina War
(1946-1954) and the Vietnam War (1955-1975).
Stretching for over 200km (124 miles) and
connecting numerous villages in the provinces, the
tunnels once housed mini-hospitals, store rooms
and factories, and were used as living quarters by
both Vietnamese fighters and local villagers.

Transportation
Air: Tan Son Nhat International Airport. **Road:**
Coach: Daily coach trip.

Contact Addresses
For more information on Cu Chi Tunnels, contact
Vietnam Tourism (see **Tourist Information** above).

P ✗ 🧺 £ 🏭

Hué Imperial Palace (Hué Cung Vua)

Hué was the political, cultural and religious capital of
unified Vietnam between 1802 and 1945. Today, the
imperial city is home to many important sites, the
most famous of which is the *Imperial Palace* (or
Citadel) situated on the north banks of the Perfume
River. Surrounded by a wall and a moat, the Citadel
can be entered via one of 10 gates and contains the
Nine Holy Cannons that used to defend the palace, the
Imperial Enclosure where the Emperor carried out his
official business, the *Palace of Supreme Harmony* and
the *Hall of the Mandarins*. It was also home to the
Purple Forbidden Palace which was reserved for use by
the Emperor himself. The whole city was recognised
as a UNESCO World Heritage Site in 1993.

Transportation
Air: Phu Bia Airport. **Rail:** Train: Reunification
Express train to Hanoi (from Ho Chi Minh City).
Road: Bus: Dong Ba Bus Station. Coach: Private
tour operators organise trips to Hué.

Contact Addresses
Vietnam Tourism, 14 Nguyen Van Cu, Hué,
Vietnam
Tel: (054) 828 316
Website: www.vn-tourism.com

P ✗ 🧺 ♿ 🏛 £ 🏭

Yemen

400km
200mls
✈ international airport

SAUDI ARABIA

Rub ' al - Khali

OMAN

•Sa'dah

YEMEN

Kamaran I.

Mareb   Shibam• •Tarim

① SANA'A   *Hadhramaut*

•Hodeida   Nisab   •Sayhut

•Ibb   •Habban •Mukalla

•Ta'izz

•Mocha

•Aden   Hadiboh

ERIT.   Socotra

Perim I.   *Gulf of Aden*   Abd al Kuri   *The Brothers*

DJIBOUTI

SOMALIA

---

1 Old City of Sana'a (al-Medina al-qadima)

Tourist Information

Ministry of Tourism and Environment
PO Box 5607, 48 Amman Street, Sana'a,
Republic of Yemen
Tel: (01) 252 319
Website: www.yenet.com/tourism

Embassy of the Republic of Yemen
57 Cromwell Road, London SW7 2ED, UK
Tel: (020) 7584 6607

Old City of Sana'a (al-Medina al-qadima)

The UNESCO-preserved site of the *Old City of Sana'a* is the largest preserved old city in the Arab world. Sana'a, which translates from Arabic as 'fortified place', has been the political capital of Yemen since the unification of the Yemen Arab Republic and the People's Democratic Republic of Yemen in 1990. It is one of the oldest continuously inhabited cities in the world, and according to Yemeni legend was founded by Shem, one of the three sons of Noah, possibly as early as the second century BC. Once an Arabian centre for Christians and Jews, the city was converted to Islam in AD 632. Apart from brief periods of Ottoman control – in the 16th century and between 1872 and 1940 – members of the Zaydi dynasty thereafter ruled Sana'a more or less continuously until 1962, when it became the capital of the newly founded Yemen Arab Republic. Surrounded by ancient clay walls which stand 6m to 9m (20ft to 30ft) high, the old city is a wonderland of over 100 mosques, 12 hammams (baths) and 6500 houses. Most of the buildings date back to the seventh and eighth centuries BC, when the city achieved prominence as an important centre for Islam, and were constructed from dark basalt stone and brick. One of the most popular attractions is the 1000-year-old *Suq al-Milh* (Salt Market), where it is possible to buy not only salt but also bread, spices, raisins, cotton, copper, pottery, silverware, antiques, and a host of other goods. The seventh century *al-Jami'al-Kabir* (Great Mosque) is one of the oldest in the Muslim world and its Persian-style minarets pierce the city's skyline. The *Liberty Gate*, formerly known as *Bab al-Yaman* (Yemen Gate) until the 1962 revolution, is one of the many points of entry through the city walls and is over 700 years old. The *National Museum* consists of three floors of displays and exhibitions, including ancient Yemeni writings, coins, jewellery and traditional costume.

Transportation
Air: Sana'a International Airport. **Road:** Car: Hodeida Way (from Hodeida); Aden Way (from Aden); Ta'izz Way (from Ta'izz); Marib Way (from Marib); Sa'dah Way (from Sa'dah).

Contact Addresses
For more information of the Old City of Sana'a, contact the General Authority of Tourism, Yemen (see **Tourist Information** above).

Key to symbols: £ Entry charged ᨈ Disabled access ◪ Man-made attraction ♥ Natural attraction ℙ Parking ✗ Restaurant ⊞ Shop ℡ UNESCO site

---

Zambia

Victoria Falls at sunset

1 Victoria Falls, Zambia

Tourist Information

Tourism Council of Zambia
PO Box 36561, Lusaka, Zambia
Tel: (01) 251 666
Website: www.zambiatourism.com

Zambia National Tourist Board
2 Palace Gate, London W8 5NG, UK
Tel: (020) 7589 6655

Victoria Falls, Zambia

Made known to the wider world by the famous British explorer Dr David Livingstone in 1855, the *Victoria Falls*, which form a natural border between Zimbabwe and Zambia, are one of Africa's best-known natural wonders and one of the world's most impressive waterfalls. The falls, which Livingstone named after Queen Victoria, were known to native Kololo tribes in the 18th century as *Mosi-oa-Tunya*, meaning 'the smoke that thunders', and the spray that they generate can be seen for miles around. The cascade is formed as the calm, 2km- (1.2 miles-) wide *Zambezi River* spills out of a flat basalt lip and plunges into the gorge below. At their highest, the Victoria Falls drop a distance of 108m (345ft), almost twice as far as the *Niagara Falls*. As much as 546,000,000 cubic metres (713,725,490 cubic yards) per minute plummet over the edge at the height of the flood season. Viewing the falls from the Zambia side means that visitors can follow a path that goes right up to the falling water. An alternative view can be had from the *Boiling Pot*, right in the depths of the gorge at the bottom of the falls. The 111m- (364ft-) high *Victoria Falls Bridge*, commissioned by British statesman Cecil Rhodes in 1900 as a railway crossing, is now a popular place for bungee jumping, and can be crossed by foot for excellent views of the falls and the winding blue-green waters of the Zambezi River. It is also possible to see an aerial view of the falls from a Micro-light or fixed-wing plane. The area around the falls is a prime game-viewing location. The best time to view the Victoria Falls is between December-July when the water levels are high.

Transportation
Air: Lusaka International Airport, Harare International Airport, Livingstone Airport (domestic flights). **Rail:** Livingstone Station. **Road:** Coach: Services from Lusaka. Car: Victoria Falls border road (from Zimbabwe); from the south on Mosi-oa-Tunya Road (from Livingstone).

Contact Addresses
Tourist Centre, Mosi-oa-Tunya Road, Livingstone, Zambia
Tel: (03) 321 404

Zimbabwe

1 Great Zimbabwe
2 Victoria Falls, Zimbabwe

Tourist Information

Zimbabwe Tourism Authority (ZTA)
PO Box CY286, Causeway, Harare, Zimbabwe
Tel: (04) 758 730
Website: www.zimbabwetourism.co.zw

Zimbabwe Tourism Office
Zimbabwe House, 429 Strand, London
WC2R OQE, UK
Tel: (020) 7240 6169

Great Zimbabwe

Great Zimbabwe was a large iron-age
settlement that existed from the 13th to 15th
centuries and lent its name to modern-day
Zimbabwe, which derives from a Shona word
meaning 'house of stone'. The *Great
Enclosure*, with its 250m (820ft) wide and
11m (36ft) high perimeter wall, is the largest

single ancient structure south of the Sahara
Desert, while the *Hill Complex* rises 79m
(260ft) above the surrounding area on a
steep, granite hill. For many years, the
origins of Great Zimbabwe and its
inhabitants were the subject of much debate;
various claims for it were made by different
groups of white colonisers following its
discovery in the 1870s, who raided it for its
many treasures and gold. However,
archaeologists have proved that it is actually
an authentic native African site, developed
by a long-dead civilisation advanced enough
to trade with people as far away as China.

Transportation
Air: Harare International Airport, Masvingo
Airport (domestic flights). **Rail:** Train:
Masvingo Station. **Road:** Bus: Services to
Morgenster Mission which is one kilometre (0.6
miles) from Great Zimbabwe (from Masvingo).
Coach: Services to Great Zimbabwe (from
Harare and Bulawayo).

Contact Addresses
For more information on Great Zimbabwe,
contact Zimbabwe Tourism Authority (see
Tourist Information above).

Victoria Falls, Zimbabwe

Made known to the wider world by the famous
British explorer Dr David Livingstone in 1855,
the *Victoria Falls*, which form a natural border
between Zimbabwe and Zambia, are one of
Africa's best-known natural wonders and one of
the world's most impressive waterfalls. The Falls,
which Livingstone named after Queen Victoria,
were known to native Kololo tribes in the 18th
century as *Mosi-oa-Tunya*, meaning 'the smoke
that thunders', and the spray that they generate
can be seen for miles around. The cascade is
formed as the calm, 2km- (1.2 miles-) wide
Zambezi River spills out of a flat basalt lip and
plunges into the gorge below. At their highest,
the Victoria Falls drop a distance of 108m
(345ft), almost twice as far as the *Niagara*

Victoria Falls

Corel©

Falls. As much as 546,000,000 cubic metres (713,725,490 cubic yards) per minute plummet over the edge at the height of the flood season. The 111m- (364ft-) high *Victoria Falls Bridge*, commissioned by British statesman Cecil Rhodes in 1900 as a railway crossing, is now a popular place for bungee jumping, and can be crossed by foot for excellent views of the falls and the winding blue-green waters of the Zambezi River. It is also possible to see an aerial view of the falls from a Micro-light or fixed-wing plane. The area around the falls is a prime game-viewing location.

Transportation
Air: Lusaka International Airport, Harare International Airport, Victoria Falls Airport (domestic flights). **Rail:** Train: Victoria Falls Station. **Road:** Bus: Services to Victoria Falls Bus Station.

Contact Addresses
For more information on Victoria Falls, contact Zimbabwe Tourism Authority (see **Tourist Information** above).

Calendar of Events

January

Australia Day	Australia
Australian Open	Australia
Brussels on Ice	Belgium
Burns' Night	United Kingdom
Celtic Connections	United Kingdom
Daily Telegraph Adventure Travel & Sports Show	United Kingdom
Festival in the Desert	Mali
Hogmanay	United Kingdom
Krakow Christmas Crib Contest	Poland
London Parade	United Kingdom
Mummers Parade	United States of America
Munich Carnival	Germany
National Western Stock Show & Rodeo	United States of America
New Year	Russian Federation
New Year's Eve	Brazil
Perth International Arts Festival	Australia
Sydney Festival	Australia
Thorri Feast	Iceland
Three Kings Parade	Spain

February

Berlin International Film Festival	Germany
Chinese New Year	United Kingdom
Dubai Shopping Festival	United Arab Emirates
Hong Kong Arts Festival	People's Republic of China
Krakow Christmas Crib Contest	Poland
Lisbon Carnival	Portugal
Madrid Carnival	Spain
Mardi Gras	United States of America
Munich Carnival	Germany
Perth International Arts Festival	Australia
Rio de Janeiro Carnival	Brazil
Sydney Gay and Lesbian Mardi Gras	Australia
Thorri Feast	Iceland
Toronto Winterfest	Canada
Venice Carnival	Italy

March

Budapest Spring Festival	Hungary
Daily Mail Ideal Home Show	United Kingdom
Dubai World Cup	United Arab Emirates
Explosion of the Cart	Italy
Festival of the Historic Centre	Mexico
Hong Kong Arts Festival	People's Republic of China
International Motor Show	Switzerland
Rio de Janeiro Carnival	Brazil
Singapore Food Festival	Singapore

Calendar of Events

St Patrick's Day Parade ....United States of America
St Patrick's Festival..Ireland
Sydney Gay and Lesbian Mardi Gras ....Australia
Ueno Cherry Blossom Festival ....Japan
Venice Biennial ....Italy

April

Boston Marathon ....United States of America
Budapest Spring Festival ....Hungary
Daily Mail Ideal Home Show ....United Kingdom
Edinburgh International Science Festival...............................United Kingdom
Flora London Marathon...United Kingdom
Grand National..United Kingdom
Hong Kong International Film Festival ....People's Republic of China
Lisbon Half Marathon ....Portugal
Queen's Day..The Netherlands
Rand Easter Show ....South Africa
Royal Easter Show ....New Zealand
Singapore Food Festival ....Singapore
Singapore International Film Festival....................................Singapore
Songkran Festival...Thailand
Ueno Cherry Blossom Festival ....Japan
Venice Biennial ....Italy
Zurich Spring Festival ....Switzerland

May

Atlanta Jazz Festival..United States of America
Bergen International Festival...Norway
Bergen Night Jazz Festival..Norway
Cannes Film Festival ....France
Cape Gourmet Festival ....South Africa
Chelsea Flower Show ....United Kingdom
Festimad Alternative Music Festival ....Spain
French Tennis Open (Roland Garros) ....France
Heineken Green Energy Festival ....Ireland
National Windmill and Pumping Station Day ....The Netherlands
Prague International Marathon ....Czech Republic
Rand Easter Show ....South Africa
San Isidro Festival ....Spain
Sanja Festival ....Japan
Vancouver International Children's Festival............................Canada
Venice Biennial ....Italy
Vienna Festival...Austria

June

Barcelona Summer Festival (GREC) ....Spain
Bergen International Festival ....Norway
Bergen Night Jazz Festival..Norway
Bloomsday Festival ....Ireland
Cardiff Festival ....United Kingdom
Carnival of the Cultures...Germany

Christopher Street Day ....Germany
City Foundation Day ....Germany
Festival of Music ....France
French Tennis Open (Roland Garros) ....France
Grant Park Music Festival ....United States of America
Historical Soccer Tournament..Italy
Holland Festival ....The Netherlands
Jewish Culture Festival ....Poland
Lisbon Festivities ....Portugal
Montréal International Jazz Festival ....Canada
Queen's Birthday Parade – Trooping the Colour ....United Kingdom
Roskilde Festival ....Denmark
Royal Highland Show ....United Kingdom
San Isidro Festival ....Spain
Swedish National Day ....Sweden
TT Races..United Kingdom
Vancouver International Children's Festival.........................Canada
Venice Biennial ....Italy
Vienna Festival..Austria
Vienna Music Film Festival ....Austria
Warsaw Mozart Festival ....Poland
Wimbledon Championships ....United Kingdom
Zurich Festival ....Switzerland

July

Arrival of the Tour de France ....France
Athens Festival..Greece
Avignon Festival..France
Barcelona Summer Festival (GREC) ....Spain
Bastille Day ....France
Calgary Stampede ....Canada
Cardiff Festival ....United Kingdom
Copenhagen Jazz Festival ....Denmark
Geneva Festival ....Switzerland
Grant Park Music Festival ....United States of America
Havana Carnival..Cuba
Independence Day ....United States of America
Jewish Culture Festival ....Poland
Krakow International Street Theatre Festival.......................Poland
Light Nights ....Iceland
Love Parade ....Germany
Montréal International Jazz Festival ....Canada
Ommegang Royal Pageant ....Belgium
Rockwave Festival ....Greece
Roman Summer ....Italy
Roskilde Festival ....Denmark
Running of the Bulls (San Fermin Festival) ....Spain
Salzburg Festival ....Austria
Summer Arts Festival ....France
Tokyo Fireworks Festival ....Japan
Venice Biennial ....Italy
Vienna Music Film Festival ....Austria

Calendar of Events

Warsaw Mozart Festival ....Poland
Wimbledon Championships ....United Kingdom
WOMAD Festival ....United Kingdom
Zurich Festival ....Switzerland

August

Amsterdam Gay Pride ....The Netherlands
Avignon Festival..France
Cardiff Festival ....United Kingdom
Copenhagen International Ballet Festival ....Denmark
Edinburgh Fringe Festival ....United Kingdom
Edinburgh International Festival..United Kingdom
Edinburgh Military Tattoo ....United Kingdom
Elvis Week ....United States of America
Geneva Festival ....Switzerland
Grant Park Music Festival ....United States of America
Havana Carnival..Cuba
Helsinki Festival ....Finland
Jaffa Nights. ....Israel
Light Nights ....Iceland
Notting Hill Carnival ....United Kingdom
Queen's Birthday Celebrations ....Thailand
Roman Summer...Italy
Salzburg Festival ....Austria
Summer Arts Festival ....France
Swiss National Day ....Switzerland
Venice Biennial ....Italy
Vienna Music Film Festival ....Austria

September

Athens Festival ....Greece
Autumn Festival ....France
Avignon Festival...France
Berlin Marathon ....Germany
Côtes du Rhône Grape Harvest ....France
Dublin Fringe Festival ....Ireland
Edinburgh International Festival..United Kingdom
Helsinki Festival..Finland
Istanbul Biennial ....Turkey
Moscow International Peace Marathon ....Russian Federation
October Festival ....Germany
Our Lady of Mercy Festival ....Spain
Prague Autumn International Music Festival ....Czech Republic
Roman Summer ....Italy
Stockholm Beer & Whisky Festival...Sweden
Venice Biennial ....Italy
Vienna Music Film Festival ....Austria

October

Autumn Festival ....France
Budapest Autumn Festival ....Hungary

Diwali ....India
Dublin Fringe Festival ....Ireland
Frankfurt Marathon ....Germany
International Festival of Authors.....................................Canada
Istanbul Biennial ....Turkey
Lord of Miracles ....Peru
Madrid Autumn Festival ....Spain
Melbourne Festival ....Australia
October Festival...Germany
Prague Autumn International Music Festival ....Czech Republic
Pushkar Fair ....India
Rome Jazz Festival ....Italy
Venice Biennial ....Italy

November

Athens Marathon ....Greece
Autumn Festival ....France
Budapest Autumn Festival ....Hungary
Ellerslie Flower Show ....New Zealand
International Festival of Advent & Christmas Music ....Czech Republic
International Film Festival of Wales ....United Kingdom
Istanbul Biennial ....Turkey
Lord Mayor's Show ....United Kingdom
Macy's Thanksgiving Day Parade ....United States of America
Madrid Autumn Festival ....Spain
Magic of Advent in Vienna ....Austria
Melbourne Festival ....Australia
Pushkar Fair ....India
Rome Jazz Festival...Italy
Stockholm International Film Festival ....Sweden
Strasbourg Christmas Market..France
Venice Biennial ....Italy

December

Autumn Festival ....France
Boston Tea Party Re-enactment ....United States of America
Brussels on Ice...Belgium
Christmas Market ....Germany
Christmas Mass in St Peter's Basilica ....Italy
European Christmas Market ....Belgium
Festival of Lights ....France
Hogmanay ....United Kingdom
International Festival of Advent & Christmas Music ....Czech Republic
Krakow Christmas Crib Contest ....Poland
Magic Night ....Portugal
Magic of Advent in Vienna ....Austria
New Year ....Russian Federation
New Year's Eve ....Brazil
New Year's Eve Gala and Ball at the Opera ....Hungary
Rome Jazz Festival...Italy
Strasbourg Christmas Market..France

Australia

Melbourne

Tourist Information
Tourism Victoria
GPO Box 2219T, 55 Swanston Street, Melbourne, VIC 3001, Australia
Tel: (03) 9653 9777
Website: www.visitvictoria.com

• January

Australian Open

The *Australian Open*, which is Australia's main tennis tournament, forms part of the Grand Slam competition, which also encorporates the *Wimbledon Championships*, the *United States Open* and the *French Open*. The record attendance for the event was set in 2005 when 60,669 people attended on the middle Saturday of the tournament. The first tennis tournament in Australia was held in Warehouseman's Cricket Ground in Melbourne in 1905 when the Australian Rodney Heath won the men's singles title. The first woman to win the women's single title was another Australian, Margaret Molesworth, in 1922. Over the years, the tournament has been played across Australia, however in 1972 it was decided to hold the tournament permanently in Melbourne. The event has grown in popularity and as a result, moved to a bigger venue at Flinders Park in 1988, with the name changing to Melbourne Park in 1996.

Event Organiser
Australian Open, Private Bag 6060, Richmond, South Victoria, VIC 3121, Australia
Tel: (03) 9286 1355
Website: www.ausopen.org

Venue
Melbourne Park.

Transport
Air: Melbourne Airport. **Rail:** Train: Richmond, Flinders Street or Jolimont stations. Tram: Public services. **Road:** Car: Melbourne Park is located on Bateman Avenue; there is, however, no public parking during the tournament and visitors are advised to use public transport.

• October-November

Melbourne Festival

Melbourne Festival is one of the most important arts festivals in Australia with performances from the worlds of dance, theatre, music, opera, visual arts and film. The event runs for 17 days each October and November and was first held in 1986, when it was headed by the composer Gian Carlo Menotti, responsible for the Spoleto Festival series, also held in Italy and the USA. The festival in Australia was originally known as the *Melbourne Spoleto Festival*, but changed its name to the *Melbourne International Festival of the Arts* in 1990 and to Melbourne Festival in 1997.

Event Organiser
Melbourne Festival, PO Box 10, Flinders Lane, Melbourne, VIC 8009, Australia
Tel: (03) 9662 4242
Website: www.melbournefestival.com.au

Venue
Theatres, cinemas and cathedrals in and around Melbourne.

Transport
Air: Melbourne Airport. **Rail:** Train: Spencer Street Station. **Road:** Coach: Greyhound Pioneer runs services to the Melbourne Transit Centre (from across Australia). Car: Western Highway (from Adelaide); Hume Highway (from Sydney).

Perth

Tourist Information
Western Australian Tourism Commission
First Floor, 16 St Georges Terrace, Perth, WA 6000, Australia
Tel: (08) 9270 331
Website: www.westernaustralia.com.au

• January-February

Perth International Arts Festival

Perth International Arts Festival is one of the highlights of Perth's cultural events calendar. Every year, the whole city comes alive with national, international and aboriginal dance, music and visual art performances. Past highlights included performances by the Perth Theatre Company and the Merce Cunningham Dance Company, as well as concerts from the WA Symphony Orchestra. This internationally-acclaimed festival has won the Western Australian Tourism Award for Best Major Festival and Special Event on three occasions (1996, 1998 and 1999) and is the longest-running and biggest international arts festival in the Southern Hemisphere.

Event Organiser
Perth International Arts Festival, UWA Festival Centre, 3 Crawley Avenue, Crawley WA 6009, Australia
Tel: (08) 6488 2000
Website: www.perthfestival.com.au

Venue
Various venues across Perth.

Transport
Air: Perth International Airport. **Rail:** Train: Perth Station or East Perth Terminal. **Road:** Coach: Greyhound and Westrail operate services to the East Perth Terminal (from across Australia).

Sydney

Tourist Information
Sydney Visitor Centre
106 George Street, The Rocks, Sydney, NSW 2000, Australia
Tel: (02) 9255 1788 *or* 132 077
Website: www.visitnsw.com.au

• January

Australia Day

Australia was formally colonised by the British First Fleet, which arrived at Sydney Cove, led by Captain Arthur Phillip, on January 26 1788. By the early 19th century there are records of celebratory events being held to mark the occasion, including formal dinners, bonfires and the consumption of large amounts of alcohol. The first official national celebrations were held on January 26 1818, the 30th anniversary of formal colonisation, when a salute of 30 guns was fired from Dawes Point, followed by a ball at Government House. Since then, the celebrations have expanded to encompass the whole nation, although Sydney remains the focal point. In the last few decades, the more formal, imperialistic *Australia Day* celebrations, such as the military parades and the re-enactment of the First Fleet landing, have been replaced with more light-hearted events recognising Australia's cultural heritage and multicultural population. Typical Sydney celebrations are many and varied, and range from free access to the city's museums to citywide galas, parades, concerts and street theatre. *Hyde Park* is the focus for family events, featuring music, wine tasting, face painting and children's entertainment, whilst The Rocks play host to jazz and blues concerts and puppet shows.

The grand finale is the *Australia Day Fireworks Spectacular* which takes place at Cockle Bay, Darling Harbour at 2100.

Event Organiser
Australia Day Council of New South Wales, PO Box 5341, Sydney NSW 2001, Australia
Tel: (02) 9513 2000
Website: www.adc.nsw.gov.au

Venue
Various locations across Sydney.

Transport
Air: Sydney Kingsford Smith International Airport. **Rail:** Train: Sydney Central Station. Cityrail: Circular Quay (to The Rocks), Town Hall (to Darling Harbour), St James (to Hyde Park), Martin Place (to Hyde Park). **Road:** Bus: Public services.

Sydney Festival

The *Sydney Festival* has been a leading light in the Australian and international arts scene for over 25 years. Every year over 2 million spectators flock to venues as diverse as the *Sydney Opera House*, the *Royal Botanic Gardens* and the *Museum of Sydney* to enjoy hundreds of performances of theatre, jazz, classical music, dance, opera, cinema and puppet shows. There are also visual art exhibitions, complemented by events ranging from guided tours of Sydney's corporate art collections to lectures by visiting artists. Past performers at the Sydney Festival have included an eclectic mix of performers ranging from Nick Cave and Beth Orton to Nederlands Dans Theater, the Russian Philharmonic Orchestra and the Catalan theatre group Els Comediants. The Sydney Festival lasts for three weeks and incorporates elements of the city's *Australia Day* celebrations, such as the free concerts in *Hyde Park* and the fireworks display in *Darling Harbour* on January 26.

Event Organiser
Level 2, 10 Hickson Road, The Rocks, Sydney, NSW 2000, Australia
Tel: (02) 8248 6500
Website: www.sydneyfestival.org.au

Venue
Various venues across Sydney.

Transport
Air: Sydney Kingsford Smith International Airport. **Rail:** Train: Sydney Central Station. Cityrail: Circular Quay (to Museum of Sydney, Sydney Opera House or Royal Botanic Gardens); Town Hall (to Darling Harbour); St James (to Hyde Park or Royal Botanic Gardens); Martin Place (to Hyde Park or Royal Botanic Gardens). **Road:** Bus: Public services.

• February-March

Sydney Gay and Lesbian Mardi Gras

Sydney Gay and Lesbian Mardi Gras began in 1978 as a parade down the city's Oxford Street to mark International Gay Solidarity Day (in commemoration of the famous Stonewall Riots in New York's Greenwich Village). The Mardi Gras name was adopted the following year and the event steadily grew in size and status during the 1980s and 1990s to become the largest gay carnival in the world, lasting for three weeks and attracting hundreds of thousands of revellers. Over 150 gay and lesbian community groups spend months creating the colourful floats and outrageous costumes for the Oxford Street parade on the final Saturday. Concerts, art exhibitions and theatre performances, all showcasing gay and lesbian talent and highlighting issues relating to sexuality, are held throughout the three weeks.

Event Organiser
Sydney Gay and Lesbian Mardi Gras, 297-299 Trafalgar Street, Petersham, NSW 2049, Australia
Postal address: PO Box 956, Petersham NSW 2049, Australia
Tel: (02) 9568 8600
Website: www.mardigras.org.au

Venue
Various venues across Sydney.

Transport
Air: Sydney Kingsford Smith International Airport. Rail: Train: Sydney Central Station. Road: Bus: Public services.

Austria

Salzburg

Tourist Information
Salzburg Tourist Board (Tourismus Salzburg GmbH)
Auerspergstraße 6, A-5020 Salzburg, Austria
Tel (43) 662 88 9870
Website: www.salzburg.info

• July-August

Salzburg Festival

Over five or six weeks each summer, the internationally-acclaimed Salzburg Festival brings together a programme of opera, plays and concerts that are staged at venues across the city. In 2006,

the 250th anniversary of Mozart's birth, the Salzburg Festival will perform all 22 of the composer's stage works which he created in his short but artistically incredible life.

Event Organiser
Salzburg Festival (Salzburger Festspiele), Hofstallgasse 1, PO Box 140, A-5010 Salzburg, Austria
Tel: (43) 662 80 4550
Website: www.salzburgfestival.at

Venue
Various venues across Salzburg.

Transport
Air: Salzburg WA Mozart Airport. Rail: Train: Salzburg Central Station. Road: Bus: Public services.

Vienna

Tourist Information
Vienna Tourist Board (Wien Tourismus)
Obere Augartenstrasse 40, 1025 Vienna, Austria
Tel: (01) 2111 4222
Website: www.vienna-tourism.at

• May-June

Vienna Festival

The Vienna Festival comprises performances of dance, music and theatre, as well as displays of visual art. The festival is renowned for its thought-provoking programmes and in the past has tackled topics such as xenophobia, national identity and the existential struggle of the individual in a socially and culturally foreign environment. Other acclaimed past performances have included Peter Brook's 'Tragedy of Hamlet', a production of the South African drama 'Le Costume', by Can Themba, and Luc Bondy's production of Händel's Baroque masterpiece. Musicians from around the world, including the Arnold Schoenberg Choir and the Vienna Symphony Orchestra, open the festival with a free concert in the Rathausplatz (Town Hall Square).

Event Organiser
Vienna Festival Office (Wiener Festwochen), Lehárgasse 11/1/1/6, 1060 Vienna, Austria
Tel: (01) 589 220
Website: www.festwochen.at

Venue
Various venues across Vienna.

Transport
Air: Vienna International Airport. **Rail:** Train: Westbahnhof Station. Underground: Rathaus (to Rathausplatz). **Road:** Bus: Public services.

• June-September

Vienna Music Film Festival

This highly popular film festival, which was first held in 1991, brings the very best in music cinema to Vienna each summer. The open-air programme includes dance, music and opera films, many of which are shown in Austria for the first time at the festival, and every year there are new innovations as well as old favourites. Recent festivals have also seen the introduction of a larger screen with improved audiovisual quality. Films begin at dusk (around 2100) every evening. Many food stalls are set up around the auditorium as part of the festival to enable filmgoers and passers-by to enjoy mouth-watering dishes from around the world.

Event Organiser
Stadt Wien Marketing Service GmbH, Kolingasse 11/13, 1090 Vienna, Austria
Tel: (01) 3198 2000
Website: www.wien-event.at

Venue
Town Hall Square (Rathausplatz).

Transport
Air: Vienna International Airport. **Rail:** Train: Westbahnhof Station. Underground: Rathaus (to Rathausplatz). **Road:** Bus: Public services..

• November-December

Magic of Advent in Vienna

Vienna's Christmas market, held each year in front of the town hall, is the perfect way to stock up on presents and soak up the festive atmosphere. There are over 140 stalls to browse and plenty to eat and drink, including candied fruit, candyfloss, maroni (roasted chestnuts) and the traditional Austrian winter warmer, *Glühwein* (mulled wine). Children will enjoy the Christmas workshop in the Volkshalle (assembly hall) of the town hall, where they can bake Christmas cookies and make their own gifts, or try out the latest games. There is an exhibition on Christmas traditions in other European countries, as well as a life-size nativity scene, and every Sunday during Advent, choirs from around the world sing Christmas carols inside the town hall. In the park next to the town halls there are pony rides

and a merry-go-round to enjoy. All the attractions are open 0900-2100 Monday-Sunday until December 23 and 0900-1700 on December 24.

Event Organiser
Wienwerbepool-City Marketing, Breitenfurter Strasse 513, 1230 Vienna, Austria
Tel: (01) 888 9933
Website: www.christkindlmarkt.at

Venue
Town Hall Square (Rathausplatz).

Transport
Air: Vienna International Airport. **Rail:** Train: Westbahnhof Station. Underground: Rathaus. **Road:** Bus: Public services.

Belgium

Brussels

Tourist Information
Tourist Information Brussels (TIB)
Hôtel de Ville, Grande-Place, 1000 Brussels, Belgium
Tel: (02) 513 8940
Website: www.brusselsdiscovery.com

• December-January

Brussels on Ice

The *Grand Place* has been the social and economic heart of Brussels since the Middle Ages and is flanked by lavish Gothic and Renaissance buildings which once served as guildhouses and now house museums, coffee shops and restaurants. It is turned into a giant ice rink over the Christmas period, allowing visitors and locals to skate in a magical open-air setting to the sounds of festive music.

Event Organiser
VO Communication, 342 chaussée d'Alsemberg, 1190 Brussels, Belgium
Tel: (02) 346 5949
Website: www.vocommunication.com

Venue
Grand Place.

Transport
Air: Brussels International Airport. **Rail:** Train: Bruxelles-Central, Bruxelles-Midi or Bruxelles-Nord stations. Underground: De Brouckère or Gare Centrale/Centraal Station. Tram: Public services to Bourse. **Road:** Bus: Public services.

• July

Ommegang Royal Pageant

Ommegang is a colourful reconstruction of the pageant held in 1549 in honour of Emperor Charles V, his son Don Philip and his sisters Eleanor of Austria and Mary of Hungary. Although the festival was essentially a religious event in Medieval Brussels, today's Ommegang celebrations are resolutely secular. The action starts in the *Grand Place* in the centre of Brussels as the royal guests, some of whom are descended from those present in 1549, take their places and the crossbow men surround the statue of *Notre Dame du Sablon*, their patron saint. Once the peasant dancers and performers have led the way, the Emperor walks the streets past the Gothic and Renaissance façades of the old guildhouses surrounded by horses, dogs, flagbearers, ladies-in-waiting and a falconry train. The costumes, which are lavish reproductions of the originals, can be up to 6m (23 feet) in height and the whole event has all the pomp and ceremony of the original pageant. The parade leaves the Sablon statue in the Grand Place at 2050 and parades through rue Lebeau and other streets until it reaches rue Charles Buls.

Event Organiser
Ommegang-Brussels, rue des Tanneurs 180, 1000 Brussels, Belgium
Tel: (02) 512 1961
Website: www.ommegang-brussels.be

Venue
Sablon statue (Grand Place) at 2050, then parades through rue Lebeau, rue Marché aux Herbes, rue Tabora, rue Midi, rue Lombard, rue Etuve and rue Charles Buls.

Transport
Air: Brussels International Airport. **Rail:** Train: Bruxelles-Central, Bruxelles-Midi or Bruxelles-Nord stations. Underground: De Brouckère or Gare Centrale/Centraal Station. Tram: Public services to Bourse. **Road:** Bus: Public services.

• December

European Christmas Market

The *Grand Place* has been Brussels's main square since the Middle Ages. For one week in December each year, the square has a very special atmosphere and a truly European flavour with the arrival of the *Christmas Market*. There are hundreds of stalls to browse, with gift ideas from many countries. The culinary choices are endless –

visitors can feast on Italian *panettone* (Christmas cake) or German speciality sausage, whilst enjoying any number of variations on mulled wine: Scandinavian *glögg*, Austrian *Glühwein* or French *vin chaud*. Alternatively, there are numerous varieties of Belgian beer available at the many bars surrounding the Grand Place. There is also entertainment from choirs from around Europe who perform traditional festive songs. The market is open 1100-1900 Monday to Thursday and 1100-2100 Friday to Sunday.

Event Organiser
For more information on the European Christmas Market, contact Tourist Information Brussels (see **Tourist Information** above).

Venue
Grand Place.

Transport
Air: Brussels International Airport. **Rail:** Train: Bruxelles-Central, Bruxelles-Midi or Bruxelles-Nord stations. Underground: De Brouckère or Gare Centrale/Centraal Station. Tram: Public services to Bourse. **Road:** Bus: Public services.

Brazil

Rio de Janeiro

Tourist Information

RioTur, City of Rio de Janeiro Tourism Authority (Empresa de Turismo do Município do Rio de Janeiro SA)
Rua da Assembléia, 10-9º andar, 20119, Centro, Rio de Janeiro, Brazil
Tel: (021) 217 7575
Website: www.riodejaneiro-turismo.com.br

• December-January

New Year's Eve

Rio de Janeiro is said to be one of the most exciting and happening places in the world at New Year (known locally as *Reveillon*). Hundreds of thousands of people gather on the city's beaches every year on December 31 to watch the giant firework display at midnight and to dance the night away. The main festivities take place on Copacabana Beach, with live music and DJ sets continuing through the night. There are also events in major hotels in the city, as well as in the many bars and restaurants. The dancing and partying goes on into the small hours, with many people staying up all night to drink a champagne breakfast at dawn.

Event Organiser
For more information on New Year's Eve, contact RioTur (see **Tourist Information** above).

Venue
The main focus is Copacabana Beach.

Transport
Air: Rio de Janeiro International Airport. **Rail:** Train: Estacao D Pedra II or Estacao Barao de Maua stations. **Road:** Coach: Novo Rio Rodoviaria Coach Station.

• February-March

Rio de Janeiro Carnival

Rio de Janeiro Carnival is one of the biggest festivals in the world, attracting hundreds of thousands of tourists and locals every year who come to participate in this incredibly lively event. Carnival is undoubtedly the biggest cultural event in Rio and an annual orgy of over-the-top fun and frivolity. The event originates from the Easter revelry tradition that took place in Portugal in the 15th century. Its date varies from year to year, usually ranging from late February to early March. It starts officially on a Saturday and goes through to the following Wednesday (*quarta-feira de cinza* – Ash Wednesday). There are many events across the city, including street parades, carnival balls and the samba school parade.

Event Organiser
For more information on Rio de Janeiro Carnival, contact RioTur (see **Tourist Information** above).

Venue
Various venues across Rio de Janeiro.

Transport
Air: Rio de Janeiro International Airport. **Rail:** Train: Estacao D Pedra II or Estacao Barao de Maua stations. **Road:** Coach: Novo Rio Rodoviaria Coach Station.

Canada

Calgary

Tourist Information
Calgary Convention & Visitors Bureau
Suite 200, 238 11th Avenue, SE Calgary, AB T2G 0X8, Canada
Tel: (403) 263 8510
Website: www.tourismcalgary.com

• July

Calgary Stampede

Calgary Stampede is one of the world's biggest celebrations of the cowboy way of life and attracts well over one million visitors each year. The event lasts for 10 days in July and includes an annual rodeo, with bull riding, bareback bronco riding and wild horse racing, as well as various stage performances, chuckwagon (chariot) races, agriculture and livestock displays and live music on the Coke Stage. This annual event dates back to 1886 and has grown to become an enormous celebration of all things related to being a cowboy.

Event Organiser
Calgary Stampede, 1410 Olympic Way SE, Calgary, AB T2P-2K8, Canada
Tel: (800) 661 1260 (toll free USA and Canada only)
Website: www.calgary-stampede.com

Venue
Stampede Park, Calgary.

Transport
Air: Calgary International Airport. **Rail:** Train: C-train routes 201 to Brentwood in the north (from Anderson Road in the south) or 202 to Tenth Street in the west (from Whitehorn in the east). **Road:** Bus: Public services.

Montréal

Tourist Information
Montréal Tourist Information
(Centre Infotouriste Tourisme Montréal)
1001 rue du Square-Dorchester, Montréal H3B 1G2, Canada
Tel: (514) 873 2015
Website: www.tourisme-montreal.org

• June-July

Montréal International Jazz Festival

The first jazz festival was held in Montréal in 1980 and attracted 12,000 spectators. Today, the event is one of the biggest jazz festivals in the world, attracting over 100,000 spectators every year to see over 120 concerts, ranging from traditional jazz through to blues and reggae.

Event Organiser
Montréal International Jazz Festival, 822 Sherbrooke Street East, Montréal, Quebec H2L 1K4, Canada
Tel: (514) 871 1881
Website: www.montrealjazzfest.com

Venue
Concert halls and cafés across Montréal.

Transport
Air: Montréal Dorval International Airport. **Rail:** Train: Gare Centrale (Central Station). **Road:** Bus: Public services.

Toronto

Tourist Information
Tourism Toronto
PO Box 126, 207 Queens Quay West, Toronto, Ontario M5J 1A7, Canada
Tel: (416) 203 2600
Website: www.toronto.com

• January-February

Toronto Wintercity Festival

Every year, Toronto organises 14 days of entertainment in celebration of Toronto's cultural diversity with a mix of free shows and events held both indoors and outside including circus acts, storytelling, musical concerts, theatre productions, ice-skating shows, dance and cultural exhibitions. There are creative hands-on activities for both children and adults at the Civic Centre and the Toronto Public Library Auditorium, including colouring contests, baking cookies, origami and pyjama parties. Winterlicious is the festival's culinary celebration where customers can enjoy the fine cuisine at over 100 of Toronto's top dining establishments.

Event Organiser
Toronto City Hall, 100 Queen Street, Ninth Floor East Tower M5H 2N2, Toronto, Canada
Tel: (416) 395 0490
Website: www.city.toronto.on.ca/special_events

Venue
Various venues across Toronto.

Transport
Air: Toronto Lester B Pearson International Airport. **Rail:** Train: Union Station. Underground: North Yorke Centre (to Mel Lastman Square or Civic Centre); Queen Station (to Nathan Phillips Square); Bloor (to Toronto Public Library). **Road:** Bus: Public services.

• October

International Festival of Authors

Toronto's *International Festival of Authors* is a literary treat for both adults and children. Every year, writers of poetry, fiction, drama and biography converge on the city's Harbourfront Centre to give readings, lectures, talks and seminars and to chat with audiences. The festival invites both new writers and international celebrities; past attendees include J K Rowling, Joanna Trollope, Candace Bushnell, Margaret Atwood, Maeve Binchy, Carlos Fuentes, Susan Sontag, Jonathan Safran Foer and David Baddiel.

Event Organiser
Harbourfront Reading Series, 235 Queens Quay West, M5J 2G8 Toronto, Canada
Tel: (416) 973 4760
Website: www.readings.org

Venue
Various venues across Toronto.

Transport
Air: Toronto Lester B Pearson International Airport. **Rail:** Train: Union Station. Tram: 510 (from Union Station). **Road:** Bus: Public services.

Vancouver

Tourist Information
Tourism Vancouver – Tourist Information Centre
Waterfront Centre, Plaza Level, 200 Burrard Street, Vancouver, BC V6C 3L6, Canada
Tel: (604) 683 2000
Website: www.tourismvancouver.com

• May-June

Vancouver International Children's Festival

Vancouver International Children's Festival was first held in 1977 to entertain, educate and inspire children and young people from Vancouver and the surrounding area. It comprises seven days of activities and events in Vanier Park, a scenic setting on Vancouver's waterfront. Every year, artists come from across Canada and around the world to entertain visitors through performances of theatre, circus, puppetry, jazz and pop music. There are colourful daily parades, as well as interactive exhibitions and a variety of hands-on activities such as kite-making, music sessions, exotic crafts, stilt-walking workshops, pottery classes and imaginative games for younger children. Special performances are staged for older children and young people, encouraging them to think about the world they live in and their place in society, whilst younger children can play in a giant sandbox full of toys.

Event Organiser
Festival Communications, 402–873 Beatty Street,
Vancouver, BC V6B 2M6, Canada
Tel: (604) 708 5655
Website: www.vancouverchildrensfestival.com

Venue
Vanier Park.

Transport
Air: Vancouver International Airport. **Water:**
Ferry: False Creek services (from Granville Island,
Aquatic Centre or Science World along the
waterfront). **Rail:** Train: Pacific Central Station.
Road: Bus: Public services.

People's Republic of China

Hong Kong

Tourist Information
Hong Kong Tourism Board
9-11th Floor, Citicorp Centre, 18 Whitfield Road,
North Point, Hong Kong, People's Republic of China
Tel: 2807 6543
Website: www.discoverhongkong.com

• February-March

Hong Kong Arts Festival

Hong Kong Arts Festival is one of the most
important cultural events in Southeast Asia. The
festival, which is the leading arts event in Hong
Kong, features numerous performances from
international stars of theatre, opera, art, dance and
classical and popular music. Past highlights
include performances by the legendary Russian
dancer Mikhail Baryshnikov, the Blind Boys of
Alabama and performances by the National
Theatre Company of China. Every year, artists
from around the world flock into Hong Kong to
take part in this internationally-renowned event.

Event Organiser
Hong Kong Arts Festival Society Ltd, 12/F Hong
Kong Arts Centre, 2 Harbour Road, Wanchai, Hong
Kong, People's Republic of China
Tel: 2824 3555
Website: www.hk.artsfestival.org

Venue
Various venues across Hong Kong including Hong
Kong Cultural Centre, Hong Kong City Hall, Hong
Kong Academy for the Performing Arts (HKAPA),
Hong Kong Arts Centre, Sha Tin Town Hall, Tsuen
Wan Town Hall, Tuen Mun Town Hall and Kwai
Tsing Theatre.

Transport
Air: Hong Kong International Airport. **Rail:** Train:
Hong Kong Station. **Road:** Bus: Public services.

• April

Hong Kong International Film Festival

Hong Kong International Film Festival, which was
first held in 1977, is an enormous annual event in
Hong Kong's calendar. Over 200 films are screened
each year at the festival including a mix of global
premieres. The festival is a non-competitive event
which comprises of four main areas: Asian
Cinema, Hong Kong Panorama, World Cinema and
Special Section Contributed by Hong Kong Film
Archive. The annual event now attracts
approximately 150,000 visitors each year, a
substantial increase on the 18,624 people who
attended the first film festival in Hong Kong in
1977.

Event Organiser
Hong Kong International Film Festival Society
Office, 21/F, Sunshine Plaza, 353 Lockhart Road,
Wan Chai, Hong Kong, People's Republic of China
Tel: 2970 3300
Website: www.hkiff.org.hk

Venue
Various cinemas across Hong Kong.

Transport
Air: Hong Kong International Airport. **Rail:** Train:
Hong Kong Station. **Road:** Car: The most
accessible places to drive to are Lantua Island,
Macau and Guangzhou; from here visitors must
take a ferry trip to get to Hong Kong.

Cuba

Havana

Tourist Information

Ministry of Tourism (Ministerio de Turismo)
Calle 19, No 710, Entre Paseo y A, Vedado,
Havana, Cuba
Tel: (07) 330 545
Website: www.cubatravel.cu

• July-August

Havana Carnival

The Cuban capital is well known for its party
spirit, and carnival time, which has been reinstated
after the hardships suffered by the communist

country since the collapse of the USSR, promises particularly colourful celebrations as the Cuban holiday period begins in earnest. The festivities begin on a Friday night in late July with a gun salute fired from the San Pedro de la Cabana fortress. The event then continues every weekend until mid-August, with shows, dancing, fireworks, floats and parades, food and drink all accompanied by traditional Cuban rhythms and Latino pop. Each Havana neighbourhood spends months designing costumes and floats for its own parties and parades, whilst the *Malecón* (seafront) is the venue for fairs and concerts.

Event Organiser
For more information on the Havana Carnival, contact the Ministry of Tourism (see **Tourist Information** above).

Venue
Malecón (seafront) and across Havana.

Transport
Air: José Marti International Airport. **Rail:** Train: Central, Egido y Arsenal Station. **Road:** Bus: Public services.

Czech Republic

Prague

Tourist Information
Prague Information Service (PIS – Pražské informační služby)
Betlemske namesti 2, 116 98 Prague 1, Czech Republic
Tel: (02) 264 022
Website: www.pis.cz

• May

Prague International Marathon

Prague International Marathon was first held in 1995, with 980 runners taking part in the main event and 10,000 runners taking part in a non-competitive race. More than 3000 runners take part in the marathon every year, with a further 13,000 and 12,000 respectively taking part in a City Run and Family Run. The marathon is billed as the most international in the world with approximately two thirds of runners coming from overseas. Spectators line the historic streets of Prague during the event, cheering on the competitors. There are also concerts and street entertainment, with music including jazz, classical, blues, reggae and rock and roll. The marathon starts at 0900 in Parízˇská Street and finishes in Old Town Square.

Event Organiser
Prague International Marathon, Záhoranského 3, 120 00 Prague 2, Czech Republic
Tel: (02) 2491 9209
Website: www.pim.cz

Venue
Streets of Prague, passing over Charles Bridge.

Transport
Air: Prague Ruzyne International Airport. **Rail:** Train: Hlavní nádráží Station (Prague Station). Underground: Staroměstká. **Road:** Bus: Public services.

• September-October

Prague Autumn International Music Festival

Prague Autumn International Music Festival, which takes place in Prague every year, is one of the most important classical music events in Eastern Europe and always attracts thousands of visitors from across Europe. The city is famous for its orchestras and boasts two of the finest in the world: Prague Philharmonic Orchestra and Prague Symphony Orchestra. Many of the festival's events take place in Dvorak Hall in Rudolfinum, which is home to Prague Philharmonic Orchestra, and overlooks the River Vltava. Located next to the famous *Mánesuv Bridge*, the venue is regarded by many to be one of the most beautiful concert venues in Eastern Europe.

Event Organiser
Prague Autumn Musical Management, Príbenická St 20, 13000 Prague 3, Czech Republic
Tel: (02) 540 484
Website: www.pragueautumn.cz

Venue
Various venues and concert halls in Prague, including Dvorak Hall in Rudolfinum, Smetana Hall in the Municipal House, State Opera Prague, St Simon and Judas Church, Lucerna and Grand Hotel Pupp Karlovy Vary.

Transport
Air: Prague Ruzyně International Airport. **Rail:** Train: Hlavní nádráží Station (Prague Station). Underground: Staromestká or Námesti Republiky. **Road:** Bus: Public services.

• November-December

International Festival of Advent & Christmas Music

The *International Festival of Advent & Christmas Music*, which was first held in Prague in 1990, begins each year on the first weekend during Advent. During the festival, there are usually a number of performances by various amateur choirs, including entries to the competition from women's choirs, men's choirs, small mixed chamber choirs, large mixed choirs and children's choirs. The choirs perform Advent and Christmas music of their choice, either a capella or with instrumental accompaniment. The competition is judged by experts in the field, both from the Czech Republic and abroad. Winners are judged on their choice of compositions and programme structure, technical level of interpretation and general artistic impression. At the end of the competition, there is singing in the *Old Town Square*, where Christmas and Advent songs are sung. There is also a competition to win the Petr Eben Prize; entrants perform a composition which has been written especially for the occasion by Petr Eben himself, who is one of the main judges.

Event Organiser
Or Fea AS, Dlouhá 10, Prague 1 110 00, Czech Republic
Tel: (02) 232 1949
Website: www.orfea.cz

Venue
Old Town Square in the centre of Prague.

Transport
Air: Prague Ruzyně International Airport. **Rail:** Train: Hlavní nádraží Station (Prague Station). Underground: Staromestká. **Road:** Bus: Public services

Denmark

Copenhagen

Tourist Information

Wonderful Copenhagen Tourist Information
Gl Kongevej 1, 1610 Copenhagen V, Denmark
Tel: 7022 2442 *or* 3325 7400
Website:
www.woco.dk

• June-July

Roskilde Festival

The annual *Roskilde Festival* is one of the biggest rock and pop music festivals in Europe. The festival began in 1971, when it featured approximately 20 bands and about 10,000 visitors. Today, as many as 170 bands perform at the event on a total of seven stages, and is watched by over 75,000 spectators. Highlights of past festivals include performances from Bob Dylan, Beck, P J Harvey, Queens of the Stone Age, Robbie Williams, Neil Young, Blondie, David Bowie, Blur, REM, Primal Scream and Cold Play. Any profit made by the festival organisers is donated to support humanitarian, cultural and non-profit making initiatives.

Event Organiser
Roskilde Festival, Havsteensvej 11, 4000 Roskilde, Denmark
Tel: 4636 6613
Website: www.roskilde-festival.dk

Venue
Roskilde Festival ground, which is 35km (20 miles) from Copenhagen city centre.

Transport
Air: Copenhagen Airport. **Rail:** Train: Trains to the festival's own train station which is located in the middle of the festival grounds (from Roskilde Station). **Road:** Bus: Public services to the festival grounds (from Roskilde Station).

• July

Copenhagen Jazz Festival

Copenhagen Jazz Festival sees around 600 concerts by Danish and international jazz artists in the city. Many concerts are performed in the city's most historic streets and squares, as well as along the banks of the canals. Clubs and small cafés in the city play host to a varied programme, ranging from New Orleans jazz and swing to experimental music. 'Giant Jazz', which is held in the old Circus Building, is one of the main events of the festival. There are also concerts at the Tivoli Gardens which attract a large audience. As well as performances from top artists there are also street parades every day, concerts and workshops for children, and other events such as midnight concerts at the National Museum. Over 100,000 attend the event in the city.

Event Organiser
Copenhagen Jazz Festival, Nytorv 3, 1450

Copenhagen, Denmark
Tel: 3393 2013
Website: www.jazzfestival.dk

Venue
Various venues in Copenhagen, including
Copenhagen JazzHouse, Circus Building and Tivoli
Gardens.

Transport
Air: Copenhagen Airport. Rail: Train: Copenhagen
Central Station. S-Bahn: Services to København H
Station. Road: Bus: Public services.

• August

Copenhagen International Ballet Festival

The annual *Copenhagen International Ballet
Festival* is held in Frederiksberg just outside
Copenhagen. This summer festival features both
classic and new performances from the
Copenhagen International Ballet Group, which
was founded by Danish ballet dancer Alexander
Kølpin. The group consists of principals and
members from the New York City Ballet, Ballet
Béjart, Lyon Opera Ballet, Royal Danish Ballet,
Momix and Hamburg Ballet. The ballets are
staged in beautiful outdoor settings, including
the courtyard of the *Royal Veterinary and
Agricultural University*, where audiences can
watch performances under the night sky.

Event Organiser
Copenhagen International Ballet, Stranezejen 451,
2938 Klanpenborg, Denmark
Tel: 3963 4900 or 3325 2107
Website: www.copeninternationalballet.com

Venue
Various outdoor venues in Frederiksberg.

Transport
Air: Copenhagen Airport. Rail: Train: Copenhagen
Central Station. Road: Bus: Public services.

Finland

Helsinki

Tourist Information
Helsinki City Tourist & Convention Bureau
(Helsingin kaupungin matkailu – ja
kongressitoimisto)
Pohjoisesplanadi 19, 00100 Helsinki, Finland
Tel: (09) 169 3757
Website: www.hel.fi/tourism

• August-September

Helsinki Festival

Helsinki Festival is a giant performing arts
festival, which is held during three weeks in
August and September every year. The festival
hosts an extensive programme of orchestral and
chamber music, opera, dance, theatre, jazz, rock,
art exhibitions and film. The festival reaches its
climax with the 'Night of the Arts', when art
galleries, museums and bookshops open their
doors, free of charge, into the small hours. A
marquee called the Huvila Festival Tent hosts
many performances and music, poetry and songs
are performed in restaurants and bars around the
city. Visitors can also try local food during the
'Piazza of Tastes' in the Senate Square, when tents
are erected, offering a range of menus, with music
playing in the background.

Event Organiser
Helsinki Festival, The Lasipalatsi, Mannerheimintie
22-24, 00100 Helsinki, Finland
Tel: (09) 6126 5100
Website: www.helsinkifestival.fi

Venue
Various venues, including Aurora Park, Finlandia
Hall, The Alexander Theatre, Helsinki City Theatre,
Senate Square, Huvila Festival Tent, The Savoy
Theatre, Kunsthalle Helsinki, Cinema Orion, Bio
Rex, Atemeum Hall and Temppeliaukio Church.

Transport
Air: Helsinki-Vantaa Airport. Rail: Train: Helsinki
Station. Road: Bus: Public services.

France

Avignon

Tourist Information
Avignon Tourist Board (Office de Tourisme
d'Avignon)
41 cours Jean Jaurès, 84000 Avignon, France
Tel: (04) 3274 3274
Website: www.ot-avignon.fr

• July-September

Avignon Festival

The *Avignon Festival* began in 1947 when French
actor and director Jean Vilar staged three works
that were previously unknown to the French
public in the *Palais des Papes* (Popes' Palace) in

the historic centre of the city. Since then the festival has become a major cultural event, attracting thousands of visitors and performers from all corners of the globe. The emphasis is on experimental theatre and presenting new theatrical works to the public, many of which then go on tour in France and abroad. Dance and musical theatre also feature in the programme. Avignon is worth visiting at this time of year just for the atmosphere created by the festival – colourful and bizarre parades wind their way through the crowds in the Place du Palais and fire eaters and jugglers entertain visitors and locals in the streets from morning until night. A parallel event called the *Festival Off* allows performers to set up stage wherever they can find space (with permission from the city council), providing an alternative theatre scene.

Event Organiser
Festival d'Avignon, 8 bis rue de Mons, 84000 Avignon, France
Tel: (04) 9027 6656
Website: www.festival-avignon.com

Venue
Various venues across Avignon.

Transport
Air: Marseille-Provence Airport, Avignon-Caumont Airport or Nîmes-Arles-Camargue Airport. Rail: Train: Avignon Station (high-speed TGV services from Paris Gare de Lyon, Montpellier, Lyon and Barcelona, Spain). Road: Bus: Public services.

• September

Côtes du Rhône Grape Harvest

Avignon is the capital of the Côtes du Rhône, one of the most well-known French wine-producing regions. The wine is harvested at the beginning of September and visitors and locals can taste the results at the many stalls in the square in front of one of the city's most spectacular buildings, the *Palais des Papes* (Popes' Palace). Entertainment is provided around the city as folk groups, jugglers and actors perform for the crowds, and at 1700 the Bacchic confraternities (wine guilds or organisations) parade through the streets in costume, followed by floats bearing barrels of wine. There are also parachutists, films, concerts, shows and exhibitions of painting and crafts to accompany the bacchanalian festivities.

Event Organiser
Compagnons du Ban des Vendanges, Hôtel de Ville, 84045 Avignon, France
Tel: (04) 9016 0032

Venue
Palais des Papes and various locations across Avignon.

Transport
Air: Marseille-Provence Airport, Avignon-Caumont Airport or Nîmes-Arles-Camargue Airport. Rail: Train: Avignon Station (high-speed TGV services from Paris Gare de Lyon, Montpellier, Barcelona and Lyon). Road: Bus: Public services.

Cannes

Tourist Information
Cannes Tourist Board (SEMAC)
Esplanade Georges Pompidou, BP 272, 06403 Cannes, France
Tel: (04) 9299 8422
Website: www.cannes-on-line.com

• May

Cannes Film Festival

In 1939, the French government chose Cannes as a suitably sunny and enchanting location for its international film festival. Initially it was merely a chance for wealthy tourists to attend the many parties organised in the luxury villas of Cannes and in the hotels and palaces along La Croisette (the main boulevard), and all films shown at the festival received a prize. Nowadays, an award at Cannes can set actors, producers and directors on the path to fame and fortune, as the festival is one of the premier events in the cultural calendar and the annual rendezvous of the international film industry. Only film professionals and journalists may attend the actual festival; however, the original air of glamour and prestige is still felt in Cannes during the two weeks, and for many it is a chance to spot the many stars and millionaires who pose in restaurants and along the expensive private beaches of La Croisette.

Event Organiser
Cannes Film Festival, 3, rue Amélie 75007 Paris, France
Tel: (01) 5359 6100
Website: www.festival-cannes.org

Venue
Palais des Festivals et des Congrès.

Transport

Air: Nice-Côte d'Azur International Airport. **Rail:** Train: Cannes Ville Station. **Road:** Bus: Public services.

Lyon

Tourist Information

Lyon Convention and Visitors Bureau (Office du Tourisme et des Congrès du Grand Lyon)
Place Bellecour, BP 2254, 69214 Lyon cedex 02, France
Tel: (04) 7277 6969
Website: www.lyon-france.com

• December

Festival of Lights

The *Festival of Lights* takes place every year in Lyon, when residents hang lights from their balconies and place candles in their windows, lighting up the city with a thousand lights. The locals congregate in the streets to admire the spectacle on December 8, which is a religious celebration dating back to 1852 honouring the statue of the Virgin Mary on *Fourvière Hill*. The festival is one of Lyon's most popular and traditional events. During the festivities, there are also a number of music performances throughout the city which is dominated by the *Fourvière Basilica*. During the Franco-Prussian war, Catholics in Lyon promised to build a giant church on Fourvière Hill in honour of the Virgin Mary, if she spared the city from the Prussian enemy. The city was spared and so the church was built in 1896.

Event Organiser

For more information on the Festival of Lights, contact Lyon Convention and Visitors Bureau (see Tourist Information above).

Venue

Fourvière Hill and various venues across Lyon.

Transport

Air: Lyon-Saint Exupéry Airport. **Rail:** Underground: Fourvière. **Road:** Bus: Public services.

Paris

Tourist Information

Paris Central Tourist Office (L'Office de Tourisme et des Congrès de Paris)
127 avenue des Champs-Elysées, 75008 Paris, France

Tel: (08) 3668 3112
Website: www.parisinfo.com

• May-June

French Tennis Open (Roland Garros)

Tennis first came across the Channel to France at the end of the 19th century and was a popular pursuit among the French upper classes. Various clubs were formed, such as the Racing Club de France and the Stade Français; the first national competition was held in 1891, with the ladies competition following in 1897. Since then, *Roland Garros* (named after a French engineer and fighter pilot shot down during World War I) has become increasingly more commercial. This is one of the grand slam championships and the hall of fame includes most of the big names in the sport. The international prestige of this tournament and its importance to world tennis, particularly in the run-up to Wimbledon a few weeks later, create an exciting atmosphere.

Event Organiser

Fédération Française de Tennis, 2 avenue Gordon Bennett, 75016 Paris, France
Tel: (01) 4743 4800
Website: www.frenchopen.org

Venue

Roland Garros Stadium (Stade Roland Garros) on the edge of the Bois de Boulogne.

Transport

Air: Paris Roissy-Charles de Gaulle Airport or Paris Orly Airport. **Rail:** Train: Paris Gare du Nord (Eurostar). Underground: Porte d'Auteuil. **Road:** Bus: Public services.

• June

Festival of Music

The *Festival of Music* (*Fête de la Musique*) is a nationwide event, although most of the major concerts take place in Paris. The city's huge variety of venues makes it an excellent place to catch a performance of virtually any style ranging from classical to reggae. The main events take place in Place de la Bastille in the fourth *arrondissement* (district), the Hôtel des Invalides in the seventh, Place de la République in the third and Parc de la Villette in the 19th. Just wandering the streets is probably the best way to enjoy this festival however, as there is music everywhere – even the *métro* stations have bands playing, as do parks, street corners, churches, cafés and museums.

Event Organiser

ADCEP (Association pour le développement de la création, études et projets), 30 rue René Boulanger, 75010 Paris, France
Tel: (01) 4003 9470
Website: www.fetedelamusique.culture.fr

Venue

Various venues across Paris.

Transport

Air: Paris Roissy-Charles de Gaulle Airport or Paris Orly Airport. **Rail:** Train: Paris Gare du Nord (Eurostar). **Road:** Bus: Public services.

• July

Arrival of the Tour de France

The *Tour de France* is widely acknowledged as the world's toughest cycling competition. Started in 1903 by Henri Desgrange, a French cyclist and journalist, the race covers both flat and mountainous terrain and travels through different regions every year in 20 stages. The 20 teams each consist of nine cyclists and the famous yellow jersey is awarded to the cyclist who has the lowest cumulative time for the race at the end of each day. In recent years the race has been dominated by American Lance Armstrong who first won the race in 1999 after overcoming cancer and went on to win the event for a record seventh consecutive time in 2005. Thousands of spectators, including film stars and celebrities, line the Champs-Elysées to see the winners speed towards the end of their three-week journey. The end often turns into a nerve-wracking sprint, followed by the cracking open of champagne and huge celebrations.

Event Organiser

La Société du Tour de France, 2 rue Rouget de Lisle, 92130 Issy-Les-Moulineaux, France
Tel: (01) 4133 1500
Website: www.letour.fr

Venue

Champs-Elysées.

Transport

Air: Paris Roissy-Charles de Gaulle Airport or Paris Orly Airport. **Rail:** Train: Paris Gare du Nord (Eurostar). Underground: Charles-de-Gaulle-Étoile, Georges V or Franklin D Roosevelt. RER: Charles-de-Gaulle-Etoile. **Road:** Bus: Public services.

Bastille Day

Towards the close of the 18th century, disenchantment with Louis XVI's monarchy, the aristocracy and the church had spread across France and was expressed, increasingly, in acts of civil unrest. On July 14 1789, several hundred ordinary Parisians marched to the Bastille prison, killed the governor and triggered the revolution that signalled the end of the monarchy in France with the pronouncement of *liberté, egalité, fraternité* (freedom, equality and brotherhood). To this day, the storming of the Bastille is commemorated across France as the *Fête de la Bastille*. The biggest celebrations are on the Champs-Elysées, with around 6000 people marching down the tree-lined avenue accompanied by military bands playing rousing music. At night there is a huge fireworks display over the city, as well as special entertainment and singing in bars and cafés throughout Paris. This is a national holiday in France, and the sense of pride that the French still feel for their republic is particularly evident on this day.

Event Organiser

For more information on Bastille Day, contact the Central Tourist Office (see **Tourist Information** above).

Venue

Champs-Elysées and various locations across Paris.

Transport

Air: Paris Roissy-Charles de Gaulle Airport or Paris Orly Airport. **Rail:** Train: Paris Gare du Nord (Eurostar). Underground: Charles-de-Gaulle-Étoile, Georges V or Franklin D Roosevelt. RER: Charles-de-Gaulle-Etoile. **Road:** Bus: Public services.

• July-August

Summer Arts Festival

For one month each summer the *Summer Arts Festival* (*Quartier d'Été*) transforms the streets of Paris into a huge open-air venue for the performing arts. Lovers of opera, jazz, theatre, classical music, circus, film and dance will all find something to entertain them – there are over 90 different events with a focus on several different countries each year. Venues range from cinemas in the bohemian Latin Quarter to the elegance of the *Jardin des Tuileries*. Parisians traditionally escape the capital for their summer holiday at this time of year, leaving more space for visitors to enjoy the show.

Event Organiser

Festival Paris Quartier d'Été, 5 rue Boudereau, 75009 Paris, France
Tel: (01) 494 9800
Website: www.quartierdete.com

Venue
Various locations across Paris.

Transport
Air: Paris Roissy-Charles de Gaulle Airport or Paris Orly Airport. **Rail:** Train: Paris Gare du Nord (Eurostar). **Road:** Bus: Public services.

• September-December

Autumn Festival

The Paris *Autumn Festival* (*Festival d'Automne*) presents a cultural mélange of literature, film, poetry and theatre from around the world. Each year a different country provides the focus for the festival with poetry, art and writing from that country. Past events have included Peter Brook's adaptation of 'Hamlet' and a staging of Boccaccio's Medieval 'Decameron' tales.

Event Organiser
Festival d'Automne, 16 rue de Rivoli, 75001 Paris, France
Tel: (01) 5345 1700
Website: www.festival-automne.com

Venue
Various venues across Paris.

Transport
Air: Paris Roissy-Charles de Gaulle Airport or Paris Orly Airport. **Rail:** Train: Paris Gare du Nord (Eurostar). **Road:** Bus: Public services.

Strasbourg

Tourist Information

Strasbourg Central Tourist Office (Office de Tourisme de Strasbourg)
17 place de la Cathédrale, 67082 Strasbourg, France
Tel: (03) 8852 2828
Website: www.strasbourg.com

• November-December

Strasbourg Christmas Market

Strasbourg Christmas Market is the biggest of its kind in France, and one of the most famous in Europe. It was first held in 1570 and is known in the local Alsatian dialect as *Christkindelsmärik*. There are hundreds of stalls selling gingerbread, spicy sausages, *vin chaud* (mulled wine), crafts and Christmas decorations around the beautiful Cathédrale Notre-Dame and along Place Broglie. A fir tree from the Vosges mountains is erected in Place Kléber in the heart of the city. There are over 50 concerts

and shows, providing musical accompaniment, and there is also an ice rink and a Christmas trail, where visitors can discover local crafts and traditions and the history of the festive season in Alsace. Children will enjoy 'chocolate cruises', which are boat rides through the city with entertainment and sweets.

Event Organiser
For more information on the Strasbourg Christmas Market, contact the Central Tourist Office (see **Tourist Information** above).

Venue
Place de la Cathédrale and various locations across Strasbourg.

Transport
Air: Euro-Airport Basel-Mulhouse-Freiburg. **Rail:** Train: Strasbourg Station. Tram: Homme de Fer or Langstrosse/Grande Rue. **Road:** Bus: Public services.

Germany

Berlin

Tourist Information

Berlin Tourist Office (Berlin Tourismus Marketing GmbH)
Am Karlsbad 11, 10785 Berlin, Germany
Tel: (030) 250 025
Website: www.btm.de

• February

Berlin International Film Festival

The *Berlin International Film Festival* was founded in 1951 as the result of an American Cold War initiative and quickly grew to become a well-established and important cultural event both in Berlin and worldwide. Film directors including Ingmar Bergman, Roman Polanski, Jean-Luc Godard and François Truffaut have all enjoyed considerable success with their films at the festival. It features an international competition, numerous film screenings, the Forum of Young Cinema and a children's film festival.

Event Organiser
International Film Festival, Potsdamerstrasse 5, 10785 Berlin, Germany
Tel: (030) 259 200
Website: www.berlinale.de

Venue
Various cinemas across Berlin.

Transport

Air: Berlin Tegel Airport. **Rail:** Train: S-Bahn trains serve the whole of Berlin. Underground: U-Bahn trains operate across Berlin. **Road:** Bus: Public services.

• June

Carnival of the Cultures

Carnival of the Cultures is a four-day street festival celebrating Berlin's cultural diversity and its ethnic communities. The carnival was established in 1996 and has grown to become one of the most important cultural events in Berlin. This huge annual street party sees thousands of performers, jugglers, musicians, dancers and DJs parade through the city's streets. The highlight of the weekend is the giant Whitsum street parade bringing together thousands of participants from around the world as they dance through the streets of the Kreuzberg district. There is also a giant programme of events during the festivities, with approximately 750 artists playing on four giant stages, and a children's party in *Goerlitzer Park*. International food, drinks and handicrafts are on sale at over 200 stalls during the four days, giving visitors the chance to sample international cuisine. Over half a million people attend the festival each year.

Event Organiser

Werkstatt der Kulturen, Wissmannstrasse 32, 12049 Berlin, Germany
Tel: (030) 6097 7022
Website: www.karneval-berlin.de

Venue

Various streets in Berlin, including Blucherplatz, Zossenerstrasse, Blucherstrasse and Gneisenaustrasse.

Transport

Air: Berlin Tegel Airport. **Rail:** Underground: Lines U1, 6 or 15 to Hallesches Tor or lines U6 or 7 to Mehringdamm. **Road:** Bus: Public services.

Christopher Street Day

Christoper Street Day is an enormous outdoor gay and lesbian party, which has been held every June in Berlin since 1979. Every year around 400,000 visitors join in the festivities, which rival gay and lesbian festivals in London, Amsterdam and San Francisco. The parade finishes at Siegessäule with a giant party and live music and DJs. Every year, there is a gigantic firework display at the end of the night, which brings the festivities to a spectacular close.

Event Organiser

Berliner CSD eV, Geschäftsführung, Michael Schmidt, Fuggerstrasse 7, 10777 Berlin, Germany
Tel: (0177) 277 3176
Website: www.csd-berlin.de

Venue

Various outdoor venues across Berlin, with parades setting off from Kurfürstendamm in the city centre.

Transport

Air: Berlin Tegel Airport. **Rail:** Underground: U9 or U15 to Kurfürstendamm. **Road:** Bus: Public services.

• July

Love Parade

The annual *Love Parade* takes place in Berlin in July (although it was cancelled in 2005 due to problems financing the huge free event). The festivities usually start at 1400 when a precession of 'lovetrucks' – many with DJs and onboard sound systems – set off on a giant parade from both *Ernst-Reuter-Platz* and *Brandenburg Tor* to Siegessäule, promoting the 'one world, one Love Parade' idea. Once they reach Siegessäule they turn around before setting off again on the big rally of the day at 1900. The first Love Parade took place on Berlin's Kurfürstendamm in 1989, when German DJ Dr Motte promoted an acid house party in the streets of Berlin to promote love and peace, and respect and understanding between nations; the event attracted 150 partygoers. The Berlin Love Parade has since grown into one of the biggest street parties in the Western world, with well over one million people attending the parade every year to watch the floats parade along the Strasse des 17 Juni, past some of Germany's most important monuments.

Event Organiser

Berlin Love Parade GmbH, Alexander Platz, 5, 10178 Berlin, Germany
Tel: (030) 284 620
Website: www.loveparade.de

Venue

Berlin city centre, starting at the Golden Angel monument in the middle of the Tiergarden and continuing down to Brandenburger Tor.

Transport

Air: Berlin Tegel Airport. **Rail:** Train: For Brandenburg Tor, S-Bahn S3, S5, S7, S9 or S75 to Friedrichstrasse Station. Underground: For Ernst-Reuter-Platz, U-Bahn 2 or 12 to Ernst-Reuter-Platz Station. **Road:** Bus: Public services.

• September

Berlin Marathon

The *Berlin Marathon* is an annual event which first took place on October 13 1974, with 284 runners from four nations starting the race. The event now attracts close to 30,000 participants. The race starts in Strasse des 17 Juni, at the *Charlottenburg Tor*, near *Ernst-Reuter Square* and ends in Kurfürstendamm. The participants run through 10 districts of Berlin: Charlottenburg, Tiergarten, Mitte, Friedrichshain, Kreuzberg, Neukölln, Schöneberg, Steglitz, Zehlendorf and Wilmersdorf, passing the *Brandenburg Gate*, the *Victory Column*, the *State Opera*, *Berlin Cathedral* and the *Botanical Gardens*. Over 60 bands and one million spectators line the streets to cheer on participants and create a truly exciting atmosphere.

Event Organiser
Berlin Marathon, SCC Running, Glockenturmstr 23, 14055 Berlin, Germany
Tel: (030) 3012 8810
Website: www.real-berlin-marathon.com

Venue
Streets of Berlin, starting at Charlottenburg Tor and ending at Kurfürstendamm.

Transport
Air: Berlin Tegel Airport. Rail: Train: S-Bahn S5 or S75 to Charlottenburg (start). Underground: U9 or U15 to Kurfürstendamm (finish). Road: Bus: Public services.

Frankfurt

Tourist Information

Frankfurt Tourist & Congress Board (Tourismus+Congress GmbH Frankfurt am Main) Kaiserstrasse 56, 60329 Frankfurt/Main, Germany
Tel: (069) 2123 8800
Website: www.frankfurt.de

• October

Frankfurt Marathon

The *Frankfurt Marathon* traditionally takes place on the last Sunday in October on a route that takes runners through the centre of the city. The marathon, which was first held in 1981, is the oldest city marathon in Germany, leading through the city centre, on to the west of the city and back through Sachsenhausen to the finish at the *Frankfurt Trade Fair Centre*. As well as the annual

42.2km (26.2 miles) marathon, there is also a 4.2km (2.6 miles) mini marathon for children and a breakfast run. The latter starts at *Frankfurt Römer*, one of the main sights in Frankfurt, and leads 5km (3.1 miles) through the city centre to the city's fairground. Visitors and spectators can also take part in a pasta party, a marathon breakfast and marathon buffet. In addition to this, there is a sportswear and sports equipment exhibition, a presentation ceremony and various course parties.

Event Organiser
Euro Marathon Frankfurt GmbH, 60135 Frankfurt am Main, Germany
Tel: (069) 9717 6330
Website: www.frankfurt-marathon.com

Venue
Starts and finishes at the Frankfurt Trade Fair Centre, in the centre of Frankfurt.

Transport
Air: Frankfurt Airport. Rail: Train: S-Bahn S3, S4, S5 or S6 to Messe Station. Road: Bus: Public services.

Munich

Tourist Information

Munich Tourist Office (Fremdenverkehrsamt München) Fraunhoferstraße 6, 80469 Munich, Germany
Tel: (089) 230 0180
Website: www.muenchen-tourist.de

• January-February

Munich Carnival

Munich Carnival (or *Fasching* as it is known in Germany) is held every year in the city, with major celebrations taking place during Germany's carnival period; this is known as the 'Fifth Season' or the 'Season of Fools', when Germans let their hair down before Lent. The first Fasching Ball was held in Munich in 1829 and was soon followed by many more masquerades and balls. Their popularity led to the establishment of a Munich carnival society in 1839 to organise annual events, marking the beginning of Fasching as it is known today. Every year, partygoers can choose from thousands of parties, balls and other festivities, which take place in the city, ranging from fancy-dress parties through to black-tie affairs. The climax of the carnival, *München Harrisch* (Mad Munich) costume parade, takes place on the

Sunday before Shrove Tuesday, with revellers partying in the streets and passing through the crowds on floats. Thousands of dancers and musicians congregate in *Marienplatz* after the parade to fill the city's beer halls. Fasching is also celebrated in other parts of Germany, such as Mainz and Düsseldorf, although Munich's Fasching lasts the longest and is the most famous.

Event Organiser
For more information on the Munich Carnival, contact the Munich Tourist Office (see **Tourist Information** above).

Venue
Various dance halls in hotels and breweries in Munich.

Transport
Air: Munich International Airport. **Rail:** Train: S-Bahn to Marienplatz. Underground: U-Bahn U3, U4, U5 or U6 to Marienplatz. **Road:** Bus: Public services.

• June

City Foundation Day

City Foundation Day is held every year to celebrate the founding of Munich, which took place on June14 1158 by the German prince, Henry the Lion, who also held the titles Duke of Saxony (1142-1180) and Duke of Bavaria (1156-1180). Every year, in commemoration, the locals drink beer and eat vast quantities of sausages during this giant street party. The festivities are accompanied by music from local bands and street performances. The event is held betweeen *Marienplatz* and *Odeonsplatz* in Munich's city centre. Many attractions, such as the *Neues Rathaus* (New Town Hall), built in the 19th century, *Altes Rathaus* (Old Town Hall), which houses a delightful toy museum, and *Frauenkirche* – Munich's cathedral, are located nearby and are well worth a visit whilst in the city.

Event Organiser
For more information on the City Foundation Day, contact the Munich Tourist Office (see **Tourist Information** above).

Venue
Between Marienplatz and Odeonsplatz in Munich city centre.

Transport
Air: Munich International Airport. **Rail:** Train: S-Bahn to Marienplatz. Underground: U-Bahn to Marienplatz. **Road:** Bus: Public services.

• September-October

October Festival

The Munich *October Festival* (or *Oktoberfest* as it is known in Germany) starts at the end of September and is one of the world's biggest public festivals. The event began in 1810 to celebrate the marriage of King Joseph Maximiliam of Bavaria to Princess Theresa of Saxony. The event was such a huge success that it has taken place ever since. The event now attracts over six million partygoers who drink around five million litres of beer. Events include the *Grand Entry of the Oktoberfest Landlords and Breweries*, the *Costume and Riflemen's Procession*, performances by Oompah bands, dancing and a giant funfair at the foot of the *Bavaria Statue*. The festivities take place in beer tents in the Theresienwiese district (a district named after Princess Theresa of Saxony).

Event Organiser
For more information on the October Festival, contact the Munich Tourist Office (see **Tourist Information** above).

Venue
Theresienwiese District.

Transport
Air: Munich International Airport. **Rail:** Underground: U-Bahn U4 or U5 to Theresienwiese. **Road:** Bus: Public services.

• December

Christmas Market

Every year, thousands of people crowd into Marienplatz to watch the Lord Mayor open the *Christmas Market* (known as *Weihnachtsmarkt* in German). This event occurs at 1700 on the Saturday before the first day of Advent, when the mayor switches on the Christmas lights on a 30m-high (98ft) Christmas tree. The market's origins can be traced back to Nicholas Market, which started in 1310, with people shopping in Nenhauserstrasse, buying toys for Christmas. In 1597, the market moved location; changing its name to Christmas Market in 1805. Since 1972, the market has taken place in Marienplatz in the centre of Munich. Every year, gifts are on sale at more than 140 market stalls. Craftsmen can also be seen at work, making gifts such as Christmas baubles and candles. There is also a *Crib Market*, based on the Nativity Crib in the Town Hall Courtyard. Folk music is played at 1730 every evening and Santa Claus greets children in the square on December 5 and 6.

Event Organiser
For more information on the Christmas Market, contact the Munich Tourist Office (see **Tourist Information** above).

Venue
Marienplatz in Munich city centre.

Transport
Air: Munich International Airport.
Rail: Train: S-Bahn to Marienplatz.
Underground: U-Bahn to Marienplatz. **Road:**
Bus: Public services.

Greece

Athens

Tourist Information
Hellenic Tourism Organisation
(Ellinikos Organismos Tourismou)
7, Tsoha, 11521 Athens, Greece
Tel: (210) 870 7000
Website: www.gnto.gr

• July

Rockwave Festival

This is Greece's major rock music event, featuring performances by groups from around the world. The festival first took place in 1996 and has attracted many big name bands since then, including Moby, Pulp, Prodigy, Blur, Garbage, Marilyn Manson and The Fun Lovin' Criminals. The event now attracts well over 50,000 people each year and there are other activities to entertain the crowd including bungee jumping, simulators and circus acts. There are also merchandise stalls and food and drink available, and festivalgoers can take time out to relax in the park.

Event Organiser
Didi Music, 3 Eptanisou Street – 2 Pipinou Street, 11257 Athens, Greece
Tel: (210) 882 0426
Website: www.didimusic.gr

Venue
Varies annually. Contact the Hellenic Tourism Organisation for more details.

Transport
Air: Athens International Airport. **Rail:** Train: Larissa or Pelopónnisos stations. Underground: Monastiraki or Theseion. **Road:** Bus: Public services.

• July-September

Athens Festival

In AD 161 the Roman ruler Herodes Atticus commissioned the *Odeon* amphitheatre at the foot of the *Acropolis* in memory of his wife, Rigilla. Decorated in marble and seating 5000 spectators, this beautiful auditorium has been used to stage performances since ancient times, when musicians, actors, poets and dancers performed to gain the favour of the gods. Since 1955, the Odeon has provided a splendid setting for the *Athens Festival*, an international celebration of theatre, music, dance and literature. The starry night sky above the amphitheatre provides the perfect backdrop for a magical evening's entertainment. Anyone wishing to try a more unusual performance might like to watch a poetry reading or avant-garde musical recital at the *Pnyx*, at the entrance to the Acropolis.

Event Organiser
Athens Festival, Athens Festival Box Office, 4 Stadiou Street, Athens, Greece
Tel: (01) 928 2900
Website: www.hellenicfestival.gr

Venue
Odeon of Herodes Atticus (at the foot of the Acropolis).

Transport
Air: Athens International Airport. **Rail:** Train: Larissa or Pelopónnisos stations. Underground: Monastiraki or Theseion. **Road:** Bus: Public services.

• November

Athens Marathon

Almost every major city in the world has its own marathon, but only Athens can claim to have the original. The event is so called after the legendary 40.2km (25 mile) journey undertaken by the messenger, Phiedippes, when he brought news of the Athenian victory over the Persians at the *Marathon* battlefield in 490 BC. The first marathon event took place at the 1896 Olympic Games in Athens and the winner was a Greek, Spyridon Louis. Today, runners must follow in the footsteps of Phiedippes, to complete a route over 42.2km (26 miles 385 yards) between the ancient battlefield in the village of Marathon and the historic *Olympic Stadium* in the centre of Athens. The standard distance for a marathon event was set in 1924, when the British Olympic Committee decided that the route for the London Games should lead from *Windsor Castle* to the royal box in the *London Olympic Stadium.*

Event Organiser
SEGAS, 137 Syngrou Avenue, 171 21 N Smirni, Athens, Greece
Tel: (01) 935 1888
Website: www.athensmarathon.com

Venue
Starts at the village of Marathon and ends at the Olympic Stadium.

Transport
Air: Athens International Airport. **Rail:** Train: Larissa or Pelopónnisos stations. **Road:** Bus: Public services.

Hungary

Budapest

Tourist Information
Tourism Office of Budapest (Budapesti Turisztikai Hivatal)
1364 Budapest PF 215, 1052 Budapest, Hungary
Tel: (01) 266 0479
Website: www.budapestinfo.hu

• March-April

Budapest Spring Festival
Although classical music predominates, the *Budapest Spring Festival* encompasses music for most tastes, as well as cinematic and theatrical events. It is the largest cultural festival in Hungary and has a growing reputation abroad. Performances take place in beautiful locations around the city including open-air events such as the *Celebration of Spring* parade. There is a vast array of classical concerts, ranging from piano recitals and string quartets to evenings of French Baroque music. Those interested in discovering traditional Hungarian culture can enjoy performances by the 100-member Budapest Gypsy Orchestra. Jazz, films, exhibitions and children's activities are also on offer each year.

Event Organiser
Budapest Festival Centre (Budapest Fesztiválközpont KHT), Egyetem tér 5, 1053 Budapest, Hungary
Tel: (01) 486 3300
Website: www.festivalcity.hu

Venue
Various locations across Budapest.

Transport
Air: Budapest Ferihegy Airport. **Rail:** Train: Eastern, Western or Southern stations. **Road:** Bus: Public services.

• October-November

Budapest Autumn Festival
The *Budapest Autumn Festival* is an experimental arts festival that aims to highlight new forms within the contemporary arts scene. Variety is the key – visitors can explore almost any genre, from high-brow literary readings and classical orchestral concerts to fun circus acts and eclectic art exhibitions. Children can join in play workshops and there are coffee shop concerts where live music can be enjoyed alongside the mouthwatering Budapest tradition of coffee and cakes. Hungarian folk dancing, jazz, film premieres, clown shows and literary sightseeing tours are also on offer.

Event Organiser
Budapest Festival Centre (Budapest Fesztiválközpont KHT), Egyetem tér 5, 1053 Budapest, Hungary
Tel: (01) 486 3300
Website: www.festivalcity.hu

Venue
Various locations across Budapest.

Transport
Air: Budapest Ferihegy Airport. **Rail:** Train: Eastern, Western or Southern stations. **Road:** Bus: Public services.

• December

New Year's Eve Gala and Ball at the Opera
This ball has taken place every year for the past decade in the opulent surroundings of the *Hungarian State Opera* House in central Budapest and is open to everyone. The Opera House was built in Italian neo-Renaissance style to designs by Miklós Ybl and was first opened in 1884. It was reopened on its 100th birthday in September 1984 after undergoing extensive restoration to return it to its former glory. Those who take part in the New Year's Eve festivities can expect to be richly entertained, with a gala concert of music and dance performed by the resident Opera House ensemble, Hungarian food and drink served on the

stage and in the box areas, and old-style Viennese ballroom dancing. For those who prefer something more contemporary, there is a piano bar and disco.

Event Organiser
Organisational Department of the Opera House, 24 Andrássy Street, VI Budapest 1061, Hungary
Tel: (01) 332 7914
Website: www.opera.hu

Venue
Hungarian State Opera House.

Transport
Air: Budapest Ferihegy Airport. Rail: Train: Eastern, Western or Southern stations. Underground: Opera. Road: Bus: Public services.

Iceland

Reykjavik

Tourist Information
(Icelandic Tourist Board) Islenska Tourist Board
Laekjargata 3, 101 Reykjavik, Iceland
Tel: 535 5500
Website: www.visiticeland.com

• January-February

Thorri Feast

Thorri is the Icelandic name for the fourth month of winter. Every year in February, Icelanders continue the ancient Viking tradition of celebrating the end of winter and the coming of spring with dancing, singing and huge feasts. The tradition all but disappeared with the advent of Christianity, but was revived in 1873 during Iceland's struggle for independence from Denmark. Traditional delicacies include *slatur* (a type of black pudding), *svith* (boiled sheep's head), *hakarl* (rotten shark meat) and *hrutspungar* (ram's testicles). For the less adventurous there are other specialities on offer, such as various kinds of bread, *lundabaggar* (lamb meatballs), *hardfiskur* (dried fish with butter) and *skyr* (curds and fresh blueberries). Restaurants in Reykjavik offer their own *Thorri Feasts*, usually as a buffet to allow guests to sample as many dishes as they can manage. This is a popular festival giving visitors the chance to experience Icelandic culture.

Event Organiser
For more information on the Thorri Feast, contact the Icelandic Tourist Board (see **Tourist Information** above).

Venue
Various locations across Reykjavik.

Transport
Air: Keflavik International Airport. Road: Car: Hwy-1 (from all coastal towns in Iceland, including Akureyri, Höfn and Isafjördur).

• July-August

Light Nights

In the 12th century, *sagnaskemmtun* (saga entertainment) was a popular way of spending evenings on Icelandic farms. Stories were passed on from generation to generation and many have been recorded in writing, although the identity of many of the authors remains a mystery. The sagas are based on legends, historical events, secular fiction and the lives of the saints, and tell the story of everyday people in a bid to give Icelanders an awareness of themselves and the society around them through the tales of their ancestors. The saga remains an important cultural tradition in Iceland and every year the audience is taken on a two-hour journey through several centuries of Icelandic history with storytelling, slides, folksongs and chants. This is a unique theatrical and cultural experience, and performances are held every Thursday, Friday and Saturday at 2100.

Event Organiser
The Travelling Theatre, Baldursgata 37, 101 Reykjavik, Iceland
Tel: 551 9181 (summer months only)
Website: www.lightnights.com

Venue
Tjarnarbíó Theatre (next to the City Hall).

Transport
Air: Keflavik International Airport. Road: Bus: Public services.

India

Delhi

Tourist Information
Government of India
Tourist Office
88 Janpath, New Delhi 110011, India
Tel: (011) 332 0005
Website: www.tourisminindia.com

• October

Diwali

Diwali is one of the most well-known Hindu festivals and is celebrated throughout India. According to Hindu legend, King Dashratha wished for his son Rama, born to his wife Queen Kaushalaya, to be the heir to his throne. Another of his wives, Queen Keykayee, used the two wishes granted to her by her husband to send Rama into exile for 14 years so that her son, Bharat, would be the future king instead. Rama is believed to have spent his years in exile in the southern tip of the Indian sub-continent killing the king of demons before returning to rule over his kingdom of Ayodhya. Diwali thus symbolises the victory of good over evil and the lifting of spiritual darkness. The Sanskrit name, 'Deepavali', is derived from two words – 'deepa', meaning 'light' and 'avali', meaning 'row', thus 'row of lights'. Diwali is commonly referred to as the 'festival of lights', and many Indians place small oil lamps, or *diyas*, outside their homes, while candles light up the city centres to welcome Lakshmi, the goddess of wealth and prosperity. Firecrackers are also burned and Hindu families hold huge feasts in their homes. Sweets are traditionally given as presents and Delhi stages its own festivities at *Lal Quila* (Red Fort) with fireworks and a funfair.

Event Organiser

For more information on Diwali, contact the Government of India Tourist Office (see **Tourist Information** above).

Venue

Various locations across Delhi with the main focus at Lal Quila (Red Fort).

Transport

Air: Indira Gandhi International Airport. **Rail:** Train: New Delhi or Old Delhi stations. **Road:** Bus: Public services.

Rajasthan

Tourist Information

Government of India
Tourist Office
Tourist Reception Centre, (RTDC), Hotel Saras, Agra Road, Rajasthan, India
Tel. (011) 22542
Website: www.incredibleindia.org

• October/November

Pushkar Fair

The spectacular *Pushkar Fair* is the largest camel fair anywhere in the world at which thousands of camels are bought, traded and paraded for the amassed crowds at this incredible week-long festival. Camels are brought from miles around, many having trekked through the hot, arid desert for several weeks to get to the festival or 'mela'. The festival also has religious significance as one of Hinduism's five major pilgrimages. As the serious business of camel trading draws to an end, the final days of the festival are devoted to fun and games including camel races and a camel beauty pageant. The festival closes with the symbolic washing in the bathing ghats of Pushkar Lake. Over 10,000 foreign tourists travel to witness the incredible festival at what is truly an awe-inspiring event.

Event Organiser

For more information on the Pushkar Fair, contact the Government of India Tourist Office (see **Tourist Information** above).

Venue

Pushkar, Rajasthan.

Transport

Air: Jaipur International Airport. **Rail:** Train: Ajmer Station. **Road:** Bus: Public services.

Ireland

Dublin

Tourist Information

Dublin Tourism
Tourism Centre, Suffolk Street, Dublin 2, Ireland
Tel: (01) 605 7700
Website: www.visitdublin.com

• March

St Patrick's Festival

St Patrick's Festival takes place in Dublin every year to remember St Patrick, who is the Patron Saint of Ireland. St Patrick was born around AD 387 and died on March 17 AD 461. He was the second bishop of Ireland and was most famous for using the shamrock to show how the Father, Son and Holy Ghost can exist as separate parts of the same body, leading to the shamrock becoming the national emblem of Ireland. Patrick is also believed to have given a sermon that drove all snakes from Ireland. To commemorate his life, there is a parade through Dublin city centre on March 17, as well as a giant carnival and celebrations during the four days of festivities. The parade begins at 1100 at *Christ Church Cathedral* and ends in O'Connell Street. St Patrick's Day, on March 17, is a bank holiday in Ireland, when the Lord Mayor of Dublin is driven through the streets in a horse-drawn carriage and is cheered on by spectators. Other events include the *Fanfare Celebration* of marching bands and the *St Patrick's Eve Night Parade* on March 16, the *Ceili Mor Celebration* of Irish dance on March 17 and *The Big Day Out* on March 19, The Big Day Out consists of more than 100 events, including street theatre, magic shows, comedy shows, puppet shows and parades. The festivities end with a giant fireworks display on March 19. St Patrick's Day celebrations take place around the world, with many major cities, including New York, Boston and Chicago, hosting their own Irish celebrations.

Event Organiser
St Patrick's Day Festival Office, St Stephens Green House, Earlsfort Terrace, Dublin 2, Ireland
Tel: (01) 676 3205
Website: www.stpatricksday.ie

Venue
Various locations across Dublin, centred around Christ Church Cathedral and O'Connell Street.

Transport
Air: Dublin Airport. **Road:** Bus: Public services.

• May

Heineken Green Energy Festival

The annual *Heineken Green Energy Festival* takes place over the May Bank Holiday weekend and showcases a host of unsigned and international bands playing in venues across the city. Over 50,000 people attend the festival each year to see a wide range of acts. Past performers have included the Black Eyed Peas, Paddy Casey and Faithless. Big names play at *Dublin Castle*, the *Olympia Theatre* and *Temple Bar Music Centre*. As well as performances from well-known international artists, unsigned groups also play gigs in Dublin and compete in the festival's band challenge.

Event Organiser
For more information on the Heineken Green Energy Festival, contact the Dublin Tourism (see **Tourist Information** above).

Venue
Various locations across Dublin, including Temple Bar Music Centre, Dublin Castle and Olympia Theatre.

Transport
Air: Dublin Airport. **Rail:** Train: Connolly or Heuston stations. **Road:** Bus: Public services.

• June

Bloomsday Festival

The *Bloomsday Festival* celebrates the life of James Joyce, who was born in 1882 and died in 1941. James Joyce is one of Ireland's most famous writers, responsible for works that include 'Ulysses' and 'Portrait of the Artist as a Young Man'. Events include a re-enactment of Paddy Dignam's funeral in Ulysses, walking tours around Dublin and various talks on James Joyce, Ulysses and Bloomsday. The actual Bloomsday celebration takes place on June 16, starting with the *Guinness Bloomsday Breakfast* which consists of 'eating with relish the inner organs of beasts and fowls', washed down with the 'foaming ebon ale', and listening to readings from the book of the day. The event is named Bloomsday after Leopold Bloom, the main character in 'Ulysses', and takes place on this day as the book was set on June 16 1904. The annual *Bloomsday Lecture & Walking Tour* also takes place on June 16, with talks by Ken Monaghan, Cultural Director of the Centre and nephew of James Joyce, and a walking tour through the city, with characters from 'Ulysses' popping up along the way. Other events include the Riverrun which celebrates the River Liffey and the women in Joyce's books and involves a bus trip to the mouth of the river and Howth Head, rounded off with readings and refreshments in the *Bloody Steam Pub*.

Event Organiser
The James Joyce Centre, 35 North Great George's Street, Dublin 1, Ireland
Tel: (01) 878 8547
Website: www.jamesjoyce.ie

Venue
Various locations across Dublin, including North Great George's Street, Westland Row train station, Temple Bar, National Library and the James Joyce Centre.

Transport
Air: Dublin Airport. **Rail:** Train: Tara Street or Connolly stations. **Road:** Bus: Public services.

• September-October

Dublin Fringe Festival

Dublin Fringe Festival first took place in 1995 and now takes place every year at the end of September. The festival, which lasts for three weeks, incorporates the best of theatre, dance, comedy and visual arts and is now Ireland's largest performing arts festival. The Fringe aims to challenge convention through exploring new ways of looking at the world through performance art and each year the Fringe venues come alive attracting thousands of visitors.

Event Organiser
Dublin Fringe Festival, 12 East Essex Street, Temple Bar Dublin 2, Ireland
Tel: (01) 679 2320
Website: www.fringefest.com

Venue
20 locations in Dublin, including Civic Theatre, Samuel Beckett Theatre, Temple Bar Square and The Crypt at Dublin Castle.

Transport
Air: Dublin Airport. **Rail:** Train: Connolly or Heuston stations. **Road:** Bus: Public services.

Israel

Tel Aviv

Tourist Information
Tel Aviv-Jaffa Tourist Information Office
New Central Bus Station, Sixth Floor, Room 6108, Tel Aviv, Israel
Tel: (03) 639 5660
Website: www.goisrael.org

• August

Jaffa Nights

Jaffa Nights is held annually in the city of Tel Aviv during mid-August. Lasting for four days, it comprises over 70 music, theatre, dance and art exhibitions, and is Israel's largest street-staged event. In the evenings, the streets of the Old Jaffa area are closed to traffic, during which time the streets come alive with music and dance performed on stages erected in the city's various squares and alleys. Tens of thousands of visitors attend the festival every year.

Event Organiser
Tel Aviv Municipality, Events Department, Tel Aviv 64162, Israel
Tel: (03) 521 8264
Website: www.tel-aviv.gov.il/english

Venue
Old Jaffa area of Tel Aviv.

Transport
Air: Ben-Gurion International Airport. **Train:** Rail: Tel Aviv Central Station. **Road:** Bus: Public services.

Italy

Florence

Tourist Information
Florence Tourist Board (Azienda di Promozione Turistica di Firenze)
Via Cavour 1r, 50129 Florence, Italy
Tel: (055) 290 832
Website: www.firenze.turismo.toscana.it

• March

Explosion of the Cart

The origins of this ritual, which is known as the *Scoppio del Carro* in Italian, go back to the time of the first Christian crusade to seize control of the Holy City of Jerusalem from the Muslims in 1095. A valiant soldier called Pazzino dei Pazzi fought bravely and was the first to scale the walls of Jerusalem, where he raised the Christian flag. For this he was rewarded with some stones from the Holy Tomb. The hero took these with him to Florence to be used by the bishop to light the fire in the cathedral on Easter morning; this fire was then distributed to every Florentine citizen. The Pazzi family then began to build a cart (or *Brindellone*, as it is called in Italian), which has been burned at this annual event for many centuries. On Easter Sunday, starting at 0950, two separate processions transport the stones and the cart (which is led by oxen) from the *Chiesa dei Santi Apostoli* (the Church of the Holy Apostles) throughout the city to the *Piazza del Duomo* (Cathedral Square), where they meet. A special Easter mass then takes place inside the cathedral. During the Gloria (the second element of Catholic mass) at 1100, a rocket, in the form of a dove, which is connected to the car, is set alight. This in turn causes the cart, which is loaded with fireworks, to explode in a mass of colour and light, watched by hundreds of spectators. According to tradition, if the ceremony goes smoothly Florence will have good harvests and a prosperous year.

Event Organiser

For more information on the Explosion of the Cart, contact the Florence Tourist Board (see **Tourist Information** above).

Venue

Piazza del Duomo in central Florence.

Transport

Air: Amerigo Vespucci Airport (Florence) or Galileo Galilei Airport (Pisa). **Rail:** Train: Firenze Santa Maria Novella Station (Florence). **Road:** Bus: Public services.

• June

Historical Soccer Tournament

Costumed football matches (now known as *Calcio Storico Fiorentino* in Italian) have long been played in the *Piazza Santa Croce* in the historic heart of Florence. The origins of the game date back at least to Roman times, with the moves involved in the game being similar to the battle order of the Roman army. It was not until centuries later that football migrated north to England and evolved into the modern game known today. The game was characterised by fights and locked battles for possession of the ball, all of which were meant to strengthen both the body and the mind of the civilians and soldiers who played. Famous players included members of prestigious Renaissance families such as Lorenzo de' Medici and Vincenzo Gonzaga. Matches were played at Carnival time and throughout the year until the end of the 18th century; the tradition was revived in 1930, the 400th anniversary of the siege of Florence, as a means of celebrating the city's resilience in the face of adversity through the centuries. Nowadays, three matches are held on the city's patron saint's day in June and players wear medieval costumes representing the four districts of the city: white for Santo Spirito, blue for Santa Croce, red for Santa Maria Novella and green for San Giovanni. The backdrop to this colourful spectacle is the celebrated Franciscan church of Santa Croce.

Event Organiser

Calcio Storico Fiorentino – Segretaria, Piazzetta di Parte Guelfa 1, 50123 Florence, Italy
Tel: (055) 261 6050
Website: www.globeit.it/caf/info.html

Venue

Piazza Santa Croce in central Florence.

Transport

Air: Amerigo Vespucci Airport (Florence), Galileo Galilei Airport (Pisa). **Rail:** Train: Firenze Santa Maria Novella Station (Florence). **Road:** Bus: Public services.

Rome

Tourist Information

Azienda di Promozione Turistica di Roma (Rome Tourist Office)
Via Parigi 11, 00185 Rome, Italy
Tel: (06) 4889 9253
Website: www.romaturismo.com

• July-September

Roman Summer

Rome's summer arts festival (*Estate Romana* in Italian) is a three-month extravaganza encompassing all manner of events. Balmy summer evenings can be spent watching some of the many Italian and foreign films showing at the open-air cinema in *Piazza Vittorio*, or enjoying a live classical music concert in one of the city's parks. The programme features a huge variety of performances including celebrating culture through classical concerts, dance, music, food and drink. The Italians are renowned for their love of children, and younger visitors will find plenty of distractions to amuse them, from sports competitions to games and cartoons.

Event Organiser

For more information on the Roman Summer, contact the Rome Tourist Office (see **Tourist Information** above).

Venue

Various locations across Rome.

Transport

Air: Rome Leonardo de Vinci Airport (Fiumicino) or Rome Ciampino Airport. **Water:** Ferry: Civitavecchia port, from where there are services to central Rome. **Rail:** Train: Roma Termini, Roma Tiburtina, Roma Ostiense or Roma Trastevere stations. **Road:** Bus: Public services.

• October-December

Rome Jazz Festival

Throughout its history, the *Rome Jazz Festival* has featured many prominent artists, including the Steve Lacy Quartet, Cuban jazz player Gonzalo

Rubalcaba, guitarist John McLaughlin and the Brad Mehldau Trio. Venues range from *Big Mama*, Rome's premier blues club, which has earned the nickname 'Home of the Blues in Rome', to *Auditorium del Massimo*, an historic cultural institute now housed in the city's ultra-modern EUR business district. Jazz and Latin American music have long been popular in Italy's capital and this festival brings together the best of both.

Event Organiser
Rome Jazz Festival, Via Salaria 292, 00199 Rome, Italy
Tel: (06) 5630 5015
Website: www.romajazzfestival.it

Venue
Various venues across Rome.

Transport
Air: Rome Leonardo de Vinci Airport (Fiumicino) or Rome Ciampino Airport. **Water:** Ferry: Civitavecchia port, from where there are services to central Rome. **Rail:** Train: Roma Termini, Roma Tiburtina, Roma Ostiense or Roma Trastevere stations. Underground: EUR Palasport (to Auditorium del Massimo). **Road:** Bus: Public services.

• December

Christmas Mass in St Peter's Basilica

One of the most moving ways to celebrate Christ's birthday is by attending this mass in the second largest church in the Christian world. Work on the *Basilica di San Pietro*, or St Peter's Basilica (so named as it is said to stand on the burial site of St Peter), was begun in 1506 during the time of Pope Julius II, and completed in 1615 under Pope Paul V. Artists and architects involved in its design and construction include famous Renaissance names such as Raphael, Bramante and Michelangelo. The fruits of their labour are awe-inspiring, with the huge interior filled with works of Renaissance and Baroque art, among them Michelangelo's 'Pietà'. Visitors who wish to join the crowds for this special occasion must book in advance by contacting the Prefettura della Casa Pontificia and stating the number of tickets they require.

Event Organiser
Prefettura della Casa Pontificia, 00120 Vatican City, Italy
Tel: (06) 6988 3114
Website: www.vatican.va

Venue
Basilica di San Pietro (St Peter's Basilica).

Transport
Air: Rome Leonardo de Vinci Airport (Fiumicino) or Rome Ciampino Airport. **Water:** Ferry: Civitavecchia port, from where there are services to central Rome. **Rail:** Train: Roma Termini, Roma Tiburtina, Roma Ostiense or Roma Trastevere stations. Underground: Ottaviano-San Pietro. **Road:** Bus: Public services.

Venice

Tourist Information
Azienda di Promozione Turistica (Venice Tourist Board)
Calle dell'Ascensione 71C, Venice, Italy
Tel: (041) 529 8711
Website: www.turismovenezia.it

• February

Venice Carnival

The wearing of masks has been a Venetian tradition since the 13th century. It was particularly popular with gamblers as a means of disguising their identity from their creditors, although the law stated that masks were not allowed during religious festivals, including Lent. They were, however, permitted from San Stefano's Day (December 26) until Shrove Tuesday and this period, the *Carnevale* (as it is known in Italian), saw huge celebrations across the city, with masked balls in the *palazzi* lining the Grand Canal and bullfights and cart-racing in the streets. Nowadays, although it does not start until February, *Venice Carnival* is one of the most famous in Europe and the age-old traditions continue to thrive. Visitors to the city can see actors and ordinary Venetians posing in opulent costumes around *Piazza San Marco* (St Mark's Square), and there are still masked balls in the historic buildings, or *palazzi*, along the canals; tickets for the *Golden Night Ball* in the Palazzo Ca' Zenobio on the last night of the carnival cost about L520,000 (£170) and, as for all balls, guests must arrive in costume. A cheaper option is to enjoy the long-standing tradition of hot chocolate and cakes in one of the city's many cafés, or listen to one of the concerts that take place during the event. Many visitors are content just to mix with the crowds and take in the festive atmosphere. On the first day of the carnival, the *Festa delle Marie* (Festival of the Brides) takes place – seven young women, representing seven brides who were kidnapped and robbed by pirates in AD 948, travel from *San Pietro di Castello* to St Mark's Square where dancing and street entertainment follow. The real climax of the carnival is the last Saturday, when thousands of people flock to the city; many of the balls take place on this night and there are concerts in St Mark's Square.

Event Organiser
Comitato per il Carnevale di Venezia Consortium, Piazzale Roma, Santa Croce 473, 30133 Venice, Italy
Tel: (041) 717 065
Website: www.carnivalofvenice.com

Venue
Various locations across Venice with the focus on St Mark's Square.

Transport
Air: Marco Polo Airport (Venice). Water: Waterbus (*Vaporetto*): 1 or 82 (from Piazzale Roma to San Zaccaria for St Mark's Square). Rail: Train: Venezia Santa Lucia or Mestre stations. Road: Bus: Public services.

• March-November

Venice Biennale

Founded in 1895, the *Venice Biennale* is a major cultural institution aimed at promoting contemporary art and culture to a wider audience by setting up permanent workshops and projects. Every two years, the Biennale presents a varied programme of art exhibitions, dance, music, cinema and theatre in the city, attracting worldwide interest and often provoking controversy. Past exhibitors have included Benetton designer Oliviero Toscani and American artist Robert Rauschenberg. The dance element of the festival (June, July and September) includes pieces choreographed by artists from Egypt, Turkey and Morocco, amongst others. The Biennial also incorporates the *Festival of Music* (May and September), the *International Film Festival* and the *International Theatre Festival* (March, May, July and September).

Event Organiser
Venice Biennale Cultural Corporation, Events Office, Palazzo Querini Dubois, San Polo 2004, 30125 Venice, Italy
Tel: (041) 272 8318
Website: www.labiennale.org

Venue
Various venues across Venice.

Transport
Air: Marco Polo Airport (Venice). Water: Waterbus (*Vaporetto*): 1 or 82 (from Piazzale Roma to San Zaccaria for St Mark's Square). Rail: Train:

Venezia Santa Lucia or Mestre stations. Road: Bus: Public services.

Japan

Tokyo

Tourist Information
Tokyo Tourist Information Center (TIC)
Tokyo International Forum, 3-5-1 Marunouchi, Chiyoda-ku, Tokyo, Japan
Tel: (03) 5221 9084
Website: www.tcvb.or.jp

• March-April

Ueno Cherry Blossom Festival

Every year thousands of people gather in *Ueno Park* in Tokyo to see over 1300 beautiful cherry blossom trees come into bloom. Cherry blossoms (or *sakura* in Japanese) are the national flower in Japan and are believed to represent beauty, as well as signifying the end of winter and the beginning of spring. During the annual *Ueno Cherry Blossom Festival*, Ueno Park is lit by lanterns every evening. People hold various parties to admire the cherry blossoms and also gather in *Sumida Park* along the Sumida River to see even more cherry blossom trees bloom.

Event Organiser
For more information on the Ueno Cherry Blossom Festival, contact the Tokyo Tourist Information Center (see **Tourist Information** above).

Venue
Ueno Park, Tokyo.

Transport
Air: New Tokyo Narita International Airport or Haneda Airport (domestic flights). Rail: Train: Tokyo Station. Underground: Ueno Station. Road: Bus: Public services.

• May

Sanja Festival

First held more than 200 years ago, *the Sanja Festival* is one of Tokyo's biggest festivals when the city's residents carry *Mikoshi* (mini-shrines) through the crowded streets surrounding the *Asakusa Shrine*. The shrine (*Asakusa-jinja* in Japanese) was founded during the 17th century and is housed in the grounds of the famous *Senso-ji Temple* in Tokyo. It is dedicated to the two fishermen who discovered the Kannon statuette, which is also housed in the Senso-ji Temple, whilst fishing in the Sumida River.

Today, the festival sees around two million people gather in Tokyo to watch the festivities, which include annual music performances, and to carry around one hundred shrines through the city to honour the famous shrine.

Event Organiser
For more information on the Sanja Festival, contact Tokyo Tourist Information Center (see **Tourist Information** above).

Venue
The streets of Asakusa, surrounding the Asakusa Shrine in Sensoji Temple.

Transport
Air: New Tokyo Narita International Airport or Haneda Airport (domestic flights). **Rail:** Train: Tokyo Station. Underground: Asakusa. **Road:** Bus: Public services.

• July

Tokyo Fireworks Festival

Tokyo Fireworks Festival, which is known as *Sumida-gawa Hanabi Taikai* in Japanese, was first held in the city in 1733 by Shogun Yoshimune who organised the display to pay respects to those who had died during a famine in 1732. It has since grown to become firmly established as Tokyo's main summer fireworks event. Around 20,000 *hanabi* (flower-fires) light up the night skies and up to one million people line the streets and river banks to watch the displays. The event is usually held on the last Saturday in July every year.

Event Organiser
For more information on the Tokyo Fireworks Festival, contact the Tokyo Tourist Information Center (see **Tourist Information** above).

Venue
Along the banks of the Sumida River.

Transport
Air: New Tokyo Narita International Airport or Haneda Airport (domestic flights). **Rail:** Train: Tokyo Station. Underground: Asakusa. **Road:** Bus: Public services.

Mali

Tourist Information
Tourist Office Mali (Office Malien du Tourisme et de l'Hôtellerie)
Rue Mohamed V., Bamako, Mali
Tel: 222 5673
Website: www.malitourisme.com

• January

Festival in the Desert

The desert Tuareg people of Mali have come together for desert gatherings for hundreds of years but it was only with the official end of the Tamashek war in 1996 that the seeds an official festival were sewn. A ceremonial burning of weapons was held to mark the end of the war and a large festival including dancing and music ensued. The first official Festival in the Desert was held in 2001 and despite the event still being in its relative infancy, it has quickly grown into a popular annual event that attracts an international crowd of revellers and curious travellers. Internationally-renowned musicians such as Robert Plant have taken part in the past but the emphasis is very much on musicians from the Sahara creating a truly unique festival experience.

Event Organiser
Festival in the Desert
Email: info@festival-au-desert.org
Website: www.festival-au-desert.org

Venue
Essakane, Mali.

Transport
Air: Bamako International Airport. **Road:** Bus: Public services.

Mexico

Mexico City

Tourist Information
Mexico City Tourist Office (Oficina de Turismo de la Ciudad de México)
Mariano Escobedo 550, Piso 7, Col Anzures, 11590 Mexico City, Mexico
Tel: (05) 2581 0941
Website: www.visitmexico.com

• March

Festival of the Historic Centre

The *Festival del Centro Histórico* (as it is known in Spanish), first held in 1985 to promote Mexico City's old quarter, is a two-week festival celebrating the best in Mexican and international culture. It has become increasingly popular and now attracts nearly 1,000,000 visitors over the two-week festival. A wide variety of events are held in churches, cloisters, squares and concert halls around the historic centre, ranging from performances of theatre, dance and opera to food and drink tastings and children's activities. There are also film screenings, art exhibitions, cultural seminars and guided tours of the historic centre, with themes such as 'Prehispanic times' and 'Jewish Life'.

Event Organiser
Festival del Centro Histórico de la Ciudad de México AC, Avenida Benjamin Franklin 176, Col Escandón, Mexico DF, 11800 Mexico
Tel: (0525) 277 9757
Website: www.fchmexico.com

Venue
Various locations across Mexico City.

Transport
Air: Mexico City International Airport. **Rail:** Train: Buenavista Station. **Road:** Bus: Public services.

The Netherlands

Amsterdam

Tourist Information
Amsterdam Tourist Office (VVV Amsterdam Kantoor Stationsplein)
Stationsplein 10, 1012 AB Amsterdam, The Netherlands
Tel: (020) 201 8800
Website: www.holand.com

• April

Queen's Day

On *Queen's Day* (which is known as *Koninginnedag* in Dutch), Amsterdamers take part in a giant street party to celebrate the Queen's birthday. Every year on April 30, people take to the streets to join in the festivities on what has been a national holiday since the end of World War II. The festivities kick off around 1800 on April 29 and last well into the small hours of the next day. People consume large amounts of alcohol and dress up in orange clothes, as the Queen is from the House of Orange; some of them even paint their faces orange in order to join in the celebrations. Queen's Day actually takes place on the Queen Mother's (Juliana) birthday as Queen Beatrix's birthday is January 31 and considered too cold for any festivities. On April 30, people also

attempt to sell their unwanted household items in the street when the city turns into a giant flea market. There is a chance to pick up a real bargain, although much of what's on sale could easily be classed as junk. Amsterdam becomes extremely crowded on Queen's Day, particularly if it is sunny, and visitors are advised to get there early.

Event Organiser
Rijks Voorlichtings Dienst (RVD), Debennenhof 20, 20001 The Hague, The Netherlands
Tel: (070) 356 4000
Website: www.koninginnedag.nl

Venue
Various locations across Amsterdam and Holland.

Transport
Air: Amsterdam Airport Schiphol. **Rail:** Train: Amsterdam Centraal Station. **Road:** Bus: Public services.

• May

National Windmill and Pumping Station Day

National Windmill and Pumping Station Day is organised every year on the second Saturday in May. Approximately 650 watermills and windmills across Holland open their doors free of charge to visitors. Many windmills also put on exhibitions and demonstrations to explain a miller's work to the general public. Mills which take part in the event can be recognised easily as they have large blue banners on display and they also all turn their sails. There are over 1000 windmills in Holland, although there are only four working windmills in Amsterdam itself. Windmills in Amsterdam include De Rieker, on the banks of the Amstel, two windmills on Haarlemmerweg (1200 Roe and De Bleom), De Gooyer, 1100 Roe and d'Admiraal.

Event Organiser
De Hollandsche Molen, Zeeburgerdijk 139, 1095 AA, Amsterdam, The Netherlands
Tel: (020) 623 8703
Website: www.molens.nl

Venue
Windmills across Amsterdam and Holland.

Transport
Air: Amsterdam Airport Schiphol. **Rail:** Train: Amsterdam Centraal Station. **Road:** Bus: Public services.

• June

Holland Festival

The *Holland Festival* takes place in Amsterdam every June and focuses on the performing arts, including opera, theatre, music and dance. The festival has grown each year and now attracts well over 100,000 visitors, with more than 50,000 attending the popular *Amsterdam Roots Festival* in the city. The festival includes numerous performances by groups from all around the world.

Event Organiser
Stichting Holland Festival, Kleine Gartmanplantsoen 21, 1017 RP, Amsterdam, The Netherlands
Tel: (020) 530 7110
Website: www.hollandfestival.nl

Venue
Across Amsterdam, in various theatres and concert halls, including the Paradiso, Theater Bellevue and the festival centre, Stadsschouwburg. There are also events around Leidesplein.

Transport
Air: Amsterdam Airport Schiphol. **Rail:** Train: Amsterdam Centraal Station. **Road:** Bus: Public services.

• August

Amsterdam Gay Pride

Amsterdam Gay Pride is one of Europe's largest gay and lesbian events and takes place in the city in the middle of summer. There is an enormous *Canal Parade*, when the city's gay and lesbian community takes to the canals in boats, wearing fancy dress and playing music. There are also numerous sport and cultural events throughout the city, as well as huge weekend parties. As well as the parade itself and the numerous parties and club nights, sports and film events also play a key part of the celebrations.

Event Organiser
Siep de Haan, Lange Niezel 7, Amsterdam, NH 1012 GS, The Netherlands
Tel: (020) 620 8807
Website: www.amsterdamgaypride.nl

Venue
Various locations across Amsterdam city centre, including festivities on the canals.

Transport
Air: Amsterdam Airport Schiphol. **Rail:** Train: Amsterdam Centraal Station. **Road:** Bus: Public services.

New Zealand

Auckland

Tourist Information

Tourism Auckland
PO Box 5561, Wellesley Street, Auckland, New Zealand
Tel: (09) 979 7070
Website: www.aucklandnz.com

• April

Royal Easter Show

The first *Royal Easter Show* was held in 1843 by the newly-formed Auckland Agricultural and Horticultural Society to promote the advantages the town could offer to prospective settlers. It has grown from its origins as a small livestock show to incorporate sporting events, family entertainment, animal shows and commercial exhibits, attracting thousands of visitors throughout the 10 days. There are equine events such as showjumping and dressage, displays of rare sheep breeds, a 'New Zealand's Strongest Man' competition, junior sporting championships including basketball and karate, craft demonstrations and exhibits featuring ceramics, photography, Chinese art and painting by mouth and foot. Various stalls are situated in the Commercial Exhibit Halls, and feature food and wine, home improvements and information and technology. Musicians, acrobats and theatre groups travel from as far afield as England to entertain the crowds, and there is also a special children's theatre, a children's art workshop and the opportunity for visitors to try their hand at milking cattle or shearing sheep.

Event Organiser
Auckland Show Grounds, PO Box 26014 Auckland, New Zealand
Tel: (09) 623 7724
Website: www.royaleastershow.co.nz

Venue
Auckland Showgrounds.

Transport
Air: Auckland International Airport. **Rail:** Train: Auckland Station. **Road:** Bus: Public services.

• November

Ellerslie Flower Show

Every summer, Auckland's 64-hectare (160-acre) *Regional Botanic Gardens* host the largest gardening and outdoor show in the Southern

Hemisphere, the *Ellerslie Flower Show*. Some 65,000 visitors come from New Zealand and around the world to enjoy floral displays, plant stalls, fruit and vegetable markets, musical concerts, food and drink and garden sculptures by top New Zealand artists, situated around the lake. Gardening enthusiasts can pick up tips from lectures and demonstrations and, on the last Sunday, materials used in the exhibits, such as paving stones and exotic flowers, are sold off to the public.

Event Organiser
Ellerslie Flower Show, PO Box 11340, Ellerslie, Auckland, New Zealand
Tel: (09) 579 6260
Website: www.ellerslieflowershow.co.nz

Venue
Auckland Regional Botanic Gardens.

Transport
Air: Auckland International Airport. **Rail:** Train: Auckland Station. **Road:** Bus: Public services.

Norway

Bergen

Tourist Information
Bergen Tourist Information
(Turistinformasjonen)
Slottsgaten 1, 2nd Floor, 5835 Bergen, Norway
Tel: (055) 552 010
Website: www.visitbergen.com

• May-June

Bergen International Festival

Bergen International Festival features numerous music, ballet and theatre performances and is the largest event of its kind in Norway and one of the premier international performing arts festivals in Europe. The festival's extensive music programme focuses primarily on Norwegian music. Over the 12 days of the festival there are close to 200 individual performances.

Event Organiser
Bergen International Festival, Box 183 Sentrum, 5084 Bergen, Norway
Tel: (055) 210 630
Website: www.fib.no

Venue
Various venues in the Bergen area, including the Grieg Hall, the Hakon Hall, the Masonic Lodge and the houses of three local composers: Edvard Grieg, Ole Bull and Harald Sæverud.

Transport
Air: Bergen Airport. **Rail:** Train: Bergen Station. **Road:** Car: E16 (from Voss); E18, E16 and E39 (from Oslo). Bus: Public services.

Bergen Night Jazz Festival

Bergen Night Jazz Festival (known as *Nattjazz* in Norway) takes place every year and is one of the longest jazz festivals in Northern Europe which lasts for almost two weeks. The festival plays host to a wide range of performances, ranging from traditional jazz to world music, rock, folk, bebop, hard pop, jazz rock, fusion and funk. The majority of events take place in venues at the *Kulturhuset USF* (*United Sardines Factory*), which can hold approximately 1600 people; they include Røkeriet USF, Sardinen USF and Scene USF. Previous artists have included John Scofield Quartet, Cesaria Evora, Kari Bremnes, Gli Impossibli and Anneli Drecker.

Event Organiser
Natt Jazz, PO Box 1957, Nordnes 5817 Bergen, Norway
Tel: (055) 307 250
Website: www.nattjazz.no

Venue
Held in an area reserved for the festival, as well as at other venues in the city. The festival area is an old sardines factory, called Kulturhuset USF, which is now used for concerts, exhibitions, theatre and cinema.

Transport
Air: Bergen Airport. **Rail:** Train: Bergen Station. **Road:** On foot: Kulturhuset USF is located on Sergels torg square in the centre of the city and can be reached easily on foot from the city centre. Bus: Public services.

Peru

Lima

Tourist Information
PromPeru
Edificio Mitince, Calle 1, 13th and 14th Floor, San Isidro, Lima 27, Peru
Tel: (01) 224 3131
Website: www.peru.info

• October

Lord of Miracles

The Lord of Miracles festival is the most important cultural event in Lima's calendar and the largest religious procession in the Americas. Hundreds of purple-clad worshippers carry an image of a black Christ through the city's streets every day during the festival to the sound of chanting and church bells. The image has hung in Lima's Church and Convent of the Nazarenes since it was painted in 1665. It is known as Neustro Señor de los Milagros (Our Lord of Miracles) since it survived several earthquakes remarkably intact. Concerts and firework displays also form part of the celebrations, which are followed throughout November by Lima's bullfighting season at Plaza de Acho, the oldest arena in the Americas dating back over 200 years.

Event Organiser
For more information on the Lord of Miracles, contact PromPeru (see **Tourist Information** above).

Venue
Various locations across Lima.

Transport
Air: Jorge Chavez International Airport (Lima). Road: Car: Pan-American Highway (from Arequipa, Trujillo, Talara or coastal cities in Chile and Ecuador).

Poland

Krakow

Tourist Information

Tourist Information Centre (Centrum Informacji Turystycznej)
ulica Pawia 8, 31-154 Krakow, Poland
Tel: (012) 422 6091
Website: www.krakow.pl

• December-February

Krakow Christmas Crib Contest

The szopki (nativity crib) is very much a part of the Polish Christmas tradition. The first ever crib was made by Jan Velita in Italy on the instruction of St Francis of Assisi three years before his death in 1225. From its simple origins, the idea was taken up by the rich merchants and noblemen who commissioned artists to create ever more elaborate versions. Krakow cribs, which can be up to 1.8m

(6ft) tall, maintain this tradition and are modelled on local buildings with their Gothic towers, Baroque onion domes and Renaissance façades. The city's first crib contest was held in 1937 and the event is organised annually by the Krakow Ethnography Museum. All entries, made by both professional craftsmen and amateurs, are put on show at the Adam Mickiewicz Monument in the Old Market for several days, and are then taken to the Ethnography Museum where they are judged; the prizewinners are announced in early December. The most exquisite and beautifully crafted cribs are then displayed in the museum for the next two months.

Event Organiser
Museum of History (Muzeum Historyczne), Rynek Gýówny 35, Krakow, Poland
Tel: (012) 422 9922

Venue
Plac Wolnica (Wolnica Square) and Muzeum Etnograficzne (Museum of Ethnography).

Transport
Air: Krakow-Balice John Paul II International Airport. Rail: Train: Krakow Station. Tram: 10 (from Main Market Square). Road: Bus: Public services.

• June-July

Jewish Culture Festival

For centuries the Kazimierz district of Krakow provided a haven for persecuted Jews in Europe. Professional, middle-class Jews contributed a lot to Polish cultural life, particularly in the fields of music and literature, and Jews were free to worship and set up their own organisations and societies. Steven Spielberg's film 'Schindler's List' famously depicts the destruction of Kazimierz during World War II, when Jewish businesses and institutions were razed to the ground and the Jews were deported from the ghetto to the concentration camps, where they were tortured and murdered. Kazimierz is once again a thriving centre for Jewish culture, and the Jewish Culture Festival has grown to become an internationally-recognised event. The streets, theatres and synagogues of Krakow host a range of events including film, dance, theatre, the visual arts, lectures and music, with the Jerusalem Jazz band, the Klezmatics and Double Edge Theatre all having performed at the festival in the past. Workshops enable visitors to learn about Jewish traditions such as paper cutting, Hebrew calligraphy, dance and cookery; the workshops are led by instructors who earn a living from such skills. This is a particularly poignant and triumphal celebration of Jewish culture and a chance for visitors to Krakow to learn more about the rich heritage of this remarkable people.

Event Organiser
Jewish Culture Festival Society, 36 Józefa Street, 31-056 Kraków, Poland
Tel: (012) 431 1517
Website: www.jewishfestival.pl

Venue
Various locations across Kazimierz.

Transport
Air: Krakow-Balice John Paul II International Airport. **Rail:** Train: Krakow Station. Tram: 13, 19 or 10 (from Krakow Station or Main Market Square). **Road:** Bus: Public services.

• July

Krakow International Street Theatre Festival

Krakow's main market square, *Rynek Glówny*, is the biggest Medieval square in Europe and every July it is the venue for the city's street theatre festival. Theatre groups from around Europe entertain the crowds each evening against the backdrop of period houses and pavement cafés. The programme for 2001 included shows from France, Poland and Ukraine, with several experimental theatre groups taking part. Performances take place between 1800 and 2200 each day.

Event Organiser
KTO Theatre, ulica Gzymsikow 8, 30-015 Krakow, Poland
Tel: (012) 623 7300
Website: www.teatrkto.pl

Venue
Rynek Glówny in Krakow's Old Town.

Transport
Air: Krakow-Balice John Paul II International Airport. **Rail:** Train: Krakow Station. Tram: 10 (from Krakow Station). **Road:** Bus: Public services.

Warsaw

Tourist Information
Tourist Information Centre
(Centrum Informacji Turystycznej)
Aleja Jerezolimsie 54, Warsaw, Poland
Tel: (022) 635 1881
Website: www.warsawtour.pl

• June-July

Warsaw Mozart Festival

Warsaw Mozart Festival began in 1991, when all 24 of the great composer's stage pieces were performed, and is the largest festival of its kind in the world. Mozart enthusiasts are able to hear oratorio, chamber, symphony and stage pieces in the Warsaw Chamber Opera Theatre. Mozart's connections with Warsaw date back to 1783, when 'Die Entführung aus dem Serail' ('Abduction from the Seraglio') was performed by the German theatre troupe Gottlieb Lorenz.

Event Organiser
Warsaw Chamber Opera, Aleja Solidarnosci 76B, Warsaw, Poland
Tel: (022) 831 2240 *or* 621 9383
Website: www.wok.pol.pl

Venue
Warsaw Chamber Opera Theatre, Solidarnosci Avenue (near Bankowy Square).

Transport
Air: Warsaw (Okecie) International Airport. **Rail:** Train: Warsaw Central Station. Tram: 17, 29 or 33. **Road:** Bus: Public services.

Portugal

Lisbon

Tourist Information
Lisbon Tourist Association
(Associação Turismo de Lisboa)
15 Rua do Arsenal, 1100-038 Lisbon, Portugal
Tel: (021) 312 700
Website: www.atl-turismolisboa.pt

• February

Lisbon Carnival

Carnival signals the end of winter and the beginning of Lent and is celebrated in Lisbon with colourful costume parades and copious amounts of food and drink. In recent years, the Portuguese festivities have taken on a Latin American flavour and many Brazilian TV stars cross the Atlantic to join in the fun. One of the best places to go to watch the celebrations is the *Parque das Naçoes*.

Event Organiser
Lisbon City Council (Câmara Municipal de Lisboa), Paços do Concelho, Praça do Município, 1100-365 Lisbon, Portugal

Tel: (021) 322 7000
Website: www.cm-lisboa.pt

Venue
Parque das Naçoes and across various locations across Lisbon.

Transport
Air: Lisbon International Airport. **Rail:** Train: Santa Apolónia, Rossio, Barreiro or Cais do Sodré stations. Tram: Estação do Oriente. **Road:** Bus: Public services.

• April

Lisbon Half Marathon

The *Lisbon Half Marathon* is watched with particular interest by those in the athletic field as it determines the world's top long distance runners before the major marathons in Boston and London later in the month. The overall race winner takes home over US$100,000 in prize money. There is a party atmosphere in the streets, with live music and entertainment. In addition, free ice cream and gifts are provided by the race sponsors at the finish line.

Event Organiser
Maratona Clube de Portugal, Bàrro Francisco Sà Caraeiro, Av. João Freitas Branco 10, Caxias, 2780 Paço de Arcos, Portugal
Tel: (021) 441 3182
Website: www.lisbon-half-marathon.com

Venue
Starts at the 25 April suspension bridge across the River Tejo and finishes at the Mosteiro dos Jeronemos in Belém via the city centre.

Transport
Air: Lisbon International Airport. **Rail:** Train: Santa Apolónia, Rossio, Barreiro or Cais do Sodré stations. Tram: 15 or 17 (to Belém). Underground: Belém. **Road:** Bus: Public services.

• June

Lisbon Festivities

Lisbon celebrates its patron saint (St Anthony) in a three-week spectacular of street parties, fireworks and entertainment known as the *Festas de Lisboa* in Portuguese. The *Marchas Populares* in mid-June are a chance to see thousands of people from the different neighbourhoods of the city march down the Avenida da Liberdade, displaying colourful costumes and banners that have taken many months to create. The festivities continue long into the night, with music, dancing and sardine barbecues. The best place to go to join one of these parties, or *arraiais*, is the *Alfama* district of the city. Throughout the whole three-week period, both visitors and locals can enjoy theatre, circus, mime and all kinds of music, from pop and ethnic to classical and jazz, in Lisbon's many squares.

Event Organiser
Empresa de Gestão de Equipamentos e Animação Cultural, Palácio Marquês de Tancos, Calçada Marquês de Tancos, 1100-340 Lisbon, Portugal
Tel: (021) 882 0090
Website: www.egeac.pt

Venue
Alfama district and various locations across Lisbon.

Transport
Air: Lisbon International Airport. **Rail:** Train: Santa Apolónia, Rossio, Barreiro or Cais do Sodré stations. **Road:** Bus: Public services.

• December

Magic Night

Magic Night (*Noite Mágica* in Portuguese) aims to create a New Year's Eve party with a difference. There is a 10-minute firework display over the *River Tejo*, which is choreographed to a specially-created musical soundtrack featuring Portuguese bands past and present. Once the show is over, there is a Latin American disco and live music that continues long into the early hours of New Year's Day. Many hotels in Lisbon also organise their own events featuring food, wine and live entertainment. The *Casino Estoril* (Estoril Casino), located 18km (11 miles) outside Lisbon, hosts various shows and an outdoor party.

Event Organiser
Lisbon City Council (Câmara Municipal de Lisboa), Paços do Concelho, Praça do Município, 1100-365 Lisbon, Portugal
Tel: (021) 322 7000
Website: www.cm-lisboa.pt

Venue
Along the River Tejo between Parque das Nações and the district of Algés.

Transport
Air: Lisbon International Airport. **Rail:** Train: Santa Apolónia, Rossio, Barreiro or Cais do Sodré stations. Tram: 15 or 17. Underground: Belém. **Road:** Bus: Public services.

Russian Federation

Moscow

Tourist Information

Ministry of Tourism (Ministerstvo Turisma)
18 ul. Kazakova, 103064 Moscow, Russian
Federation
Tel: (095) 207 7117 *or* 207 3891
Website: www.rossport.ru

• December-January

New Year

On December 31 every year, revellers party in the
streets of Moscow to see in the *New Year*.
Traditionally Moscovites used to celebrate New
Year's Eve (which is known as *Noivy God* in
Russian) at home before taking to the streets after
midnight to visit friends and neighbours and drink
vast amounts of alcohol until the early hours.
Increasingly, more and more people gather in Red
Square to hear the stroke of midnight from the
Kremlin, and to drink champagne in the city
centre. Many people also dress in fancy dress,
either as 'Grandfather Frost' or the 'Snow Maiden',
as they go about the city wishing a happy new
year to fellow revellers.

Event Organiser

For more information on New Year, contact the
Ministry of Tourism (see **Tourist Information**
above).

Venue

Red Square and across the city.

Transport

Air: Moscow Sheremetyevo International Airport.
Rail: Train: Kiev Station. Underground: Kitay-
Gorod. **Road:** Bus: Public services.

• September

Moscow International Peace Marathon

The annual *International Peace Marathon* takes
place in September on the streets of Moscow,
starting at 1100 at Red Square in front of St
Basil's Cathedral. The course runs along the
Moscow River, past many of the city's finest
historic monuments, including the Kremlin, the
Cathedral of Christ the Saviour and the Peter the
Great Monument in Gorky Park. The event
finishes in front of the Rossya Hotel, near St
Basil's Cathedral. On the day before the
marathon, there is a *Marathon Expo* conference
for runners and a lottery draw. In the evening,
there is a pasta party at the Golden Hill
restaurant in the Rossya Hotel, with musical
performances from folk bands.

Event Organiser

For more information on Moscow International
Peace Marathon, contact the Ministry of Tourism
(see **Tourist Information** above).

Venue

Starts at Red Square through the streets of
Moscow, and finishes at the Rossya Hotel, near St
Basil's Cathedral.

Transport

Air: Moscow Sheremetyevo International Airport.
Rail: Train: Kiev Station. Underground: Kitay-
Gorod. **Road:** Bus: Public services.

Singapore

Singapore

Tourist Information

Singapore Tourism Board
Tourism Court, 1 Orchard Spring Lane, Singapore
247729
Tel: (65) 736 6622
Website: www.visitsingapore.com

• March-April

Singapore Food Festival

First held in 1994, *Singapore Food Festival* is a
giant culinary event that allows visitors to taste
food from around the world. During the month-
long event, visitors can sample culinary delights
from as far afield as Italy, Turkey and Japan, as
well as taste the best of Chinese and Asian cuisine.
They can also take part in food tours and wander
through the streets of Singapore, which are filled
with the aromatic smells of different dishes. The
festival usually kicks off with a three-day opening
celebration which is a carnival of food and
entertainment, featuring live music, as well as
food and drink from around the world.

Event Organiser

Singapore Tourism Board, Events Marketing
Division, Tourism Court, 1 Orchard Spring Lane,
Singapore 247729
Tel: (65) 6780 4681
Website: www.singaporefoodfestival.com.sg

Venue

Various locations across Singapore.

Transport
Air: Singapore Changi Airport. **Rail:** Train: Singapore Station. **Road:** Bus: Public services.

• April

Singapore International Film Festival

Singapore International Film Festival is one of the most important celebrations of Asian cinema in the world, with more than 300 films from over 45 countries shown in Singapore during the event. The festival was first held in 1987 to allow film enthusiasts to view films which would not normally be given a mainstream release. The festival also awards Silver Screen Awards which were introduced in 1991 and are given to the best Asian film, as well as to the best actor, actress and director.

Event Organiser
Film Festival Pte Ltd, 45A Keong Saik Road, Singapore 089149
Fax: 6738 7578
Website: www.filmfest.org.sg

Venue
Golden Village (GV) cinemas in the city, such as Golden Village Grand, as well as the Goethe Institut and Alliance Française de Singapour.

Transport
Air: Singapore Changi Airport. **Rail:** Train: Singapore Station. **Road:** Bus: Public services.

South Africa

Cape Town

Tourist Information

Cape Town Tourism
103 Louis Building, 4 Regent Road, Sea Point, Cape Town, South Africa
Tel: (021) 434 1750
Website: www.cape-town.org

• May

Cape Gourmet Festival

Every May, Cape Town plays host to two weeks of events celebrating the indulgent world of food and wine. The central focus is the Good Food and Wine Show on the last weekend of the festival, with culinary demonstrations and masterclasses, wine-tasting sessions, stalls selling olive oil, cheeses and local wines and appearances by celebrity chefs. Chefs come from around the world to exchange ideas and prepare gastronomic delights in the city's restaurants, and a whole host of hotels and eating establishments organize their own special menus and events, from international food-tasting evenings to jazz concerts.

Event Organiser
Cape Gourmet Festival, 50 Tennant Road, Kenilworth, Cape Town 8001, South Africa
Tel: (021) 797 4500
Website: www.gourmetsa.com

Venue
Good Hope Centre (Good Food and Wine Show) and various venues across Cape Town.

Transport
Air: Cape Town International Airport. **Rail:** Train: Cape Town Station. **Road:** Bus: Public services.

Johannesburg

Tourist Information

Tourism Johannesburg
Upper Shopping Level, Village Walk Shopping Centre, corner of Rivonia Road and Maud Street, Rosebank, Johannesburg, South Africa
Tel: (011) 784 1354
Website: www.joburg.org.za

• April-May

Rand Easter Show

The **Rand Easter Show** is one of the biggest exhibitions in Southern Africa, attracting around half a million visitors each year. The show has developed from its origins as an agricultural event in 1894, when it was hosted by Witwatersrand Agricultural Society, to become a giant consumer fair and entertainment show. As well as merchandise on display from almost 600 South African exhibitors and over 100 foreign exhibitors from nine different countries, the show also features live music, as well as sporting events and an amusement park.

Event Organiser
Kagiso Exhibitions Pty Ltd, Private Bag X 383, Cresta, 2118, South Africa
Tel: (011) 661 4000
Website: www.randshow.co.za

Venue
Expo Centre, which is located in the Nasrec area of Johannesburg.

Transport
Air: Johannesburg International Airport. **Rail:** Train: Trains stop at the grounds (from Park Station). **Road:** Bus: Public services.

Spain

Barcelona

Tourist Information

Barcelona Tourist Office (Turisme de Barcelona)
Plaça de Catalunya 17-S, 08008 Barcelona
Tel: (093) 368 9740
Website: www.bcn.es

• January

Three Kings Parade

The story of the Three Kings is recorded in the Bible, in St Matthew's Gospel, and tells of three wise men who travelled from the east to Bethlehem to present gifts of gold, frankincense and myrrh to the infant Jesus. Epiphany, as Twelfth Night (January 5) is known in the Christian church, commemorates the journey of the Three Kings and is widely celebrated throughout Europe. At the end of each year, Catalan children post their wish lists to the Three Kings in special boxes in stores around Barcelona. On the night of January 5, they then place a shoe on the balcony of their house for the Three Kings to fill with sweets, as well as a bucket of water and food for the camels. Every January 5, for the *Cabalgata de los Reyes Magos*, or *Three Kings Parade*, the Three Kings arrive at the harbour at *Moll de Fusta* with their entourage and sacks full of presents, and are greeted by city officials and excited children before going about their annual duties. The kings arrive at 1800 in the harbour and it is advisable to arrive as early as possible to get the best view.

Event Organiser

For more information on the Three Kings Parade, contact Barcelona Tourist Office (see **Tourist Information** above).

Venue

The stalls are mainly located along Gran Vía; the Three Kings arrive at the harbour.

Transport

Air: Barcelona Airport. **Rail:** Train: Central-Sants Station. **Underground:** Tetuan or Monumental (to Gran Vía); Drassanes or Barceloneta (to harbour). **Road:** Bus: Public services.

• June-July

Barcelona Summer Festival (GREC)

The *Teatre Grec* amphitheatre, built into the

mountainside at *Montjuic*, is the birthplace of the *Barcelona Summer Festival* (popularly known as GREC), which started when a group of disillusioned actors and directors got together to produce a small fringe theatre festival in 1976. It has since grown to become the biggest and most popular festival in Barcelona. Every summer for around six weeks, tourists and locals are treated to a huge variety of events, from theatre, dance and cinema to classical music, rock and circus. The venues are just as varied, with Gothic chapels, vast modern theatres and concert halls all hosting events. At the open-air *Picornell* swimming pool it is even possible to watch a film whilst relaxing in the water.

Event Organiser

For more information on the Barcelona Summer Festival, contact Barcelona Tourist Office (see **Tourist Information** above).

Venue

Various venues across Barcelona (for further information, contac the Spanish Tourist Office (see **Tourist Information** above).

Transport

Air: Barcelona International Airport. **Rail:** Train: Central-Sants Station. **Road:** Bus: Public services.

• September

Our Lady of Mercy Festival

According to legend, *La Mercé* (Our Lady of Mercy, or the Virgin Mary) once saved Barcelona from a plague of locusts, and thus became the patron saint of the city. A wide range of activities takes place during the festival, such as musical concerts and theatre performances in outdoor theatres, food and wine fairs, and sports activities. The main events are a huge fireworks display, the *Dance of the Giants* and the *Correfac*, when demons, dragons and other devilish creatures run amock through the streets of the city's old quarter, throwing firecrackers.

Event Organiser

For more information on the Our Lady of Mercy Festival, contact Barcelona Tourist Office (see **Tourist Information** above).

Venue

Various locations across Barcelona.

Transport

Air: Barcelona Airport. **Rail:** Train: Central-Sants Station. **Road:** Bus: Public services.

Madrid

Tourist Information

City Tourist Office (Oficina Municipal de Turismo)
Plaza Mayor 3, 28012 Madrid, Spain
Tel: (091) 588 2900
Website: www.esmadrid.com

• February

Madrid Carnival

In February each year, before the beginning of Lent, a week of festivities brightens up the streets of the Spanish capital as the centuries old tradition of *Carnaval* (Carnival) comes to town. There is a procession of carriages and a costumed parade through the streets of Madrid with a fancy dress competition adding to the fun. The party ends with a peculiar ritual known as *El Entierro de la Sardina* (the Burial of the Sardine). This ritual involves people in black cloaks and top hats following a coffin that contains an effigy of a sardine, which is then buried at the 18th-century hermitage of *San Antonio de la Florida* near the city centre. However, the mood is not entirely sombre as the procession stops at *tavernas* on the way for a drink or two.

Event Organiser

For more information on the Madrid Carnival, contact the City Tourist Office (see **Tourist Information** above).

Venue

Calle de Cádiz, San Antonio de Florida and various locations across Madrid.

Transport

Air: Madrid Barajas Airport. **Rail:** Train: Chamartín or Atocha stations. **Road:** Bus: Public services.

• May

Festimad Alternative Music Festival

Visitors to *Festimad* can catch the latest in the alternative music scene in a beautiful 350 sq metres (325 sq ft) of parkland. The two days of events that have been held each summer since 1995 attract over 20,000 spectators who come to be entertained by a whole host of rock and indie bands, DJs and other performers. Concerts in the past have featured groups such as Metallica, Marilyn Manson and the Black Crowes. The site is turned into a music village with facilities including bars, restaurants, a supermarket and showers for those who wish to camp.

Event Organiser

Festimad, Gran Vía 68, 5E 28013 Madrid, Spain
Tel: (091) 547 2385
Website: www.festimad.es

Venue

El Soto de Móstoles, which is located 20km (12.4 miles) from central Madrid.

Transport

Air: Madrid Barajas Airport. **Rail:** Train: Chamartín or Atocha stations. Underground: El Soto (the festival site can then be accessed on foot). **Road:** Bus: Public services.

• May-June

San Isidro Festival

San Isidro is the patron saint of Madrid and every year, from mid-May to mid-June, festivities known as the *Fiestas de San Isidro* in Spanish, take place throughout the city. According to tradition, all those from Madrid must make a pilgrimage to the shrine on the banks of the River Manzanares on the spot where the saint is said to have miraculously caused a spring to open up from the ground. Traditional dress is worn and specialities such as *barquillos* (rolled wafers), *buñuelos* (fritters) and *rosquillas* (doughnuts) are sold throughout the city. The famous *taurina* (bullfighting fair) is part of the Fiestas and fights take place every day at the historic *Plaza Monumental Las Ventas* bull ring.

Event Organiser

Plaza Monumental Las Ventas, Calle Acalá 237, 28028 Madrid, Spain
Tel: (091) 356 2200
Website: www.las-ventas.com

Venue

Various locations across Madrid.

Transport

Air: Madrid Barajas Airport. **Rail:** Train: Chamartín or Atocha stations. Underground: Ventas (to Plaza Monumental Las Ventas). **Road:** Bus: Public services.

• October-November

Madrid Autumn Festival

This festival brings a huge variety of cultural performances to Madrid and encompasses theatre, jazz, musical theatre, dance, literature and art. Groups come from as far afield as Cuba, India and the USA to take part, and the festival offers a welcome diversion for *Madrileños* and visitors alike as the nights grow darker and the weather colder.

Event Organiser
For more information on the Madrid Autumn Festival, contact City Tourist Office (see **Tourist Information** above).

Venue
Various locations across Madrid.

Transport
Air: Madrid Barajas Airport. **Rail:** Train: Chamartín or Atocha stations. **Road:** Bus: Public services.

Pamplona

Tourist Information
Navarra Tourist Office
Servicio de Turismo Gobierno de Navarra, Edificio Fuerte del Principe 2, 4a Planta, Plaza Tomás Caballero 1, 31005 Pamplona, Spain
Tel: (948) 20 70 35
Website: www.navarra.es

• July

The Running of the Bulls (San Fermin Festival)
Made famous by Ernest Hemingway who wrote about the Running of the Bulls in his cult 1926 novel, 'Fiesta: The Sun Also Rises', the event is a central part of the nine-day *San Fermin Festival* that's celebrated each July in Pamplona. The festival begins on July 6 and ends on July 14 each year with the traditional bull run taking place at 0800 each day from the second day onwards. The city of Pamplona is packed out to celebrate the festival of St Fermin, the town's patron. Locals and visitors alike take to the streets to run with the bulls dressed in the traditional white clothing with red neckerchiefs. Copious amounts of alcohol are consumed during the festival and parties usually continue late into the night. Fatal gorings have happened in the past and the very real danger involved in the run is not to be taken lightly. In 2005, the town's authorities coated the streets in a non-slip paint to try and minimise the risk of serious injury to the thousands of revellers who flock here to take part in the festival each year.

Event Organiser
For more information about the Running of the Bulls, contact the Navarra Tourist Office (see **Tourist Information** above).

Venue
San Fermin.

Transport
Air: Bilbao Airport. **Water:** Ferry: Bilbao Port. **Rail:** Train: Pamplona Station. **Road:** Bus: Public services.

Sweden

Stockholm

Tourist Information
Stockholm Information Service
Hamngatan 27, Kungsträdgården, 10327 Stockholm, Sweden
Tel: (08) 508 28508
Website: www.stockholmtown.com

• June

Swedish National Day
Every year on June 6, Skansen Open-air Museum in the heart of Stockholm hosts the *Swedish National Day* celebrations. The event is attended by the Swedish Royal family: King Carl XVI Gustaf, Queen Silvia, Crown Princess Victoria, Prince Carl Philip and Princess Madeleine. King Carl XVI Gustaf is the 74th King of Sweden who came to the throne in 1973. On this patriotic day, when Swedes remember their heritage, highlights include songs, speeches and flag-waving. The festivities are transmitted live on Swedish national television, allowing an even wider audience to see the day's events.

Event Organiser
Stiftelsen Skansen, Post Box 27807, 115 93 Stockholm, Sweden
Tel: (08) 442 8000
Website: www.skansen.se

Venue
Skansen Open-air Museum in Stockholm city centre.

Transport
Air: Stockholm Arlanda Airport. **Rail:** Train: Stockholm Central Station. Tram: From Norrmalmstorg to Skansen. **Road:** Bus: Public services.

• September

Stockholm Beer & Whisky Festival

The annual *Stockholm Beer & Whisky Festival* takes place in Stockholm in September. The festival, which began in 1992, is the leading festival for beer, cider and whisky in Scandinavia. Approximately 500 different varieties of beer are available for the public to sample and vote for in an awards ceremony, with a further 100 varieties of whisky and cider also on offer. Every year, more than 150,000 visitors attend the festival to taste different varieties of beer, whisky and cider. Highlights of the event include beer tastings, tutorings and the annual beer awards. Awards are given to the best fresh beer, best blond lager, best porter, best ale and best Swedish beer.

Event Organiser
Stockholm Öl & Vin AB, Karlavägen 75B, 114 49 Stockholm, Sweden
Tel: (08) 662 9494
Website: www.stockholmbeer.se

Venue
Nacka Strand in Stockholm.

Transport
Air: Stockholm Arlanda Airport. **Road:** Bus: Public services.

• November

Stockholm International Film Festival

The *Stockholm International Film Festival*, which is one of the most important film festivals in Northern Europe, takes place in the city each November. The festival, which was set up in 1990 by two Swedish film enthusiasts, is attended by more than 70,000 people every year who view some 150 films on offer. Many entries are received from directors making their first, second or third film, as well as from directors of short films. The festival also focuses on different regions and screens films ranging from American independent films through to Asian cinema. Many famous names have attended the festival in previous years, including Dennis Hopper and Quentin Tarrantino.

Event Organiser
Stockholm International Film Festival, PO Box 3136, 103 62 Stockholm, Sweden
Tel: (08) 677 5000
Website: www.filmfestivalen.se

Venue
Various cinemas in Stockholm.

Transport
Air: Stockholm Arlanda Airport. **Rail:** Train: Stockholm Central Station. **Road:** Bus: Public services.

Switzerland

Geneva

Tourist Information
Geneva Tourism (Genève Tourisme)
Rue du Mont-Blanc 18, PO Box 1602, 1211 Geneva 1, Switzerland
Tel: (022) 909 7070
Website: www.geneva-tourism.ch

• March

International Motor Show

The *International Motor Show* takes place in Geneva every March. Over 700,000 visitors attend the annual event which first began in 1930. Leading car manufacturers, including BMW, Audi, Ferrari, Ford, Jaguar, Mercedes-Benz and Porsche, are all present at the fair, eager to show off their new cars to the world. Around 900 makes of car are exhibited, from over 35 different countries, by 275 exhibitors. Cars are exhibited in numerous sectors, which include cars, fun cars, converted cars, special bodywork, equipment, accessories and components for cars, garage equipment and electric vehicles.

Event Organiser
ORGEXPO, Foundation for the promotion and organization of exhibitions and conferences – PO Box 112, 1218 Grand-Saconnex, Geneva, Switzerland
Tel: (022) 761 1111
Website: www.salon-auto.ch

Venue
PalExpo Exhibition Centre in Geneva.

Transport
Air: Geneva International Airport. **Rail:** Train: Cornavin Station to Geneva Airport Station, which is 300m (328 yards) from PalExpo Hall 7. **Road:** Bus: Special buses run from Geneva city centre during the exhibition.

• July-August

Geneva Festival

The *Geneva Festival* begins at the end of July and is one of Switzerland's biggest parties, with street parades, floats, techno parties and theatre performances. There are also various performances by folk groups and live concerts featuring international stars, as well as numerous operatic shows. Children are kept entertained by a giant clown parade, as well as a funfair on children's day at the end of July. Food from around the world is also on sale at street stalls during the festivities. More than 1,500,000 visitors attend the annual festivities and join the great outdoor party which also includes spectacular firework displays over Lake Geneva.

Event Organiser

For more information on the Geneva Festival, contact Geneva Tourism (see **Tourist Information** above).

Venue

In and around Geneva harbour, Parc des Eaux-Vives, Théatre de Verdure and Grand Casino de Genève.

Transport

Air: Geneva International Airport. **Rail:** Train: Cornavin Station. **Road:** Car: N1 (from Lausanne).

• August

Swiss National Day

Swiss National Day takes place on August 1 every year to celebrate the union of three former Swiss states, Uri, Schwyz and Unterwalden on this date in 1921. Every year, Geneva holds celebrations, which include fireworks at the *Mur des Réformateurs*, a traditional bonfire and dancing after dark in the streets. On this day, which has been a national holiday since 1993, the Swiss drink large amounts of wine and eat local sausages cooked on barbecues. There are also plenty of speeches and a rendition of the national anthem. Other celebrations take place at the *Parc des Bastions* in Geneva's Old Town. In villages throughout Switzerland, the locals also join in the festivities to celebrate their national day, with children lighting coloured lanterns and parents dancing around the bonfire.

Event Organiser

For more information on Swiss National Day, contact Geneva Tourism (see **Tourist Information** above).

Venue

Mur des Réformateurs and the Parc des Bastions in Geneva. Celebrations also take place across Switzerland.

Transport

Air: Geneva International Airport. **Rail:** Train: Cornavin Station. **Underground:** Place Neuve Station. **Road:** Bus: Public services.

Tourist Information

Zurich Tourist Office (Zürich Tourismus)
Bahnhofbrücke 1, 8023 Zurich, Switzerland
Tel: (01) 215 4000
Website: www.zuerich.com

• April

Zurich Spring Festival

Zurich Spring Festival, which is known locally as *Sechseläuten*, celebrates the end of the cold winter weather and the start of spring. The festival begins with a children's parade on April 22, with more than 2000 children taking part. This is followed by the main events on April 23, when members of various guilds (or societies) eat a midday meal at their respective Guildhouses, before taking part in the *Parade of the Guilds* at 1515. Thousands of spectators line the streets of the city's Old Town to watch more than 7000 participants parade through the city. The highlight of the festival, the *Burning of the Böögg*, begins on the stroke of 1800 on April 23. At the moment the bells of St Peter signal an end to winter in the city, a giant Böögg bonfire (in the shape of a snowman, representing the figure, Old Man Winter) is lit on Sechseläuten Field.

Event Organiser

Zentralkomitee der Zünfte, Herr Pit Wyss, Gumpenwiesenstrasse 13, 8157 Dielsdorf, Switzerland
Tel: (01) 853 1777
Website: www.sechselaeuten.ch

Venue

Sechseläutenwiese (Sechseläuten field) at Bellevue.

Transport

Air: Zurich Airport. **Rail:** Tram: Opernhaus or Bellevue Tram to Sechseläutenwiese, which is in front of Zurich's opera house. **Road:** Car: A1 (from Geneva).

• June-July

Zurich Festival

Every summer, Zurich's three main arts institutions – the *Opera*, the *Tonhalle* (concert hall) and the *Kunsthalle* (art gallery) – join forces to transform the city into a hive of cultural activity, with high-quality performances of opera, jazz, classical music, theatre, cinema and ballet, alongside exhibitions of art and literature. The main events are staged at the Zurich Opera House and the city's chapels and churches host smaller concerts.

Event Organiser
Zürcher Festpiele, Falkenstr 1, 8008 Zürich, Switzerland
Tel: (01) 269 9090
Website: www.zuercher-festspiele.ch

Venue
The Opera House, the Kunsthalle, the Tonhalle, and various other venues across Zurich.

Transport
Air: Zurich Airport. **Rail:** Train: Zurich Station. Tram: Opernhaus or Bellevue (to Opera House). **Road:** Car: A1 (from Geneva).

Thailand

Bangkok

Tourist Information
Tourism Authority of Thailand (Kan Tong Teow Hang Prated Thai)
1600 New Phetburi Road, Makkasan, Rajatevee, Bangkok 10310, Thailand
Tel: (02) 250 5500
Website: www.tourismthailand.org

• April

Songkran Festival

Songkran, meaning 'to pass' or 'to relocate', heralds the arrival of the Thai New Year (when the sun exits Pisces and enters Aries), which is celebrated throughout the country. Bangkok festivities are centred on *Sanam Luang* (Royal Palace Ground), close to *Phra Barom Maha Rajcha Wang* (Royal Grand Palace), where an image of the Buddha is worshipped and bathed by religious elders and devotees; *Wat Phra Kaeo* (Temple of the Emerald Buddha) is another important site where worshippers gather during Songkran to receive blessings from elders. Water fights take place throughout the city, in particular in the old commercial district of *Bang Lamphu*. There are concerts and other forms of cultural entertainment on offer along the Khao San Road, where a *Miss Songkran* beauty pageant is also held.

Event Organiser
For more information on Songkran, contact the Tourism Authority of Thailand (see **Tourist Information** above).

Venue
Various locations across Bangkok.

Transport
Air: Bangkok International Airport. **Rail:** Train: Hualampong Station. **Road:** Bus: Public services. Taxi: Taxis or *tuk tuks* (three-wheeled taxis) are the best way to get around Bangkok.

• August

Queen's Birthday Celebrations

Thailand's present queen, Queen Sirikit, was born M R Sirikit Kitiyakara on August 12 1932. She enjoys a great deal of popularity in the country due to her humanitarian approach and the projects she has established to revive traditional arts and crafts. Every year, Thais celebrate her birthday by erecting portraits decorated with flowers on Ratchadamnoen Avenue near the *Royal Grand Palace* (Phra Barom Maha Rajcha Wang). The palace itself is festooned with coloured lights and other decorations, as are many other public buildings and private homes.

Event Organiser
For more information on the Queen's Birthday Celebrations, contact the Tourism Authority of Thailand (see **Tourist Information** above).

Venue
Various locations across Bangkok. For further information, contact the Tourism Authority of Thailand (see **Tourist Information** above).

Transport
Air: Bangkok International Airport. **Rail:** Train: Hualampong Station. **Road:** Bus: Public services. Taxi: Taxis or *tuk tuks* (three-wheeled taxis) are the best way to get around Bangkok and can be haled from the street.

Turkey

Istanbul

Tourist Information
Tourism Bureau (Turizm Danisma Burosu)
Sultanahmet Square, Istanbul, Turkey
Tel: (0212) 518 1802
Website: www.turizm.gov.tr

• September-November

Istanbul Biennial

The first *Istanbul Biennial* was organised in 1987 by the Istanbul Foundation for Culture and the Arts, and every two years presents a showcase of international contemporary art. The works of art are displayed in a variety of venues across the city, which have in past years included the beautiful *Topkapi Palace* gardens, the historic *Yerebatan Cisterns*, Ottoman warehouses and even Istanbul Atatürk Airport. Past exhibitors at the festival included British Turner Prize winners Gillian Wearing and Gavin Turk.

Event Organiser
Istanbul Foundation for Culture and Arts, Istiklal Caddesi 146, Beyoglu 34435, _Istanbul, Turkey
Tel: (0212) 334 0700
Website:
www.iksv.org

Venue
Various venues across Istanbul. For further information, contact the Istanbul Foundation for Culture and Arts (see above).

Transport
Air: Istanbul Atatürk Airport or Istanbul Sabiha Gökçen International Airport. Rail: Train: Sirkeci or Haydapasa stations. Road: Bus: Public services.

United Arab Emirates

Dubai

Tourist Information

Department of Tourism and Commerce Marketing (DCTM) Welcome Bureau
Beni Yas Square, Deira, Dubai, UAE
Tel: (04) 228 5000
Website: www.dubaitourism.co.ae

• February

Dubai Shopping Festival

Dubai has established itself in recent years as a mecca for duty-free shopping, and every March, visitors to the glittering Arab city can find even more bargains. The *Dubai Shopping Festival* features special discounts on a whole host of goods, from Rolls Royce cars to perfumes and jewellery, in shops across the city. In addition, visitors have the opportunity to win hundreds of prizes in shopping malls and department stores. There is also a Global Village, with pavilions selling goods from countries including Bangladesh, Vietnam and the Czech Republic. Once the purse is empty, there are many events and shows on offer, such as street theatre, fireworks and fashion shows.

Event Organiser
Dubai Shopping Festival Secretariat, PO Box 25425, Dubai, UAE
Tel: (04) 223 5444
Website: www.mydsf.com

Venue
Various venues across Dubai.

Transport
Air: Dubai International Airport. Road: Coach: Public services to Gold Souk Bus Station or Al-Ghubaiba Bus Station.

• March

Dubai World Cup

The *Dubai World Cup*, held in late March each year, is one of the most glamorous events in the sporting calendar, and certainly the richest. The two-kilometre (1.3-mile) sand and dirt track is floodlit for the thousands of spectators who come to watch the thoroughbred horses and their jockeys compete for the million dollar prize money. Unsurprisingly, the race attracts some of the best in the field and is closely watched by all involved in the sport. The total prize money for the race exceeded US$15 million at the 2005 event.

Event Organiser
Dubai Racing Club, Suite 206, City Tower 1, PO Box 9305, Dubai, UAE
Tel: (04) 332 2277
Website: www.dubaiworldcup.com

Venue
Nad Al Sheba Race Track.

Transport
Air: Dubai International Airport. Road: Coach: Public services to Gold Souk Bus Station or Al-Ghubaiba Bus Station.

> # Need More Information on UAE / Consult
> the World Travel Guide

United Kingdom

Cardiff

Tourist Information
Cardiff Visitors Centre
16 Wood St, Cardiff CF10 1ES, UK
Tel: (029) 2022 7281
Website: www.visitcardiff.info

• June-August

Cardiff Festival

The seven-week *Cardiff Festival* takes place in Wales's capital city with events taking place from June through until August. This giant outdoor event attracts hundreds of thousands of people every year to its various free events. The festival features the best in street theatre, live music and comedy in numerous events which take place across the city. The festivities kick off with *Celtic Food & Drink* in Cardiff Bay's Oval Basin. There are various concerts from the Welsh Proms, and the city's streets around Queen Street are brought to life with *Fiesta Nights*, which sees street performances from international artists. There's also a *Children's Festival* in June. Queen Street is the scene of more celebrations at the end of July when the *International Street Festival* brings the best of street theatre to the city. One of the most popular events during the festival is *MAS Carnival* which usually takes place on the last Saturday in July when hundreds of partygoers, including stilt walkers, dancers and samba bands from all over the world join in the celebrations. The festival comes to a climax at the beginning of August, with the free, open-air *Big Weekend*, which attracts more than 750,000 visitors. Highlights of the weekend festival include a free music festival, free entry to the National Museum's exhibitions, the Lord Mayor's Parade, a giant funfair and a dance party.

Event Organiser
Cardiff County Council, County Hall, Atlantic Wharf, Cardiff CF10 4UW, UK
Tel: (029) 2087 3690 (festival information hotline)
Website: www.cardiff.gov.uk

Venue
Various locations across the city. The festival ends in the city's Civic Centre with the Big Weekend.

Transport
Air: Cardiff International Airport. **Rail:** Train: Cardiff Central Station. **Road:** Car: M4 (from London, Reading, Swindon, Bath, Bristol and Swansea).

• November

Cardiff Screen Festival

The *Cardiff Screen Festival* (formerly *International Film Festival of Wales*) takes place each year in November. During the event, more than 100 short, feature-length and animated films are screened in various venues across the capital. The festival attracts thousands of visitors every year, including members of the public, industry professionals and film enthusiasts, and there are many film premieres during the event. The festival culminates in the presentation of the prestigious DM Davies Short Film Award, one of the largest prizes for a short film competition in Europe.

Event Organiser
Cardiff Screen Festival, 10 Mount Stuart Square, Cardiff CF10 5EE, UK
Tel: (029) 2033 3324
Website: www.iffw.co.uk

Venue
Various cinemas and other venues across Cardiff, including Chapter Canton, Chapter Globe and UCI cinemas.

Transport
Air: Cardiff International Airport. **Rail:** Train: Cardiff Central Station. **Road:** Car: M4 (from London, Reading, Swindon, Bath, Bristol and Swansea). Bus: Public services.

Edinburgh

Tourist Information
Edinburgh and Lothians Tourist Board
3 Princes Street, Edinburgh EH2 2QP, UK
Tel: (0131) 473 3800
Website: www.edinburgh.org

• December-January

Hogmanay

Edinburgh is undoubtedly one of the most exciting cities in the world to be at New Year, with celebrations taking place throughout the city over a five-day period. Traditional *Hogmanay* celebrations in Scotland date back to 1560 when the Protestant Reformation meant that many religious events, including Christmas, were banned. This meant that the Scots focused on celebrating non-Catholic days, such as New Year, as these were spared a religious ban. Edinburgh's Hogmanay celebrations began in 1992 when the Summit in the City and the European Union Heads of State Conference were held in the city. The festival has grown to be one of the world's largest New Year celebrations, attracting over half a million visitors, with performances from over 400 artists in around 60 venues. Edinburgh's Hogmanay mixes tradition with modern performances and appeals to all age groups. Highlights include the *Concert in the Gardens*, the *New Year Revels*, the *Winter Wonderland* ice rink in West Princess Street Gardens and the *Candlelit Concert* in the Cathedral. Fireworks are let off around the city every year at midnight to celebrate Hogmanay.

Event Organiser
Edinburgh's Hogmanay Box Office, The Hub, Castle Hill, Royal Mile, Edinburgh EH1 2NE, UK Tel: (09069) 150 150 (information; calls cost £1 per minute) *or* (0131) 473 2000
Website: www.edinburghshogmanay.org

Venue
Various locations across Edinburgh, with the main festivities taking place in the area around Princes Street and Edinburgh Castle.

Transport
Air: Edinburgh International Airport. **Rail:** Train: Waverley or Haymarket stations. **Road:** Bus: Public services.

• January

Burns' Night

Every year, Scotsmen and women around the world gather to eat a traditional Burns' Supper to celebrate the life and works of the great Scottish poet, Robert Burns. He was born on January 25 1759 and died on July 21 1796. The National Bard of Scotland is most famous for poems which include 'To a Haggis', 'To a Daisy', 'Halloween' and 'To a Mouse'. He is also famous for writing the traditional New Year's Song, 'Old Langs Syne', as well as 'Scots Wha Hae', 'A Red, Red Rose' and 'Comin' Through the Rye'. On his birthday, people around Scotland remember his life and celebrate Scottish culture by eating a traditional meal of tatties (potatoes), neeps (turnip) and haggis (a mutton, oatmeal and onion mix, cooked in a sheep's stomach bag) and by consuming large quantities of Scotch whisky. It is customary to hear 'To a Haggis' recited during the celebrations; this famous poem is read by the evening's host. As he reads the line 'an cut you up wi' ready slight', he cuts open the haggis and the meal begins. *Burns' Night* celebrations range from formal

gatherings, where Burn's most well-known poems are recited, to informal parties, where drunken revellers sing his most famous songs.

Event Organiser
For more information on Burns' Night, contact the Edinburgh and Lothians Tourist Board (see **Tourist Information** above).

Venue
Various venues, restaurants and bars across Scotland.

Transport
Air: Edinburgh International Airport or Glasgow International Airport. **Rail:** Train: Waverley Station (Edinburgh) or Glasgow Central Station (Glasgow). **Road:** Bus: Public services.

• April

Edinburgh International Science Festival

The *Edinburgh International Science Festival* takes place in April each year. The festival celebrates all aspects of science and technology, and has a wide appeal to all age groups. Visitors can take part in many interesting events, including lying on a bed of nails and floating in the Dead Sea Loch. Every year, approximately 175,000 visitors enjoy shows, workshops, exhibitions, talks and tours across Edinburgh. At the beginning of the 1990s, there were around 100 events at the festival, which attracted approximately 60,000 visitors. Today, there are around 300 events, attracting visitors from the UK and across Europe.

Event Organiser
Edinburgh International Science Festival, 4 Gayfield Place Lane, Edinburgh EH1 3NZ, UK Tel: (0131) 558 7666
Website: www.go-edinburgh.co.uk/science

Venue
Various venues, including many of Edinburgh's art galleries.

Transport
Air: Edinburgh International Airport. **Rail:** Train: Waverley or Haymarket stations. **Road:** Bus: Public services.

• June

Royal Highland Show

The *Royal Highland Show* takes place every year in June, just outside Edinburgh. The show attracts approximately 160,000 visitors who come to see over 5000 livestock and 2000 exhibitors. The highlights of the show are the displays of cattle, sheep and horses, as well as the *Food From Scotland* exhibition, which is the largest display of Scottish food and drink in the world. There is also a giant flower display, a crafts show and one of the largest displays of agricultural machinery in the UK.

Event Organiser
Royal Highland & Agricultural Society of Scotland, Royal Highland Centre, Ingliston, Edinburgh EH28 8NF, UK
Tel: (0131) 335 6200
Website: www.rhass.org.uk

Venue
Royal Highland Centre, outside Edinburgh.

Transport
Air: Edinburgh International Airport. There is a free bus service to the show (from the airport). **Rail:** Train: Waverley Station. **Road:** Bus: Public services. Car: M9 or M90 (from the north); M8 (junction 2) (from Glasgow); A8 via Gogar Roundabout (from the east and south).

• August

Edinburgh Fringe Festival

The *Edinburgh Fringe Festival* is held in August every year in parallel with the *Edinburgh International Festival*. The first Edinburgh Fringe Festival was held in 1947 and has since grown to become one of the largest arts festivals in the world. In 1947, eight theatre groups turned up uninvited to the Edinburgh International Festival, but were unable to perform at the event. Finding themselves on the 'fringe' of the event, they found alternative venues at which to perform. The Fringe Festival has continued every year and has developed into an enormous festival where amateur and unknown artists are able to perform. The festival sees many performances in unconventional locations in the city by any artist who is prepared to hire a venue for the night.

Event Organiser
The Fringe Office, 180 High Street, Edinburgh EH1 1QS, UK
Tel: (0131) 226 0026
Website: www.edfringe.com

Venue
Various venues in Edinburgh city centre, including Holyrood Park, La Belle Angele, George Square Theatre, Randolph Studio and Edinburgh College of Art.

Transport
Air: Edinburgh International Airport. **Rail:** Train: Waverley Station (Edinburgh). **Road:** Bus: Public services.

Edinburgh Military Tattoo

The *Edinburgh Military Tattoo* is a well-established, world-renowned event, attracting visitors from around the globe. The Tattoo was first performed in 1950 as the Scottish Army's contribution to the *Edinburgh International Festival*. The word 'tattoo' comes from the cry used by innkeepers in the Low Countries in the 17th and 18th centuries to signal closing time. Every year, hundreds of performers from more than 30 countries, including India, the USA, Norway, Australia and Pakistan, take part in this event, which is watched by an audience of 200,000. The Tattoo is also shown on television in around 30 countries to an annual television audience of 100 million. The event sees international musical performances, theatre and dance, as well as marching by the Army in the spectacular grounds of Edinburgh Castle. Other highlights include the sounds of the Massed Pipes and Drums, music from the Massed Military Bands, the Guards of His Majesty The King of Norway and a Highland Dance display. At the end of each day's events, a lone piper plays a haunting lament on the castle's ramparts, before all the day's performers march off the *Esplanade* to the sounds of the famous pipe melody 'The Black Bear'.

Event Organiser
Edinburgh Military Tattoo, The Tattoo Office, 32 Market Street, Edinburgh EH1 1QB, UK
Tel: 08707 555 118
Website: www.edinburgh-tattoo.co.uk

Venue
Castle Esplanade, Edinburgh Castle.

Transport
Air: Edinburgh International Airport. **Rail:** Train: Waverley Station. **Road:** Bus: Public services.

• August-September

Edinburgh International Festival

The *Edinburgh International Festival* provides audiences with impressive arts performances, ranging from theatrical productions through to opera, dance and music. Every year, this giant festival attracts visitors from all over the globe to see many of the world's greatest artists perform at this renowned festival. The first Edinburgh International Festival took place in 1947 to celebrate the end of World War II.

Event Organiser
Edinburgh International Festival, The Hub,

Castlehill, Edinburgh EH1 2NE, UK
Tel: (0131) 473 2001 (bookings) *or* 473 2099
(administration)
Website: www.eif.co.uk
Venue
Various venues across Edinburgh, including Usher
Hall, Festival Theatre and The Hub.

Transport
Air: Edinburgh International Airport. **Rail:** Train:
Waverley or Haymarket stations. **Road: Bus:** Public
services.

Glasgow

Tourist Information
Greater Glasgow & Clyde Valley
Tourist Board
11 George Street, Glasgow G2 1DY, UK
Tel: (0141) 204 4400
Website: www.seeglasgow.com

• January

Celtic Connections

Celtic Connections is a celebration of traditional
and contemporary Celtic music and culture
from Scotland, Ireland and Brittany, as well as
other Celtic places around the world. The event
takes place across Glasgow during January. The
festival first took place in 1993 to fill a
scheduling gap in the Glasgow Royal Concert
Hall's winter season and has grown into a 19-
day event taking place at venues across the
city. The festival focuses predominantly on
Scottish traditional music but is truly
international with performances by artists from
all over the world.

Event Organiser
Glasgow Royal Concert Hall, 2 Sauchiehall Street,
Glasgow G2 3NY, Scotland
Tel: (0141) 353 8000
Website: www.celticconnections.com

Venue
Venues across Glasgow, including the Piping
Centre, Old Fruitmarket, Tron, Glasgow Cathedral,
St Aloysius Church, St Mary's Cathedral and the
Central Hotel; many events take place in Glasgow
Royal Concert Hall.

Transport
Air: Glasgow International Airport. **Rail:** Train:
Glasgow Central Station. **Road: Bus:** Public
services.

Isle of Man

Tourist Information
Isle of Man Department of Tourism and Leisure
Sea Terminal Buildings, Douglas, Isle of Man IM1
2RG, UK
Tel: (01624) 686 801
Website: www.visitisleofman.com

• June

TT Races

The origins of the legendary *TT Races* date back to
1904 when the isle hosted the Gordon Bennett car
trials because it was not possible to close public
roads to allow racing in England. New legislation
was brought in to make this a regular event and
three years later in 1907 the first TT Races involving
motorbikes were held. The event has grown over the
years and many see the Isle of Man as the Road
Racing Capital of the world which attracts
thousands of visitors each year. In 1988 race
organisers also introduced the Pre-TT Classic Races
where motorbikes of yesteryear race along the 6.8-
km (4.25-mile) Billown Course in May each year.

Event Organiser
For more information on the TT Races, contact the
Isle of Man Department of Tourism and Leisure
(see **Tourist Information** above).

Venue
Courses on the Isle of Man.

Transport
Air: Isle of Man Airport (Ballasalla). **Water:** Ferry:
Douglas Ferry Port. **Rail:** Scenic steam railway
travels south from Douglas. The Manx Electric
Railway travels north from Douglas. **Road: Bus:**
Public services.

Liverpool

Tourist Information
Liverpool Tourist Information Centre
Queen Square Centre, Queen Square, Liverpool L1
1RG, UK
Tel: (0845) 601 1125
Website: www.visitliverpool.com

• April

Grand National

The *Grand National* at *Aintree Racecourse* is one
of the best-known and best-loved horse racing
meets in the UK. The first races at Aintree date

back to 1829 but the first Grand National (now often abbreviated to the National) wasn't held until 1839 in which Lottery became the first horse to win the National. A maximum of 40 riders race in the Grand National which traditionally is the final race in the three-day meeting. The course is notorious for its 16 fences and the 494-yard (452m) sprint to the finish line. The Grand National is one of the most prestigious meetings on the horse racing calendar which has traditionally been the biggest day in the year for British betting. Aintree itself is currently undergoing a £30m renovation project due for completion in 2007.

Event Organiser
Aintree Racecourse, Ormskirk Road, Aintree, Liverpool L9 5AS, UK
Tel: (0151) 523 2600
Website: www.aintree.co.uk

Venue
Aintree Racecourse, Liverpool.

Transport
Air: Liverpool John Lennon Airport or Manchester Airport. Rail: Train: Mainline services to Liverpool Lime Street Station then local services to Aintree from Liverpool Central Station. Road: Bus: Public services. Car: Aintree is signposted from the M6.

London

Tourist Information
London Tourist Board & Convention Bureau Accommodation Booking Service
1 Warwick Row, Victoria, London SW1E 5ER, UK
Tel: (020) 7932 2020
Website: www.visitlondon.com

• January

Daily Telegraph Adventure Travel & Sports Show

The *Daily Telegraph Adventure Travel & Sports Show* began in 1995 and has grown into one of the leading travel shows in the UK bringing together tour operators, travel gear stockists and adventure companies under one roof at the Olympia exhibition hall in London. In addition to over 250 exhibitors there's also a packed programme of lectures and personal appearances by well-known explorers, adventurers, travel writers and presenters. There are also usually live demonstrations, simulators and an indoor climbing wall where visitors can try their hand at

new sports. The show also usually features a team of travel experts who can help visitors plan their trip details.

Event Organiser
Ats Events Limited, Lower Dane, Hartlip, Kent ME9 7TE, UK
Tel: (01795) 844400
Website: www.adventureshow.co.uk

Venue
Olympia Exhibition Centre, Hammersmith Road, Kensington, London W14 8UX, UK

Transport
Air: London Heathrow Airport. Rail: Train: Kensington Olympia Station (mainline). Underground: Kensington Olympia underground station (District Line). Road: Bus: Public services.

• January

London Parade

The *London Parade* takes place in central London on January 1 each year. During this giant, free party, spectacular marching bands parade through the streets, along with thousands of cheerleaders, clowns and vintage cars. The parade first took place in the city in 1987, when a few hundred performers from the USA and the UK paraded through London's streets to celebrate the New Year. The event was first called the *Lord Mayor of Westminster's Big Parade*, but was renamed the London Parade in 1994, by which time thousands of professional cheerleaders from the USA had joined the procession. Today, the parade features almost 10,000 participants from all over the world and attracts around one million spectators who line the streets of central London to watch the show. Every year, the event raises large amounts of money for charity. The parade sets off from Parliament Square at 1200 and continues for 3.5km (2.2 miles) through the streets of central London, finishing in Berkeley Square, off Piccadilly and Regent Street.

Event Organiser
London Parade, Research House, Fraser Road, Greenford, Middlesex UB6 7AQ, UK
Tel: (020) 8566 8586
Website: www.londonparade.co.uk

Venue
Central London, beginning in Parliament Square and finishing in Berkeley Square.

Transport
Air: London Heathrow Airport. Rail: Train: London Charing Cross Station. Underground:

Westminster (start); Piccadilly Circus (Piccadilly or Bakerloo lines) or Green Park (Jubilee, Piccadilly or Victoria lines) (finish). **Road:** Bus: Public services.

• February

Chinese New Year

Chinese New Year festivities take place every year in London's Chinatown, which is located in the Soho district of the city. The festival, which is known as *Spring Festival* in its native country, is the oldest and most important festival in China. The Chinese New Year takes place on a different date every year as the Chinese calendar is based on lunar and solar movements. A leap month is added in every couple of years, thus changing the date of the New Year, which takes place on the first day of the new moon every year. The Chinese use 12 animals to represent a 12-year cycle, with a different animal representing each Chinese Year. In London, New Year festivities take place in Gerrard Street, between Soho and Leicester Square, and also spread into nearby *Covent Garden*. There are numerous parades during the festivities, as well as music, Chinese opera, kung fu, and lion and dragon dances. There are also many food stalls in the area selling traditional Chinese cuisine, as well as around 60 Chinese restaurants located in Soho.

Event Organiser
For more information on Chinese New Year, contact the London Tourist Board & Convention Bureau (see **Tourist Information** above).

Venue
Gerrard Street, between Leicester Square and Soho.

Transport
Air: London Heathrow Airport. **Rail:** Train: London Victoria Station. Underground: Leicester Square (Piccadilly and Northern lines) or Piccadilly Circus (Piccadilly and Bakerloo lines). **Road:** Bus: Public services.

• March-April

Daily Mail Ideal Home Show

The *Daily Mail Ideal Home Show* is a major event in the UK calendar, taking place every year in London's Earls Court. The show, which began in 1908, attracts thousands of keen homemakers every year, who are drawn to see inspirational homes from both the past and future. One of the most famous features of the show is the *House of the Future* display which sees leading designers give their impressions of the shape of things to come. Homes from previous decades are also on display and attract huge crowds of people.

Event Organiser
Daily Mail Ideal Home Show, Dmg World Media, Equitable House, Lyon Road, Harrow, Middlesex HA1 2EW, UK
Tel: (020) 8515 2000
Website: www.idealhomeshow.co.uk

Venue
Earls Court Exhibition Centre, SW5, London.

Transport
Air: London Heathrow Airport. **Rail:** Train: West Brompton Station (from Clapham Junction). Underground: Earls Court (District or Piccadilly lines) or West Brompton (District Line). **Road:** Bus: Public services.

• April

Flora London Marathon

The *Flora London Marathon* is a 42.2km (26.2 mile) race, which first took place on March 29 1981. Around 7750 runners took part in the first London Marathon, with approximately 6250 completing the race successfully. The event takes place around the streets of central London, starting in Greenwich Park and ending in the Mall. Runners pass many major London sites, including the Cutty Sark, Canary Wharf, the Tower of London, Buckingham Palace and Big Ben. Nearly 100,000 people applied to run the race in 2005 with more than 30,000 competitors eventually taking part, including top athletes from around the world, as well as thousands of fun runners. The majority of amateur competitors also raise money for charity and many of them take part in fancy dress. Spectators line the streets, joining in the festivities and cheering on the runners, in what has become one of London's biggest street parties.

Event Organiser
Flora London Marathon, Suite 3, Waterloo Court, 10 Theed Street, London SE1 8ST, UK
Tel: (020) 7902 0200
Website: www.london-marathon.co.uk

Venue
Central London, starting in Greenwich Park and ending in the Mall.

Transport
Air: London Heathrow Airport. **Rail:** Train: Greenwich, Maze Hill or Blackheath stations (start), Charing Cross Station (finish). Docklands Light Railway: Cutty Sark or Greenwich (start)

(from Bank). Underground: Charing Cross (Bakerloo or Northern lines), Green Park (Jubilee, Piccadilly or Victoria lines) or St James's Park (District or Circle lines) (finish). **Road:** Bus: Public services.

• May

Chelsea Flower Show

The *Chelsea Flower Show* is one of the most famous garden displays in Europe. Every year, visitors from all over the world flock to London to see this spectacular event which was first held in 1913. Displays range from modern sculptured displays through to wild, untamed gardens. The show includes a *Lifelong Learning in the Garden* feature, explaining how gardens grow, and Royal Horticultural Society experts are on hand to offer advice about gardening to visitors.

Event Organiser
Royal Horticultural Society, 80 Vincent Square, London SW1P 2PE, UK
Tel: (020) 7834 4333
Website: www.rhs.org.uk

Venue
Showgrounds at the Royal Hospital, Chelsea.

Transport
Air: London Heathrow Airport. **Rail:** Train: Victoria Station. Underground: Sloane Square (District or Circle lines). **Road:** Bus: Public services.

• June

Queen's Birthday Parade – Trooping the Colour

Trooping the Colour takes place every year in central London to celebrate the Queen's birthday. The ceremony takes place on *Horse Guards Parade* in Whitehall and is watched by thousands of spectators, as well as invited guests and members of the Royal Family. Queen Elizabeth II was actually born on April 21, although her birthday is officially celebrated in summer. Troops from the Household Division parade down the ranks, escorting regimental colours, before giving the Queen a royal salute at *Buckingham Palace*. A musical 'troop' is also performed, prior to the Queen carrying out an inspection of the troops. The word 'trooping' can be dated back to the origins of the ceremony in the early 18th century, when the colours of the battalion were carried (or trooped) down the ranks on parade to the soldiers. The parade has been a celebration of the Sovereign's official birthday since 1748, although the Sovereign has officially only taken part in the ceremony since the time of Edward VII's reign.

Event Organiser
Household Divisions Headquarters, Horse Guards, Whitehall, London SW1A 2AX, UK
Tel: (020) 7414 2479.
Website: www.royal.gov.uk

Venue
Horse Guards Parade, London SW1.

Transport
Air: London Heathrow Airport. **Rail:** Train: London Charing Cross Station. Underground: Charing Cross (Bakerloo or Northern lines) or Westminster (District, Circle or Jubilee lines). **Road:** Bus: Public services.

• June-July

Wimbledon Championships

The *Wimbledon Championships* is an internationally-renowned tennis tournament, which attracts leading tennis professionals from around the world. The first *Lawn Tennis Championships* was held at The All England Croquet and Lawn Tennis Club in 1877, with the introduction of the Men's Singles which was won by Englishman Spencer Gore. The first Ladies' Singles event was held in 1884 and was won by Englishwoman Maud Watson; the Men's Doubles was also started in the same year. Every year the event is attended by thousands of spectators, as well as by members of the British Royal Family. Traditionally the event is plagued by rain, with play called off due to the weather; it is also traditional to eat strawberries and drink champagne. The youngest man to win the championships was Boris Becker of Germany in 1985, who at 17 was also the first German to win the title. The youngest female to win the title was Martina Hingis of Switzerland, who was just 16 years old when she won the Ladies' Singles event in 1996.

Event Organiser
The All England Lawn Tennis & Croquet Club, Church Road, Wimbledon, London SW19 5AE, UK
Tel: (020) 8944 1066
Website: www.wimbledon.org

Venue
All England Lawn Tennis & Croquet Club Grounds, Wimbledon, SW19.

Transport
Air: London Heathrow Airport. **Rail:** Train:
Wimbledon Station (from Waterloo Station).
Underground: Southfields (District Line). **Road:**
Bus: Shuttle buses from Southfields Station,
Victoria Station and Marble Arch.

• August

Notting Hill Carnival

The *Notting Hill Carnival* takes place every year
in West London. The first Notting Hill Carnival
took place in 1964, when Caribbean immigrants
introduced the Carnival to London to unite the
inhabitants of the area, which had suffered
racial tensions. The event has grown from its
origins as a small procession of people in
costume carrying steel drums to an enormous
multicultural festival which is attended by more
than two million people every year. There are
five disciplines to the carnival; these are Mas,
Steelband, Calypso, Soca and static sound
systems. There is a procession of costumes, soca
and steel bands along a 4.8km (3 miles) route
and 40 licensed static sound systems, playing
different types of music, including jazz, soul,
funk and reggae. Hundreds of street stalls sell
food from around the globe, as well as
numerous arts and crafts. There are two live
stages, featuring local bands and international
artists, which have in the past included Eddie
Grant, Jamiroquai, Wyclef Jean, Burning Spear
and Finley Quaye. The motto of the carnival is
'Every Spectator is a participant – Carnival is
for all who dare to participate'.

Event Organiser
The Notting Hill Carnival Trust, 332 Ladbroke
Grove, London W10 5AH, UK
Tel: (020) 8964 0544
Website: www.mynottinghill.co.uk

Venue
Streets around Ladbroke Grove and Notting Hill.

Transport
Air: London Heathrow Airport. **Rail:** Train:
London Victoria Station. Underground:
Westbourne Park (Hammersmith & City Line),
Notting Hill Gate (Central, District or Circle
lines) or Latimer Road (Hammersmith & City
Line). Ladbroke Grove (Hammersmith & City
Line) is usually closed during the weekend and
other underground stations close if they
become overcrowded. **Road:** Bus: Public
services.

• November

Lord Mayor's Show

The *Lord Mayor's Show* takes place in the City of
London every year when the Lord Mayor of
London parades through the streets as a show of
allegiance to the Crown. The position of Lord
Mayor of London was created by King John in
1215, as a way of showing thanks to the City for
its support. The City is an area around the Bank of
England covering 1.6 sq km (one sq mile) which
was developed by the Romans and is today the
financial heart of the capital. The Lord Mayor (not
to be confused with the new title Mayor of
London) was originally selected by the people of
London in 1215, making this one of the first
elected posts in the world. Every year the Lord
Mayor must swear loyalty to the Crown in person;
the show is a celebration which evolved from his
journey. In the evening, fireworks are launched by
the Lord Mayor over the River Thames, bringing a
spectacular end to the day's festivities.

Event Organiser
Lord Mayor's Show, PO Box 270, Guildhall,
London EC2P 2EJ, UK
Tel: (020) 7332 1456
Website: www.lordmayorsshow.org

Venue
Central London parade route between Mansion
House and Aldwych.

Transport
Air: London Heathrow Airport or London City
Airport. **Rail:** Train: London Blackfriars or London
Bridge stations. Underground: St Paul's (Central
Line), Mansion House (District or Circle lines),
Bank (Central, District, Circle or Northern lines) or
Blackfriars (District or Circles lines). **Road:** Bus:
Public services.

Reading

Tourist Information
Reading Visitor Centre and Travel Shop
Church House, Chain Street, Reading RG2 7HD, UK
Tel: (0118) 956 6226
Website: www.readingtourism.org.uk

• July

WOMAD Festival

The *WOMAD Festival* (World of Music, Art and
Dance) began back in 1990 as an alternative to the
UK's mainstream music festivals showcasing the

very best acts and performers from the world music scene. The three-day event usually takes place over the last weekend in July each year and attracts thousands of revellers. The festival has a strong family emphasis and there's a children's fun park and area with a circus feel and face painting tents. Past performers have included Robert Plant, Asian Dub Foundation, Youssou N'Dour and reggae legend Jimmy Cliff. WOMAD host similar festivals around the world throughout the year.

Event Organiser
WOMAD, Millside, Mill Lane Box, Wiltshire SN13 8PN, UK
Fax: (01225) 743481
Website: www.womad.org

Venue
The Rivermead, Richfield Avenue, Caversham, Reading RG1 8EQ, UK

Transport
Air: London Heathrow Airport or London City Airport. **Rail:** Train: Reading Station. **Road:** Bus: Public services. Car: Signposted from the M4 and car parking facilities at the festival site.

United States of America

Atlanta

Tourist Information
Atlanta Convention & Visitors Bureau
Suite 100, 233 Peachtree Street NE, Atlanta, GA 30303, USA
Tel: (404) 521 6600
Website: www.atlanta.net

• May

Atlanta Jazz Festival

The month-long *Atlanta Jazz Festival* is a music event featuring many of the world's great jazz legends, as well as rising international stars. The festival, which has been running for nearly 30 years and is the largest free jazz festival in the USA, sees hundreds of entertainers perform every year at the festival in Piedmont Park. There are also concerts in various other parks across Atlanta, as well as night performances in local bars and clubs. A wide selection of food is on sale in Piedmont Park and a large arts and crafts market is held during the festival. Up to 50,000 people attend the festival each year.

Event Organiser
Atlanta Jazz Festival, City Hall East, Fifth Floor, 675 Ponce de Leon Avenue, Atlanta, GA 30308, USA
Tel: (404) 817 6851
Website: www.atlantafestivals.com

Venue
Piedmont Park and various other venues in Atlanta.

Transport
Air: Hartsfield Atlanta International Airport. **Rail:** Train: Brookwood Station. **Road:** Bus: Public services.

Boston

Tourist Information
Greater Boston Convention & Visitors Bureau
2 Copley Place, Suite 105, Boston, MA 02116, USA
Tel: (617) 536 4100
Website: www.bostonusa.com

• April

Boston Marathon

The *Boston Marathon* is the world's oldest annually contested marathon and was first held in 1897 by the Boston Athletic Association, who were inspired by the revival of the marathon event at the 1896 Olympic Games in Athens. The winner of the 1897 marathon was John J McDermott of New York, who completed the 39.4-km (24.5-mile) route from Boston's Irvington Oval to Metcalf's Mill in Ashland in 2 hours, 55 minutes and 10 seconds to earn his place in marathon history. The standard distance of 42.2km (26 miles 385 yards) for a marathon event was set in 1924, when the British Olympic Committee decided that the route for the London Games should lead from Windsor Castle to the royal box in the London Olympic Stadium. The Boston Marathon is held on Patriot's Day, the third Monday in April and a Massachusetts public holiday, which gives the event a party atmosphere. The liveliest places with the best views for spectators are at Boston College or Beacon Street before the race ends at Boylston Street.

Event Organiser
Boston Athletic Association, 40 Trinity Place, 4th Floor, Boston, MA 02116, USA
Tel: (617) 236 1652
Website: www.bostonmarathon.org

Venue
The marathon starts at Irvington Oval and finishes at Metcalf's Mill, Ashland passing through the streets of central Boston.

Transport
Air: Boston Logan International Airport. Rail: Train: South or Back Bay stations. Underground: Boston College or Cleveland Circle. Road: Bus: Public services.

• December

Boston Tea Party Re-enactment

On the night of December 16 1773, a group of American patriots, called the Sons of Freedom, disguised themselves as Mohawk Indians and boarded three tea clippers – Eleanor, the Dartmouth and the Beaver – belonging to the ailing British East India Company. They then threw the cargo into the waters of Boston Harbour in protest at the taxes levied upon tea and other goods by the British colonists and the perceived monopoly granted to the East India Company by the British Parliament. Every year, visitors to Boston can see a re-enactment, performed by the Massachusetts Council of Minutemen and Militia, of what is generally considered to be the single most important event leading up to the American Revolution. The events start with a recreation of the town meeting in the city's South Meeting House where the Tea Party was planned. From there, the band of actors, accompanied by cheers from the assembled crowd, proceed down Congress Street to Beaver II, the replica of one of the original East India Company ships that now serves as a permanent Tea Party Museum, where they ceremonially throw tea chests into the water.

Event Organiser
Boston Tea Party Ship and Museum, 380 Dorchester St., Boston, MA 02127, USA
Tel: (617) 269 7150
Website: www.bostonteapartyship.com

Venue
Various locations in central Boston, focusing on the South Meeting House and Boston Tea Party Ship.

Transport
Air: Boston Logan International Airport. Rail: Train: South or Back Bay stations. Underground: South Station. Road: Bus: Public services.

Chicago

Tourist Information

Chicago Office of Tourism
78 East Washington Boulevard, Chicago IL 60602, USA
Tel: (312) 744 2400 or (0800) 487 2446
Website: www.cityofchicago.org/tourism

• March

St Patrick's Day Parade

Chicago is well known for its parades, and the city's large Irish population means that the St Patrick's Day Parade is one of the biggest and the best. The parade, which features floats decorated with huge shamrocks and leprechauns, live bands, Irish step dancers in traditional costume and even Irish dog and horse breeds, begins at 1200 at Balbo Drive and ends at Monroe Street at around 1700. Other activities, which last well into the evening, include Celtic dancing in churches, and pipe bands by the Chicago River.

Event Organiser
St Patrick's Day Parade Committee, 1340 West Washington Boulevard, Chicago IL 60607, USA
Tel: (312) 942 9188
Website: www.chicagostpatsparade.com

Venue
Balbo Drive to Monroe Street.

Transport
Air: Chicago O'Hare International Airport or Midway Airport (domestic flights). Rail: Train: Chicago Union Station. Underground: Balbo. Road: Bus: Public services.

• June-August

Grant Park Music Festival

Grant Park Music Festival was founded by the Chicago Park District in 1935. The concept grew from a desire to allow Chicagoans of all backgrounds to enjoy live classical music and for professional live musicians, who were suffering due to the rise in popularity of recorded music, to gain secure employment. Today, the festival is the only free, municipally funded, outdoor classical music festival in the USA, and continues to offer an excellent opportunity to enjoy symphonic concerts in a beautiful open-air setting in the heart of the 'Windy City'. Over 40 performances are held for two months each year, mainly at the Petrillo Music Shell (named after

James C Petrillo, the former president of the Chicago Federation of Musicians who convinced the park authorities to hold the event on an annual basis) on the Lake Michigan side of Grant Park, but also in churches and community centres around Chicago. The Grant Park Orchestra and Chorus and Chicago Children's Choir perform a variety of concerts most Wednesdays and Sundays, including opera, folk music, classical music made popular by films, songs from musicals and jazz. Composers featured include Beethoven, Strauss, Rachmaninoff, Sibelius, Rodrigo, Verdi and Britten.

Event Organiser
Grant Park Music Festival, 205 E. Randolph Drive, Chicago, IL 60601, USA
Tel: (312) 742 7638
Website: www.grantparkmusicfestival.com

Venue
Grant Park.

Transport
Air: Chicago O'Hare International Airport or Midway Airport (domestic flights). **Rail:** Train: Chicago Union Station. Underground: Jackson. **Road:** Bus: Public services.

Denver

Tourist Information
Denver Metro Convention & Visitors Bureau
1555 California Street, Suite 300, Denver, CO 80202, USA
Tel: (303) 892 1112 *or* (800) 233 6837 (toll free USA and Canada only)
Website: www.denver.org

• January

National Western Stock Show & Rodeo

Denver's *National Western Stock Show & Rodeo* attracts over 400,000 cowboys every year and is the largest festival in Colorado. It was first held in 1907 in a tent; it has since grown, however, to become a huge annual event which now attracts more than 630,000 visitors. The show aims to preserve the western lifestyle through a giant agricultural festival, which includes livestock displays and an annual horse show. Every year, there are events for all the family, including the *Indoor Rodeo of the Year* event and *The Super Bowl of Cattle Shows*, when cattle are judged to win the *National Western Grand Champion* prize.

Event Organiser
National Western Stock Show, 4655 Humboldt Street, Denver, CO 80216, USA
Tel: (303) 297 1166
Website: www.nationalwestern.com

Venue
National Western Complex, off I-25 and I-70.

Transport
Air: Denver International Airport. **Rail:** Train: Union Station. **Road:** Bus: Public services.

Memphis

Tourist Information
Memphis Convention & Visitors Bureau
47 Union Avenue, Memphis, TN 38103, USA
Tel: (901) 543 5300
Website: www.memphistravel.com

• August

Elvis Week

Elvis Week, which takes place in Memphis every August, is a celebration of the music and life of the late Elvis Presley. Every year, fans of the singing legend gather in Memphis to take part in this major event and pay homage to the star. During the week-long festival, there are many concerts and individual events around Memphis. There are also events at Elvis's former home, *Graceland*, the highlight of which is the *Candlelight Vigil* on August 15, the anniversary of his death in 1977, where fans have the chance to pay their respects to 'The King'.

Event Organiser
Elvis Presley Enterprises Inc, PO Box 16508, 3734 Elvis Presley Boulevard, Memphis, TN 38186, USA
Tel: (901) 332 3322 *or* (800) 238 2000 (toll free USA and Canada only)
Website: www.elvis.com

Venue
The main festivities take place at Graceland, the former home of Elvis.

Transport
Air: New Orleans International Airport. **Rail:** Train: Memphis Central Station. **Road:** Bus: A free shuttle bus departs from Elvis Presley's Memphis (a downtown restaurant) daily from 1130 onwards.

New Orleans

Tourist Information

New Orleans Metropolitan Convention & Visitors Bureau Inc
1520 Sugar Bowl Drive, New Orleans, LA 70112, USA
Tel: (504) 566 5011
Website: www.neworleanscvb.com

• February

Mardi Gras

Mardi Gras, which was first held in New Orleans in 1837, is today a giant celebration, with elaborately decorated floats, marching bands, parades, parties and lots of live music. The day itself, Mardi Gras (or *Fat Tuesday*), takes place on a different date each year, although it always ends on Mardi Gras day (46 days before Easter) with enormous parades through the streets. Every year, hundreds of thousands of visitors descend upon the city to join in the festivities, which also include private masked balls. Many partygoers dress up in fancy dress costumes during Mardi Gras, often wearing the official festival colours – purple, green and gold. These colours, which represent justice, faith and power respectively, were chosen by the King of the Carnival (known as Rex today) in 1872. This started a carnival tradition and every year a King and Queen is chosen to ride on the largest float, dressed in flamboyant costumes.

Event Organiser
For more information on Mardi Gras, contact New Orleans Metropolitan Convention & Visitors Bureau Inc (see **Tourist Information** above).

Venue
New Orleans Convention Centre and various venues across the city.

Transport
Air: New Orleans International Airport. Rail: Train: New Orleans Station. Road: Coach: Public services.

New York

Tourist Information

NYC & Company
810 Seventh Avenue, between 52nd and 53rd Streets, New York NY 10019, USA
Tel: (212) 484 1200
Website: www.nycvisit.com

• November

Macy's Thanksgiving Day Parade

Macy's Thanksgiving Day Parade is one of the Big Apple's most dynamic and colourful events. Its origins can be traced back to the 1920s when the city's European immigrant population decided to celebrate the American *Thanksgiving Day* holiday (which celebrates the harvest) with the sort of festivities they had known in their homelands. Hundreds of immigrant workers marched from 145 Street to 34th Street in costume, accompanied by floats, live animals on loan from Central Park Zoo and music bands. The parade attracted over 250,000 spectators and the Thanksgiving Day Parade quickly became a New York institution. Trademark giant balloons of cartoon characters were introduced for the first time in 1927, with Felix the Cat. The only interruption to the tradition came during World War II, but the festivities were soon revived and are now as popular as ever, with millions of people lining the streets from 0900–1200 to see the balloons, floats, marching bands and clowns and enjoy the holiday atmosphere.

Event Organiser
For more information on Macy's Thanksgiving Day Parade, contact NYC and Company (see **Tourist Information** above).

Venue
West 77th Street and Central Park West to Macy's Department Store, 34th Street and 6th Avenue.

Transport
Air: New York La Guardia International Airport or New York John F Kennedy International Airport.
Rail: Train: Grand Central Station. Underground: West 81st Street (for West 77th Street) or 34th Street (for Macy's). Road: Bus: Public services.

Philadelphia

Tourist Information

Philadelphia Visitors Center
Love Park, 1515 Market Street, Philadelphia, PA 19103, USA
Tel: (215) 636 1666
Website: www.phillyvisitor.com

• January

Mummers Parade

Philadelphias's extravagant *Mummers Parade* heralds the New Year and, like *Macy's Thanksgiving Day Parade* in New York, can trace its origins back to customs and traditions brought over from Europe by the city's immigrant workers. Mummers plays were performed at Christmas time by troupes of actors in towns and villages in Medieval England and told the story of a dead warrior brought back to life by a doctor, loosely based on the story of St George and the Dragon. 'Momerie' was also a popular form of winter entertainment in Europe from the 13th to the 16th century, where groups of masked performers would enter houses to dance or play dice, and the German word for mask, 'Mumme' is thought to derive from this practice. The earliest known Philadelphia mummers band was the Chain Gang, formed in the 1840s and other bands soon formed in other parts of the city. In 1876 these bands of mummers staged their own individual parades, and marched to *Independence Hall* in the heart of the city; it was not until 1901, however, that the first official Mummers Parade was organised. Today's Parade lasts for 11 hours, and the city's various troupes of mummers start their lively march down Market Street or Broad Street at around 0800. There are four divisions: 'Comics' (clowns who impersonate public figures); 'Fancies' (fancy dress costumes developed around a given theme); 'String Bands' (combining fancy dress and music); and 'Fancy Brigades' (mummer troupes who give indoor performances at City Hall and Philadelphia Convention Center). There are prizes for the best costumes and music, awarded by a panel of judges, guaranteeing high standards and plenty of imagination.

Event Organiser
Mummers Museum, 1100 S. 2nd Street, Philadelphia, PA 19147, USA
Tel: (215) 336 3050
Website: www.mummers.com

Venue
Fifth & Market Street to City Hall.

Transport
Air: Philadelphia International Airport. **Rail:** Train: 30th Street Station. Underground: 5th & Market Street, 15th Street or City Hall. **Road:** Bus: Public services.

• July

Independence Day

Philadelphia, founded by Quaker William Penn in 1682, is regarded as the birthplace of the United States. It was here that the Declaration of Independence was signed in 1776 and the city also served as the country's first capital from 1790-1800. It is therefore fitting that the city's *Independence Day* celebrations should be some of the most impressive and significant in the USA, starting with the presentation of the Liberty Medal in *Independence Hall* where the Declaration was first adopted on July 4 1776 (but not signed until July 8). The Liberty Medal is presented to foreign or US citizens who have advanced the cause of freedom; past recipients include Polish trade unionist, Solidarity leader and former president Lech Walesa and former South African president and freedom fighter Nelson Mandela. The commemoration of the importance of this day in American history continues, when at 1300 a group of descendants of the signatories of the Declaration attend a simple ceremony at the Liberty Bell. After this, the fun begins, in the form of parades, concerts and picnics, as Philadelphia celebrates its place in American history and indulges in proud displays of patriotism. A fireworks display over the Delaware River lights up the evening sky to provide a magnificent finale.

Event Organiser
For more information on Independence Day, contact the Philadelphia Visitors Center (see **Tourist Information** above).

Venue
Independence Hall and various locations across Philadelphia.

Transport
Air: Philadelphia International Airport. **Rail:** Train: 30th Street Station. Underground: Fifth Street. **Road:** Coach: Public services.

Index

D

E

F

I

J

K

L

COLUMBUS
WORLD TRAVEL
DICTIONARY

The aim of the title is to provide clear, accurate and concise definitions of over 4,000 words and phrases that are commonly used within the travel industry and in the materials it produces for its clients. This latter consideration has led to the inclusion of a number of terms in areas such as geography, history, cartography, religion and insurance which are widely used in guide books, brochures and web-sites but often without their meanings being clearly explained.

The following points are worth bearing in mind when using this dictionary:

- Many of the terms have many more possible definitions than those offered here. In such cases, the dictionary has generally limited itself to usages specific to, or common in, the travel industry.

- Words or phrases used in the definitions which are themselves defined elsewhere have not been cross-referenced. At the end of some definitions, however, reference has been made to complementary or related entries. These are indicated by >.

- Terms that are proper nouns, or are generally regarded as such, have been capitalised: otherwise, lower-case has been used. This sometimes gives rise to more than one definition for the same term.

- Countries and capital cities have only been defined where an ambiguity needs to be clarified, such as where there are two or more with similar names.

- The description (UK), (US), (Canada) or (Australia) indicates that the definition that follows is specific to that country, although it may also be correctly understood elsewhere.

- Some commonly used abbreviations and alternative spellings of terms are provided: others may exist, particularly where the term has been translated from another language or transliterated from another alphabet.

- For consistency, all acronyms that are defined have been written in capitals with no punctuation, although where they appear in the definitions they may be in lower case if this is an acceptable usage. Where these are abbreviations of phrases, rather than abbreviations of organisations, they can generally be written in lower case or in capitals, and with or without full stops.

- Imperial units of measurement (miles, inches and the like) have generally been written in full: metric units (km, cm and the like) have generally been abbreviated.

- Many aspects of English writing, such as the use of capital letters, inverted commas, hyphens and apostrophes, are open to individual interpretation. The usages in this book represent the Editor's preferences and not necessarily those of any other organisation. In many cases, there is no 'correct' usage.

- Throughout, British, rather than American, spelling has been used, except where American terms are being defined or American usages quoted. See Appendix 6 for more on these points.

Many individuals and organisations have provided specialist assistance in the preparation of the Columbus World Travel Dictionary, and these are all thanked by name on the credits page. Two particular debts of gratitude are owed: firstly to Graeme Payne, whose considerable knowledge and experience of the travel trade was so invaluable during the updating; and secondly to Richard English, who edited the first two editions of this title and on whose excellent work the subsequent editions have been based.

Any suggestions as to how the title can be further improved for future editions will be gratefully received. Please contact the Editor at the email address shown on the credits page at the font of this publication.

A a

A clamp A device fitted to air hose, manifold or regulator which may be attached to a diving cylinder pillar valve.

A flag A small blue and white pennant used in the seafaring 'international code of signalling' which represents the letter A. When flown independently above any craft, this flag also denotes diving is in progress – translated as 'stand well clear, I have divers down'. Also called flag alpha.

à la carte 1. A restaurant menu that lists a wide range of choices, individually priced.
2. A term often used by tour operators to denote a higher class of package holiday, possibly one that can be varied to meet a customer's individual tastes. > *tailor-made.*

A sizes One of the ranges in the international system of metric paper sizes, used virtually everywhere in the world except in North America. A sizes are used mainly for stationery, books and magazines. The most commonly used size is A4 (297mm x 210mm).

AA Automobile Association. *See Appendix 5a.*

AAC Association of ATOL Companies. *See Appendix 5a.*

AAS Alternative air source.

Abacus A GDS operated by a consortium of Far Eastern airlines.

abaft The stern half of a ship.

ABC 1. *See Advance Booking Charter.*
2. An informal term for the Caribbean islands of Aruba, Bonaire and Curaçao.

abeam On a line at right-angles to the length of a ship or aircraft.

ABLJ *See adjustable buoyancy life-jacket.*

aboard On or in a ship, aircraft, train or bus.

Aboriginal (or **Aborigine**) Of or relating to the original inhabitants of Australia before the arrival of European settlers.

aboriginal The original inhabitant of a place.

ABP Able bodied passenger. Usually selected to sit near the emergency exits on an aircraft.

ABPCO Association of British Professional Conference Organisers. *See Appendix 5a.*

abroad A foreign country. From wherever a person happens to live, other countries are abroad.

abseiling The act of making a controlled descent of a cliff or other steep ground by sliding down a rope. Also known as rappelling.

absolute pressure The total pressure exerted at any depth (including atmospheric pressure).

ABTA Association of British Travel Agents. *See Appendix 5a.*

ABTA Association of British Travel Agents. *See Appendix 5a.*

ABTA Travel Agents Certificate An examination-based qualification developed by ABTA and TTC Training, operated in conjunction with City & Guilds.

ABTOF Association of British Tour Operators to France. *See Appendix 5a.*

ABTOT Association of Bonded Travel Organisers Trust Ltd. *See Appendix 5a.*

abyss An exceptionally deep chasm.

AC 1. An abbreviation for air conditioning, in a car, train, hotel room, coach or other enclosed space.
2. *See alternating current.*

ACAV Associació Catalana d'Agencies de Viatges. *See Appendix 5c.*

accident An unexpected event causing physical injury. Most insurance policies can offer cover against the various consequences of an accident while travelling (including curtailment, disablement, medical expenses and repatriation). The conditions under which such a claim can be made will be set out in the small print and will vary from policy to policy. > *travel insurance.*

ACCKA Association of Czech Travel Agencies. *See Appendix 5c.*

acclimatisation The process of gradually adjusting the body to a different environment, such as a lower level of oxygen at higher altitudes. By limiting the amount of ascent each day and resting frequently, the body can adapt to live normally at altitudes up to around 5,000m. > *altitude sickness.*

acclimatise To become accustomed to new or changed conditions.

acclivity An upward slope.

accommodation 1. A hotel or other similar facility.
2. Specifically, the provision made in such a facility for its guests' sleeping arrangements.
3. Sleeping space and facilities available for

A
B
C
D
E
F
G
H
I
J
K
L
M
N
O
P
Q
R
S
T
U
V
W
X
Y
Z

passengers in a form of transport such as a ferry or a train. This can range from a reclining seat to a private cabin.
4. The term used by the WTO to quantify the amount of sleeping space available in a country, defined as 'the total capacity in rooms of establishments offering accommodation available in the entire country'.

accommodation grading and listing organisations The bodies that operate classification schemes for hotels and other accommodation. These include:
• *Government-run bodies.* Some governments operate an official registration scheme. The department responsible will allocate an official classification, and may impose certain conditions on the establishment's operation. When government classifications exist, registration is normally obligatory.
• *Transport-related organisations.* These include the AA and the RAC in the UK and the Michelin Guides in France. Other organisations such as airlines and railways may also produce lists of recommended establishments. Inclusion criteria will vary from guide to guide.
• *Consumer organisations.* Perhaps the best known in the UK is the series of *Which?* guides that give details of a wide range of properties.
• *Commercial organisations.* Several publishers specialise in hotel guides. The most-used by the UK travel trade is DG&Gtravel information's, online, *Hotel Gazetteers Plus.* Such guides use a grading system that incorporates other 'official' grades in place.
• *Holiday companies.* Most tour operators try to give their customers an indication of the quality of the accommodation they are considering and indeed, it is a requirement of the ABTA Code that the 'official' classification (if one exists) is shown. However, many operators will also provide their own description and rating. > *accommodation grading systems.*

accommodation grading systems Any method by which different hotels or other properties are compared by examining factors such as facilities, room sizes, number of staff and location and, as a result, allocating each property one of several grades: these are either named or given a rating by symbol, such as stars or crowns. There are many different accommodation grading systems in use in the world: by far the most important are those which relate to hotels. Some systems are international, some national, some regional. Some cover a wide range of properties, some only those certain types. Some have been developed by publishers, some by national tourist offices and some by hotel chains. While each is useful enough in its way, comparisons between properties listed in different sources may be impossible to draw: even if both use the same grade names (such as one to five stars), each might be based on different criteria. > *accommodation grading and listing organisations.*

accommodations (US) Accommodation.

accredited agent A passenger sales agent that has met the necessary conditions specified by the appropriate organisation (such as IATA).

ACE Association for Conferences and Events. *See Appendix 5a.*

Acela Express The high-speed train service running between Boston and Washington via New York in the USA.

acre An imperial measurement for an area of land equal to 4,840 square yards (approximately 0.405 hectare).

acronym A name, such as ABTA and UK, which is made up of the initial letters of other words.

Act of God An event, such a natural disaster, over which a travel provider or insurer has no control and therefore no legal responsibility.

ACTA Association of Canadian Travel Agents. *See Appendix 5c.*

activity holiday Any holiday that involves some type of structured or organised activity. There are many holidays offered by tour operators to meet the special needs of enthusiasts for the various different types of activity.

actual flying time The time an air journey takes, disregarding local time differences. This expression is gradually replacing the earlier 'EFT' (elapsed flying time), which has the same meaning.

ACV *See hovercraft.*

AD 1. Agent's discount. On air tickets, the letters will appear with a secondary code to indicate the amount of discount allowed. For example, AD75 = 75% discount.
2. *Anno Domini* (the year of our Lord), describing the dates of the Christian Era. It is written before the date in question, but is generally only used when there might otherwise be a confusion with BC. > *BC.*

ad hoc Anything that is arranged for a specific (usually exclusive) purpose. Typically, ad hoc arrangements will be made at relatively short notice to suit the needs of an organisation or individual.

ad hoc charter A one-off arrangement by which a vehicle, usually an aircraft, is hired in order to meet special demand or cover an unforeseen circumstance.

ADA room (US) A room complying with the requirements of the Americans with Disabilities Act.

add-on An expression, more common in North America, that means anything that can be bought by a customer that is an extra to the basic cost of the holiday or other arrangement. Shore excursions for cruise passengers are an example. In the UK the term optional extra is more commonly used.

add-on fare An amount added to the fare to a gateway in order to construct a through fare to a final destination. For example, a London to New York fare would require an add-on for a passenger wishing to continue their journey on another flight to Norfolk, Virginia.

adjoining rooms Rooms in a hotel or similar establishment which are next to each other.

adjustable buoyancy life jacket An inflatable collar, worn by divers, that can be partially inflated and then deflated to suit underwater buoyancy requirements. When fully inflated at the surface it also act as a lifejacket.

administration The management of a bankrupt company under a court order, often with the intention of finding a purchaser for it. Such a company is said to be in administration.

administrative county Any of the various and successive sub-divisions of England, Wales or Scotland created as a result of administrative reforms since the 1880s. In some cases these adopted the names, and sometimes the frontiers of, the far more ancient geographical counties which still exist for some non-administrative purposes. > *geographical county.*

administrative office The principal office of an accredited agent.

Adirondack The rail service between New York in the USA and Montréal in Canada.

adult A person who will normally have to pay the full charge for a travel facility. Normally this will be anyone over 12 years of age, although this varies from service to service. > *child.*

advance booking charter An obsolete type of charter flight previously available to customers booking in advance.

advance purchase rate A lower price charged to someone who is prepared to pay in advance for a product or service, such as a hotel room, where post-payment is more common.

AEA Association of European Airlines. *See Appendix 5d.*

AEDAVE Asociación Empresarial de Agencias de Viajes Españolas. *See Appendix 5c.*

AEO Association of Exhibition Organisers. *See Appendix 5a.*

aerodrome An obsolete term for airport, still occasionally used to describe a small airport.

aero-engine (UK) An aircraft engine.

aerofoil Any one of the curved surfaces on an aircraft designed to give lift.

aerophobe A person who is afraid of air travel.

aeroplane (or **airplane**) A heavier-than-air flying machine with fixed and non-rotating wings.

aerostat An airship or balloon, especially one that is tethered.

aero-towing The act of towing a glider in the air by means of a powered aircraft.

aerotrain A train supported on its track by a cushion of air.

affinity card A card that identifies members of an affinity group.

affinity group A group of people linked by a common interest or purpose. Some suppliers and brokers offer special rates for affinity groups.

Africa One of the world's continents. As with most continents, opinions differ as to its exact composition and area. > *continent.*

aft Towards the stern of a vessel. When a person or object moves toward the stern of a vessel they will be going aft.

AFTA Australian Federation of Travel Agents. *See Appendix 5c.*

after On a ship, nearer to the stern or aft.

agency list The list maintained by a trade body of their members.

agent A person or organisation that acts for another. Technically, an agent should be paid for the facilitation of the transaction regardless of its outcome. In practice, the term is often used to describe those, such as travel agents, who are paid by the supplier on the basis of sales made. Consultancy fees are beginning to erode this practice. > *travel agent.*

agent's coupon The coupon of a ticket or voucher that is retained by the issuing agent.

agonic line An imaginary line joining the north and south magnetic poles, along which a magnetic compass will point without deflection.

agriculture One of the three types of profession (manufacturing and services being the others) into which economic activity is generally divided for statistical purposes.

agri-tourism Holidays spent working on a farm.

aground The situation of a ship having run into the bottom of an area of water.

Agulhas Current A very strong north-south current off the south-west coast of Africa.

AH&LA American Hotel & Lodging Association. *See Appendix 5b.*

A

ahead When used as a nautical term means to move forward, as in 'full steam ahead'.

AIDS See HIV.

aiguille A sharp peak of rock, especially in the Alps.

aileron The hinged part of the wing of an aircraft used to control lateral balance.

air brake 1. A brake operated by compressed air, commonly used on larger vehicles.
2. A movable flap or other surface used to reduce an aircraft's speed.

air bridge (UK) The removable walkway set against an aircraft for transferring passengers to and from the departure gate.

air corridor A route to which aircraft are restricted, especially when flying over a foreign country.

air hostess (UK) A female aircraft cabin attendant.

air mile A nautical mile when used as a measure of distance flown.

Air Miles A passenger loyalty programme operated in conjunction with British Airways and its associated companies. The term is sometimes more loosely used to describe such loyalty programmes generally.

air pocket A region of low pressure that can cause an aircraft to lose height suddenly.

air rage An act of violence on an aircraft, directed either at cabin crew or other passengers.

air sickness A feeling of nausea when flying, usually caused by a combination of nervousness and turbulence.

air taxi A small aircraft that can be chartered for one-off journeys. Most air taxis are relatively small (generally carrying less than 20 passengers) and the journeys they undertake relatively short (generally less than 250 miles).

air terminal 1. (UK) The location in a town or city from which passengers travel to and from the airport.
2. One of the passenger buildings at an airport.

air testing The analysis of an air sample to ascertain whether it conforms to the appropriate air purity standards.

air traffic control The system or organisation responsible for the safe routing of aircraft while in flight.

Air Travel Organiser's Licence (ATOL) A certifying document which any company in the UK must have obtained before it can operate any form of package-style travel arrangement by air.

air-boat A vessel propelled by an enclosed fan or propeller, used for travelling over shallow water and marshland.

Airbus Originally an aircraft designed to carry large numbers over relatively short routes. Now used to describe many types made by the Airbus Industrie consortium.

aircraft Any machine that flies. Nowadays the term almost always refers to an aeroplane or helicopter, rather than to lighter-than-air vehicles such as balloons and dirigibles.

airfield An area, possibly grass-covered, where aircraft can take off and land.

airfoil (US) Aerofoil.

airframe The body of an aircraft.

airline A carrier providing regular public air transport.

airline accounting code The unique three-digit code which is allocated to and used by each airline. This appears before the ticket number on tickets and other travel documents. The accounting code is distinct from the more widely used *airline code*.

airline code The unique code – usually of two letters, sometimes of a number and a letter, and (rarely) of three letters – which is allocated to and used by each airline, and which appears as a prefix to the flight number. Occasionally two airlines will have been allocated the same code but these will be in different geographical locations. Often one of these operators will be a passenger airline while the other is a cargo carrier. This is known as a controlled duplication. In recent years, as the number of new airlines in the market has exhausted the supply of two-letter prefixes available, some codes have become partly numerical. Some airlines have a three-letter identification but these are rarely used as they may be confusing when used next to the city and airport codes described above. Such codes are only seen on the departure indicators at some Spanish airports.

airliner A large passenger aircraft.

air-miss When two or more aircraft get closer to one another than safety regulations permit.

airplane See aeroplane.

airport The complex of buildings, runways, car parks and administrative areas that make up the overall facility for the handling of civil aircraft.

airport code The unique three-letter code which is allocated to and used by each airport in the world. This is often the first three letters of the city's name, such as ALG for Algiers, but it is not always the case: Toronto, for example, even though it is in a major city, has a code of YYZ. It is important to remember

that where a city has more than one airport, each airport will have its own code, and these, rather than the city's code, will be the ones used on ticketing. Thus London, England (LON) has Heathrow (LHR), Gatwick (LGW), Stansted (STN), Luton (LTN) and London City (LCY).
Apart from airports, other travel destinations such as major railway and bus stations have also been allocated three-letter codes, although these will very rarely bear any resemblance to the city or the name of the station. Thus Birmingham Colmore Row Bus Station in the UK has a code of ZBC, and Berlin's Friedrichstrasse Rail Station of QWE.

airport surcharge An additional charge which may apply for hiring a vehicle at certain airport locations.

airport transfer The transport provided for passengers between their arrival or departure airport and their accommodation or other specified points.

airscrew An old-fashioned term for an aeroplane's propeller.

airship A powered aircraft that is lighter than air. The first ever passenger air service was operated by the German airline DELAG, before the First World War, using Zeppelin airships.

airside The area of an airport reached after passing through immigration and other security controls.

airspace The part of the sky available for aircraft to fly in, especially that part subject to the jurisdiction of a particular country.

airspeed An aircraft's speed relative to the surrounding air.

airstrip An area of land suitable for aircraft take off and landing which has few of the facilities normally provided at airports.

AITO Association of Independent Tour Operators. *See Appendix 5a.*

AKA Also known as.

Al Andalus A luxury six-day rail cruise in Spain which starts and finishes in Seville and visits Antequera, Granada and Ronda.

Alaska Standard Time One of the time zones used in North America, nine hours behind UTC.

Aleutian/Hawaiian Standard Time One of the time zones used in the Aleutian Islands and Hawaii, ten hours behind UTC.

Algarve Portugal's southern coast and the country's main resort area. The main towns include Lagos, Albufeira, Faro and Tavira.

alien A person from a foreign country.

all hands The entire crew of a ship.

all-aboard time The time (generally 30 minutes before sailing) by which all passengers should be on board ship at a port of call.

alleyway A passageway or corridor on board a ship.

all-inclusive A package holiday, resort, ship or hotel which includes accommodation, meals and certain drinks, entertainment and sporting facilities. These will generally be pre-paid. > *inclusive resort.*

allocation Space or accommodation reserved in advance by a principal for an intermediary, such as a tour operator, for onward sale to a customer. Space held on allocation will not be sold directly by the principal without reference to the allocation holder. Sometimes known as an allotment.

allotment *See allocation.*

aloft At or near the top of the mast.

alongside Beside a pier, dock or other landing area, or another vessel.

alp A high mountain, generally snow-capped.

alpenglow The rosy light at sunrise and sunset seen on high mountains.

alphabetical The ordering of information by the first and, if necessary, subsequent letters of the alphabet. Confusions can be caused with entries that begin with numbers or with abbreviations such as 'St', with names such as 'McDonald' or 'MacDonald', and with acronyms.

alpine Of or relating to high mountains, particularly the Alps.

alpine skiing The main form of modern downhill skiing as practised by most people visiting ski resorts, invented in the early 20th century.

Alps The main mountain range in Europe, extending from southern France to western Austria, and from northern Italy to southern Germany.

alternating current (AC) An electrical supply that varies in voltage from zero to a peak, then to zero, then to a trough, then back to zero many times a second. Such a complete cycle is known as a Hertz. Most countries have an AC supply at either 50 Hertz (such as the UK) or 60 Hertz (such as the USA). Travellers need to ensure their appliances work on the different frequencies. > *direct current.*

alternative dining An eating facility, offered on a ship, which is not in the normal sitting arrangement. *This usually takes the form of a bistro, Pizzeria or fine-dining option.*

altimeter An instrument that shows a pilot the height of an aircraft.

A

altitude The height of an object or place, normally measured from sea level. Altitude will directly affect its air pressure and will have implications for any activities undertaken.

altitude sickness (or **mountain sickness, AMS**). A variety of physical problems caused by the lack of oxygen in the air at altitude. It can occur anywhere above 2,500m if proper acclimatisation procedure is not followed and may manifest itself up to 36 hours after travel to height. Symptoms include headache, nausea, vomiting, poor appetite, insomnia a racing heart and extreme fatigue. If untreated, it may develop into its more rare but life-threatening forms, HACE and HAPE. The only cure is rest and descent. > *acclimatisation*.

AM Ante meridiem – used in 12-hour clocks and timetables for the period between midnight and midday. Most transport schedules in the United States are listed using am and pm. Note that IATA regulations require that am and pm be written without full stops.

Amadeus A GDS operated by a consortium of European airlines.

AMAV Asociacion Mexicana de Agencias de Viajes. *See Appendix 5c.*

ambient Local, immediately surrounding. The term is often used in relation to pressure and temperature.

amenity 1. A pleasant or useful feature, often mentioned in sales literature to stimulate interest. 2. (US) Kitchen facilities in a property.

amenity kit A pack provided by some airlines, generally to premium passengers, containing such items as slipperettes, eyeshades and washing kit.

America 1. The Americas. *See the Americas, continent.* 2. A commonly used unofficial term for the USA.

American Of or relating to the Americas. Without qualification, the term is generally taken to relate to North America and often specifically to the United States of America.

American Civil War The conflict in the USA (1861 to 1865) between the newly former Confederate Southern States of America which had declared their secession from the Union and the eventually victorious northern states.

American plan A hotel rate that includes accommodation and all meals. Also known as full board.

Americas The land mass comprising North, Central and South America. > *continent.*

amidships (US amidship) The longitudinal centre part of a boat or ship.

amphibian A mode of transport that can operate on land or water.

amusement park *See theme park.*

anchor The heavy fluked metal weight used to moor a ship to the sea bed.

anchor ball A black ball hoisted above the bow of a ship to show that it is at anchor.

anchorage A place where a ship may be anchored.

anchorage port A port of call where a ship drops anchor and remains positioned off-shore. Passengers are then transferred by tender to land.

ancient monument (UK) An old building or similar, often preserved under government control.

ancillary services In travel, extra services provided such as visas, foreign exchange and insurance.

Andean Of or relating to the Andes mountains of South America.

Andes The main mountain range in South America, extending along the entire western coast.

anemometer A wind speed gauge.

anemometer An instrument for recording the speed or direction of the wind.

Anglo 1. Used as a prefix to denote anything of English or British origin.
2. (US) A person of British or Northern European origin.

Anglophile A person who is well disposed towards England or the English.

Anglophobe A person who dislikes or distrusts England or the English.

Anglo-Saxon 1. Of English descent.
2. (US) The modern English language, especially when referring to a plain form of it.
3. Of or relating to the language, people and culture of England between the unification of the 9th century and the Norman Conquest of 1066.

annexe A separate or added building giving extra accommodation in a hotel or similar.

annular eclipse *See eclipse.*

Antarctic Of or relating to the continent of Antarctica.

Antarctic Circle The parallel of latitude at 66° 30' S, which marks the southernmost point at which the sun can be seen during the southern hemisphere's winter solstice. Any point south of this will experience at least one period of 24 hours without a sunrise and a similar period without a sunset.

Antarctic Circumpolar Current The ocean current that runs around Antarctica.

Antarctic Travellers' Code A set of regulations, enforced by the expedition cruise companies operating in this area, designed to prevent pollution and to preserve the continent's eco-systems.

Antarctica One of the world's continents, a vast, ice-bound landmass surrounded by the Southern Ocean and containing the South Pole. > *continent.*

antebellum (US) Existing before the American Civil War.

anticyclone A system of winds rotating outwards from an area of high pressure, usually producing fine weather.

Antilles 1. *See Greater Antilles, Lesser Antilles.* 2. *See French Antilles, Netherlands Antilles.*

antimacassar Paper or cloth placed on the headrests of aircraft or other seats.

antipasto The Italian equivalent of hors d'oeuvre.

antipodes The opposite point on the earth to where one is. From the UK, the antipodes is Australasia.

anti-trust (US) A collective term for the state and federal legislation in the USA designed to protect consumers from anti-competitive behaviour by companies.

ANTOR Association of National Tourist Office Representatives. *See Appendix 5a.*

ANVR Algemeen Nederlands Verbond van Reisondernemingen. *See Appendix 5c.*

AOA Airport Operators Association. *See Appendix 5a.*

aparthotel A hotel in which the accommodation is provided as self-catering apartments or suites with additional communal facilities.

apartment A room or collection of rooms. When used as holiday accommodation it will normally be rented out on a self-catering basis.

APAVT Associação Portuguesa das Agências de Viagens e Turismo. *See Appendix 5c.*

APEX Advance Purchase Excursion Fare. A type of advance booking fare.

appetiser A small amount of food or drink, taken before a main meal, to stimulate the appetite.

appointment The situation of a travel agent being authorised by a supplier to sell its products or services in exchange for a commission or a consultancy fee. > *travel agent.*

approved location A location for the sale of passenger tickets, including head offices, branch offices and satellite printers, that appears on the appropriate agency list.

après ski The social activities taking place after a day's skiing.

apron The hard surfaced area of an airfield used for loading and unloading aircraft. Also known as a ramp.

APTG Association of Professional Tourist Guides. *See Appendix 5a.*

aqualung Portable breathing apparatus for use underwater. > *scuba.*

aquapark A water-orientated amusement park.

aquarium A place where fish and other marine species are kept in captivity for scientific study or the enjoyment of visitors.

aqueduct A bridge, similar to a viaduct, but designed to carry water.

Arab 1. A member of the Semitic peoples originally inhabiting the area around what is now Saudi Arabia. 2. Of or relating to Saudia Arabia, the Arabian peninsula, or the Arabs.

Arabian Gulf *See Persian Gulf.*

Arabian peninsula The geographical region comprising Bahrain, Oman, Qatar, Saudi Arabia, United Arab Emirates and Yemen.

Arabian Sea The area of the Indian Ocean between the Indian sub-continent and the Arabian peninsula.

Arabic civilisation Of or relating to the culture of Arabia and the Arab peoples. Arabic influence extended from the Pyrenees to the Indian sub-continent as a result of the spread of Islam in the centuries following Mohammed's death in AD632.

Arabic numerals The figures 1, 2, 3, 4 and so on. > *Roman numerals.*

arboretum An area devoted to the cultivation, study and preservation of trees, often operating as a visitor attraction.

arc Part of the circumference of a circle or other curve. Since the Earth is spherical, a 'straight line' journey between any two points is actually an arc.

archipelago A group of many islands.

Arctic Circle The parallel of latitude at 66° 30' N, which marks the northernmost point at which the sun can be seen during the northern hemisphere's winter solstice. Any point north of this will experience at least one period of 24 hours without a sunrise and a similar period without a sunset.

A
B
C
D
E
F
G
H
I
J
K
L
M
N
O
P
Q
R
S
T
U
V
W
X
Y
Z

A

Arctic Ocean *See oceans.*

arête A sharp mountain ridge.

arrival tax Taxation raised on passengers arriving at a port or airport. Arrival taxes do not only apply to international arrivals but may on occasions be raised on domestic arrivals as well.

arrondissement An administrative division of a French city or *departement.*

Art Deco A style of architecture that flourished in the 1930s, characterised by geometric shapes and symmetrical patterns. Supreme examples include the Chrysler Building in New York and the Art Deco District in Miami Beach.

ARTA Association of Retail Travel Agents. *See Appendix 5b.*

artificial respiration A means of resuscitation by re-oxygenating the blood of an unconscious person.

Aryan A member of the peoples speaking any one of the languages of the Indo-European family.

ASAP As soon as possible.

ASATA Association of South African Travel Agents. *See Appendix 5c.*

Ascension Day A festival in the Christian religious calendar, celebrated 39 days after Easter.

ascent The process of rising towards the water's surface from any depth.

ASEAN The Association of South East Asian Nations. A regional organisation comprising: Brunei, Laos, Malaysia, Myanmar, the Philippines, Singapore, Thailand and Vietnam.

Ash Wednesday A festival in the Christian religious calendar, celebrated 46 days before Easter. It marks the start of Lent.

ashore Towards or on the shore or land.

Asia One of the world's continents. As with most continents, opinions differ as to its exact composition and area. > *continent.*

Asian Of or relating to the continent of Asia.

ASIRT The Association for Safe International Road Travel. *See Appendix 5b.*

ASPIRE A conference, organised by the Association of Travel and Tourism (ITT), normally held every March in the UK designed to cater for those new to the travel industry.

ASR Bundesverband mittelstndischer Reiseunternehmen.

See Appendix 5c.

ASTA American Society of Travel Agents. *See Appendix 5b.*

astern A nautical term meaning the rear of a vessel. When a ship goes astern it will go backwards.

ASVA Association of Scottish Visitor Attractions. *See Appendix 5a.*

asylum, political Protection given by a state to political refugees from another country.

ATA Air Transport Association. *See Appendix 5b.*

ATB *See automated ticket and boarding pass.*

ATC *See air traffic control.*

Athens Convention An international agreement that limits the liability of shipping companies in respect of loss or damage to passengers and their luggage.

Athens of... A term used to market a town or city by virtue of its cultural heritage (such as the 'Athens of the North' or the 'Athens of America').

ATII Association of Travel Insurance Intermediaries. *See Appendix 5a.*

Atlantic Ocean *See oceans.*

Atlantic Standard Time One of the time zones used in North America, four hours behind UTC.

atlas A book composed entirely or principally of maps.

Atlas Mountains The main mountain range in North Africa, extending from the Atlantic coast of Morocco to Tunisia.

ATM (US) Automated Teller Machine: an automatic cash dispensing machine. (UK cashpoint).

ATOC Association of Train Operating Companies. *See Appendix 5a.*

ATOL *See Air Travel Organiser's Licence.*

atoll A ring shaped island formed by a coral reef.

atrium A central open area in a hotel, ship or other building. There will often be access to natural light, either through an opening or a transparent roof.

atrium view Accommoadation on a ship from which the window looks onto the atrium.

attraction In tourism terms, something that a tourist wants to see or visit. Attractions are generally regarded as being natural or man-made. For more information, consult the Columbus *Attractions & Events of the World* section in this publication.

auberge A French inn.

AUC Air Transport Users Council. *See Appendix 5a.*

auditor's coupon The coupon of a ticket or voucher that is used for accounting purposes. Usually it will be submitted to the principal with the sales return.

Aurora Australis The southern hemisphere's equivalent to the Aurora Borealis that can be seen regularly below 70° south. Also known as the southern lights.

Aurora Borealis Spectacular luminous phenomena caused by electrical solar discharges and visible every dark night in the higher latitudes above 70° north but less frequently the nearer an observer is to the Equator. London can expect a maximum of seven sightings a year. Also known as the northern lights.

Australasia One of the world's continents. As with most continents, opinions differ as to its exact composition and area. > *continent.*

auto 1. An abbreviation for automatic transmission (on a car). Standard in the USA; an extra in most other countries.
2. (US) An abbreviation for automobile.

autobahn The German word for motorway.

autogiro An aircraft with rotating wings, somewhat similar to a helicopter, but where the rotors are turned by their motion through the air and not by an engine. Autogiros were the first successful type of rotating-wing aircraft.

automated ticket and boarding pass A document containing details of a passenger's flight booking and seat allocation.

autopilot A device that maintains the course and, in the case of an aircraft, the attitude of a vehicle without the pilot's intervention.

autopista The Spanish word for motorway.

autoroute The French word for motorway.

autostrada The Italian word for motorway.

auxiliary A sailing boat with an additional source of power, such as an engine.

avalanche A rapid, dangerous and often unpredictable fall of snow and ice down a mountain.

avalanche corridor *See couloir.*

avalanche transceiver A radio transmitter, used by skiers travelling off-piste, which sends a signal that can help rescuers locate users in the event of their being buried in an avalanche.

AVE The Spanish high-speed rail service, operating between Madrid and Seville via Cordoba.

aviation The skill or practice of operating aircraft.

avionics The electronic systems used in navigating and flying aircraft.

awning A cover, usually of canvas, set up to provide temporary protection against sun or rain. Often used over an open deck of a ship.

AWTE Association of Women Travel Executives. *See Appendix 5a.*

axis The imaginary straight line around which something rotates. In the case of the earth, this imaginary line joins the poles.

Azores A group of nine islands in the Atlantic, west of, and politically part of, Portugal.

Aztec The dominant civilisation in Mexico before the Spanish conquest in the 16th century.

B b

B sizes One of the ranges in the international system of metric paper sizes, used virtually everywhere in the world except in North America. B sizes are used mainly for posters.

B&B *See Bed and Breakfast.*

BAA British Airports Authority. *See Appendix 5a.*

Babylonic Of or relating to the ancient Babylonian civilisation (c.1500BC until 538BC).

BACD British Association of Conference Destinations. *See Appendix 5a.*

backcountry (US) An area away from settled districts.

backdate The often illegal practice of issuing a ticket or voucher later than the date shown in the issuing stamp box. This is usually done to circumvent the regulations covering advance purchase restrictions.

backhaul A fare construction rule that states that it is not possible to apply normal fare rules to journeys that double back on themselves. This rule prevents the undercutting of fares to a more distant point than that where the journey ends.

backing Change of wind direction in an anti-clockwise manner.

back-pack 1. A ruck-sack.
2. A harness attached to a diving cylinder, comprising shoulder and waist straps, that allows the diver to wear the cylinder.

back-to-back 1. The principle on which a charter flight series works. The flight taking a group out to a destination will return with those travellers who have finished their holiday, and so on.
2. The combination of two restricted return tickets to create a fare that undercuts the cost of a full-priced journey.

backwash 1. The wave of waters created by a vessel's passage.
2. A similar wave of air caused by the passage of an aircraft.

badlands Extensive, uncultivatable tracts of land, usually arid and bare of vegetation.

Baedecker One of the first travel guides published. The term is still sometimes used as a generic term for a guide book.

Baffin Bay The area of the North Atlantic Ocean between northern Greenland and northern Canada.

baggage The luggage and personal effects that a traveller might reasonably carry on a journey.

baggage allowance The amount of luggage which a passenger may take with them without additional charge. This is most commonly encountered in air travel, where the usual baggage allowance is 20kg (44 pounds) in economy class and 30kg (66 pounds) in first class. Most other forms of public transport have a limit of some kind, although this is generally very high and few travellers will exceed it.

baggage check (US) A receipt for baggage. > *baggage tag (1).*

baggage claim area The part of an airport where arriving passengers collect their baggage.

baggage tag 1. The labels, usually adhesive, that are issued at check-in to identify checked baggage. One part will be given to the traveller as a receipt.
2. The label noting the passenger's name and destination address which should be attached to each item of luggage before starting a journey.

BAHA British Activity Holiday Association Ltd. *See Appendix 5a.*

Bahama Islands The group of islands comprising the Commonwealth of the Bahamas and the Turks and Caicos Islands.

BAHREP British Association of Hotel Representatives. *See Appendix 5a.*

bail bond The security paid to an authority to enable someone to be released from custody pending trial. Some insurance companies offer bail bond cover.

bailiwick The district or area of jurisdiction of a bailee or bailiff. The administrative areas of Guernsey and Jersey in the Channel Islands are bailiwicks.

baksheesh A term of Middle Eastern origin meaning a tip or gratuity.

balconette A small balcony, rarely more than a few inches deep, generally outside French windows.

balcony A platform or terrace on the outside of a building with access from the room.

Balearic Islands A group of three islands situated in the western Mediterranean, politically part of Spain.

Balkans The geographical region of the Balkan Peninsula (bordered by the Adriatic Sea to the west, the Aegean and Black Seas to the east and the Mediterranean to the south). The countries in this region are generally known as the Balkan States and comprise Albania, Bosnia-Herzegovina, Bulgaria, Croatia, Greece, the former Yugoslav Republic of Macedonia, Romania, Slovenia, Serbia & Montenegro (formerly the Federal Republic of Yugoslavia) and the European part of Turkey.

ball lightning A very rare natural phenomenon where a glowing mass of energised air moves around until it strikes an earthed object, whereupon it discharges and disappears.

ballast 1. Heavy weights put in the hold of a vessel to give stability. They are often used when a voyage is being made without cargo or passengers.
2. The stone chippings on which railway lines are laid.

balloon A lighter-than-air vehicle that cannot be steered. Now often used for sightseeing trips in such places as game parks where their quietness and slow speed avoid disturbance to wildlife.

BALPA British Airline Pilots Association. *See Appendix 5a.*

Baltic Sea The area of sea between Scandinavia and the coasts of north-eastern Germany, Poland and the Baltic States.

Baltic States Any country with a coastline on the Baltic Sea. However, the term normally refers to Lithuania, Latvia and Estonia.

bamboo curtain The political and cultural divide that exists between communist China and the rest of the world. > *Iron Curtain.*

banana republic A derogatory term for a state, often in a deprived area, dependent on one type of trade (such as banana growing).

bangstick A long rod containing an explosive-charged head (normally a shotgun cartridge) which detonates on contact. It is used by divers to repel sharks.

bank holiday (UK) A day when the banks are officially closed and which is generally designated a public holiday.

bank settlement plan The previous name for billing and settlement plan.

banqueting rooms Rooms set aside in a hotel or similar for private and public functions.

bar 1. A place that serves alcoholic drinks and, on occasions, simple food. This can be within a hotel, ship or similar, or a place in its own right.
2. (UK) As definition 1, but the term does not usually include pubs.
3. (UK) Any one of the various public rooms in a pub.
4. A barrier of sand or sediment, usually caused by tidal action, near to shore or in the mouth of a river.
5. An abbreviation for barometric, used as a unit of pressure.
6. To forbid someone from entering a particular place, now or in the future.

BAR UK Ltd Board of Airline Representatives in the UK. *See Appendix 5a.*

Barbary An old name given to the western part of North Africa, now preserved in the name of the monkeys living on the Rock of Gibraltar known as Barbary Apes.

Barbary Coast The coast of North Africa from Morocco to Egypt, named after the infamous Barbary Corsairs who once preyed on ships in the Mediterranean.

bareboat charter A form of charter whereby the vessel is provided without supplies or crew.

barge A cargo vessel, usually towed, that plies rivers and canals. The expression is often used (technically incorrectly) to describe the narrow boats common on British inland waterways.

barograph A barometer that records its readings.

barometer An instrument for measuring air pressure. .

baroque A highly ornate and extravagant style, popular in the 17th and 18th centuries. Commonly used to describe architecture of that period.

barotrauma Internal physical damage to human body caused by expanding or contracting air. Divers are most at risk from such damage, which can include burst ears, air embolism, emphysema and spontaneous pneumothorax.

barque A type of sailing ship, usually with four masts.

barrage A structure built across a tidal river or estuary to control the flow of water. In some countries the word is synonymous with dam.

basement A storey in a building that is below ground level.

basin A geographical term meaning a portion of land that is lower than the surrounding area. The term may also be applied to an area drained by a river.

bassinet A little-used term that describes a cot provided for a baby on an aircraft.

BATA British Air Transport Association. *See Appendix 5a.*

bathometer An instrument used to measure the depth of water.

bathometric Of or relating to the depth of water.

bathroom 1. (UK) A room containing a bath and other washing facilities.
2. (US) A lavatory.

batten down To secure the hatches of a ship against bad weather. The term derives from the original practice of using wooden battens to secure the tarpaulin covers over a ship's holds.

bay A part of an ocean or sea that is partly or mainly surrounded by land.

Bay Area The urban area surrounding San Francisco Bay. Includes San Francisco in the west, Oakland in the east and San Jose and Silicon Valley in the south.

Bay of Bengal The area of the Indian Ocean between the Indian sub-continent and Indochina.

Bay of Biscay The area of the Atlantic Ocean between the northern coast of Spain and the western coast of France.

bayou A name given to a marshy creek or tributary in the southern USA.

bazaar An oriental market.

bourne (or **bourn**) A small stream or brook, all or part of which may flow only at certain seasons.

BC Before Christ, describing the dates before the Christian Era. It is written after the date in question, and is generally used with all such dates to avoid confusion with AD. > *AD*.

BCH Bonded Coach Holiday Group. *See Appendix 5a.*

beach The area of rocks, sand or shingle making up the shore of a lake, sea or river.

beach buggy A small, wide-wheeled motor vehicle used mainly for recreation, for travelling on sand or similar.

beam The width of a vessel at its widest point.

beamy A ship that is broad in the beam.

beanery (US) A slang expression for a cheap restaurant.

bearing The direction of a journey, usually expressed as an angle relative to magnetic north.

beating the lung A diving term that means breathing at a rate faster than an aqualung is able to deliver air.

Beaufort scale The scale used to measure wind speed. In the USA an extension of the scale, up to scale 17, is sometimes used. The levels are:

0	Calm	Less than 1 knot
1	Light air	1 - 3 knots
2	Light breeze	4 - 6 knots
3	Gentle breeze	7 - 10 knots
4	Moderate breeze	11 - 16 knots
5	Fresh breeze	17 - 21 knots
6	Strong breeze	22 - 27 knots
7	Near gale	28 - 33 knots
8	Gale	34 - 40 knots
9	Strong gale	41 - 47 knots
10	Storm	48 - 55 knots
11	Violent storm	56 - 63 knots
12	Hurricane	Over 64 knots

becalm To deprive a ship of wind.

bed and breakfast 1. A guest house providing simple accommodation and breakfast.
2. A hotel rate or arrangement which includes accommodation and breakfast.

Bedouin A nomadic Arab people, usually living in the desert.

beerhouse (UK) A public house licensed to sell only beer and wine, not spirits.

bell boy (US) A page or porter in a hotel.

bell captain (US) The head porter of a hotel.

bell hop *See bell boy.*

bells A method of recording the passage of time on board a ship, with one bell measuring each progressive half-hour to a total of eight. The series starts at half past the hours of 4, 8 and 12. Each 4-hour period makes up a watch.

below Anything beneath the main deck of a ship.

beltway (US) A ring road.

bend A knot used for joining two pieces of rope.

bends, the The common term for decompression sickness, so named because the patient is often found bent over with pain.

benefit An insurance term describing the amount that will be paid to the insured in the event of a successful claim for a specific incident. The term is often used to describe any such payment from an insurance company, but more properly refers to payments which are made on a fixed scale, usually reflecting some degree of inconvenience (such as £30 per 12-hour period for a delayed departure), rather than those which are made to cover a quantifiable loss or expenditure covered under the policy. > *travel insurance.*

Benguela Current A cold-water current running northwards up the coast of West Africa and then westwards into the south Atlantic ocean. Its significance is the up-welling of nutrient-bearing water it brings from the seabed that supports vast numbers of fish in the area.

berg A South African term for mountain.

berg wind A hot dry wind blowing from the interior of Africa to coastal districts.

Bering Sea The area of the North Atlantic Ocean between eastern Siberia and Alaska.

Bering Strait The narrow channel where the Bering Sea meets the Arctic Ocean, between eastern Siberia and Alaska.

Berlin The capital of the Federal Republic of Germany. and previously the capital of Germany between 1871 and 1945. During the period when the country was divided, Bonn was the capital of West Germany (the Federal Republic of Germany). The eastern part of Berlin (East Berlin) was the capital of East Germany (the German Democratic Republic), divided from West Berlin by the infamous Berlin Wall between August 1961 and November 1989. After reunification, Berlin was once again declared to be the German capital, but the process of moving the functions from Bonn took the rest of the decade to complete. > *Germany.*

Berliner 1. A resident of Berlin.
2. A type of yeast bun with a jam filling.

berm A narrow path or earthwork beside a slope, road or canal.

Bermuda Agreement An air travel agreement developed in the 1940s that restricted air travel between Britain and the USA to the services of the national carriers. The agreement was substantially modified in the 1970s and few such restrictions now exist.

Bermuda plan A hotel rate that includes accommodation and full breakfast.

Bermuda Triangle A triangular area of the Atlantic Ocean stretching between Bermuda in the north-east, Puerto Rico in the south-east and south Florida in the south-west, in which there is supposed to have been a disproportionately high number of unexplained disappearances of ships and aircraft. The area first gained its reputation following the mysterious loss of several US warplanes in the 1940s.

berth 1. A bed on a ship or train. Berths can usually be folded against the wall when not in use and can be situated one above another. Obviously an upper berth can be inconvenient to passengers who are not fully able.
2. The name given to an area where a ship ties up when in port.

BH&HPA British Holiday & Home Parks Association Ltd. *See Appendix 5a.*

BHA British Hospitality Association. *See Appendix 5a.*

BIBA British Insurance Brokers' Association. *See Appendix 5a.*

Bibby cabin A cabin that has a narrow corridor leading to a porthole, thus getting some natural light and fresh air. It had the advantage of being away from the ship's side and was thus cooler when the plates are heated by the sun. The term is now rarely used.

Bible Belt The parts of the United States where Fundamentalist Christianity exerts a dominating influence on local politics and culture. The term was first used in the 1920s to describe rural communities and small towns in the South. Parts of the South-west and the Midwest are now often included in the term.

Big Foot A large ape-like creature reputedly living in the mountains of North America.

big foot A short fun-ski, shaped like a giant foot.

bight 1. A curve or recess in a coastline or river.
2. A loop in a rope.

bike A two-wheeled vehicle driven by pedal power. > *cycle.*

bilateral agreement An agreement between two parties (for example, countries). Often used in connection with airlines' agreements with each other.

bilge The lowest part of the hull of a ship.

bilharzia A disease of the tropics caused by a parasitic flatworm.

bilingual 1. A person who can speak two languages fluently.
2. Something that is written in, or spoken in, two languages.

bill of fare *See menu.*

billabong (Australia) A branch of a river forming a backwater.

billing and settlement plan (BSP) An IATA payment system whereby agents hold one type of ticket, rather than separate documents for each airline. Payment for all tickets sold is made through a bank in the agent's own country and BSP arranges for the airlines to be paid. Agents do not therefore have to make individual payments to airlines participating in the scheme.

bin The enclosed luggage container situated above the seats of an aircraft.

binding 1. A clip that fixes the ski or snowboard to the ski boot or snowboard boot. They are normally designed to release the user in a fall to minimise the risk of injury and can be set according to the ability of the skier.
2. Any of the methods by which the pages of a magazine, book or similar are held together.
3. An explicit agreement which generally cannot be retracted from without some form of penalty.

binnacle A receptacle for a ship's compass.

biodiversity The variety of animal and plant life that exists within a particular region.

bioinvasion The phenomenon whereby indigenous species of plants and animals are being invaded by other types carried in by travellers. Many fragile ecosystems, such as the Florida Everglades, are under threat from bioinvasion. The effects of this phenomenon are known as biopollution.

biopollution *See bioinvasion.*

biosphere That part of the earth in which life exists.

biplane An aeroplane with two pairs of wings. Biplanes can usually operate at lower speeds than monoplanes and are thus still used in regions where STOL capabilities are important.

bird flu A virus mainly contracted by and spread between birds, particularly poultry, which during 2004 was reported to have spread to humans in South-East Asia and led to a number of deaths. The extent to which this poses a threat to humans on a wider scale is still unclear.

bisque Fish soup.

bistro A small, often informal, restaurant.

BITOA British Incoming Tour Operators Association. *See Appendix 5a.*

bitumen (Australia) A tarred road.

bivi *See bivouac.*

bivouac (or **bivi**) An overnight stop in the middle of a climbing or mountaineering route without the benefit of a tent.

black box *See flight recorder.*

black diamond run *See black run.*

black ice Thin, hard, transparent and shiny ice, dangerous to climbers and motorists alike.

black run The grading given by most ski areas to the most difficult, and usually the steepest, of ski runs. In North America the toughest runs are called black diamond runs.

Black Sea The sea between the Mediterranean, Ukraine, the Caucasus and Turkey.

black tie (UK) The name given to the mode of formal evening dress for men that involves the wearing of a dinner jacket and bow tie.

black-water rafting An extreme sport that involves rafting down underground streams in the dark.

blimp A non-rigid airship.

blizzard A violent snowstorm with high winds.

bloc A combination of parties, governments or other groupings sharing a common purpose or ideology.

Blue Badge Guide (UK) The highest category of professionally qualified tourist guide.

blue channel *See customs clearance.*

Blue Flag beach (UK) A beach that meets the strict environmental requirements set by FEEE. These cover water quality, environmental education and information, environmental management, and safety and services. Each beach is inspected annually, and any blue flags are awarded only for one year.

Blue Peter A blue flag with a white square, raised on a ship when leaving port.

blue run The very easiest ski run category in Austria and German-speaking Switzerland. In France and Italy it is the second easiest category after a green run. In North America this is defined as green circle trail.

blue square trail (US) A ski run of moderate difficulty in North American resorts. > *red run.*

Blue Train The luxury rail service in South Africa which operates regularly between Pretoria and Cape Town, and less frequently on other routes, including the Garden Route (to Port Elizabeth), the Valley of the Olifants (to Neispruit and Hoedspruit) and the service to the Victoria Falls in Zimbabwe.

blue water The open sea.

bluff A steep cliff or headland.

BMC British Mountaineering Council. *See Appendix 5a.*

board 1. To get onto or into a vehicle.
2. Food and lodging.

boarding card *See boarding pass.*

boarding house (UK) An old-fashioned term for a private home whose owner rents out rooms and may provide meals. The term 'guest house' is now more commonly used.

boarding pass 1. A document given to a passenger that proves their entitlement to board an aircraft or other vehicle subject to immigration and security clearance, and (where applicable) indicates their class of service and seat allocation.
2. A card given to a passenger at the beginning of a cruise that acts an identity card on disembarkation and rembarkation at ports of call and which is used as a charge card for on-board purchases.

boardroom seating plan A common configuration at meetings, conferences or seminars whereby the delegates are seated around one main table.

boardwalk 1. A wooden walkway across a sandy or marshy area.
2. (US) A seaside promenade.

boat A small water-borne vessel. The distinction between a large boat and a small ship is vague but any vessel that is large enough to have more than one lifeboat is probably a ship.

boat deck The deck of a ship on which the lifeboats are located.

boat drill *See lifeboat drill.*

boat stations The designated meeting points for passengers prior to the lowering of the lifeboats.

boat train A train transporting passengers to or from a ship.

boatel (Also **botel**.)
1. A waterside hotel with facilities for mooring boats.
2. A floating vessel converted to a hotel.

boatswain Pronounced, and sometimes spelt, bosun. The ship's officer in charge of equipment and crew.

bodega A shop selling wine and food, especially in Spanish speaking countries.

bog An area of wet, spongy ground.

bogie A wheel set on a locomotive or other railway vehicle.

Bohemian 1. Of or relating to Bohemia, a former kingdom in central Europe, roughly corresponding to the area of Slovakia and the Czech Republic.
2. A socially unconventional person.

boiler The tank fitted to a steam engine in which the water is boiled into steam.

bollard A stout post, either on shore or on board ship, used for fixing mooring lines.

bond A guarantee of repayment in the case of financial failure of the bondholder. Most travel principals require a bond to protect themselves against loss through the financial failure of a travel agent. Many insurance companies will arrange a bond in consideration of an appropriate premium.

book To make a reservation of some kind.

booking form Originally an essential document, completed and signed by customers to show in writing the arrangements requested. These days many bookings are made on the telephone or electronically and booking forms are not usually needed by principals. However, it is good practice for agents to hold a written and signed copy of a customer's request, since, in the event of a later dispute, this may avoid arguments about what was agreed or requested at the time.

booking reference A name, number, letter or a combination of any or all of these that identifies a specific booking. Ideally a booking reference should enable immediate access to the reservation in question without any need for cross-referring.

boom A spar that supports the base of the sail.

booster 1. A further vaccination after the initial one that prolongs the period of immunity.
2. A type of seat for small children, usually strapped onto a chair for use at meal-times.

Bora A strong, cold, dry north-easterly wind blowing in the Adriatic region.

Borneo An island in the Malay Archipelago divided between Brunei, Indonesia (the provinces of Central, East, South and West Kalimantan) and Malaysia (the states of Sabah and Sarawak).

borough (UK) A large town.

Borough One of the administrative divisions of London (32) or New York (5), and some other cities.

botel *See boatel.*

bottom time The duration between commencing a dive (i.e. leaving the surface) and beginning the final ascent.

bouldering A climbing activity that takes place on large boulders. Ropes and other climbing gear are not generally used.

Bourbon 1. Of or relating to the kings of France between 1589 and 1793 (and, less commonly, also between 1815 and 1848), and to those periods of French history generally (particularly the former).
2. Of or relating to the kings of Spain between 1700 and 1808 and 1831 to 1931, and to those periods of Spanish history generally (particularly the former).

boutique hotel A generally small hotel offering a high level of service and often a particular and individual style of décor and atmosphere.

bow The front of a ship. Usually used as the plural, bows.

bow thruster A screw mounted at the front of a ship, facing sideways, that assists docking. Many car ferries use bow thrusters.

bow wave The wave set up by the bows of a moving ship or other vessel.

bowsprit A spar projecting from the bows of a boat or ship.

BPA British Ports Association. *See Appendix 5a.*

BR *See British Rail.*

BRA British Resorts Association. *See Appendix 5a.*

brae A Scottish term for a steep bank or hillside.

Brahman (or **Brahmin**) A member of the highest Hindu caste.

branch office location An accredited agent's place of business, other than its head office, listed on the appropriate agency list as a branch office location.

breakaway A short holiday.

break-even point The number of sales required on a given service to cover the direct costs of its operation. Profit will not be made until sales in excess of the break even are made.

break-out room (US) A smaller room adjacent to a larger room or hall which might be used at conferences or meetings when an event needs to fragment into small groups.

breakwater A barrier built out into the sea to mitigate the force of waves and currents.

bridge 1. A structure built to carry a road or railway across an obstruction.
2. The control point of a ship.

bridleway A route or track intended for the use of horse-riders.

A
B
C
D
E
F
G
H
I
J
K
L
M
N
O
P
Q
R
S
T
U
V
W
X
Y
Z

brig A two-masted, square-rigged ship.

British Of or relating to the British Isles, its inhabitants and culture.

British Crown Dependency *See British Overseas Possessions.*

British English The form of English spoken in the UK, rather than in, say, the USA.

British Isles The geographical region comprising the United Kingdom, the Republic of Ireland, the Isle of Man and the Channel Islands. > *Great Britain, UK.*

British National Grid A cartographic referencing system, designed by the Ordnance Survey in the UK, providing numeric locations on maps. This does not use longitude and latitude to indicate positioning but a special grid based on the Transverse Mercator projection. > *Ordnance Survey, map projection.*

British Overseas Possessions The various former British colonial possessions which now enjoy varying degrees of autonomy. Since the 2002 British Overseas Territories Act, the nomenclature of these has been simplified. There are now three British Crown Dependencies (Guernsey, Jersey and the Isle of Man) and 14 British Overseas Territories. For more information, please consult the Columbus *World Travel Guide.*

British Overseas Territory *See British Overseas Possessions.*

British Rail The former name for the rail network of the United Kingdom prior to its break-up into a track authority and several private train operating companies.

British Summer Time The daylight saving time used in the UK. > *daylight saving time.*

British Virgin Islands *See Virgin Islands.*

Britisher A term, used by races other than the British, to refer to a British subject or someone of British descent.

Briton 1. A member of the peoples that inhabited the southern part of Britain before the Roman conquest. 2. A native or inhabitant of Great Britain.

broad gauge A railway track gauge of more than the standard four feet eight and a half inches.

brochure The catalogue issued by tour operators and others that gives details of the products on offer.

BSP *See billing and settlement plan.*

BSP Committee A committee composed of representatives of IATA members, established in accordance with the Provisions for the Conduct of IATA Traffic Conferences and having general responsibilities with respect to Standard Bank Plans.

BSP Coordinator A person appointed by the plan management as required, to act in accordance with its rules on behalf of airlines and IATA members.

BSP Panel A panel composed of IATA members who operate services, or issue traffic documents through agents, in the country or area of a Billing and Settlement Plan. The panel also includes non-IATA airlines which participate in Billing and Settlement Plans.

BSP Steering Panel The IATA panel which, in accordance with the instructions and directions of the BSP committee, is charged with the implementation and certain supervisory aspects of BSP.

BST *See British Summer Time.*

BTA British Tourist Authority. *See Appendix 5a.*

bubble car (US) *See observation car.*

Bucharest The capital of Romania. Not to be confused with Budapest, the capital of Hungary.

buck (US) A colloquial term for a US dollar.

bucket shop A now redundant term for a travel agency which specialised in selling discounted air tickets. In the past, many fares created by these outlets were contrary to IATA rules, and the bucket shops themselves were often perceived as being untrustworthy. Such operations have ceased to exist now that almost all travel agents are able to offer reduced priced tickets.

bucket-and-spade A term used to describe a traditional type of family holiday, typically at a beach resort and with young children, taken in a relatively low-price destinations.

buckshee (UK) A slang expression meaning free of charge.

Budapest The capital of Hungary. Not to be confused with Bucharest, the capital of Romania.

Buddhism The philosophy or belief observed by the followers of Guatama Buddha, who lived in India during the 5th century BC. > *religion.*

buddy In sub-aqua terms, a fellow diving companion.

buffet 1. An eating establishment, often on a railway station, where customers serve themselves from a counter. 2. The food service system where customers help themselves from a counter or table.

buffet car The carriage on a train which is wholly or partly devoted to providing snacks and beverages for passengers.

buffeting An irregular oscillation of an aircraft, caused by air turbulence.

bulkhead A vertical partition or wall in a ship or aircraft.

bulkhead seats Seats in an aircraft or other form of transport that either face or back on to a bulkhead. The former may have more leg room, but less storage space; the latter may not recline. Families with babies are usually seated immediately behind a bulkhead.

bullet train A general term for the high-speed passenger trains in Japan running on Shinkansen lines.

bulwarks The sides of a ship above the top deck.

bumboat A small boat plying between ships and the shore with provisions.

bump 1. The act of denying carriage to a passenger with a confirmed booking. This happens when the service is overbooked and the customer is requested to travel on a later flight, usually in exchange for compensation.
2. (US) A ridge on a ski slope.

bundling The act of combining a number of different products or services together and selling them at a single price.

bungaloft (Can) A bungalow with a loft area on the upper storey providing additional sleeping accommodation.

bunk A sleeping berth, especially one projecting from a wall or partition, often in pairs.

bunkering The taking on of fuel by a ship.

bunkers The space on ship where the fuel is stored.

buoy A floating marker that indicates a channel or hazard.

buoyancy compensator An inflatable jacket worn by divers which can be partially inflated or deflated to suit underwater buoyancy requirements.

bure A South Pacific term used to describe a thatched-roof bungalow, especially in Fiji.

burst lung A condition brought about by the diver holding his or her breath during ascent, thus causing the air in the lungs to expand dangerously.

bus 1. A large passenger-carrying road vehicle. In the UK a distinction is made between buses, which operate short-distance scheduled services, and coaches, which operate longer-distance and chartered services. This distinction is not applied in many other parts of the world.
2. The act of transporting passengers by bus.

busboy (US) A person on a cruise ship or in a restaurant in North America who assists the waiter during a meal.

business centre A room for business travellers, usually including telecommunications equipment, secretarial assistance and other office facilities.

business class An airline class of service in which passengers are offered extra comforts compared to economy class, but not to the luxurious standards of first class.

business house An obsolete term for business travel agent or implant.

business travel agent See travel agent.

business traveller A traveller who makes a journey for the purpose of trade or commerce, rather than for leisure or other personal reasons.

bustitution (US) The act of making a journey by bus rather than (generally) by train because of some problem with the rail service.

button lift See drag lift.

BVRLA British Vehicle Rental & Leasing Association. See Appendix 5a.

BW British Waterways. See Appendix 5a.

bwana A polite form of address used in many African countries. From the Swahili for 'sir'.

bypass A route, usually a road, that avoids a town centre or other congested area.

byway A minor road.

Byzantine Of or relating to the Eastern Roman Empire (AD325 to 1453), and in particular to the highly decorated style of art and architecture which flourished there.

C c

C card The diver certification card issued by each authority responsible for awarding qualifications in scuba diving.

C sizes One of the ranges in the international system of metric paper sizes, used virtually everywhere in the world except in North America. C sizes are used mainly for envelopes. The number corresponds to the A-sized sheet it is designed to hold. Thus a C5 envelope is designed to hold an A5 sheet.

c. (or **circa**) Approximately.

CAA Civil Aviation Authority. *See Appendix 5a.*

cab An alternative name for a taxi. > *minicab.*

cabaña A US and South American term for a beach hut.

cabin 1. A small hut or shelter.
2. A room for sleeping on a ship.
3. The interior of an aircraft.

cabin bag A small bag suitable for carriage in the passenger cabin of an aircraft.

cabin baggage *See hand baggage.*

cabin class An obsolete expression denoting a class on a ship that is between first and tourist.

cabin crew Those members of an airline's staff who are responsible for the comfort and safety of the passengers on board the aircraft.

cabin cruiser A large motor boat with living accommodation.

cable A nautical measure of length equal to 100 fathoms (600 feet).

cable car 1. A large cabin attached to a cable along which it travels. They are able to travel up steep gradients, and are thus much used in ski resorts.
2. (US) A tram.

cable railway A railway along which a train is drawn by means of an endless cable. Examples can be found in Llandudno (Wales), Hong Kong and San Francisco.

Cabo da Roca The westernmost point of mainland Europe, west of Lisbon, in Portugal.

cabotage 1. The navigation and movement of ships in coastal waters.
2. Air travel between territories of the same sovereign state. This may be between points within the same country (such as London to Manchester) or between a country and its dependencies (such as London to Gibraltar). The air fares for cabotage journeys are not governed by the normal international fare agreements.
3. The act of reserving such air travel to the exclusive control of the state concerned.

caddy A person who carries golf clubs on a golf course and otherwise assists a golfer.

café 1. (UK) A small, relatively informal, eating establishment, usually not serving alcohol.
2. (US) A bar or night-club.

cafeteria 1. The full name for café, to which it is usually abbreviated.
2. A self-service restaurant.

caique A small rowing boat used on the Bosphorus.

cairn A mound of stones built as a monument or landmark.

Cajun Country The area of southern Louisiana settled by a group of people of French origin, expelled from Nova Scotia in the 18th century by the British.

Caledonian Of or relating to Scotland.

calendar 1. The system by which the start, finish, duration and sub-divisions of years are fixed. The most widely used is the western (Gregorian) calendar However, there are several other systems, of which the Chinese, Jewish and Muslim are the most important.
2. A table of dates for a year, usually showing festivals and events important to a particular occupation or interest group.

California Current A wide, cold and sluggish current that runs north to south off the west coast of the USA.

California Zephyr The rail service between Chicago and San Francisco in the USA.

calm *See Beaufort scale.*

Camino de Compostela The medieval pilgrim routes from south-western France to the tomb of St James in Santiago de Compostela. The monuments and churches erected along the way, and the route as a whole, have now become tourist attractions. Also known as the Way of St James.

campground *See campsite.*

camping holiday A holiday where holidaymakers stay in temporary accommodation such as tents or caravans.

camping site *See campsite.*

campsite An area where campers can pitch their tents or where static tents can be rented. In the USA most sites will accept motorhomes and caravans, but in the UK this is not always the case.

Canadian 1. Of or relating to Canada.
2. The rail service between Toronto and Vancouver in Canada.

Canadian Technology Triangle An area south-west of Toronto, Canada, famous for its concentration of high-tech industries.

canal An artificial waterway. Most canals were originally built for goods traffic, but many are now used by leisure travellers.

Canary Current An extension of the North Atlantic Drift flowing south along the north-west African coast and moderating temperatures in the coastal region.

Canary Islands A group of seven islands in the Atlantic off the north-west coast of Africa and politically part of Spain.

cancel To release, withdraw or revoke a reservation.

cancellation and curtailment insurance *See travel insurance, curtail.*

cancellation charge A fee charged to a customer who cancels a booking. In general, the more notice is given of the cancellation, the more money will be refunded. Since it is always difficult to collect such charges, it is important for agents to collect in advance an amount sufficient to cover any likely charges. The scales of cancellation charges can be complex, and it is important that travel staff do not refund any part of a pre-payment without having proper authority from the principal involved.

canoe A small, narrow boat usually propelled by paddling.

cantina A Spanish term, especially common in Mexico, for a bar or wine-shop.

Canuck A Canadian, especially a French Canadian.

canx. A commonly used abbreviation for 'cancelled'.

canyon A deep valley or ravine with steep sides.

canyoning *See gorge walking.*

cap As applied to commission, to place a ceiling or limit on the maximum amount that can be earned.

capacity The maximum number of people, or amount of goods, that a vehicle, hotel, room or similar can physically, or legally, accommodate.

cape A point of land projecting into a body of water, usually a sea or ocean.

Cape Agulhas The southernmost point of the African continent, in South Africa.

Cape Cod A long, sandy peninsula in Massachusetts, USA.

Cape Comorin The southernmost point of India, south of Nagercoil.

Cape Doctor A strong south-easterly wind experienced in South Africa.

Cape Farewell The southernmost point of Greenland.

Cape Horn The southernmost point of the South American continent, in Chile.

Cape of Good Hope A headland in South Africa, south of Cape Town.

Cape Sable The southernmost point mainland Florida, USA.

Capetian Of or relating to the kings of France between AD987 and 1328, and to that period of French history generally.

capital The city or town of a country, province or state which is the administrative centre and which has officially been designated as such. The capital may be the largest city, but this by no means always the case: only three of the world's ten most populous cities are capitals; only four of the world's ten most populous countries have their largest city as the capital; and out of Europe's 19 urban agglomerations with a population of over 2 million, only seven are capitals. In some cases (such as the USA, Canada and Australia), the capital was deliberately not established in the largest city in order to counterbalance its influence, and the same policy was adopted by many US States (such as New York, California and Florida). In recent times, some countries (such as Nigeria, Côte d'Ivoire and Brazil) have established new capital cities away from the major centres, and others may do so in the future. A few countries (such as South Africa, Bolivia and Sri Lanka) have administrative, legislative or judicial pre-eminence split between more than one capital. > *Appendix 1.*

Capital Region USA A US regional marketing organisation covering the states surrounding Washington DC. > *US regional marketing organisations..*

Capsian Of or relating to the Palaeolithic culture of North Africa and Southern Europe.

capsize Of a boat, to overturn or upset.

capstan A thick revolving spindle used for winding a rope or hawser, commonly found on marine vessels to haul in mooring ropes.

capsule hotel Accommodation, commonly used in Japan, that provides sleeping compartments in drawer-like capsules, just large enough for one person.

captain The person in charge of a waterborne vessel or aircraft.

car 1. (UK) A private motor vehicle having three or more wheels.

2. A railway carriage.
3. Any passenger compartment in a vehicle such as a lift.

car ferry A vessel, usually a ship, designed to carry vehicles as well as passengers.

car hire *See vehicle rental.*

car rental *See vehicle rental.*

carafe An open-topped glass jug used for serving water or wine in a restaurant.

caravan Originally a trailer vehicle providing accommodation, but now also applied to many types of semi-permanent accommodation on special sites.

caravan park *See caravan site.*

caravan site An area where caravans may be parked. Sites may be semi-permanent, where the caravans may be parked for months or years, or short-stay.

caravanette A motor-caravan.

cardboarding A method of falsifying the audit coupons of a manually issued ticket. It is, of course, fraud and thus a criminal offence.

Cardinal The rail service between Chicago and Washington DC in the USA.

cargo Goods, other than a passenger's personal effects, carried on board a ship or aircraft.

carhop (US) A colloquial expression for a waiter at a drive-in restaurant.

Caribbean A general term used to describe the islands of the Caribbean Sea and, in many cases, the parts of the countries of Central and South America which have a Caribbean coastline. For convenience, the term may also include the Bahamas and the Turks and Caicos Islands.

Caribbean Sea The area of the Atlantic Ocean between South America, Central America and the Antilles.

carnet 1. A term of French origin that describes an official document that allows the temporary importation of goods without payment of duty.
2. On some transport networks (including the London Underground and the Paris Métro) a book of tickets sold at a discount.

Carnival of Colour *See Holi.*

Caroline Islands An archipelago in the western Pacific Ocean. The islands comprise the Federated States of Micronesia and Palau.

Carolingian Of or relating to the kings of France between AD751 and AD987 and the Holy Roman Emperors between AD800 and AD911, and those periods of those countries' history generally.

carousel 1. A rotating delivery system for the collection of luggage, especially at an airport.
2. (US) A merry-go-round at a funfair or similar.

carriage 1. (UK) A passenger vehicle on a railway.
2. Transportation between two points by a company existing for that purpose.

carriageway That part of a road intended for vehicles.

carrier A generic term for any transport operator.

carrier identification plate A small embossed plate that is fitted into a ticket validating machine and which endorses the name of the carrier onto the ticket or other document. Also known as a plate.

carsickness Nausea caused by travelling in a car or other road vehicle.

cartel An association or group of manufacturers or suppliers that seeks to control prices and other aspects of its members' trading. It is common practice for cartels to fix prices at a high level. Although cartels are now illegal in many countries, it is often difficult to detect and prevent their activities.

cartogram A map with statistical information in diagrammatic form.

cartography The art and practice of map-making.

carving skis A current design of skis, shorter than the skiier and wider at the tip and tail than was previously popular, which helps the skis to turn more easily. They are sometimes called shaped skis or hourglass skis: particularly wide models are sometimes known as fat boys.

casbah *See kasbah.*

cascade A small waterfall.

cash basis A method of payment for goods or services where no credit facilities are offered and settlement must be made in full before the goods or services are provided. The term 'cash' can in certain cases include a banker's draft or a cheque.

cashless system An arrangement adopted on cruise ships and at hotels whereby a credit card is registered on arrival and exchanged for an identity card against which purchases are charged.

casino A building used for gambling, especially roulette, sometimes attached to a hotel.

casita A bungalow, especially in Mexico.

Caspian Sea The inland sea in west central Asia, bordered by Russia, Kazakstan, Turkmenistan, Iran and Azerbaijan.

caste system The system practised in the Hindu culture whereby different personal levels of purity or pollution are said to be inherited. In a strict caste system, members of different levels will have no contact with each other.

casual dress A dress code whereby women wear a simple dress or skirt/slacks and blouse, and men wear trousers and open-necked shirts. In many establishments, jeans, shorts and trainers are unacceptable.

CAT Clear air turbulence. The disturbance caused to an aircraft when flying through inclement weather or air pockets.

cat's paw A very slight breeze that just ripples the surface of water.

catacomb An underground cemetery, generally Roman.

catamaran A boat with twin parallel hulls.

cataract A large waterfall or cascade, often with a relatively slight drop.

catchment area The area from which an attraction or resort derives most of its customers.

cathedral A principal place of Christian worship, in which there is a Bishop or Archbishop in residence.

Caucasian Of or relating to the white or light-skinned division of humankind.

Caucasus The range of mountains between the Black Sea and the Caspian Sea.

causeway A raised road or tract across low or wet ground or shallow water.

cave A large hollow in the side of a hill or cliff or underground.

cave tubing See *black-water rafting*.

caveat emptor A Latin expression meaning 'let the buyer beware', used to point out that the buyer is responsible for their satisfaction with a purchase.

cavern A cave, usually large.

cay A small island (sometimes spelled key, as in the Florida Keys).

CBT See *Certificate in Business Travel*.

CDW See *vehicle rental insurance*.

ceiling 1. The maximum height at which an aircraft can fly under a given set of conditions.
2. The inside planking of a ship's hull.

Celebes Also known as Sulawesi, an island in the Malay Archipelago and politically part of Indonesia.

Celsius See *centigrade*.

Celtic Of or relating to the pre-Roman inhabitants of Britain and Gaul and their descendants.

centi- A prefix commonly found in the metric system, meaning one-hundredth part of. Thus a centilitre is one hundredth of a litre.

Centigrade The temperature scale in which water freezes at $0°$ and boils at $100°$. A quick way approximately to convert Centigrade to Fahrenheit is to double the Centigrade figure and add 30. Thus $25°C \times 2 = 50 + 30 = 80°F$. Also known as Celsius.

centimetre A unit of measurement in the metric system, equal to approximately 0.4 of an inch.

Central America The geographical region comprising Belize, Costa Rica, El Salvador, Guatemala, Honduras, Nicaragua and Panama.

Central Standard Time 1. One of the time zones used in North America, six hours behind UTC.
2. One of the time zones used in Australia, nine and a half hours ahead of UTC.

Certificate in Business Travel (CBT) The qualification run by the Guild of Business Travel Agents and validated by City and Guilds. It is an examination-based qualification at several levels designed for those working, or intending to work, in business travel.

Ceylon An island off the south-east coast of India, now Sri Lanka.

chain 1. An obsolete imperial measurement of distance equal to 66 feet (one eightieth of a mile). The railways of Britain were surveyed using chains and certain measurements may still be referred to in these units.
2. A group of shops, restaurants, hotels or other retail businesses owned by the same person or organisation.

chair lift A lift with one to eight seats, common in ski resorts but sometimes used at other visitor attractions. Chairs are carried on a constantly moving cable up a slope. The oldest and slowest lifts typically seat one or two people, and are known as single and double chairs. The most modern and fastest lifts detach from a faster moving cable at the bottom of the lift, moving on a slower cable and thus allowing the chair to move slowly to pick up users. The same process takes place in reverse for dismounting. These modern chairs typically seat four (quad chairs), six (six-pac) or eight people in a row.

chalet A small, wooden house or bungalow, usually with an overhanging roof. Traditional in Switzerland and Austria and often used as accommodation for winter sports enthusiasts.

chambermaid A housemaid in a hotel.

champagne powder Very light powder snow, typically falling in western North America. The name has been trademarked by Steamboat resort.

channel 1. An expanse of water, wider than a strait, joining two larger areas of water.
2. A navigable passage between two or more areas of shallows in a waterway.
3. Any one of group of radio frequencies used to broadcast television images or similar.

Channel Islands A group of islands off the north-west coast of France comprising Alderney, Guernsey, Herm, Jersey, Sark and Jethou. They are British Crown Dependencies and not part of the United Kingdom, although close ties are maintained.

Channel Tunnel The under-sea tunnel that provides a direct rail link between England and France, carrying Eurostar (passenger) and Eurotunnel (vehicle and freight) services.

Channel, the (UK) The English Channel.

Chanukah (or **Hanukah**) A festival in the Jewish religious calendar, lasting for eight days, generally in December.

chapel A place of Christian worship, smaller than a church, and often currently or formerly attached to a private house or an institution, such as a school, or created as a distinct part of a cathedral.

charabanc An old-fashioned term for a motor coach.

charge card Similar to a credit card, although the extended payment facility is not automatically offered.

chart An alternative name for map, usually applied to the very accurate navigational maps used on aircraft and ships.

charter The act of a person or organisation paying for the exclusive use of part of or the whole of a vehicle. The term is usually applied to aircraft but can apply to any form of transport. An ad hoc charter is a one-off arrangement; a series charter is several journeys between the same points; a time charter is when the vehicle is chartered for a period of time.

chasm A deep, wide fissure or opening in the earth or rock, either on land or under water.

chauffeur The paid driver of a motor car.

chauffeur-drive A vehicle rented with a driver.

check (US) A cheque.

check digit A number, following a document number, that bears a mathematical relationship to that number. It is used to verify the accuracy of the number and thus identify any transcription errors. Also known as check sum.

check sum See check digit.

checked baggage Baggage that is registered to a traveller's destination and is conveyed in a special container or in the aircraft's hold.

check-in 1. The process of registering at a hotel or other accommodation.
2. The process of completing formalities before boarding a flight or other transportation.
3. The location or time at which a vehicle rental ends, and the formalities associated with this. Also known as drop-off.

check-in time The time by which a person must have checked in. In the case of accommodation, this may also refer to the earliest time at which the guest may take possession of the room.

check-out 1. The process of removing luggage and finalising the bill when a guest vacates a hotel or other accommodation.
2. The location or time at which a vehicle rental begins, and the formalities associated with it. Also known as pick-up.

check-out time The time by which a person must have checked out. In the case of accommodation, this is rarely later than noon. Late check-out, which may incur an additional charge, should ideally be agreed with the establishment in advance.

check-point A place where traffic is stopped for inspection and clearance.

chef A cook in a restaurant or similar establishment.

cheque (UK) A written order to a bank, usually on a pre-printed sheet, to pay a specified sum of money to a specified person or organisation. The increasing use of credit and debit cards has led to a decline in their use. Furthermore, cheques are generally not acceptable outside their country of issue. > travellers' cheques.

cheque card (UK) A card that guarantees payment of a cheque up to a stated amount.

chevron seating plan See herringbone seating plan.

chevron seating plan See herringbone seating plan.

Chicago Convention The international agreement that defined the freedoms of the air in 1944. > freedoms of the air.

child In travel, a young person who will not have to pay the full fare, but who may be entitled to a reduced one. The age at which a child ceases to be an infant, and the age at which a child becomes an adult, will vary from service to service, but for most airlines these cut-offs are 2 and 12 years respectively. Some organisations, such as amusement parks, will define a child by height, not age. > adult, infant.

chill factor The perceived lowering of temperature caused by wind. The chill factor is often more important in determining comfort than is the actual temperature.

chimney A wide crack, generally with three sides, that can accommodate a climber (or most of one).

China, People's Republic of The official name for mainland China. Not to be confused with the Republic of China (ROC), the term used by Taiwan to describe itself.

chine A deep narrow ravine, especially in the Isle of Wight or Dorset.

Chinook 1. A warm dry wind that blows east of the Rocky Mountains.
2. A warm wet southerly wind that blows west of the Rocky Mountains.
3. A make of helicopter.

chit A note, memorandum or similar document.

chocks Blocks placed either side of an aircraft's nose-wheel. Exact departure and arrival times are usually determined by the time at which the chocks are taken off or put on.

cholera An infectious intestinal disease transmitted by water and endemic in countries with poor standards of sanitation. Current WHO policy advises that immunisation is not effective in stopping the spread of the disease. > *health precautions.*

chondola The name for a modern ski lift that can carry either chairs or cabins.

chopper A colloquial term for a helicopter.

Christian 1. A person believing in or following Christianity.
2. A general term for countries or areas where Christianity is the dominant religion, particularly with reference to the aspects of its culture which Christianity has influenced. > *religion.*

christian name A person's first or given name. This term is not generally used in countries where Christianity is not the main religion and the expression 'given name' may be better understood.

Christianity The religion based on and following the teachings of Jesus Christ and his disciples. > *religion.*

Christmas A festival in the Christian religious calendar, generally celebrated on 25 December, but on 6 January by the Orthodox church.

chronological The ordering of information by date, usually with the most recent appearing last. Confusions can be caused when dates written in the date-first system are sorted using the month-first, and vice-versa. > *date order.*

chronometer An instrument that measures time, particularly at sea. Accurate navigation across meridians of longitude was not possible until the invention of the chronometer by the Englishman, John Harrison.

Chunnel A colloquial term for the Channel Tunnel. *See Channel Tunnel.*

church 1. A place of Christian worship, larger than a chapel but smaller than a cathedral.
2. A collective term for the Christian community regarded in general, or for the various officials and institutions concerned with the propagation and administration of the Christian religion.

chute 1. A narrow, short, steep ski run, off-piste in Europe.
2. An inflatable slide used as a means of emergency exit from an aircraft.
3. A very steep gully.

CIMTIG Chartered Institute of Marketing Travel Industry Group. *See Appendix 5a.*

Cinque Ports The ports of Sandwich, Dover, Hythe, Romney and Hastings on the south-east coast of England. From the 11th century they were granted privileges in exchange for defensive obligations. The term is retained today for ceremonial and touristic purposes.

CIP *See commercially important person.*

circle trip A return journey which is continuous back to its starting point and via two or more intermediate points, each of which carries a different fare.

circuitous A journey that is indirect and usually a long way around. Such routes are often discouraged or prohibited by many carriers.

circumnavigate To sail around, especially around the world.

circumpolar Around or near to one of the earth's poles.

cirque A deep, bowl-shaped hollow at the head of a valley or on a mountain.

cirrus A form of white, wispy cloud found at high altitude. Often known as 'mare's tails'.

CIS *See Commonwealth of Independent States.*

citizen A native or naturalized inhabitant of a country.

city 1. (UK) A large town which has formally been designated as a city by Royal Charter.
2. In most of the world, a large town. > *urban agglomeration.*
3. *See City, the.*

city terminal A point in a town or city where airline or boat passengers may check in for flights or sailings rather than at the airport or docks. Passengers may be taken into a city terminal at the end of their journeys.

City, the 1. The administrative area of the City of London.
2. The financial institutions which exist in and around the City of London.

claim To submit a request for compensation or reimbursement.

claimant A person making a claim.

clan A group of people with a common ancestor, especially in Scotland.

class In travel, the segregation of passengers according to the fare paid. Once simply first, second and third, the demands of marketing have resulted in many special names for the different classes. Some are unique to one carrier, and all may be subject to change.

classroom seating plan A common configuration at meetings, conferences or seminars whereby the delegates are seated at rows of tables arranged one behind the other.

clearance 1. The specific permission granted to an aircraft or other mode of transport to allow it to begin or continue with its journey.
2. The act of being allowed through customs.
3. The act of moving funds from one bank account to another, and the time taken to do this.
4. An amount of space needed for the safe passage of two objects, such as a lorry and a bridge, or two ships.
5. The activity of reducing prices of goods, including holidays, in order to create space for new products, as in the phrase 'clearance sale'.

clearing house The bank or other organisation appointed under BSP to perform various functions, including: receipt of sales transmissions; extraction and processing of data; rendering of billings to agents; receipt of payments from agents.

clearstory (US) *See clerestory.*

cleat 1. A projecting piece on a spar or gangway to give secure footing.
2. A clip to which a rope may be secured.

clerestory (or **clearstory**) (US) A raised-roof section of a building or railway carriage that contains windows and ventilators. Rarely seen these days on transport.

CLIA Cruise Lines International Association. *See Appendix 5b.*

cliff A steep rock face.

climate The general condition of an area in terms of its temperature, rainfall, humidity and other meteorological factors, arrived at by compiling weather statistics over a period of time (generally at least 30 years) and averaging the results. Unlike weather, variations in climate are relatively regular and predictable.

climate zones The climatic types, in approximately ascending order of average temperatures over a 24-hour period are:
• *Polar.* Extreme cold with vicious winds. Rainfall or snowfall is low, but as there is little evaporation, polar regions are snow-covered for much of the year.
• *Mountain.* Each rise in altitude of 15,000 feet (4,500 m) has the same effect as a change in latitude towards a pole of around 15°. At the tops of the tallest mountains, the climate is often as cold as at the poles, even in equatorial latitudes.
• *Tundra.* The area of cold, coniferous forests that extends across the northern parts of Siberia, Europe and North America, with long, cold winters and brief, warm, summers. There is relatively little rainfall. Tundra only occurs in the northern hemisphere since there are no large land masses at the equivalent southern latitudes.
• *Temperate.* Temperature and rainfall are reasonably evenly distributed throughout the year and there are no extremes of either. Temperate regions are characterised by very changeable day-to-day weather. The UK is in a temperate region.
• *Mediterranean.* Hot, dry summers and warm wet winters characterise the climate of west-facing coastal regions between the temperate and desert latitudes. Mediterranean climates can be found in every continent except Antarctica and all are popular with holidaymakers.
• *Savannah.* Areas such as the prairies of North America, the pampas of Argentina and the veldt of southern Africa are all screened from the moisture-laden sea air. There is only enough rainfall to support grass and similar plants.
• *Hot desert.* Areas with high daytime temperatures and little rainfall. With irrigation, desert areas can be made fertile.
• *Subtropical.* High temperatures throughout the year but with marked seasonal variations in rainfall.
• *Tropical.* High day and night temperatures and high rainfall give rise to luxuriant growth of many types of vegetation. Where unchecked this results in a typical rain forest.

climatic Of or relating to climate.

climbing clinic (US) A climbing school.

climbing grades A way of describing the relative difficulty of different kinds of climbing trips. While each operator tends to rank the various climbs featured in their programmes in some way, there is no common system, even within one country, such as exists with skiing. This makes direct comparisons difficult. Most companies will grade climbs into one of between three and six levels, with the higher number or letter generally being the hardest. In addition, some will have two grading systems: one referring to the technical difficulty of the climb and the amount of equipment needed; the other referring to level of fitness required by the climber. The second is at least as important in deciding whether a particular trip is suitable for a particular person. These issues also apply to trekking, hill walking, scrambling, ice climbing and mountaineering, each of which will have its own grades. A grade-three walk, for example, is thus a very different proposition from a grade three climb.

climbing school An institution where rock climbing is taught at all grades. Often called a climbing clinic in the USA.

clime An alternative and old-fashioned name for a region or climate.

clip The act of removing a small piece from a ticket (usually one for rail travel) to show that it has been used.

clip-joint A slang expression for a night club or similar establishment that swindles its guests by overcharging.

clipper A large, fast sailing vessel.

cloakroom 1. A room where outer garments and baggage can be left.
2. A lavatory.

closed dates Days for which reservations can no longer be taken due to unavailability.

closed-U-shape seating plan A common configuration at meetings, conferences or seminars whereby the delegates are seated around the outside of tables arranged together in a hollow rectangle.

cloud The visible masses of condensed water vapour floating in the atmosphere.

club car (US) A railway carriage equipped with a lounge and other amenities.

clustering The situation whereby a number of hotels or other similar travel-related establishments are grouped closely together in a certain area.

coach 1. (UK) A motor vehicle carrying a large number of passengers and used mainly for longer distance journeys and tours.
2. (US) Economy class.
3. A railway carriage.

coach class (US) Economy class.

coaming Small raised partitions at the doorways and around the hatches on a ship that prevent the access of water.

coast The border of the land near the sea.

coastal region An area on or close to a coast generally with a unifying factor such as dialect, topography or historical associations. In tourism terms, a coastal region will generally comprise a number of resorts and will have a name (such as 'English Riviera' or 'Costa del Sol'). The principal ones are described separately.

coaster A ship that travels along the coast from port to port.

coastguard A person or organisation keeping watch on the coasts and on local shipping to maintain safety and prevent smuggling.

coastline The line of the seashore, especially as regards its shape and characteristics.

cockpit 1. The part of an aircraft where the flight controls are located.
2. The control position of a yacht or motor launch.

code-share An arrangement whereby two or more airlines are allocated seats on the flight and sell them independently under their own airline prefix, although the actual aircraft will be operated by another airline.

co-development The situation where a plot of land, a building or other feature is jointly constructed or modified by two or more commercial partners (such as a hotel and a sports club) engaged in complementary business activities.

co-extensive Having the same extent, frontiers or limits.

coffee shop A small informal restaurant in a hotel or similar.

cog railway A form of railway used on steep gradients where the normal friction between wheels and track would give insufficient grip. An extra toothed wheel engages with a toothed rack on the track.

col The lowest passage between two mountain tops.

collection charge *See delivery charge.*

collision damage waiver *See vehicle rental insurance.*

colonial Of or relating to a colony or colonies. The term is also used pejoratively to describe a patronising attitude towards other cultures.

colony A group of settlers in a country, subject to a mother country.

colours The national flag or emblem flown by a ship.

commercially important person (CIP) Similar to VIP, but where the traveller's importance derives from commercial or business activities rather than status. > *VIP.*

commis A junior waiter or chef.

commission The amount paid by a principal to its agents for selling their products or services, usually calculated as a percentage of the sum paid by the client.

commissionable Any product or service the sale of which will result in a commission being paid to the seller.

common carrier A carrier that undertakes to transport any person or goods in a specified category or categories.

common-rated The name given to two or more destinations to which the fare is the same.

commonwealth A nation, viewed from the point of view of all its members having a stake or interest in it. The term was originally coined to help express a political philosophy, but has survived in the name of some international institutions, and also as part of the formal title of some countries.

Commonwealth Games A major international athletics event, which takes place every four years in a different Commonwealth city on each occasion. Accommodation and transport arrangements may need to be made months, and sometimes years, in advance.

Commonwealth of Independent States (CIS) The short-lived political entity in the 1990s which was created after the demise of the USSR and lasted until the establishment of its constituent republics as independent states. It included all the republics of the USSR except Estonia, Latvia and Lithuania.

Commonwealth, The A free association of independent states (currently 53) most of which were at one time under British administration.

communicating cabins The shipboard equivalent of connecting rooms.

communism The political and economic philosophy derived from Marxism, the main principles of which include the common ownership of property, the central control of economic and political activity and the subordination of the individual to the common good. In various forms, communism formed the guiding philosophy of many countries in the 20th century although has survived in only a few (notably China, Korea DPR and Cuba).

commuter Anyone who travels regularly on a route, usually to and from work.

commuter aircraft An aircraft, usually with fewer than 30 seats, that operates on relatively short routes.

comp. See *complimentary ticket.*

companionway A staircase on a ship, technically to a cabin, but often used loosely to refer to any stairway on board.

compartment 1. A small separate section in a railway carriage. On railways in Britain, these days compartments tend to be restricted to use by holders of first-class (or equivalent) tickets.
2. A watertight division in a ship.

compass An instrument used to determine direction. Magnetic compasses point to the magnetic north: other types, such as giro compasses, can give a true north reading.

compatriot A fellow countryman.

compensate To make restitution for loss or damage.

compensation An amount of money or other reimbursement made as restitution.

complement (or **full complement**) The number of persons required to fill or crew a ship or other conveyance.

complimentary ticket A free ticket given as thanks for a service provided or to be provided, or possibly as compensation.

complimentary upgrade The situation whereby a passenger or customer is upgraded to a higher class of accommodation, facility or service without additional payment.

comprehensive Complete or all-inclusive. Often used to describe insurance cover.

compressor A pump used to compress air to the high pressure necessary to charge diving cylinders.

computerised reservation system (CRS) The former name for *global distribution system.*

concierge A term of French origin that refers to a person in a hotel who provides information and arranges the transfer of the guests and their luggage to their rooms.

Concorde The world's first and to date only supersonic passenger aircraft. An Anglo-French co-operative venture, it made its maiden flight in March 1969: regular trans-Atlantic services started in May 1976. Only 20 were ever built, though the original plan was for over 300. On 25 July 2000, an Air France Concorde crashed on take-off from Paris with the loss of 113 lives. Although services were resumed the following November the aircraft was no longer considered viable. The last commercial flight took place between New York and London on 24 October 2003.

concourse An open area in a large building, station or airport, where people can wait for a short while before moving on.

conditions of carriage The special terms and conditions under which principals will carry passengers and their baggage. The purchase of a ticket is deemed to indicate acceptance of these terms and conditions, even if the passenger is not familiar with them. Many conditions of carriage exclude the rights that people have under the law.

condominium 1. (US) A block of flats or apartments, often rented out on a long term or timeshare basis. Often abbreviated to 'condo'.
2. A region administered by two or more powers.

conducted tour A tour led by a guide on a predetermined and fixed itinerary.

confederation A union or alliance of states.

conference The generic name for any sort of medium to large gathering for discussion, especially one held annually.

conference rooms Rooms set aside for business and similar meetings.

confidential tariff The rates offered by principals, such as hotels and excursion companies, for the use of agents and premium customers when arranging travel.

configuration The way in which the seats and other parts of an aircraft's interior are laid out.

confirmation A written, emailed or printed document that verifies the existence and details of a booking. Many travel bookings are now no longer confirmed in writing, although under CAA regulations, package holidays still must be.

confluence A place where two rivers meet and join.

Congo, Democratic Republic of A country in central West Africa formerly known as Zaire. Not to be confused with the Republic of Congo.

Congo, Republic of A country in central West Africa. Not to be confused with the Democratic Republic of Congo.

conjunction tickets The issuing of multiple flight tickets to cover a complex itinerary. A journey of four or more sectors cannot be fitted onto one ticket and in such instances, two or more tickets will be issued 'in conjunction' to cover the entire itinerary.

connecting rooms Two or more rooms in a hotel that have a private connecting door, so that occupants can move from one room to another without using the external corridor.

connecting service A flight or other service that links with another to provide a transfer, whereby a passenger completes a journey to a final destination travelling on two or more scheduled services with a change at the intermediate point/s.

consequential loss An insurance term meaning a loss arising from an original loss, for example loss of business incurred by a traveller as a result of a delayed flight. Partly because it is so difficult to evaluate, consequential loss is often excluded from cover in travel policies.

conservation area A region protected against damage or undesirable change. Many tourist destinations such as safari parks are also conservation areas.

consol. fare *See consolidation (2).*

consolidation 1. The action whereby a charter flight or tour operator combines two or more departures, thus maximising the passenger load.
2. The general term for the practice of selling discounted air tickets. Various regulations prohibit the public sale of air fares at a discount, but airlines often wish to maximise their profits by selling off surplus seats. They circumvent the various rules by selling their surplus seats, at heavily discounted rates, to a 'consolidator'. The consolidator then sells the seats on to agents or travellers at a price that includes his profit, but which is far lower than the official fare. These fares are colloquially known as 'consolidation' or 'consol.' fares.

consolidator A person or organisation dealing in discounted airfares, especially those made available by scheduled carriers. > *consolidation (2).*

consortium An association of companies or other organisations usually with the aim of enabling the members to increase their buying power or to share resources.

constellation A group of stars whose outline or appearance in the sky is considered to represent the outline of a figure or mythical being.

consul A government official, stationed in a foreign country, who represents the interests of the nationals of the represented country when they are in that foreign country. Consuls can render assistance to travellers who find themselves in difficulty, but generally only to the extent of ensuring they are treated in the same way as nationals of the country in question.

consulate The office where the consul works.

consultancy fee A mark-up that a travel agent adds to the price when no commission is paid by the supplier.

contents gauge A gauge which indicates the pressure of air inside a diving cylinder.

contents, table of A list, in order of appearance, of the items appearing in a book or manual.

contiguous Neighbouring, touching or in contact with. The 48 states of the USA (excluding Alaska and Hawaii, but generally also including Washington DC) are sometimes described as the contiguous states, and Alaska and Hawaii as the non-contiguous ones.

continent The Earth's landmass is divided into eight (some say five, six or seven) continents. These are:
• Africa
• Europe
• North America
• South America
• Asia
• Australasia
• Oceania
• Antarctica
Australasia and Oceania are often bracketed together, as are (less commonly) North and South America. For obvious reasons, Antarctica is often ignored altogether. Sometimes, still other divisions are used, reflecting the needs and usages of the particular sector or industry being addressed.
Despite being what might be termed the largest objects in the world, there is – with the exception of Antarctica – no universally accepted agreement as to the exact composition or area of any of the continents. One organisation will employ its own definitions which are, if consistently applied, as valid as those used by another. Turkey and Russia, for example, can reasonably be seen as being in either Europe or Asia, or both, and a

similar problem exists with Panama, Egypt, Greenland and Papua New Guinea. The whole of Central America (sometimes including Mexico) is often regarded as a separate entity, as is the Caribbean, and the widespread use of the term Latin America only adds to the confusion. Terms such as 'the Caribbean', 'the Middle East' and 'the Mediterranean' are often more widely used – and useful – in the travel industry than are the names of the continents (sometimes more than one) in which these regions are to be found. Some places, such as French Guiana, Hawaii and the Canary Islands, are politically fully part of one country but geographically somewhere else altogether. Organisations such as IATA and the WTO will often use names such as 'Europe' or 'Asia' in a specific sense which might conflict with the generally understood area of that name. So too do many other high-profile organisations with no connection with the travel industry, such as international sporting bodies. For more information, see the Columbus *World Travel Atlas*. (This book divides the world into six continents – Europe; Africa; Asia; Australasia & Oceania; Latin America & the Caribbean; and the USA & Canada.)

continental breakfast A light breakfast, generally of rolls, coffee and fruit juice.

continental plan A hotel rate that includes accommodation and continental breakfast.

contour lines Lines drawn on a map to connect points of equal height.

contour map A map that shows heights and depths by means of contour lines.

contraband Items that are illegal to export or import.

contrail An abbreviation of **condensation trail**. The visible trail of condensation left by a high-flying aircraft.

contremarque A term of French origin meaning a simple document issued to identify passengers, usually those travelling by rail, on a group ticket. This avoids the necessity for issuing separate tickets to each passenger.

contribution An insurance term for the principle that any liability is shared between all insurers involved.

control tower The building at an airport from which aircraft movements are controlled.

controlled duplication See *airline code*.

conurbation An extended urban area, often when several towns and their suburbs merge.

convenience A public lavatory.

convention 1. A widely held agreement about standards of behaviour and dress in specific circumstances.
2. A formal meeting or conference.
3. A formal agreement about standards and practices (such as the Montréal Convention, relating to air travel).

Convention and Visitors' Bureau (CVB) (US) A tourist office, generally regional or local.

convertible 1. A car with a roof that can be folded down.
2. An aircraft whose layout can be changed rapidly from cargo to passenger configuration and vice-versa.
3. A currency for which a market exists, and which can thus easily be exchanged.

cooling-off period The period of time during which the purchaser of a service, such as an insurance policy, may cancel the agreement and obtain a full refund. This will vary depending on the type of service, the policy of the individual company and the rules of any regulatory authority.

cooperative (1) A group of individuals of organisations that have joined together, permanently or temporarily, formally or informally, to maximise their negotiating, marketing or buying power.
(2) An organisation that is run for the mutual benefit of all its members.

co-pilot The second pilot of an aircraft.

coracle A small boat made of wickerwork and covered with watertight material. Used on Welsh and Irish lakes and rivers.

coral The shells of various marine animals. When laid down over time, these form reefs, islands and atolls.

Coral Coast The northern coast of Tunisia, the main town of which is Bizerte.

Coral Sea The area of the Pacific Ocean between the Great Barrier Reef and Melanesia.

cordillera A chain of mountains, especially one (such as the Andes) that forms the axis of a large land mass.

cordon bleu Cookery of the highest possible standard of preparation and presentation.

corduroy road A road made of tree trunks and laid across an unsound area such as a swamp.

Corinth Canal The canal that connects the Aegean Sea with the Ionian Sea, running through southern Greece.

Corinthian 1. Of or relating to ancient Corinth in southern Greece.
2. An amateur in sport; and the attitude of doing something for its own sake, rather than for profit, associated with this.

corkage The sum a restaurateur may charge customers who wish to bring their own drinks into their establishment.

corked The result of the contents of the bottle reacting with the cork and spoiling the wine.

corkscrew The movement of a ship or boat when it is both pitching and rolling as it meets oncoming waves.

corniche A road cut into the face of a cliff, often with spectacular views.

Coromandel Coast The coast of south-east India. The main ports include Nellore, Chennai (Madras), Pondicherry, Cuddalore and Nagappattinam.

corona A ring of light that appears closely around the moon or sun under certain meteorological conditions. > *halo*.

corporate Of or relating to a business, generally or specifically.

corporate rate Specially discounted rates offered to major purchasers of travel products. These rates are usually offered by hotels and car rental operators, although other principals are now adopting the idea.

corridor (UK) The passage in a railway carriage from which compartments can be accessed. > *korridorzuge*.

cosmopolitan Of, or knowing, many parts of the world.

Cossack One of the people of southern Imperial Russia, originally famous for their military skill.

Costa Blanca 'White coast': the resort area on the eastern coast of Spain from Denia to Torrevieja. The main town is Alicante: other resorts include Calpe and Benidorm.

Costa Brava 'Wild coast': the coast of the province of Gerona, north of Barcelona, with many popular tourist resorts. The coast south of Blanes is strictly speaking the Costa del Maresme.

Costa Calida 'Warm coast': the coast in the provinces of Andalucia and Murcia in Spain between Cabo de Gata and Cartagena.

Costa de Almería The eastern part of the Costa del Sol in southern Spain. The main town is Almería.

Costa de la Luz 'Coast of light': the Atlantic coast of southern Spain, principal towns are Huelva and Cádiz. More popular with the Spanish than with foreign tourists, the main resorts are Sanlúcar de Barrameda, Rota and Chipiona.

Costa de Lisboa The resort coast around Lisbon in Portugal, also known as the Costa do Sol or the Costa do Estoril. The main resorts are Cascais and Estoril.

Costa de Prata 'Silver coast': the Portuguese coast stretching from Oporto in the north to the Costa de Lisboa in the south. The main resorts include Figuera da Foz and Nazaré.

Costa del Azahar 'Orange-blossom coast': the Spanish resort area on the Mediterranean coast between the Costa Dorada in the north and the Costa Blanca in the south. The main town is Castellón de la Plana.

Costa del Maresme *See Costa Brava*.

Costa del Sol 'Coast of the sun': the resort region of southern Spain, stretching along the Mediterranean coast from Tarifa in the west to Cabo de Gata in the east, with the main concentration of resorts between Marbella and Motril. The main town is Málaga: resorts include Marbella, Fuengirola, Torremolinos, Nerja, Almuñécar, Salobreña and Almería.

Costa do Estoril *See Costa de Lisboa*.

Costa do Sol *See Costa de Lisboa*.

Costa Dorada 'Golden coast': the coastal resort area in Catalonia south of the Costa Brava. The main centres are Barcelona and Tarragona.

Costa Dourada 'Golden coast': Portuguese coastal region between Lisbon and the Algarve. The main towns are Sines and Vila Nova de Milfontes. Also known as the Costa de Ouro.

Costa Verde 'Green coast': the resort coast in Portugal north of Oporto. Also the Spanish coast of the Asturias region, principal town Gijón.

cost-of-living allowance A payment which is made to compensate employees to offset the higher costs in staying or living in certain cities, regions or countries compared to those of their home country.

cot A small bed, often folding, and usually only suitable for a child.

Côte d'Argent 'Silver coast': the coastal area in south-west France running from Arachon to the Spanish border. The main resorts include Vieux-Boucau-les-Bains, Mimizan, Bayonne and Biarritz.

Côte d'Azur 'Azure coast': the coast of south-east France, also known as the French Riviera. The main towns include St Tropez, St Raphaël, Cannes, Antibes, Nice and Monte Carlo. > *Riviera*.

Côte d'Emeraude 'Emerald coast': the coastal region in Brittany in north-east France between St Malo and Cap Fréhel, including Dinard.

Côte d'Opale 'Opal coast': the coast of north-east France in the Nord-Pas-de-Calais region, centred on Boulogner.

Côte des Calenques 'Coast of rocky inlets': the section of coast between Hyères and Marseilles in southern France.

Côte des Landes 'Coast of moors': the section of coast in south-west France, running from the Gironde estuary to Cap Ferret.

Côte Vermeille 'Ruby-red coast': the coast of south-western France between the Etang de Leucate and the Spanish frontier.

co-tidal line A line on a map connecting points at which tidal levels (such as high or low tide) appear simultaneously.

couchette A type of sleeping accommodation offered on European trains, which provides six fold-down berths to each standard class compartment. Only basic bedding is supplied and there is no segregation of the sexes. Couchettes are not used on UK rail services.

couloir A steep gully on mountainside that can be used as a transit route, which are sometimes prone to avalanching. Also known as an avalanche corridor.

count (**countess** when feminine) A noble of high rank. Where the term survives, it is mainly honorific.

counterfeit A document, bank note or similar that has been forged.

counterfoil Part of a receipt, ticket or other document retained by the issuer.

country 1. The territory of a nation with its own independent government, and recognised as such by other countries and international bodies. In practice, the definition of what is and what is not a country is not clear-cut. There are several areas of confusion:
• *Overseas territories that are politically part of another country.* These include Hawaii, the Canary Islands and French Guiana. These are administratively part of another country from which they are geographically separated. This may result in their being treated as if they were separate countries in some cases, particularly where they are seen as wholly separate travel destinations.
• *Overseas dependencies, with some degree of self-government.* There are over 30 of these. Most are islands or groups of islands, and most were previously directly administered by another country. These include Gibraltar, Wallis and Futuna, Guam, Greenland and the Cook Islands. For the same reasons as the overseas territories above (although with more justification) these are also often regarded as separate countries.
• *Countries within a federal union.* Before 1991, the republics of the USSR were examples of this, but nowadays, the United Kingdom provides the best instance. England, Scotland, Wales and Northern Ireland are in many ways separate countries and are generally marketed as separate destinations, and yet all are politically united.
• *Countries which are attempting to gain, or are in the process of gaining, independence.* By their nature, such places are in a state of some turmoil and are thus of less importance for the travel industry. These include Palestine NAR, East Timor and Western Sahara. Throughout the world there are many other separatist movements at work which may, in the future, result in the formation of new countries.
• *Countries which are de facto independent but are not recognised by a sizeable number of other states.* These places will generally have a bitter dispute with neighbouring countries which may claim some or all of the territory. The significance here is that travel to the countries with which the dispute exists may be impossible if the traveller has an entry visa for the disputed country or shows any other strong connection

with it. These include Israel, the Turkish Republic of Northern Cyprus and Taiwan. > *Appendix 1.*
2. The term 'country' is often used as part of a region created for travel marketing purposes, such as 'Shakespeare Country' and 'Mississippi River Country'.

county 1. Any of the territorial divisions of a country (or in the USA, a state), forming the main unit of local administration.
2. The territory of a count or countess. Where the term survives it is mainly honorific.

coupé A car with a sloping roofline and usually with two doors and limited seating in the rear. The term coupe (pronounced coup) is generally used in the USA. Note that different manufacturers and rental companies may use these and other descriptive terms to mean slightly different vehicles.

coupe See *coupé.*

coupon 1. A page of a multi-part ticket. Such tickets will have at least four types of coupon:
• *Exchange coupons* which are presented in exchange for the service;
• *Passenger coupons* which are the passenger's record and details of conditions of carriage;
• *Agency coupons* which are for the agent's records;
• *Audit coupons* which are used for accounting purposes.
2. A marketing term that refers to that part of an advertisement which is designed to be returned to the advertiser as a request for further information.
3. A discount voucher offering a price reduction on a specified item or service.

courier 1. See *tour guide.*
2. A person who delivers messages or portable items.

courier flight A journey undertaken by a messenger carrying documents, samples and the like.

course The direction in which a vehicle is heading.

courtyard An area, enclosed by walls or buildings, often with access to a street.

cove An inlet from a sea or other body of water, smaller than a bay.

cover charge An extra charge levied in some restaurants and night-clubs.

coxswain 1. The person who steers a boat. Usually pronounced cox'n.
2. (UK) The senior petty officer on a small ship.

CPT Confederation of Passenger Transport UK. See *Appendix 5a.*

CRAC Continental Rail Agents Consortium. See *Appendix 5a.*

crachin A light rain that falls in the coastal regions and mountains of Vietnam.

craft A general term for any boat or plane.

crag A steep or rugged rock.

crampons Metal devices with spikes fitted to boots to give a grip on hard packed snow and ice. For personal safety it is better to receive training in the use of crampons before embarking for areas where their use may be required.

crater The mouth of a volcano.

creative ticketing A term describing the means by which an agent seeks to obtain a lower fare by taking advantage of what are sometimes perceived as ambiguous or unenforceable fare regulations. If detected by carriers or their agents, this can result in denied travel and the imposition of financial or other penalties.

credit card A small plastic card that identifies a customer and allows the purchase of goods or services. Payment for the goods or services is made to the credit card company, which generally allow the debt to be discharged over a period of time if required. Interest is charged for this facility.

creek A small bay or harbour.

Creole 1. A descendent of European settlers in the West Indies or Central or South America.
2. A white descendent of French settlers in the southern United States.
3. A person of mixed European and African descent.
4. A former pidgin that has developed into a formalised language.

Crescent The rail service between New Orleans and New York in the USA.

crest The very top of a ridge or arête.

crevasse A deep crack, especially in a glacier.

crew Those who work on board a ship, aircraft or similar vehicle.

crewed charter A form of charter whereby the vessel is provided complete with supplies or crew.

cross trees A pair of horizontal timbers at the top of a lower mast of a ship, supporting the topmast.

cross-border ticketing The practice of issuing a ticket to start from a country other than that of the passenger's home or real origin. This is done to take advantage of a more favourable fare structure or exchange rate and is obviously discouraged by carriers.

cross-country skiing A method of skiing on generally flat land, as opposed to Alpine or downhill skiing. Cross-country skis are long, thin and light, connected to a lightweight shoe at the toe only, unlike downhill ski equipment which involves heavier, rigid boots connected at toe and heel to the ski.

crossroad (US) A road that joins or crosses a main road.

crossroads An intersection of two roads.

croupier A person who operates the gaming table at a casino.

crow's nest A small lookout position, near the top of the mast of a ship.

Crown Colony The former name for what is now a British Crown Dependency. *See British Overseas Territories.*

CRS *See Computerised Reservation System.*

cruise A voyage taken for pleasure, rather than purely for the purpose of transport.

cruising area The part of the world in which a cruise ship generally operates.

Crusader states Any of the four territories in the Middle East (the Kingdom of Jerusalem, the Principalities of Antioch and Tripoli and the County of Edessa) established by the Christians in the aftermath of the First Crusade (1098-1100), some of which survived in some form until 1291. Many castles and churches in the area date from this period.

CTA China Tourism Association. *See Appendix 5c.*

CTC Coach Tourism Council. *See Appendix 5a.*

CTO Caribbean Tourism Organisation. *See Appendix 5a.*

CTT Council for Travel & Tourism. *See Appendix 5a.*

cultural attraction An attraction that capitalises on its importance as a centre for cultural pursuits.

culture 1. The distinctive characteristics, achievement, attitude or way of life of a group or nation.
2. A general term for artistic, intellectual, musical or literary activities.

cumulus A type of cloud, generally dense and with sharp outlines, looking rather as if it were made of cotton wool.

cupola A rounded dome forming all or part of the roof of a building.

curfew A restriction on the public movement of people, typically during the hours of darkness. Curfews are usually imposed during periods of conflict or civil unrest.

currency Money in circulation in a specific country or countries in which it is officially recognised as a means of exchange for goods and services. In general, each country has its own currency which is used only within its borders (although it can often be exchanged elsewhere). Sometimes, however, a common currency may be used within a geographical or political area, even if each constituent country produces its own design of notes and coins: the Eastern Caribbean dollar, the CFA franc and, most recently, the euro are examples of this. In some cases, currencies of one country may be very widely accepted in others in addition to their own: some countries do not have their own currencies at all, but instead use a foreign hard currency as the preferred means of exchange. Such places are often dependant territories or former possessions. The US dollar and, to a lesser extent, the pound sterling are examples. The US dollar could fairly be described as a global currency, being widely accepted throughout the world, often in preference to local money.

currency exchange The act of converting one currency into another, such as through a bank or a bureau de change.

currency restrictions Controls put in place by governments to restrict the flow of money into and out of their countries.

current 1. A flow of water.
2. The measure of flow of electricity usually rated in amperes (generally abbreviated to amps). UK appliances are usually protected by a fuse in the plug rated at 3, 5 or 13 amps. Travellers should be aware that, if they adjust an appliance to run on a lower voltage, the fuse may need to be upgraded. This is because a halving of the voltage will lead to a doubling of the current drawn.

curtail To cut short. Most insurance policies can offer cover in the event that a holiday or other trip abroad needs to be curtailed. The conditions under which such a claim can be made will be set out in the small print and will vary from policy to policy. > *travel insurance.*

customer profile Information stored by business travel agents and similar organisations about their clients, such as class of travel, passport details and credit card details. Such information will generally be protected by legal restrictions as to its future use, particularly with regard to its sale or rental to a third party.

customs 1. The manners, morals and behavioural patterns of a country or society.
2. The government agency that seeks to control the movement of goods into and out of a country, particularly those which are prohibited or subject to customs duty.

customs clearance The act of passing through customs control when entering a country. This is normally facilitated by a series of channels, usually colour-coded: red generally indicates the traveller has goods to declare; green usually indicates that the traveller has no goods to declare; blue is used for people travelling within the EU (but not the Canary Islands, the Channel Islands or Gibraltar) who have no goods to declare. Whichever channel is used, travellers may be stopped by a customs officer and searched. If goods that are prohibited, restricted or in excess of the appropriate customs allowances are discovered, travellers risk heavy fines and possibly a prison sentence. Customs regulations vary from country to country and should be established in advance.

customs duty A tax levied on goods being imported.

cut-off date The last date by which an arrangement must be confirmed or completed.

cutter A small boat, other than a lifeboat, carried by a ship.

cutting An excavated channel through high ground for a railway or road.

CVB *See Convention and Visitors' Bureau.*

cyber butler *See technology butler.*

cycle Technically any wheeled vehicle, but usually used to refer to lightweight vehicles such as bicycles.

cycle route A track or path reserved for the use of those on pedal cycles.

cyclone 1. A circular storm revolving around a relatively calm centre.
2. An area of winds rotating inwards towards an area of low pressure, usually causing bad weather.

cylinder *See diving cylinder.*

Cyprus 1. A large island in the eastern Mediterranean, the southern part of which is the Republic of Cyprus, and the northern part the Turkish Republic of Northern Cyprus, an entity not recognised by most governments.
2. The Republic of Cyprus.

Cyrillic The alphabet used by the Slavonic people of the Orthodox Church, especially in Russia and Bulgaria. > *Appendix 8.*

D d

Dakar The capital of Senegal. Not to be confused with Dhaka, the capital of Bangladesh.

Dalmatia The Adriatic coast of most of former Yugoslavia, stretching from Zadar, Croatia in the north to Montenegro in the south, generally barren but with some excellent harbours. Principal towns are Zadar, Split and Dubrovnik.

dam An artificial barrier built across a river or other watercourse to hold back water and create a reservoir.

DAN Divers Alert Network. A US-based, non-profit organisation which provides emergency medical advice and assistance for scuba divers all over the world.

Danelaw The parts of northern and eastern England administered by the Danes in the 9th, 10th and early 11th centuries.

dangerous activity Any one of a range of hazardous sports and pastimes, such as winter sports, scuba diving and mountaineering, participation in which may invalidate an insurance policy unless specifically included in it. The conditions under which such a claim can be made will be set out in the small print and will vary from policy to policy. > *travel insurance.*

Dark Ages The period of European history from the collapse of the Roman Empire in the 5th century AD to the emergence of nation states and the revival of trade in the 10th century.

data Information of any kind. These days the term is commonly used in connection with information stored on a computer.

date order The convention for expressing dates as numbers. Most countries in the world, with the important exception of the USA, use the date-first system, whereby 9th August 1998 is written 9/8/98. In some computer systems and on some forms, leading zeros must be used (09/08/98); in others, the year must be written in full (09/08/1998). In the USA, however, the convention is month-first: 9th August 1998 would thus be written 8/9/98 (or 08/09/98, or 08/09/1998). In the USA, the month is generally expressed first even when written or spoken in full (August 9th rather than 9th August). IATA regulations require that all travel documents be written using the date-first system, but other communications between companies in the USA and the rest of the world can be fraught with confusion as a result of this difference of usage. If space permits, dates in such communications should ideally have the month written out, or abbreviated (Aug.).

davit A special crane built into a ship for loading and unloading goods and for lowering lifeboats or cargo.

day care (US) *See Ski Kindergarten.*

day delegate rate A rate offered by a hotel or similar venue to organisers of conferences and training events. The rate usually includes room hire, refreshments and lunch, as well as basic meeting facilities and equipment.

day out (UK) A short trip or excursion completed in a single day.

day rate A rate offered by a hotel or similar to a guest wishing to stay for a short time and not overnight.

day return A fare, often discounted, that is valid for travel out and back during the same day. Day return fares are usually cheaper than the single and therefore may not be used for a one-way journey. In cases where the non-usage of the return is detected (for example on a cross-Channel car ferry), the principal may retrospectively charge the full fare.

day trip *See day out.*

daylight saving time (DST) A practice observed in many countries, generally outside the tropics, whereby clocks are advanced by one hour in the local spring and put back by one hour in the local autumn. Countries which observe DST do not always do so across the whole of their territories (USA, Brazil, and Australia are examples). Nor will all countries that observe DST necessarily make their changes on the same day; moreover, the dates of change will differ from year to year to reflect national circumstances. Countries may have names, such as British Summer Time, to describe this change of time. > *time zones.*

daylight time (US) Time adjusted for daylight saving. > *daylight saving time.*

DC 1. *See direct current.*
2. District of Columbia, the Federal District of the USA, co-extensive with the national capital, Washington.

DCA *See deposit collection advice.*

DCS *See decompression sickness.*

deluxe The term usually applied to the very best accommodation or facility. It has no official meaning unless it is related to other terms within the classification to which it belongs.

dead calm No measurable wind.

dead reckoning A method of calculating a vessel's position from existing data when fresh observations are not possible.

deadheading (US) The circumstance of a vehicle or crew operating without passengers or payload. When aircrew travel on flights as passengers in order to position for another flight, they are said to be deadheading.

deadlight 1. A cover for a ship's porthole fixed to prevent the entry of light or sunlight. Deadlights may also be fitted to the portholes of the lowest decks in stormy weather conditions.
2. (US) A skylight that cannot be opened.

debark To land from a ship.

debit card A card, similar in size and shape to a credit card, but which takes money directly from its holder's bank account.

deck A horizontal division of a ship. The upper decks are often given names such as sun deck, boat deck and lido deck. Lower decks tend to be numbered or lettered. There is, however, no standard system.

deck plan A diagram showing the layout of cabins and public rooms on a ship.

deckhand A person employed to do jobs on the deck of a ship.

decompression 1. The sudden loss of cabin pressure in an aircraft.
2. The reduction in pressure experienced by divers when ascending, during which dissolved gases such as nitrogen escape from the body tissues.

decompression sickness A physical condition caused by a sudden or too rapid reduction in pressure, thus allowing dissolved nitrogen to form bubbles within the body tissues.

decompression tables A published list of stages at various depths of water at which a diver must pause and wait in order to allow for decompression to occur safely within the body.

Deep South The south-eastern states of the USA. Often considered as an area embodying traditional southern culture and values. > *South, the.*

deep vein thrombosis (DVT) A potentially fatal condition, which can affect those undergoing a prolonged period of inactivity, such as on a long flight, in which blood clots form in deep veins. Certain groups. including the overweight, those with heart problems and pregnant women, have an increased risk of DVT, but it can affect anyone. During a long flight, the risks can be reduced by taking regular exercise and drinking plenty of water. The condition has also been dubbed 'economy class syndrome', as it is argued that passengers in cramped conditions are less easily able to move during the flight and are thus more at risk. Some airlines have recently increased the seat pitch on certain long-distance services in response to this. > *health precautions, seat pitch.*

deep-sea Used to describe activities, such as diving or fishing. in the deeper parts of a sea or other body of water.

degree A measurement of angle denoted by the symbol °. There are 360 degrees in a circle. All bearings and positional measurements on a sphere (such as the earth) or a circle are expressed in degrees measured from a base line or point. Each degree is subdivided into 60 minutes (symbol '), and each minute into 60 seconds (symbol").

delivery charge The charge for delivering a vehicle to, or collecting a vehicle from, an address requested by the renter.

delta An area of land, usually roughly triangular, at the mouth of a river. This will have been formed from the sediment deposited from the river and its flatness will allow the river to create a large number of small channels.

delta wing An aircraft wing of triangular shape.

demand valve A regulator that supplies air as demanded by the diver.

demi-pension A hotel rate which includes room, breakfast and one other meal. Also known as half-board or modified American plan.

democracy A system of government whereby power is vested in elected representatives, and any state so governed.

demographics The factors concerning the characteristics of a population. Demographics can include aspects such as age, income, family size and employment.

demurrage An amount payable to the operator of a cargo vessel because of failure to load or unload a cargo by an agreed time.

dengue A tropical viral disease, transmitted by mosquitoes.

denied-boarding compensation The compensation to which passengers are generally entitled when they have a confirmed reservation for a flight but for which the airline cannot provide a seat, usually due to overbooking. The amount of compensation will vary according to a number of factors, including the carrier, the type of service and the length of the delay.

denizen An inhabitant or occupant of a place.

denomination The range of values of coins or banknotes in a particular currency.

departure The act of going away from a place, and specifically the time or place at which this journey begins.

departure delay insurance *See travel insurance.*

departure tax Taxation raised on passengers leaving a port or airport. The tax can be collected either at the time of ticketing or at the time of departure. Departure taxes do not only apply to international departures and may on occasions be raised on domestic departures as well.

dependency A country or province that is controlled by another.

deplane (US) To get off an aircraft.

deportation The lawful forced removal of a foreign national from a country. At the point of attempted entry this is often because of the lack of correct documentation; at other times often because of violation of local laws or of the conditions of their visa.

deportee A person who is being deported.

deposit A partial payment made to hold space or show goodwill.

deposit collection advice A document issued by travel agents to confirm collection of a customer's deposit. Agents will be billed at agreed periods for the total value of deposits collected. DCAs are becoming less common as electronic payment systems take over.

deposit reservation A reservation for which a hotel has received pre-payment for at least one night and is committed to holding the room, regardless of the guest's actual arrival time. This policy varies from hotel to hotel.

depot 1. (UK) A storage place.
2. (US) An alternative name for a terminal or station.

depression A low pressure air circulation in temperate latitudes. The condition is usually associated with wet weather.

depressurisation *See decompression.*

depth gauge An instrument used by divers which measures changes in pressure and calibrates these in terms of depth.

derail When a railway locomotive or its train leaves the tracks, usually as a result of an accident.

deregulation The term given to the gradual removal of government controls over an industry, such as air travel.

desert A dry and barren area, often sandy, and characterised by its lack of water and vegetation. > *climate zones.*

desolate Of a place, abandoned, uninhabited or neglected.

destination The end point of a journey.

destination wedding A wedding that takes place away from the bride or groom's country of residency, usually in a location perceived to be romantic.

detour 1. A deviation, voluntary or otherwise, from a planned route.
2. A voluntary deviation from the most direct route.

detrain (US) To alight from a train.

developing country A poor or underdeveloped country that is seeking to become more advanced.

devolution The act of certain legislative, administrative or judicial powers being relinquished by a central government and handed over to a regional authority to exercise. This has recently happened to some degree in the UK, particularly in relation to Scotland and Wales.

Dhaka The capital of Bangladesh. Not to be confused with Dakar, the capital of Senegal.

dhow A lateen-rigged ship used on the Arabian Sea.

dialect A form of speech peculiar to a particular region or group.

diarchy A region governed by two independent authorities.

diarise The act of recording an item in a diary or other scheduling system.

dictator A ruler who is not restricted by laws, a constitution, free elections or an effective opposition, and who governs in an arbitrary or tyrannical fashion.

dictatorship A state ruled by a dictator, or the government of such a state.

diesel engine An internal combustion engine in which the heat of compression of the air in the cylinders ignites the fuel.

diesel-electric A vehicle propelled by electricity generated by a diesel powered generator, carried on the same vehicle.

diesel-hauled A railway train that is pulled by a diesel-powered locomotive.

dig The site of an archaeological excavation.

digs (UK) A slang term for cheap lodgings.

diligence A legal term referring to the attention and care required in a given situation.

diner 1. (US) An informal roadside restaurant.
2. (US) A restaurant car on a train.
3. A person dining in a restaurant.

dinghy A small boat, often carried by a ship.

dining car (UK) A restaurant car on a train.

dinner jacket (UK) Formal evening wear for men comprising a jacket (usually black) and trousers, worn with a shirt and bow tie. The expression 'dinner jacket' does not refer simply to the jacket but generally to the whole ensemble. Both the jacket individually, and the outfit collectively, are also known as a tuxedo.

diphtheria An acute contagious bacterial disease, endemic worldwide, causing severe inflammation of the throat. Children are particularly at risk. > *health precautions.*

direct current An electrical supply whose direction does not alter. Battery-operated appliances run on DC, whereas most mains appliances run on AC. Travellers must take care in countries where DC supplies still exist as AC equipment may be damaged if it is used. > *alternating current.*

direct sell *See disintermediation.*

direct service A flight or other journey that does not require a passenger to change services. A direct service is not necessarily non-stop.

directional fare A fare that only applies in one direction of travel.

dirigible A steerable, lighter-than-air, aircraft. Also known as an airship.

disclaimer A clause, or series of clauses, in or appended to a contract or other form of agreement, which limits the right of one or other party (usually the purchaser) from making certain claims, for example for compensation.

discount A reduction given from the published fare, price or tariff.

Discover New England A US regional marketing organisation covering some of the states of New England. > *US regional marketing organisations.*

disembark To get off an aircraft, ship, train or other method of transport.

disintermediation The act of selling a product or service directly to the ultimate consumer, without recourse to a middle man. In travel, the middle man is generally the travel agent. The practice has long existed, with some tour operators specialising in direct selling. In recent times it has become more popular due to the information and purchasing possibilities of the internet.

displaced person A person who has been forced to leave his or her home country because of persecution, disease, famine, war or other serious problem.

displacement effect A tourism term given to the phenomenon where workers move from primary jobs (such as agriculture) to tourism-related jobs, such as hotel work.

distribution channel A means by which a product or service is made available to customers. Tour operators, for example, can choose either to use travel agents as their distribution channel, or maybe to sell via the internet.

distributory A branch of a stream that does not return to the main channel once having left it.

district 1. A territory or region marked off for special administrative purposes.
2. A part of a town or city.

ditch 1. A long, narrow gully that provides drainage.
2. To bring an aircraft down in the sea.

diuretic A substance that increases the amount of water passed in urine. Coffee, tea and alcohol are examples. Diuretics should be avoided as far as possible on long flights due to the low relative humidity of aircraft cabins. > *humidity, jet lag.*

Divers Alert Network *See DAN.*

diving cylinder A metal container designed to hold air at high pressures underwater. Sometimes called bottle or tank.

Diwali A festival in the Hindu religious calendar, celebrated at the time of the new moon in late October or early November.

docent (US) A guide, usually voluntary, in a museum, art gallery or similar.

dock (1) An area designed for the safe mooring of ships and the handling of their passengers and cargoes.
(2) The act of a ship coming to rest at a dock, harbour or other designated place.

doldrums A region of unpredictable weather near the Equator. In the days of sail the doldrums were feared because of the possibility of long periods of completely calm weather.

Dolphin Coast The stretch of coast in South Africa from Durban in the south to the Tugela river in the north.

domain An area owned by, ruled by or under the influence of a person, government or organisation.

dome car (US) *See observation car.*

Domesday Book A record of the land and property in England made on the orders of William the Conqueror after the Norman Conquest and completed in 1086. Many places stress their antiquity by claiming to have been mentioned in it.

domestic Within one's own country. Domestic tourism

is tourism within the country where a person lives; domestic flights are those within the airline's own country.

domestic inbound tourism A term defined by the WTO as comprising 'any person residing in a country, who travels to a place within this same country. The unit of measure used to quantify this concept is the number of nights by resident.' Note that the term 'tourism' refers to travellers generally, rather than those travelling purely for pleasure. > *tourism*.

domestic tourism *See tourism.*

domicile A person's own home or dwelling place.

Dominica, Commonwealth of One of the Lesser Antilles in the Caribbean. Not to be confused with the Dominican Republic.

Dominican Republic A country occupying the eastern part of the island of Hispaniola in the Caribbean. Not to be confused with the Commonwealth of Dominica.

dominion *See domain.*

doorman An employee of a hotel, restaurant, club or other similar, and usually high-class, establishment, who will be responsible for such services as greeting guests, hailing taxis, providing directions and assisting with luggage.

dory A small flat-bottomed fishing boat with high sides.

douane The French word for a customs post.

double An abbreviation for a double room.

double chair *See ski lift.*

double room A room with one double (large) bed. The term is sometimes used casually to describe any room that can accommodate two people, even if it has two small beds, but this is not strictly correct. > *twin*.

double-booking When two or more reservations are made for the same seat, accommodation or service. When done in an attempt to maximise load factors, it is usually known as over-booking. *See over-booking.*

double-decker A bus with an upper and lower deck.

double-double A room with two double (large) beds.

double-headed A train hauled by two locomotives.

downgrade To move to a lower grade of accommodation or service.

downriver At or towards the mouth of a river.

downtown (US) The lower or more central part of a town or city, particularly where this forms a distinct area or is associated with commerce.

down-under A colloquial term for Australia or New Zealand.

downwind In the direction in which the wind is blowing.

drag The air resistance a vehicle, such as an aircraft, is subjected to when in motion.

drag lift The commonest type of ski lift which pulls a skier or snowboarder uphill by means of an attachment to a moving cable. Common types include button lifts (also known as Poma lifts after the main manufacturer), or as surface tow lifts in North America. Another type is the T-bar named after its shape which, unlike the single-person button lift, can drag two skiers per T-bar side by side.

dram A small drink of spirits.

draught The depth of water a ship draws. In effect, the minimum depth that is required for it to float clear of the bottom.

drayage The charge levied for transporting goods.

dress code The standard of dress which is expected, required, or prohibited at an event or in an establishment.

DRF Danmarks Rejsebureau Forening. *See Appendix 5c.*

drift Deviation from the set course, due to the effect of side-winds or currents.

drift diving A dive where divers allow the current to move them along.

drive-in (Also **drive-through**) (Mainly US) Of a place, such as a bank or fast-food restaurant, into which customers may drive and obtain goods or services without leaving their vehicles.

drive-on A ferry or similar, onto which vehicles are loaded by their own drivers, rather than by a crane or other method.

drive-through *See drive-in.*

drophead (UK) A car with a collapsible fabric roof.

drop-off *See check-in (3).*

drop-off charge The name given to the charge levied by a car rental company in connection with a one-way rental.

droshky A Russian small four-wheel open horse-drawn carriage.

DRV Deutscher Reisebüro- und Reiseveranstalter Verband e.V. *See Appendix 5c.*

dry dock A structure large enough to contain a ship and from which the water can be emptied. Dry docks allow work to be undertaken on those parts of the hull of a vessel that would normally be submerged.

dry grassland   *See savannah.*

dry lease   The rental of a vehicle, such as an aircraft, without supplies or crew. > *wet lease.*

dry suit   A diving suit which keeps its wearer dry by means of neck, wrist and possibly ankle seals.

DST   *See daylight saving time.*

duchy   The territory of a duke or duchess. Where the term survives it is mainly honorific.

dude ranch   (US) A ranch converted to a holiday centre.

duke   (**duchess** when feminine) A noble of high rank and, in the past, at times independent (such as the Dukes of Normandy). Where the term survives it is mainly honorific.

dumb terminal   A computer connected to a mainframe on which its files and often its programmes are stored.

dune   A hillock or mound formed of sand. Sand dunes can move with the wind and have been known to engulf large features.

dune-buggy   *See beach-buggy.*

duplex   A hotel suite with two floors.

Dutch   1. Of or relating to the Netherlands.

2. (US) The region of Pennsylvania, mainly Lancaster County, settled by Amish people and others originally from Germany. 'Dutch' is, in this case, a corruption of 'Deutsch'.

dutiable   subject to duty > *duty.*

duty   The tax levied on certain goods, especially alcohol and tobacco.

duty manager   A person in charge of an establishment at a given time.

duty-free   Goods bought in a place where duties are not levied, such as ships or aircraft in transit in international waters or airspace.

duty-free allowance   The number, amount or value of goods, bought duty-free, that may be brought into a country without payment of duty.

duty-free shop   A retail outlet, usually at an airport, selling goods free of its country's duties and taxes.

DVT   *See deep vein thrombosis.*

DVW   Damage-to-vehicle waiver. Similar to collision damage waiver (CDW). > *vehicle rental insurance.*

DWT   Dead-weight tonnage. The total weight of everything carried on a vehicle or ship, equal to the difference between the laden and the unladen weight.

dyke   (or **dike**) A long wall or bank built to prevent flooding.

E e

EANx *See nitrox.*

ear clearing The process of equalising the pressure inside the ear with the outside pressure caused by increased depths. Also called Valsalva Manoeuvre.

earl (**countess** when feminine) A noble of high rank. Where the term survives it is mainly honorific.

earldom The territory of an earl or countess. Where the term survives it is mainly honorific.

earlybird Originally a proprietary term used to describe advance booking discounts offered by certain principals. Now often used as any form of advance purchase product attracting a discount, especially package holidays.

easement 1. A right of passage over another's land. 2. A relaxation in routing restrictions, especially on local rail journeys.

east One of the four cardinal points of the compass, 90° clockwise from north and 180° from west; on the right of maps where (as is normal) north is at the top. > *north.*

East China Sea The area of the Pacific Ocean between China, Korea, Taiwan and Japan.

East Greenland Current A cold current running down the east coast of Greenland, bringing Arctic waters in the Atlantic.

East Indies A general geographical term used for the area comprising India and the Malay Archipelago. Not commonly used these days.

Easter A festival in the Christian religious calendar celebrated in March or April on the Sunday following the first full moon after the vernal equinox.

Eastern & Oriental Express The luxury rail service which runs between Bangkok and Chang Mai in Thailand; and between Bangkok and Singapore via Kuala Lumpur in Malaysia.

eastern hemisphere The half of the earth to the east of 0° longitude and to the west of 180° longitude.

Eastern Mediterranean Terms Yacht charter terms under which the fee includes the charter of the yacht with all equipment; basic consumables for engine-room, deck and cabins; the crew's wages and food; insurance for the yacht itself, for third party claims and employer's liability insurance for the crew; fuel for three to five hours cruising per day (depending on yacht and averaged throughout the charter); half board for the guests (breakfast and lunch); berthing dues and other harbour charges (except Corinthian

Canal dues); and water or electricity taken from the shore. Other costs, such as fuel for the ski boats, the client's food and drink, berthing and harbour expenses outside the yacht's normal cruising area, laundry and radio telephone and other communication costs, must be paid by the client. These terms may vary.

Eastern Standard Time 1. One of the time zones used in North America, five hours behind UTC. 2. One of the time zones used in Australia, ten hours ahead of UTC.

eatery A colloquial expression for a restaurant or other eating place, often an informal one.

ebb The movement of the tide back out to sea.

EBTA European Business Travel Association. *See Appendix 5a.*

EC European Community, the previous name for what is now the EU.

echo sounder An instrument which measures the depth of water by timing the echo of a pulse as it bounces back from the seabed.

eclipse The total or partial obscuring of one celestial body by another, and the period of time during which this occurs. A solar eclipse is caused by the moon passing between the earth and the sun; a lunar eclipse is caused by the earth passing between the sun and the moon. A solar eclipse, which is what is mainly meant by the word, results in varying degrees of darkness on parts of the earth's surface. During a total solar eclipse, when the sun appears to be totally obscured, the area in complete shadow is called the umbra; the penumbra is the area of partial shadow surrounding this. An annular eclipse is when the apparent size of the moon is too small to fully cover the sun, resulting in a ring of sunlight remaining round the moon. Timings and locations of eclipses can be predicted with complete accuracy. Total solar eclipses over populated areas are comparatively rare.

ecology The study of the interaction of people with their environment.

economy class Usually the cheapest available class on a service and with the most basic level of comfort.

economy class syndrome *See deep vein thrombosis*

economy of scale The savings that might be made when larger quantities of a product or service are supplied. For example, a 12-coach train will incur the same driver costs as a two-coach one.

ecotourism Tourism that considers or encourages the preservation of the environment. Sometimes called green tourism.

ECTAA Group of National Travel Agents' and Tour Operators' Associations within the EU. *See Appendix 5d.*

eddy A small circular movement of air or water.

educational *See familiarisation trip.*

educational trip *See familiarisation trip.*

EEC European Economic Community, the original name for what became the European Community, and what is now the EU. *See European Union.*

effendi A man of standing and respect in many eastern Mediterranean and Middle Eastern countries, occasionally used as a term of respect to a visitor.

efficiency (US) Accommodation, such as a small apartment, with some cooking facilities.

EFT Elapsed flying time. *See actual flying time.*

EFTPOS *See electronic funds transfer at point of sale.*

Egyptiac The civilisation of the ancient Egyptians (c.4000BC to AD280).

EIBTM *See European Incentive and Business Travel Market.*

Eid al-Adha A festival in the Islamic religious calendar marking the culmination of the Hajj.

Eid al-Fitr A festival in the Islamic religious calendar marking the end of Ramadan.

Eight Degree Channel The marine frontier between the Lackshadweep Islands (India) and the Maldives.

Eire A former name for the Republic of Ireland.

EJT Elapsed journey time. *See actual flying time.*

El Niño A change in the ocean-atmosphere system in the eastern Pacific that contributes to significant weather changes throughout the world. El Niño is characterised by an increase in water temperatures in the equatorial regions of the central and eastern Pacific. El Niño is a recurrent phenomenon, first recorded in 1567 and the most recent occurrence prior to the 1990s was in the early 1940s.

El Transcantábrico A seven-day luxury rail cruise running along Spain's northern coast.

elapsed time The actual time taken to travel between two points, taking local time changes into account.

electric storm A thunderstorm.

electrified A railway line with electrical conductors, using either overhead lines or an extra rail. Electrified railways usually provide a faster and more reliable service than those operated by steam or diesel locomotives.

electronic funds transfer at point of sale A payment system by which funds are drawn electronically from a customer's bank account as soon as a transaction has been authorised.

electronic ticketing (or **e-ticketing**) The system by which passengers can travel without holding a conventional ticket. Their details are stored on a computer system: on reaching their departure point and identifying themselves, passengers will be given authority to check in. Increasingly, this facility applies to most low-cost airlines and UK ferry companies. Passengersmay sometimes check in at a machine and choose their own seat.

elevator 1. The moveable part of an aircraft's tailplane that controls vertical motion.
2. (US) A lift used for carrying people.

Elizabethan Of or relating to the period of English history during the reign of Elizabeth I (1558 to 1603).

Elsan A British proprietary brand of portable chemical lavatory, sometimes used to describe any such appliance.

embankment An earth or stone bank for carrying a railway or road over a depression. Embankments and other earthworks are necessary for railways since they lose efficiency very rapidly if faced with gradients.

embargo 1. A prohibition preventing suppliers from dealing with a country or organisation.
2. A period during which, or for which, bookings may not be taken.

embark To get on board.

embassy The residence and offices of a ambassador. Embassy staff can often provide assistance to travellers.

Emerald Coast The stretch of coast in north-west Florida. The main resorts are Destin and Fort Walton Beach.

Emerald Isle Ireland.

emigrant A person who leaves their native country permanently.

emigrate To leave one's native country permanently.

émigré An emigrant, particularly a political exile.

emir An independent ruler or chieftain in Islamic countries, and sometimes also a military commander.

emirate The domain of an emir.

empire An extensive group of states or countries under the control of one supreme power (an emperor or empress).

Empire Builder The rail service between Chicago and Seattle/Portland in the USA.

emplane *See enplane.*

empty leg The operation of a journey without passengers on board.

en bloc All together. Sometimes used in travel to denote an action taken for a group. > *group.*

en fête Holding or getting ready for a holiday or celebration.

en route Actually travelling on a journey.

en suite Forming a single unit. Often used to describe a bedroom with a connecting bathroom.

endemic A disease which is generally present in a given area.

end-on construction A fare construction method whereby a fare from point A to point B is added to the fare from point B to point C. Since this type of construction is usually resorted to by those wishing to undercut an advertised through fare, there are many ways by which its use is restricted. > *split ticketing.*

endorsement 1. A signature or other entry on a document to indicate that it has in some manner changed.
2. (UK) A record of a driving conviction entered into a driving licence.

engine A colloquial term for a railway locomotive.

engineer (US) The driver of a railway locomotive.

England One of the constituent countries of the United Kingdom of Great Britain and Northern Ireland. > *Great Britain, United Kingdom.*

English breakfast Full cooked breakfast in the English style.

English Channel The body of water between northern France and Southern England and one of the busiest shipping lanes in the world. Its narrowest point is the Strait of Dover.

English Civil War A collective name for the series of conflicts in England (1642 to 1651) between the Royalists and the Parliamentarians. After the execution of Charles I in 1649, a Commonwealth was established for 11 years. Charles' son, Charles II, was restored to the throne in 1660.

English Riviera The resort coast of south Devon centred on Torquay, Brixham and Paignton.

enplane To get onto an aircraft.

enriched air *See nitrox.*

ensign 1. A banner or flag, especially one used on a ship.
2. A junior naval officer.

entente cordiale A friendly understanding between nations or states. It is particularly applied to the relationship between the UK and France.

entrain To get onto a train.

entrée 1. (UK) A dish served before the main course.
2. (US) The main course.

entrepôt A warehouse for the temporary storage of goods in transit.

entresol A mezzanine floor.

entry permit 1. A form, often needing completion immediately prior to arrival, which must be presented to the immigration officer.
2. The stamp or other endorsement made in a passport showing the date of the traveller's arrival in the country.

entry visa *See visa.*

envelope The covering of a balloon or airship.

environment 1. The physical surroundings and conditions of an area, especially as they relate to people's lives.
2. The natural world in general.

environs The area surrounding or in the vicinity of a particular place.

enzootic A disease affecting animals which is generally present in a given area.

EP 1. *See European Plan.*
2. *See extended protection.*

epidemic A widespread occurrence of a disease.

Equator An imaginary line at 0° latitude dividing the earth into its two hemispheres, northern and southern.

equatorial At or near the Equator. > *latitude.*

Equatorial Counter-current The current in the tropics that flows in the opposite direction to the trade winds.

Equatorial Guinea A country in West Africa. Not to be confused with Guinea, Guinea-Bissau, New Guinea or Papua New Guinea .

equinox Either of the two times of the year (around 21 March and 23 September) when the sun passes directly over the Equator and when days and nights throughout the world are of equal length. The equinox which occurs in that hemisphere's autumn is known as the autumnal equinox: the one that occurs in that hemisphere's spring is known as the vernal equinox.

ERA European Regional Airlines Association. *See Appendix 5d.*

escalator A staircase powered by a motor consisting of an endless chain of steps continuously ascending or descending.

escarpment A steep slope at the edge of a plateau.

escort 1. *See tour guide.*
2. A person hired by an individual to provide company for an agreed period of time. The term can also refer to a prostitute.

escorted tour A tour, often on a coach, that is accompanied by a tour leader or guide.

escrow account A bank account established to hold a customer's payment to a supplier until such time as specified goods or services have been delivered or performed.

ESITO Events Sector Industry Training Organisation. *See Appendix 5a.*

Eskimo Of or relating to the peoples inhabiting northern Canada, Alaska, Greenland and Siberia. > *Nunavut, Inuit, Inupiat, Inupiak.*

Eskimo civilisation (Also **Inuit civilisation**) The civilisation that started in the Aleutian Islands around 1100BC and lasted until around AD1850.

esplanade A long level area for walking, usually between the beach and road.

estaminet A French term for a small café selling alcoholic drinks.

estate car (UK) A car with an extended rear luggage area.

estuary The mouth of a river that is relatively long and wide. Estuaries are considered to begin at the upstream point where the tidal effect can be detected.

ETA Estimated time of arrival.

ETC English Tourism Council. *See BTA, Appendix 5a.*

ETC European Travel Commission. *See Appendix 5d.*

ETD Estimated time of departure.

Etesian Wind A wind blowing from the north and north-west in the eastern Mediterranean and the Aegean, often creating rough seas.

ethnic Belonging to a group, region or nation having a distinctive cultural tradition.

ethnic minority An ethnic group living in a country or area where they are significantly outnumbered by the majority of the population.

ethnocentric The evaluation of the culture and traditions of other races by criteria relating to one's own.

e-ticket *See electronic ticketing.*

E-tickets The increasingly common system whereby travel tickets are not issued in printed form but are confirmed and stored electronically. On production of the correct passport, credit card, booking reference number or other specified identification, boarding cards or other appropriate documents are issued at the point of departure.

ETOA European Tour Operators Association. *See Appendix 5a.*

Etruscan Of or relating to ancient Etruria in Italy, especially its pre-Roman civilisation.

EU *See European Union.*

Eurasian Of mixed European and Asian parentage.

euro The currency now used by 12 member states of the EU, but not currently the UK. It was introduced in January 2002 and replaced the previously used local currencies. Each country issues its own notes and coins, all of which are legal tender in all 12 countries.

Europe 1. One of the world's continents. As with most continents, opinions differ as to its exact composition and area. > *continent.*
2. Sometimes used, generally in a political or economic context, to refer to the European Union. *See European Union.*

European City of Culture An initiative run by the European Union since 1985 to reflect, promote and celebrate Europe's wide cultural diversity. Until 1999, only one city a year was selected, but the millennium year of 2000 there were nine (Avignon, Bergen, Bologna, Brussels, Cracow, Helsinki, Prague, Reykjavik and Santiago de Compostela), and two in both 2001 (Oporto and Rotterdam) and 2002 (Bruges and Salamanca). 2003's European City of Culture was Graz and 2004's were Genoa and Lille. 2005's is Cork. The UK's only representative to date has been Glasgow in 1990.

European Community The former name, replacing European Economic Community (EEC), for what is now known as the European Union (EU). *See European Union.*

European Incentive and Business Travel Market An exhibition and conference held every December in Barcelona.

European Plan A hotel rate including accommodation only and no meals.

European Union An economic and political association currently comprising the countries of Austria, Belgium, Denmark, Finland, France, Germany, Greece, Ireland,

Italy, Luxembourg, the Netherlands, Portugal, Spain, Sweden, the United Kingdom, Poland, Hungary, Czech Republic, Slovak Republic, Slovenia, Estonia, Latvia, Lithuania, the Republic of Cyprus and Malta. Other countries are scheduled to join in the future. For more information, see the Columbus *World Travel Atlas*.

Eurostar The high-speed train service that links London with Paris, Lille and Brussels via the Channel Tunnel. Seasonal services also operate to southern France and to the Savoy area for winter sports.

Eurotunnel The rail shuttle service that carries cars, lorries, coaches and motor cycles, and their passengers, through the Channel Tunnel. This was formerly called Le Shuttle.

Eustachian tube The passageway which connects the middle ear and the back of the throat.

even keel When a ship is in an upright position.

ex gratia A payment or reimbursement made as a favour, rather than by legal obligation.

exceptions and exclusions An insurance term that refers to the risks that an insurance policy does not cover. Certain exclusions are common to most policies: for example radioactive contamination. Others will depend on the insurance company's business decisions: for example, some cover motorcycling, some do not. Many companies will cover sports such as scuba diving and skiing only if an additional premium is paid.

excess An amount that may be deducted from an insurance claim prior to payment by the insurer. For example, if a baggage cover section had an excess of £35, then a claim for £100 would be reduced to £65 on settlement. This discourages policyholders from making very small claims.

excess baggage Baggage that is larger or heavier than the baggage allowance. On airlines, where space is at a premium, passengers carrying excess baggage generally have to pay extra. Traditionally the standard charge was set at 1% of the first class one-way fare for each kilo of excess, but some carriers have now changed their charging structure.

exchange coupon The coupon or coupons of a ticket or voucher that are exchanged for the service provided.

exchange order See *voucher*.

exchange rate The rate at which money can be converted from one currency to another.

excise duty The tax payable on certain goods, typically alcohol and tobacco.

exclusive Originally accommodation or other facility the use of which is restricted to a select few. Now frequently used as a marketing term implying that a particular offer is special and restricted, even though this may not always be strictly true.

excursion 1. A trip taken as an extra while on holiday, often to a place of special interest.
2. A short trip away, usually for a day or less.

excursion fare A discounted fare with restrictions designed to discourage its use by business travellers.

executive floor A hotel floor reserved for business travellers, usually at a premium rate and often for members of the hotel's loyalty club.

executive lounge The general name given to a room, especially at an airport, that provides extra facilities to those passengers who have paid a premium fare.

exit permit A document or a passport stamp which allows a traveller to leave a country.

exit visa A visa that allows a traveller to leave a country.

exotic A destination, resort or hotel that is strikingly different and glamorous. The term sometimes implies that the destination is also far away.

expatriate A person living in a country other than that of their origin.

expedition A journey made for a specific purpose, such as exploration or scientific research.

exploration A journey made with the intention of discovery.

expo An abbreviation for exposition.

export To take or send items out of a country.

exposition A large international exhibition.

express A faster than normal method of transport or delivery.

express train A train stopping at few intermediate stations or none at all.

expressway (US) An urban motorway.

extended protection See *vehicle rental insurance*.

extras Items or services not included in the basic price and which are usually charged for separately.

extreme sport A generic name given to any sport or activity that involves more than the normal amount of hazard and/or discomfort.

exurb (US) The district outside a town or city, especially a prosperous area beyond the suburbs.

F f

face-mask A mask with a glass port that fits over the eyes and nose of a diver to facilitate underwater operation.

Fahrenheit The temperature scale in which water freezes at 32° and boils at 212°. A quick way to approximately convert Fahrenheit to centigrade is to deduct 30 and halve the result. Thus, 70°F - 30 = 40. Divide by 2 = 20°C.

fairway 1. A navigable channel.
2. The mown part of a golf course between the tee and the putting green.

fall (US) Autumn.

fam trip See *familiarisation trip*.

familiarisation trip A visit, usually by a group of travel agents, to a resort, hotel, region or other similar organisation body, in order that they can better understand and sell the destination to their clients. They are sometimes called fam trips or educationals.

family cabin A cabin on a ship with sufficient accommodation for a family, usually assumed to be two adults and two children.

family fare A special fare offered to families travelling together.

family plan A special rate for family groups at a hotel or similar establishment.

family room A hotel room with sufficient accommodation for a family, usually assumed to be two adults and two children.

fan jet A type of jet aircraft engine where the incoming air is compressed by a fan.

fantail The overhang at the stern of a ship.

Fantasia A GDS used by some Far Eastern airlines.

Far East A general geographic term describing East and South-East Asia and including Brunei, Cambodia, China, Indonesia, Japan, Democratic People's Republic of Korea (North Korea), Republic of Korea (South Korea), Laos, Malaysia, Myanmar, the Philippines, Singapore, Taiwan, Thailand, Vietnam. Sometimes the definition is taken to include Mongolia and the eastern Siberian region of the Russian Federation.

Far Eastern civilisation The civilisation of the Far East in general, but particularly that of Japan and Korea (c.AD645 to date).

fare 1. The amount that a passenger must pay to be conveyed on a vehicle providing public transport.
2. The range of food and beverages provided in a restaurant.

fare basis The type of fare used for a particular ticket and the code that indicates this.

fare construction point The point where a fare ends or the point of tunaround. This is usually, but not always, the most distant point on the journey.

fast-food A type of food which is provided, typically by large multi-national chains, on demand, without delay and generally at low cost. > *slow food*.

fast-track Any system that allows a more rapid completion of a task. Typically used to describe special airline check-in and airport transit systems that allow more rapid processing, generally for first- and business-class passengers.

fat boys See *carving skis*.

fathom A measure of water depth. A fathom is 6 feet (1.82m).

fathometer A device for measuring the depth of water.

fauna The animal life of a region.

favela A Brazilian shack or shanty town.

FB See *full board*.

FCU See *fare construction unit*.

FE See *foreign exchange*.

federal 1. A system of government in which several states form a unity but remain to a greater or lesser extent independent in their internal affairs, such as Switzerland and the USA.
2. The name commonly given to the central government of a federal country and its agencies.

fee-based pricing See *management fee*.

feeder service A service that carries passengers from a smaller originating point to a main hub, and back.

FEEE The Foundation for Environmental Education in Europe. One of its functions is to administer the Blue Flag Campaign for beaches. See *Blue Flag beach*.

fell A stretch of hills or moorland, especially in northern England.

felucca A small Mediterranean coastal vessel with oars and/or lateen sails. They are also sometimes seen on the Nile around Aswan.

fen A low, marshy or flooded area of land.

fender 1. A piece of rubber or other resilient substance hung over the side of a ship or boat to prevent damage when mooring or coming alongside another vessel.
2. (US) The wing (or sometimes the mudguard) of a motor vehicle.

ferry 1. A boat, ship or aircraft used for conveying passengers and goods on a regular and relatively short journey.
2. To transfer an aircraft between two points without passengers.

FHA Family Holiday Association. *See Appendix 5a.*

FIAVET Federazione Italiana Associazioni Imprese Viaggi e Turismo. *See Appendix 5c.*

fiesta A public holiday, usually in Latin countries, often associated with a particular saint or other religious figure.

fifth freedom *See freedoms of the air.*

fin The vertical control surface of an aircraft, usually at the rear, that governs its side to side motion.

fine dining A general term used to describe superior service, presentation and food quality in a restaurant.

firm up To make definite.

first class One of the best categories for transport or accommodation, exceeded in comfort only by de luxe.

first floor 1. (UK) The floor above the ground floor of a building.
2. (US) The ground floor of a building.

first quarter 1. The phase of the lunar cycle, seven days after the new moon, when the moon appears as a half-circle.
2. The first quarter of any type of year (such as calendar, financial or accounting), usually beginning on the first day of a month. Quarters are commonly used periods for measuring company performances.

first sitting The earlier of two meal times on a train or cruise ship.

First World War The global conflict (1914 to 1918) between the Central Powers (Germany, Austro-Hungary, the Ottoman Empire and Bulgaria) and the eventually victorious Allies (France, Russia, the UK, Italy and the USA) that led to a dismantling of several major European empires and the end of absolutist monarchy.

firth An inlet or estuary.

FIT Fédération de l'Industrie du Tourisme. *See Appendix 5c.*

Five Pillars of Islam The five central tenets of the Islamic religion: the profession of faith; the turning towards Mecca five times a day for prayer; the giving of alms; the fasting during the month of Ramadan; and the pilgrimage to Mecca.

fixed wing aircraft The traditional type of heavier-than-air aircraft, where the wings project from the fuselage and do not move.

fjord A narrow sea inlet, usually bounded by high cliffs.

flag A graphic device, usually rectangular and colourful, used to represent a country, state, county, city, town, international organisation or other body. Many countries have more than one flag – some have as many as six – which are generally more ornate variations on a simple basic theme, each of which is used for specific civil, military, ceremonial or governmental purposes. The designs of flags are subject to variation from time to time. Even in official usage, the colours of the same flag may vary considerably from one example to the next, particularly where these appear on different materials or are printed by different processes.

flag alpha *See A flag.*

flag carrier The name given to the national airline of a country or state.

flag of convenience The practice whereby ship owners will register their ships in a country other than their home country where the taxes, wage rates, standards and other aspects may be more favourable.

flagpole *See flagstaff.*

flagship The most prestigious hotel, ship or service of a supplier.

flagstaff 1. Any pole set up to fly a flag.
2. On a ship, the pole at the stern that flies the flag of the ship's country of registry. Also known as a jackstaff.

flaps Extendible, hinged surfaces on an aircraft's wings that control the amount of lift generated.

flat light A condition common in skiing resorts after the sun has gone down. At this time it is difficult to make out the conditions of a run because the various shades all blur to grey.

flight attendant A member of an aircraft's cabin crew.

flight code The unique code that is allocated to every flight and which identifies it throughout the duration of the journey. Flight codes are made up an airline identifier (such as BA for British Airways) and a number that denotes the route. > *airline code.*

flight coupon An exchange coupon from a ticket that is valid for a flight.

flight deck   The name used for the cockpit on larger aircraft.

flight path   The course of an aircraft.

flight recorder   An automatic device fitted to all commercial passenger aircraft that records the technical data recorded or received during a flight. In the event of an accident this data can help establish the cause. Popularly known as a 'black box' although they are usually painted bright orange.

float plane   *See seaplane.*

floatel   A hotel that is on a boat, or built over water.

flood tide   An exceptionally high tide.

floodplain   A low lying flat area of land around a river that is subject to flooding.

flora   The plant life of a region.

flotilla   A collection of boats sailing together.

flotilla charter   An arrangement whereby a group of chartered boats leave one harbour and sail to another, following a pre-arranged itinerary but their own time-table, with support, assistance and ground arrangements being provided by the charter company.

flotsam   Wreckage and other objects found floating on water. Often used in conjunction with jetsam.

fly-cruise   A package holiday that includes flights and a cruise.

fly-drive   A package holiday that includes flights and car hire.

flyer   A printed sheet containing advertising or promotional information.

flying boat   A large aircraft designed to operate from water. Prior to the widespread construction of airports, flying boats maintained many of the longer distance services.

flying wing   An aircraft with little or no fuselage and containing its passenger and cargo accommodation within the wings. Although aircraft of this configuration have flown, none has yet entered regular service.

fo'c'sle   *See forecastle.*

FOB   Free on board. Delivered without charge to a carrier's vehicle (typically a ship or railway wagon).

FOC   Free of charge. Issued or provided without charge.

fog   Any cloud of moisture touching the ground that reduces visibility to less than one kilometre.

Föhn   1. A hot, southerly wind on the northern slopes of the Alps.
2. A warm dry wind on the lee side of a mountain.

folklore   The traditional customs, beliefs, stories, songs and other cultural traditions of a group of people, usually passed down orally over many generations.

foot   A unit of measurement in the imperial system equal to 12 inches (0.305 m). Usually abbreviated ft or '. (Note that the latter symbol is also used to denote a minute of a degree.)

foot passenger   A passenger without a vehicle travelling on a car-carrying ferry service.

footfall   A marketing expression that refers to the number of people entering a place. It does not indicate the numbers who spend, only those who enter. > *footprint.*

foothill   A small hill or range of hills around the bottom of a mountain or range of mountains.

footpath   1. (UK) A path for pedestrians, especially between buildings.
2. A track, generally in the countryside.

footplate   (UK) The cab of a railway locomotive.

footprint   A marketing expression describing the evidence that a person leaves after having visited a place. Thus the footprints of an international visitor might include visa applications, air tickets, credit card payments, hotel registrations, landing cards and currency transactions, all of which can be used to help build up a statistical picture of travel patterns. > *footfall.*

ford   A shallow point in a river or stream where it may be crossed by wading or by driving through.

fore   Towards the front of an aircraft or ship.

forecastle   Pronounced 'foke-sul'.
1. The forward part of a ship where the crew has its quarters.
2. A raised deck at the bow of a ship.

foreign   Of, from or situated in a country other than one's own.

foreign exchange   A term used to refer to any commercial transaction relating to the supply, exchange or purchase of currency other than that of one's own country.

Foremost West, Four Corners   A US regional marketing organisation covering the states of Wyoming, Utah and New Mexico. > *US regional marketing organisations.*

foreshore   That part of the shore that lies between high and low water.

forest A large area covered with trees and undergrowth. In tropical areas forests can be extremely dense and inhospitable.

form of indemnity An airline form which a passenger must complete to indemnify a carrier against loss. It is often used in the case of a lost ticket, where the carrier may replace the ticket without charge providing the passenger agrees to repay any loss incurred by the airline should the lost ticket later be fraudulently used.

formal dress 1. A dress code whereby women wear an evening or cocktail dress, and men a dinner jacket and bow tie. In some cases, the term may as appropriate refer to traditional costume. > *dinner jacket.* 2. (US) Evening dress.

former GDR *See Germany.*

former Soviet Union The countries of Armenia, Azerbaijan, Belarus, Estonia, Georgia, Kazakhstan, Kyrgyzstan, Latvia, Lithuania, Moldova, Russian Federation, Tajikistan, Turkmenistan, Ukraine and Uzbekistan. The term has no current political or administrative significance, but is sometimes used to describe these countries collectively.

former Yugoslavia *See Yugoslavia, Macedonia.*

Formosa *See Taiwan.*

fortnight (UK) Two weeks.

Four-thousander A term used to describe a mountain of over 4,000m. Normally used in the Alps.

foyer The main lobby or entrance hall of a hotel or theatre (or sometimes a cruise ship).

FP Full pension. *See full board.*

Franc Zone Those countries whose currencies were linked to the French franc at a fixed exchange rate, and are now linked to the euro. The member countries are: Benin, Burkina, Cameroon, Central African Republic, Chad, Comoros, Congo, Côte d'Ivoire, Equatorial Guinea, Gabon, Guinea-Bissau, Mali, Niger, Senegal and Togo.

franchise A formal authorisation granted to an individual or organisation (the franchisee) by another (the franchisor), that gives the former right to sell the latter's products or services and to use its brand name. Many catering outlets, especially fast-food ones, are run as franchises.

franchisee *See franchise.*

franchisor *See franchise.*

Francophile A person who is well disposed towards France or the French.

Francophobe A person who dislikes or distrusts France or the French.

Frank A member of the Germanic peoples who invaded and occupied Gaul in the sixth century. The term was used throughout the Middle Ages by eastern Europeans and Muslims to describe western Europeans generally.

frank An official mark or stamp put on a document, usually the stamp on an envelope, to record payment; and the act of so doing.

free ascent When a diver ascends towards the water's surface without the use of additional air supply.

free house (UK) A drinking establishment, usually a pub, not owned by a brewery which is thus free to sell beers from several suppliers. > *tied house.*

free port A port where goods in transit are not subject to taxes or duties.

free trade The philosophy of allowing trade between nations without governmental regulations, controls or duties.

freeboard The space between the lowest open deck and the waterline of a vessel.

freedoms of the air In the Chicago Convention on Civil Aviation of 1944, it was agreed that airlines would have five 'levels' of freedom under which they could operate. The higher the level of freedom afforded, the greater the level of flexibility the airline will enjoy. A sixth freedom has since been added. The levels are:
• 1. The right to fly over a country.
• 2. The right to land in a country for technical reasons such as refuelling.
• 3. The right to off-load freight, mail or passengers from an aircraft of the country from which they originated.
• 4. The right to load freight, mail or passengers onto an aircraft of the country from which they originated or for which they are destined.
• 5. The right to load or off-load freight, mail or passengers onto or from an aircraft other than that of the country for which they are destined.
• 6. The right of an airline of one country to carry passengers between two other countries, providing it travels via its home country.

freesale A system whereby an agent can sell a facility without reference in advance to the principal. Reservations made in this way will have to be reported to the principal in accordance with specified procedures.

freeskiing A term adopted to cover the increasingly wide range of options available to skiers since the late 1990s. This includes skis of different shape and length (but always shorter and wider than traditional skis) and different types of skiing, such as on terrain parks.

A B C D E F G H I J K L M N O P Q R S T U V W X Y Z

freeway (US) An express highway, the equivalent of a motorway.

freighter In shipping, a vessel operating line services for freight. Some of these vessels carry a limited number of passengers.

French Antilles The Caribbean islands of Martinique; and Guadeloupe and five smaller islands. Each forms a Départements d'Outre-Mer (Overseas Department) of France.

French Overseas Possessions The various former French colonial possessions which now enjoy varying degrees of autonomy. There are four Départements d'Outre-Mer; three Territoires d'Outre-Mer; two Collectivités Territoriales; and one overseas country. For more information, consult the Columbus *World Travel Guide*.

French Revolution The conflict in France (1789 to 1799) which led to the overthrow of the absolutist monarchy, the execution of Louis XIV and the establishment of the First Republic. This in turn was overthrown by Napoleon Bonaparte in 1799.

frequent flyer programmes Incentive loyalty clubs operated by airlines on behalf of customers who use their services regularly. Travellers accumulate points in proportion to the number and value of their journeys and these can be exchanged for gifts of various types, including free flights.

fresh breeze *See Beaufort scale.*

front of house The reception area of a hotel.

frontier The border between two countries, states, provinces or any other significant administrative division.

fruit machine *See one-armed bandit.*

FSU *See former Soviet Union.*

FTI Federatie van de Toeristische Industrie. *See Appendix 5c.*

FTO Federation of Tour Operators. *See Appendix 5a.*

full board A hotel rate including three meals daily. Also called American Plan.

full foliage (US) The time in the fall when the colours of leaves of trees, especially in New England, are at their most vivid.

full house The situation when all availble accommodation has been taken up.

full moon The phase of the lunar cycle, 14 days after the new moon, when the moon appears as a complete circle.

full pension *See full board.*

full-face mask A face-mask that covers the whole face, including the mouth, eyes and nose.

fumarole An opening in or near a volcano from which hot gases emerge.

funicular A mountain railway, usually one operated by cable.

funitel *See gondola (3).*

funnel The smokestack on a ship. Originally it carried the large quantities of smoke and steam from the engines but these days is more likely to carry diesel exhaust.

furlong An unit of measurement in the imperial system equal to one eighth of a mile. Now rarely used, except for when describing the length of horse races.

furlough (US) A temporary laying-off of employees.

fuselage The main body or an aircraft to which the wings and tailplane are fitted.

FX An abbreviation for foreign exchange. *See foreign exchange.*

A B C D E F G H I J K L M N O P Q R S T U V W X Y Z

G g

Gaelic Any of the Celtic languages spoken in Ireland, Scotland and the Isle of Man.

gale *See Beaufort scale.*

Galileo A multi-national GDS used by a number of European airlines and travel agents.

galley A ship's or aircraft's kitchen.

game lodge Accommodation in a game reserve or safari park.

game reserve An area in which game animals, especially large ones, are kept in protected but natural environments. Usually they may be viewed by visitors under controlled conditions.

gangplank A movable plank, often with cleats, used to board a vessel.

gangway 1. (UK) A passage between rows of seats. 2. A bridge laid from ship to shore to enable embarkation and disembarkation.

Garden Route A scenic stretch of the South African coast stretching from Mossel Bay in the west to Storms river in the east. The main resorts are Knysna and Plettenberg Bay. Other attractions include Tsitsikamma National Park and the Wilderness Lakes.

garden side A room in a hotel or similar establishment on the same level as the garden and which opens onto it.

garden view A room in a hotel or similar establishment that overlooks the garden but which has no direct access to it.

Garúa A heavy mist on the Pacific slope of the Andes in a normally very dry part of the coast.

gasthaus A small hotel or inn in German-speaking countries.

gasthof A hotel or inn in German-speaking countries, larger than a gasthaus.

gate The part of an airport, usually specified by a number, via which passengers board or leave an aircraft.

gateway A point of access to a country or region. A gateway will usually be an airport or seaport, although certain frontier points and railway stations can be given the designation. In general a gateway is the point served most directly from the originating point, which usually implies that it accepts international traffic.

gauge The distance between the rails of a railway track. In most countries of the world this is the British-invented gauge of four feet eight and a half inches (167 cm).

GAVL Groupement des Agences de Voyages du Grand-Duché du Luxembourg. *See Appendix 5c.*

gazetteer A geographical index or dictionary.

gazpacho A Spanish vegetable soup, served cold.

GB *See Great Britain.*

GBCO Guild of British Coach Operators. *See Appendix 5a.*

GBTA Guild of Business Travel Agents, the former name of the Guild of Travel Management Companies. *See Appendix 5a.*

GBTAI Guild of Business Travel Agents Ireland. *See Appendix 5d.*

GDS *See global distribution system.*

GEBTA Guild of European Business Travel Agents. *See Appendix 5d.*

geisha A Japanese hostess trained to entertain male guests with dancing, songs and conversation. Can also refer to a Japanese prostitute.

general sales agent The authorised representative of a principal, particularly in cases where a principal does not have its own office in a country and wishes to appoint a GSA to handle its promotion, sales and enquiries. A GSA may represent several principals.

gentle breeze *See Beaufort scale.*

gentlemen's agreement An unwritten understanding between two parties, the observance of which is more a matter of honour than of legal obligation.

geographic pole *See poles.*

geographical county One of the original counties of England, Wales and Scotland (such as Rutland, Pembroke and Buteshire), many of which have been in existence for over a thousand years. Some have seemed to disappear as a result of administrative reforms since the 1880s, although they still exist for some ceremonial, touristic, sporting and other purposes, > *administrative counties.*

geographical mile *See nautical mile.*

geography The study of the earth's physical features, resources and climate as well as aspects of its population and their activities.

geology The study of the earth's structure and composition.

George A colloquial term for the automatic pilot on an aircraft.

George Town The capital of the Cayman Islands. Not to be confused with Georgetown, the capital of Guyana, or St George's, the capital of Grenada.

Georgetown The capital of Guyana. Not to be confused with George Town, the capital of the Cayman Islands, or St George's, the capital of Grenada.

Georgian 1. Of or relating to the period of English history during the reigns of the first four Georges (1713 to 1830) particularly with regard to architecture.
2. Of or relating to the country of Georgia.
3. Of or relating to the state of Georgia in the USA.

Germany A country in central Western Europe, officially the Federal Republic of Germany. Between 1945 and 1991, it was divided between the Federal Republic of Germany (West Germany) and the German Democratic Republic (East Germany). The term 'eastern Germany' generally refers to the eastern part of the country in the present, generally co-extensive with the former GDR. The term 'East Germany' generally refers to the former GDR in the past, or to its legacy today. The distinction is often made when referring to the infrastructure, which in East Germany is in many cases still of a lower standard than that in the former West Germany. > *Berlin.*

geyser A volcanic phenomenon causing the eruption of hot water and steam, often at regular intervals.

Ghan The rail service in Australia between Adelaide and Darwin.

ghetto Part of a town or city (usually a rundown area) occupied by a minority or deprived group.

Ghibli The local name for the Sirocco in Libya. *See Sirocco.*

ghost town A deserted town or settlement, usually found in areas that have experienced a short-lived boom (such as from mining).

gig 1. A light, two-wheeled horse-drawn carriage.
2. A musical performance, generally by a folk, rock or jazz group or similar.

gimbals A device to keep something horizontal on a ship, regardless of any pitch or roll.

GIT *See group inclusive tour.*

gite A French expression meaning a holiday dwelling, usually situated in the countryside and rented on a self-catering basis.

glacier A slowly moving sheet of ice. Some glaciers can be several kilometres wide.

Glacier Express A spectacular alpine rail service in Switzerland, running between St Moritz and Zermatt.

Glass Country An area in south-east Småland, Sweden, famous for glass-making.

glen A narrow valley.

glider An engineless heavier-than-air aircraft, often one that is towed by a powered aeroplane to assist take-off.

global distillation The phenomenon whereby cold areas, such as the Arctic, are polluted by emissions produced far away. Such emissions can be carried far from their source and not be deposited until they condense in the colder atmosphere.

global distribution system (GDS) The generic name given to a range of computer systems that enable agents to make bookings with principals. They were formerly known as computerised reservations systems (CRS). The earliest of these were developed during the mid-1970s, and thus have claim to be the first functioning e-commerce systems in the world.

global indicator A code shown against the fare on an air ticket that indicates the general route of a long distance flight.

global price tickets Tickets, often rail, that include a package of facilities, for example, travel, sleeping accommodation and a meal.

globe The planet earth or a representation of it.

glühwein Mulled wine popular in Switzerland, Austria and Germany. It is often served in ski resorts.

GMT Greenwich Mean Time. The former name for Universal Time Co-ordinate (UTC). *See UTC.*

goggles 1. A device used as an aid to seeing under water. Unlike the face mask, goggles cover the eyes only and are for use by surface swimmers.
2. A device used by skiers to protect their eyes against wind, sun and snow.

Gold Coast 1. Australia's largest resort area, situated to the south of Brisbane. The main resorts include Southport, Surfers Paradise and Coolangatta.
2. The section of the Florida coastline around Palm Beach and Miami with numerous resorts.
3. The coastal strip of Ghana, originally named after the gold mined in the area.
4. *See Kona Coast.*

Golden Coast The coastal region in south-west Sweden stretching from Strömstad in the north to Laholm in the south. The main centres are Gothenburg and Halmstad.

Golden Horseshoe The area around the western end of Lake Ontario containing over 20% of Canada's population. The main towns are Oshawa, Toronto, Hamilton and St Catharines.

Golden Ring The area to the north-east of Moscow with many towns of great historical, architectural and spiritual significance, including Suzdal, Vladimir and Yaroslavl.

Golden Triangle 1. An area in northern India with many ancient sites and important monuments, with Delhi to the north, Agra to the south-east and Jaipur to the south-west.
2. A region in South-East Asia on the borders of Laos, Myanmar and Thailand. Notorious for the production of opium.

Golfo de California The long gulf in the Pacific Ocean separating the Baja California from the Mexican mainland.

gondola 1. A traditional vessel used on canals, especially in Venice.
2. The passenger-carrying cabin on an airship or balloon.
3. A type of lift common in larger ski resorts and in some other large leisure facilities in hilly or mountainous areas. It is sometimes known in the UK by its French name of *télécabine*. Gondolas differ from cable cars in that they normally contain several dozen cabins, each holding two to eight passengers, that connect to a continually moving cable. Larger gondolas have appeared recently that can hold more than 20 people in each cabin, often standing. Some of these are known as funitels and are suspended from two parallel cables for added stability.

gondolier The oarsman of a gondola.

Good Friday A festival in the Christian religious calendar, celebrated two days before Easter.

google To make a search for information on the internet, whether by using the Google search engine or any other method.

gorge A deep, narrow canyon.

gorge-walking The pastime of travelling down streams and along water filled gorges in mountain areas without the aid of boats. The method of progress may require various types of equipment including that used for climbing and caving. Unless experienced in this it is usual to be part of a guided party. Also known as canyoning.

go-show A passenger who arrives for a flight without a reservation.

Goth A member of the Germanic tribe that invaded the Roman Empire in the 3rd to the 5th centuries.

Gothic An architectural style common in Europe in the 12th to 16th centuries.

gourmand A glutton.

gourmet A person who appreciates the finest things, especially food and drink.

gourmet meal Food and drink prepared to exacting standards.

GPU *See ground power unit.*

grade crossing (US) A level crossing.

gradient The slope of a road or railway. Gradients can be measured in percentages or as a ratio. A slope of 10% is equivalent to a ratio of 1 in 10, whereby for every ten feet of progress forward a vehicle would gain one foot in height.

Grain Coast The coastal strip of West Africa situated in Liberia.

Granada A city in Andalucia in southern Spain. Not to be confused with the Grenadines or Grenada.

Grand Tour A historical term given to the practice of sending wealthy young aristocrats on a circuit of the major cultural centres of Europe. The fashion started in the 17th century and is one of the foundations of modern travel.

graticule The intersecting lines of latitude and longitude which are usually used as a basis for drawing a map. These will usually be described as representing progressive increments of degrees north or south, and east or west. Depending on the map projection and the scale, these will appear as straight lines or curves. These may be also be used as a map reference. > *longitude, latitude, map, map projection, map reference.*

gratis Free of charge.

gratuity A tip for service. Theoretically it is for service over and above that expected but is now often demanded as a right by many providers. It is often added to a bill in a restaurant or on a ship, usually at a rate of 10 or 15%.

greasy spoon (UK) A slang expression meaning a cheap, often inferior, restaurant.

Great Barrier Reef A coral reef, the largest in the world, off the north-eastern coast of Australia.

Great Britain The political unit comprising England, Scotland and Wales. Some organisations, such as travel insurance companies, may use a slightly different definition of the term 'Great Britain'. > *United Kingdom.*

great circle The shortest distance between two points

on a sphere. A piece of string stretched between two points on a model globe will follow the great circle route and this route will often be significantly different from a straight line on a map projection.

Great Dividing Range The main mountain range in Australia, extending along almost the entire eastern part of the continent.

Great Lakes A group of five lakes in central North America: Lakes Superior, Huron, Erie, Ontario and Michigan. The first four are divided by the border between the USA and Canada; Lake Michigan is entirely in the USA.

Great Lakes of North America A US regional marketing organisation covering the states that border the Great Lakes, and Ontario in Canada. > *US regional marketing organisations.*

Great Plains The area of the USA to the east of the Rocky Mountains.

Great Rift Valley The most extensive and dramatic rift in the earth's surface, creating a chain of mountains, volcanoes and escarpments extending from Syria to Mozambique, but most strongly associated with Kenya and Tanzania.

Greater Antilles The group of Caribbean islands comprising the Cayman Islands, Cuba, Hispaniola, Jamaica and Puerto Rico.

Greek Terms Yacht charter terms under which the fee includes the charter of the yacht with all equipment; basic consumables for engine-room, deck and cabins; the crew's wages and food; insurance for the yacht itself, for third party claims and employer's liability insurance for the crew; sufficient fuel and lubricants for four hours cruising per 24 hours; harbour dues and pilotage within Greek waters; and water and ship's laundry. Other costs, such as the client's food and drink, Corinthian Canal dues where applicable and port taxes and harbour dues outside Greek waters must be paid by the client. These terms may vary.

green card 1. A certificate issued by an insurance company that provides evidence of cover (especially of motor insurance) outside the UK.
2. A work permit issued to residents of the USA who are not US citizens.

green channel *See customs clearance.*

green circle trail (US) The easiest ski run in North American resorts. > *green run, blue run.*

green fee The cost of playing a round of golf. Green fees are charged per person playing and are usually quoted for a round of 18 holes. All-day green fees may also be available.

green run The very easiest ski run category in Italy,

France and French-speaking Switzerland. Rarely used in other parts of Europe where blue run is the easiest category. In North America defined as 'green circle' trail. > *blue run, green circle trail.*

green tourism *See ecotourism.*

Greenwich Mean Time The former name for Universal Time Co-ordinate (UTC). *See UTC.*

Greenwich meridian The meridian of longitude that passes through Greenwich in London from which all the meridians are calculated. Generally this appears in or near the centre of a typical world map. It is also known as the prime meridian or the zero meridian. > *UTC, time zones, GMT, British Summer Time, Daylight Saving Time, International Date Line.*

Grenada The southernmost of the Windward Islands in the Caribbean. Not to be confused with the Grenadines or Granada.

Grenadines, the The string of islands between St Vincent and Grenada in the Windward Islands in the Caribbean, politically part of St Vincent and the Grenadines. Not to be confused with Grenada or Granada.

gringo A slang expression used in Spanish-speaking countries for a foreigner, especially one from North America.

gross registered tonnage A measure of the capacity of a ship. One GRT is equivalent to 100 cubic feet of enclosed space. The expression derives from the word tun (a type of barrel) and has nothing to do with weight. > *tonnage.*

grotto A cave, often one part filled with water.

ground arrangements The additional facilities such as airport connections, accommodation and excursions that may be required by air travellers when they arrive at their destinations.

ground content The part of a travel arrangement, such as a package holiday, that comprises services provided after arrival at the destination, such as airport transfers, accommodation and guided tours.

ground floor (UK) The lowest floor of a building.

ground handling agent A provider of ground arrangements.

ground operator *See ground handling agent.*

ground power unit A small engine, separate from the main engines, that maintains an aircraft's air conditioning and other services while it is on the ground.

ground speed An aircraft's speed relative to the ground.

ground staff The members of the staff of an airline who are responsible for ground duties such as check-in and ticketing as well as general passenger welfare.

group A party of travellers whose travel arrangements as regards departure point, transport details, arrival point and ground arrangements are identical or broadly similar and have been arranged en bloc. Economies of scale, for the travellers in terms of cost and for the various travel organisations in terms of convenience, often result from group arrangements.

group desk A counter or office, usually at an airport, for facilitating the processing and onward arrangements of groups.

group inclusive tour Travel arrangements made in bulk for a group.

groyne A low wall built out into the sea to help prevent erosion of the shore.

GRT *See gross registered tonnage.*

GRTG The Guild of Registered Tourist Guides. *See Appendix 5a.*

GSA *See general sales agent.*

GSM Grams per square metre, the most common measurement of paper weight outside North America.

GTMC Guild of Travel Management Companies, the new name for the Guild of Business Travel Agents. *See Appendix 5a.*

GTOA Group Travel Organisers Association. *See Appendix 5a.*

GTT The Guild of Travel and Tourism. *See Appendix 5a.*

guarantee An agreement by a principal to provide accommodation, even though the exact type, reference or category cannot be advised at the time.

guaranteed reservation Usually applicable to hotels, where a client or agent will guarantee payment for the accommodation booked, even if the client is a no show.

guaranteed upgrade An arrangement whereby passengers of major commercial importance to an airline or hotel are offered a complimentary upgrade to higher class of accommodation than that paid for.

guard (UK) A railway employee who rides on a train and is responsible for passenger safety, reservation and ticket inspection, timely departure from stations and sometimes luggage. Many trains no longer have guards as such, and their various functions are now discharged by other officials before, during or after the journey.

guard's van (UK) The coach or compartment on a train occupied by the guard.

guardianed hut A mountain hut that is owned or managed by a person or a family. Food is purchased from the guardian and self-catering is not permitted.

guest A person resident in a hotel or other accommodation.

guest beer (UK) A beer which is avialable in a pub or similar for a limited period of time.

guest house A more modern term for boarding house.

guest list The list of people invited to a function.

guest worker A person with a temporary entitlement to work in a foreign country.

guide 1. A person who guides or escorts groups. The duties of the various types of guide vary considerably and the official definitions, where they exist, are shown under their respective headings. 2. A book or other reference manual that gives details of an attraction, resort, country or other place or area.

Guinea A country in West Africa. Not to be confused with Guinea-Bissau, Equatorial Guinea, New Guinea or Papua New Guinea.

Guinea Current An extension of the Equatorial Counter-current that flows southwards down the north-west coast of central Africa.

Guinea Monsoon A warm humid wind blowing from the southwest in West Africa between April and September, associated with the rainy season.

Guinea-Bissau A country in West Africa. Not to be confused with Guinea, Equatorial Guinea, New Guinea or Papua New Guinea .

gulch (US) A ravine.

gulet (Also **gulett, gullette**) A beamy Turkish sailing vessel built mainly of wood on traditional lines. Commonly used for flotilla type holidays.

Gulet Terms Yacht charter terms, mainly used in Turkish waters, under which the fee includes the charter of the yacht with all equipment; basic consumables for engine-room, deck and cabins; the crew's wages and food; insurance for the yacht itself, for third party claims and employer's liability insurance for the crew; sufficient fuel and lubricants for four hours cruising per 24 hours; harbour dues and pilotage in Turkish waters; and water and ship's laundry. Other costs, such as the client's food and drink and port taxes and harbour dues outside Turkish waters, must be paid by the client. These terms may vary.

gulf Similar to a bay, but generally larger.

Gulf Coast The stretch of coastline on Florida's west coast between Cedar Key in the north and Marco Island in the south. Developed as a resort area separately from Miami's Gold Coast.

Gulf of Aden The gulf between the Red Sea, the Indian Ocean, Somalia and Yemen.

Gulf of Alaska The area of the North Atlantic Ocean to the south of Alaska.

Gulf of Guinea The area of the South Atlantic Ocean between the southern coast of West Africa and the coast of Central Africa.

Gulf of Mexico The area of the Atlantic Ocean between the USA, Mexico and Cuba.

Gulf States Any of the countries with a coastline on the Persian Gulf.

Gulf Stream A warm-water current that moves from the Gulf of Mexico to the North Atlantic. The warmth of the Gulf Stream has a moderating effect on British winters.

Gulf, the *See Persian Gulf.*

gunnel *See gunwale.*

gunwale Pronounced (and sometimes spelt) 'gunnel'. The very top of a ship's sides. Thus, 'full to the gunwales' means there's no more space whatsoever.

Guru Gobind Singh's Birthday A festival in the Sikh religious calendar, celebrated in December.

Guru Nanak A festival in the Sikh religious calendar, celebrated at the time of the full moon in July.

Gypsy A member of the nomadic people of central Europe, of Hindu origin, speaking a language related to Hindi.

gyrocompass A non-magnetic compass working by the action of a gyroscope. A gyrocompass can be set to indicate true north.

gyroplane An aeroplane deriving its lift from a freely spinning overhead rotor. > *autogiro.*

gyrostabiliser A stabiliser using the steadying effect of a gyroscope to maintain the stability of a ship or other vessel.

H h

habitat The indigenous or actual location of a plant or animal species. Destruction or modification of habitats is a frequent consequence of tourism development.

habitué A regular visitor or resident.

HACE *See High Altitude Cerebral Edema*

hachures The parallel lines shown on some maps to indicate the steepness of gradients.

hacienda In Spanish-speaking countries, an estate or plantation with accommodation.

hackney carriage (UK) The original term for a taxi. No longer in common use but still the official term for a licensed taxi in the UK.

ha-ha (UK) A dry ditch, usually with a wall on its inner side, used as a boundary that does not spoil the view.

hairpin bend A sharp U-shaped curve in a road.

hajj (or **hadj, haj**) The Islamic pilgrimage to the Sacred Mosque at Mecca in Saudi Arabia.

hajji (**hajja** when feminine) A Muslim who has undertaken the hajj.

halal Food and drink prepared in accordance with Islamic law.

half pipe Originally a horizontal, semi-circular structure used for skateboarding, but now a common feature at ski resorts. They are particularly popular with snowboarders, but also with skiers using the latest short skis. A half pipe is built from snow on a ski slope and is typically around 100m (350 feet) long and 5m (16 feet) wide.

half round trip A fare construction based on the sum of half the two return fares to a destination. This type of construction is useful when, for example, a passenger travels outward on a peak date and returns off peak.

half-board *See demi-pension.*

half-pension *See demi-pension.*

hall porter (UK) The member of hotel staff in charge of messages, passing of information and baggage. > *concierge.*

halo A ring of light that appears around the sun or moon under particular meteorological conditions. Haloes differ from coronæ, appearing very much further away from the object they surround. > *corona.*

halocline The boundary between waters of differing salinity.

halt (UK) A minor station on a railway line.

hamlet (UK) A small village, usually one without a church.

hand baggage Bags and other items, usually those of airline passengers, that are carried on board rather than being checked in. All carriers have strict limits on the size and weight of hand baggage, which must usually be able to be stored under a seat or in an overhead locker. Sometimes referred to as 'carry on' baggage. > *baggage allowance, excess baggage.*

hand luggage *See hand baggage.*

hand spear A spear, used for catching fish, which does not include any form of propulsive gun.

handicap An official rating of a golfer's ability. The lower the handicap the better the player. Maximum handicaps (the handicaps given to beginner golfers) are usually 28 for men and 36 for women. In continental Europe, it is not uncommon for clubs to allocate handicaps above 28 and 36. Travel agencies should be prepared to provide golf clubs with the handicaps of their client golfers. Many clubs have a handicap limit whereby only golfers of a certain standard will be allowed to play. > *handicap certificates.*

handicap certificate The official proof of the golfer's handicap. Some golf courses will require to see a golfer's official handicap card before allowing them onto the course. > *handicap.*

handle tow A simple form of ski lift comprising a continually moving cable that skiers simply catch hold of..

handling agent 1. An organisation that provides services to incoming visitors on behalf of a travel agent or tour operator. The rates for such services are contained in a confidential tariff.
2. A company that looks after the needs of passengers and their baggage at an airport on behalf of an airline.

handling fee A fee paid to an agent for working on a ticket that is sold by another and on which no further commission may be earned.

hangar A large building used to house aircraft.

Hanoverian 1. Of or relating to the kings and queens of England between 1714 and 1901, or to that period generally.
2. Of or relating to the city of Hanover in Germany.

Hanseatic League A medieval political and commercial league of north German towns.

hansom A two-wheeled, horse-drawn cab. The term is still in use in some areas to denote a horse-drawn sightseeing vehicle.

Hanukah *See Chanukah.*

HAPE *See High Altitude Pulmonary Edema.*

Hapsburg (or **Habsburg**) Of or relating to the most widespread, successful and long-lived royal family in medieval and early modern Europe, branches of which provided, amongst numerous other rulers, the kings of Spain (and much of the New World) between 1516 and 1700, the Holy Roman Emperors (rulers of Germany) between 1438 and 1806, and the emperors of Austria from 1804 until 1919; also to those periods of the history of those countries and regions generally.

harbour A bay or other protected area where ships can anchor in safety.

hard copy Data which is printed on paper rather than supplied digitally.

hard currency A currency that is sought after and has a relatively high rate of exchange.

hard shoulder (UK) An emergency stopping area along the edge of a motorway.

hard-top A car with a hard but detachable roof.

Harmattan A dry, dusty land wind of the West African coast, occurring from December to February.

HATA Hong Kong Association of Travel Agents. *See Appendix 5c.*

hatch An opening, usually covered when at sea, on a ship's deck that gives access to the holds.

hatchback *See coupé.*

HATTA Hellenic Association of Travel and Tourist Agencies. *See Appendix 5c.*

haute cuisine A French expression meaning food of the highest quality, usually, but not invariably, served in expensive and elegant surroundings.

haven A harbour or port, often considered a refuge.

Hawaiian Sling A hand-held diver's spear with an additional tube-like device and rubber band which enables the user to propel the spear in a catapult fashion.

hawker A person who sells unsolicited goods or services. In some places, the authorities have tried to control the number of hawkers by enforcing a system of licenses or tickets.

hawker stand A small booth or stall selling food or drink, particularly in Singapore. These are frequently grouped together with a common seating area.

hawse That part of a ship's side where the hawse holes are situated.

hawse hole The opening in a ship's side through which the anchor chain passes.

hawser A cable used to tow or secure a ship.

hazardous activity *See dangerous activity.*

HBAA Hotel Booking Agents Association. *See Appendix 5a.*

HCA Holiday Centres Association. *See Appendix 5a.*

head office location An IATA-accredited agent's place of business that is also an approved location.

heading A direction or bearing.

headland A promontory.

headline city The main city of entry in a timetable, beneath and following which services to other places are listed.

headwaters The streams flowing from the source of a river.

headway The rate of progress of a ship.

health precautions The preventative measures which a traveller should take before embarking on a foreign trip. Travellers need to be aware of the possible dangers of disease or other health hazards. Details of risks are published by several organisations, and under the terms of the EU Directive on Package Travel, travel agents are obliged to inform their customers of them. Travellers abroad are at risk from a range of unfamiliar situations and infections. Changes in food and water and insects and insect-borne diseases are probably the two most important problems a traveller will encounter, but other issues including heat, stress, jet-lag and excessive alcohol consumption can also be significant. Many of these risks can, with the right advice and precautions, be minimised or eliminated. Specific advice on which diseases are present in countries to be visited is likely to be complicated. A practical starting point for the traveller seeking advice is to consider which diseases can be prevented by immunisation, prophylactic tablets, or other measures, and decide whether it is appropriate to do so in each case.
An unpredictable environment is a particular problem for overland travellers who plan their own journeys, and who need greater knowledge of disease prevention and management than the air or sea traveller whose environment, food and drink are largely in the hands of the operator. Unforeseen changes in timetables may lead to stays in accommodation not of the expected standard. Delays at airports, particularly out-of-the-way ones, can take place in overcrowded and unhygienic conditions

where the facilities have not kept pace with increased demand. Jet-lag and exhaustion may prompt a traveller to take risks with food and drink. More experienced travellers tend to have fewer health problems. Better planning, immunisations and experience in prevention may all play a part, as well as salutary lessons learnt on previous occasions. A recent survey of returning travellers (most of whom had been to Europe, especially the Mediterranean countries) showed that half had had diarrhoea or respiratory symptoms while abroad. Excessive alcohol, sun and late nights can add to the problems. About 1% of package holidaymakers who take out a health insurance policy make a claim. Diarrhoea and sunburn are principal reasons, but accidents are also common. Injuries occur especially in and around swimming pools, to pedestrians forgetting on which side of the road the traffic drives, to motorists on unfamiliar roads, and to users of unfamiliar equipment such as gates on lifts. Sexually transmitted diseases may be contracted and may require urgent treatment. Long-stay travellers may adapt to these initial problems, but then find themselves suffering from diseases endemic in their chosen country, such as malaria, hepatitis, diarrhoea and skin problems. The traveller should be insured against medical expenses and most policies include the cost of emergency repatriation when appropriate. Such insurance, however, rarely covers a service overseas similar to that available at home. Language and administrative differences are likely to present problems. Reciprocal arrangements between countries differ and money may have to be paid and then reclaimed in the visited country itself, which can be time-consuming. Extra provision should be made for such emergencies.

Brief information on the major diseases and other health risks are given under individual entries elsewhere in this Dictionary. For more detailed information, please consult the Health appendix of the latest edition of the Columbus *World Travel Guide*, which includes listings of specialist sources of further advice.

heartland The central or most important part of an area.

heat-stroke A feverish sickness caused by over-exposure to high temperatures.

heave The up and down motion of a vessel at sea.

heave to To stop in the water without anchoring or mooring.

heavier-than-air Of an aircraft, one that weighs more than the air it displaces. Such aircraft can only remain in the air through the power of their engines.

Hebrew 1. Of or relating to the Semitic people originally from ancient Palestine.
2. The official language of Israel.

hectare An area equal to 10,000 sq m (2.47 acres).

hedging The act of entering into forward-buying arrangements for foreign currency in order to offset the effect of subsequent unfavourable movement in exchange rates.

HEDNA Hotel Electronic Distribution Network Association. *See Appendix 5b.*

heel When a vessel at sea tilts to port or starboard.

helicopter An aircraft with rotating wings. Helicopters can take off and land vertically and are thus often used for flights to destinations where there are no runways. Helicopters are slower than planes and so are mainly used for short journeys.

heliport The equivalent of an airport, but used for helicopters. As they need no runways, heliports are much smaller than ordinary airports.

heli-skiing A holiday arrangement where skiers are taken to the skiing area, frequently on a mountaintop, by helicopter. This has obvious advantages for those who wish to ski in areas not served by lifts.

helium An inert, light gas used these days to give buoyancy to lighter-than-air aircraft.

Hellenic The civilisation of ancient Greece (c.1300BC to 146BC).

helm The mechanism by which a ship is steered. Originally this was a wheel directly connected to the rudder. Nowadays it is often a small computer-controlled wheel.

hemisphere In geography, one half of the earth's surface, each separated from the other by the Equator or by the line of 0°/180° longitude.

hepatitis A potentially fatal infection of the liver causing jaundice. There are two main types of infectious hepatitis, A and B. A is caused eating contaminated food or drink; B by contaminated blood products or sexual contact. Apart from the obvious precautions, short-term immunity can be obtained by a pre-journey injection. > *health precautions*.

heritage A general expression that describes anything that has a link with some past event or person.

heritage attraction An attraction that capitalises on its connection with heritage.

heritage tourism Holidays taken with the sole or principal aim of exploring the history and culture of the region being visited. The phrase is sometimes used pejoratively.

herringbone seating plan A common configuration at meetings, conferences or seminars whereby the delegates are seated in rows of chairs separated by a central aisle which slants in a V-shape, with the speakers' table at the open end of the V.

Hibernian Of or relating to the island of Ireland.

Hibiscus Coast The coastal area in South Africa near Port Shepstone, the main resort of which is Margate.

hidden city ticketing The discouraged practice of issuing a ticket to a more distant point with a lower fare than the intended change point and suggesting that the passenger end the journey at the change point.

High Altitude Cerebral Edema (HACE) High Altitude Cerebral Edema (sometimes spelled Oedema). A very serious condition caused by swelling of the brain due to fluid accumulation as a result of high altitude exposure. It is characterised by blinding headaches and loss of co-ordination (ataxia), and requires immediate descent and medical attention. > *HAPE.*

High Altitude Pulmonary Edema (HAPE) High Altitude Pulmonary Edema (sometimes spelt Oedema). A very serious condition caused by liquid collecting in the lungs as a result of high altitude exposure. It is characterised by extreme shortness of breath (even after rest) and gurgling or bubbling sounds in the lungs, and requires immediate descent and medical attention. > *HACE.*

high latitudes The areas of the earth near the poles.

high road A main road.

high seas The open seas, not within the jurisdiction of any state or country.

high season The busiest time for the use of a travel facility.

high tide *See high water.*

high water The tide at its fullest.

high water mark An indicator showing the level reached at high water.

higher intermediate points An airline fare construction principle that applies if a multi-sector journey passes through a point to which, from the point of origin, the fare is higher than it is to the ultimate destination. In such cases, an adjustment to the fare may need to be made.

highway (US) A public road.

hijacking The taking control by force of a vehicle, usually an aircraft.

hill A raised area of ground, less high than a mountain.

hill station A government settlement, originally used for officials' holidays during the summer, in the higher areas of India, Malaysia and Sri Lanka.

hill walking The activity which involves exploring countryside, moorland, wilderness or mountain terrain by foot, generally following established pathways and making use of equipment such as hiking boots and waterproofs and skills such as navigation and route planning.

hill walking grades *See climbing grades.*

Himalayas The mountain range in Asia that separates the Indian sub-continent from China.

Hinduism The religion of the Hindus, based on the belief in Brahma as the absolute, all-embracing spirit, mainly followed in the Indian sub-continent. > *religion.*

hinterland 1. The geographical area beyond a coast or river banks.
2. An area served by a port or other transport hub.

Hispaniola An island in the Greater Antilles in the Caribbean, divided between the Dominican Republic and Haiti.

historical attraction Any attraction that derives interest from its historical significance.

hitchhike To travel by soliciting lifts in passing vehicles. This is against the law in some places.

Hittite The civilisation of ancient Turkey (c.2000BC to c.1200BC).

HIV A complex, infectious and often fatal viral disease, endemic worldwide but particularly prevalent in parts of sub-Saharan Africa, passed on by sexual intercourse and contaminated blood. > *health precautions.*

HMA Hotel Marketing Association. *See Appendix 5a.*

HMS When placed in front of a ship's name means Her/His Majesty's Ship: used for vessels in the Royal Navy.

hold The area in a ship or aircraft where the baggage or cargo is stored.

hold baggage Baggage that is checked in by an air passenger and generally placed in the hold.

Holi A festival in the Hindu religious calendar, also known as the Carnival of Colour, celebrated at the time of the full moon in March.

holiday Any time away from the normal working environment, or a trip taken away during such time.

holiday camp Now usually referred to as holiday centres. Mainly a UK phenomenon which developed after the 1935 Holiday Pay Act. Holiday camps or centres now offer a high-grade product, with many entertainment and other facilities included.

Holiday Care *See Appendix 5b.*

holiday centre *See holiday camp.*

holiday complex *See holiday camp.*

holidaymaker A person on holiday.

Home counties The counties immediately surrounding London.

home port The port from which a ship originates.

home town The town of one's birth, early life or fixed residence.

homeland A person's native land.

Hong Kong A Special Administrative Region of the People's Republic of China since 1997, although it is still often regarded as a separate travel destination.

horizon The point at which the earth and sky appear to meet.

horizontal integration The expansion of an organisation by its move into associated areas of activity, but not those areas connected with the work done by its suppliers or distributors. In travel, for example, an airline might decide to buy a hotel chain.

Horn of Africa The part of north-eastern Somalia which protrudes into the Gulf of Aden, and which is the easternmost part of the African mainland.

hors d'oeuvres The first course of a meal.

horse latitudes The two regions of calm located at 30° north and at 30° south of the Equator.

hospitality 1. Those people and organisations that are involved in the accommodation and catering sectors. 2. The business of entertaining others, generally for commercial gain.

hospitality suite A hotel room used for entertainment or meetings, rather than sleeping.

host location A head office or branch office to which a satellite ticket printer is connected and controlled.

hostal A Spanish term for a small hotel or guest house.

hostel A form of comparatively basic and generally non-serviced accommodation available throughout the world. The sleeping arrangements are usually in dormitory-style. Self-catering facilities may also be available. > *youth hostel.*

hostelry 1. (UK) A colloquial term for a pub. 2. (US) A small inn.

hot desert *See climate zones.*

hot line A telephone service providing direct access to a source of help, sales or expertise.

hotel 1. An establishment providing accommodation

and meals. A hotel would be expected to provide a greater and/or superior range of facilities than establishments such as guest houses. 2. (Australia & New Zealand) A public house.

hotel register The list of guests who are staying or have stayed at a hotel. These days it is usually computerised, although written ledgers still exist.

hotel representative An organisation that represents a number of hotels. This enables travel agents and independent brokers to obtain information and make bookings more easily.

hotelier A hotel manager, operator or owner.

hourglass skis *See carving skis.*

house limit The maximum amount of credit, goods or services that will be extended to a guest at a hotel or similar, or a casino, before full or partial payment of the amount owing is requested.

house wine Wine, often of average quality and usually the cheapest on the restaurant's list, sold in bottles or carafes.

houseboat A boat fitted out as living accommodation.

house-flag The flag indicating to which company a ship belongs.

hovercraft Otherwise known as an air cushion vehicle (ACV). A vehicle that travels on a cushion of air, constrained by a flexible skirt, rather than being in contact with ground or water. Although hovercraft are considered to be flying vehicles, they are only able to travel at a maximum height of a few feet, as determined by the skirt depth.

hoverport A port for hovercraft.

hovertrain A tracked air cushion vehicle.

HTF *See SSC, Appendix 5a.*

hub and spoke The use of a central base (the hub) from which connecting transport links operate to outlying areas (the spokes). > *interchange point.*

Hudson Bay 1. A large bay in north-eastern Canada. 2. The previous name for the rail service between Winnipeg and Churchill in Canada.

hull The body or frame of a ship or aircraft.

human geography The branch of geography that deals with the effects of human activity on the earth's surface and vice versa.

Human Immunodeficiency Virus *See HIV.*

Humboldt Current A cold current flowing north along the west coast of South America and cooling the coastal region as far as the Equator.

humidity A measure of the amount of moisture in the air. Higher levels of humidity are uncomfortable since sweat is less able to evaporate from the skin and its cooling effect is therefore reduced. The relative humidity of the air is expressed as a percentage, with 100% being the maximum amount of moisture the air can hold at a given temperature. As hot air can hold more moisture than cold air, 100% humidity at 30°C contains more moisture than 100% at 15°C. Various medical bodies have described the comfort level for an average person as being between 30 and 70% relative humidity, within which range many places (both indoor and outdoor) comfortably sit. One environment that falls well short of this standard is the passenger cabin of a typical aircraft at cruising altitude, where the relative humidity can fall to as low as 1%.

hummock A small hill.

hurricane A storm with winds in excess of 64 knots. Hurricanes usually occur in tropical areas, since they need plenty of sun to provide their power. > *Beaufort scale.*

hydraulic test The process of pressure-testing a diving cylinder in order to assess its suitability for further use as a container of high pressure gas.

hydrofoils 1. The foils or wings attached to the hull of a specially designed vessel. Once sufficient speed has been attained, the vessel rises until its hull is clear of the water and is supported on the wings.
2. A ship or boat fitted with hydrofoils. Such vessels can travel at much higher speeds than conventional ships.

hydrogen A light, highly inflammable gas that was originally the first choice for giving buoyancy to lighter-than-air aircraft. Accidents caused by fire were common and hydrogen is no longer used for this purpose.

hydrography The science of surveying the waters of the earth and the adjacent land area, usually for the purpose of producing navigational maps and charts.

hydroplane A light, fast motorboat designed to skim over the water.

hypersonic Over five times the speed of sound.

hyperventilation Unusually deep or rapid breathing, often a result of panic.

hypothermia Reduced body core temperature.

hypoxia Reduced levels of oxygen within the body. A risk to travellers at extreme altitudes or in certain diving situations.

I i

IAGTO International Association of Golf Tour Operators. *See Appendix 5a.*

IATA International Air Transport Association. *See Appendix 5d.*

IATA Traffic Area *See Area.*

IATAN International Airlines Travel Agent Network. *See Appendix 5b.*

IATM International Association of Tour Managers. *See Appendix 5a.*

Iberia The peninsula in Western Europe occupied by Andorra, Gibraltar, Portugal and Spain.

Iberian Of or relating to Iberia.

ICCA International Congress and Conference Association. *See Appendix 5d.*

ICE The high-speed inter-city train services connecting many of the major cities in Germany.

ice axe A tool used to assist climbers. There are 'walking', 'climbing' and 'general mountaineering' axes. Walking axes are usually longer than the others and are used more as a walking stick is used and provide added security when travelling on snow or ice. The others are shorter and not suitable for walking on level ground, and need some instruction to be used safely.

ice climbing The ascent of cliffs, crags, icefalls and mountains by means of climbing steep sections of snow, ice (and sometimes rock), requiring the use of specialist tools like ice axes and crampons. Usually regarded as more dangerous than rock climbing due to instabilities in snow or ice, winter weather conditions and lack of 'gear' placements.

ice gully A gully that has become frozen and can now only be accessed with appropriate climbing tools.

ice-boat A boat-like vessel mounted on runners and able to travel on ice.

ice-climbing grades *See climbing grades.*

IDL *See International Date Line.*

IFTO International Federation of Tour Operators. *See Appendix 5a.*

IFTTA International Forum of Travel and Tourism Advocates. *See Appendix 5b.*

igloo A dome-shaped house made of ice, as built by the Inuit (Eskimo) peoples.

IIT Independent inclusive tour. A tailor-made arrangement put together to meet the specific needs of a customer.

ILAM Institute of Leisure and Amenity Management. *See Appendix 5a.*

ILTM *See International Luxury Travel Market.*

immigrant A person living or working in a country other than their own.

immigration 1. The act of entering a country with the intention of settling there permanently. 2. The area in an airport or other international transport terminal where passengers show their identity and travel documents and are given permission to enter or leave the country.

imperial 1. Of or relating to an empire or similar state. 2. Of or relating to the non-metric system of weights and measures, a form of which is still officially used in the USA. Some aspects of it (such as pints and miles) are still officially used in the UK; unofficially, so are many others. > *Appendix 6.*

implant A business travel agency employee working in the customer's own location, usually to undertake that customer's business travel exclusively.

import To bring items into a country.

inaugural The first time of use of a new aircraft, route or similar product, service or vehicle.

inboard Within the sides or towards the middle of a ship, aircraft or other vehicle.

inbound 1. A flight or other travel service arriving at an airport, port or other transport terminus. 2. The return leg of a package holiday flight.

inbound tour operator *See incoming tour operator.*

Inca Of or relating to the South American Indian people whose empire, centred on Peru, lasted from c.1100 to the 1530s.

incentive commission A bonus commission paid to an agent in order to encourage extra sales. Usually such commission will be paid once an agreed sales target is reached

inch A unit of measurement in the imperial system equal to approximately 2.5 cm. Usually abbreviated to in. or ". (Note that the latter symbol is also used to denote a second of a minute of a degree.)

incidentals Minor items of expenditure that are too small to be worth detailing.

inclusive rate A tariff for a hotel room, meal or similar in which all costs such as taxes, gratuities and cover charges are included.

inclusive resort An accommodation and leisure complex which aims to satisfy as many of the requirements of its visitors as possible on the one site.

inclusive tour See package holiday.

inclusive tour excursion fare A fare designed to be part of an inclusive package which would, in theory, also include accommodation.

incoming tour operator A tour operator that specialises in supplying services, such as ground arrangements, for visitors to a country.

incoming tourism Tourism coming into a country from another country.

Indaba A Zulu word for a gathering. Now also used as the name for an annual tourism marketplace held in South Africa.

indemnify To make good a loss.

indemnity Compensation for a loss. > travel insurance.

indemnity basis A principle used by the insurance business for valuing a lost or stolen item, and generally regarded as the replacement cost less wear-and-tear.

independent 1. (UK) A travel agency group with less than five outlets.
2. A traveller who makes his own ground arrangements rather than travelling as part of a package or tour.
3. A hotel or other property not a member of or affiliated to a group pr chain.

index An alphabetical list of entries in a book.

Indian Ocean See oceans.

Indian Pacific The rail service between Sydney and Perth in Australia.

Indic 1. The civilisation of the region around the Indus and Ganges rivers (c.3000BC to c.AD500).
2. The language of this group.

indicator See global indicator.

indigenous Belonging to or originating from a country or region.

indirect routing A routing going via a point or points that it need not necessarily take. Indirect routings may be made necessary through lack of suitable services or through passenger inclination.

Indochina The geographical region comprising Cambodia, Laos, peninsular Malaysia, Myanmar, Singapore, Thailand and Vietnam.

industrial attraction A tourist attraction that capitalises on its connection with industry, usually historical.

ineligible Not entitled or allowed.

infant A child who has not yet reached the age at which child fares will be charged and who may be allowed to travel free. This will vary from service to service, but for most airlines an infant is anyone under two years old. > child.

inflatable (or **inflatable dinghy**) A small boat made from rubber or a similar material that can be easily carried and is inflated when needed for use.

in-flight catering The food and beverage services provided on board an aircraft. On most airlines the cost is included in the fare, but on some no-frills airlines an extra charge is made.

in-flight entertainment Those services, such as films, music and magazines which are available to passengers during a flight.

informal Without ceremony or formality. When referring to an event it usually refers to the style of dress expected.

informal dress A dress code whereby women wear smart dresses or trouser suits, and men wear a suit and tie.

information display Any system for making information available to a customer or an audience.

information technology The use of computers for recording, storing, analysing and displaying information.

infrastructure The underlying, man-made framework of a place, such as buildings, roads, railways, telecommunication lines, sewers, and water and power supplies.

inhabit To dwell in or occupy.

inhospitable Uninviting or otherwise unwelcoming.

in-house Provision of goods or services from within a company or institution.

inland Situated in the interior of a country or state.

inlet A small arm of water penetrating the land.

inn (UK) A public house which may also provide accommodation.

inoculation An alternative name for vaccination.

in-plant See implant.

insalubrious Of a climate or place, unhealthy.

inshore At sea, but close to the shore.

inside cabin A ship's cabin that has no window or porthole and thus no natural light.

insular Like or relating to an island.

insurable interest The insurance principle that states that a person cannot insure against a risk in which they have no direct interest.

insurance premium The sum taken by an insurance company from a proposer in order to accept the risk. As a rule, the higher the risk the greater the sum required.

Inter-American Highway The section of the Pan-American Highway between Nuevo Laredo in Mexico and Panama City. > *Pan-American Highway.*

interchange point Any point on a public transport network where passengers may change services. > *hub and spoke.*

inter-city Existing or travelling between cities. Sometimes used as a generic term for transport services offering rapid conveyance between major points.

intercontinental Existing, involving or conducted between two or more continents.

interior Inland and remote from the coast or frontier.

interline A co-operative administrative arrangement between two or more carriers. This facilitates more streamlined ticket sales, flight connections, check-in and baggage handling.

internal Existing, involving or conducted within a single nation or state.

internal combustion engine An engine, using petrol or diesel fuel, that develops its power by means of controlled burning of the fuel in enclosed cylinders. Most cars and motorcycles are driven by internal combustion engines.

international Existing, involving or conducted between two or more nations.

International Date Line (IDL) An imaginary line, based on the line of 180° longitude, which runs through the Pacific Ocean, on the east side of which the date is one day earlier than on the west. The IDL does not follow the line of 180° exactly but deviates to avoid cutting through certain countries, in the same way that many other time zones do. > *UTC, time zones, Greenwich meridian, GMT.*

international departures *See international outbound tourism.*

International fare expenditure A term defined by the WTO as being 'any payment made to carriers registered abroad by any person resident in the compiling country'.

International fare receipts A term defined by the WTO as being 'any payment made to the carriers registered in the compiling country of sums owed by non-resident visitors, whether or not travelling to that country.'

International Luxury Travel Market An exhibition and conference held every December in Cannes.

international outbound tourism (Also **international departures**) A term defined by the WTO as being 'the visits that each person makes from their country of usual residence to any other country for any purpose other than exercising a remunerated activity in the country visited'. Note that the term 'tourism' refers to travellers generally, rather than those travelling purely for pleasure. > *tourism, international visitors.*

international tourism *See tourism.*

international tourism expenditure A term defined by the WTO as being 'expenditure of outbound visitors in other countries including their payments to foreign carriers for international transport.' This is normally expressed in US$. For various reasons, fare payments are often expressed as separate items on many travel and tourism statistics. Each country may have different ways of calculating expenditure. Note that the term 'tourism' refers to travellers generally, rather than those travelling purely for pleasure. International tourism expenditure is classed as an export by the country concerned. > *tourism.*

international tourism receipts A term defined by the WTO as being 'expenditure of international inbound visitors including their payments to national carriers for international transport. They should also include any other prepayments made for goods and services received in the destination country'. This is normally expressed in US$. For various reasons, fare receipts are often expressed as separate items on many travel and tourism statistics. Each country may have different ways of calculating receipts. Note that the term 'tourism' refers to travellers generally, rather than those travelling purely for pleasure. International tourism receipts are classed as imports by the country concerned. > *tourism.*

international tourists *See international visitors.*

international visitors (Also **international tourists**) The official distinction between 'visitors' and 'tourists' is problematic for many reasons and open to many different interpretations. The WTO defines an international visitor as being 'any person who travels to a country other than that in which she/he has her/his usual residence but outside her/his usual environment for a period not exceeding 12 months and whose main purpose of visit is other than the exercise of an activity remunerated from within the country visited'. The distinction between people who visit wholly for pleasure, those who visit wholly for business and the people who mix both cannot easily be separated by this definition. Where they bother to do so, different countries will have different ways of attempting to record these differences. The WTO subdivides international visitor into: a) a tourist (overnight visitor) – a visitor who stays at least one night in collective or private accommodation in the country visited; and b) a same-day visitor – a visitor who does not spend the night in a collective or private accommodation in the country visited. For some countries, same-day visitors will be particularly numerous, and may therefore inflate the arrival statistics out of proportion to the amount of time or money actually spent by visitors in the country in question.

In addition, it must be remembered that WTO figures relate to the number of arrivals and not to the number of persons. The same person who makes several trips to a given country during a given period will be counted as a new arrival each time, while a person who travels through several countries on one trip is counted as a new arrival at each frontier crossing.

Due to the different methods used by different countries to collect data, international visitors may sometimes be determined by international arrivals at frontiers (including or excluding same-day visitors), or by international tourist arrivals at hotels and similar establishments. The abolition of frontier controls as a result of such developments as the Schengen Agreement (affecting, amongst others, France, Italy and Spain, three of the four most visited countries in the world) has made the problems of statistical calculation more acute. > *tourism*.

Internationale Tourismus-Börse *See ITB.*

internet A global communications network providing a wide range of communication and information services to its users. By some estimates, there are close to one billion internet users worldwide and this is expected to increase by 35% by 2007. The internet has revolutionised the way in which companies in the travel trade and elsewhere sell their products and services. The internet is also known as the world-wide web, or the web.

interoceanic Between or connecting two or more oceans.

interprovincial Existing, involving or conducted between two or more provinces.

interstate 1. (US) A motorway crossing a state boundary. In the USA, interstates that have a two-digit even number tend to run east-west; those that have a two-digit odd number tend to run north-south; and those that have a three-digit odd number are beltways around cities.
2. Existing, involving or conducted between two or more states.

intranet A communications network similar to the internet but with restricted access, usually within a company or organisation.

Inuit Of or relating to the Eskimo people, particularly those of northern Canada, and their language.

Inupiaq The Eskimo-Aleut languages spoken in northern Canada, Alaska and Greenland.

Inupiat Of or relating to the Eskimo people of Alaska.

invalid 1. Not valid for use (pronounced in-*valid*).
2. A person who is less able through disease or injury and will need special help or care when travelling (pronounced *in*-valid).

invalidate To make a document invalid for use.

invisible exports Items, such as services, that require the transfer of funds into a country but that do not involve the actual movement of goods. Incoming tourism is an example of an invisible export since such tourists bring funds into the country.

invisible imports Items, such as services, that require the transfer of funds out of a country but that do not involve the actual movement of goods. Outgoing tourism is an example of an invisible import since such tourists take funds out of the country.

involuntary change An alteration to an airline passenger's journey that has been brought about by circumstances beyond their control. The passenger should not lose the benefit of any special fares or concessions granted, even if the involuntary change results in the ticket being invalidated.

IPA International phonetic alphabet. *See phonetic alphabet.*

Ireland 1. An island situated in the west of the British Isles, which includes the Republic of Ireland and the six counties of Northern Ireland, politically part of the United Kingdom.
2. The Republic of Ireland.

Irminger Current The northernmost arm of the Gulf Stream.

Iron Curtain The name given to the division of Europe along ideological grounds which existed between 1945 and the early 1990s.

Islam The religion of the Muslims, based on the teachings of the Prophet Mohamed. > *religion*.

island A piece of land, other than a continent, entirely surrounded by water.

island-hop To travel from island to island.

Isle of Man An island in the Irish Sea between Great Britain and Ireland. It is a British Crown Dependency and not part of the United Kingdom, although close ties are maintained.

islet A small island.

isobar A line drawn on a weather map that joins points of equal barometric pressure.

isolated Remote or cut off.

isopleth A line on a weather map joining points with an equal incidence of a particular meteorological feature.

isotherm A line drawn on a weather map joining points of equal temperature.

Israeli Of or relating to the modern state of Israel.

issue Of documents, to prepare by writing or printing, ready for handing over to a customer.

issuing carrier The airline or other operator whose ticket is issued, or in whose name it is issued.

isthmus A narrow strip of land joining two larger land masses.

IT 1. *See inclusive tour.*
2. *See information technology.*

ITAA Irish Travel Agents Association. *See Appendix 5c.*

ITB *Internationale Tourismus-Börse*, one of the most important travel exhibitions in the world, held in Berlin in March each year. Attendance is generally restricted to persons connected with the travel industry.

itinerary 1. A journey.
2. The details of a customer's travel arrangements such as modes of transport, dates, times and destinations.

ITM Institute of Travel Management. *See Appendix 5a.*

ITMA Incentive Travel & Meetings Association Ltd. *See Appendix 5a.*

ITOA Irish Incoming Tour Operators Association. *See Appendix 5a.*

ITT Institute of Travel & Tourism. *See Appendix 5a.*

ITX *See inclusive tour excursion fare.*

Ivory Coast 1. The coast of Côte d'Ivoire, formerly popular with traders in ivory.
2. The former name of Côte d'Ivoire.

J j

jack A ship's flag, especially one flown from the bow. It generally indicates the ship's nationality.

jackstaff A small mast set at the bow of a ship on which a jack is hoisted.

Japan Current A warm-water current in the Pacific Ocean, the equivalent of the Atlantic's Gulf Stream.

Japanese encephalitis A viral disease transmitted by mosquitoes and endemic in certain parts of Asia. > *health precautions.*

JATA Japan Association of Travel Agents. *See Appendix 5c.*

jeepney A small bus especially common in the Philippines. Many were originally built from old US Jeeps.

Jerusalem One of the three holy cities of Islam (Mecca and Medina being the others), and also of central importance to both Christianity and Judaism, situated between the Mediterranean Sea and the Dead Sea.

jet age The era of travel by jet aircraft, beginning in the 1950s.

jet aircraft An aircraft powered by jet engines. The first jet airliner was the De Havilland Comet, introduced in the 1950s, but it was the adoption of larger jets like the Boeing 707, and the rapid increase in runway length and airport facilities to accommodate them, that created a dramatic increase in worldwide air travel.

jet engine An engine that relies on the continuous burning of fuel to provide thrust and/or power to drive a propeller. The jet turbine engine was invented in the 1930s but the first jet aircraft did not fly until the end of the Second World War.

jet lag A temporary discomfort suffered by passengers who fly across a number of time zones in one journey. Dehydration, disruption of sleep patterns, lack of exercise and daylight, too much food and too many diuretics such as tea, coffee and alcohol can all contribute to this.

jet set A colloquial term for groups of wealthy and socially prominent people who supposedly travel from place to place by jet in search of enjoyment.

jet ski A water vehicle designed to carry one or two persons and propelled by a jet of water. These are usually controlled by handlebars similar to those on a motorcycle, and are thus often referred to as 'wet bikes'. Since they have no wheels, this expression is obviously nonsensical.

jet stream A high-speed air current, generally at high altitude. Pilots often take advantage of jet streams to increase the speed of their aircraft without having to burn extra fuel.

jetfoil A hydrofoil vessel, powered by water jets.

jetsam Discarded material thrown overboard at sea, especially when deliberately jettisoned to lighten the vessel. Normally used in conjunction with flotsam.

jetty 1. A pier or breakwater. A landing jetty is one that passengers can use for embarkation and disembarkation. 2. The extensions at airports where aircraft park and load. These are sometimes called bridges.

Jew A person of the Jewish faith.

jib A triangular sail extending from the outer end of the bowsprit to the top of the mast of a boat or ship.

John O'Groats The north-easternmost point of mainland Britain, in Caithness, Scotland.

jolly-boat A type of ship's boat, smaller than a cutter.

journey To travel from one place to another for any reason, and the act of so travelling.

joystick A colloquial name for the control column of an aircraft.

Judaic Of or relating to Jews or Judaism.

Judaism The religion of the Jews. > *religion.*

jumbo jet The colloquial term applied to large, wide-bodied aircraft, in particular the Boeing 747.

jump jet A jet aircraft that can take off vertically.

jump seat An aircraft seat, often foldaway, used by crew members during take-off and landing.

junction A point where a road or railway meet, join or cross.

jungle An area of very dense vegetation, especially in tropical areas.

jungle fever Severe malaria.

junior suite Accommodation usually with one room with a sitting area at one end.

junk A flat-bottomed sailing vessel typically used in China.

junket A slang expression for a trip offered at the expense of a principal to thank its customers and hopefully gain new business.

junta A political or military group or faction that takes power after a revolution or coup d'état.

K k

kala-azar A tropical parasitic disease transmitted by sandflies.

Karoo (or **Karroo**) An elevated, semi-desert, plateau in South Africa.

kasbah The Arab quarter surrounding a North African castle.

kayak Originally an Eskimo canoe, but now used to describe any similar type of vessel.

keel A horizontal structure, usually of steel, that runs the length of the bottom of a ship. It could be considered the ship's backbone and is the base from which all other parts are built.

keelboat 1. A yacht with a permanent keel.
2. (US) A large flat riverboat

keelson A line of timber fastening a ship's floor-timbers to the keel.

Kelvin A scale of temperature with the same graduations as those used in centigrade, but with absolute zero (minus 273°C) used as its starting point. The freezing point of water is 273°K.

kerosene 1. (US) Paraffin, as used in some domestic heaters.
2. The fuel used by jet aircraft.

key *See cay.*

key card A small card, similar to a credit card, used instead of a room key in some hotels.

Khamsin An oppressive, hot, south or south-easterly wind occurring in the eastern Mediterranean which can contribute to dust storms.

Kharif The rainy season in northern India and Arab countries.

Khmer 1. The civilisation of ancient Cambodia (c.AD100 to 1432).
2. A native of modern Cambodia.

kibbutz A communal settlement in Israel.

Kiel Canal The canal which connects the North Sea with the Baltic Sea, running through northern Germany.

kilo- A prefix commonly mound in the metric system, meaning one thousand times. Thus a kilowatt is 1,000 watts.

kilogram (or **kilo**) A weight of 1,000 grams, or approximately 2.2 imperial pounds.

kilometre A length of 1,000m or approximately 0.62 of a statute mile.

king *See monarch.*

king room A hotel room with a king-sized bed.

kingdom A country with a monarch as its head of state.

Kingston The capital of Jamaica. Not to be confused with Kingstown, the capital of St Vincent & the Grenadines.

Kingstown The capital of St Vincent & the Grenadines. Not to be confused with Kingston, the capital of Jamaica.

klong A canal in Thailand.

kloof A steep-sided ravine in South Africa.

knap The summit of a hill.

knoll A small hill.

knot Nautical miles per hour. 20 knots is approximately 23 mph.

Kona Coast Part of the south-west coast of the island of Hawaii, also known as the Gold Coast.

Korea, Democratic People's Republic of The official name for North Korea.

Korea, Republic of The official name for South Korea.

korridorzuge A term used in German-speaking countries for a type of train service in that travels through another country in a special 'corridor' of track, within which it may not stop to pick up or set down passengers. This type of routing will avoid the circuitous journey that would otherwise be necessary, such as that from Innsbruck to Salzburg.

kosher Food and drink prepared in accordance with the Jewish law. The term is often used loosely to describe anything that is true or genuine.

kremlin A citadel within a Russian town.

Kremlin The seat of the Russian government in Moscow.

Kurds The Aryan peoples living in parts of Iraq, Iran, Turkey and Syria.

Kuroshio A warm current that brings tropical waters northward past Japan. Almost the equivalent of the Atlantic's Gulf Stream.

kyle A Scottish name for a narrow channel between an island and another island or the mainland.

L l

La Niña The opposite phenomenon to El Niño that also causes significant global climatic changes. La Niña is characterised by unusually cool water temperatures on the equatorial regions of the central and eastern Pacific.

La Palma One of the Canary Islands. Not to be confused with Las Palmas de Gran Canaria, capital of the island of Gran Canaria, also in the Canary Islands.

Labrador Current A current bringing cold water and icebergs down from Baffin Bay. Where it meets the Gulf Stream of Newfoundland, the mixing of the waters gives rise to the fogs that affect the Grand Banks for around 120 days each year.

Labrador Sea The area of the North Atlantic Ocean between southern Greenland and Labrador in Canada.

ladder The form of fare construction box on airline tickets in which the calculations are shown vertically.

lagoon An enclosed body of water, usually sea, such as the centre of an atoll.

lake A large body of fresh water surrounded by land.

Lake Shore Ltd A train service in the USA running between Chicago, and New York and Boston.

lanai A Hawaiian term for a room with a balcony or patio, usually overlooking water or gardens.

land arrangements Another name for ground arrangements.

land breeze A breeze blowing off the land onto the sea.

land bridge A neck of land joining two land masses.

land mass A single large body of land, such as a continent.

Land of the Midnight Sun See *Lapland*.

land yacht A vehicle with wheels and a sail used for recreational purposes on beaches and sand flats. Sometimes called a sand yacht.

Land's End The south-westernmost point of mainland Britain, in Cornwall, England.

landau A four-wheeled enclosed horse-drawn carriage with a rear hood that can be lowered.

landfall The first sighting of land after a sea journey.

landing card A document which sometimes needs to be completed by passengers before arrival at a foreign destination to facilitate progress through immigration.

landing gear The wheels of an aircraft. Also known as the undercarriage.

landing stage A platform, often floating, onto which passengers may disembark from a vessel.

landing strip An aircraft runway, often small and away from an airport and possibly grass-covered.

landlocked A country or region with no coastline.

landmark A conspicuous building or topographical feature that is easily recognised from a distance.

landscape The natural scenery or view of an area.

landside That part of an airport open to any legitimate visitor; the area before customs and other controls.

landward Towards the land.

langlauf Cross-country skiing.

Lapland A region of Northern Europe mainly within the Arctic Circle, traditionally the home of Father Christmas. It consists of the northern parts of Norway, Finland, Sweden and the Russian Kola Peninsula. Also sometimes known as the Land of the Midnight Sun.

Lapp A member of the nomadic Mongol peoples of northern Scandinavia. The term Sami is now the preferred name.

Las Palmas (Las Palmas de Gran Canaria) The capital of the island of Gran Canaria in the Canary Islands. Not to be confused with the nearby island of La Palma.

Lassa fever A serious viral disease of tropical Africa.

last quarter 1. The phase of the lunar cycle, 21 days after the new moon, when the moon appears as a half-circle.
2. The last quarter of any type of year (such as calendar, financial or accounting), usually beginning on the first day of a month. The term fourth quarter is often used for this. Quarters are commonly used periods for measuring company performances.

last seat availability The facility available on GDSs to give information regarding limited availability of airline seats.

late booking A vague term that means any booking that is made only a short while before travel. The period will vary according to the service booked. For example, an inclusive holiday booked a week before departure would probably be considered late; an air ticket from London to Paris booked by a business traveller at similar notice would probably not.

lateen sail A triangular sail on a long yard at an angle of 45° to the mast. Commonly used on Arab dhows.

Latin 1. The language of the Roman Empire, medieval Europe and still, for some purposes, of the Roman Catholic church.
2. A general description of anything relating to the peoples or countries using languages which developed from Latin.

Latin America All of the Americas south of the USA. The term sometimes excludes the few countries in this area where Spanish or Portuguese are not the official languages.

latitude, lines of (or **parallels of**) Any of the imaginary circles drawn around the earth at right angles to earth's axis. The lines of latitude are expressed in relation to the Equator, which runs around the globe at its widest point and is approximately 40,076 km (24,902 miles) in length. This is said to be at 0° latitude: the other lines of latitude run parallel to the Equator and are numbered in degrees north or south. Both the northern and southern parallels end at the poles at 90° north and 90° south respectively. Lines of latitude are parallel to each other, but are not all of equal length. Each division of one degree (divided into 60 minutes) is 60 nautical miles (approximately 110 km or 69 miles) apart; their lengths progressively diminish as they approach the poles. > *longitude, lines of.*

launch A motor boat, sometimes used to carry passengers from ship to shore.

lavatory Another name for a toilet or rest-room.

lay-by (UK) An area by a road where vehicles may stop.

layover A long (often regarded as more than two hours) period of rest or waiting time between one part of a journey and the next, such as while waiting for a connecting flight.

LCA Leading Cruise Agents of the UK. *See Appendix 5a.*

LDW *See vehicle rental insurance.*

Le Shuttle *See Eurotunnel.*

le surf A French expression for snowboarding.

league 1. A group of people, cities, nations or other organisations combining for a particular purpose.
2. An old-fashioned measure of distance equal to three miles.

lee The direction away from the wind. Sometimes referred to as leeward.

leeward *See lee.*

Leeward Islands The group of Caribbean Islands that includes: Anguilla, Antigua and Barbuda, Dominica, Guadeloupe, Monserrat, Saba, St. Eustatius, St. Kitts & Nevis and St. Maarten/St Martin.

leeway 1. The sideways drift of a ship to the lee of its desired course.
2. An allowable deviation or freedom of action.

left luggage (UK) Luggage temporarily deposited in a storeroom or locker specially designated for that purpose.

left, driving on the The practice followed by traffic in the UK, the Channel Islands, the Isle of Man, Ireland, Malta, the English-speaking states of the Caribbean Sea, the Indian Ocean and the Atlantic Ocean, Surinam, Guyana, most of East and Southern Africa, the Indian sub-continent, Australia, New Zealand, Hong Kong, Macau, Japan, parts of South-East Asia, and most of the states of the South Pacific; over 60 countries, territories and dependencies in all. Traffic elsewhere drives on the right.

leg The journey between two consecutive scheduled stops.

legal advice and expenses insurance *See travel insurance.*

legend 1. An event or story which has no provable basis in fact.
2. A panel on or near a map or chart which provides explanations of any symbols and abbreviations used.

lei A Polynesian garland of flowers, traditionally placed around the necks of visitors to these Pacific islands.

leishmaniasis Any one of a number of parasitic diseases cause by the bite of sandflies.

leisure Free time or time at one's disposal.

leisure travel agent A travel agent dealing mainly with holidaymakers, rather than business travellers. > *travel agent.*

leisure traveller A traveller who is not travelling on business or for some other obligatory reason.

Lent A period of 40 weekdays between Ash Wednesday and Easter Eve, traditionally a time of fasting and self-denial among Christians.

leprosy A slightly contagious disease that affects the nerves causing loss of sensation and consequent damage and disfigurement through unfelt injury. Still common in some Third World countries although easily treatable.

Lesser Antilles The group of Caribbean Islands comprising the Leeward Islands, the Virgin Islands, the Windward Islands and the small chain of Venezuelan islands east of Bonaire, and also the islands of Aruba, Barbados, Curaçao and Trinidad & Tobago.

Levant A former name for the area of the eastern Mediterranean now occupied by Syria, Lebanon, Israel and Palestine NAR.

Leveche A hot, dry and dusty wind in southern Spain which blows from the Sahara. > *Sirocco.*

levee (US) An embankment alongside a river, or surrounding a field that is to be irrigated.

level crossing An intersection where a railway crosses a road on the level.

levy A tax or toll.

LGV The dedicated high-speed lines (*lignes à grande vitesse*) on which French high-speed trains operate some of their services. (Some are also run on normal track). >*TGV.*

liability insurance supplement *See vehicle rental insurance.*

licensed premises (UK) A place such as a pub that is permitted to sell alcoholic drinks.

lido deck The deck of a ship that contains the swimming pool and sunbathing area.

lien A right over another's property in order to protect a debt.

life jacket A buoyant outer garment that keeps the wearer afloat in water.

lifebelt (UK) *See lifebuoy.*

lifeboat A small boat carried on board a ship to evacuate passengers in the case of serious emergency. It is a maritime regulation that all ships must carry enough lifeboats to accommodate all those aboard.

lifeboat drill An obligatory demonstration of the safety procedures on board a ship.

lifebuoy A buoyant support, often a ring, that will keep a person afloat in water.

lifeline A line which connects a diver to a point on the surface.

life-raft A raft carried on board a ship to provide an alternative or additional safety measure.

life-support systems The systems of air-conditioning, pressurisation, heating and the like that allow passengers to survive in a hostile environment, such as at a high altitude.

lift 1. The force generated by an aircraft's wings that enables it to fly.
2. (UK) An elevator, used for people or goods.

lift pass *See lift ticket.*

lift ticket (or **lift pass, ski pass**) (US) A ticket that allows the holder to use some or all of the lifts at one or more ski areas for an agreed period of time, sometimes for the entire season. Lift tickets are increasingly sophisticated and the latest versions electronically open turnstiles to allow access to a lift without needing to be removed from the user's pocket. Some act in the same way as credit cards and can be used in mountain restaurants, recharged with credit, sometimes using the internet or a mobile telephone. The terms lift pass and ski pass are more widely used in the UK and Europe.

light air *See Beaufort scale.*

light breeze *See Beaufort scale.*

light railway A railway, often narrow gauge, constructed to less demanding standards than normal and designed to cope only with light traffic.

lighter A small boat used to transfer goods between ships or to the shore.

lighter-than-air An aircraft that weighs less than the air it displaces: in other words, one that can float in the air. Such aircraft can remain in the air indefinitely without the need for engine power.

lightning A high-voltage, naturally occurring electrical discharge between clouds and other clouds or the earth.

limited 1. Of accommodation generally, when only a small amount of space remains available for sale.
2. A service, often rail, where the number of passengers is restricted to the amount of seating or other accommodation available. Usually such services require advance reservation. In the US the name is sometimes given to any long-distance luxury rail service.
3. A common form of company incorporation whereby the liability of the directors for the company's debts is limited to the extent of their investment.

limited mileage A car rental tariff whereby a certain number of miles or kilometres is included in the cost of the rental, each additional mile or kilometre thereafter being charged for at a fixed rate.

limo A colloquial term for limousine.

limousine An enclosed motor car, originally one with a division between driver and passengers, but the term is now often used casually to refer to any luxurious vehicle.

liner A large passenger ship, traditionally used for long-distance voyages.

link span A type of complex loading bridge used at ports and harbours which can be adjusted to allow for tidal height variations, such as occur in the Channel ports of Dover and Calais.

liqueur A spirit, usually sweetened and highly flavoured, traditionally drunk after meals.

liquor 1. (US) Alcoholic drink.
2. The broth, sauce or gravy in which meat has been cooked.

lithosphere The scientific name for the earth's crust or surface.

live-aboard A sea-going craft, designed for or adapted for use by scuba divers with facilities for guests to eat and sleep on-board. Also called safari boat.

live-in A person who sleeps at their place of employment.

live-out A person who sleeps away from their place of employment.

livery The distinctive colour scheme used by a carrier to identify its vehicles.

llano A treeless plain, especially in South America.

load factor The percentage of occupancy of seats or other accommodation. A100% load factor means full occupancy.

load line *See Plimsoll line.*

lobby An entrance or reception area of a hotel, typically of a hotel.

local 1. Belonging to a particular place or region.
2. Of or belonging to the neighbourhood.
3. (UK) A colloquial term for a pub.

local service A transport service operating in and around the local area.

local time The time as reckoned in a particular place. Most timetables are expressed in local times, even where a journey spans more than one time zone.

locality A district or neighbourhood.

location The place or position where something is situated.

locator A unique reference number given to a travel reservation in order that it may be accessed quickly at a later date.

loch A Scottish expression for a lake or arm of the sea.

lock A separate section of a canal or river fitted with gates to control the flow of water, thus allowing vessels to change levels.

lockjaw *See tetanus.*

locomotive A vehicle designed to haul a train or (more rarely) another form of transport.

lodge card A charge card 'lodged' in the care of an agent (usually a business travel agent) against which travel facilities may be charged. This system allows the cardholder a credit facility without the necessity for opening an account directly with the agent.

log The official record of the progress and happenings on board a ship or aircraft.

log cabin A hut or similar dwelling built from tree trunks.

loggia An open-sided extension to a building.

long vacation (UK) The extended summer holiday taken by students at British universities.

long weekend A weekend holiday extended by a day or days on either side.

longboat The largest boat used on a sailing ship.

long-haul An inexact term that is usually applied to journeys between continents.

longitude, lines of (or **meridians of**) Any of the imaginary great circles drawn around the earth from pole to pole. The meridians of longitude are expressed in relation to the 'Greenwich (or 'prime', or 'zero') meridian' which runs through Greenwich in London. This is said to be at 0°/180° longitude: the other lines of longitude also form great circles from pole to pole and are numbered in degrees east or west of it. Meridians of longitude are all equal in length, but not parallel to each other. At the Equator each division of 1 degree (divided into 60 minutes) is 60 nautical miles (approximately 110 km or 69 miles) apart: the distance between them gets progressively less as they get closer to the poles. > *latitude, lines of.*

loss damage waiver *See vehicle rental insurance.*

lounge A seating area designed to accommodate people for a short period while they are waiting to move to another area or facility.

Low Countries The geographical region comprising Belgium, Luxembourg and the Netherlands.

low latitudes Regions at or near the Equator.

low season The period during which there is the least demand for a product or service.

low tide *See low water.*

low water The tide at its lowest.

low-cost airlines A general term used to describe the wave of new airlines, particularly in North America, Europe and, increasingly, Asia, which offer lower fares than the traditional 'flagship' airlines, but also a generally lower level of service.
The term 'low-cost' is slightly arbitrary: 'no-frills' and 'budget' are also used, and are in many ways more accurate; while 'full-service' is often employed to

describe other carriers. In reality, the distinction is starting to blur, for most other airlines now compete on cost. The picture is further complicated by established airlines starting their own low-cost operations, some of which (like Buzz and Go) have since been taken over by the very companies with which these were designed to compete.

Low-cost airlines have continued the job started by airline deregulation by providing competition, and thus lower fares, on many routes. To do this, they had to build a radically different kind of airline. The ones that have succeeded best – principally Ireland's Ryanair and the UK's easyJet – entered the market afresh, adapting the model of USA's Southwest: 'low-cost' thus applies as much to their overheads as to their prices. Their main distinctive features, and areas of cost-saving, are:

• Flying from or to under-used airports, so reducing landing fees.
• Tending to use one kind of aircraft, so reducing training and maintenance costs.
• Cutting back on free meals, so reducing purchases.
• Operating in general point-to-point, so reducing the risk of unprofitable empty legs.
• Selling flights over the internet, so avoiding agency commissions.

The first four factors also reduce delays and turn-around time, so offering further advantages. This combination, together with bold marketing and the commercial flexibility that so often accompanies low overheads, saw the new airlines prosper even through the dark days of late 2001. Many low-cost airlines are now far more profitable than the larger carriers with which they compete, although they generally only threaten these airlines' short-haul routes.

lower deck   Generally the lowest deck of a ship, immediately above the hold.

loyalty club   An incentive programme for frequent users of a supplier's services. > *frequent flyer programmes and frequent stay programmes.*

luau   A Hawaiian outdoor feast with entertainment.

lubber line   A line marked on a compass showing a ship's forward direction.

luggage   Another term for baggage.

lugger   A small ship with two or three masts with a lugsail on each.

lugsail   A four-sided sail.

lunar   Of or relating to the moon.

lunar eclipse   *See eclipse.*

lunar month   A period of 28 days reckoned from the new moon.

lunar year   A period of 12 lunar months, about 354.3 days.

M m

Macau Part of the People's Republic of China since 1997, although it is still often regarded as a separate travel destination.

Macedonia 1. A division of northern Greece.
2. A district in south-western Bulgaria.
3. One of the former constituent republics of Yugoslavia, now independent. Officially known as the Former Yugoslav Republic of Macedonia. > *Yugoslavia*.
4. An ancient kingdom in northern Greece, ruled most famously by Alexander the Great in the 4th century BC.

Mach number A measure of speed as compared to the speed of sound. Mach 1 is the speed of sound; Mach 2 is twice the speed of sound, and so on.

Madeira An island in the Atlantic off the north-west coast of Africa and politically part of Portugal.

magic carpet A simple ski lift in the form of a moving walkway. Often used on beginners' and children's ski slopes.

maglev From magnetic levitation. A train supported slightly clear of its track by magnetic repulsion.

magnetic compass A compass that indicates direction in relation to a magnetic pole by means of a magnetised pointer.

magnetic pole Either of the two variable points of the earth's surface, near to but not exactly corresponding to the geographical North and South Poles, where the lines of force of the earth's magnetic field are vertical. According to which hemisphere one is in, the needle of a magnetic compass will indicate the north or the south magnetic pole. Magnetic poles move slowly around the geographic poles and a constantly varying adjustment must be made to a magnetic compass reading if a true bearing is needed. > *poles*.

Magyar Of or relating to the Ural-Altaic peoples now predominant in Hungary.

maiden voyage The first journey of a new ship, traditionally after some form of ceremony.

main course The principal course of a meal.

main deck The upper deck between the forecastle and the poop of a merchantman.

main line A primary railway line, generally with express as well as stopping services. Dedicated high-speed lines are often shown separately on timetables and maps.

main mast The principal mast on a vessel.

main road A major highway, generally including motorways.

main sail The sail fixed to the main mast of a vessel.

Mainland 1. The largest island in Orkney and in Shetland in the UK.
2. A colloquial term for the South Island of New Zealand.

mainland A large continuous piece of land, excluding its associated islands.

mainplane The main wing of an aircraft.

mainsheet A line that controls and secures the mainsail.

maitre d'hôtel A French term describing the head waiter in a restaurant. Used world-wide and often abbreviated to maître d'.

mal de mer Seasickness.

Malabar Coast The coastal region of the states of Karnataka and Kerala in south-west India. The main ports are Calicut, Cochin and Trivandrum.

malaria Formerly known as marsh fever. One of the most common diseases to which travellers are exposed. It is prevalent in many areas of Asia, Africa and Latin America. It is caused by plasmodium parasites that live inside the anopheles mosquito. It is difficult to cure and travellers should protect themselves by avoiding mosquito bites and by taking suitable anti-malarial drugs. Mosquitoes have developed resistance to some drugs in some parts of the world. > *health precautions*.

Malay Archipelago The largest island group in the world, off the south-east coast of Asia and between the Indian and Pacific Oceans. Major islands in the group include Borneo, Sulawesi (Celebes), Jawa (Java), New Guinea and Sumatera (Sumatra). The countries within the archipelago are Brunei, Indonesia, Malaysia (East), Papua New Guinea and the Philippines.

management fee An amount paid by a corporate customer to a business travel agent. There are two main systems:
1. A management fee is agreed for a specified period, regardless of the number of transactions taking place.
2. A fee is charged for each transaction, regardless of the period over which they are completed.
Occasionally the two systems may be combined. Management fees have now become the normal way of trading between travel agents and corporations rather than relying on commission from suppliers. > *travel agent*.

management information system A term used to denote the statistical and other data supplied by business travel agents to their customers in order to monitor spend and travel trends.

mañana An expression of Spanish origin literally meaning tomorrow, but implying later or possibly never.

Manche, la Literally 'the sleeve', the French name for the English Channel.

manifest The official list of passengers or cargo being carried on a vehicle, ship or plane.

manifold A connecting pipe between two or more sources of high pressure gas.

manual issue A document which is hand-written, rather than computer-processed and printed.

manufacturing One of the three types of profession (agriculture and services being the others) into which economic activity is generally divided for statistical purposes.

Manx Of or relating to the Isle of Man.

Maori The inhabitants of New Zealand and the Cook Islands before the arrival of European settlers.

map A flat representation of all or part of the earth's surface generally showing political and/or physical features, or illustrating a particular theme.
Two important features of maps are their scale (determining how much detail can be included); and their function (determining what kind of features are concentrated on). Only maps of very small areas can clearly display all the physical and man-made features. A map produced for motorists will show roads more prominently and comprehensively than railways, while one illustrating diving sites will be more concerned with bathometric (sea-depth) contours than with the altitude of the land. Also, local significance can be of more importance than absolute size. A mountain of 2,000m in the Himalayas or a town of 50,000 people near Paris would probably not merit inclusion on many maps of those areas: the same sized feature in a comparatively flat or under-populated area (like England or central Australia) probably would.
Maps which have been designed to display one theme exclusively may have no consistent scale or may distort the shape of the area being covered and the relative positions of the places marked on it. A good example of this is the map of the London Underground. In the same way, a map showing ferry services in Europe might distort land shapes in order to maximise the length of the coastlines and the area of the sea.

MAP *See modified American plan.*

map projection The method by which all or part of the world's surface can be represented in two dimensions. The term is also used to describe the name of the particular projection used.
Because the earth is spherical, displaying its surface in two dimensions requires some distortion, the effects of which become greater as the area of coverage increases. In the case of town plans and maps of small countries or regions, this distortion is insignificant; on maps of large countries, continents or the entire world, it is very significant indeed.
Different projections address this problem in different ways and, as a result, the shape and respective sizes of landmasses may vary from one map to another. To a greater or lesser extent, on most world map projections the further a place is from the Equator, the larger it will appear to be. Greenland, for instance, is roughly two-thirds the size of India; yet because of their respective positions on the earth's surface Greenland appears on many maps to be considerably bigger. For this reason, scale bars are often omitted from maps showing very large areas, as a fixed distance (say 1cm) on the page will, in different parts of the map, represent a different distance on the ground.
As a general rule, the more similar the latitude between two places (whether north or south of the Equator), the more accurate their respective sizes will be. Thus two places, one at 40° north and one at 40° south will be in proportion: two places, one at 10° north and one at 55° north, will not.

map reference Two sequences of numbers and/or letters, one running along the horizontal edge of a map and one along the vertical, which together help locate a particular place or feature. On some maps, the graticule lines will fulfil this function. > *graticule.*

Maple Leaf The rail service running between Toronto in Canada and New York in the USA.

Mardi Gras 1. Shrove Tuesday in many Catholic countries.
2. The celebration often associated with this, most famously in Nice, Rio de Janeiro and New Orleans.

marina A harbour, often specially constructed, with moorings and, generally, associated facilities for small boats and yachts.

marine Of or relating to the sea or shipping.

mariner A seaman.

market 1. A public place, often in a town centre, where goods are bought and sold.
2. A group of people or a place with a demand for a certain service or commodity.

marketing The business of promoting and selling a product or service.

mark-up 1. The amount added to a net price to arrive at a selling price.
2. The act of correcting a proof.

Marlin Coast An area of coast in northern Queensland, Australia, centred on Cairns.

maroon To abandon or leave stranded in a place, generally abroad.

marsh Low land flooded for much of the year.

marsh fever *See malaria.*

Mascarene Islands The group of volcanic islands in the Indian Ocean, east of Madagascar, that includes Réunion and Mauritius.

mask clearing An underwater process whereby the mask is held firmly to the forehead whilst the diver exhales through the nose. The exhaled air rises to the top of the mask and forces water out at the bottom thus clearing the mask.

Mason-Dixon Line The division between the northern and southern states in the American Civil War, broadly following the line of 40° N along the southern border of Pennsylvania before turning south to follow the frontier between Maryland and Delaware. The line has its origins in the settlement of a property dispute before the American War of Independence. > *American Civil War.*

massif A compact group of mountains.

mast A tall pole, usually fixed to the hull of a ship. On sailing vessels masts will be high and substantial to take the weight and thrust of the sails. On powered vessels, they may carry little more than the ensigns and wireless aerials.

masthead The highest point of a mast.

maximum permitted mileage The maximum number of miles that may be flown within each IATA fare component. The MPM is usually about 20% greater than the actual ticketed point mileage (TPM). For example, the ticketed point (or flown) mileage from London to New York is 3,458 but the MPM is 4,149. The mileage concept often permits a traveller to make stopovers at intermediate points without having to pay a higher fare.

Mayan The civilisation of ancient Mexico and Guatemala (c.2500BC to c.AD1550), one of the longest surviving civilisations in history.

mayday The standard international radio distress call.

MC Master of ceremonies.

MCO *See miscellaneous charges order.*

MCS Mountaineering Council of Scotland. *See Appendix 5a.*

MCT *See minimum connecting time.*

MDR-TB Multiple Drug Resistant Tuberculosis. An increasingly common and very serious disease with mortality rates in excess of 50%. > *health precautions.*

meadow An area of grass and small flowers.

mean sea level The level of the sea midway between high and low tides.

meander 1. A section of a river that has a series of curves or bends.
2. A slower or less direct route taken by planes to satisfy air traffic restrictions, or by ships to avoid rough seas or to arrive in port at a specific time.

Mecca (Also **Makkah**) One of the three holy cities of Islam (Medina and Jerusalem being the others), 80 km from the Red Sea in Saudi Arabia. > *hajj.*

media The collective term for the various methods of mass communication, including the press, television, radio and the internet.

medical expenses insurance *See travel insurance.*

medieval (or **mediæval**) Of or relating to the Middle Ages (broadly speaking from the 10th to the 15th centuries).

Medina One of the three holy cities of Islam (Mecca and Jerusalem being the others), 338 km north of Mecca.

medina The old Arab quarter of a North African town.

Mediterranean 1. The sea between Southern Europe, North Africa and Western Asia.
2. Of or relating to the islands of the Mediterranean Sea and the countries bordering it.
3. A type of climate. *See climate zones.*

Mediterranean Yacht Brokers Association An organisation which represents and regulates yacht charter companies in Europe, and which has developed standard terms and contracts for yacht chartering in various parts of the world.

meet and greet The provision of a service to meet and assist passengers on arrival at their destination port, station or airport. This term is often used by car parking companies who meet their customers at the airport and park their car for the duration of a trip.

megalopolis A very large city or conurbation.

Melanesia The collective name given to the group of islands in the south-west Pacific Ocean, south of the Equator and north-east of Australia. It includes Fiji, Nauru, New Caledonia, Papua New Guinea (excluding the New Guinea mainland), Solomon Islands and Vanuatu.

melt water Water formed from the melting of ice, especially from a glacier.

Meltemi *See Etesian Wind.*

member A term used to describe an airline, travel agent or tour operator which subscribes to an association such as IATA, ABTA or AITO. *A list of many travel-related bodies may be found in Appendix 5.*

memsahib A polite form of address used in India when referring to a woman.

menagerie A collection of wild animals for exhibition, generally privately owned.

meningitis A potentially fatal disease caused by inflammation of the brain or spinal cord. Meningoccal meningitis is endemic in certain parts of the world, including the southern fringes of the Sahara and the Indian sub-continent. > *health precautions.*

menu 1. A list of food and drink available in a restaurant.
2. A list, on a computer screen, giving a choice of actions that may be taken.

Mercator projection A type of map projection, designed originally for navigation purposes, in which lines of latitude and longitude are shown as parallel intersecting straight lines. > *map projection, latitude, longitude.*

merchant marine (US) *See merchant navy.*

merchant navy (UK) A nation's commercial shipping fleet.

merchantman A ship used for merchant (or passenger and mixed cargo) purposes, as opposed to military or tanker use.

meridian *See longitude, lines of.*

mesa A high, steep-sided plateau.

Meso-American Of or relating to the area stretching from Central Mexico to Nicaragua or the various pre-Columbian civilisations which flourished there.

mestizo A Spanish expression meaning a person of mixed parentage, especially Spanish or Portuguese and Native American (Indian).

meteograph An instrument that records a number of different meteorological phenomena simultaneously.

meteorology The science of the study of weather.

metric The decimal-based system of weights and measures, used throughout most of the world except for the USA. > *Appendix 6.*

metro A name used in many parts of the world to describe an urban railway system in general, and that of some cities in particular. Apart from Paris (see below), the urban railways of Madrid, Barcelona,

Lisbon, Washington DC and Moscow (as well as many others) are known as the Metro. Names for other systems include BART in San Francisco, DART in Dublin, U- and S-Bahn in many German cities including Berlin, MRT in Singapore, MTR in Hong Kong, and Subte in Buenos Aires.

Métro The underground railway network in Paris. It is sometimes taken also to include the RER, the city's deep-level express network.

Metroplex The metropolitan area of Dallas-Fort Worth in Texas. The cities between Dallas and Fort Forth are described as the Mid-Cities: the largest of these is Arlington.

metropolis A large, important city, generally the principal city of a country or region.

metropolitan area A general term for a built-up area comprising more than one city or town which have largely grown together.

mezzanine A low storey between two others in a building, usually the first and ground floors.

MIA Meetings Industry Association. *See Appendix 5a.*

mic (pronounced 'mike') An abbreviation for microphone.

Micronesia A collective name for the islands in the west part of the Pacific Ocean, north of the Equator and east of the Philippines. It includes Guam, Kiribati (western part), the Marshall Islands, Federated States of Micronesia, Northern Mariana Islands and Palau.

Micronesia, Federated States of One of the island countries in the area known generally as Micronesia.

Middle America 1. Mexico, Central America and the Caribbean
2. The middle classes in the USA.

Middle East A general geographic term describing a loosely defined area comprising the countries of the Arabian Peninsula, Egypt, Iran, Iraq, Israel, Jordan, Lebanon, Palestine NAR and Syria. It is often extended to include Algeria, Morocco, Sudan, Tunisia, Cyprus, Libya and Turkey.

midnight sun The sun as seen in polar regions, at midnight during that hemisphere's summer.

Midnight Sun Coast The eastern coast of Sweden from Gavle to the Finnish border.

midships *See amidships.*

midtown (US) That part of a town or city midway between the uptown and downtown districts, particularly where this forms a distinct area.

migration The movement of people or animals, either

temporarily or permanently, from one place to another.

mike An abbreviation for microphone.

mile *See statute mile, nautical mile.*

milli- A prefix commonly found in the metric system, meaning one thousandth part of. Thus a millimetre is one thousandth of a metre.

millibar The international unit for measuring atmospheric pressure.

millimetre A unit of measurement in the metric system, one-tenth of a centimetre. > *centimetre.*

mini-bar A small cabinet or fridge found in a hotel room containing drinks and snacks. A charge is usuually added to the room bill for those used.

minibus (UK) A small bus, usually for fewer than twelve passengers.

minicab (UK) A car available for hire which cannot by law be hailed in the street but which must be ordered by phone. They are less tightly regulated than taxis.

minimum connecting time (MCT) The minimum amount of time that a passenger may allow between flights or any other mode of transport. Every major airport in the world has set MCTs

minimum rated package A UK term for an inclusive tour by air that provides 'nominal' accommodation in order to comply with regulations. > *seat only.*

minimum stay The shortest time a passenger can stay before using the return portion of a ticket. Return before this time will usually involve a surcharge. The most used minimum stay requirement is the 'Sunday Rule' whereby travellers may not return from their point of turnaround until after 0001 on the Sunday following the day of arrival.

miniple (UK) A travel agency group with between five and 20 outlets.

minivan 1. (US) See minibus.
2. (UK) A small van.

Minoan Of or relating to the civilisation, language and people of Crete (c.3000BC to c.1200BC).

minute 1. One sixtieth of an hour; sixty seconds.
2. One sixtieth of a degree of arc. > *nautical mile*

mirage An optical illusion, most commonly seen in deserts and other very hot places, usually caused by the refraction of light in warm air.

MIS *See management information system.*

miscellaneous charges order (MCO) An airline voucher

that can be used for almost any type of service. For example, a passenger might choose to have an MCO issued to cover excess baggage charges. Nowadays replaced by MPDs (multi-purpose documents).

Mississippi River Country A US regional marketing organisation covering the states that border the Mississippi river. > *US regional marketing organisations.*

mist Water vapour near the ground limiting visibility to between one and two kilometres.

mistral A cold, northerly wind that blows down the Rhone valley and southern France into the Mediterranean.

mixed route A climbing route from one point to another that involves differing types of terrain. Normally used to denote that one will encounter rock as well as snow and/or ice while ascending this route.

mobile home 1. A large caravan permanently parked and used as a residence.
2. (US) A recreational vehicle (RV).

moderate breeze *See Beaufort scale.*

modified American plan Also known as half-board or *demi pension.* A hotel rate which includes room, breakfast and one other meal.

Mogul (or **Mughal**) 1. An alternative form of *Mongol*
2. Of or relating to the dynasty which ruled an empire in India from the 16th to 19th centuries.

mogul 1. A bump on a ski slope.
2. An influential or important person.

momentarily 1. (UK) Lasting for a very short time.
2. (US) Shortly.

monarch A king or queen ruling as a head of state, often by right of hereditary succession, with powers ranging from the absolute to the purely ceremonial.

monarchy 1. A country with a monarch as its head of state.
2. A general collective term for the role and office of a monarch and its associated dignities, traditions, constitutional status and functions.

Mongols The peoples of Central Asia who made considerable conquests in the 13th century under Gengis Khan and Kublai Khan. > *Mogul.*

monitor A computer screen.

mono-hull A vessel with a single hull. Most vessels are constructed in this way.

monolingual 1. A person who can speak only one language.
2. Something that is written in, or spoken in, only one language.

monoplane An aeroplane with one pair of wings, the conventional arrangement for modern aircraft.

monorail A railway whose track consists of a single rail.

monoski A single, straight ski, used with both feet locked to it in a parallel position.

monsoon 1. A wind in southern Asia blowing from the south-west in summer and from the north-east in winter.
2. The rainy season associated with the monsoon.

Montréal Convention A mandate which came into force on June 28th 2004 that replaced the outdated Warsaw Convention. The mandate sets out procedures and compensation packages to which airlines must conform in the case of delayed flights and damaged or lost baggage. The new rules fall in favour of the passenger as the maximum claim for lost baggage was increased from £280 to approximately £850 depending on prevailing exchange rates. In addition, under the previous agreement a bag was regarded as lost after six weeks but compensation has to now be paid after 21 days. Many low-cost carriers are fearful that compensation payments will be, in some cases, far in excess of the fare paid. > *Warsaw Convention*.

monument A structure generally intended to commemorate a person or event. For descriptions of a selection of the more notable monuments throughout the world, consult the Columbus *Tourist Attractions & Events of the World*.

moor 1. To secure a vessel to the land, or to a buoy at sea.
2. A tract of open, uncultivated land.

Moor A member of the Muslim peoples of mixed Berber and Arab descent.

mooring A place where a vessel can be moored.

moraine An area of rocks and other debris deposited by a glacier. The ground is often loose and stony and can be uncomfortable to walk on.

Moresque Architecture in the Moorish style.

Morse code An early communications system using a combination of dots and dashes to represent the different letters of the alphabet. The increasing power and sophistication of modern communication systems has rendered it obsolete.

mosque A Muslim place of worship.

motel Originally a hotel designed for overnight stays by car travellers, often with limited facilities. The name is also given to more traditional types of hotel, whose guests arrive by other means.

motion sickness Nausea caused by the movement of any form of transport.

motor bike *See motor cycle*.

motor boat A boat powered by an engine, usually internal combustion.

motor coach 1. (US) A large passenger-carrying road vehicle, generally equipped with toilet facilities.
2. A passenger coach on an electrified railway which has its own motor.

motor cycle A cycle, usually with two wheels, powered by an engine.

motor scooter A small motor cycle with additional weather protection.

motor ship A ship powered by internal combustion engines, usually diesel. Usually denoted by the abbreviation MS in front of its name.

motor yacht A yacht powered by a motor.

motorail Originally a proprietary term for the vehicle-carrying services operated by the former British Rail. Now often used to denote any such service.

motorway (UK) A high-speed multi-carriageway road with special regulations.

motu A term used in the South Pacific for a very small island or islet.

mountain A large elevation of the earth's surface, taller and generally steeper than a hill. Mountains generally occur in ranges, of which the three largest in area are the Himalayas (Asia), the Rockies (North America) and the Andes (South America). Traditionally a mountain has to be over 1,000 feet (305m) in height to be considered as such. The world's ten tallest mountains are all to be found in the Himalayas. For a list of the tallest mountains in each continent, consult the Columbus *World Travel Atlas*.
2. A type of climate. *See climate zones*.

mountain hut A refuge available in areas popular with climbers designed for overnight accommodation. They can be anything in size from places that sleep half a dozen people to those that can accommodate over one hundred.

mountain sickness *See altitude sickness*.

Mountain Standard Time One of the time zones used in North America, seven hours behind UTC.

mountaineering The ascent of mountains (normally with the aim of reaching the summit) by a combination of hill walking, trekking, scrambling, via ferrata, rock climbing or ice climbing. As well as the obvious risks, additional dangers result from practising the above techniques in remote areas subject to extreme weather conditions and altitude

problems. > *altitude sickness and acclimatisation.*
2. A type of climate. *See climate zones.*

mouth 1. The opening of a cave.
2. The point where a river enters the sea.

mouthpiece That part of the aqualung or snorkel which enters the mouth and through which the wearer may breathe.

Mozambique Channel The area of the Indian Ocean between Mozambique and Madagascar.

MPD Multi-Purpose Document. *See MCO.*

MPM *See maximum permitted mileage.*

MPV Multi Purpose Vehicle.

MS When placed in front of a ship's name means Motor Ship.

mudéjar A style of architecture found in Iberia dating from the late middle ages, a blend of Gothic and Arabic styles.

Mughal *See Mogul.*

MUISZ Association of Hungarian Travel Agencies. *See Appendix 5c.*

mull The Scottish word for a promontory.

multi-hull A vessel with several hulls.

multi-lateral agreement An agreement between three or more parties.

multi-lingual 1. A person who can speak three or more languages fluently.
2. Something that is written in, or spoken in, three or more languages.

multiple (UK) A travel agency group with a large number of branches, generally accepted to be 20 or more. A company with five to 20 outlets is generally referred to as a miniple and smaller groups as independents.

multiple dives More than one dive taken within a relatively short space of time.

multiple entry visa A visa valid for several visits.

multiplier effect The term used to describe the way in which expenditure by tourists affects the local economy by a greater amount than the value of the initial expenditure might suggest.

multi-sector A journey that involves several separate legs.

municipal golf course A golf course open to the public. A municipal or public golf course is usually open to all visitors, although some of the world's top municipal courses have special booking procedures.

municipality A town or area having its own local government.

mural A painting executed directly onto a wall or, less commonly, a ceiling, usually part of some larger scheme of decoration.

Muslim (also **Moslem**) Of or relating to the Islamic religion, its followers or the customs and culture associated with it.

muster station An area of a ship where passengers are instructed to gather in the event of an emergency.

MV When placed in front of the name of a boat or ship means Motor Vessel.

MY When placed in front of the name of a boat or ship means Motor Yacht.

MYBA See Mediterranean Yacht Brokers Association.

Mycenaean Of or relating to the late Bronze Age civilisation of ancient Greece.

mystery client One of the terms used to describe a person who visits a retail outlet such as a travel agency pretending to be a client, but whose real purpose is either to discover pricing or other information for a rival company, or to assess the levels of knowledge and service for a feature in a trade publication.

mystery tour (UK) A coach excursion on an unknown route to an unknown destination.

N n

N/A 1. Not available.
2. Not applicable.

NACOA National Association of Cruise Oriented Agencies. *See Appendix 5b.*

NACTA National Association of Commissioned Travel Agents.

nadir The lowest point. Typically used to describe the fortunes of a person or organisation.

NAITA National Association of Independent Travel Agents. *See Appendix 5a.*

named driver A person, specified on a rental agreement or an insurance document, who is permitted to drive a particular vehicle.

Napoleonic Of or relating to the period when Napoleon I was ruler of France (1799 to 1815).

narks A colloquial term for nitrogen narcosis.

narrow boat A vessel used on a canal, mainly in Great Britain, these days for leisure although there are a few commercial services. Often incorrectly referred to as a barge.

narrow gauge A railway track gauge of less than the standard four feet eight and a half inches.

narrow seas (UK) The English Channel and the Irish Sea.

narrow-bodied The traditional kind of aircraft design with a single centre aisle.

nation A community of people of mainly common descent, history, language and culture, generally when organised within a political state.

national 1. A person who has a citizen of the country or state in question.
2. Of, belonging to or conducted within a nation.

national park An area of natural beauty or interest protected by a state for the use and enjoyment of the general public.

National Rail (UK) The brand name used to promote, emplain and sell the rail services of the UK generally. > *Railtrack, Network Rail.*

national tourist office An government-run organisation which exists to promote tourism that country to the consumers and the travel trade, both directly and through their network of overseas branches.

nationality The status of belonging to a particular nation.

native A person born in or living in a particular place.

natural attraction A tourist attraction that is not man-made.

naturalise To admit a person to the citizenship of a country.

nature reserve A tract of land left in its natural state to preserve its fauna and flora.

nature trail A signposted track through an area of countryside, whose natural attractions it is designed to show off.

nautical Of or relating to the sea, sailors or navigation.

nautical mile The length of one minute of an arc of a great circle round the Earth, equal to 1,852m (2,025 yards, or approximately 1.15 statute miles). > *statute mile.*

navigable A river or other stretch of water that allows the passage of vessels.

navigation 1. The act of plotting the course of a vehicle and ensuring that it keeps to it.
2. A river artificially modified to improve its ability to convey commercial traffic such as barges or narrow boats.

NEA National Exhibitors Association. *See Appendix 5a.*

neap tide A tide occurring just after the first and third quarters of the moon, when there is the least difference between high and low water and when the tidal streams run least strongly.

Near East A general geographical term, now rarely used, that describes an area of south-west Asia that includes the Arabian Peninsula, Cyprus, Israel, Jordan, Lebanon, Syria and Turkey. Often extended to include Egypt and the Sudan.

near gale *See Beaufort scale.*

negative buoyancy The state of being heavier than water, and therefore prone to sinking in it.

neighbourhood 1. The region in or near to a place.
2. A district in a built-up area.

net fare Any non-commissionable fare to which an agency must add its own consultancy fee.

net rate A wholesale rate to holiday organisers who would be expected to add their own mark-up.

net registered tonnage A measure of the capacity of a ship. As with GRT, it is the measure of the enclosed space in a ship, but the calculation is made after spaces such as crew quarters, engine room have been deducted. In other words, it is a measure of the space that can be used for paying passengers' accommodation.

Netherlands Antilles Those islands of the West Indies administered by the Netherlands. They comprise Bonaire, Curaçao, Saba, St Eustatius and St Maarten. Aruba was a part of the Netherlands Antilles until it became a separate dependency of the Netherlands in 1986.

netiquette 'net etiquette', the (ever-shifting) rules and conventions that define what is and what is not acceptable in on-line communications.

Network Rail (UK) The company which took over the functions of Railtrack in managing key aspects of the UK's railways in 2002. > *Railtrack, National Rail.*

neutral buoyancy The state of being the same weight as water, and therefore neither sinking in it nor rising to the surface.

neutral unit of construction An artificial currency used to construct IATA air fares and to exchange funds between airlines. It is necessary to have one unit of currency (NUC) against which each actual currency has an exchange rate. As a result, IATA can pass funds between members by use of NUCs, rather than a multitude of local currencies.

New Guinea A large island north of Australia, divided between the Indonesian state of Irian Jaya and Papua New Guinea.

new moon The phase of the lunar cycle when the moon appears as a thin crescent, or not at all.

new tourist A recent term describing tourists who exhibit a number of travel characteristics including independence, experience, environmental awareness, flexibility, health-consciousness and a demand for quality.

New World North and South America collectively, as regarded by the Old World.

Newfoundland Standard Time One of the time zones used in North America, three and a half hours behind UTC.

nimbostratus Low, dense, grey cloud from which rain often falls.

NITB Northern Ireland Tourist Board. *See Appendix 5a.*

nitrogen narcosis A condition sometimes experienced by divers where sufferers become insensible, in a manner similar to being drunk. It is caused by the effects on the body of nitrogen when under pressure. Symptoms vary with each individual.

nitrox An abbreviation taken from the words nitrogen and oxygen and used in relation to the contents of a gas cylinder containing a mixed gas for breathing underwater where the oxygen content has been increased beyond 21%, thus reducing the Nitrogen content in order to reduce susceptibility to DCS. Also termed enriched air and enriched air nitrox (EANx).

nitrox course Formal training in the use of nitrox.

nitrox diving Scuba diving using nitrox instead of ordinary breathing air.

no show The failure to use a confirmed hotel room or airline seat reservation without having cancelled. On many short flights the proportion of no-shows can reach 20%, which explains why airlines overbook.

no-frills A basic service or product providing the minimum to meet a customer's requirements.

no-go area (UK) An area to which access by unauthorised people is forbidden.

no-man's land An area assigned to no particular owner. Often used to describe the stretch of land between the frontiers of adjoining territories, particularly (as in Korea and Cyprus) where there is a strong military presence.

non-aligned A state that does not side with any other particular state or country or international alliance.

non-commissionable A product or service that carries no agent's commission.

non-op Non-operational or not operating.

nonref An airline code that officially means 'refund restricted' but that is often and incorrectly assumed to mean non-refundable.

non-resident 1. Someone who is not permanently domiciled in a particular country.
2. Someone who is not staying at a particular hotel or other accommodation. In many cases, some facilities are not available to non-residents, or are only available if paid for.

non-smoking A compartment or area where smoking is not permitted.

non-stop A trip that is continuous from beginning to end.

non-transferable A ticket, voucher, reservation or other travel service that can only be used by the person for whom it was originally provided.

normal fare A fare carrying no special restrictions of validity or use.

Norman 1. A native or inhabitant of Normandy.
2. Of or relating to the peoples of Scandinavian origin who settled in Normandy in the 10th century and

invaded England in 1066 (ruling until 1154). They also founded states in Sicily and the Middle East.

3. The style of Romanesque architecture introduced to Britain by the Normans.

north One of the four cardinal points of the compass, 90° clockwise from west and 180° from south. Most maps have north at the top, although in some cases the orientation might be twisted slightly (for example, to show all of a given land mass at a suitable scale). In such cases, the direction of north will be illustrated with a compass arrow.

North America One of the world's continents. As with most continents, opinions differ as to its exact composition and area. > *continent*.

North Atlantic Drift The northern extension of the Gulf Stream that warms the coasts of Iceland, Norway and Spitzbergen.

North Korea A widely used, though unofficial, term for the Democratic People's Republic of Korea.

North Pacific Current The Pacific equivalent of the North Atlantic Drift. It brings the warm waters of the Kuroshio to the north-west coast of North America.

North Pole The northernmost point of the earth.

North Sea The sea between the British Isles, Scandinavia and the Netherlands.

northern hemisphere That part of the earth north of the Equator.

Northern Ireland One of the constituent countries of the United Kingdom of Great Britain and Northern Ireland. > *Great Britain, United Kingdom*.

northern lights See *aurora borealis*.

nose The projecting front of an aircraft or other vehicle.

nose wheel The front landing wheel of an aircraft.

nouvelle cuisine A style of cooking that avoids traditional heavy sauces in favour of lighter and fresher ingredients and pays particular attention to the presentation of the food.

NRT See *net registered tonnage*.

NT National Trust. See *Appendix 5a*.

NTO National Tourist Office. See *tourist office*.

NTS National Trust for Scotland. See *Appendix 5a*.

NUC See *neutral unit of construction*.

null and void Invalid, not binding.

nullify To invalidate.

Nunavut The new name for the eastern (Inuit) part of Canada's Northwest Territories, from which it was separated in 1999. Nunavut is an Inuit word meaning 'Our Land'. It covers an area of around one million square miles (2,560,00 square kilometres), approximately 20% of Canada's land area.

nursery See *ski kindergarten*.

nursery slope A gentle ski run used to teach the art of skiing or snowboarding.

O o

OAG A publisher of airline and other travel-related information derived from the original Official Airline Guide.

OAP (UK) *See old age pensioner.*

oasis A fertile spot in a desert, often around a pool of water.

observation car A carriage on a train built to allow a good view. Also known in the US as a bubble car or dome car.

occidental Of or relating to the western nations and culture.

occupancy The number of people using a particular facility.

occupancy rate 1. The number of people occupying a room in a hotel. If one person stays in a double room, they may be charged a low occupancy rate. 2. A measurement of the percentage of the total number of beds in a hotel that are actually occupied on a given night. Thus an occupancy rate of 50% suggests that the hotel is half full.

ocean A large sea. There are five oceans: Arctic; Atlantic (sometimes split into North and South); Indian; Pacific; and Southern. For obvious reasons, the boundaries between them are not always easy to define. Many oceans contain areas that are known as seas, bays, gulfs or similar (such as the South China Sea, the Bay of Biscay and the Gulf of Mexico) a selection of which have their own entries elsewhere in this book. Roughly 70% of the surface of the world is covered by oceans.

oceanarium A large seawater aquarium.

ocean-going Of a ship. One designed to cross large stretches of water.

Oceania 1. One of the world's continents. As with most continents, opinions differ as to its exact composition and area. > *continent.* 2. Sometimes used to describe the world's oceans and seas generally and collectively.

oceanic Of, relating to or near an ocean.

octopush A form of underwater hockey played in a swimming pool.

off season Another name for low season.

off-line carrier A carrier whose flights are being booked on another carrier's reservation system.

off-line point A city not served by a particular carrier.

offload To remove a person from, or refuse to carry a person on, a flight or other means of transport. This may be a result of overbooking, although there are other reasons, such as unacceptable behaviour.

off-peak A period of low demand for a product or service.

off-piste Away from the prepared ski-runs. Many travel insurance policies do not cover off-piste skiing due the sharply increased level of risk.

off-season *See off-peak.*

offshore At sea some way from the shore.

OK The official abbreviation on most travel documents for a confirmed seat, room or other booking.

old age pensioner (UK) An elderly person. This expression tends to be considered derogatory these days and terms such as senior citizen are often preferred. Persons of pensionable age can usually obtain discounts on most forms of travel.

Old World Europe, Asia and Africa.

Olympic Games The world's major international multi-sport event (known also as the Summer Olympics) which takes place in a different city every four years, lasting about three weeks and first held (in the modern era) in 1896. The 2000 event took place in Sydney and the 2004 event in Athens. Future Summer Olympic Games will be held in Beijing in 2008 and in London in 2012. The Winter Olympics (which take place also every four years, two years apart from the Summer Olympics) cover the full range of winter sports. The 1998 event took place in Nagano (Japan) and the 2002 event in Salt Lake City. Future Winter Olympics will be held in Turin in 2006 and Vancouver in 2010. Accommodation and transport arrangements may need to be made months, and sometimes years, in advance.

omnibus *See bus.*

OMT *See WTO*

on board When a person has boarded a ship or other vessel.

one-armed bandit A coin- or token-operated slot machine used for gambling.

one-class A means of transport where all passengers have access to all facilities and public areas. On one-class ships there may still be significant differences between the quality of sleeping and eating accommodation, but the communal areas (such as spas, restaurants, bars and decks) will be available to everyone.

one-way rental A car rental that terminates at a location other than that at which it started. In many cases an additional one-way rental charge will be payable by the hirer. One-way rentals may not always be offered at a particular vehicle rental location.

one-way rental charge *See drop-off charge.*

one-way trip A journey from origin to destination with no return booking.

on-line carrier The carrier whose system is being used to make a booking.

on-line connection An arrangement of flight connections between services of the same carrier.

on-line marketing The promotion of goods or services using the internet or other electronic media.

onshore 1. On land, rather than on water.
2. A wind blowing from the sea to the land.

open A booking for which confirmed reservations have not yet been made. > *open-ended, open date, ticket (1), reservation.*

open bar A catering arrangement whereby drinks are not charged to those who consume them (but may be to the organiser of the event).

open date Any date on a booking that is awaiting a confirmed reservation. > *open-ended, open, ticket (1), reservation.*

open sea An expanse of sea away from the land.

open skies The philosophy or policy of total deregulation allowing unrestricted access to airspace by any carrier.

open-ended A booking with a return portion that is awaiting a confirmed reservation. > *open, open date, ticket (1), reservation.*

open-jaw A return journey that has different originating and terminating points, or with different turnaround points. For example, London to Montreal, returning to Manchester; or London to Montreal, then returning from Vancouver to London.

open-sitting An eating arrangment whereby guests dine at any time within the restaurant's opening hours. >

option (UK) A provisional booking, usually for a holiday, held without payment while a customer decides whether to go ahead with the purchase.

option date The deadline by which a whole or partial

payment must be made, a contract signed or a reservation confirmed in order to secure the product or service in question.

optional extra Anything bought by a customer that is additional to the basic holiday or other arrangement. This has the same meaning as the term 'add on', which is more common in North America.

Ordnance Survey The UK's national mapping agency, founded in the 1790s, which produces a wide range of maps of the UK (such as the 1:625,000 Route, the 1:250,000 Road, the 1:50,000 Landranger and the 1:25,000 Explorer series) and of many other countries worldwide.

organiser Under the EC (now EU) Package Travel Regulations, anyone who organises, other than 'occasionally', a package holiday. This does not have to be a commercial organisation; an individual, even if arranging a package on a purely voluntary basis, is still bound by the regulations.

Orient Express The rail service which, between the 1880s and 1977, operated services from London to Istanbul via Paris, Milan, Venice, Belgrade, Sofia and Athens. Today it is an ordinary train running between Paris and Venice. The name may be dropped in the near future. > *Venice-Simplon Orient Express.*

oriental Of or relating to the eastern nations and culture.

origin 1. The starting point for a journey.
2. The place from where a person initially comes.

orthodox A person who strictly adheres to the forms and observances of a particular religion, such as Judaism.

Orthodox Of or relating to the family of Christian churches (including Russian, Greek and Romanian) which originated in Eastern Europe and Western Asia and separated themselves from the Roman Catholic church in the 11th century.

ÖRV Österreichischer Reisebüro- und Reiseveranstalter Verband. *See Appendix 5c.*

Ottoman Of or relating to the Turkish dynasty founded in 1300 and lasting until 1922, and the empire that it ruled.

outback The remote bush country of Australia.

outboard A motor attachable to the outside of the stern of a boat.

outbound 1. A flight or other mode of transport leaving from an airport, port or other terminus.
2. The outward sector of an air package holiday.

outcrop A stratum of rock emerging from the surface of the soil.

outfall The mouth of a river, stream, drain or other waterway where it empties.

outing A short trip or excursion, especially from one's home.

outlying Remote.

out-of-date A document whose validity has expired.

outrigger 1. A beam or spar projecting from the side of a ship or boat to add stability.
2. A boat fitted with outriggers.
3. A part of a map which projects beyond the frame in order to show an outlying part of the area being considered. Maps of the UK, for example, may require an outrigger to show the whole of the Cornish mainland.

outside cabin A cabin on a ship with a window or porthole. A cabin on the outside of a ship without a porthole or window is not considered to be 'outside'.

overbooking The situation in which more people with reservations for a flight turn up for it then there are seats available. This is known as overselling in the US.

over-capacity A surplus of seats or beds or other accommodation above what is needed to meet the needs of customers.

Overland The rail service between Melbourne and Adelaide in Australia.

overpass A road or railway that passes over another by means of a bridge.

overriding commission (or **override**) Officially, the extra commission paid by principals to their general sales agents to enable them to pay full commission to other agents. The term is often used to describe any commission paid in excess of the 'standard' amount.

overseas Foreign or abroad.

overselling (US) *See overbooking.*

Oyashio The Pacific's equivalent of the East Greenland Current, flowing south through the Bering Strait.

ozone layer A part of the upper atmosphere which provides protection from the sun's ultra-violet rays. Recent depletion of the ozone layer, particularly in the southern hemisphere, demands that people take even more precautions to avoid over-exposure to the sun.

P p

Pacific Ocean *See oceans.*

Pacific Rim Those countries and regions surrounding the Pacific Ocean, especially the eastern Asian nations.

Pacific Standard Time One of the time zones used in North America, eight hours behind UTC.

package holiday The term is generally used to describe a travel product that includes transportation, usually by air, and accommodation. However, it now has a strict definition in EU legislation, as follows: 'The pre-arranged combination of not fewer than two of the following when sold or offered for sale at an inclusive price and when the service covers a period of more than 24 hours or includes overnight accommodation: (a) transport; (b) accommodation; (c) other tourist services not ancillary to transport or accommodation and accounting for a significant proportion of the package'. In simple language, any arrangement that includes something more than just travel is likely to be a package. It can also be referred to as an inclusive tour.

Package Travel, Package Holidays & Package Tours Regulations 1992 The regulations, made under the EC Council Directive 90/314 and colloquially known in the trade as the 'EU Directive', were introduced in an attempt to harmonise consumer protection throughout the EC. The legislation is backed up by UK law and contravention of its provisions is a criminal offence.

Padania A name claimed for the area of Italy from Umbria and Tuscany northwards. A local political party, the Northern League, would like to see the area become an independent country within the EU.

paddle steamer A vessel propelled by paddles, either on its side or at its stern.

page To call for someone in a hotel or similar environment. Originally done by means of a page who called the person's name, nowadays it is usually done by means of a public address system.

pagoda A Hindu or Buddhist temple or sacred building, usually a tower with many tiers, most common in Far Eastern countries.

PAI (personal accident insurance) *See travel insurance.*

painter A short length of rope used to tie up a boat.

pairings The names of golfers who wish to play together. A maximum of four golfers can play together at one tee-time. The golf club may request to know the names of the golfers playing at each tee-time. These are referred to as the pairings. > *tee-time.*

Palace on Wheels The luxury rail service in India which provides services between Delhi and major tourist centres in Uttar Pradesh and Rajasthan, including Agra and Jodhpur.

palatial 1. Of or relating to a palace. 2. Very luxurious.

pampas A large treeless plain in South America.

Pampero A strong, cold wind in South America, blowing from the Andes to the Atlantic.

Panama Canal The canal that connects the Atlantic Ocean with the Pacific Ocean, running through Panama.

pan-American encompassing the continents of North and South America.

Pan-American Highway A system of highways stretching from Fairbanks, Alaska to Ushuaia, Argentina. > *Inter-American Highway.*

pandemic A disease prevalent throughout a given region.

panhandle (US) A narrow strip of land projecting from one state or country into another.

panorama An unbroken view of the surrounding area, usually from a high point.

pantheon A temple, usually ancient, dedicated to or used for the worship of more than one god.

Papal States The territories, mainly in Central Italy and at times very extensive, which were for many centuries under the political control of the Papacy. All that now remains of these is the Vatican City.

Papua New Guinea A country occupying the eastern part of the island of New Guinea. Not to be confused with Guinea, Equatorial Guinea or Guinea-Bissau.

par of exchange The official term to denote the recognised value of one currency in terms of another.

parador A Spanish hotel owned by the government. Often converted from castles or other old buildings, they offer a high standard of accommodation, frequently in areas where normal commercial provision might not be feasible.

paragliding An sport in which participants jump from a height with a parachute-like canopy strapped to their backs.

parallel *See latitude, lines of.*

paramotoring An aerial sport in which the user flies wearing a paraglider canopy and is propelled by a pusher propeller.

parasailing An aerial sport in which participants, wearing parachutes, are towed though the air by a motor boat.

parascending A generic term for the main parachuting sports. *See parasailing, paragliding, paramotoring.*

paratyphoid A disease resembling typhoid, caused by different but related agents. > *health precautions.*

parish 1. A district having its own church and clergy. 2. A district constructed for the purposes of local government.

parkway (US) An open, landscaped highway.

part charter An arrangement whereby a tour operator contracts some of the seats on an aircraft, rather than booking the whole aircraft.

partial pressure The pressure exerted by any single constituent gas within a mixture of gases.

partner fare A special fare issued to an accompanying partner at a reduced rate.

partnership A business, owned and operated by two or more people, without limited liability. > *limited.*

party An alternative term for group.

pass 1. The lowest passage between two mountain tops. 2. A permit, usually free, giving access to an amenity.

passage An alternative term for journey, particularly one by sea.

passenger A person, other than the driver or crew, travelling in or on some form of vehicle.

passenger coupon The coupon or coupons of a ticket or voucher that are retained by the passenger. Passenger coupons will usually give outline details of the conditions of carriage and occasionally also act as a baggage check.

passenger mile One passenger carried for one mile. When the number of passengers carried is multiplied by the number of miles travelled, a total passenger mile figure is obtained for that carrier.

passenger name record (PNR) A unique code used by an airline to store and recognise a booking.

passenger sales agent A travel agent appointed to sell passenger (as opposed to freight or cargo) tickets and services.

passenger space ratio (PSR) A shipping term for the GRT divided by the passenger capacity of a vessel. The lower the number the higher the density and the less space there is likely to be for each passenger. A vessel with a PSR of 20 is likely to be more crowded than one with a PSR of 40. Only the most luxurious ships would have PSRs in excess of 50.

passenger transport authority A public organisation set up to control public passenger transport services.

Passover A festival in the Jewish religious calendar, lasting for eight days in March or April.

passport An identity document that allows its bearer to travel abroad.

passport control The point at an airport, port or border where travellers have to show their passports. This may also be known as immigration control.

passport photograph The photograph of the bearer that appears inside a passport. Most issuing bodies have specific requirements regarding size, background and authentication.

PATA Pacific and Asian Travel Agents Association. *See Appendix 5d.*

path 1. A small track or trail. 2. A determined route along which something moves (e.g. flight path).

patio 1. A paved area adjacent to a house 2. An inner courtyard in a Spanish or Latin American house.

patois The dialect or slang of the locals in an area, that might differ significantly from the official language of the country.

patriality Having the right by birth to live in the UK.

pavement 1. (UK) The area on one or both sides of a road reserved for pedestrians. Referred to as a sidewalk in the USA. 2. (US) The roadway or its surface.

pax A common abbreviation for 'passengers'.

payload The proportion of the total weight of a vehicle that can produce revenue. Payload can be of passengers, cargo or both.

PC 1. Any desktop computer. 2. A desktop computer running on the Windows, rather than the Macintosh (Mac), operating system. Transferring data between these two platforms is now far less troublesome than was once the case. In general, PC-to-Mac poses fewer problems than does Mac-to-PC. Macs are particularly common in the print and design industries.

PDF file A widely used format for supplying designed pages electronically to clients or to printers which does not require their having the programme in which the document was created.

peak season Another name for high season.

ped Xing (US) Abbreviation for 'pedestrian crossing'.

pedalo A small, pedal-operated pleasure boat.

pedicab A pedal-operated rickshaw.

pedometer An instrument, carried or worn by a walker, that measures the distance travelled.

pedway (US) A route built for pedestrians in an urban area.

pelican crossing *See zebra crossing.*

penalty fare A fare charged, often with a surcharge, to a passenger on board public transport without a valid ticket or authority to travel in the class and/or on the route travelled.

peninsula An area of land surrounded by water or projecting into the sea and connected to the mainland by a relatively small area.

peninsular Of or relating to a peninsula.

pension A European term for a small hotel. Some grading systems require certain minimum facilities from establishments before they can be categorised as hotels and in cases where these standards are not met, a pension designation may be given.

penthouse An apartment on the roof of a building. Often used by hotels to denote their highest (and usually best) accommodation.

penumbra *See eclipse.*

peoples Persons making up a community, tribe, race, nation or similar.

per diem *See diem.*

perestroika A Russian expression meaning the practice of restructuring or reforming a political system. Its application in the former Soviet Union has lead to the emergence of many new or revived states and countries.

perishability Anything that is perishable will deteriorate if it is not used. In travel, an unsold seat or room or an unhired car perishes as soon as bookings close.

permafrost Subsoil that is permanently frozen, as found in extreme northern and southern latitudes.

permanent way (UK) The completed track of a railway.

Perpendicular A form of Gothic architecture, popular in England in the 15th and 16th centuries, characterised by the vertical tracery in the larger windows.

Persian Gulf (or **the Gulf, Arabian Gulf**) The gulf which separates the Arabian peninsula from Iran.

personal accident insurance (PAI) *See travel insurance.*

personal liability insurance *See travel insurance.*

personal money Currency carried for an individual's use. Depending on the context, this can refer to cash only, or also to other forms of exchange such as travellers' cheques and vouchers, and even admission or travel tickets. Most insurance policies can offer cover against loss of personal money while travelling. The conditions under which such a claim can be made will be set out in the small print and will vary from policy to policy.

personal money insurance *See travel insurance.*

personal possessions insurance *See travel insurance.*

Peru Current *See Humboldt Current.*

pet passport *See Pet Travel Scheme.*

Pet Travel Scheme (PETS) Introduced in 2000, this allows cats and dogs to travel between the UK and a number of European and long-haul destinations (though currently not North America) without the need for a six-month stay in quarantine on arrival in the UK. In order to comply with the scheme, pets must be micro-chipped, be issued with an appropriate pet passport, and have a valid vet's certificate certifying vaccination against rabies.

PETS *See Pet Travel Scheme.*

PEX A promotional excursion fare which carries a number of restrictions regarding dates and times of flights.

phaeton 1. An open four-wheeled horse-drawn carriage.
2. (US) A vintage touring car.

Phoenician Of or relating to the Semitic peoples of ancient Phoenicia in southern Syria and the Lebanon.

phonetic alphabet A list of words starting with successive letters of the alphabet for confirming the spellings of words. Each major language has at least one, but for travel and tourism by far the most important is the English one, as that is the industry's language. The most widely used English phonetic alphabet is as follows: Alpha, Bravo, Charlie, Delta, Echo, Foxtrot, Golf, Hotel, India, Juliet, Kilo, Lima, Mike, November, Oscar, Papa, Quebec, Romeo, Sierra, Tango, Uniform, Victor, Whisky, X-ray, Yankee, Zulu. *For a list of phonetic alphabets in French, Spanish, German and Italian, and a pronunciation guide for the alphabets and numbers in these languages, please see Appendix 7.*

physical feature Any feature that is a part of the landscape, either created naturally (such as a mountain) or man-made but seeming to be natural (such as a canal).

physical geography The branch of geography that deals with physical features.

piazza A public open square, especially in Italy.

pick-up *See check-out (2).*

picnic A meal eaten out of doors, often without tables or chairs.

picnic site A place where travellers may stop to have a picnic.

pictogram An informative sign or symbol created by means of a stylised image rather than words, and generally internationally recognised irrespective of language.

pictograph 1. *See pictogram.*
2. Ancient hieroglyphic writing in picture form.

pidgin A simplified language, often containing words from several languages, used to communicate between people having no common language.

pidgin English A pidgin, the main language of which is English.

piece concept The airline baggage system where the free allowance is based on the size and number of items, rather than their weight.

pied-à-terre A dwelling. kept for occasional use.

piedmont A gentle slope leading from the foot of the mountains to a region of flat land.

pier 1. A bridge-like structure, raised on piles and leading out over water.
2. A projection from an airport terminal building leading towards an aircraft stand.

pilgrim A person who visits a sacred place for religious reasons.

pilgrimage A journey taken by a pilgrim or group of pilgrims.

pillar valve The valve attached to one end of a high pressure diving cylinder used to gain access to the contents.

pilot 1. A person who flies an aircraft.
2. A person licensed to navigate ships into and out of ports and harbours who will join a ship to advise the captain on its handling during these procedures.

pinnace A ship's small boat, usually motor-driven.

Pioneer Club A body of specialist UK travel agents who have undertaken a USTTA (subsequently Visit USA) training programme.

PIR *See property irregularity report.*

piste (UK) A marked ski run down a mountain. It is usually formed of compacted snow, but some resorts prefer to leave the snow ungroomed.

piste basher *See piste groomer.*

piste groomer A large tractor with very wide caterpillar tracks designed to flatten ski runs. Also known as piste basher or snow cat.

piste map (UK) A map showing all the ski runs and lifts in a ski resort's ski area. Known as a trail map in North America.

piston engine An internal combustion engine similar to the type used in cars, generally only used by small or old aircraft.

pitch 1. The distance between the front edge of an aircraft seat and the front edge of the seat behind.
2. The fore and aft motion of a ship.

pizza pie (US) *See snowplough (2).*

plage The French word for a beach.

plague Any deadly disease spreading rapidly over a wide area.

plague, the Bubonic plague, a contagious bacterial disease, usually transmitted by rat fleas.

plain A level tract of land, especially one with few trees.

Plan Management The department of IATA responsible for the administration, management and development of the Billing and Settlement Plan.

plane 1. An aircraft.
2. The action of a boat travelling at speed and rising in the water so that the front part of the hull is clear of the surface.

Plantagenet Of or relating to the kings of England between 1154 and 1399 (some say 1485).

plat du jour The chef's daily recommendation in a restaurant.

plate 1. A small embossed metal sheet used in a ticket validating machine. Each plate gives details of the carrier and the issuing agent.
2. A large part of the earth's crust. *See plate tectonics.*
3. The sheet metal forming the outer shell of a ship.
4. A polished metal sheet used in offset lithographic printing on which the image has been engraved.
5. (US) The main course of a meal served on one dish.

plate tectonics The science of the movement of the earth's plates upon its fluid interior that lead to phenomena such as volcanoes and earthquakes.

plateau A large, flat, elevated area of land.

platform 1. The raised area of a railway station where passengers embark and disembark.
2. A raised area in an auditorium or similar from which a speaker may address an audience.

playa The Spanish word for a beach.

plaza A market place or open square in a town in Spanish speaking countries.

Plimsoll line A series of lines, painted on the outside of a ship's hull to indicate the various safe levels to which the vessel may be loaded. There are several lines denoting the levels for varying situations such as water salinity and season.

Plimsoll mark *See Plimsoll line.*

ply To travel regularly between two or more points, generally on water.

ply for hire To offer the services of a vehicle, typically a taxi, to members of the public on an ad hoc basis.

PM Post meridiem – used in 12-hour clocks and timetables for the period between midday and midnight. Most transport schedules in the United States are listed using am and pm. Note that IATA regulations require that am and pm be written without full stops.

PNR *See passenger name record.*

podium A raised platform used for public speaking.

point-of-sale display Material used to promote a product or service at the place where it can be bought.

point-to-point air fare A fare that is valid only between a specified pair of plates and which allows no stopover en route.

polar 1. Of, at or relating to the poles.
2. A type of climate. *See climate zones.*

polder An area of land reclaimed from the sea. These are especially common in low-lying countries such as Holland.

pole star A star in the constellation of Ursa Minor that appears in the direction of true north.

poles The most northerly and southerly points of the Earth's surface, at 90° north and 90° south, and the points about which the earth rotates (also known as geographic poles). True north and true south are calculated from these points. Magnetic north and south are the points towards which compasses point and are not the same are true north and south. > *magnetic poles.*

poliomyelitis (or **polio**) An infectious viral disease that can cause paralysis. > *health precautions.*

political geography The study of the boundaries, divisions and possessions of states.

pollution The spoiling of the environment by the impact of harmful things such as effluents and noise.

polyglot 1. Of or relating to many languages.
2. A multi-lingual person.

Polynesia The collective name for the islands of the central and south Pacific ocean including American Samoa, Cook Islands, Easter Island, French Polynesia, Hawaii, Kiribati (east), New Zealand, Niue, Pitcairn Islands, Tokelau, Tonga, Tuvalu, Wallis and Futuna and Western Samoa.

Polynesian civilisation The civilisation of Samoa and Tonga (c.500BC to c.1775).

Poma One of the world's main lift manufacturers, responsible for the Millennium Wheel in London. Also the common name for a particular type of ski lift. > *drag lift.*

pond 1. A very small, enclosed body of water.
2. A colloquial term for the Atlantic Ocean, particularly used by people who fly across it frequently.

pontoon 1. A floating support for a temporary bridge.
2. A flat-bottomed boat.

pony cylinder A small high-pressure diving cylinder normally strapped to the side of the main diving cylinder capable of providing a small amount of breathing air in an emergency.

pool agreement An arrangement where two or more carriers agree to serve a route and accept each other's tickets. The revenue earned is 'pooled' and divided between the carriers in proportion to the number of seats sold.

pool side A room in a hotel or similar establishment on the same level as the swimming pool and which opens onto it.

pool view A room in a hotel or similar establishment that overlooks the swimming pool but which has no direct access to it.

poop The aftermost and highest deck of a ship.

pooped When a following wave overtakes a boat and breaks over its stern, possibly swamping it.

population The inhabitants of a place referred to collectively.

port 1. An originating, en-route or destination point for a vessel, usually a ship.
2. The left-hand side of a vessel when one is looking towards the forward end. Denoted by a red light.

port of call A scheduled stop on the itinerary of a cruise or line service.

port surcharge A fee charged to rental companies delivering or collecting hire vehicles at a port or airport.

port taxes Charges levied on passengers arriving or departing from a port, similar in principle to airport taxes.

porter 1. A person employed to carry luggage and generally give assistance at an airport or railway station.
2. (US) A sleeping car attendant.

porthole The circular window in a ship or boat.

POS *See point of sale.*

posada A small Spanish roadhouse or restaurant.

positioning The movement of an aircraft, ship or other vehicle from where it is to where it can begin to earn revenue. Positioning is costly and some carriers, particularly cruise lines, seek to defray these costs by offering positioning voyages for which they can sell accommodation at particularly attractive rates.

positive buoyancy The state of being lighter than water, and therefore floating on the surface of it.

positive space A confirmed hotel reservation.

post code (UK) The mail sorting code appearing at the end of the address.

post-date To date a document (such as a cheque) later than its date of issue. Usually done to delay payment to the carrier and thus generally frowned upon or prohibited.

post-panamax A cruise ship, usually in excess of 100,000 grt, which is too wide to transit the Panama Canal..

pothole A deep hole or system of caves.

pound 1. A unit of weight in the imperial system, equal to c.454 grams.
2. The unit of currency used in the UK and in some dependant territories, divided into 100 pence. Also known as pound sterling.

pourboire A French term for a tip or gratuity.

pousada A Portuguese government-owned hotel, built in the local style.

pousse-café A French term for a liqueur, taken with or after coffee.

powder snow Light, fluffy snow, often recently fallen, most commonly found in dry climates.

powerboat A powerful motor vessel, often used for racing.

powwow A conference or meeting for discussion, originally between North American Indians.

pp 1. per person.
2. on behalf of (when used at the end of a letter).

prairie A large area of treeless grassland, mostly found in North America.

pre-boarding An arrangement by which those with special needs may be allowed onto an aircraft before other passengers.

pre-book To reserve in advance.

precinct 1. An enclosed or clearly defined area, such as a pedestrian precinct in a town (from which vehicles are excluded).
2. (US) A police district.

precipice A steep cliff.

precipitation The falling of rain, sleet, hail or snow.

pre-existing condition An insurance term relating to a condition, such as an illness, that existed before the insurance was contracted. Many companies will not cover claims so arising.

Préfect The chief administrative officer of a *departement* in France.

Préfecture A district under the control of a préfect.

preferred supplier A principal with which a travel agency has a special agreement. This is usually that it will give extra sales support in return for additional commission or other incentives.

premier First in class, style or importance.

premium The amount payable in consideration for a contract of insurance.

premium traffic The name given to those, such as business travellers, paying the most expensive prices for a service.

prepaid ticket advice A notification to a distant point that a passenger has paid for a ticket. Usually used if a passenger wishes to collect the document from a point other than that of payment (at the airport of departure, for example).

pre-payment Payment made in advance for a service.

president 1. The elected head of a republic.
2. (US) The head of a company or corporation.

pressurisation The stabilisation of the air pressure in an aircraft's cabin. Modern aircraft fly at heights where the air is too thin to be breathed comfortably, and most cabins are thus pressurised to a degree that is safe both for the passengers and the structure of the plane. Generally this is set to the equivalent of atmospheric pressure at around 6,000 to 8,000 feet.

prestige Of a higher class or standard than normal.

prevailing wind The wind direction that occurs most frequently at a place. In the UK, the prevailing winds are generally from the west.

price grid The way in which prices are often displayed in travel literature, such as brochures. Commonly the details of the holiday are listed on one axis of the chart and the departure dates on the other. The intersection points on the grid show the price for that holiday at that time. The same principle is used for timetables where different fares apply at different times.

price-fixing An agreement between suppliers to maintain prices at an agreed level. This is now illegal in many countries, including the the USA and the UK.

price-ring See price-fixing.

prime meridian The meridian of longitude at 0° that passes through Greenwich. > Greenwich meridian, longitude, lines of.

prince (**princess** when feminine) A non-reigning male member of a royal family, or the monarch of a small territory (such as Monaco).

principal See supplier.

principality A country, territory or state governed by a prince (such as Monaco).

priority boarding See pre-boarding.

private 1. Accommodation in a private dwelling
2. Individual arrangements made personally by a traveller.
3. Having sole use of vehicle or other travel component, such as a balcony or a swimming pool.
4. A form of company incorporation whereby the company's shares are owned by a small number of people closely connected to it, and not traded publicly.

private facilities The provision of washing and toilet facilities in a hotel room.

private golf club A membership-based golf club. Some private golf clubs only allow club members and their guests access to the course. Others may allow visitors to play for on payment of a green fee, although access may be restricted to certain days of the week or times of the day. > green fee.

private island A small island which has purchased by or leased to a travel supplier, such as a cruise line, for the sole use of its own cutomers.

private transfer An arrangement whereby passengers are transported from the arrival point at a resort to their accommodation by taxi or light aircraft rather than on a bus used by other people.

pro rata In proportion. A pro rata payment would be made in proportion to the rest of the payment.

pro tem For the time being or temporarily.

program 1. (US) A pre-determined series of events.
2. (US) The printed document used to describe this.
3. A piece of computer software, and the act of writing or editing it.

programme 1. (UK) A pre-determined series of events.
2. (UK) The printed document used to describe this.

projection See map projection.

promenade (UK) A public walkway along the seafront.

promenade deck An upper deck on a ship that is designed for passengers to walk around.

promontory A piece of high land jutting into the sea.

promotional fare A specially reduced fare designed to attract customers.

propeller A large screw-shaped device that provides thrust for an aircraft or ship. The action of the screw forces water or air to the rear thus creating the thrust.

property irregularity report (PIR) A form used by airlines to record details of a problem with a passenger's property, such as its loss or damage.

propjet An aircraft with propellers that are driven by a jet turbine engine.

protectorate A state that is controlled and protected by another.

province A principal administrative division of some countries. See Appendix 3 for a list of Canadian Provinces.

provisional booking A reservation that has not yet been confirmed by the agent or passenger and where space is being held pending a decision. > option.

provisioned charter The rental of a boat or yacht or similar vessel that includes fuel and provisions but not crew.

prow The pointed or projecting part of the front of a ship.

PSA Passenger Shipping Association Ltd. See Appendix 5a.

PSARA Passenger Shipping Association Retail Agents Scheme. See Appendix 5a.

PSR See passenger space ratio.

PSV (UK) See public service vehicle.

PTA 1. *See prepaid ticket advice.*
2. *See passenger transport authority.*

pub (UK) *See public house (1).*

public bar (UK) The name often given to the less well-appointed bar in a pub (the other often being called the 'saloon').

public golf course *See municipal golf course.*

public holiday A day when most commercial premises and government departments are closed. > *bank holiday.*

public house 1. (or **pub**) (UK) A place designed for the sale and consumption of alcoholic drinks, and sometimes food. These often (but not always) are owned by a brewery, and often (but not always) have two bars.
2. In some countries, a brothel.

public service vehicle A vehicle, such as a bus, operated to serve the needs of the public.

public transport Vehicles travelling on fixed routes and offering carriage to the public, usually on payment of a fare.

publican 1. (UK) The keeper of a pub.

2. (Australia) The keeper of a hotel.

published fare The fare shown in a carrier's official tariff.

Pullman Luxury train carriages without sleeping berths. Few now remain except on special services, such as the UK portion of the Venice-Simplon Orient Express. The original Pullman was an American railroad company that ran luxury services with sleeping accommodation.

pullman berth A name sometimes given to an upper berth that can be folded away when not in use.

punt A narrow, flat-bottomed boat used mainly on rivers and generally propelled by means of a long pole.

Purim A festival in the Jewish religious calendar, celebrated four weeks before Passover (in February or early March).

purser The person who looks after the administration of the passengers on board a ship or aircraft.

put about Of a ship or boat, to turn around.

Pyrenees The mountain range in Europe that separates the Iberian peninsula from France.

Q q

quad An abbreviation for quadricycle. > *cycle.*

quad bike A small four-wheeled motorcycle used for recreation and sport.

quad chair *See chair lift.*

quad room A hotel room suitable for sleeping four people.

quadricycle 1. A four-wheeled cycle.
2. An alternative name for quad bike.

quagmire A marsh or bog.

quarantine A period of time during which animals or people, who may possibly have been exposed to a disease, are isolated from others to avoid the chance of transmitting infection. Until recently, animals imported into the British Isles had to undergo a six month quarantine period although the introduction of micro-ships and pet passports means that this is now not always necessary. *See Pet Travel Scheme.*

quarter-deck Part of the upper deck of a ship, situated towards the stern, usually reserved for officers.

quay A wharf or pier.

quayside The land near a quay.

queen *See monarch.*

queen room A hotel room with a queen-sized bed (about 5 feet 6 inches wide).

Queenslander 1. A native of the state of Queensland in Australia.
2. The rail service between Brisbane and Cairns in Australia.

queue 1. (UK) A line of people waiting for something.
2. The making available of an item on an agent's computer terminal. For example, if an agent has made a request for a reservation that cannot immediately be confirmed (possibly because the service is full), the request is queued. When space becomes available, the agent's computer is automatically accessed by the principal and the details advised.

quick release A style of belt buckle that allows for quick removal. It is particularly favoured by divers as it facilitates the swift removal and jettison of weight belts and cylinders. It is also worn by cabin crew on aircraft.

quicksand Loose wet sand into which an object or person is likely to sink.

quid (UK) A colloquial term for a pound sterling.

quin room A hotel room for sleeping five people.

quota 1. The maximum permitted amount or number (for example of passengers).
2. The target to be reached (for example of sales).

quote A price calculated for a service and advised to a potential customer so that they may decide whether to accept the offer.

R r

rabies A contagious and usually fatal virus disease of dogs and other mammals. It can be transmitted to humans through saliva. Endemic in most of the world although not in the British Isles where quarantine (and now the Pets Travel Scheme) has kept it out. > *health protection, Pet Travel Scheme.*

RAC Royal Automobile Club. *See Appendix 5a.*

race Each of the major divisions of humankind, distinguished by variations in physical characteristics.

rack railway *See cog railway.*

rack rates The rates advertised by hotels and other principals before any discounts. So called because these are the prices on the leaflets in the racks.

racking policy The marketing decisions taken by a travel agency as to which brochures it will display and how prominently it will display them.

radar Radio detection and ranging. A system for detecting the range and presence of objects. Now an integral part of all transport systems.

raft A flat, floating construction of timber and other buoyant materials.

rail *See terrain park.*

rail map A map showing the railway routes of a country or area.

railcar A railway vehicle consisting of a single powered carriage.

railcard (UK) One of various types of card that allows its holder discounted rail travel fares.

railhead The start or end of a railway.

railroad (US) A railway.

Railtrack The organisation responsible for running the track, signals, tunnels, bridges, level crossings and some principal stations on the railways of Britain between the rail privatisation in 1996 and Railtrack's bankruptcy in 2002 following the Hatfield train crash of 2000. Its functions have now largely been taken over by Network Rail. > *Network Rail, National Rail.*

railway A means of transport in which the vehicles run on metal rails.

rain forest Luxuriant and dense jungles growing in tropical areas.

rain shadow A region sheltered from rainfall, usually by mountains.

Raj The period of British rule in India, ending in 1947.

rajah An Indian ruler or dignitary.

rake-off Commission or share on a deal, often an underhand one.

Ramadan The ninth month of the Muslim year, during which fasting is observed from dawn to dusk. As the Islamic calendar is determined by sightings of the new moon, the dates of Ramadan (and all other Islamic months) change each year. Generally, it falls eleven days earlier each year.

ramjet A type of jet engine in which the air is drawn in and compressed by the forward motion of the vehicle, rather than by a fan.

ramp *See apron.*

Randstad The most populous part of the Netherlands, including the cities of Amsterdam, Rotterdam and The Hague.

range The distance a vehicle can safely travel in normal conditions before needing to refuel.

ranger (US) An employee of a National Park, usually working mainly outdoors.

rapid transit A system or vehicle designed for high speed transport of passengers in urban areas.

rapids A section of a river where the water runs very fast, often over rocks.

rappelling *See abseiling.*

rate The charge for an item or service, generally where this involves rental rather than purchase. It is often expressed as a specific amount for a specific period of time.

Rath Yadra A festival in the Hindu religious calendar, celebrated at the time of the first full moon in November.

ravine A deep narrow gorge.

reasonable care The duty placed on an insured person to act in a prudent manner, often defined as behaving as if there were no insurance in place.

rebate A discount or an amount refunded.

re-book To reinstate a booking or to book a passenger again.

receiver A person appointed by a court to handle the affairs of, and realise the assets of, a bankrupt company.

receiving agent *See incoming tour operator.*

reception 1. The area in a hotel or other public building where visitors report on arrival.
2. An occasion designed to welcome a person or group or to celebrate an event.

receptionist A person working in reception.

receptive agent *See incoming tour operator.*

réchauffé Food that has been warmed up.

recompression The act of re-pressurising a diver, usually in a recompression chamber after the onset of decompression sickness.

recompression chamber Pressurised steel chamber used for the compression, decompression and recompression of the occupants at air pressures which equate to various depths of water.

reconfirmation The requirement that passengers who break an air journey for more than 72 hours may need to advise the airline of their intention of using their next reservation. There are many variations to this procedure, which is now only followed by a small number of airlines, particularly in Asia.

record locator The identification for a file or record in a computer.

recreational vehicle (RV) (US) A general term used to denote any motorhome.

red carpet Preferential treatment afforded to an important visitor or traveller. Traditionally a red carpet was laid for the person to walk upon.

Red Centre The heart of the Australian outback, centred on Alice Springs.

red channel *See customs clearance.*

Red Crescent An international aid organisation, mainly active in Muslim countries.

Red Cross An international aid organisation, mainly active in Christian countries.

red ensign The flag of the British merchant navy.

red run A ski run of moderate difficulty suited to intermediate or advanced level skiers and snowboarders. Known as a blue square trail in North America.

Red Sea The gulf that separates the Arabian peninsula from Africa.

red-eye A colloquial expression for an overnight flight, especially from the west coast to the east coast in the USA.

red-light district An area of a town or city where brothels and other aspects of the sex industry are located.

reef A ridge, often of coral, at or just under the surface of the sea.

re-embark To get back on board a vessel.

re-entry visa A visa that allows a traveller back into a country.

refuelling service A service provided by some vehicle rental companies whereby a customer can return a vehicle without a full tank of fuel, the cost of the fuel required being taken from their credit card.

refuelling stop A stop required en route, generally by a plane, solely for the purpose of taking fuel on board. Passengers cannot join or leave at a refuelling stop.

Regency Of or relating to the period of English history during the regency at the end of George III's reign (1811 to 1820).

regime A method or system of government. The term tends to be used in a derogatory way about governments that are not well thought of.

region An area of land having more or less definable boundaries.

register The official record, maintained by hotels, of the names and other details of guests.

registered baggage Baggage that has been put into the care of a carrier who will undertake to handle and convey it until arrival at the passenger's destination.

regulator Also called demand valve. A valve that reduces the high pressure contained in an aqualung cylinder to a usable pressure so that the diver is able to breathe.

reissue 1. To issue a document again, usually after having made changes to it.
2. A document so reissued.

relative humidity *See humidity.*

relief map A map showing the height or depth of physical features by means of bands of colour rather than contour lines.

relief road (UK) A road taking traffic around a congested area.

religion Any of the systems of belief in a controlling superhuman power or powers demanding obedience, reverence and worship, often associated with a structured or ritualistic system of organisation, and often professing a comprehensive moral and ethical code intended to guide or govern all aspects of the lives of its adherents.

The number of religions, past and present, and the various denominations and sects within them, are almost beyond count. Most would agree that there are five which have had a particularly profound influence on the world, on other religions, and on each other. These are, in order of antiquity, Hinduism (c.4000BC), Judaism (c.2000BC), Buddhism (c.560 BC), Christianity (c.AD30) and Islam (c.AD622); and, in order of number of estimated present-day adherents, Christianity (c.2 billion), Islam (c.1.3 billion), Hinduism (c.900 million), Buddhism (c.360 million) and Judaism (c.15 million). If one adds Sikhism (which developed in northern India in the 16th century, and which has c.23 million adherents), and the traditional religions of China and Africa (c.225 million and c.95 million respectively), nearly five out of six of the world's population are thus accounted for. Of the 1.1 billion who remain, most (c.850 million) are estimated as being non-religious. Other religions, all of which are estimated to have less than 15 million adherents, include Spiritism, Baha'i, Jainism, Shinto, Cao Dai, Tenrikyo, Neo-Paganism, Unitarian-Universalism, Rastafarianism, Scientology and Zoroastrianism. Finally, there is Juche, the official philosophy of Korea DPR (North), which is for sociological reasons sometimes regarded as a religion. Further information on the main customs and beliefs of the world's major religions can be found in the Columbus *World Travel Guide.*
Two aspects of religion are likely to affect the day-to-day life of the travel trade professional. The first is that many holidays, or excursions within a holiday, are influenced by a desire to witness some aspect of religious life, whether this be a pilgrimage to Lourdes, Puri, Mecca or the Wailing Wall or a recreational visit to Khajuraho, Notre Dame, Thimpu or the Blue Mosque. Some knowledge on the part of the travel arranger of the religious beliefs which underpin the allure of these places will often be useful. Secondly, some religious adherents will have strict views on a number of matters, while others may find themselves needing to avoid the consequences of the strict views of others. The travel arranger may thus find clients specifying unacceptable carriers or transit stops, essential or prohibited days or dates of travel or specific dietary requirements.
Brief details for selection of the main religious festivals for a selection of the major religions may be found throughout the text. In most cases, their dates change from year to year.

remark A note or endorsement on a document to convey a special instruction.

Renaissance Of or relating to a loosely defined period during the 14th to 16th centuries in Europe during which there was a revival of art and literature using classical models. With a qualification, the term is also used to describe similar artistic revivals at other times and in other places (such as the Carolingian Renaissance in France and Germany or the Celtic Renaissance in Ireland).

rental day A 24-hour period starting at the time the vehicle was rented, often rounded to nearest hour or half-hour. Any rental period which exceeds the rental day may incur an additional charge.

renter The person, usually but not always the driver, who is responsible for paying for a vehicle rental agreement and who is liable for any obligations under it.

rep *See representative.*

repatriation The bringing home of a traveller from abroad, usually for reasons of sickness or emergency.

representative Anyone who represents a company or organisation. In travel, the expression usually refers to a tour operator's employee, retained in a resort to attend to the needs of its customers.

republic A country with an elected representative, rather than a monarch, as head of state.

Republic of China *See ROC.*

request 1. Where a facility has been asked for but not confirmed.
2. The circumstance of a potential passenger being placed on a waiting list for a flight in case of cancellations. The code RQ is officially used for this. Because of the possible confusion between meanings, some travel clerks use the abbreviation WL for a waiting list, but this is not an official airline abbreviation.

request stop (UK) A stop at which a vehicle, usually a bus, will only stop on the instruction of a passenger or potential passenger.

re-route To change the routeing on a ticket or itinerary.

reservation 1. In general, a booking made for a particular accommodation, transport, entertainment or other service.
2. The act of booking, or receiving confirmation for, space on a particular transport service. Although many tickets (such as most air journeys) have reservation and travel details shown on the one document, on some services (such as most rail journeys) a ticket only shows that a passenger has paid for travel and a separate reservation document may be necessary.

reservation system Any system that is set up to control the booking of flights, holidays and other travel products and services. Most reservation systems are now computerised.

reserve To make a booking. > *reservation.*

reserved Space that has been booked or set aside for a customer or group.

resort A city, town, village or other development visited by holidaymakers, often for a specific reason. Since individual preferences vary, almost anywhere can be considered a resort. However, major centres such as London, although attracting large numbers of visitors, are not usually called resorts. In the USA, the term is now often used to describe a large-scale hotel and leisure complex, or even a large hotel with extensive grounds and facilities.

resort complex A concentration of specifically constructed and largely self-contained holiday facilities.

resort condominium A block of separately owned apartments in a North American resort complex.

rest house A place for travellers to rest in, possibly overnight. Typically found in the Indian subcontinent.

restaurant An eating establishment offering a range of food, often with table service.

restaurateur (or **restauranteur**) A person who owns or runs a restaurant.

Restoration Of or relating to the period of English history following the restoration of Charles II after the English Revolution, and generally associated with his reign (1660 to 1685).

restroom (US) A lavatory.

retail travel agent A company or individual which makes and sells travel services. > *travel agent*.

re-time To set a new schedule for a service.

return ticket (UK) A ticket bought for a journey to one or more places, returning to the originating point. It is known as a round-trip ticket in the USA.

revaccination A repeat vaccination to boost or reinforce the original.

revalidation The process of amending a detail of a ticket or reservation. The expression usually refers to airline tickets, on which agents may only change flights or dates of travel.

revalidation sticker A sticker which is attached to a ticket to show that certain details have been amended and recorded.

reverse thrust The system by which the exhaust of a jet engine can be directed forward into the direction of travel. This can be used to reverse an aircraft on the ground or to create a powerful braking effect after landing.

RHIB (or **RIB**) A rigid-hulled inflatable boat.

ría A long narrow inlet formed by the submergence of a river valley, especially in north-west Spain.

Richter scale A logarithmic scale that records the severity of earthquakes. Its values range from 0 to 9. The most severe earthquake ever recorded (at Gansu in China in 1920) measured 8.6.

rickshaw A light two- or three-wheeled vehicle usually drawn by a person or people on foot. In some parts of the world, such as southern India, they may be motorised.

ridge A long narrow hilltop or similar.

ridgeway A road or track along a ridge.

rift valley A steep-sided valley caused by subsidence of the earth between two faults. The river Jordan lies at the bottom of the deepest rift valley on dry land.

rig 1. (US) A vehicle, particularly a lorry.
2. The arrangement of sails ands masts on a boat.
3. To make a boat ready for a voyage.
4. To fix, control or manipulate fraudulently.

rigging The arrangement of sails and ropes on a sailing ship.

right of abode (UK) A person's right to take up residence in a country.

right of way 1. A right established to travel across another's land.
2. A path having such a right.
3. The order of precedence of a ship or other vehicle.

right, driving on the *See left, driving on the.*

ring road (UK) A road that encircles a town or city, such as the Périphérique around Paris or the M25 around London.

rip A stretch of rough or fast running water in the sea or a river, caused by the meeting of currents.

river A substantial stream of water, flowing to an ocean or sea (or sometimes to a lake). For a list of the world's longest rivers, consult the Columbus *World Travel Atlas*.

riviera Any coastal region with a sub-tropical climate, especially in southern France and north-west Italy.

Riviera The popular tourist region in south-east France and north-west Italy bordering the Mediterranean Sea. The coastal strip stretches from Cannes to La Spezia. The French Riviera is also known as the Côte d'Azur: main coastal resorts include Cannes, Antibes, Nice and Monte-Carlo. The Italian Riviera is divided into the Riviera di Ponente in the west and the Riviera di Levante in the east. The main resorts include Genoa and La Spezia.

road A generic term for any path or way with a specially prepared surface and intended for the use of pedestrians, animals or vehicles.

road map A map showing the roads of a country or area, sometimes to the exclusion of some other features such as railways.

road train A large road locomotive pulling a number of trailers, commonly used in Australia.

road warrior Marketing jargon for a business traveller, especially one who demands special facilities in hotels.

roadhouse An inn or similar establishment on or near a road.

roadside The strip of land next to a road.

roadway The part of a bridge used for traffic.

roaring forties Areas of high wind at approximately 40° to 50° north and south of the Equator.

ROC 1. The Republic of China, or Taiwan. The term Taiwan (ROC) is often used by that country to describe itself. It is not to be confused with the People's Republic of China, the official name for mainland China.
2. A ticketing abbreviation meaning record of change.

rock climbing The ascent of boulders, cliffs, crags and mountains by means of climbing steep sections of rock, requiring the use of hands and feet for progress and technical safety equipment such as a rope, harness and 'gear' – machined metal items that can be temporarily lodged in the rock to safeguard progress.

rock climbing grades *See climbing grades.*

Rocky Mountaineer A luxury tourist train running between Vancouver and Jasper or Calgary in Canada.

Rocky Mountains The main mountain range in North America, extending from Alaska to New Mexico.

Rocky Mountains International A US regional marketing organisation covering the states of Idaho, Wyoming, South Dakota and Montana. > *US regional marketing organisations.*

RoE Rate of exchange. Used when calculating prices quoted in foreign currencies into local money or in a bureau de change.

ROH *See run of house rate.*

roll The side to side movement of a ship.

roll on, roll off The system used on most car ferries that allows vehicles to be driven on and driven off, as opposed to being loaded by crane.

rolling stock 1. The locomotives, carriages, goods wagons and other vehicles used on a railway.
2. (US) The road vehicles of a company.

Roman numerals The system of numbering, now most commonly employed for preliminary pages in books, that uses letters and letter combinations. They can be used either in capitals or in lower case. The units are I=1, V=5, X=10, L=50, C=100, D=500 and M=1000.

Where a lower number is placed before a higher number, the former is subtracted from the latter: thus IV is 4 and XC is 90. Where a lower number is placed after a higher number, the two are added together: thus VI is 6 and CX is 110. Multiples of 1,000 are sometimes indicated by a horizontal line over the letter/s to be multiplied. No zero is used in the Roman numbering system. > *Arabic numerals.*

Romanesque A style of architecture prevalent in Europe between 900AD and 1200 with massive vaulting and rounded arches.

Romantic Road A tourist route in Germany between Wurzburg and Füssen, passing through areas of great scenic and historic interest.

Romany *See Gypsy.*

rondavel A round hut or similar simple building, especially in South Africa.

room night One room occupied for one night.

room only Hotel accommodation provided without any meals included.

room service The provision of drinks, meals and other services in a hotel room.

roomette 1. (US) A single compartment in a railway sleeping car.
2. (US) A small room available for letting.

rooming list A list giving details of clients booked, usually when a group is involved.

ro-ro *See roll on, roll off.*

Rosh Hashanah A festival in the Jewish religious calendar celebrating the new Year. It takes place in September or October.

rostrum *See podium.*

rotating wing aircraft An aircraft whose wings rotate in flight to provide lift. This is usually a helicopter or similar.

rough passage A crossing over rough seas.

round the world (RTW) 1. A journey round the world.
2. An air fare using this construction.

round trip 1. (US) A journey to one or more places and then back to the originating point.
2. An airline term meaning a return trip comprising two fare components only, the fares for which are the same, but with different routes. > *circle trip.*

roundabout 1. An interchange where roads converge in a circular junction. in general, the traffic already on the junction has priority over that waiting to enter it, although in many French-influenced countries the reverse is the case. Roundabouts are very rare in the USA.

2. A merry-go-round at a funfair or similar.

rounding The act of adjusting a figure, usually a price, to the nearest convenient or specified unit. Fares for most transport operators are calculated to a nearest whole unit. In the case of UK rail, for example, this is usually five pence. Any calculation must be rounded to the specified unit before the fare is used. Population and area figures for countries are often rounded to the nearest 1,000.

Route 66 The first long-distance paved highway in the USA, immortalised in song and popular legend. It was completed in 1926 and fully paved by 1937, and ran from Chicago to Los Angeles via Springfield, Oklahoma City, Amarillo, Albuquerque and Flagstaff. With the opening of Interstate 40 in 1984, Route 66 was decommissioned, but a Route 66 Association now exists to recall its heyday as 'the main street of America'. As a result, many old road signs and landmarks along the route have been replaced or restored.

routing The way or course taken on a journey. Many fares will be available by a specific route or routes and the restriction as to what route is available for any ticket will be shown somewhere on the document.

rover ticket A ticket allowing unlimited travel in a particular area for a specified time. Usually restricted to the services of one carrier or its commercial partners.

Royal Orient The luxury rail service in India which provides services between Delhi and major tourist centres in Rajasthan, Gujarat and Daman & Diu including Udaipur and Sasan Gir.

Royal Scotsman The luxury rail service running from Edinburgh to various towns in Scotland.

royalty 1. The amount, usually a percentage, of sales revenue paid to the owner of a product or service.

2. Persons belonging to a royal family.

RQ A code used to indicate that a passenger's booking is on request or waitlisted. > *request.*

RT *See round trip.*

RTW *See round the world.*

rubberneck A derogatory term for a tourist or sightseer.

rudder The part of a ship or aircraft that controls its direction.

running gear The suspension and wheels of a vehicle.

running lights Sometimes called navigation lights. The lights that a vessel must display when travelling at night.

run-of-the-house rate A reduced price at which a hotel has agreed to offer rooms.

runway A long, straight, flat and wide paved pathway from which aircraft take off and onto which they land.

rural Of or relating to the countryside.

Russian Revolution The conflict in Russia (1917) which led to the overthrow of the monarchy, the execution of Tsar Nicholas II and the establishment of the Soviet Union.

Rust Belt The areas of the north and north-eastern United States characterised by older, heavy industry, particularly the steel and auto industries.

RV *See recreational vehicle.*

ryokan A Japanese term for a traditional wayside inn.

S s

Sabbath The day of rest and religious observance kept by Jews on a Saturday. Agents should be aware of the possible implications on travel arrangements.

sabbatical Leave granted at intervals to a university teacher for study or travel, originally every seven years. The term is now often used to denote any extended leave period granted to an employee.

Sabre A GDS sponsored by American Airlines.

saddle The lowest passage between two mountain tops.

safari A trip into a wildlife area, such as a game reserve, for photography or occasionally hunting.

safari boat *See live-aboard.*

safari park *See wildlife park.*

safety announcement Instructions in the use of the safety and evacuation equipment on board a ship or aircraft given by the crew soon after the start of a journey, usually with the aid of a video.

safety deposit A facility offered by hotels for the safekeeping of their guests' valuables.

sahel A semi-arid region which forms a transitional area between deserts and more fertile areas such as savannahs and forests

Sahel, the The area of sahel on the southern borders of the Sahara.

sahib A polite form of address used in India when referring to a man.

sail The large piece of material, traditionally canvas, fixed to a ship's mast to catch the wind.

sailboard A small boat with a mast and sail used in windsurfing.

sailboat (US) A sailing boat.

sailing boat (UK) A boat propelled by sails.

sailing list An obsolete term that meant a shipping line's timetable. Where they exist, shipping lines now call them timetables.

sailing ticket A passenger or vehicle control document used on some shipping and ferry services that experience very heavy peak demand.

sailplane An engineless heavier-than-air aircraft used for sustained unpowered flight. Originally sailplanes differed from gliders in that gliders needed a permanent tow and sailplanes could fly using upward wind currents. Nowadays the distinction is rarely made.

sales agency agreement An agreement for the sale of a principal's services. Most principals will have a specific form or structure for such agreements.

salinity The concentration of salt in a liquid, typically the sea. The higher the salinity the more buoyant the water.

saloon 1. A public room on a ship.
2. (US) A bar.
3. (UK) The name often given to the better-appointed bar in a pub (the other often being called 'public')
4. (UK) An enclosed motor car with no partition between driver and passengers. *(US: sedan)*
5. (UK) A railway carriage serving as a lounge.

saloon keeper (US) A bartender.

salt A sailor (often 'old salt' to imply knowledge and experience).

salt flat The dried up bed of a salt lake that leaves a plain covered in salt.

salt lake A lake of salt water.

salubrious Of a climate or place, healthy.

salvage The rescue of a ship or other vessel or its property following an accident or similar.

salvage tug A tug designed to rescue disabled vessels.

samovar A Russian urn used for making tea. and at one time a standard provision on Russian long-distance trains.

sampan A small boat used in the Far East.

sample room A room that displays merchandise.

sand yacht *See land yacht.*

sandbank A deposit of sand forming a shallow place in the sea or a river.

sandbar *See bar (2).*

SAR Search and Rescue.

Sargasso Sea An area of the North Atlantic in which large clumps of sargasso seaweed are found on or near the surface.

SARS Severe Acute Respiratory Syndrome, an air-borne disease caused by the corona virus, linked to the common cold. The first reported case was in Hanoi in

February 2003 and it subsequently spread widely, causing havoc in the travel industries of south-east Asia and Canada (after several infected people were identified as having flown to Toronto). By July 2003 the situation had largely stabilised and the last official World Health Organization guidelines on its treatment and surveillance were issued in October 2004.

satellite printer location   The place in which a satellite ticket printer is located. The official IATA definition is: 'An accredited agent's place of business in one country, controlled by a host location in the same country: (a) which is located on the premises of a customer of the agent, such customer not being an agent or tour operator; (b) which is not accessible to the general public; (c) whose sole purpose is the issuance, by means of a satellite ticket printer, of traffic documents to the customer or its employees; and (d) which is entered on the agency list as a satellite ticket printer location.'

satellite state   A small country dependent on or controlled by another.

satellite ticket printer   A ticket printer located away from an agency that can be used to print out traffic documents in a distant location. Satellite ticket printers can only be controlled by the agency.

satellite town   A small town dependent on a nearby larger town or city.

SATH   1. The Society for the Advancement of Travel for the Handicapped (UK). *See Appendix 5a.*
2. The Society for the Advancement of Travel for the Handicapped (USA). *See Appendix 5b.*

satnav   Satellite navigation. A navigation system using data from satellites, common on ships and aircraft.

saturation diving   Diving for long periods whereby body tissues are saturated with dissolved nitrogen to the maximum extent for the depth in question.

savannah   (or **savanna**) The tropical grasslands bordering on the equatorial rain forests in both the northern and southern hemispheres. > *climate zones.*

Saxon   Of or relating to the Germanic peoples that conquered parts of England in the 5th and 6th centuries.

scale   The ratio between the a distance on a map and the corresponding distance on the ground. This is normally expressed in one of two ways: numerically (for example 1:5,000, meaning that 1 unit on the map represents 5,000 of the same units on the ground); or as a series of graduated marks on a line, each indicating what distance on the ground is represented by the appropriate distance on the map. See also *maps* and *map projections.*

Scandinavia   The geographical region comprising

Denmark, Norway and Sweden. Often extended to include Finland and, more rarely, Iceland.

scenery   The general appearance of the natural features of a landscape, particularly where this is pleasing.

scenic   Picturesque or attractive as regards its view.

schedule   An alternative name for a timetable.

scheduled carrier   A carrier that operates a scheduled service.

scheduled flight   *See scheduled service.*

scheduled service   A service, generally by air, which is available to all passengers, and which operates at advertised set times between set points, regardless of demand.

Schengen   The agreement which in 1995 abolished most frontier controls between participating member countries, which comprises all the current members of the EU except the UK and Ireland, and some associate non-EU members including Norway and Iceland.

schooner   1. A fore-and-aft rigged sailing ship with two or more masts.
2. (US) A tall beer glass.
3. (UK) A large-measure glass, particularly for sherry.

schuss   A straight downhill ski-run.

Scotland   One of the constituent countries of the United Kingdom of Great Britain and Northern Ireland. > *Great Britain, United Kingdom.*

scrambling   The activity which is a combination of usually rough and strenuous walking and technically easy rock climbing, sometimes requiring use of the hands (or even basic rock climbing equipment) and generally taking place in very exposed situations such as cliff tops or narrow ridges. Generally graded from 1 to 3, with 1 being the easiest.

scrambling grades   *See climbing grades.*

scree   Loose rocks and stones that cover a slope, usually below a cliff.

screw   A ship's propeller.

scrub   An area of low bushes or stunted forest growth.

scuba   Self-contained underwater breathing apparatus. An aqualung.

scupper   1. An opening in the side of a ship that allows any accumulation of water to escape.
2. To sink a vessel deliberately.

scuttle   1. A hole in a ship's deck fitted with a cover.
2. To sink a ship deliberately, usually by letting in water through the sea cocks.

SDMA Scottish Destination Management Association. *See Appendix 5a.*

sea A large body of water, usually salt. Many seas, such as the South China Sea, are contained within oceans.

sea anchor A device dragged from a ship to control its drift.

sea breeze A breeze blowing off the sea onto the land.

sea cock A valve situated below the waterline in a ship to let water in or out.

sea facing A room in a hotel or similar establishment that faces the sea but may not have a view of it, perhaps due to an abundance of vegetation. > *sea view.*

sea legs The ability to walk properly on the decks of a ship, even when it is pitching and rolling. It usually takes a day or two for a passenger to acquire their sea legs.

sea travel Travelling by ship, hovercraft, hydrofoil or other seaborne vessel.

sea view A room in a hotel or similar establishment that has a view of the sea. Since such rooms are preferred by many guests, a supplement is usually payable. > *sea facing.*

sea wall A wall or embankment constructed to prevent encroachment by the sea.

seafront That part of a coastal town or resort that faces onto the shore.

seaplane An aircraft that can operate from water.

seashore That part of the land close to the sea.

seasickness A temporary illness suffered on rough seas when the body's balance is disturbed.

season 1. Any division of the year characterised by clearly identifiable climatic characteristics. The differences between the seasons, particularly as regards temperature and sunlight, become more pronounced as one moves towards the poles.
2. In travel, a particular time of the year during which demand or activity is at a certain and identifiable level.

season ticket A ticket available for a series of journeys or admissions in a given period.

seasonality The variation for demand for products and services that is due to different seasons.

seat belt A retaining device fitted to many vehicles that holds passengers in their seats in the event of accident or violent movement. The use of seat belts in cars and coaches is obligatory in many countries while their use in aircraft is universal.

seat configuration The arrangement of the seats in a particular aircraft, coach, train, ship or other mode of transport. This will vary from service to service and from carrier to carrier. Aircraft seat configurations may change from time to time, particularly as a result of the controversy surrounding DVT. > *seat pitch, DVT.*

seat pitch The term used to describe the distance between aircraft seats. Note that the figure does not give the amount of legroom, but the distance occupied by the seat and the legroom combined (in other words, the distance between any position on one seat and the same position on the seat immediately in front of or behind it). Seat pitch varies according to the class of travel, and for many travellers is the main reason for paying a higher fare. Although the CAA's legal minimum is 26 inches, recent policy (particularly in the light of the controversy over DVT) has been for airlines to increase the pitch on economy class services. Typically, the seat pitch in economy class will be around 31 inches; in full-fare economy around 37 inches; in business class around 48 inches; and in first class around 60 inches. All seat pitches will vary from carrier to carrier and from aircraft to aircraft.

seat plans Diagrams of an aircraft showing the location of seats, galleys and other services.

seat rotation A system used on coach tours where passengers change seats at intervals to ensure that everyone has an opportunity to occupy the better seats.

seating plan A diagram showing the layout of seats, such as on a vehicle or in a hall.

seatmate (US) Each of a set of people who share a seat.

seat-only (UK) A seat on an air charter service for which no associated hotel accommodation is provided.

seaward Towards the sea.

seaway An ocean or estuarial traffic lane.

second 1. A sixtieth of a minute of time.
2. A sixtieth of a minute of an angle. > *degree.*

second class A level of service, accommodation or transport that is less good than first class. It is now rarely employed as an official designation, terms such as 'standard' and 'economy' being preferred.

second floor 1. (UK) The floor of a building two levels above the ground floor.
2. (US) The floor of a building immediately above the ground floor.

second sitting The later of two meal times on a train or cruise ship.

Second World War The global conflict (1939 to 1945, although the Asian phase began in 1937) between the Axis Powers (principally Germany, Italy and Japan) and the eventually victorious Allies (principally the UK,

France and Poland, later joined by the USSR and the USA) that led to the breaking up of the European colonial empires, the rise of the USA and the USSR and global super-powers and the formation of the European Economic Community (now the European Union).

sector A complete portion of an itinerary or journey, which can comprise several legs or segments.

security tax A charge levied to cover the cost of screening of passengers and their luggage to try to detect acts of terrorism.

sedan 1. An enclosed chair carried by two porters to provide transport.
2. (US) A saloon car.

segment That portion of a passenger's journey from boarding to disembarking. Since a vehicle may stop several times en route, a segment could comprise several legs. > *leg*.

seiche A fluctuation in the water level of a lake or other enclosed body of water caused by changes in barometric pressure, rather than by tidal influences.

seif A long narrow sand dune.

self-catering Any type of accommodation that allows or expects guests to arrange their own meals.

self-drive A vehicle driven by the person who has hired it, or their named driver/s, rather than by a chauffeur.

self-righting A characteristic of a small boat which has been designed to return automatically to its upright position after a capsize.

selling point A feature or aspect of a holiday or other arrangement that makes it of particular interest or benefit to a prospective customer.

semaphore 1. An early signalling method using hand-held flags, each position representing a letter.
2. A signal, usually on a railway, that makes use of a moving arm, rather than coloured lights.

semi-basement A storey in a building that is partly below ground level.

semi-tropical *See sub-tropical.*

senior citizen An elderly or retired person. *See old-age pensioner.*

SEO Society of Event Organisers. *See Appendix 5a.*

sepulchre A tomb cut into rock, or built of stone or rock.

serein Fine rain that occasionally falls from cloudless skies in the tropics.

serial number The number or code on a document that indicates its position in the batch.

series charter A charter based on the use of a vehicle, usually an aircraft, for several journeys between the same points.

service 1. A scheduled transport link provided between one place and another.
2. Public religious worship conducted according to a prescribed form, generally in a place designed or designated for that purpose.
3. The act of waiting at a table, bar or similar, and the manner in which this is done. > *silver service*.
4. Alternative term for service charge. *See service charge.*
5. The set of dinner plates, bowls, cutlery and the like which is used for serving meals.
6. The serving of a meal at any one of a number of separate sittings, often on a train or a ship.
7. A thin cord used as a binding around a rope on a ship to prevent rotting or unravelling.
8. One of the three types of profession (manufacturing and agriculture being the others) into which economic activity is generally divided for statistical purposes. (Generally 'services' in such cases.)
9. The regular checks and overhauls given to a mechanical object, such as a car or a plane.

service area An area by a road, usually for the supply of fuel, refreshments and other services and facilities.

service bus (Australia) A motor coach.

service charge An additional amount added to a bill to cover the cost of service, as opposed to a discretionary tip.

service industry An industry, such as travel, that provides services rather than goods.

service road A road running parallel to a main road giving access to shops or buildings set back from it.

service station An establishment selling fuel and other goods.

serviced accommodation Any accommodation provided by an organisation, such as a hotel, that provides a range of additional services.

set down To offload passengers.

set jetter A person who makes holiday destination decisions based wholly or partly on being able to visit the sets or locations of films or novels.

set meal A meal with no choice of dishes.

seven seas The oceans of the world, or the whole world generally. > *ocean*.

sex tourism Tourism that attracts visitors to destinations where they may seek sexual encounters. Although this is frowned on by many, the practice is widespread in some countries.

sextant An instrument that measures angular distance, used in navigation.

SFT Swiss Federation of Travel Agencies. *See Appendix 5c.*

SGTP Society of Government Travel Professionals. *See Appendix 5b.*

shakedown cruise The first cruise operated after a ship has been built or re-fitted. It is intended to identify any flaws before the vessel enters full service.

Shamal A hot dry wind which blows from the north-west in Iraq and the Persian Gulf.

Shangri La An imaginary paradise on earth, supposedly located somewhere in Tibet.

shanty A small, crudely built dwelling.

shantytown A residential area made up of shanties, often found on the outskirts of large conurbations, and often occupied by immigrant workers or those originating from the countryside.

shaped ski *See carving skis.*

Sharav *See Khamsin.*

shark billy Short stick with pointed end used for fending off sharks.

Shavuot A festival in the Jewish religious calendar, celebrated seven weeks after Passover (in May or June).

shebeen An unlicensed house that sells alcohol, especially in Ireland and Scotland.

sheikh (or **sheik**) The head of a region, village or family in Muslim countries. The term can also refer to a religious leader. It is also used as a title of respect.

sheikha (or **sheika**) The wife of a sheikh. It is also used as a title of respect.

sheikhdom A country or state ruled by a sheikh.

shingle Small stones or pebbles.

Shinkansen The high-speed train network in Japan, connecting most of the main cities in Honshu and Kyushu. > *Bullet Trains.*

ship 1. A large waterborne vessel, often of many thousands of tons and hundreds of feet in length. 2. (US) An aircraft.

ship canal A canal large enough to take seagoing vessels.

ship density *See passenger space ratio.*

ship of the desert A camel.

shipboard A term that means anything that is used or occurs on board a ship.

shipping lane A busy track across the sea or ocean, such as the Straits of Dover.

shipwreck Any derelict vessel or part thereof abandoned at or on the coast. A shipwreck may be found floating, ashore or on the seabed in either a submerged or partly submerged condition.

shire (UK) A county.

shooting brake (UK) An estate car.

shore The land along the edge of a body of water.

shore excursion A trip taken by passengers whilst a ship is in port.

short break A short duration trip usually taken in addition to a main holiday. Many short breaks are to cities or similar destinations that boast a wide range of attractions.

short haul An inexact term that is applied generally to journeys within one continent.

short takeoff and landing Any aircraft that can operate from a shorter runway than is needed for conventional types.

shoulder season The period between high season and low season.

Shrove Tuesday A festival in the Christian calendar, the day before Ash Wednesday. Also known as Pancake Day.

shuttle service A transport service that simply plies back and forth between two points.

Siberia A vast region of Russia, extending from the Ural Mountains to the Bering Sea and from the Arctic Ocean to Mongolia.

sick flag *See yellow flag.*

sickbay The part of a ship used as a hospital.

sidereal time Time measured by the apparent motion of the stars. A sidereal day is about 20 minutes 23 seconds longer than a solar day.

side-road A road joining or leaving a main road.

sidewalk (US) The area on one or both sides of a road reserved for pedestrians. Referred to as a pavement in the UK.

siding 1. An area of track on a railway used for the marshalling and storage of rolling stock. 2. (US) External cladding material for a building.

sierra A mountain range.

Sierra Madre The continuation of the Rocky Mountains in Mexico, divided into the Orientale (east) and Occidentale (west).

siesta A rest taken in the middle of the afternoon. Once common in hot countries, it is becoming less so with the advent of air conditioning and the demands for full-time working.

sightseeing trip A visit to one or more tourist attractions.

signal box (UK) A building from which the signals and points of a railway are controlled.

signal tower (US) *See signal box.*

Sikhism The religion of the Sikhs. > *religion.*

Silicon Valley An electronics and computer research and manufacturing area in the Santa Clara Valley, California, stretching from Palo Alto in the north to San Jose in the south.

Silk Road 1. A general term for the various ancient trade routes which for many centuries linked China with Europe.
2. A WTO Regional Promotional Project, launched in 1994. It aims to revitalise through tourism the ancient highways used by Marco Polo and the caravan traders who came after him. The Silk Road stretches 12,000 km from Asia to Europe. Sixteen Silk Road countries have joined forces for this project: Japan, Republic of Korea, DPR Korea, China, Kazakstan, Kyrgyzstan, Pakistan, Uzbekistan, Tajikistan, Turkmenistan, Iran, Azerbaijan, Turkey, Georgia, Greece and Egypt. Joint promotional activities include publicity material, familiarisation trips and special events at major tourism trade fairs.

Silver Meteor A rail service running between New York and Miami in the USA.

silver service Restaurant service where the food is brought to the table on large dishes from which it is served in portions to meet the needs of each diner.

Silver Star A rail service running between New York and Miami in the USA.

single 1. A hotel room for one person only.
2. A one-way ticket.

single chair A chair lift designed to carry only one person.

single entry visa A visa valid for one visit only.

Single European Currency *See euro.*

single occupancy rate A special rate charged to a lone guest occupying a multiple bedded room. It would usually be more than the price for a single room, but less than the full rate for the multiple bedded room

single supplement An extra amount payable by a person occupying accommodation for sole use.

single-decker (UK) A bus or coach with only one deck.

Sinic The ancient Chinese civilisation (c.1600BC until AD220).

Sino- Of or relating to China or the Chinese, generally used as a prefix.

Sirocco (or **Scirocco**) A hot dusty wind blowing towards Europe from North Africa. Known as the Ghibli in Libya and Leveche in Spain. Its origins are the same as the Khamsin or Sharav. On the northern Mediterranean coast, particularly in southern Italy, the wind is moist after crossing the Mediterranean.

Site of Special Scientific Interest (SSSI) (UK) An area designated as being of special scientific importance and thus often having restricted access.

sitting One of several meal times.

six pac *See chair lift.*

sixth freedom *See freedoms of the air.*

sked (US) *See schedule.*

Skeena The rail service running between Prince Rupert and Jasper in the Canadian Rockies.

Skeleton Coast The desert coast of Namibia between Walvis Bay and the Angolan border. A national park and part of the Namib Desert, the name comes from the number of ships wrecked on its treacherous rocks or lost in the fogs created by the cold Benguela current.

skerry A Scottish term for a reef or rocky island.

ski area A part of a mountain where ski lifts and ski runs create an area where it is possible to ski or snowboard. All ski resorts have ski areas next or near to them but may also exist where there is no resort nearby.

ski boot A special boot for skiers, normally with a rigid plastic shell which holds the ankle firm to protect from injury and help the skier control the ski. The boot connects to the ski by means of a binding which is fixed to the ski.

ski évolutif A method of learning to ski where beginners start with special short skis, graduating to longer ones as they improve.

ski kindergarten A facility by which younger children (typically aged four to ten) are offered a mixture of supervised indoor play and meals and well as ski or snowboard lessons in ski resorts. Known as day care in North America and sometimes offered without an outdoor element.

ski lift Any one of a number of types of device to carry skiers up a slope.

ski pass See lift ticket.

ski poles The two metal rods held by a skier to assist propulsion and manoeuvrability.

ski report See snow report.

ski resort A mountain destination developed for the dedicated use of those taking skiing and other winter-sports holidays.

ski run See piste.

ski season The months when ski resorts typically have enough snow on their slopes and operate their ski lifts and prepare their ski runs. In the northern hemisphere this is often from the end of November to mid-April but most tour operators will only run tours from mid-December to late-March to increase the likelihood that there will be adequate snow cover.

ski slope See piste.

ski sticks See ski poles.

skiable vertical The vertical distance that a skier can ski down without having to take a lift up.

ski-bob A single track vehicle, similar in layout to a bicycle, but with skis instead of wheels.

Skidoo A brand name for a make of snowmobile, often used as a generic name for all such vehicles.

ski-jump A man-made slope with a sharp drop from which skiers jump.

ski-plane An aircraft with skis rather than wheels.

skipper A colloquial expression for the captain of a ship or aircraft.

skipper charter A form of charter whereby the vessel is provided with a skipper, but otherwise without supplies or crew.

skirt The flexible surround that contains the air of a hovercraft or similar vehicle.

ski-run A slope prepared for skiing.

skis 1. A pair of long narrow devices fitted to the underside of a pair of special boots, that allow rapid travel over snow. Initially made of wood, modern skis are made from increasingly complex compounds of hi-tech materials.
2. The act of using a pair of skis.

skyjack See hijack.

slack water The time when the tide is turning, especially at low tide.

Slave Coast The coastal areas of present-day Togo, Benin and western Nigeria. The name comes from the trade in slaves between the 16th and 19th centuries.

Slave Route A WTO Regional Promotional Project, launched in 1995 as part of the United Nations' International Year of Tolerance. It aims to boost cultural tourism to West African nations. Its immediate goals are to restore monuments, enhance history museums and launch joint promotional campaigns in selected tourism-generating markets, which will motivate foreign visitors to learn about the history of these countries and to discover their roots. The project is expected to be expanded in the future to include other nations in East and Southern and Africa, as well as countries in the Caribbean.

sleeper 1. A railway sleeping car. On UK railways, it is generally a single or two-berth sleeping compartment. UK sleepers have proper beds and bed linen and sexes are segregated.
2. The wooden or concrete transverse supports that hold the metals of a railway track in proper alignment. Known as ties in the USA.

sleeping car See sleeper (1).

sleeping policeman (UK) A specifically constructed bump in the road designed to slow down traffic.

sleigh A sledge, especially one for riding on, often drawn by horses or reindeer.

SLI See supplementary liability insurance.

slip (US) An artificial slope in a marina or dock where boats can be brought into or out of the water.

slip road (UK) A road that enters or leaves a motorway or similar.

slipstream A current of air or water driven back by a moving vehicle.

sloop A small single-masted vessel with foresail and jib.

slot An allocated time of departure or arrival at an airport. Slots are at a premium in busy airports.

Slovak Republic A country in Central Europe, formerly part of Czechoslovakia and sometimes referred to as Slovakia. Not to be confused with Slovenia.

Slovenia A country in the Balkans, formerly part of Yugoslavia. Not to be confused with the Slovak Republic.

slow food Food which is prepared using traditional methods and ingredients and which is designed to be eaten in a leisurely way. The phrase, and the organisation of the same name, originated in Italy in the 1980s as a reaction to the fast food outlets which were threatening to destroy culinary individuality. > fast food.

SMAL Suomen matkatoimistoalan liitto. *See Appendix 5c.*

small print An informal but widely used expression for the terms, conditions, exclusions, exceptions, definitions and the like that apply to a particular agreement, such as an insurance policy or a package holiday.

smallpox A once deadly, contagious viral disease that has now been eliminated in the wild although strains are still kept in a few laboratories.

SMB *See surface marker buoy.*

smog Fog mixed with smoke.

smokestack *See funnel.*

smorgasbord A Swedish-style buffet or meal, often featuring open sandwiches.
2. An assortment, medley or variety.

smuggle To attempt to bring in goods to a country secretly and illegally.

SNAV Syndicat National des Agences de Voyages. *See Appendix 5c.*

snorkel (or **schnorkel**) A J-shaped tube that enables a diver to breathe ordinary air at the surface without having to raise the face out of the water.

snorkelling The act of swimming face down in the water using a snorkel to breathe.

Snow 24 *See Appendix 5a.*

snow blindness A condition, usually temporary and avoided by wearing adequate goggles or sunglasses, caused by looking at the glare of sunlight on snow.

snow cat *See piste groomer.*

snow cover The parts of a ski area that have enough snow on which to ski or snowboard.

snow depth A measurement of the depth of snow given in snow reports, typically at the bottom, middle and top of the mountain.

snow garden A separate and enclosed part of a ski area reserved for younger children. Snow gardens are particularly common in France but similar areas exist under different names at ski resorts in other countries. Snow gardens may contain special lifts and attractions for children and be attached to ski kindergartens.

snow making A process which enables machines to create snow from stored water piped to the slopes. This is particularly common at low-altitude ski areas to ensure snow cover through the season.

snow permanent Snow, usually at high altitudes, which never disappears completely before fresh snow is deposited.

snow report A report produced by a ski resort or an independent agency that advises on the depth of snow and quality and status of ski runs.

snowbird (US) A slang term for a person from a northern region or country who often travels south during the winter.

snowboard A wide, single ski.

snowboard boot A special boot worn by snowboarders that fixes to their board with a special binding. Snowboard boots are softer, lighter and more comfortable than ski boots.

snow-cap A mountain-top covered with snow.

snowdrift A bank of snow heaped up by the wind.

snowfield A wide expanse of snow, generally present year-round. The term is also colloquially used to describe non-permanent expanses that commonly melt in the summer.

snowline 1. The height above which snow never entirely melts.
2. In skiing, the height where the snow begins and ends on a mountain at a particular time, according to season and weather conditions.

snowmobile A powered vehicle fitted with skis on the front and caterpillar tracks at the rear, used for moving over snow.

snowplough 1. A device for clearing or moving snow.
2. The name given to the commonest way of teaching people to ski. It is derived from the inverted V-shape made by the skis in the 'snowplough' position.

snowshoe A tennis-racquet shaped device that straps over ordinary boots to allow the wearer to walk on snow without sinking.

soft spikes A type of cleat worn on a golfer's shoes, using rubber rather than metal spikes. Some golf courses only permit soft spikes.

soirée (or **soiree**) Originally, a French term for an evening party, particularly in a private house. Now widely used to describe any evening event.

sojourn A temporary stay.

solar Of or relating to the sun.

solar day The length of a day as measured by the apparent movement of the sun. The normal measurement of time on earth.

solar eclipse *See eclipse.*

solstice The two days in a year which have the most and the least hours of daylight. In the northern hemisphere the summer solstice is on 21 June and the winter solstice on 22 December: in the southern hemisphere the reverse is the case. The further from the Equator one is, the greater will be the difference between the hours of daylight on these two dates.

Somali Current The warm current that runs off the north-east coast of Africa flowing north in June, July and August and south during other times of the year.

sommelier The person in charge of the wine in a restaurant.

son et lumière From the French 'sound and light', an entertainment making use of illuminations and music. Often used at historic man-made attractions, such as the Pyramids.

SOS An international distress signal, using letters in Morse code that were easily transmitted and recognised.

souk A market place in Arabic countries.

sound 1. A narrow passage of water connecting two other bodies of water.
2. To test the depth and quality of the bottom of a body of water.

south One of the four cardinal points of the compass, 90° clockwise from east and 180° from north; at the foot of maps where (as is normal) north is at the top. > *north.*

South America One of the world's continents. As with most continents, opinions differ as to its exact composition and area. > *continent.*

South China Sea The area of the Pacific Ocean between Indochina, the Philippines, Borneo and China.

South Equatorial Current Originating close to the Equator and flowing westward, this current is diverted northwards by the Brazilian coast and feeds the source of the Gulf Stream.

South Korea A widely used, though unofficial, term for the Republic of Korea.

South Pole The southernmost point of the earth.

South Sea (Also **South Seas**) The southern Pacific Ocean.

South, the The parts of the USA south of Pennsylvania and the Ohio river, and in particular those states south of the Mason-Dixon line that fought on the Confederate side in the American Civil War. > *Mason-Dixon Line.*

South-East Asia A general geographic term describing the area comprising Maynmar, Laos, Thailand, Vietnam, Cambodia, Malaysia, Singapore, Brunei and the Philippines. Sometimes also taken to include Indonesia, Taiwan and the southern coastal areas of China including Macau and Hong Kong.

South-East, the The south-eastern corner of England, including Kent, Sussex, Surrey and London, and sometimes other home counties.

Southern Cone The region of South America comprising Brazil, Paraguay, Argentina and Uruguay.

Southern Cross A distinctive cross-shaped constellation visible only in the southern hemisphere.

southern hemisphere That part of the earth south of the Equator.

southern lights *See aurora australis.*

Southern Ocean *See oceans.*

Southwest Chief The rail service between Chicago and Los Angeles in the USA.

Southwest Effect An airline time, named after the pioneering low-cost Southwest Airlines in the USA, to describe the effect on fares (falling), passenger numbers (rising) and the market share of neighbouring airports (falling) when a low-cost carrier begins operations at a specified airport.

souvenir A memento bought as a reminder of a journey or visit. Souvenirs are a major earner of foreign exchange in most resorts.

sovereign A supreme ruler, especially a monarch.

spa 1, A resort or other establishment which specialises in hydrotherapy treatments.
2. Any resort or hotel which caters for or appeals to health-conscious guests.
3. A facility within a resort or hotel which offers hydrotheraputic treatments such as Turkish baths or saunas.

SPAA Scottish Passenger Agents Association. *See Appendix 5a.*

space available basis *See standby.*

Space Coast An area of coastline east of Orlando, Florida, stretching from New Smyrna Beach in the north to Palm Bay in the south. It encompasses many sites relating to the US space programme, as well as numerous beach resorts and wildlife reserves.

space ratio *See Passenger Space Ratio.*

spaghetti junction (UK) A motorway junction having several levels and complex interchanges. The original is to the east of Birmingham in the UK where the M6, the M42, the A446 and the A452 intersect.

spar 1. A pole used for the mast, yard, boom or other rigid part of the rigging of a ship.
2. The main structural member of an aircraft's wing.

Spartan The civilisation of ancient Laconia (c.900BC to

AD396). The Spartans were reputedly very hardy, and the term now also refers to anything, such as accommodation, that is bare, austere or unadorned.

spear gun A device for propelling a spear at speed through the water.

special-interest attraction Any tourist attraction that is designed to appeal to a specific hobby or interest.

special-interest holidays A holiday arrangement which caters for those following particular interests or hobbies.

special-needs accommodation Accommodation designed for guests with disabilities.

speed bump *see sleeping policeman.*

speedboat A small, fast boat.

SPF *See sun protection factor.*

SPH Skiers per hour. *See uplift capacity.*

Spice Islands The former name for the Moluccas, or Maluku, Islands, in eastern Indonesia.

spinnaker A large triangular sail.

spit A point of land projecting into a body of water.

split charter An arrangement whereby two or more different companies or individuals hire different parts of the same vehicle.

split season Travelling out and back in different seasons.

split ticketing The issuing of separate tickets for a multi-sector journey to undercut the through fare.

sporting attraction An attraction that capitalises on its ability to offer visitors the chance to participate in or watch a sport.

spot height A specific height marked on a map, for example, the summit of a mountain.

spouse A husband or wife. At one time carriers' special fares for accompanying partners were restricted to spouses. These days such fares are usually available to any partner.

spouse fare *See partner fare.*

spring tide The tide just after the new and the full moon, when there is the greatest difference between high and low water and during which the tidal streams run most strongly.

squall A sudden and violent gust or storm of wind.

square-rigged A form of rigging where the principal sails are arranged at right angles to the length of the ship and extended by horizontal yards attached to the masts.

SRF Svenska Resebyråforeningen. *See Appendix 5c.*

SS When placed in front of a ship's name means steamship.

SSC Sector Skills Council. *See Appendix 5a.*

SSSI *See site of special scientific interest.*

SST *See supersonic transport.*

St Christopher & Nevis The country in the Leeward Islands in the Caribbean now known as St Kitts & Nevis.

St George's The capital of Grenada. Not to be confused with Georgetown, the capital of Guyana, or George Town, the capital of the Cayman Islands.

St Maarten *See St Martin.*

St Martin One of the Leeward Islands in the Caribbean, divided into the French St Martin (administratively part of Guadeloupe) and the Dutch St Maarten (one of the Netherlands Antilles).

stabilisers A mechanism used on cruise ships to provide a smoother journey in rough seas.

stage decompression A specific depth at which the diver must remain before completing the journey to the surface to enable accumulated nitrogen to escape from the body without danger of contracting decompression sickness.

stagecoach Historically, a large, closed horse-drawn coach running to a timetable between various points. Sometimes still used to describe similar motor coach services.

stalactite A deposit of crystallised minerals hanging from the roof of a cave or cavern caused by mineral-laden water seeping through the cavern roof. Most resemble a stone icicle.

stalagmite A deposit of crystallised minerals rising from the floor of a cave or cavern caused by drops of mineral-laden water falling from a stalactite.

stall The condition that occurs when the airflow over an aircraft's wings is insufficient to maintain lift.

stamp To endorse a ticket or other items by means of a rubber or metal stamp.

Standard Caribbean Terms Yacht charter terms under which the fee includes the charter of the yacht and all associated costs, including full board for the client, although generally excepting drinks. Other costs, such as cruising taxes and radio telephone and other communication costs, must be paid by the client. These terms may vary.

Standard Eastern Mediterranean Terms Yacht charter terms under which the fee includes the charter of the yacht with all equipment; basic consumables for engine-room, deck and cabins; the crew's wages and food; insurance for the yacht itself, for third party claims and employer's liability insurance for the crew; fuel for up to five hours cruising per day (averaged throughout the charter); berthing dues and other harbour charges (except Corinthian Canal dues); and water or electricity taken from the shore. Other costs, such as fuel for the ski boats, the client's food and drink, berthing and harbour expenses outside the yacht's normal cruising area, laundry and radio telephone and other communication costs, must be paid by the client. These terms may vary.

standby fare A general term for a discounted fare offered to passengers who are prepared to wait until the last minute to obtain a seat.

starboard The right-hand side of a vessel when one is looking towards the forward end. Denoted by a green light.

state 1. An organised political community under one sovereign government.
2. An organised political community forming part of a federal republic. *See Appendix 2 for a list of US states and appendix 4 for a list of Australian states.*

stateless A person who has no nationality or citizenship.

stateroom 1. A state apartment in a palace or hotel.
2. A private room on a ship. Originally the term was reserved for the best cabins, but some shipping lines refer to all their sleeping accommodation as staterooms.
3. (US) A private compartment on a train.

station A stop or terminus for trains or buses.

station wagon (US) An estate car.

status box The space on an air ticket that indicates whether a reservation has been confirmed or not.

statute mile A unit of measurement in the imperial system equal to 1,760 yards or approximately 1.6 kilometres. > *nautical mile.*

steam engine An engine that produces its power by burning fuel in a boiler to produce steam, which drives a piston or turbine. Steam engines are now used mainly in large static installations such as power plants. However, in transport they can still be found in larger liners and on a few railways.

steamer *See steamship.*

steam-hauled A train pulled by a steam-powered

locomotive: usually only found on preserved lines or tourist trains.

steamship A ship powered by steam engines. Usually denoted by the abbreviation SS in front of its name.

steerage Historically the cheapest accommodation on a ship, situated far aft.

stem An alternative name for a ship's bow.

steppe A level, grassy plain with extreme temperature variations.

sterling *See pound (2).*

stern The rear part of a ship.

steward A male passenger attendant on a ship, aircraft or train.

stewardess (UK) A female steward.

STF School Travel Forum. *See Appendix 5a.*

stock 1. The unissued tickets and other documents held pending use.
2. *See rolling stock.*

STOL *See short take off and landing.*

Stone (UK) A unit of measurement of weight, equal to 14 pounds, only used for expressing the weight of a person.

stopoff *See stopover.*

stopover A deliberate interruption to a journey, agreed in advance, between the origin and destination points. Many discounted fares do not allow stopovers.

storey A floor of a building.

storm *See Beaufort scale.*

stowaway A person who has hidden aboard a vehicle in the hope of obtaining free transport.

STP *See satellite ticket printer.*

STP location *See satellite printer location.*

strait A narrow passage of water joining two seas or other larger areas of water.

Strait of Dover The narrowest part of the English Channel between Calais and Dover.

stratus A type of cloud characterised by its generally low, flat base and grey colour.

stream A small river or similar flowing body of water.

street A public road in a town or village.

street furniture The various signs and other artefacts provided in a road or street to assist the public.

streetcar (US) A tramcar.

strong breeze *See Beaufort scale.*

strong gale *See Beaufort scale.*

Stuart (or **Stewart**) Of or relating to the kings and queens of Scotland between 1371 and 1714 and of England between 1603 and 1714, or to those periods generally.

studio A one-bedroomed apartment.

sub-aqua Relating to any underwater activity, especially diving.

sub-continent A large land mass, smaller than a continent, such as the Indian sub-continent.

subject to load The situation when a carrier agrees to convey a passenger if space is available. Most discounted tickets are subject to load and the greater the discount the lower the priority of the holder of the subload ticket. Often abbreviated to 'subload' or 'standby'. > *standby.*

subload *See subject to load.*

submarine 1. Beneath the sea.
2. A vessel capable of operating beneath water. Submarine excursions are now common in resorts where there are underwater attractions, such as coral reefs.

subsonic Less than the speed of sound (approximately 1,225 kph or 760 mph at sea level).

sub-temperate The cooler parts of a temperate climatic zone. > *climate zones.*

subterranean Under ground.

subtropical A climate zone slightly cooler than tropical. *See climate zones.*

suburban Often abbreviated to suburb. The area around a city.

subway 1. (UK) An underground passage, often beneath a road.
2. (US) An underground railway. > *metro.*

Subway, the The urban rail system in New York, and several other cities including Seoul and Tokyo.

Succot A festival in the Jewish religious calendar, celebrated five days after Yom Kippur.

Suez Canal The canal that connects the Mediterranean Sea with the Red Sea, running through Egypt.

suite Accommodation comprising one or more connecting rooms.

Sulawesi *See Celebes.*

sultan A Muslim sovereign.

sultanate A state ruled by a sultan.

sultry Of the weather, hot or oppressive.

Sumerian The civilisation of ancient Sumeria (c.3500BC to c.1700 BC).

Summer Olympics *See Olympic Games.*

summer solstice *See solstice.*

summit The highest point of a feature, especially a hill or mountain.

summit The top of a mountain.

sumptuous Particularly lavish or costly.

sun deck The deck of a ship designed for sunbathing.

sun protection factor The indicator of the effectiveness of sun creams and lotions, often described as a number: the higher the number, the better the protection.

sunbelt An area receiving more than the average amount of sunshine.

Sunbelt, the The areas of south and south-west United States (mainly Florida, Arizona and southern California) made popular by holidaymakers and those in retirement.

sunblock An alternative term for sunscreen, but often referring to the maximum level of sunscreen protection available. > *sun protection factor.*

sunlust The desire to travel to a sunny destination.

sunscreen 1. A screen providing protection against the sun.
2. A lotion or cream rubbed into the skin to prevent damage from the sun's rays. > *sun protection factor.*

Sunset Ltd The rail service between Orlando and Los Angeles in the USA.

Sunshine Coast The resort coast north of Brisbane, Australia, stretching from Bribie Island to Tin Can Bay, less developed than the Gold Coast to the south.

sunstroke Acute exhaustion or collapse caused by over-exposure to the sun.

suntrap (UK) A place designed to catch the sun, generally also sheltered from the wind.

sunup (US) Sunrise.

superelevation The amount by which the outer edge of a road or railway is above the inner edge.

superhighway 1. (US) A particularly fast main road with multiple carriageways in each direction.
2. An abbreviation of the information superhighway, the means by which information can be transferred rapidly between computers by means of the internet and similar networks.

superior A high class or category of accommodation, usually attracting a supplement.

supersonic Travelling faster than the speed of sound (approximately 1,225 kph or 760 mph at sea level).

superstructure Any structure built onto another structure. Thus the superstructure of a ship will include all the cabins and entertainment facilities built onto the hull.

supplement A fee for an extra, or higher, grade of product or service.

supplementary liability insurance See *vehicle rental insurance*.

supplier An individual or organisation in the travel industry responsible for organising or supplying some sort of facility. This might be transport: airlines, shipping lines, railways, car rental companies and bus and coach operators are examples. Providers of accommodation, such as hotels, motel and holiday centres are also principals. Other principals provide services which may be less obvious, such as travel insurance companies.

surcharge An extra charge on a customer's bill, enforced by a hotelier or tour operator.

surface demand Air supplied to a diver underwater through tubes from a source of air at the surface.

surface lift See *drag lift*.

surface marker buoy A small buoy floating on the surface of the water attached to the end of a long line and pulled by the submerged diver to indicate their presence.

surface tow See *drag lift*.

surface travel A generic term that can denote any form of travel that is not by air, but usually refers to travel over the ground rather than the sea.

surfboard A long narrow buoyant board on which riders are carried over the surf.

surrender Of a ticket or other document, to give it up on demand.

surrey (US) A light four-wheeled horse-drawn carriage often used for sightseeing.

sustainable tourism Tourism that has a minimal or manageable effect on the natural and cultural environment of the area visited.

swallow An area where a river appears to sink into the ground, only to reappear later.

swamp An area of waterlogged land.

sweepback The angle at which an aircraft's wings are set back from the right-angle.

swell The heaving of seas that do not break into waves, often after a storm.

A
B
C
D
E
F
G
H
I
J
K
L
M
N
O
P
Q
R
S
T
U
V
W
X
Y
Z

T t

T junction A road junction where one road joins another at right angles without crossing it.

TAANZ Travel Agents Association of New Zealand TAANZ. *See Appendix 5c.*

table d'hôte A menu in a restaurant that is available at a fixed price and which contains relatively few choices.

table top *See terrain park.*

tableland An extensive elevated region.

tables *See decompression tables.*

tachograph A device fitted to vehicles such as coaches that measures the speed, duration of stops and number of hours a driver works.

tack The direction in which a sailing vessel moves as determined by its own direction and that of the wind.

taffrail The rail around a ship's stern.

taiga 1. A stretch of cold, swampy coniferous forest, especially in Siberia.

tail wind A wind blowing in the same direction as a vehicle is travelling.

tailor-made A holiday or other arrangement designed especially for a particular client.

tailplane The smaller horizontal projections from the fuselage of an aircraft, situated towards the rear. These serve to stabilise the machine and provide most of the control.

Taiwan The island off the south-east coast of China (formerly known as Formosa) and the country known variously as Taiwan, Taiwan (ROC) and the Republic of China, > *China, People's Republic of, ROC.*

take a chance A marketing device used by some cruising companies. By taking a chance on the exact cabin and cruise, prospective passengers can pay a substantially reduced fare. Their accommodation will then be allocated around a month before sailing.

take off The moment when an aircraft leaves the ground and starts to fly.

taking air The act of leaving the snow and jumping into the air, intentionally or not, while skiing or snowboarding. Also known as taking big air.

tall ship A sailing ship with a tall mast or masts.

tandem A bicycle designed for two people.

tannoy A brand name for a type of public address system, but often used in the UK to denote any such system.

tapas Small savoury dishes, often served at a Spanish bar.

taproom A room in which alcoholic drinks, usually beer, are served.

tariff 1. A rate or charge, generally displayed as a list. 2. An alternative name for an air fare.

tarmac A paved surface such as a road or runway.

tarn A small lake.

Tasman Sea The area of the Pacific Ocean between Australia and New Zealand.

tavern An old fashioned name for an inn.

taverna A Greek name for an eating place or sometimes a small hotel.

taxi 1. A car or similar vehicle licensed to ply for hire. 2. The movement of an aircraft on the ground.

taxi way Paved tracks on which aircraft move between the parking and loading area and the runway.

taximeter The device that calculates the distance travelled and the fare payable for a cab journey.

TBA *See to be advised.*

T-bar *See drag lift.*

TBN To be notified. > *to be advised.*

tech stop *See technical stop.*

technical stop A planned stop on an air journey that is not scheduled for passenger pick up or drop off. Usually this will be for refuelling or crew change. Passengers may not need to leave the aircraft, but this will depend on local restrictions.

technology butler (US) A member of staff in a hotel or similar organisation whose job is wholly or partly to assist guests with their technology-related problems.

tee-time The time booked for golfers to begin playing their round. Golfers may wish to know what tee-time has been booked for them in advance of travel, particularly on arrival and departure days. Groups of more than four golfers may be allocated more than one tee-time. It is important for the golfers to know all the tee-times allocated to their group.

télécabine *See gondola.*

téléférique Another name for a cable car, commonly used in France and Switzerland.

Telemark skiing A method of downhill skiing that predates Alpine skiing by approximately 40 years. It was developed in the Telemark region of Norway in the 1860s. The technique has gained popularity worldwide over the past decade following the fragmentation of winter sports holiday options. Telemark skiing uses boots only connected to the ski at the toe.

temperate A type of climate. *See climate zones.*

temperature-humidity index A value that gives the measure of discomfort experienced due to the combined effects of the temperature and humidity of the atmosphere.

tempest A violent, windy storm.

temple 1. A place of worship, particularly for Hindus or Buddhists.
2. A term sometimes used to describe a Christian place of worship, such as by Mormons or protestants in France and French-speaking countries.
3. A place of worship in ancient pagan cultures, such as those of the Romans and Greeks.
4. (US) A synagogue.

tender 1. A small boat used to transfer passengers from a cruise ship to the land when it is not possible to dock.
2. The putting in of a bid for business. Business travel agents who are often expected to re-tender for a company's travel account at regular intervals.

tent A portable, temporary dwelling made of canvas or similar. Often the cheapest form of accommodation, although many modern tents are quite luxurious.

tentalow A cross between a tent and a bungalow, typically a canvas structure on a solid base and often with electricity and plumbing laid on.

terminal 1. A building at an airport, bus station or similar that is used to process arriving and departing passengers.
2. The computer screen and associated equipment in a travel agency that is connected to a GDS or other system.

terminus (UK) The station at the end of a railway line or bus route.

terra firma Solid earth (as opposed to air or sea).

terra incognita An unknown or unexplored area.

terrace 1. A raised, flat area outside a house or similar.
2. A flattened area of hillside, often in progressive steps supported by stone walls, used for cultivation.

terrain The physical features of an area. > *topography.*

terrain park An area of a ski slope, often fenced off from the rest of the ski area, where terrain features are created for snowboarders and increasingly also skiers using the latest short skis. Terrain parks may include a half pipe, rails (a steel rail to slide along above the snow), table top (a flat area of metal or snow) and other features carved from snow.

terrestrial 1. Of or relating to the earth, as opposed to the air. In some cases, its meaning includes all the surface of the earth, including the seas, in others merely to the land.
2. Of or relating to telecommunication systems that do not make use of satellites.

territorial waters The waters under the jurisdiction of a country or state, especially that part of the sea a stated distance from the country's shore.

territory Any piece of land belonging to, or under the jurisdiction of, a state or country.

test pressure The maximum pressure to which a diving cylinder may be safely charged for testing purposes. The process should only be undertaken by a competent testing authority.

tetanus (or **lockjaw**) An acute infectious disease, endemic worldwide, caused by bacterial infection of a wound. > *health precautions.*

Texas Eagle The rail service between Chicago and San Antonio in the USA.

TGV The French high-speed trains (*trains à grande vitesse*) which operate services within France from their Paris hub, and also into Belgium, Switzerland, Germany and Italy. Not all TGV trains run on dedicated high-speed lines. > *LGV.*

Thalys The high-speed train service running between Paris, Brussels, Amsterdam and Cologne.

theatre-style seating plan A common configuration at meetings, conferences or seminars whereby the delegates are seated in rows as in a theatre, usually with a raised stage for the speakers at the front of the hall.

theft protection See *vehicle rental insurance.*

theme cruise A cruise designed to appeal to a specific interest group.

theme park An entertainment centre, usually spread over a large area with a number of separate entertainment facilities, generally based on a particular special interest.

themed attraction Any tourist attraction that has chosen a particular special subject or topic on which to base its activities and displays.

thermocline The boundary between waters of differing temperature.

third age The period in life of active retirement, often a time when many people travel extensively.

third class The third-best category of travel or accommodation.

Third World That part of the world that is less advanced or developed than the global average.

third-party insurance The cover against claims made by another person, in respect of injury, damage, death or other loss. > *travel insurance.*

thoroughfare A road or path open at both ends for the passage of traffic.

through fare A fare for travel between two points. Usually through fares will allow en route stopovers, unlike point-to-point fares. The publication of a through fare for a journey does not mean that a through service exists.

through passenger Any traveller who is not transiting or disembarking at a specific stop.

through service A service that does not require a passenger to change. Through services are not necessarily non-stop services, even by air. In cases where a flight makes an intermediate stop or stops, the entire flight through to the final destination will have the same flight number for every leg of the journey.

throughway 1. A thoroughfare.
2. (US) (often thruway) a motorway.

throwaway (US) Any element of a travel package which is bought but, for whatever reason, not used.

thrust The force generated by an aircraft engine.

thunder The sound of lightning caused by the rapid heating of air by the electrical discharge. The sound of thunder is generated at the same time as the lightning and the interval between the two is caused by the different speeds at which light and sound travel. Each five-second delay between seeing the lightning and hearing the thunder is equal to about a mile.

thunderbolt A flash of lightning with an almost simultaneous crash of thunder, caused by the nearness of the storm.

thundercloud A tall cumulus cloud, producing thunder and lightning.

thunderstorm A storm producing rain, thunder and lightning.

TIAA Travel Industry Association of America. *See Appendix 5b.*

TIC *See tourist information centre.*

tick-borne encephalitis A viral infection caused by tick bites, generally confined to forested areas of Central Europe and Scandinavia. > *health precautions.*

ticket 1. A document that proves entitlement to travel on a specific journey, subject to the conditions of carriage and the discretion of the airport or airline authorities. It is not the same as a reservation, in that in itself it does not guarantee passage at any particular time. > *reservation.*
2. A document allowing entry to an event or place.
3. A colloquial term for a citation given by a police officer or other authorised person for a motoring offence. In the UK, it generally refers only to a fin for a parking offence.

ticket agent A person or office that sells tickets, such as for entertainment or ground transportation.

ticket collector A person who checks tickets or travel documents, usually on a train or at the barrier of a station.

ticket fraud The defacement, non-purchase, re-sale, forgery or other misuse of a ticket.

ticket inspector A person responsible for checking travel tickets during a journey, usually to detect ticket fraud on trains. They may be in plain clothes, with identification, and may be authorised to levy on-the-spot fines.

ticket office A place where tickets are issued.

ticket on departure A ticket which is collected at the departure point, rather than the purchasing point. > *prepaid ticket advice, E-ticket.*

ticket printer A printer that prints the details on automated tickets.

ticket tout A person who obtains tickets, usually for a concert or sporting event, hoping to re-sell them at a profit.

ticketed point mileage (TPM) The published mileage between the origin and destination points of a journey by air. > *MPM.*

ticket-holder A person who has legitimately obtained and carries a ticket for a journey or facility.

ticketless travel *See electronic ticketing.*

tidal stream The flow of water caused by the tides.

tidal wave A dangerous and destructive wave, usually produced by an earthquake.

tide The regular rise and fall of the surface of seas and oceans that occurs about every 12 hours 25 minutes.

tidetable A table indicating the times of high and low tides.

tideway The channel in which a tide runs, especially the tidal part of a river.

tied house (UK) A pub owned by a brewery and thus usually obliged to sell primarily the brewery's own products. > *free house*.

tiller The horizontal handle fitted to a boat's rudder by which it is turned.

Timbuktu A town in Mali. The term is often used to denote a distant or inaccessible place.

time charter A charter based on the use of a vehicle, usually an aircraft, for an agreed length of time.

time zones The bands into which the earth is divided, within each of which the local time is the same. Time zones are numerically expressed as variations of hours from the bench-mark of UTC (GMT) time: +3.5, -7 and so on. There are 360 degrees of longitude and 24 hours in a day. 360 divided by 24 is 15; and thus the local time generally advances by one hour for every 15° one moves east, and decreases by one hour for every 15° one moves west. In practice, time zones do not follow this rigid 15° changeover, for some would otherwise cut through the middle of countries, perhaps even of cities. Time zones tend to follow national frontiers. Not counting offshore islands like the Canaries and the Azores, only a handful of countries (including the USA, Canada, Brazil and Australia) span more than one time zone. By contrast, China (despite its size) spans only one.
Due to the operation of daylight saving time in some regions, mainly outside the tropics, it is possible that some countries which are in the same time zone may, for about half the year, have different times. Additionally, some countries have time zones in fractions of an hour. Nepal, for example, is five and three-quarter hours ahead of UTC while Newfoundland in Canada is three and a half hours behind. In general, however, the world's time is divided into segments of roughly 15°, each generally corresponding to one hour's difference in local time. There are 36 time zones in all, but the ones which are more than UTC+12 or which contain differences of a fraction of an hour are generally limited to only one country or island group. The local time zones are often given names, such as Central European Time and Pacific Standard Time. > *daylight saving time*.

time-and-mileage A car rental tariff that is calculated on a combination of the period of time for which the vehicle is hired and the distance it is driven.

timeshare The concept where people 'buy' a period of time in a particular accommodation. This time is then reserved for their use year-on-year. Other customers will buy other time slots in the same accommodation and all will share maintenance costs.

timetable A list of departure and arrival times of a mode of transport or various inter-connecting modes of transport, usually limited to a specified region.

Timor Sea The area of the Indian Ocean between Indonesia and Australia.

tip See *gratuity*.

TIPTO Truly Independent Professional Travel Organisation. See *Appendix 5a*.

TMC See *travel management company*

TMI Tourism Management Institute.

to be advised (TBA) An expression used to express the fact that a particular and generally important item of information for the completion of a travel arrangement is not available at that time but will be supplied later. Commonly used by agents when they are awaiting details about a customer (the passport number, for example). Principals may also use the expression if they are unable to give full details about a booking, such as a timing or accommodation details.

TOC See *train operating company*.

TOD See *ticket on departure*.

token 1. A staff or similar object carried by the driver or guard of a train to control access to a section of single track taking two-way traffic.
2. A metal disc, used in some cases instead of a coin, for example in slot machines or on some urban transport systems.

toll 1. A fee charged for the use of a road, bridge or similar.
2. (US) The charge for a long-distance telephone call.

toll booth The place where a road or bridge toll is collected.

toll free (US) A telephone call where the charges are paid not by the caller but by the person or (more commonly) the organisation being called.

tonnage 1. A general term referring to the total number of ships in the region, fleet, class or season being considered.
2. A measurement of a ship's capacity with four different meanings: (a) gross registered tonnage or GRT; (b) net registered tonnage or NRT; (c) displacement tonnage, which is the weight of water displaced by a vessel (and thus its actual weight); and (d) dead-weight tonnage is the carrying capacity by weight. Most passenger shipping companies quote GRT in their brochure since this is the most useful measurement when determining a ship's likely comfort. Displacement tonnage is usually quoted for warships (and sometimes for US merchantmen). Dead-weight tonnage is usually quoted for tankers.

topography That variety or mix of natural or artificial features that make up a landscape.

topside The side of a ship above the waterline.

tor A rocky peak or hill, particularly in the west country of England.

tornado A violent storm, covering a relatively small area and characterised by whirlwinds (revolving, funnel-shaped clouds).

torrent A rushing stream of water.

torrid Extremely hot and dry weather.

total eclipse *See eclipse.*

totalitarian Of or relating to a centralised and dictatorial form of government.

touch of the sun A colloquial expression for a feeling of sickness caused by exposure to too much sun. Less severe than sunstroke.

touchdown The moment when an aircraft lands.

tour A trip that visits a number of exhibits, venues, attractions or other locations. Tours are often operated by coach and frequently have a guide. Tours with guides are usually known as escorted tours.

tour conductor *See tour guide.*

tour escort *See tour guide.*

tour guide Someone who escorts a tour. Also known as guide, courier, tour escort, escort, tour conductor or tour leader.

tour leader *See tour guide.*

tour manager A person who manages and supervises a pre-established tour itinerary, using the services of hotels, airlines, local guides and couriers, ensuring that it is carried out according to schedule and to standard.

tour operator An organisation that puts together an inclusive holiday for sale to the public, usually combining transportation, accommodation and ground services. > *organiser.*

tour organiser *See tour operator.*

tourism The all-embracing term for the movement of people to destinations away from their place of residence for pleasure (or – see below – for business), and the many other activities associated with this. Tourism is defined by the WTO as being 'the activities of persons travelling to and staying in places outside their usual environment for not more than one consecutive year for leisure, business and other purposes.' Note the use of the word 'business': the distinction between 'leisure' (or touristic) and 'business' travel is, statistically, very hard to draw on an international level. For a travel organiser, the differences in expectations, carriers, flexibility, accommodation and other details will be obvious; yet, once arrived, the nature and extent of the consumption of goods and services of the two types of traveller will generally be statistically impossible to distinguish, particularly as many travellers will mix business with pleasure. Moreover, many countries or organisations are unable, or unwilling, to separate these reasons for travel in the figures they report; and, even if they do, they do not apply the same criteria in differentiating them. The fact that the WTO, which tends to define 'travel' generally as 'tourism', is the only internationally accepted statistical source of such data, has further confused this distinction. So too has the reduction of border controls within the EU, within which many of the world's most visited countries (for whichever reason) are to be found. For many countries, domestic tourism is also vastly important to the national economy, although statistically very hard to measure. International tourism involves the traveller leaving more 'footprints' which can more easily create statistical records; for obvious reasons, it also tends to involve the expertise of the travel professional to help make the necessary arrangements, particularly in the case of countries such as the UK or the USA where the act of reaching all or some international destinations involve flights or sea crossings. The cost or length of the journey is, however, not always the key factor: a ten-kilometre car ride from France to Belgium, involving no prior arrangements, is an international journey, while a flight of many thousands of miles from New York to Hawaii, crossing five time zones and probably requiring the services of a travel arranger, is a domestic one.

tourism apartheid The situation where discrimination exists against local people in favour of free-spending foreign tourists.

tourist 1 A person who engages in tourism. > *tourism.* 2. On some airlines, an alternative term for economy class. > *economy class.*

tourist attraction *See attraction.*

tourist card A document required by certain countries before travellers will be allowed to enter it. The requirements for obtaining a tourist card are similar to, but usually less onerous than, those required for obtaining a visa.

tourist class *See economy class.*

tourist enclave An area of separate tourist accommodation, often provided for security reasons.

tourist generating country A country from which large numbers of tourists originate.

tourist guide A person who possesses an area-specific tourist guide qualification recognised by the appropriate public authority in the country concerned. The tourist guide's role is to guide visitors from home or abroad, in languages of their choice, interpreting the natural and cultural heritage of the area.

tourist information centre (UK) An office, usually run by a tourist board or local authority, which gives information about a destination.

tourist office An office which exists to promote tourism to a country or region and usually funded by the governments of the countries they promote.

tourist receiving country A country that large numbers of tourists visit.

tourist region An area visited by tourists that has a specific name or identity. This will often differ from the name for the region used geographically. For example, the stretch of coast between Valencia and Alicante is officially in the Comunidad de Valenciana, but holidaymakers know it as the Costa Blanca.

tourist trap A scathing expression for a destination or attraction that is reputedly overcrowded with visitors and often offering poor value-for-money.

tow path A path alongside a canal or navigable river, originally used by draught horses to haul barges.

town A large urban area with a name and boundaries, not large enough to be classed as a city.

TP See theft protection.

TPI See third party insurance.

TPM See ticketed point mileage.

track 1. A rough path through countryside.
2. A railway line.
3. The course of an aircraft in flight.

track-laying A vehicle such as a tank that that lays its own tracks as it progresses, often used for haulage where the ground is poor or slippery.

tract A region or area of indefinite size.

trade body (Also **trade association**.) An organisation created by or on behalf of the members of a particular industry which generally exists to further the interests of its members, to lobby on their behalf, to provide codes of standards and practice and to organise events where the members may meet socially and professionally. The travel trade has many such organisations, and a selection of these are listed in Appendix 5. The international nature of the industry means that many will have an international membership and, consequently, that many of their conferences and the like will be held in countries other than that in which the trade body is based.

trade discount A discount given by one business to another, generally in the same industry, for purchasing its products of services.

trade fair (Also **trade show**) An event set up to meet the interests of people and organisations involved with a particular industry (such as travel) and to provide commercial opportunities. There are many each year throughout the world. Some are international; some national; some regional. Some cater for specialist areas, such as cruising or winter sports; others are industry-wide. Two of the largest are the World Travel Market in London in November, and the ITB in Berlin in March.

trade mission A tour arranged for business or government representatives to visit a destination with a view to obtaining more business.

trade show See trade fair.

trade winds The steady winds that blow across the oceans from about 30° north to about 30° south. In the northern hemisphere they blow from north-east to south-west; in the southern, from south-east to north-west. .

traffic In travel, any movement of people and or vehicles between two points, by any means of transport.

Traffic Area IATA's division of the world into three areas.
• TCA 1 is North and South America (sub-divided into North, Mid and South Atlantic)
• TCA 2 is Europe and Africa (sub-divided into Europe, Middle East, Africa and East Africa)
• TCA 3 is Asia and Australasia (sub-divided into Asia and South-west Pacific)

traffic calming The deliberate reduction or slowing of road traffic by the construction of obstacles, such as humps or chicanes, in the roadway or by restricting or charging the vehicles which may access a given area.

Traffic Conference Area See Traffic Area.

traffic document A passenger ticket or similar document. Traffic documents may be issued manually, mechanically or electronically and are generally produced using either the carrier's own forms or those of its handling agents. Such documents include: passenger ticket and baggage check forms; automated ticket/boarding passes; miscellaneous charges orders; multiple-purpose documents; agent's refund vouchers; and on-line tickets supplied by the carrier to accredited agents.

traffic evaporation The effect by which the closure of a road or an intersection, or the introduction of measures such as congestion charging, have been observed to have the effect of making drivers switch to other forms of transport. This is in contrast to the policy of building more roads to solve congestion, which tends to attract more vehicles and thus creates similar congestion but on a larger scale.

traffic rights Usually applicable to air travel, but can apply to any form of transport. In a journey between two points, A and B, a carrier may travel via one or more intermediate points, say C and D. The carrier will have the right to carry passengers between A and B, but not necessarily between A and C or C and D. > *freedoms of the air.*

trail 1. A path created for leisure use.
2. (US) A piste. The term is now increasingly widely used in the UK. *See piste.*

trail map *See piste map.*

trailer 1. An unpowered vehicle drawn by a powered vehicle.
2. (US) A caravan.

train A collection of vehicles linked together. Generally only used for rail travel, but also to be found for road travel, particularly in Australia. > *road trains.*

train ferry A ferry designed to carry railway vehicles across water.

train operating company One of the various (currently about 25) private companies operating UK rail services.

tram 1. (or tramcar) (UK) A vehicle that uses a tramway.
2. (US) a cable-car.

tramp steamer A cargo vessel that travels from point to point on an ad hoc basis, as determined by the demands for cargo.

tramway 1. (UK) A light railway, often running along the roads and penetrating into the very heart of towns.
2. (US) An alternative name for a cable car.

transaction fees *See management fees.*

transatlantic Across the Atlantic.

trans-canal A cruise or other sea voyage that passes through a canal, usually the Panama Canal.

Trans-Caucasus The region between Russia, Iran, the Black Sea and the Caspian Sea, comprising Azerbaijan, Armenia and Georgia.

transcontinental Across a continent.

transfer The transport provided for passengers between their point of arrival and their accommodation.

transferable Capable of being transferred, such as a ticket or other travel document that can be passed on to another (which is not usual).

transit 1. A stop en route to a final destination at an intermediate airport or port.
2. (Mainly US) Public passenger transport.

transit line A line joining two fixed objects in order to determine one's position, such as by aligning a church spire in the foreground with another prominent feature in the distance. Used by mariners when offshore.

transit lounge A room at an airport for transit passengers.

transit passenger A passenger who has disembarked at an intermediate point, usually to change services, and who will be continuing on a connecting service. In most countries, transit passengers on international flights do not need to undertake immigration and customs clearance provided they stay in a designated transit area.

transit stop A stop at an intermediate airport or port en route to a final destination.

transit visa *See visa.*

transliteration The act of transcribing the letters of a word from one alphabet into another. As there will be often be cases where a particular sound in one alphabet can be rendered in several ways in another, this can give rise to spelling variations, for example of place names, from one publication to another.

Trans-Manchurian Express An unofficial name for the rail service from Moscow to Beijing via Harbin.

Trans-Mongolian Express An unofficial name for the rail service from Moscow to Beijing via Ulan Bator.

transocean Across an ocean.

transom A vertical strong point, forming the rear of a boat, onto which an outboard motor may be attached.

transpacific Across the Pacific.

transport The movement of passengers or goods. Along with accommodation and entertainment, transport is one of the three main elements of travel and tourism. Transport or transportation is usually categorised as surface, sea or air.

transportation order An IATA term for an agent's own order form authorised by a carrier for use by the agent, against which the airline issues its ticket.

trans-ship To transfer from one form of transport to another.

Trans-Siberian Express A British-operated luxury train service running on the Trans-Siberian Railway.

Trans-Siberian Railway The railway from Moscow to Vladivostok via Irkutsk, a distance of some 5,800 miles (9,300 kilometres). The principal train on the route is the Rossiya.

trattoria An Italian restaurant, generally small and informal.

travel agent A broker of travel services, acting as an intermediary between the purchaser and the supplier, traditionally receiving a commission from the supplier but sometimes now receiving a fee from the purchaser. A travel agent can be a company or an individual. Apart from the term 'travel agent' to describe the person who works in a travel agency, many other titles are used. These include travel clerk, travel counsellor, travel consultant and travel arranger. Travel agencies can operate from a home or a shop, or be located in vast travel hypermarkets in retail parks. They can also be virtual, with their customer contact being via the internet, a call centre or a television channel. Different countries enforce different levels of professional standards, financial security and regulatory controls. A selection of the major travel agency associations in the UK, the USA and worldwide may be found in Appendix 6, from whom more specific information about that country's industry may be obtained.

At one time, travel agents would undertake bookings for all types of traveller, whether travelling on holiday or for business reasons. Now, it is common to find that many agencies tend to specialise. The two main distinctions are between retail (or leisure) travel, and business travel.

• *Business travel agents* (some of which may located within large companies to conduct their travel arrangements exclusively) usually charge their customers a fee for the maintenance of the travel account. This fee will allow for the provision of large amounts of information on the customer's travel patterns and spend and will also enable the agent to spend time and effort in negotiating preferential travel deals. The business travel agent who charges such a fee is, in effect, acting as an agent for the customer. Many business travel agents are now known as travel management companies. *See management fee, implant, travel management company.*

• *Leisure travel agents* will generally sell a wide range of holiday travel products (particularly package tours), but increasingly many are specialising in certain sectors. These include special interest holidays (such as skiing), rail travel and cruising. This drift towards specialisation has been encouraged by the recent revolution in communications and information technology: for, as a result, people no longer expect to visit an agency in person. A specialist can thus service a very wide geographical area. Another emerging trend is for some leisure travel agents to move towards charging a consultancy fee, rather than receiving a commission from suppliers. They then offer their clients discounted prices and a range of other travel-related services (such as visa procurement) and advice (such as on destination information). This is already fairly common in the business-travel sector (see above).

travel agents' commissions *See commission.*

travel bureau Another name for a travel agent, less commonly used nowadays. *See travel agent.*

travel clerk *See travel consultant.*

travel consultant The name usually given to those working in a travel agency and dealing directly with customers over the counter, on-line or by phone.

travel counsellor *See travel consultant.*

travel hypermarket A large outlet for various travel-related products and services on one site, usually in a retail park.

travel industry The overall global business of travel and tourism, including variously either the organisations directly involved in it (such as airlines, hotels and travel agencies) or also the organisations which are connected to it indirectly (such as fuel companies, electricians and printers). By many reckonings, it is the largest industry in the world.

travel insurance The various policies which are available to protect the traveller against matters such as theft, delays, illness, injury and third-party claims, and the industry which exists to provide these. All prudent travellers purchase insurance. It is a criminal offence under the terms of the EU Package Travel legislation for travel agents not to advise their customers about this matter.

Most travel insurance policies in the UK are broadly similar, although each will differ in details described in the small print that may be significant for the individual traveller. These include: the precise terms used to describe areas of cover; the amount of cover; the limits (per single article or overall value); the excesses; the exclusions; the special conditions; the age limits of the insured party or parties; and the premiums. Many policies have been designed specifically for certain types of trip, such as winter sports, business, frequent travellers and families. Some are limited to one trip, while others provide cover for a whole year.

The main areas of cover are as follows (not all policies may cover all the examples given below, or may only do so as optional extras):

• *Medical cover*, including medical expenses, personal injury, hospital benefit and repatriation.

• *Personal effects*, including baggage, valuables, personal items, money and travel documents.

• *Cancellation of travel.*

• *Travel delay*, including withdrawal of services, curtailment and missed departures.

• *Personal liability*, including legal expenses and third-party claims.

• *Specialist cover*, including dangerous activities and search and rescue.

Most policies do not cover the financial failure of scheduled airlines or tour operators.

travel management company A business travel agency, generally operating on a contract rather than a commission basis, which will offer a comprehensive service managing the travel patterns, arrangements and expenditure on behalf of one or more corporate clients. Business travel agencies are increasingly offering such enhanced levels of service. > *travel agent.*

travel publication A book which has been written with the sole or principal intention of providing information on a country, a region or a travel-related theme, usually with an objective stance.

Some travel publications are aimed mainly, but not exclusively, at consumers; other mainly but not exclusively at the travel trade. Particularly of the former kind, there is a vast range available. Most bookshops have a large area devoted to the subject, and a few specialise in nothing else. All budgets and tastes, from backpackers to luxury honeymooners and from birdwatchers to dangerous sports enthusiasts, are catered for, often in exhaustive detail. Increasingly, travellers will supplement information that they receive from a travel agent about a particular destination with what they have themselves researched, which has both advantages and disadvantages for the travel trade professional.

Many of the specialist travel trade titles, such as those dealing with the precise details of accommodation rates or flight timetables, are of little or no interest to those unconnected with the day-to-day running of the industry, except perhaps for a brief glance during discussions about travel arrangements. These have been supplemented by on-line sources of information through which reservations can also be made, such as GDSs.

A list of useful publications, both consumer and trade, can be found in Section 4.2 of the Columbus *Travel Planning Workbook*.

As an addition to both of these categories, the internet looms ever large. Rather than replace the printed page, as many at one time hoped or feared, it has rather opened up new opportunities for direct access to knowledge, particularly when the user is searching for information too whimsical or occasional to merit the purchase of a book, or where up-to-the-minute details are required, such as on health, visas and travel security.

travel sickness Nausea caused by motion while travelling.

Travel South USA A US regional marketing organisation covering the south-eastern states of the USA. > *US regional marketing organisations.*

traveller 1. A person who goes from one place to another.
2. A colloquial term to describe those who travel independently, as opposed to 'tourists' who use pre-arranged facilities.

travellers cheques A form of money that is more secure than cash. The principle of the travellers cheque is that it is purchased for a specific value and then signed by the purchaser. When it is accepted by a vendor of goods or services, the purchaser signs it again and the signature match proves validity. The recent increase in the use and international acceptability of credit and debit cards have made travellers cheques less popular and necessary than previously.

traverse A horizontal passage across rock, ice or mountains.

travolator A level or inclined moving walkway, without the steps used on an escalator.

trekking A more strenuous form of hill walking which generally takes place at higher altitude and for many days continuously, and may include ascending a high but technically easy mountains such as Kilimanjaro. > *altitude sickness, acclimatisation.*

trekking grades See *climbing grades.*

tributary A river or stream flowing into a larger river or a lake.

trike An abbreviation for tricycle. > *cycle.*

trilingual 1. A person who can speak three languages fluently.
2. Something that is written in, or spoken in, three languages.

trimaran A three-hulled catamaran.

trip An informal term for a journey.

triplane An aeroplane with three pairs of wings. The configuration is no longer used.

triple A hotel room suitable for sleeping three people.

triple chair See *chair lift.*

tripper A person on a trip, usually for pleasure.

triptyque A term of French origin that describes a customs permit allowing passage of a motor vehicle.

trishaw A three-wheeled, man-powered rickshaw.

trolley 1. A bus propelled by electricity, drawing its current from an overhead wire.
2. (US) A tramcar.

Tropic of Cancer The parallel of latitude at 23° 28' N, where the sun appears directly overhead at noon during the northern summer solstice.

Tropic of Capricorn The parallel of latitude at 23° 28' S, where the sun appears directly overhead at noon during the southern summer solstice.

tropical See *climate zones.*

tropical storm A severe storm, but not as fierce as a hurricane or cyclone.

tropics Those areas of the world situated between the tropics of Cancer and Capricorn.

true north North according to the earth's axis, not as indicated by a magnetic compass. See *poles.*

true south South according to the earth's axis, not as indicated by a magnetic compass. See *poles.*

TS The Tourism Society. *See Appendix 5a.*

tsunami A tidal wave, usually caused by an earthquake, such as that which affected coastal areas in the Indian Ocean on 26 December 2004.

TTA Travel Trust Association Ltd. *See Appendix 5a.*

Tube The name given to the underground railway network in London. > *metro.*

tubing A reinforced rubber ring used to slide down ski slopes and often provided as an alternative activity by ski resorts. Often special tubing runs are created with bumps and turns to increase the fun.

Tudor Of or relating to the kings and queens of England between 1485 and 1603, or to that period generally.

tug 1. (Also **tugboat**) A small, powerful boat used to tow ships into and out of their moorings.
2. A small, heavy tractor used to move aircraft around an airport.

tugboat *See tug (1).*

tuk-tuk A small three-wheeled scooter taxi, common in India and Thailand. Also called a rickshaw.

tundra A large, treeless arctic region, usually having a marshy surface with underlying permafrost. > *climate zones.*

turboprop 1. A jet engine designed to drive a propeller rather than rely solely on jet thrust.
2. An aircraft equipped with turbo-prop engines.

turbulence The violent movement of air. This can cause an aircraft to shake, sometimes violently, which is why airlines recommend that passengers keep their seat belts loosely fastened at all times during a flight.

turnaround The period when an aircraft or other vehicle, following its arrival, prepares for its next journey.

turnpike (US) A toll road.

turnstile A special form of gateway that will admit only one person at a time. Turnstiles allow control of access and exit and can be designed to provide additional functions such as cash collection and usage counts.

Turquoise Coast A coastal resort region in southern Turkey. The main town is Antalya: other resorts include Alanya and Side.

TURSAB Turkiye Seyahat Acentalari Birligi. *See Appendix 5c.*

tuxedo (US) *See dinner jacket.*

twelve-hour clock The method of determining time whereby each day is divided into two segments of 12 hours each, running from 12 am midnight to 12 pm noon, and from 12 pm noon to 12 am midnight. Although the travel industry throughout most of the world now uses the 24 hour clock, there are still some countries, most importantly the USA, where the 12 hour clock is still used. In such cases, IATA regulations demand that the terms 'am' and 'pm' be written without full stops. > *twenty-four-hour clock.*

twenty-four-hour clock The method of determining time whereby each day is regarded as one period of 24 hours, the distinctions of am and pm thus being redundant. With the notable exception of the USA, the travel industry uses the twenty-four hour clock. In this system, times between midnight and noon are counted from 0000 to 1200 (no dots or hyphens should be used) and times thereafter from 1201 to 2359. > *twelve-hour clock.*

twenty-four-hour delegate rate A rate offered by a hotel or similar venue to organisers of conferences and training events. The rate usually includes room hire, refreshments, three meals and overnight accommodation, as well as basic meeting facilities and equipment.

twin A hotel room with two beds.

Twin Cities The two cities of Minneapolis and St Paul situated either side of the Missouri river, USA.

twin double Another name for a double double room.

twin screw A description of a vessel having two propellers, one on each side of its keel.

twin towns An initiative developed in Europe after the Second World War, and now promoted by the EU, by which towns in different countries establish links to promote social, educational, commercial and cultural exchanges. Some towns may have more than one twin.

twin-set An aqualung with two diving cylinders.

twister (US) A colloquial expression for a tornado.

typhoid An infectious bacterial fever endemic worldwide, usually spread by contaminated food or water. > *health precautions.*

typhoon A violent tropical storm. The Pacific region's equivalent to an Atlantic hurricane.

U u

UAE The United Arab Emirates, a federation of seven autonomous emirates on the Persian Gulf coast of the Arabian peninsula. Abu Dhabi is the largest: the others – Dubai, Sharjah, Fujairah, Umm al Qaiwain and Ras al-Khaimah – are known collectively as the Northern States.

UATP *See universal air travel plan.*

UFTTA Universal Federation of Travel Agents Associations. *See Appendix 5d.*

UK *See United Kingdom.*

Ulster The geographical region comprising the six counties of Northern Ireland and the counties of Cavan, Donegal and Monaghan in the Irish Republic. It is often used informally, and technically incorrectly, to describe Northern Ireland as a whole.

ultima thule A far-away, unknown region.

UM An airline code used to indicate an unaccompanied minor. > *unaccompanied minor.*

umbra *See eclipse.*

umiak An Eskimo open boat made from skins stretched over a wooden frame.

UMTS *See universal mobile telecommunications system.*

UN *See United Nations.*

unaccompanied minor An underage traveller taking a trip on his or her own. All carriers have their own minimum and maximum ages for unaccompanied minors, which can be as low as two years and as high as 15, and each will have its own procedures and regulations regarding their travel arrangements.

uncharted An area that has not been explored or mapped.

unchecked baggage *See hand baggage.*

under canvas A colloquial term for accommodation in tents.

under way In motion. Often used to refer to a ship moving under its own power.

undercarriage The wheels and associated landing mechanisms of an aircraft.

undercart A colloquial term for undercarriage.

underdeveloped A country or region that has not yet reached
its potential level of economic development.

Underground The name given to the mainly sub-surface or deep-level railway networks in London (also known as the Tube) and Glasgow. > *metro.*

underground railway A railway that has a significant part of its route below ground. Commonly used in large towns and cities. > *metro.*

underpass A road or railway that passes under another by means of a short tunnel.

undertow When the current below the surface of a stretch of water flows in an opposite direction from that on the surface. This is especially dangerous to swimmers from a beach when the direction of the undertow is away from the land.

UNESCO The United Nations Educational, Scientific and Cultural organisation, a specialised agency of the UN. Its purpose is to contribute to peace and security by promoting collaboration amongst nations by education, science and culture. UNESCO also selects, promotes and helps to safeguard natural and cultural heritage sites world-wide. > *UNESCO World Heritage Sites.*

UNESCO World Heritage Sites A register of world sites considered to be of global importance either because of their natural heritage or their significant man-made contribution to world culture. Countries which are signatories to the World Heritage Convention can submit potential sites to UNESCO, which considers each proposal under strict criteria and lists each site where one or more natural or cultural criteria have been met. > *UNESCO.*

ungroomed The condition of a piste or trail where the snow has not been compacted but left in a more-or-less virgin condition.

UNICEF United Nations Children's Fund.

unicycle A cycle with only one wheel.

Union flag The United Kingdom's national flag, often referred to as the Union Jack (technically, the latter term is only correct when the flag is flying from a jackstaff).

Union Jack *See Union flag.*

unique selling point A selling point that is unequalled by other providers or products.

United Arab Emirates *See UAE.*

United Kingdom The country comprising England, Scotland, Wales and Northern Ireland. The full title is United Kingdom of Great Britain and Northern Ireland. The Channel Islands and the Isle of Man are not part of the United Kingdom although they retain very close links with it. Some organisations, such as travel insurance companies, may use a slightly different definition of the term 'United Kingdom'. > *Great Britain*.

United Nations An international body established in the aftermath of the Secomd World War in 1945 to promote world-wide peace and security.. It is based in New York and has many specialist agencies. Every independent state in the world is a member except for Switzerland and Taiwan. > *UNESCO*.

United States of America The country comprising the 50 states and the District of Colombia. The USA also has very close ties of various natures with Puerto Rico, the US Virgin Islands, Guam and certain other Pacific Islands.

universal air travel plan (UATP) The credit card scheme operated by IATA.

universal mobile telecommunications system A proposed new high-capacity system that will allow the genuinely universal use of portable telephones.

Universal Time Coordinate *See UTC*.

unlade To unload a ship, generally of its cargo.

unladen A vehicle without passengers or cargo.

unlimited mileage A car rental tariff whereby the hirer has paid a set amount to cover a duration of hire and where no extra amount is payable whatever the distance travelled.

unmapped *See uncharted*.

UNO United Nations Organisation. *See United Nations*.

unpressurised An aircraft without a pressurised cabin. Usually only found on smaller aircraft that fly at relatively low altitudes or in less developed countries where older aircraft are still in service.

UNPROFOR United Nations Protection Force.

unpublished fare A fare that is not advertised in tariffs. Often an air fare made available through a consolidator.

UNRWA United Nations Relief and Works Agency.

unscheduled Not in the advertised schedule. Often used to describe a stop on a journey that has become necessary through abnormal operational circumstances.

unsurfaced A road without a suitable all-weather surface suitable for vehicles.

up-anchor *See weigh anchor*.

up-country Toward the interior of a country.

upgrade The switching of a passenger or guest to accommodation in a higher class than that originally paid for. > *complimentary upgrade*.

uplift capacity The number of skiers a lift, or the total numbers of lifts in a resort, can carry up a slope in one hour.

upmarket Of a holiday or other travel arrangement, towards or relating to the more expensive.

upper works That part of a ship that is above water when it is fully laden.

upscale (US) *See upmarket*.

uptown (US) The residential or more sophisticated part of a town or city, particularly where this forms a distinct area.

Ural Mountains The main mountain range in Russia, running roughly north-south to the north of the Aral Sea, and forming what is often regarded as the geographic frontier between the European and Asiatic parts of the country.

urban Living in, situated in or relating to a city. *See city*.

urban agglomeration A contiguous area inhabited at a consistently urban density of population, but ignoring any administrative boundaries. The urban agglomeration of New York thus includes Jersey City, Newark, Patterson and Yonkers even though these span more than one state. According to UN estimates, in 2000 there were worldwide exactly 100 urban agglomerations with a population in excess of 3 million, the largest of which, at over 28 million, was Tokyo. In 1900, there were three (London, New York and Paris).

urban tourism Tourism concentrated in urban areas.

US 1. An abbreviation for United States (of America), particularly when used as an adjective.
2. (UK) Unserviceable.

US external territories Scattered throughout the world, mainly in the Pacific, are various US possessions which enjoy varying degrees of autonomy. For more information, please consult the Columbus *World Travel Guide*.

US regional marketing organisations One of currently eight bodies which exist to co-ordinate regional tourism issues in the USA. Participation by each state is voluntary. A state may be represented in more than one region, or none, and membership is subject to change.

US Virgin Islands *See Virgin Islands*.

USA *See United States of America*.

useful load The load that can be carried by a vehicle in addition to its own weight.

user-friendly Any system or procedure that is designed to be easy to understand and use.

U-shape seating plan A common configuration at meetings, conferences or seminars whereby the delegates are seated around tables arranged together in the shape of a U.

USP *See unique selling point.*

USSR Union of Soviet Socialist Republics, the former state (also known as the Soviet Union) dominated by the Russian Republic. It has now fragmented into 15 independent states. > *former Soviet Union.*

USTI United States Tourism Industries. *See Appendix 5b.*

UT *See UTC.*

UTC Universal Time Co-ordinate. Formerly known as Greenwich Mean Time (GMT), a term which is still widely used and understood. UTC is the time on the Greenwich meridian and in the time zone associated with it. Other time zones are expressed as their variation behind or in advance of this. UTC is used throughout the world for airline and marine navigation. It is sometimes known as 'Zulu'. > *time zones, Greenwich meridian, British Summer Time, Daylight Saving Time, International Date Line.*

Utopia An imaginary perfect place or situation.

UV Ultra-violet.

V v

vacancy The availability of space or accommodation.

vacate To leave accommodation.

vacation (US) A holiday.

vaccination The process of introducing a vaccine into a person's body. > *health precautions.*

vaccine A protective substance made from the organisms that cause a particular disease. It will stimulate the production of antibodies in humans and thus afford them protection from that disease. > *health precautions.*

valet A personal servant or (more commonly in the travel industry) services provided by an hotel or similar organisation such as car parking or laundry.

validation The act of making a ticket good for travel, usually by stamping or imprinting. A validation stamp will contain, at least, the name of the issuing office and the date of issue of the document.

validator A machine for endorsing an agency's name and other details when validating documents.

validity The condition of a document being good for use. The most common use of the term refers to the period of validity – the dates or times between which it can be used. London Tube tickets, for example, are only valid for use on their day of purchase, and many airline tickets are only valid for a particular flight.

valise A suitcase, generally small.

valley A long and often narrow depression in the land, usually between two ranges of hills or mountains. Many valleys have, or once had, a river running along the bottom.

Valley of the Kings A region of great archaeological significance near Luxor in Egypt, about 500km south of Cairo.

Valley of the Olifants *See Blue Train.*

Valley of the Queens A region of great archaeological significance near Luxor in Egypt, about 500km south of Cairo.

Valley of the Sun The valley in which Phoenix, Arizona is situated, together with most of its major suburbs including Mesa and Scottsdale. It is one of the fastest-growing parts of the Sunbelt.

Valois Of or relating to the kings of France between 1328 and 1589, and to that period of French history generally.

Valsalva manoeuvre The term for a method for equalising the pressure inside the ear-drum with that on the outside. It is achieved by holding the nose firmly closed and then trying to breathe out through it, until the ears are felt to gently 'pop' The technique is typically used by divers but some find it useful when travelling by air, especially during descent.

valuables Items of high worth, such as jewellery, computer equipment and cameras. Most insurance policies can offer cover in the event that valuables are lost, damaged or stolen. The conditions under which such a claim can be made will be set out in the small print and will vary from policy to policy. Insurance for valuables often includes a limit on the repayment per single article, and on the overall value of all such items claimed for. > *travel insurance.*

Value Added Tax A form of indirect taxation on many goods and services with the retailer paying the taxable value to the government less what they have themselves paid out in Value Added Tax to others. In some cases, on following appropriate formalities, foreign visitors can reclaim such taxes on goods purchased while abroad. Value Added Tax rates vary from country to country. In the UK, it is 17.5%.

van 1. An enclosed vehicle designed for the conveyance of goods.
2. (UK) The railway carriage provided for the use of the guard and the conveyance of luggage.

vaporetto A small motor boat, especially one used on the canals of Venice.

vapour trail *See contrail.*

VAT *See Value Added Tax.*

VDU Visual Display Unit. A monitor or similar used to display computer data.

vegan A person who abstains from eating any food of animal origin, including fish, eggs and dairy products.

vegetarian A person who abstains from eating meat, but who will eat eggs and dairy products, and possibly also fish.

vehicle Any machine designed for the transport of passengers or goods.

vehicle hire *See vehicle rental.*

vehicle rental The act of hiring a car for a specified period of time, and the industry which exists to provide this. The term generally refers to self-drive vehicles, but also can include those hired with a chauffeur. > *vehicle rental insurance.*

vehicle rental insurance The various insurance policies that are available for anyone renting a vehicle. There are many different types of cover: the terms used to describe them, and the conditions that apply to each, will vary from agency to agency and from country to country. Many of these, such as third-party cover, will be obligatory, although in some cases it may be possible for the renter to show that cover is already in place under existing insurance policies.
• *Damage to the car* is covered by what is normally termed collision (or loss) damage waiver (CDW/LDW), which will cover the cost of repair or replacement in the event of an accident, less an excess which will have to be paid by the renter. The excess, although fixed, will sometimes be quite high, but can sometimes be reduced or eliminated on payment of a further premium.
• *Third-party insurance* covers claims made by someone else against the renter. In some countries, particularly the USA, it is advisable to top up this insurance with some form of additional cover: supplementary liability insurance, extended protection and liability insurance supplement are some of the terms used for this kind of additional protection.
• *Injury to the driver and passengers* will be covered by a personal accident insurance policy. Some renters may have this as part of general travel insurance that might be in place.
• *The theft or attempted theft of the vehicle* is covered by a theft protection cover, on which an excess might apply.
• *The theft of personal possessions from the vehicle* can, in some cases, be covered by a personal effects cover. This may also cover time spent in accommodation en route. Some renters may already have this as part of general travel insurance that might be in place.
Non-compliance with the terms of the rental agreement (such as leaving the car unlocked or driving dangerously) may result in the cover being invalidated. It is also worth remembering that almost all rental agreements require the renter to pay the full cost of any damage caused by the vehicle striking overhead or overhanging objects, such as bridges.

veld (or **veldt**) A South African term for open country or grassland.

velocity Speed.

velodrome A stadium designed mainly or exclusively for bicycle racing.

vendor (US) Anyone who sells a product or service to another.

Venice of... A term used to market a town or city anywhere in the world by virtue of the number or splendour of its canals.

Venice-Simplon Orient Express The luxury rail service which has operated since 1982 between London and Venice via Paris. Occasional journeys also run to Prague, Rome or Istanbul.

veranda (or **verandah**) A raised platform, sometimes roofed, along the side of a house.

verify To check the accuracy of something.

vernal equinox *See equinox.*

vertical drop The difference in height between the top of the highest lift in a resort and the bottom of the lowest lift. This is one of the most important indicators as to how much skiing is likely to be available in an area.

vertical integration The term used to describe the ownership, by one organisation, of both the means of production and the means of distribution of a commodity. In travel, for example, the same organisation could own an airline, a tour operator and a travel agency.

vertical take off and landing Of an aircraft that can take off vertically, for example, a helicopter

vessel A waterborne vehicle.

vestibule 1. A hall or ante-chamber.
2. (US) An enclosed entrance to a railway carriage.

vexillology The study of flags.

VFR *See visiting friends and relatives.*

via By way of.

via ferrata Literally 'the iron roads', these are long scrambling routes equipped with ladders, metal spikes and safety rails to enable passage over sections that would otherwise require technical rock climbing. The routes exist mainly in Italy France and Spain, but require more specialised equipment than that needed for regular scrambles. See also *scrambling.*

viaduct A bridge, often constructed of a number of short spans, that conveys a road or railway across a valley.

vicinity The local area.

victoria A low, light four-wheeled horse-drawn carriage with a collapsible top.

Victorian Of or relating to the period of English history during the reign of Queen Victoria (1837 to 1901).

video-conference A meeting conducted with the participants in different locations but linked by visual communication via the internet or another communication device.

view That which can be seen from a particular point, usually with the implication that it is attractive.

viewdata Any computerised information and booking service, generally using on-line communication: In the

UK, Prestel was the first widely available system, but it has long-since been replaced by far more sophisticated networks such as the various GDSs.

Viking The Scandinavian seafaring pirates, and later settlers and traders, who were active in Northern Europe between the 8th and 11th centuries.

villa Self catering accommodation, usually in a private, detached house or bungalow. The name originally applied to prestigious houses privately owned and rented to selected guests. Now however, a villa may be in a specially built complex containing many similar properties

village A group of houses and other buildings, larger than a hamlet and smaller than a town.

violent storm *See Beaufort scale.*

VIP Very Important Person. The designation is usually reserved for public figures who might appreciate, require or expect special treatment and additional security. > *CIP.*

Virgin Islands A group of islands in the Leeward Islands in the Caribbean, to the east of Puerto Rico. They are divided politically into the US Virgin Islands (an Unincorporated Territory of the USA) and the British Virgin Islands (a British Overseas Territory).

visa The physical evidence of the granting of permission for travel to or via or out of a country. This generally takes the form of a stamp in a passport, although in some cases (particularly where evidence of travel to or from that country might cause the traveller problems when later trying to enter another country) it is recorded on a piece of paper which can removed from the passport after use. Charges are often made for issuing visas, and the procedure can take a long time. Visas are generally of three types:
• *Entry visa.* This gives the traveller the right to travel to the country, although the right to enter it will be at the discretion of the immigration officials. Entry visas will generally be valid for use within a specified period from the date of issue, and valid for a specified length of visit, or number of visits, from the first date of entry. In some cases there may be restrictions as to the part/s of the country that can be visited or the activities that can be engaged in. Different types of visas may be required depending on the purpose of travel: business travellers, for example, often need to undergo different formalities. The definition of what exactly is meant by business travel will vary from country to country.
• *Transit visa.* This gives the traveller the right to pass through the country for a specified period of time, generally because of the need to change planes. Transit visas generally do not permit the traveller to leave a designated area in the airport.
• *Exit visa.* In rare cases, countries may require travellers to obtain an exit visa before departure,

although this is generally applied to nationals of the country in question where travel restrictions apply.

visibility The greatest distance at which an object can be seen against its background.

Visigoth A member of the branch of the Goths who settled in France and Spain during the 5th century, ruling Spain until the early 8th century.

visit 1. To go to a place for a short period. 2. (US) A chat.

Visit Scotland *See Appendix 5a.*

visiting friends and relatives (VFR) A term used to describe travellers whose main purpose for their journey is to visit friends or relatives who live abroad.

visitor One who is undertaking a visit.

visitor attraction *See attraction.*

visitor's book A register in which visitors to a hotel, an attraction or similar record their names and comments.

vista A long narrow view, especially between trees.

void An endorsement on a ticket that shows that the particular section is not to be used.

volcano A mountain formed through the expulsion of lava from the earth's interior. Volcanoes can be active, that is, still likely to erupt, dormant (inactive) and therefore unlikely to erupt, or extinct and very unlikely to erupt.

voltage The pressure of an electrical supply. In most of Europe the mains supply is delivered at between 220 and 250 volts. In most of the Americas it is delivered at 110 volts. Travellers must take care when using appliances in other countries since poor operation or damage can arise if suitable adjustment or adaptation is not made.

voluntary changes Changes to an itinerary that are made at a passenger's own request.

voucher A document that may be exchanged for services such as meals or accommodation, in the same way that a ticket may be exchanged for travel. The terms 'voucher' and 'ticket' are often used interchangeably.

voyage A journey, especially one by sea.

voyager A person on a voyage.

V-shape seating plan *See herringbone seating plan.*

VTOL *See Vertical Take Off and Landing.*

W w

W pattern A pattern of aircraft operation designed to maximise fare-paying usage and to avoid ferry mileage. For example, an aircraft may take passengers from Gatwick to Palma, pick up passengers there and take them to Cardiff, pick up more passengers there and take them to Palma then pick up a further load and take them back to Gatwick. This type of intensive utilisation is generally more common with short-haul charter operations than it is with long-haul or scheduled services.

wadi A rocky watercourse, usually in Arabia, that is dry for most of the year.

Wagon-Lit A European sleeping car. They are more comfortable than a couchette and usually more expensive.

wait list (or **waiting-list**) A record of potential travellers or customers for a particular service or product that is currently fully booked. Once the waiting list reaches such a length that it is unlikely that all those on it will be accommodated, the principal will refuse to add further names and the waiting list is said to be closed.

waiter 1. (UK) A man employed to serve customers in a restaurant or similar establishment with food, drinks or other requirements.
2. (US) A person of either sex providing waiting services as described above.

waiting room A room provided, especially at a railway or bus station, for passengers waiting for the arrival of their service.

waiting-list *See wait-list.*

waitress (UK) A woman employed to perform the same job as a waiter.

waive To refrain from insisting on or making use of a right or claim. The term is usually used in connection with a legally binding document.

waiver A clause in a contract or agreement by which one or more parties agrees to waive their right to make a specific claim, usually in exchange for some compensation in cash or kind. If, for example, a damage waiver is paid to a car rental company, the company will waive its right to charge if the car suffers damage. > *vehicle rental insurance.*

wake The waves caused by the motion of a ship through water.

Wales One of the constituent countries of the United Kingdom of Great Britain and Northern Ireland. > *Great Britain, United Kingdom.*

walk-in 1. A guest who arrives without having made a reservation.
2. A service not requiring a prior appointment or reservation.
3. A wardrobe or other storage space large enough for a person to enter.

walking tour A holiday on foot, usually of several days.

walk-on (UK) A traveller who purchases a ticket just prior to departure.

walk-out (US) A passage, doorway or other exit that provides outdoor access.

walk-through A building or room that can be entered from either end.

walk-up 1. (US) A floor of a building that can only be reached by stairs, rather than a lift.
2. (US) A traveller who purchases a ticket just prior to departure.

walkway A passage or path, often a raised passageway connecting parts of a building or similar.

wall bed A bed designed to be folded away against the wall when not in use.

Wallace's line A hypothetical boundary between Asia and Oceania, following zoogeographical rather than political divisions. It runs between the Indonesian islands of Bali and Lombock, through the Macassar Strait (between Sulawesi and Borneo) and to the south-east of the Philippines.

wanderlust The desire to travel or explore.

warrant A document, often issued by the military or a government department, that can be exchanged for tickets or other travel documents.

Warsaw Convention An international agreement, ratified in 1928, which limits the liability of airlines for loss or damage to international passengers and their baggage. Its provisions have been considerably modified over the years. In 1999, it was effectively replaced by the Montréal Convention. > *Montréal Convention.*

wash-out A breach in a road or railway track caused by flooding.

washroom (US) A room with washing and lavatory facilities.

wat A Buddhist temple.

WATA World Association Of Travel Agents. *See Appendix 5d.*

watch A period of duty for a seaman, usually four hours.

water bus A boat carrying passengers on a regular service on a river, lake or canal. Usually the journeys will be fairly short.

water closet A lavatory with a means for flushing. Usually abbreviated to WC.

water park A recreational area where the facilities are mainly based on activities involving water.

water taxi A small boat, usually motor-driven, taking passengers on a casual basis. Commonly used in cities such as Venice.

watercourse A stream or artificial channel.

waterfall A stream or river flowing over a precipice. Waterfalls are often spectacular and are therefore significant tourist attractions.

waterfront The area adjacent to water, often a dock or harbour.

watering hole 1. A place at which animals regularly drink. Often a focal point for visitors to game reserves.
2. A colloquial term for a bar or pub.

waterline The point on a ship's hull up to which the water reaches.

waterman A boatman plying for hire.

water-ski A sport whose participants are towed across a stretch of water, usually by a speedboat, with special skis attached to their feet.

waterspout An up-welling of water caused by a tornado.

watertight doors Heavy doors that, when closed, divide a ship into a series of separate compartments. This minimises the risk of sinking following damage to the hull.

waterway Any route used for travel by water, but usually applied to rivers and canals.

watt A measurement of power. In an electrical appliance it will be shown on the data plate. Dividing the power rating of the appliance by the voltage at which it is being operated will give an indication of the current that will be drawn.

wave The undulations in the sea, caused by wind and tides.

wave machine A device for producing waves in a swimming pool.

Way of St James *See Camino de Compostela.*

way station (US) A minor railway station.

waybill A list of passengers or goods on a vehicle.

wayside The edge of a road or other land route.

WC A universal term for a lavatory or toilet.

weather The day to day variations of temperature, rainfall, humidity and other indicators. Unlike climate, which indicates the overall situation of a region, weather can be variable and unpredictable. The UK is an example of a region with a mild and temperate climate but with very unpredictable weather. > *climate.*

web *See internet.*

weddings abroad These have become increasingly popular in recent years. Several companies now specialise in organising such events, and many hotels, resorts and cruise lines worldwide are actively promoting themselves as wedding venues. The formalities required will vary from country to country and these will require attention before departure. The Columbus *World Travel Guide* contains a dedicated section on this subject, including details of necessary documentation and procedures for a selection of popular wedding destinations.

week Officially a period of seven days, nowadays generally regarded to run from midnight at the end of the traditional day of rest: thus in Christian countries, most would agree that the week runs from Monday to Sunday. In travel it usually means a period of seven days from the start of a provided facility. In airline timetables, the days are generally given numeric codes: 1 (Monday) through to 7 (Sunday). 'Dly' indicates that the service operates daily, while an X preceding a number or numbers indicates that it does *not* operate on those days: thus X35 means that the service operates every day except Wednesday and Friday.

weekday A day other than at the weekend.

weekend The days at the end of the normal working week when many businesses are shut. In most of Europe and the USA it falls on Saturday and Sunday:. Moslems observe Fridays, and Jews Saturdays.

WEF (UK) With effect from.

weigh anchor To raise the anchor of a ship prior to sailing.

weir A small dam built across a river to raise its level or regulate its flow.

well-appointed Accommodation having fixtures and fittings to a good and suitable standard.

well-travelled A person who has travelled a great deal and who is, by implication, knowledgeable about travel procedures and terminology.

west One of the four cardinal points of the compass, 90° clockwise from south and 180° from east; on the left of maps where (as is normal) north is at the top. > *north*.

west country The western part of any country, and particularly the area including the counties of Cornwall, Devon and Somerset (and sometimes others) in England.

West Highland Line A spectacular railway journey in Scotland between Glasgow and Mallaig.

West Indies The islands enclosing the Caribbean Sea including the Bahama Islands and the Greater and Lesser Antilles. Also known as The Caribbean.

West, the Generally used to refer to Europe and North America.

Westerlies The winds that blow from mainly west to east, between latitudes 30° and 70°. In the northern hemisphere their prevailing direction is from the south-west; in the southern hemisphere it is from the north-west.

western hemisphere The half of the earth to the west of 0° longitude and to the east of 180° longitude.

Western Mediterranean Terms Yacht charter terms under which the fee includes the charter of the yacht with all equipment; basic consumables for engine-room, deck and cabins; the crew's wages and food; and insurance for the yacht itself, for third party claims and employer's liability insurance for the crew. Other costs, such as fuel, the client's food and drink, berthing charges, laundry and radio telephone and other communication costs, must be paid by the client. These terms may vary.

Western Standard Time One of the time zones used in Australia, eight hours ahead of UTC.

Western States Tourism Policy Council An informal US regional marketing organisation covering many of the western states of the USA. > *US regional marketing organisations*.

wet bar (US) A small area in a hotel room or similar where drinks can be mixed and served.

wet bike *See jet ski*.

wet lease To hire a vehicle, usually a ship, boat or aircraft, with all its crew and supplies.

wet suit A protective rubber suit worn by divers that allows water to enter the suit before being largely retained in place. The layer of water thus formed provides an extra layer of insulation.

wetland A marsh, bog or similar area.

wharf A structure projecting into water to which vessels can be moored.

wherry 1. A light rowing boat. 2. (UK) A large, light barge.

whirlpool A powerful circular eddy in water.

whirlwind A tornado.

whirlybird A colloquial term for a helicopter.

whistle-stop 1. (US) A small, unimportant railway station. 2. A very fast tour or journey with few and brief stops.

Whit Sunday A festival in the Christian religious calendar, celebrated seven weeks after Easter.

white ensign The flag of the British Royal Navy and the Royal Yacht Squadron.

white night A night in extremely high latitudes when it never gets properly dark.

white tie A name given to the very formal mode of evening dress for men that involves the wearing of a tail coat and white bow tie.

white-out A condition, often caused by blizzard conditions, where it is impossible to see anything except white snow in the air and on the ground.

white-water rafting An extreme sport involving taking a raft or similar vessel through a stretch of very rough water such as rapids on a river.

wholesaler An organisation that buys in bulk from a manufacturer to sell to retailers. In travel, this is usually a tour operator.

wide-bodied aircraft An large passenger aircraft with two or more aisles. The Boeing 747 is probably the best known example.

Wild Coast The scenic coastal area between East London and Port Shepstone in South Africa.

Wild West The western USA during its historical period of lawlessness.

wilderness A wild or undeveloped region.

wildlife attraction Any attraction, such as a wildlife park, where animals, birds or other fauna are on view to visitors.

wildlife park A place where exotic animals are kept in a semi-wild state in conditions that allow them to be viewed by visitors, often at close quarters. Sometimes known as a safari park.

WIN Worldwide Independent Travel Network. *See Appendix 5a*.

wind chill The extent to which the speed of the wind reduces the perceived temperature of the air.

wind force The force of the wind as measured by the Beaufort scale. *See Beaufort Scale.*

wind shear A sudden downward rush of air, often experienced in storm conditions. Wind shear has caused several aircraft accidents.

windbound When a sailing vessel is unable to operate because of contrary winds.

windjammer A merchant sailing vessel.

windward On the side from which the wind is blowing.

Windward Islands The group of Caribbean islands including Grenada, Martinique, St Lucia and St Vincent and the Grenadines.

wine bar A bar or small restaurant serving drink and food.

wine waiter A waiter in larger restaurants whose sole responsibility is the provision of the wine and other drinks.

wing 1. One of the projections from the fuselage of an aircraft that create the lift that support it during flight.
2. (UK) The side panels of a car.
3. Any protruding part of a hotel or other large building.

wingspan The measurement across the wings or an aircraft.

Winter Olympics *See Olympic Games.*

winter solstice *See solstice.*

winter sports Sports performed on snow and ice, such as skating, sledging and skiing.

wipe out 1. A colloquial term given by winter sports enthusiasts to a crash or fall from a snowboard or skis.
2. A similar accident from a surfboard.

withdrawal of services insurance A 'loss of enjoyment' insurance cover paid when a pre-arranged service or facility was not provided, regardless of any financial loss. > *travel insurance.*

workday (US) A day on which work is usually done.

working pressure The maximum pressure to which a diving cylinder should be normally charged for everyday use.

World Athletics Championships A major international athletics event, which takes place every four years in a different city on each occasion. Accommodation and transport arrangements may need to be made months, and sometimes years, in advance.

world cup Any of the regular international competitions for national teams in a particular sport, taking place at regular intervals in a different country or countries on each occasion. Many sports now organise a world cup; the three most important are cricket (generally every four years since 1975), rugby union (every four years since 1987) and, largest of all, football (1930, 1934, 1938 and every four years since 1950). Accommodation and transport arrangements may need to be made months, and sometimes years, in advance.

World Heritage Site *See UNESCO World Heritage Site.*

World Tourism Organization *See WTO.*

World Travel Market One of the most important travel exhibitions in the world, held in London, in November each year. Attendance is generally restricted to persons connected with the travel industry.

Worldspan A GDS sponsored by Delta and other airlines.

Worldwide Fund for Nature One of the world's largest private nature conservation organisations. Its aim is to conserve the natural environment by preserving species and ecosystem diversity. Formerly known as the World Wildlife Fund.

world-wide web *See internet.*

WP *See working pressure.*

WP Word processor.

wreck *See shipwreck.*

write out To issue a document manually.

WTB Wales Tourist Board. *See Appendix 5a.*

WTM *See World Travel Market.*

WTO World Tourism Organisation. *See Appendix 5d.*

WTO World Tourism Organization. The WTO describes itself as: 'The World Tourism Organization (WTO/OMT), a specialized agency of the United Nations, is the leading international organization in the field of tourism. It serves as a global forum for tourism policy issues and practical source of tourism know-how. With its headquarters in Madrid, Spain, the WTO plays a central and decisive role in promoting the development of responsible, sustainable and universally accessible tourism, with the aim of contributing to economic development, international understanding, peace, prosperity and universal respect for, and observance of, human rights and fundamental freedoms. In pursuing this aim, the Organization pays particular attention to the interests of developing countries in the field of tourism. The WTO plays a catalytic role in promoting technology transfers and international cooperation, in stimulating and developing public-private sector partnerships and in encouraging the implementation of the Global Code of Ethics for Tourism, with a view to ensuring that member countries, tourist destinations and businesses maximize the positive economic, social and cultural effects of tourism and fully reap its benefits, while minimizing its negative social and environmental impacts. In 2005, the WTO's membership is comprised of 145 countries, seven territories and more than 300 Affiliate Members representing the private sector, educational institutions, tourism associations and local tourism authorities.' The WTO is the source of the most comprehensive and authoritative statistics on global travel and tourism. *See Appendix 5d.*

WTO Regional Promotional Projects Specialised initiatives organised by the WTO to promote tourism to a group of member countries. The Silk Road and the Slave Route are currently two of these.

WWF *See Worldwide Fund for Nature.*

X x

x Conventionally used to indicate an unknown quantity, price, time or other numeric variable.

x axis The horizontal axis of a chart or graph.

Xanadu A place of unattainable splendour and luxury.

xebec A small, three-masted Mediterranean sailing vessel.

xenophile A person who likes foreign things or people.

xenophillia The state of liking foreign things or people.

xenophobe A person who fears or distrusts foreign things or people.

xenophobia The fear or distrust of foreign things or people.

xeric Characterised by dry climate.

Xmas A commonly used abbreviation for Christmas.

x-rays Short-wave radiation that can pass through many solid materials. X-rays are sometimes used for baggage screening at airports and other sensitive places. Since they can affect photographic film, travellers should ask for their baggage to be hand-searched if they are concerned as to the impact of the screening equipment.

Y y

y axis The vertical axis of a chart or graph.

yacht 1. A small sailing vessel used for pleasure.
2. A large and generally luxurious motor vessel.

yard 1. A unit of measurement in the imperial system equal to three feet (0.9144m).
2. A spar slung across a mast to hold a sail.
3. (UK) Any piece of uncultivated land around a commercial or domestic property.
4. (US) Any piece of land around a commercial or domestic property, regardless of whether it is cultivated or not.

yaw The failure of a ship or aircraft to hold a straight course; veering from side to side.

yawl A two-masted sailing vessel.

yellow fever A tropical disease caused by a virus, and difficult to cure. Travellers should ensure that they are vaccinated before visiting endemic zones (Central Africa and the northern part of South America). Certificates of vaccination may be required when travelling to or from countries in these areas. > *health precautions*.

yellow flag A flag displayed by a vessel in quarantine.

Yellow Sea The area of the Pacific Ocean between China and Korea.

Yemen A country in the Arabian peninsula, officially the Republic of Yemen. Between 1970 and 1990, it was divided between the Republic of Yemen (North Yemen) and the People's Democratic Republic of Yemen (South Yemen).

Yeti A large, ape-like creature reputedly living in the Himalayas.

yield A term covering various ways of expressing the financial gain from specified activities, including the percentage return on a total amount invested, the profit derived per item sold, or the income resulting from the allocation of seats and accommodation to different market sectors. Different organisations will often have different ways of calculating this. Airlines, for example, may refer to yield in terms of operating revenue per kilometre , a figure which will vary depending on measurable factors such as the revenue from the ticket sales, operating costs and distance flown.

yield management The control of the way in which space is used on aircraft and other means of transport. Typically a carrier will adjust the ratio of accommodation available at various rates so as to maximise the load factor and revenue of a service.

yogwan A traditional Korean inn.

Yom Kippur A festival in the Jewish religious calendar, celebrated ten days after Rosh Hashanah.

youth A young person, generally aged between the early teens and early twenties.

youth fare A fare offered to people up to the age of approximately 25 years.

youth hostel An inexpensive form of accommodation originally restricted to young people. Most youth hostels will now accept travellers of any age.

Yugoslavia The name by which two former Balkan states were commonly known. The first of these, the Federal People's Republic of Yugoslavia, was established after the Second World War and dissolved in the early 1990s and comprised the modern-day states of Bosnia-Herzegovina, Croatia, Slovenia, Macedonia, Serbia and Montenegro. Subsequently the Federal Republic of Yugoslavia, comprising Serbia and Montenegro, was briefly established. This country changed its name to the Republic of Serbia & Montenegro in March 2003.

Z z

Zaire The former name for the African country now called the Democratic Republic of Congo.

zawn (UK) A deep and narrow fold or inlet in a sea cliff.

zebra crossing (UK) A pedestrian crossing, marked on the road with black and white stripes and often on the kerb with flashing orange lights. Once on the crossing, the pedestrian has right of way. Crossings in other countries that look similar to this will not necessarily give the pedestrian right of way, but may merely indicate that this is a place where they are permitted to cross the road.

zenith The highest point, often used to describe a period of prosperity.

zephyr A soft, gentle breeze.

Zeppelin A German manufacturer of airships, whose name is still sometimes used as a generic term for this type of aircraft.

zero emission vehicle A vehicle that produces no emissions at the point of operation. At present the only successful ZEVs are electrically or cable operated.

ZEV *See zero emission vehicle.*

ziggurat A tiered temple used by the ancient Babylonians and Assyrians.

zip code (US) The mail sorting code appearing at the end of the address.

zócalo A Mexican term for the main square and focal point of a town.

zone An area or region having particular properties that make it special or identifiable.

zoo (or **zoological garden, zoological park**) A place where visitors can see animals in captivity, often as well as other attractions. Many zoos are now finding a new role in the conservation and preservation of endangered species.

zoogeographical Of or relating to the study of animals according to their geographical distribution.

zorbing An extreme sport invented in New Zealand in 1996 that involves being strapped into a large plastic ball that is then rolled down a steep hill.

Appendix 1

Countries

The chart below gives a selection of information for every country in the world.

The matter of deciding what is and what is not a country is by no means clear-cut, but no political or other subjective stance has been adopted. Some of the places listed below are not truly independent, but have been included separately because they are generally regarded as being separate travel destinations. In general, figures for places that are fully integrated into another state – such as Hawaii (USA), the Balearic and Canary Islands (Spain) and the Azores and Madeira (Portugal) – have been included in those for the main country. For more information on countries worldwide, consult the most recent editions of the Columbus World Travel Guide or World Travel Atlas. The latter title provides a more detailed version of this chart, and includes a range of economic indicators and travel statistics as well as world rankings for each category.

The **country** names are rarely the full official title. Some have been shortened for reasons of space. The **region** for each entry does not follow any official divisions, but is merely a guide for locating the country on a map. For a few countries, the matter of what is the **capital** causes some confusion: these will be referred to in the notes below the chart. **Area** figures ('000 sq km) relate to land area and disregard major lakes. **Population** figures ('000) are 2005 estimates from the CIA World Factbook. **Population density (P.D.)** is population divided by area, and is rounded to the nearest whole number for figures above 10, to one decimal point for figures under 9.5 and to two decimal points for figures under 1. Under **nationality** the chart lists the term that is most commonly used to describe the country or its citizens. In many cases this can be used as an adjective ('a French resort') and as a noun ('the French'). Only one such word as been listed per country. In many cases, others also exist: these include spelling variations, local expressions, slang, feminine and plural forms, and separate terms for the place and for the people. A few terms describing the smaller parts of federal countries have been provided in the footnotes. Where no term is given, this is because research has failed to discover a commonly accepted one. Finally, the **main language/s** spoken have been listed. In addition to these, many countries have many other widely-spoken languages and dialects; sometimes over a hundred.

Country	Region	Capital	Area	Pop.	P.D.	Nationality	Main language/s
Afghanistan	Asia W	Kabul	652.1	29,929	46	Afghan	Dari, Pashtó
Albania	Europe E	Tirana	28.7	3,563	124	Albanian	Albanian, Greek
Algeria	Africa N	Algiers	2,381.70	32,532	14	Algerian	Arabic, French
American Samoa	Pacific E	Pago Pago	0.2	58	289	Samoan	Samoan, English
Andorra	Europe W	Andorra la Vella	0.45	71	157	Andorran	Catalan, French, Spanish
Angola	Africa S	Luanda	1,246.70	11,827	9.5	Angolan	Portuguese
Anguilla	Caribbean	The Valley	0.16	13	83	Anguillan	English
Antigua & Barbuda	Caribbean	St John's	0.44	69	156	Antiguan (12)	English
Argentina	America S	Buenos Aires	2,780.40	39,538	14	Argentine	Spanish

Country	Region	Capital	Area	Pop.	P.D.	Nationality	Main language/s
Armenia	Asia W	Yerevan	29.8	2,983	100	Armenian	Armenian, Russian
Aruba	Caribbean	Oranjestad	0.18	72	398	Aruban	Dutch, Papiamento, English, Spanish
Australia	Australasia	Canberra	7,682.30	20,090	2.6	Australian	English
Austria	Europe W	Vienna	83.9	8,185	98	Austrian	German
Azerbaijan	Asia W	Baku	86.6	7,912	91	Azerbajani	Azerbajani, Russian
Bahamas	Caribbean	Nassau	13.9	302	22	Bahamanian	English
Bahrain	Asia W	Manama	0.71	688	970	Bahraini	Arabic, English
Bangladesh	Asia S	Dhaka	148.4	144,320	973	Bangladeshi	Bengali
Barbados	Caribbean	Bridgetown	0.43	279	649	Barbadian	English
Belarus	Europe E	Minsk	207.6	10,300	50	Belorussian	Russian, Belorussian
Belgium	Europe W	Brussels	30.5	10,364	340	Belgian	Flemish, French
Belize	America C	Belmopan	23	281	12	Belizian	English, Spanish
Benin	Africa W	Porto Novo	112.6	7,649	68	Beninese	French
Bermuda	Atlantic N	Hamilton	0.05	65	1,307	Bermudan	English
Bhutan	Asia S	Thimphu	46.5	2,232	48	Bhutanese	Dzongkha
Bolivia	America S	(1)	1,098.60	8,858	8.1	Bolivian	Spanish
Bosnia–Herzegovina	Europe E	Sarajevo	51.1	4,430	87	Bosnian	Serbo-Croat and Croato-Serb
Botswana	Africa S	Gaborone	581.7	1,640	2.8	Tswana	English, Setswana
Brazil	America S	Brasilia	8,547.40	186,113	22	Brazilian	Portuguese
British Virgin Is.	Caribbean	Road Town	0.13	23	174	Virgin Islander	English
Brunei	Asia SE	Bandar Seri Begawan		5.8	372	64	Bruneian Malay, English
Bulgaria	Europe E	Sofia	111	7,450	67	Bulgarian	Bulgarian
Burkina	Africa W	Ouagadougou	274.1	13,492	49	Burkinese	French, Moré, Dioula, Peulh
Burundi	Africa E	Bujumbura	27.8	7,795	280	Burundian	Kirundi, French
Cambodia	Asia SE	Phnom Penh	181	13,636	75	Cambodian	Khmer, Chinese, Vietnamese
Cameroon	Africa W	Yaoundé	475.4	16,988	36	Cameroonian	French, English
Canada	America N	Ottawa	9,970.60	32,805	3.3	Canadian	English, French, Inuktitut
Cape Verde	Atlantic E	Praia	4	418	105	Cape Verdean	Portuguese, Creole, English
Cayman Is.	Caribbean	George Town	0.26	44	170	Cayman Islander	English
Central African Rep.	Africa C	Bangui	622.4	4,238	6.8		French, Sangho
Chad	Africa C	Ndjaména	1,284.00	9,657	7.5	Chadian	Arabic, French, Sara
Channel Is.	Europe W	(2)	0.2	156	780	Channel Islander	English, Norman-French dialect

Country	Region	Capital	Area	Pop.	P.D.	Nationality	Main language/s
Chile	America S	Santiago	736.9	15,981	22	Chilean	Spanish
China	Asia E	Beijing	9,536.70	1,306,314	137	Chinese	Mandarin, Cantonese
China: Hong Kong	Asia E	-	1.1	6,899	6,272		Cantonese, English
China: Macau	Asia E	-	0.02	449	22,460	Macanese	Cantonese, Portuguese
Colombia	America S	Bogotá	1,141.70	42,954	38	Colombian	Spanish
Comoros	Indian Ocean	Moroni	1.9	671	353	Comoran	French, Arabic
Congo, Rep.	Africa W	Brazzaville	341.8	3,602	11	Congolese	French, Lingala, Kilcongo
Congo, Dem. Rep.	Africa C	Kinshasa	2,344.90	60,764	26	Congolese	French, Lingala, Kilcongo
Cook Is.	Pacific E	Avarua	0.23	21	93	Cook Islander	Cook Islands Maori, English
Costa Rica	America C	San José	51.1	4,016	79	Costa Rican	Spanish
Côte d'Ivoire	Africa W	(3)	320.8	17,298	54	Ivorian	French
Croatia	Europe E	Zagreb	56.5	4,496	80	Croatian	Croatian (Croato-Serb)
Cuba	Caribbean	Havana	110.9	11,347	102	Cuban	Spanish
Cyprus	Europe E	Nicosia	9.3	780	84	Cypriot	Greek, Turkish, English
Czech Rep.	Europe E	Prague	78.9	10,241	130	Czech	Czech
Denmark	Europe N	Copenhagen	43.1	5,432	126	Dane	Danish, English
Djibouti	Africa E	Djibouti	23.2	477	21	Djiboutian	Arabic, French, Afar, Somali
Dominica	Caribbean	Roseau	0.75	69	92	Dominican	English, Creole
Dominican Rep.	Caribbean	Santo Domingo	48.4	9,050	187	Dominican	Spanish
East Timor	Asia SE	Dili	14.6	1,041	71	Timorese	Tetum, Portuguese, English
Ecuador	America S	Quito	275.8	13,364	48	Ecuadorian	Spanish
Egypt	Africa N	Cairo	997.7	77,506	78	Egyptian	Arabic, English, French
El Salvador	America C	San Salvador	21	6,705	319	Salvadorean	Spanish
Equatorial Guinea	Africa W	Malabo	28.1	529	19	Guinean	Spanish, Fang, Bubi
Eritrea	Africa E	Asmara	93.7	4,670	50	Eritrean	Arabic, Tigrinya, Italian
Estonia	Europe E	Tallinn	45.2	1,333	29	Estonian	Estonian, Russian, English
Ethiopia	Africa E	Addis Ababa	1,104.30	73,053	66	Ethiopean	Amharic, English
Falkland Is.	Atlantic S	Stanley	12.2	3	0.24	Falkland Islander	English
Faroe Is.	Europe N	Tórshavn	1.4	47	34	Faroese	Danish
Fiji Is.	Pacific W	Suva	18.3	893	49	Fijian	Fijian, Hindi
Finland	Europe N	Helsinki	338.1	5,223	15	Finn	Finish, English
France	Europe W	Paris	549.1	60,656	110	French	French
French Guiana	America S	Cayenne	85.5	196	2.3	Guianese	French, Creole
French Polynesia	Pacific E	Papeete	4.2	270	64	Tahitian	Tahitian, French

Country	Region	Capital	Area	Pop.	P.D.	Nationality	Main language/s
Gabon	Africa W	Libreville	267.7	1,394	5.2	Gabonese	French, Fang
Gambia, The	Africa W	Banjul	10.7	1,595	149	Gambian	English
Georgia	Asia W	Tbilisi	69.7	4,677	67	Georgian	Georgian, Russian
Germany	Europe W	Berlin	357	82,431	231	German	German
Ghana	Africa W	Accra	238.5	21,946	92	Ghanaian	English
Gibraltar	Europe W	Gibraltar	0.006	28	4,647	Gibraltarian	English, Spanish
Greece	Europe E	Athens	132	10,668	81	Greek	Greek
Greenland	Atlantic N	Nuuk	2,166.10	56	0.03	Greenlander	Greenlandic, Inuit, Danish
Grenada	Caribbean	St George's	0.34	90	263	Grenadian	English
Guadeloupe	Caribbean	(4)	1.7	449	264	Guadeloupian	French, Creole
Guam	Pacific W	Agaña	0.54	169	312	Guamanian	English, Chamorro
Guatemala	America C	Guatemala City	108.9	12,014	110	Guatemalan	Spanish
Guinea	Africa W	Conakry	245.9	9,453	38	Guinean	French, Susu, Malinké, Fula
Guinea–Bissau	Africa W	Bissau	36.1	1,413	39	Guinean	Portuguese, Guinean Creole
Guyana	America S	Georgetown	215	765	3.6	Guyanese	English
Haiti	Caribbean	Port-au-Prince	27.8	8,122	292	Haitian	French, Creole
Honduras	America C	Tegucigalpa	112.1	7,168	64	Honduran	Spanish, English
Hungary	Europe E	Budapest	93	10,007	108	Hungarian	Hungarian
Iceland	Europe N	Reykjavik	103	297	2.9	Icelander	Icelandic, Danish, English
India	Asia S	New Delhi	3,065.00	1,080,264	352	Indian	English plus 14 other official languages
Indonesia	Asia SE	Jakarta	1,919.40	241,974	126	Indonesian	Bahasa Indonesian (Malay)
Iran	Asia W	Tehran	1,648.00	68,018	41	Iranian	Persian (Farsi), Arabic
Iraq	Asia W	Baghdad	438.3	26,075	59	Iraqi	Arabic, Kurdish
Ireland	Europe W	Dublin	70.3	4,016	57	Irish	English, Gaelic
Israel	Asia W	Jerusalem	21.9	6,277	287	Israeli	Hebrew, Arabic, English
Italy	Europe W	Rome	301.3	58,103	193	Italian	Italian
Jamaica	Caribbean	Kingston	11.4	2,736	240	Jamaican	English
Japan	Asia E	Tokyo	377.8	127,417	337	Japanese	Japanese
Jordan	Asia W	Amman	91.9	5,760	63	Jordanian	Arabic, English
Kazakstan	Asia C	(5)	2,717.30	15,186	5.6	Kazakh	Kazakh
Kenya	Africa E	Nairobi	582.6	33,830	58	Kenyan	Kiswahili, English
Kiribati	Pacific E	Bairiki	0.72	103	143	Kiriwinian	Kiribati, English
Korea, DPR (North)	Asia E	Pyongyang	122.8	22,912	187	Korean	Korean

Country	Region	Capital	Area	Pop.	P.D.	Nationality	Main language/s
Korea, Rep. (South)	Asia E	Seoul	99.4	48,641	489	Korean	Korean
Kuwait	Asia W	Kuwait City	17.8	2,336	131	Kuwaiti	Arabic, English
Kyrgyzstan	Asia C	Bishkek	199.9	5,146	26	Kyrgyz	Kyrgyz, Russian
Laos	Asia SE	Vientiane	236.8	6,217	26	Laotian	Lao, French, Vietnamese
Latvia	Europe E	Riga	64.6	2,290	35	Latvian	Latvian, Russian
Lebanon	Asia W	Beirut	10.5	3,826	364	Lebanese	Arabic, French, English
Lesotho	Africa S	Maseru	30.4	2,031	67	Mosotho	Sesotho, English
Liberia	Africa W	Monrovia	99.1	2,900	29	Liberian	English, Bassa, Kpelle, Kru
Libya	Africa N	Tripoli	1,775.50	5,766	3.2	Libyan	Arabic
Liechtenstein	Europe W	Vaduz	0.16	34	211	Liechtensteiner	German, Alemmanish
Lithuania	Europe E	Vilnius	65.3	3,597	55	Lithuanian	Lithuanian, Russian
Luxembourg	Europe W	Luxembourg	2.6	469	180	Luxembourger	French, German, Letzeburgesch
Macedonia, FYR	Europe E	Skopje	25.7	2,045	80	Macedonian	Macedonian
Madagascar	Indian Ocean	Antananarivo	587	18,040	31	Madagascan	Malagasy, French
Malawi	Africa S	Lilongwe	118.5	12,707	107	Malawian	English, Chichewa
Malaysia	Asia SE	Kuala Lumpur	329.8	23,953	73	Malaysian	Bahasa Malay
Maldives	Indian Ocean	Malé	0.3	349	1,164	Maldivian	Dhiveli
Mali	Africa W	Bamako	1,248.60	11,415	9.1	Malian	French
Malta	Europe W	Valletta	0.32	399	1,245	Maltese	Maltese, English
Marshall Is.	Pacific W	Majuro	0.18	59	328	Marshall Islander	English
Martinique	Caribbean	Fort-de-France	1.1	433	394	Martiniquan	French, Creole
Mauritania	Africa W	Nouakchott	1,030.70	3,087	3.0	Mauritanian	Arabic, French
Mauritius	Indian Ocean	Port Louis	2	1,231	615	Mauritian	English, Creole, Hindi, Bojpuri
Mayotte	Indian Ocean	Dzaoudzi	0.37	194	523		Mahorian, French
Mexico	America N	Mexico City	1,967.20	106,203	54	Mexican	Spanish, English
Micronesia, Fed. States	Pacific W	Palikir	0.7	108	154	Micronesian	English, Micronesian languages
Moldova	Europe E	Chisinău	33.7	4,455	132	Moldavian	Moldavian (Romanian), Russian
Monaco	Europe W	Monaco-Ville	0.002	32	16,205	Monégasque	French, Monégasque
Mongolia	Asia E	Ulan Bator	1,565.00	2,791	1.8	Mongolian	Mongolian Khalkha
Montserrat	Caribbean	Plymouth (6)	0.1	9	93	Montserratian	English
Morocco	Africa N	Rabat	458.7	32,726	71	Moroccan	Arabic, Berber, French
Mozambique	Africa S	Maputo	799.4	19,407	24	Mozambican	Portuguese

Country	Region	Capital	Area	Pop.	P.D.	Nationality	Main language/s
Myanmar	Asia SE	Yangon (7)	676.6	46,997	69	Burmese	Burmese
Namibia	Africa S	Windhoek	824.3	2,031	2.5	Namibian	English
Nauru	Pacific W	Yaren District	0.02	13	652	Nauruan	Nauruan, English
Nepal	Asia S	Kathmandu	140.8	27,677	197	Nepalese	Nepali, Maithir, Bhojpuri
Netherlands	Europe W	Amsterdam (8)	41.5	16,407	395	Dutch	Dutch
Netherlands Antilles	Caribbean	Willemstad	0.8	220	275		Dutch, Papiamento
New Caledonia	Pacific W	Nouméa	18.6	216	12	New Caledonian	French, Polynesian, Melanesian
New Zealand	Australasia	Wellington	270.5	4,035	15	New Zealander	English, Maori
Nicaragua	America C	Managua	130.7	5,465	42	Nicaraguan	Spanish
Niger	Africa C	Niamey	1,186.40	12,163	10	Nigerian	French, Hausa
Nigeria	Africa W	Abuja (9)	923.8	128,766	139	Nigerian	English
Niue	Pacific E	Alofi	0.26	2	8.3	Niuean	Niuean, English
Northern Mariana Is.	Pacific W	Saipan	0.46	80	175		English, Chamorro, Carolinian, Japanese
Norway	Europe N	Oslo	323.8	4,593	14	Norwegian	Norwegian, Lappish
Oman	Asia W	Muscat	309.5	3,002	9.7	Omani	Arabic, English
Pakistan	Asia S	Islamabad	796.1	162,420	204	Pakistani	Urdu, English
Palau	Pacific W	Koror	0.51	20	40	Palauan	Palauan, English
Palestine NAR	Asia W	Jerusalem (9)	6.2	3,762	607	Palestinian	Arabic
Panama	America C	Panama City	75.5	3,140	42	Panamanian	Spanish, English
Papua New Guinea	Australasia	Port Moresby	462.8	5,545	12	Papuan	English, Pidgin English, Hiri Motu
Paraguay	America S	Asunción	406.8	6,348	16	Paraguayan	Spanish, Guaraní
Peru	America S	Lima	1,285.20	27,926	22	Peruvian	Spanish, Quechua
Philippines	Asia SE	Manila	300	87,857	293	Filipino	Filipino (Tagalog), English
Poland	Europe E	Warsaw	312.7	38,558	123	Pole	Polish
Portugal	Europe W	Lisbon	91.9	10,566	115	Portuguese	Portuguese
Puerto Rico	Caribbean	San Juan	8.9	3,911	439	Puerto Rican	Spanish, English
Qatar	Asia W	Doha	11.4	863	76	Qatari	Arabic
Réunion	Indian Ocean	Saint-Denis	2.5	777	311		French, Creole
Romania	Europe E	Bucharest	236.4	22,330	94	Romanian	Romanian
Russian Federation	Europe E	Moscow	17,075.40	143,420	8.4	Russian	Russian
Rwanda	Africa S	Kigali	26.3	8,441	321	Rwandan	Kinyardwanda, French, Kiswahili

Country	Region	Capital	Area	Pop.	P.D.	Nationality	Main language/s
St Helena	Atlantic S	Jamestown	0.12	7	62	St Helenian	English
St Kitts & Nevis	Caribbean	Basseterre	0.26	39	150	Kittitian (13)	English
St Lucia	Caribbean	Castries	0.62	166	268	St. Lucian	English, French patois
St Pierre et Miquelon	America N	St Pierre	0.24	7	29		French, English
St Vincent & the Gren.	Caribbean	Kingstown	0.39	118	301	Vincentian	English
Samoa	Pacific E	Apia	2.8	177	63	Samoan	Samoan, English
San Marino	Europe W	San Marino	0.06	29	481	San Marinese	Italian
São Tomé e Príncipe	Atlantic E	São Tomé	1	187	187	São Tomean	Portuguese, Fôrro, Agolares
Saudi Arabia	Asia W	Riyadh	2,200.00	26,418	12	Saudi	Arabic
Senegal	Africa W	Dakar	196.2	11,706	60	Senegalese	French, Wolof
Serbia & Montenegro	Europe E	Belgrade	102.2	10,829	106	Serbian (14)	Serbo-Croat
Seychelles	Indian Ocean	Victoria	0.46	81	176	Seychellois	Creole, English, French
Sierra Leone	Africa W	Freetown	73.3	5,867	80	Sierra Leonean	French, Krio
Singapore	Asia SE	Singapore	0.65	4,426	6,809	Singaporean	Mandarin, English, Malay, Tamil
Slovak Rep.	Europe E	Bratislava	49	5,431	111	Slovakian	Slovak
Slovenia	Europe E	Ljubljana	20.3	2,011	99	Slovenian	Slovene
Solomon Is.	Pacific W	Honiara	28.4	538	19	Solomon Islander	English, Pidgin English
Somalia	Africa E	Mogadishu	637.7	8,592	13	Somali	Somali, Arabic
South Africa	Africa S	(10)	1,224.70	44,344	36	South African	English, Afrikaans
Spain	Europe W	Madrid	504.8	40,341	80	Spaniard	Spanish, Catalan, Galician, Basque
Sri Lanka	Asia S	(11)	65.6	20,065	306	Sri Lankan	Sinhala, Tamil, English
Sudan	Africa N	Khartoum	2,505.80	40,187	16	Sudanese	Arabic
Surinam	America S	Paramaribo	163.8	438	2.7	Surinamese	Dutch, Sranan Tongo (Creole)
Swaziland	Africa S	Mbabane	17.4	1,138	65	Swazi	English, Siswati
Sweden	Europe N	Stockholm	450	9,002	20	Swede	Swedish, Lapp, English
Switzerland	Europe W	Bern	41.1	7,489	182	Swiss	German, French, Italian
Syria	Asia W	Damascus	185.2	18,449	100	Syrian	Arabic, French, English
Taiwan	Asia E	Taipei	36.2	22,894	632	Taiwanese	Mandarin
Tajikistan	Asia C	Dushanbe	143.1	7,164	50	Tajik	Tajik, Russian
Tanzania	Africa S	Dodoma	945	36,766	39	Tanzanian	Swahili, English
Thailand	Asia SE	Bangkok	513.1	64,186	125	Thai	Thai, English, Malay, Chinese (Tachew)
Togo	Africa W	Lomé	56.8	5,400	95	Togolese	French, Ewe, Watchi, Kabiyé

Country	Region	Capital	Area	Pop.	P.D.	Nationality	Main language/s
Tonga	Pacific W	Nuku'alofa	0.75	112	150	Tongan	Tongan, English
Trinidad & Tobago	Caribbean	Port of Spain	5.1	1,075	211	Trinidadian (15)	English
Tunisia	Africa N	Tunis	154.5	10,075	65	Tunisian	Arabic, French
Turkey	Asia W	Ankara	779.5	69,661	89	Turk	Turkish
Turkmenistan	Asia C	Ashgabat	488.1	4,952	10	Turkoman	Turkmen
Turks & Caicos Is.	Caribbean	Cockburn Town	0.5	21	41	Turks & Caicos Islander	English
Tuvalu	Pacific W	Funafuti	0.02	12	582	Tuvaluan	Tuvaluan, English
Uganda	Africa E	Kampala	241	27,269	113	Ugandan	English, Luganda, Kiswahili
Ukraine	Europe E	Kyyiv (Kiev)	603.7	46,997	78	Ukrainian	Ukrainian
United Arab Emirates	Asia W	Abu Dhabi	83.7	2,563	31		Arabic
United Kingdom	Europe W	London	243.5	60,441	248	British	English
United States	America N	Washington DC	9,372.60	295,734	32	American	English, Spanish
US Virgin Is.	Caribbean	Charlotte Amalie	0.35	109	311	Virgin Islander	English, Spanish, Creole
Uruguay	America S	Montevideo	176.2	3,416	19	Uruguayan	Spanish
Uzbekistan	Asia C	Tashkent	447.4	26,851	60	Uzbek	Uzbek
Vanuatu	Pacific W	Port Vila	12.2	206	17	Vanuatuan	Bislama (Pidgin English)
Venezuela	America S	Caracas	916.5	25,375	28	Venezuelan	Spanish
Vietnam	Asia SE	Hanoi	331.7	83,536	252	Vietnamese	Vietnamese, English, French
Wallis & Futuna	Pacific W	Matu Utu	0.24	16	67		French
Western Sahara	Africa N	al-Aioun	252.1	273	1.1	Sahrawi	Arabic
Yemen	Asia W	San'a	555	20,727	37	Yemeni	Arabic
Zambia	Africa S	Lusaka	752.6	11,262	15	Zambian	English
Zimbabwe	Africa S	Harare	390.7	12,161	31	Zimbabwean	English, Shona, Ndebele

Notes:

1 Bolivia – La Paz (seat of government); Sucre (judicial).

2 Channel Islands – St Peter Port (Guernsey); St Helier (Jersey).

3 Côte d'Ivoire – Yamassoukro (official); Abidjan (administrative & commercial).

4 Guadeloupe – Basse-Terre (administrative); Pointe-à-Pitre (commercial).

5 Kazakstan – Astana (Almaty until December 1998).

6 Montserrat – Plymouth was largely destroyed in 1997 by volcanic eruption. A temporary administrative centre has been established at Brades.

7 Myanmar – Formerly called Rangoon.

8 Netherlands – Amsterdam (capital); The Hague (seat of government).

9 Palestine NAR – Jerusalem, as declared by Palestinian Authority.

10 South Africa – Pretoria (administrative), Cape Town (legislative), Bloemfontein (judicial). This arrangement is currently under review.

11 Sri Lanka – Colombo (administrative & commercial); Sri Jayewardenepura Kotte (legislative).

12 Barbuda – Barbudan.

13 Nevis – Nevissian.

14 Montenegro – Montenegrin.

15 Tobago – Tobagan.

Appendix 2

US States

ISO* Abbr.	State	Nickname	Date of admission to the Union	State Capital
AL	Alabama	Heart of Dixie	14th Dec 1819	Montgomery
AK	Alaska	The Last Frontier	3rd Jan 1959	Juneau
AZ	Arizona	Grand Canyon State	14th Feb 1912	Phoenix
AR	Arkansas	The Natural State	15th June 1836	Little Rock
CA	California	Golden State	9th Sept 1850	Sacramento
CO	Colorado	Centennial State	1st Aug 1876	Denver
CT	Connecticut	Constitution State	9th Jan 1788 †	Hartford
DE	Delaware	First State/Diamond State	7th Dec 1787 †	Dover
DC	District of Columbia	– *Federal District, coextensive with the city of Washington*		
FL	Florida	Sunshine State	3rd Mar 1845	Tallahassee
GA	Georgia	Empire State of the South/Peach State	2nd Jan 1788 †	Atlanta
HI	Hawaii	Aloha State	21st Aug 1959	Honolulu
ID	Idaho	Gem State	3rd July 1890	Boise
IL	Illinois	Land of Lincoln	3rd Dec 1818	Springfield
IN	Indiana	Hoosier State	11th Dec 1816	Indianapolis
IA	Iowa	Hawkeye State	28th Dec 1846	Des Moines
KS	Kansas	Sunflower State	29th Jan 1861	Topeka
KY	Kentucky	Bluegrass State	1st June 1792	Frankfort
LA	Louisiana	Pelican State	30th Apr 1812	Baton Rouge
ME	Maine	Pine Tree State	15th Mar 1820	Augusta
MD	Maryland	Old Line State	28th Apr 1788 †	Annapolis
MA	Massachusetts	Bay State	6th Feb 1788 †	Boston
MI	Michigan	Great Lakes State	26th Jan 1837	Lansing
MN	Minnesota	Gopher State/North Star State	11th May 1858	St Paul
MS	Mississippi	Magnolia State	10th Dec 1817	Jackson
MO	Missouri	Show Me State	10th Aug 1821	Jefferson City
MT	Montana	Treasure State	8th Nov 1889	Helena
NE	Nebraska	Cornhusker State	1st Mar 1867	Lincoln
NV	Nevada	Silver State	31st Oct 1864	Carson City
NH	New Hampshire	Granite State	21st June 1788 †	Concord
NJ	New Jersey	Garden State	18th Dec 1787 †	Trenton
NM	New Mexico	Land of Enchantment	6th Jan 1912	Santa Fe
NY	New York	Empire State	26th July 1788 †	Albany
NC	North Carolina	Tar Heel State	21st Nov 1789 †	Raleigh
ND	North Dakota	Flickertail State/Peace Garden State	2nd Nov 1889	Bismarck
OH	Ohio	Buckeye State	1st Mar 1803	Columbus
OK	Oklahoma	Sooner State	16th Nov 1907	Oklahoma City
OR	Oregon	Beaver State	14th Feb 1859	Salem
PA	Pennsylvania	Keystone State	12th Dec 1787 †	Harrisburg
RI	Rhode Island	Ocean State	29th May 1790 †	Providence
SC	South Carolina	Palmetto State	23rd May 1788 †	Columbia
SD	South Dakota	Mount Rushmore State	2nd Nov 1889	Pierre
TN	Tennessee	Volunteer State	1st June 1796	Nashville
TX	Texas	Lone Star State	29th Dec 1845	Austin
UT	Utah	Beehive State	4th Jan 1896	Salt Lake City
VT	Vermont	Green Mountain State	4th Mar 1791	Montpelier
VA	Virginia	Old Dominion State	25th June 1788 †	Richmond
WA	Washington	Evergreen State	11th Nov 1889	Olympia
WV	West Virginia	Mountain State	20th June 1863	Charleston
WI	Wisconsin	Badger State	29th May 1848	Madison
WY	Wyoming	Cowboy State/Equality State	10th July 1890	Cheyenne

* *International Organisation for Standardisation.*
† *Original 13 states: date of ratification of the Constitution.*

Appendix 3

Canadian Provinces and Territories

ISO Abbr.	State	Language*	Date of admission to the Dominion	State Capital
AL	Alberta	English	1st Sept 1905	Edmonton
BC	British Columbia	English	20th July 1871	Victoria
MN	Manitoba	English	15th July 1870	Winnipeg
NB	New Brunswick	English †	1st July 1867	Fredericton
NF	Newfoundland & Labrador	English	31st March 1949	St John's
NT	Northwest Territories	English	15th July 1870	Yellowknife
NS	Nova Scotia	English	1st July 1867	Halifax
NU	Nunavut (Territory)	Inuktitut	1st April 1999	Iqaluit
OT	Ontario	English	1st July 1867	Toronto
PE	Prince Edward Island	English	1st July 1873	Charlottetown
QU	Québec	French	1st July 1867	Québec
SA	Saskatchewan	English	1st Sept 1905	Regina
YT	Yukon Territory	English	13th June 1898	Whitehorse

* Although Canada is officially bilingual (English & French), this column indicates the most commonly-spoken language in each region.
† Approx. 35% of the population are French-speaking.

Appendix 4

Australian States and Territories

ISO Abbr.	State	Nickname	Date of granting of responsible Government	State Capital
AC	Australian Capital Territory	Nation's Capital	1911	Canberra *
CL	Coral Sea Territory *(External Territory bordering the Queensland coast and the Great Barrier Reef)*			
NS	New South Wales	Premier State	1788 †	Sydney
NT	Northern Territory	Outback Australia	1911 **	Darwin
QL	Queensland	Sunshine State	1859	Brisbane
SA	South Australia	Festival State	1856	Adelaide
TS	Tasmania	Holiday Isle	1856	Hobart
VI	Victoria	Garden State	1855	Melbourne
WA	Western Australia	State of Excitement	1890	Perth

* Canberra became the seat of the Australian government on 9th May 1927.
† Date of first settlement: New South Wales originally covered the whole island with the exception of Western Australia.
** Transferred to Commonwealth from South Australia in 1911, self-government within the Commonwealth granted 1978.

Appendix 5a

Travel Associations: UK

This section provides details of a selection of travel trade associations in the UK. The descriptive text was supplied by, or with the approval of, the organisation concerned.

AA
Automobile Association
AA Travel
Fanum House
Basingstoke
Hampshire RG21 4EA
Tel: 0870 544 8866
Web: www.theaa.com
Provides an information, support and breakdown service for motorists.

AAC
Association of ATOL Companies
5th Floor
Regal House
70 London Road
Twickenham TW1 3QS
Tel: 020 8288 1430
Web: www.aac-uk.org
Keeps members abreast of current legislation as it affects their business, and provides a platform for members to voice their views to opinion formers.

ABPCO
Association of British Professional Conference Organisers
6th Floor Charles House
148-9 Great Charles Street
Birmingham B3 3HT
Tel: 0121 212 1400
Fax: 0121 212 3131
Email: info@bacd.org.uk
Web: www.abpco.org
A trade association offering advice and services to professional conference organisers.

ABTA
Association of British Travel Agents
68-71 Newman Street
London W1T 3AH
Tel: 020 7637 2444
Fax: 020 7637 0713
Email: abta@abta.co.uk
Web: www.abta.com
Promotes and regulates the activities of its members, and protects the interests of consumers.

ABTOF
Association of British Tour Operators to France
PO Box 54
Ross-on-Wye HR9 5YQ
Tel: 01989 769140
Fax: 01989 769066
Email: info@abtof.org.uk
Web: www.holidayfrance.org.uk
Promotes travel to France and represents the interests of its member companies.

ABTOT
Association of Bonded Travel Organisers Trust Ltd
Tower 42
Old Broad Street
London EC2N 1HQ
Tel: 0845 3456 078
Fax: 0845 2411 235
Email: tgic.mail@travel-general.com
Web: www.travel-general.com
A simple, economical and fully DTI-approved bonding scheme, enabling travel organisers to provide financial protection for their non-licensable arrangements.

ACE
Association for Conferences and Events
Riverside House
High Street
Huntingdon
Camb PE29 3SG
Tel: 01480 457595
Fax: 01480 412863
Email: ace@martex.co.uk
Web: www.martex.co.uk/ace
Provides a service to, and forum for, its members who are involved in various aspects of the conference and meetings industry.

AEO
Association of Exhibition Organisers
119 High Street
Berkhamstead
Herts
HP4 2DJ
Tel: 01442 873331
Fax: 01442 875551
Email: info@aeo.org.uk
Web: www.aeo.org.uk
Works to increase the significance of exhibitions within the marketing mix, and to satisfy an increasing number of visitors.

AITO
Association of Independent Tour Operators
133a St Margaret's Road
Twickenham
TW1 1RG
Tel: 020 8744 9280
Fax: 020 8744 3187
Email: info@aito.co.uk
Web: www.aito.co.uk
Represents the specialist tour operator to the trade and the public through joint marketing and promotional activities.

ANTOR
Association of National Tourist Office Representatives
37 Peter Avenue
London NW10 2DD
Tel: 020 8459 4052
Email: antor@ukonline.co.uk
Web: www.tourist-offices.org.uk
Promotes travel and tourism worldwide, to the trade and to the public, and represents its member tourist organizations.

AOA
Airport Operators Association
3 Birdcage Walk
London
SW1H 9JJ
Tel: 020 7222 2249
Fax: 020 7976 7405
Email: enquiries@aoa.org.uk
Web: www.aoa.org.uk
Trade association for British airports representing views on legislative and regulatory matters.

APTG
Association of Professional Tourist Guides
40 Bermondsey Street
London SE1 3UD
Tel: 020 7939 7690
Fax: 020 7939 7049
Email: aptg@aptg.org.uk
Web: www.aptg.org.uk
www.touristguides.org.uk
The professional body of London's 'Blue Badge' guides. It seeks to promote the highest possible standards in tourism in general and guiding in particular.

ASVA
Association of Scottish Visitor Attractions
Argylls Lodgings
Castle Wynd
Stirling FK8 1EG
Tel: 01786 475 152
Fax: 01786 474 288
Email: info@asva.co.uk
Web: www.asva.co.uk.
Improves the quality and viability of visitor attractions in Scotland, and assists with tour development by identifying appropriate places to visit.

ATII
Association of Travel Insurance Intermediaries
C/O Voyager Insurance Services LTD
13-21 High Street
Guilford
Surrey GU1 3DG
Tel: 01483 562 662
Fax: 01483 569 676
Email: info@atii.co.uk
Web:www.atii.co.uk
An association of travel insurance intermediaries committed to high standards in travel insurance. Amongst its members are Lloyds Brokers, regulated insurance brokers and intermediaries.

ATOC
Association of Train Operating Companies
3rd Floor 40 Bernard Street
London WC1N 1BY
Tel: 020 7904 3033
Email: Anthony.ewers@atoc.org
Web: www.atoc.org
Represents the interests of the train operating companies to government and key opinion-formers, as well as managing a range of network services, products and responsibilities on their behalf.

AUC
Air Transport
Users Council
CAA House K2
45-59 Kingsway
London WC2B 6TE
Tel: 0207 240 6061
Fax: 020 7240 7071
Email: admin@auc.caa.co.uk
Web: www.auc.org.uk
As the Civil Aviation Authority's official
consumer watchdog, protects the interests of
users of aviation services.

AWTE
Association of Women
Travel Executives
C/O Monika Warburton
G&O Public Relations
Coppice Lane
Reigate
Surrey RH2 9JG
Tel: 01737 247 033
Fax: 01737 225 305
Email: monika@working.co.uk
Web: www.awte-london.co
Provides a social forum for female executives
employed in the travel industry.

BAA
British Airports Authority
130 Wilton Road
London SW1V 1LQ
Tel: 020 7834 9449
Fax: 020 7932 6699
Email: mark_mann@baa.com
Web: www.baa.com
Manages airport facilities at various airports in
the UK and overseas.

BACD
British Association of
Conference Destinations
6th Floor Charles House
148-9 Great Charles Street
Birmingham B3 3HT
Tel: 0121 212 1400
Fax: 0121 212 3131
Email: info@bacd.org.uk
Web: www.bacd.org.uk
Represents and promotes all the major British
conference destinations, providing information,
venue finding and related services in respect of
3,000 venues countrywide.

BAHA
British Activity Holiday Association Ltd
Morritt House
58 Station approach
South Ruislip
Ruislip
Middlesex HA4 6SA
Tel: 020 8842 1292
Fax: 020 8842 0090
Email: info@baha.org.uk
Web: www.baha.org.uk
Works towards improving quality and safety in
the activity holiday industry.

BALPA
British Airline Pilots Association
81 New Road
Harlington UB3 5BG
Tel: 020 8476 4000
Fax: 020 8476 4077
Email: balpa@balpa.org
Website: www.balpa.org
The professional union representing pilots and
flight engineers in the UK

BAR UK Ltd
Board of Airline Representatives in the UK
5 Hobart Place
London SW1W 0HU
Tel: 020 7393 1261
Fax: 020 7393 1206
Email: office@bar-uk.org
Web: www.bar-uk.org
Trade association representing full-service
scheduled airlines doing business in the UK.

BATA
British Air Transport Association
Artillery House
11-19 Artillery Row
London SW1P 1RT
Tel: 020 7222 9494
Fax: 020 7222 9595
Email: admin@bata.uk.com
Website: www.bata.uk.com
Encourages the safe, healthy and economic
development of UK civil aviation.

BCH
Bonded Coach Holiday Group
Imperial House
15-19 Kingsway
London WC2B 6UN
Tel: 020 7240 3131

Fax: 020 7240 6565
Email: bch@cpt-uk.org
Website: www.cpt-uk.org/cpt
Provides a government-approved bonding scheme for the operators of coach holidays.

BH&HPA
British Holiday & Home Parks Association Ltd
6 Pullman Court
Great Western Road
Gloucester GL1 3ND
Tel: 01452 526911
Fax: 01452 508508
Email: enquiries@bhhpa.org.uk
Website: www.ukparks.com
Represents the parks industry including caravans, chalets, tents and self-catering accommodation.

BHA
British Hospitality Association
55-56 Queens House
Lincoln's Inn Fields
London WC2A 3BH
Tel: 020 7404 7744
Fax: 020 7404 7799
Email: bha@bha.org.uk
Website: www.bha_online.org.uk
Protects and develops the interests of its members in the British hospitality industry.

BIBA
British Insurance Brokers' Association
BIBA House
14 Bevis Marks
London EC3A 7NT
Tel: 020 7623 9043
Fax: 020 7626 9676
Email: enquiries@biba.org.uk
Website: www.biba.org.uk
Trade association for insurance brokers, mainly on the commercial side.

BMC
British Mountaineering Council
177-179 Burton Road
Manchester
M20 2BB
Tel: 0870 010 4878
Fax: 0161 445 4500
Web: www.thebmc.co.uk
Represents and promotes the interests of climbers, hill walkers and mountaineers in England and Wales, encourages sustainable development and conservation, promotes good

practice and training, supports events and specialist programmes and provides information and services for members.

BPA
British Ports Association
Africa House
64-78 Kingsway
London WC2B 6AH
Tel: 020 7242 1200
Fax: 020 7430 7474
Email: info@britishports.org.uk
Website: www.britishports.org.uk
Lobbies the government on behalf of ports and harbours in the UK.

BRA
British Resorts Association
Crown Building
Eastbank Street
Southport
Merseyside PR8 1DL
Tel: 0151 934 2286
Fax: 0151 934 2287
Email: bresorts@sefton.u-net.com
Website: www.britishresorts.co.uk
A national organisation promoting the mutual interests of all member resorts (inland and coastal) and tourist regions.

BTA
British Tourist Authority
Thames Tower
Blacks Road
London W6 9EL
Tel: 020 8846 9000
Fax: 020 8563 0302
Web: www.visitbritain.com
Promotes tourism to Britain, and ensures that the national and regional tourist boards respond effectively to the needs of government, the industry and the public. (The English Tourism Council has now merged with the BTA.)

BVRLA
British Vehicle Rental & Leasing Association
River Lodge
Badminton Court
Amersham HP7 0DD
Tel: 01494 434 747
Fax: 01494 434 499
Email: info@bvrla.co.uk
Website.www.bvrla.co.uk
Represents the short- and long-term vehicle

rental, leasing and contract hire industry, and presents their views to government.

BW
British Waterways
Willow Grange
Church Road
Watford, WD17 4QA
Tel: 01923 226422
Fax: 01923 201400
Email: enquiries.hq@britishwaterways.co.uk
Web: www.bitishwaterways.co.uk
Cares for over 2,000 miles of Britain's canals and rivers.

CAA
Civil Aviation Authority
CAA House
45-59 Kingsway
London WC2B 6TE
Tel: 020 7379 7311
Fax: 01293 573 999
Email: tom.hamilton@srg.caa.co.uk
Provides regulates the civil aviation industry including the licensing of air travel organisers, and advises government on civil aviation.

CIMTIG
Chartered Institute of Marketing Travel Industry Group
Home Cottage
Old Lane
Tatsfield
Westerham TN16 2LN
Tel: 01959 577469
Fax: 01959 577469
Email: ugo@cimtig.org
Website: www.cimtig.org
Improves the success and profitability of its members and their organisations by understanding and applying modern marketing techniques, and offering networking opportunities.

CPT
Confederation of Passenger Transport UK
Imperial House
15-19 Kingsway
London WC2B 6UN
Tel: 020 7240 3131
Fax: 020 7240 6565
Email: admin@cpt-uk.org
Website: www.cpt-uk.org
Represents the views of bus, coach and light rail

operators to government, the European Union and the media and protects the commercial environment of the industry.

CRAC
Continental Rail Agents Consortium
C/O Gerry Harris
Ultima Travel
424 Chester Road
Little Sutton
South Wirral CH66 3RB
Tel: 0151 339 6171
Fax: 0151 339 9199
Represents the interests of those selling European rail travel and provides a forum for discussion with European rail principals

CTC
Coach Tourism Council
Berkeley House
18 Elmfield Road
Bromley
BR1 1LR
Tel: 020 8461 8325
Fax: 020 8461 8326
Email: info@coachtourismcouncil.co.uk
Website: www.coachtourismcouncil.co.uk
Promotes travel and tourism by coach.

CTO
Caribbean Tourism Organisation
42 Westminster Palace Gardens
Artillery Row
London SW1P 1RR
Tel: 020 7222 4335
Fax: 020 7222 4325
Email: cto@carib-tourism.com
Represents its members from the travel and tourism industry, and promotes travel to and within the Caribbean region.

CTT
Council for Travel & Tourism
LGM House
Mill Green Road
Hayward's Heath
Sussex RH16 1XL
Tel: 01444 452277
Fax: 01444 452244
Email: info@ctt-online.co.uk
Provides a forum for member organisations to exchange information, news and views on current developments, and lobbies government on issues of concern to the travel and tourism industries.

ESITO
Events Sector Industry Training Organisation
Tetford House
Tetford
Lincolnshire LN9 6QQ
Tel: 01507 533 639
Fax: 01507 533 491
Email: esito@righttrack.co.uk
Acts as the forum for training and development in the events industry, and to pursue issues with government, education and other bodies.

ETC
English Tourism Council
See British Tourist Authority.

ETOA
European Tour Operators Association
6 Weighhouse Street
London W1K 5LT
Tel: 020 7499 4412
Fax: 020 7499 4413
Email: info@etoa.org
Web: www@etoa.org
A trade association representing the interests of its members – mostly tour operators, but also including other sectors of the travel industry.

FHA
Family Holiday Association
16 Mortimer Street
London
W1T3JL
Tel: 020 7436 3304
Fax: 020 7436 3302
Email: info@fhaonline.org.uk
Website: www.fhaonline.org.uk
A charity providing holidays for families in need.

FTO
Federation of Tour Operators
First Floor
Graphic House
14-16 Sussex Road
Haywards Hearth
West Sussex
RH16 4EA
Tel: 01444 57900
Fax: 01444 457901
Website: www.fto.co.uk
Works with tour operators to bring about change and improvement in all areas affecting customers' holidays on the journey and in resort.

GBCO
Guild of British Coach Operators
The Administrator
Guild of British Coach Operators
P O Box 5657
Southend on Sea
Essex SS1 3WT
Tel: 01702 588590
Fax: 0870 1399469
Email: admin@coach-tours.co.uk
Web: www.coach-tours.co.uk
A consortium of independently owned and quality-driven coach operators.

GRTG
The Guild of Registered Tourist Guides
Guild House
52d Borough High Street
London
SE1 1XN
Tel: 020 7403 1115
Fax: 020 7378 1705
Email: guild@blue-badge.org.uk
Acts as the national professional association of registered guides in the UK.

GTMC
Guild of Travel Management Companies Limited
Queens House
180-182 Tottenham Court Road
London W1T 7PD
Tel: 020 637 1091
Fax: 020 7580 6593
Email: info@gtmc.org
Web: www.gtmc.org
Provides a forum for business and corporate travel agencies, and seeks the highest standards for its members and their clients.

GTOA
Group Travel Organisers Association
28a Rectory Close
Carlton
Bedford MK43 7JY
Tel: 01234 720784
Fax: 01234 720784
Email: yvonne@hodsony.freeserve.co.uk
Website: www.gtoa.co.uk
Enhances the status and professionalism of group travel organisers and represents their interests in dealing with industry suppliers and official bodies.

GTT
The Guild of Travel and Tourism
Suite 193
Temple Chambers
3-7 Temple Ave
London EC4Y 0DB
Tel: 020 7583 6333
Fax: 01895 834028
Email: Nigel.bishop@traveltourismguild.com
Web: www.traveltourismguild.com
Acts as a forum for anyone in the travel, tourism or transport sectors, to provide benefits for its members, and to lobby for industry issues of concern.

HBAA
Hotel Booking Agents Association
Association House
South Park Road
Macclesfield SK11 6SH
Tel: 01625 267887
Fax: 01625 267879
Email: secretariat@hbaa.org
Website: www.hbaa.org.uk
A leading professional and ethical body representing the hotel and conference agency community for the benefit of its members, hotels, venues and corporate buyers.

HC
Holiday Care
Sunley House
4 Bedford Park
Croydon CR0 2AP
Tel: 0845 124 9971
Fax: 0845 124 9972
Minicom: 0845 124 9976
Email: holiday.care@virgin.net
Web: www.holidaycare.org.uk
A registered charity and the UK's central source of holiday information for people with disabilities.

HCA
Holiday Centres Association
Pillars
Eastacombe Lane
Heanton Punchardon
North Devon EX31 4DG
Tel: 01271 816696
Fax: 01271 817411
Email: holidaycentres@aol.com
Web: www.holidaycentres.com

Represents all of the major and independent holiday centres in the UK that provide inclusive accommodation, entertainment, sporting and leisure activities packages.

HMA
Hotel Marketing Association
The Old Mill
High Street
Selbourne
Alton GU34 3LG
Tel: 0845 758 5435
Fax: 0845 758 5435
Email: alyryan@aol.com
Website: www.hotelmarketingassociation.com
Promotes a good marketing practice in the hotel industry, through educational events, industry-wide research studies and recognition of hotel marketing excellence.

IAGTO
International Association of Golf Tour Operators
1 Trafalgar House
Grenville Place
London, NW7 3SA
Tel: 020 8906 3377
Fax: 020 8906 8181
Email: info@iagto.com
Web: www.iagto.com
The global trade association of the golf tourism industry with over 700 member companies and organisations in more than 60 countries, including 195 golf tour operators in 35 countries.

IATM
International Association of Tour Managers
397 Walworth Road
London SE17 2AW
Tel: 020 7703 9154
Fax: 020 7703 0358
Email: iatm@iatm.co.uk
Web:www.iatm.co.uk
Recognises, represent and promote tour managers in the UK and internationally.

IFTO
International Federation of Tour Operators
First Floor Graphic House
14-16 Sussex Road
Haywards Hearth
West Sussex RH16 4EA
Tel: 01444 57900

Fax: 01444 457901
Email: ifto@fto.co.uk
Enables tour operators throughout Europe to cooperate in order to solve the major problems which confront package holiday makers.

ILAM
Institute of Leisure and Amenity Management
ILAM House
Lower Basildon
Reading RG8 9NE
Tel: 01491 874800
Fax: 01491 874801
Email: info@ilam.co.uk
Website: www.ilam.co.uk
The professional body for the leisure industry.

ITM
Institute of Travel Management
Waters Green House
Waters Green
Macclesfield
Cheshire SK11 6LF
Tel: 01625 430472
Fax: 01625 439183
Email: secretariat@itm.org.uk
Website: www.itm.org.uk
Provides networking opportunities for members, comprising travel managers within corporations and suppliers.

ITMA
Incentive Travel & Meetings Association Ltd
26-28 Station Road
Redhill
Surrey RH1 1PD
Tel: 01737 779928
Fax: 01737 779749
Email: info@itma-online.org
Website: wwww.itma-online.org
Represents the UK event-management industry.

ITOA
Irish Incoming Tour Operators Association
19 Kerrymount Rise
Dublin, 18
Tel: 00 353 1-289 9366
Fax: 00 353 1-289 9369
Email: info@itoa-ireland.com
Website: www.itoa-ireland.com
Represents over 34 incoming operators which provide professional services for overseas travel trade.

ITT
Institute of Travel & Tourism
ITT PO BOX 217
Ware
Herfordshire SG12 8WY
Tel: 0870 7707960
Fax: 0870 7707961
Email: admin@itt.co.uk
Website: www.itt.co.uk
Develops the professionalism of its members within the industry.

LCA
Leading Cruise Agents of the UK
The Guild of Professional Cruise Agents
23 Portland Street, Hull,
HU2 8JX
Tel: 01292 316820
Fax: 01292 311953
Email: lca.info@virgin.net
Website: www.thelca.com
Represents a group of over 50 travel agents who concentrate on the sale of cruises, each achieving cruise sales in excess of £250,000 per year.

MCS
Mountaineering Council of Scotland
The Old Granary
West Mill Street
Perth
PH1 5QP
Tel: 01738 638 227
Fax: 01738 442 095
Email: info@mountaineering-scotland.org.uk
Web: www.mountineering-scotland.org.uk
Represents and promotes the interests of climbers, hill walkers and mountaineers in Scotland, encourages sustainable development and conservation, promotes good practice and training, supports events and specialist programmes and provides information and services for members.

MIA
Meetings Industry Association
PO Box 6984
Wellingborough
NN29 7WU
Tel: 0845 230 5508
Fax: 0845 230 7708
Email: info@mia-uk.org
Leading professional trade association for the meetings and conference industries in the UK and Ireland.

NAITA
National Association of Independent Travel Agents
Kenilworth House
79-80 Margaret Street
London W1W 8TA
Tel: 020 7323 3408
Fax: 0171 323 5189
Email: naita@advantage4travel.com
Enables independent agents to compete with the 'multiples' without losing their personal service and independent management.

NEA
National Exhibitors Association
29a Market Square
Biggleswade SG18 8AQ
Tel: 01767 316255
Fax: 01767 316430
Email: info@seoevent.co.uk
Web: www.seoevent.co.uk
A national organisation of exhibiting companies, offering information and seminars on all aspects of exhibiting.

NITB
Northern Ireland Tourist Board
St Anne's Court
59 North Street
Belfast BT1 1NB
Tel: 028 9023 1221
Fax: 028 9024 0960
Email: info@nitb.com
Web: www.discovernorthnireland.com
Promotes tourism to and within Northern Ireland.

NT
National Trust
PO Box 39
Warrington WA5 7WD
Tel: 0870 458 4000
Fax: 020 8466 6824
Email: enquiries@thenationaltrust.org.uk
Web: www.nationaltrust.org.uk
Promotes the permanent preservation, for the benefit of the nation, of lands and buildings of beauty or historic interest.

NTS
National Trust for Scotland
28 Charlotte Square
Edinburgh EH2 4ET
Tel: 0131 243 9300
Fax: 0131 243 9301
Email: information@nts.org.uk
Web: www.nts.org.uk
The conservation charity that protects and promotes Scotland's natural and cultural heritage for present and future generations to enjoy.

People 1st
2nd Floor
Armstrong House
38 Market Square
Uxbridge
UB1 1LH
Tel: 0870 060 2550
Fax: 0870 060 2551
Email: info@people1st.co.uk
Web: www.people1st.co.uk
An employer-led organisation, responsible for driving up levels of skills, productivity and employability across the hospitality, leisure, travel and tourism sector.

PSA
Passenger Shipping Association Ltd
Walmar House
288-292 Regent Street
London W1B 3AL
Tel: 020 7436 2449
Fax: 020 7636 9206
Email: admin@psa-psara.org
Web: www.the-psa.co.uk
Represents member organisations from the cruising and ferry industries.

PSARA
Passenger Shipping Association Retail Agents Scheme
Walmar House
288-292 Regent Street
London,W1R 5HE
Tel: 020 7436 2449
Fax: 020 7636 9206
Email: admin@psa-psara.org
Web: www.psa-psara.org
The training arm of the PSA (see above).

RAC
Royal Automobile Club
RAC Motoring Services
Great Park Road
Bradley Stoke
Bristol BS32 4QN
Tel: 0800 029 029
Web: www.rac.co.uk
Provides information, support and breakdown services for motorists.

SATH
**Society for the Advancement
of Travel for the Handicapped**
Whiteridge
Chalkpit Lane
Marlow SL7 2JE
Tel: 01628 487494
Fax: 01628 487494

*Creates a forum for the exchange and
development of information within the travel
industry and to promote barrier-free access to
travel for those with disabilities.*

SDMA
**Scottish Destination
Management Association**
14 Learmonth Terrace
Edinburgh EH4 1PG
Tel: 0131 343 3770
Fax: 0131 343 1368
Email: scot.dest.man@btinternet.com
Web: www.scotland-sdma.org.uk

*Official body that represents incoming tour
operators and destination management
companies in Scotland.*

SEO
Society of Event Organisers
29a Market Square
Biggleswade SG18 8AQ
Tel: 01767 316255
Fax: 01767 316430
Website: www.seoevent.co.uk

*A membership group of organisations involved in
event organising , offering advice, publications
and seminars.*

Snow 24
The Snow Centre
21 Camault Muir
Kiltarlity
Inverness IV4 7JH
Fax: +44 (0)1463 741802
Email: info@snow24.com
Web: www.snow24.com

*An information service providing up-to-date
details on virtually every winter sport resorts
throughout the world.*

SPAA
Scottish Passenger Agents Association
22 Dunveran Avenue
Gourock
PA19 1AE

Tel: 01475 639924
Fax: 01475 635408
Email: alistairt@aol.com

*A trade association representing the interests of
retail travel agents in Scotland.*

STF - School Travel Forum
STS School Travel Service Limited,
Lees House, 21 Dyke Road, Brighton, Sussex, BN1
3GD, UK.
Tel: 01273 775 776
Fax: 01273 772 735
Website: www.ststravel.co.uk

*Provides a forum for businesses within the school
travel industry, and a focus for members to
explore and act on industry issues.*

TIPTO
**Truly Independent Professional Travel
Organisation**
Lockwood House
Lockwood Park
Brewery Drive
Huddersfield HD4 6EN
Tel: 01484 345028
Fax: 01484 345030
Email: tipto@thenetwork-uk.com
Web: tipto.co.uk

*A marketing organisation of independent tour
operators and travel-service providers which is
able to offer independent travel agents an
unrivalled choice of holiday options under one
banner.*

TMI
Tourism Management Institute
18 Cuninghill Avenue
Inverurie
Aberdeenshire AB51 3TZ
Tel: 01467 620 769
Email: cathguth@aol.com
Web: www.tmi.org.uk

*The professional body for tourism destination
management in the United Kingdom, aiming to
advance the profession and its standing, and to
be an independent voice for its members.*

TS
The Tourism Society
1 Queen Victoria Terrace
Sovereign Court
London E1W 3HA
Tel: 020 7488 2789

Fax: 020 7488 9148
Email: admin@tourismsociety.org
Web: www.tourismsociety.org
A leading tourism membership body promoting professionalism in travel and tourism.

TTA
Travel Trust Association Ltd
Albion House
High Street
Woking
Surrey
GU21 6BD
Tel: 0870 889 0577
Fax: 01483 730746
Email: contact@traveltrust.co.uk
Web: www.traveltrust.co.uk
Trade association that licenses travel agents and tour operators to trade within the industry, providing financial protection for their customers.

Ukinbound
British Incoming Tour Operators Association- UKinbound
Victory House
14 Leicester Place
London
WC2H 7BZ
Tel: 020 7734 9569
Fax: 020 7287 3217
Email: info@ukinbound.org
Web: www.ukinbound.org
Represents members of the inbound tourism industry and provides them with services such as research, lobbying and training.

Visit Scotland
Oceanpoint 1
94 Ocean Drive]
Edinburgh EH6 6JH
Tel: 0131 332 2433
Fax: 0131 472 2250
Email: info@visitscotland.com
Web: www.visitscotland.com
Promotes tourism to and within Scotland.

WIN
Worldwide Independent Travel Network
C/O Advantage Travel Centre
Kenilworth House
79/80 Margaret Street
London W1W 8TA
Tel: 020 7323 3408
Fax: 020 7323 5189
Email: neil.armorgie@win-travel.org
An international commercial and marketing organisation for over 7,000 independent travel agents around the world.

WTB
Wales Tourist Board
Brunel House, 2 Fitzalan Road
Cardiff CF2 1UY
Tel: 02920 499909
Fax: 02920 485031
Email: info@visitwales.com
Web: www.wtbonline.gov.uk
Promotes tourism to and within Wales. This section provides details of a selection of travel trade associations in the USA. The descriptive text was supplied by, or with the approval of, the organisation concerned.

Appendix 5b

Travel Associations: USA

AH&LA
American Hotel & Lodging Association
1201 New York Avenue N.W.
Suite 600, Washington DC 20005
Tel: 202 289 3100
Fax: 202 289 3199
Email: info@ahla.com
Web site: www.ahla.com
A federation of state lodging associations which provides operational, technical, educational, marketing and communications services, plus governmental-affairs representation to the lodging industry.

ARTA
Association of Retail Travel Agents
3161 Custer Drive, Suite 8
Lexington KY 40517-4067
Tel: 859.269.9739
Fax: 859.266.9396
Email: artalexhdq@aol.com
Web site: www.artaonline.com
The largest non-profit travel-trade association in North America that represents travel agents exclusively.

ASIRT
The Association for Safe International Road Travel
11769 Gainsborough Road
Potomac MD 20854
Tel: 301 983 5252
Fax: 301 983 3663
Email: asirt@erols.com
Web: www.asirt.org
An international, non-profit organisation that promotes road safety through education and advocacy. Alerts individuals and corporations to road conditions in 150 countries.

ASTA
American Society of Travel Agents
1101 King Street
Alexandria VA 22314
Tel: 703 739 2782
Fax: 703 684 8319
Email: asta@astahq.com
Web: www.astanet.com

Enhances the professionalism and profitability of members worldwide through effective representation in industry and government affairs, education and training, and by identifying and meeting the needs of the travelling public.

ATA
Air Transport Association
1301 Pennsylvania Avenue,
Suite 1100
Washington DC 20004-1707
Tel: 202 626 4000
Fax: 202 626 4181
Email: prata@airlines.org
Web: www.airlines.org
Advocates and supports measures to enhance air transport safety, ensures efficiency, fosters growth and promotes economic health of the travel industry.

CLIA
Cruise Lines International Association
500 5th Avenue
Suite 1407
New York
NY 10016
Tel: 212 921 0066
Fax: 212 921 0549
Email: CLIA@cruising.org
Web: cruising.org
Represents the North American cruise industry, and works to expand and promote cruise holidays.

HEDNA
Hotel Electronic Distribution Network Association
333 John Carlyle Street
Suite 600
Alexandria
VA 22314
Tel: 703 837 6181
Fax: 412 781 2871 703 548 5738
Email: info@hedna.org
Web site: www.HEDNA.org
Promotes the use of electronic distribution in the booking of hotel rooms.

IATAN
International Airlines Travel Agent Network
300 Garden City Plaza, Suite 342
Garden City NY 11530
Tel: 516 747 4716
Fax: 516 747 4462
Email: no general address
Web site: www.iatan.org
Promotes professionalism, administers business standards, and provides a vital link between the supplier community and the US travel distribution network.

IFTTA
International Forum of Travel and Tourism Advocates
2107 van Ness Avenue, Suite 200
San Francisco CA 94109
Tel: 415 673 3333
Fax: 415 673 3548
Email: anolik@travellaw.com
Web site: www.tay.ac.uk/iftta or
www.travellaw.com
Travel law attorneys, professors and industry personnel dealing with legal issues from 40 countries worldwide.

NACOA
National Association of Cruise Oriented Agencies
7600 Red Road
Suite 128
Miami FL 33143
Tel: 305 663 5626
Fax: 305 663 5625
Email: nacoafl@aol.com
Web site: www.nacoa.com
Non-profit trade association dedicated to the cruise product and the cruise professionals who sell it.

NACTA
National Association of Commissioned Travel Agents
1101 King Street
Suite 300
Alexandria VA 22314
Tel: 703 739 6826
Fax: 703 739 6861
Email: nacta@aol.com
Web: www.nacta.com
National association of travel agents whose members include independent contractors, outside sales agents, cruise- and tour-orientated agents and their host agency partners.

SATH
The Society for the Advancement of Travel for the Handicapped
347 5th Avenue, Ste 610
New York
NY 10016
Tel: 212 447 7284
Fax: 212 725 8253
Email: sathtravel@aol.com
Web: www.sath.org
A non-profit organisation which assists and advises on travel arrangements of all kinds for people with disabilities.

SGTP
Society of Government Travel Professionals
6935 Wisconsin Avenue,
Bethesda MD 20815-6109
Tel: 301 654 8595
Fax: 301 654 6663
Email: govtvlmkt@aol.com
Web: www.government-travel.org
National association focusing on research, education, buyer/seller opportunities, networking, mentoring and advocacy.

TIA
Travel Industry Association of America
1100 New York Avenue NW
Suite 450 West
Washington DC 20005
Tel: 202 408 8422
Fax: 202 408 1255
Web: www.tia.org
The national, non-profit organisation representing all components of the US travel industry which promotes and facilitates increased travel to and within the US.

USTI
United States Tourism Industries
Office of Travel and Tourism Industries
14th & Constitution Avenue
NW Suite 7025
Washington DC 20230
Tel: 202-482-0140
Fax: 202-482-2887
web: www.tinet.ita.doc.gov
The National Tourism Office for the United States of America, providing research, technical assistance and policy guidance on the international travel market to and from the USA.

Appendix 5c

Travel Agency Associations: Global

This section provides details of the travel agency associations for a selection of countries of major importance for travel and tourism.

Australia

AFTA
*(Australian Federation
of Travel Agents)*
309 Pitt Street
3rd floor
Sydney
NSW 2000
Australia
Tel: 00 61 29 2643299
Fax: 00 61 - 29 2641085
Email: afta@afta.com.au
Web: www.afta.com.au

Austria

ÖRV
*(Österreichischer Reisebüro- und
Reiseveranstalter Verband)*
Wiener Kongreßzentrum Hofburg
Heldentplatz
- Postfach Box 113
A - 1014 WIEN
Tel: 00 43 1 587 36 66-24
Fax.: 00 43 1 532 26 91
Email: office@oerv.at
Web: www.oerv.at

Belgium

FIT/FTI
*(Fédération de l'Industrie du Tourisme
– Federatie van de Toeristische Industrie)*
Avenue de la Métrologie, 8
B - 1130 Bruxelles
Tel: 00 32 2 240 16 69
Fax.: 00 32 2 245 20 50
Email: piet.vintevogel@fti-fit.be
Web: www.fti-fit.be

Canada

ACTA
(Association of Canadian Travel Agents)
130 Albert Street
Suite 1705
Ottawa
K1P 5G4
Canada
Tel: 00 1 - 613 237 3657
Fax: 00 1 - 613 237 7052
Email: actacan@acta.ca

China

CTA
(China Tourism Association)
9A Jianguo-Mennei Dajie
Beijing 100740
China
Tel: 00 86 10 6512 2907
Fax: 00 86 10 6513 5383
Email: cta@cnta.gov.cn
Web: www.cnta.gov.cn

China – Hong Kong

HATA
(Hong Kong Association
of Travel Agents)
Room 1003
Tung Ming Building 40
Des Voeux Road
Central
Hong Kong
Tel: 00 852 2869 8624
Fax: 00 852 2869 8632
Email: gloriadr@att.net.hk
Web: www.hata.org

Czech Republic

ACCKA
(Association of Czech Travel Agencies)
Vinohradska 46
Prague 2
Tel: 00 42 02 2158 0256
Email: secretariat@accka.cz

Denmark

DRF
(Danmarks Rejsebureau Forening)
Falkoner Allé 58 b
DK - 2000 Frederiksberg
Tel: 00 45 31 3566 11
Fax.: 00 45 31 3588 59
Email: drf@travelassoc.dk
Web: www.drf-dk.dk

Finland

SMAL
(Suomen matkatoimistoalan liitto)
Vilhonkatu, 4B
FIN – 00100 Helsinki
Tel: 00 358 9 4133 3500
Fax.: 00 358 9 4133 3555
Email: smal@smal.fi
Web: www.smal.fi

France

SNAV
(Syndicat National des Agences de Voyages)
15, Place du Général Catroux
F – 75017 Paris
Tel: 00 33 1 44 0199 90
Fax.: 00 33 1 440199 99
Email: contact@snav.org
Web: www.snav.org

Germany

DRV
*(Deutscher Reisebüro- und
Reiseveranstalter Verband e.V.)*
Albrechtstrasse 10
D - 10177 Berlin
Tel: 00 49 30 284 060
Fax: 00 49 30 284 0630
Email: info@drv.de
Web: www.drv.de

ASR
*(Bundesverband mittelstndischer
Reiseunternehmen)*
Mainzer Landstrae 82-84
60327 Frankfurt/Main
Tel: 00 49 69 756 0540
Fax: 00 49 69 756 05420
Email: geschaeftsstelle@asr-online.de
Web: www.asr-online.de

Greece

HATTA
*(Hellenic Association of Travel
and Tourist Agencies)*
11 losif Rogon Street
GR – 11743 Athens
Tel: 00 30 1 9223522
Fax.: 00 30 1 9233307
Email: hatta@hatta.gr
Web: www.hatta.gr

Hungary

MUISZ
(Association of Hungarian Travel Agencies)
PO Box 267
1364 Budapest
HUNGARY
Tel: 00 36 1 318 4977
Fax: 00 36 1 318 4977
Email: muisz@mail.selectrade.hu

Ireland

ITAA
(Irish Travel Agents Association)
32, South William Street
IE – Dublin 2
Tel: 00 353 1 679 40 89
Fax.: 00 353 1 671 98 97
Email: info@itaa.ie
Web: www.itaa.ie

Italy

FIAVET
*(Federazione Italiana Associazioni
Imprese Viaggi e Turismo)*
Via Ravenna 8
I– 00161 Roma
Tel: 00 39 6 44 02 552
Fax.: 00 39 6 44 02 205
Email: fiavet.nazionale@fiavet.it
Web: www.fiavet.it

Japan

JATA
(Japan Association of Travel Agents)
Zen-Nittu Kasumigaseki Bldg. 3-3
Kasumegaseki 3
Chome Chiyoda-ku
Tokyo 100
Japan

Tel: 00 81 3 35921271
Fax: 00 81 3 35921268
Email: jata@jata-net.or.jp
Web: www.jata-net.or.jp

Luxembourg

GAVL
*(Groupement des Agences de Voyages
du Grand-Duché du Luxembourg)*
31, Boulevard Konrad Adenauer,
Kirchberg BP 482
L – 2014 Luxembourg
Tel: 00 352 43 94 44
Fax.: 00 352 43 94 50
Email: info@clc.lu
Web: www.clc.lu

Mexico

AMAV
(Asociacion Mexicana de Agencias de Viajes)
Calle Guanajuato 128
Colonia Roma Sur
Mexico DF 06700
Mexico
Tel: 00 52 5 5849300
Fax: 00 52 5 5849933
Email: amav_nacional@uole.com

Netherlands

ANVR
*(Algemeen Nederlands Verbond van
Reisondernemingen)*
Rijnzathe 8d
NL - 3454 ZH De Meern
Tel: 00 31 30 669 7033
Fax: 00 31 30 669 7034
Email: info@anvr.nl
Web: www.anvr.nl

New Zealand

TAANZ
(Travel Agents Association of New Zealand)
Level 5
79 Boulcott Street
1888 Wellington
DX SX 10033
New Zealand
Tel: 00 64 4 4990104
Fax: 00 64 4 499 0786
Email: info@taanz.org.nz
Web: www.taanz.org.nz

Portugal

APAVT
*(Associação Portuguesa das Agências
de Viagens e Turismo)*
Rua Sousa Martins n° 21, 5 audor
P – 1050-217 Lisboa
Tel: 00 351 21 355 30 10
Fax.: 00 351 21 314 50 80
Email: apavt@apavtnet.pt
Web: www.apavtnet.pt

South Africa

ASATA
(Association of South African Travel Agents)
11 Wellington Road
Parktown
2193 Johannesburg
South Africa
Tel: 00 27 11 484 05 80
Fax: 00 27 11 484 08 28
Email: general@asata.co.za
Web: www.asata.co.za

Spain

AEDAVE
*(Associación Empresarial de
Agencias de Viajes Españolas)*
Plaza de Castilla, 3-9° A
E – 28046 Madrid
Tel: 00 34 91 314 18 30
Fax.: 00 34 91 31418 77
Email: aedave@aedave.es
Web: www.aedave.es

ACAV
*(Associació Catalana
d'Agencies de Viatges)*
Avda. Roma 13-15, entres 2A
E - 08029 Barcelona
Tel: 00 34 93 321 97 29
Fax.: 00 34 93 322 12 04
Email: acav@acav.net
Web: www.acav.net

Sweden

SRF
(Svenska Resebyråforeningen)
Kammakargatan 39
P.O. Box 1375
S–111 93 Stockholm

Tel: 00 46 8 762 74 60
Fax.: 00 46 8 212 555
Email: kansli@srf-travelagent.se
Web:: www.srf-travelagent.se

Switzerland

SFT

(Swiss Federation of Travel Agencies)
Secretariat
Etzelstrasse 42
CH-8038 Zurich
Switzerland
Tel: 00 411 487 330 0
Fax: 00 41 1 480 09 45
E.mail: mail@srv.ch
Web: www.srv.ch

Turkey

TURSAB

(Turkiye Seyahat Acentalari Birligi)
Dikilitas
Asik Kerem Sokak 48-50
Besiktas
Istanbul - 80690
Turkey

Tel: 00 90 212 2598404
Fax: 00 90 212 2590656 & 2363978
Email: tursab@sim.net.tr
Web: www.tursab.org.tr

UK

ABTA

(Association of British Travel Agents)
68-71 Newman Street
London
W1T 3AH
Tel: 020 7637 2444
Fax: 020 7637 0713
Email: abta@abta.co.uk
Web: www.abta.com

USA

ASTA

(American Society of Travel Agents)
1101 King Street
Alexandria VA 22314
Tel: 703 739 2782
Fax: 703 684 8319
Email: asta@astahq.com
Web: www.astanet.com

Appendix 5d

Travel Associations: Global

This section provides details of a selection of regional or international travel trade associations.

AEA
Association of European Airlines,
350 Avenue Louise,
Postfach 4,
B-1050 Brussels
Belgium
Tel: 00 32 2 639 8989
Fax: 00 32 2 639 8999
Email: aea.secretariat@aea.be
Web: www.aea.be

ECTAA
Group of National Travel Agents' and Tour Operators' Associations within the EU,
Rue Dautzenberg 36,
Box 6,
B-1050 Brussels
Belgium
Tel: 00 32 2 6443450
Fax: 00 32 2 6442421
Email: ectaa@skynet.be
Web: www.ecta.org

ERA
European Regional Airlines Association,
The Baker Suite,
Fairoaks Airport,
Chobham,
Surrey GU24 8HX
UK
Tel: 00 44 1276 856495
Fax: 00 44 1276 857038
Email: info@eraa.org
Web: www.eraa.org

ETC
European Travel Commission,
61, rue du Marche aux Herbes,
B-1000 Brussels
Belgium
Tel: 00 32 2 504 0303
Fax: 00 32 2 514 1843
Email: etc@planetinternet.be
Web: www.etc-europe-travel.org

GBTAI
Guild of Business Travel Agents Ireland
12 South Leinster Street,
Dublin 2
Ireland
Tel : 00 353 1 607 9944
Fax : 00 353 1 676 7830
Email: gillian.neenan@neenantrav.ie

GEBTA
Guild of European Business Travel Agents
Rue Dautzenberg 36/38,
Boite 6,
Brussels B-1050
Tel: 00 32 2 6442187
Fax: 00 32 2 6442421
Email: gebta@gebta.org

ICCA
International Congress and Conference Association,
Entrada 121,
NL-1096
EB Amsterdam,
The Netherlands
Tel: 00 31 20 398 1919
Fax: 00 31 20 699 0781
Email: icca@icca.nl
Web: www.icca.nl

IATA
International Air Transport Association,
800 Place Victoria
PO Box 113
Montréal
Québec
H42 1M1
Canada
Tel: 00 1 514 0202
Fax: 00 1 514 874 9632
Web: www.iata.org

PATA

**Pacific and Asian Travel
Agents Association,**
Unit B1
Siam Tower
989 Rama I Road
Pathumwan
Bangkok 10330
Thailand
Tel: 00 66 2 658 2000
Fax: 00 66 2 658 2010
Email: patabkk@pata.th.com
Web: www.pata.org

WATA

**World Association
of Travel Agents,**
11 Ch. Riant-Coteau
1196 Gland
Switzerland
Tel: 00 41 22 995 1545
Fax: 00 41 22 995 1546
Email: wata@wata.net
Web: www.wata.net

WTO

World Tourism Organisation
Capitán Haya 42
28020 Madrid
Spain
Tel: 00 34 91 567 81 00
Fax: 00 34 91 571 37 33
Email: omt@world-tourism.org
Web: www.world-tourism.org

UFTAA

**Universal Federation of
Travel Agents Associations**
1, avenue des Castelans
MC98000
Monaco
Tél. : 00 377 92 05 28 29
Fax : 00 377 92 05 29 87
Email : uftaa@uftaa.org
Web: www. uftaa.org

Appendix 6

British and American English

The English language has evolved in different ways in the various parts of the world where it has taken root. Probably the most important variations, and those that concern this section, are between the forms of English used in the UK and in the USA. While important differences in meaning, style, spelling and pronunciation do exist, these are often overstated. Indeed, considering how long the two countries have been politically separated, and the distance between them, and the lack (until recently) of regular mass communication across the pond (whether digitally or by air), it is perhaps surprising that the two forms of the language are as similar as they are. Since the Second World War, a shared popular culture and increased trans-Atlantic travel have helped bridge a linguistic gulf that in the mid-20th century seemed to growing at an alarming rate. It is probably true to say that the two variations of English are now more mutually understandable than ever before.

None the less, important areas of confusion remain, and this section has tried to address those that are of particular relevance to the travel industry. The interpretations are shown both from UK to US English and vice versa although some terms will appear in only one interpretation. The presence of an interpretation does not necessarily mean that the original term is quite unknown in the other country: 'soccer', for example, is universally understood in the UK, but 'football' is the official and generally preferred term.

In general, words which are substantially the same in both but are spelled differently (ax/axe, color/colour, for example) have not been included, as only a few of the spelling variations affect the respective meanings. As a general rule, where spelling variations exist, the American word tends to be the shorter.

The main differences are as follows:

- Words ending *–ise* (such as enterprise) in UK English are generally spelled *–ize* in America. In UK English either ending is acceptable for most constructions. However, words ending *–yse* (such as analyse and paralyse) will be spelt analyze and paralyze in US English; this usage is not acceptable in UK English.

- In UK English the ending *–ise* usually denotes a verb (to license), and the ending *–ice* a noun (a licence). This distinction does not usually apply in US English where the *–ise* ending is commonly used for both. There are exceptions, most notably practise and practice, which in US English form the opposite parts of speech from their UK English equivalents.

- Words ending *–our* (such as colour or flavour) are generally spelt *–or* (color or flavor) in US English.

- The French-derived ending using a double consonant followed by 'e' (such as cigarette or programme), common in UK English, is not normally used in US English. The usual US ending is a single consonant (cigaret, program). It should be noted, though, that the US spellings are now accepted in cases where the word is applied to a US-originating term. An example is the word program, spelled the US way in both countries when used to describe a computer program but spelled programme in the UK when used to describe a sequence of events or the document that lists them.

- In UK English, the letter 'l' in a word is usually doubled if it follows a single vowel, such as in labelled or travelled. In US English this does not occur and labeled or traveled would be used.

- The UK English ending *-re* is usually replaced by *-er* in US English. Thus, centre becomes center and theatre becomes theater.

The alphabets are the same in both forms of the language, except for Z. This is pronounced zed in the UK, and zee in the USA.

Numbers are the same in both forms. Americans prefer using the word 'zero': the British tend to say 'oh', 'nought' and 'zero' more indiscrimately, but this is generally clearly understood in the USA. The American billion (a thousand million) has ousted the British billion (a million million), and is now universally used. Fractions are now very rarely used in British documents but are more common in American ones: this can sometimes cause problems when a text has been emailed from the USA and needs to be printed out in the UK.

Americans usually show dates in the form month/day/year, not day/month/year as is the case in the rest of the world. See the entry for *date order* in the main listing for more information on this point.

The metric system is not widely used or understood in the USA, and weights and measures are expressed in a form of what is known in Britain as the imperial system (which, apart from pints and miles, has been phased out of official life in the UK: in general, the younger a British person is, the less likely they will be to use or understand it). In addition, there are some important differences between the British and the American usages. A US pint is about 20% smaller than a British one, which has a knock-on effect on the respective sizes of quarts and gallons. Americans always express personal weights in pounds; the UK stone of 14 pounds is not used. Thus a 14-stone man would be referred to in the USA as being 196 pounds. For weightier matters, the UK ton is 240 pounds heavier than the US one.

Weights and measures thus reflect the UK/US English differences as a whole: two languages superficially similar and with most terms identical, but with some that are unique and often mutually incomprehensible, and others that seem familiar but which in fact mean something quite different. Language changes fast – English more than most – and any suggestions as to how this section can be updated, refined or expanded for future editions will be gratefully received.

British to American

British ....American	British ....American

A

accommodation ....accommodations
aerial ....antenna
afters ....dessert
air hostess ....flight attendant (female)
aluminium ....aluminum
American muffin ....muffin
anorak ....parka
antenatal...prenatal
anticlockwise ....counterclockwise
articulated lorry ....tractor-trailer
aubergine...eggplant
autumn ....fall

B

baby's dummy ....pacifier
baggage reclaim ....baggage claim
bank holiday ....public holiday
banknote ....bill
bap ....hamburger bun
barrister ....trial lawyer, attorney
bath ....bathtub, tub
beetroot ....beet
big dipper ....roller coaster
bill (in restaurant) ....check
bin liner ....trash bag
biscuit (savoury) ....cracker
biscuit (sweet)...cookie
Black Maria ....paddy wagon
blancmange ....vanilla pudding
blind (roller) ....shade
boiler suit ....overalls, coveralls
bonnet (car) ....hood
boot (car)..trunk
braces...suspenders
bubble and squeak ....cabbage and potato
bumbag ....fanny pack
busker ....street performer

C

cake shop ....bakery, pastry shop
candy floss ....cotton candy

car park ....parking lot
car silencer ....muffler
caravan ....motorhome, trailer, campervan, RV
carriageway ....highway
carry on ....continue, drive on
cashpoint ....ATM (Automated Teller Machine)
casualty unit ....hospital emergency room
cat's eyes (on road) ....reflectors
central reservation (of a highway) ....median strip
chemist's shop ....pharmacy, drugstore
cheque..check
chest of drawers ....dresser
chips (potato)...............................French fries
cinema (building) ....moviehouse, movie theater
cinema (in general) ....movies
cloakroom ....check room
coach (railway) ....car (railroad)
coach...bus
collection (car rental) ....pickup
condom ....rubber
confectionery...candy
conserves, jams ....jams, jellies, preserves
constable ....police officer
cooker..oven
corn ....grain
cot ....crib
courgette ....zucchini
crèche..nursery
crisps ....chips
crossroads ....intersection, crossroads
crumpet ....unknown in the USA
cul-de-sac...dead end
cupboard (in a kitchen) ....cupboard
cupboard (such as for clothes).......................closet
current account...........................checking account
cuttings (newspaper) ....clippings

D

demister...defroster
deposit account ....savings account
dialling code ....area code
dialling tone ....dial tone
dinner jacket ....tuxedo
dipped headlights ....low beam
diversion ....detour

British ....American

double glazing...................................storm windows
draught ....draft
drawing pin ....thumb tack
dressing gown ....bathrobe
driving licence ....driver's license
dual carriageway ....divided highway,
two-lane highway
dummy (for child) ....pacifier
dustbin ....trashcan, garbage can
duvet ....comforter

E

eiderdown ....comforter, quilt
elastic band.......................................rubber band
elastoplast ....band aid
electric fire...electric heater
electrical socket ....outlet
encircle ....circle
engaged..busy, occupied
ensuite (bathroom) ....private (bathroom)
entitle ....title
entrecôte steak ....rib steak, prime rib
estate agent ....realtor, real estate agent

F

filling station ....gas station
film (noun)..movie
fire brigade ....fire department
fire station...fire house
first floor...second floor
fishmonger ....fish market
flat (dwelling)...apartment
flyover ....overpass
football..soccer
fortnight ....two weeks
front stalls................................orchestra seats
full headlights ....high beams, brights
full stop (punctuation)....................................period
funfair ....amusement park

G

gammon ....ham, hamsteak
gas fire ....gas heater
gear lever...gearshift
gearbox...transmission

British ....American

gents ....men's room
greaseproof paper ....wax paper
grilled (meat) ....broiled
ground floor ....first floor
guard (on a vehicle) ....conductor
guard's van...caboose

H

hand luggage ....carry-on bags,
carry-on luggage
handbag ....purse, pocket book
headmaster, head teacher ....principal
high street..main street
hoarding (advertising)...............................billboard
hockey ....field hockey
holiday ....vacation
(but 'holiday' for public or religious holidays)
holidaymaker.......................................vacationer
hood (of a convertible car)....................................top
horse riding ....horseback riding
housing estate ....housing development
housing project

I

ice lolly...popsicle
indicator (vehicle)....................................turn signal

J

jam (clear)...jelly
jam (with fruit) ....jam
jelly ....jello
jumper...pullover, sweater

K

kerb ....curb
kipper....................................smoked herring
knickers ....panties

L

ladies' ....women's restroom
laundrette ....laundromat
lavatory ....bathroom
lay on...provide, arrange for
lay-by ....pull-off, rest stop
left-luggage office ....baggage room, storage

British	American
letterbox	mailbox (or letterbox)
level crossing	train crossing, grade crossing
lift (for freight)	lift
lift (for people)	elevator
limited (company)	incorporated
liqueur	after-dinner drink (or liqueur)
lobster tail and steak	surf-and-turf
loo	bathroom, rest room
lorry	truck
lost property	lost-and-found
luggage trolley	baggage cart

M

British	American
mackintosh	raincoat
main course	entrée
maize	corn
mange-tout	snow pea
marrow	squash
metalled (road)	paved
meter (electricity meter)	meter
metre (unit of measurement)	meter
mileometer	odometer
mince	ground meat
minibus	minivan
motorway	highway, expressway, freeway, interstate, turnpike
mudguard	fender
muesli	granola
muffin	English muffin

N

British	American
nappy	diaper
near-side lane	the lane furthest from the center of the road
neat (drink)	straight
newsagent	news stand
nil	nothing, zero
note (banknote)	bill
number plate	license plate

O

British	American
off-licence	liquor store
off-side lane	the lane nearest the center of the road
on offer	for sale, offered
on show	on display, displayed
on stream	on line
one-off	one-of-a-kind (or one-off)
open day	open house
orbital road	beltway
out-of-hours	after-hours
overtaking	passing

P

British	American
pack of cards	deck of cards
paddle steamer	side wheeler
paddle-steamer with rear propulsion	sternwheeler
page (in a hotel)	bell-hop, bell boy
pants	underwear, jockey shorts
paracetamol	acetaminophen
paraffin, aviation fuel	kerosene
pardon?	excuse me?, pardon me?
pavement	sidewalk
pelican crossing	pedestrian crossing
penknife	pocket knife
petrol station	gas station
petrol	gasoline, gas
phone box	pay-phone
pickle	relish
pillar box	mailbox
plimsolls	deck shoes
plus-fours	knickers
porridge	oatmeal
porter (in a building)	superintendent, super
porter	janitor
post	mail
post box	mailbox
postcode	zip code
postman	mailman
practice (noun)	practise
practise (verb)	practice
pram	baby carriage
prawn	shrimp
prom	a walkway, or kind of musical concert
proper	standard
pub	bar
public school	private school
pull down (demolish)	tear down
pulses	legumes
puncture	blowout, flat
purpose built	built to order, specially designed
purse	coin purse, wallet
put paid to	finish, put an end to

British ....American

Q

queue (verb) ....stand in line
queue ....line

R

railway goods wagon......................................boxcar
railway station ....train station
railway...railroad
rasher...slice
rates (domestic).......................local property taxes
read (for a degree) ....study
rear lights..tail lights
reception ....front desk
recovery vehicle ....tow truck
redundant...laid off
return ticket ....round trip ticket)
reverse-charge telephone call...............collect call
ring (to telephone) ....call
ring road ....beltway
rise (in salary) ....raise
roadside embankment ....berm
roadworks ....construction
roast beef, entrecôte steak ....prime rib
roundabout ....traffic circle
rowing boat ....rowboat
rubber (pencil) ....eraser
rubbish bin ....garbage can
rucksack ....backpack

S

sack (dismiss from a job) ....fire
sailing boat...sailboat
saloon (car)..sedan
self-catering ....efficiency apartment, efficiency
sellotape ....scotch tape
semi-detached ....duplex
shorts...short pants
sideboard ....buffet
sign-posted ....marked, well-marked
silencer (car) ....muffler
single ticket ....one-way ticket
situated, situation.......................located, location
sledge ....sled
sleeper (railway) ....railroad tie

British ....American

sleeping car ....pullman, sleeper
sleeping policeman...............................speed bump
smoked salmon...lox
socket (electrical) ....outlet
soft drink ....soda
solicitor..lawyer, attorney
spanner...wrench
speciality ....specialty
spirits (drinks) ....liquor
squash (drink)..........................juice concentrate
stalls (theatre)...........................orchestra seats
starter ....appetizer
steam train driver..engineer
steward (aircraft) ....flight attendant
stewardess ....flight attendant
sticking plaster.................adhesive tape, band-aid
stone (weight, of people only) ....14 pounds
stop lights ....traffic lights (or traffic lights)
stopover ....layover
subway (pedestrian) ....underground
(or pedestrian) passageway
surname, family name..............................last name
suspenders ....garter belt
sweet (confectionery) ....candy

T

take-away (meal) ....take-out
tap (noun) ....faucet
tariff ....rate-sheet
taxi rank ....taxi stand
tea towel ....dish towel
teat (baby's bottle) ....nipple
telephone box ....telephone booth, pay-phone
term (academic year) ....semester
terminus ....terminal
tights ....panty-hose
till ....cash register
tinned ....canned
toilet..restroom
toll road ....turnpike
torch ....flashlight
tower block ....high rise
traffic jam ....backup
traffic lights ....stop lights
train driver ....engineer
trainers (footwear) ....sneakers
tram..trolley, streetcar
transport..transportation
treacle ....molasses, syrup

British ....American	British ....American
trolley ....baggage cart	WC ....toilet, restroom
trousers ....pants, slacks	Wellington boots ....gumboots
tyre ....tire	white coffee ....light coffee
	windscreen......................................windshield
U	wing (car) ....fender
	wing mirror......................................rear-view mirror
underground ....subway	woman's handbag ....purse
unsurfaced road ....dirt road, unpaved road	
	Y
V	
	yard ....an uncultivated area
van...............................minibus (or more likely van)	around a property.
venue ....arena (or venue	Y-fronts ....one kind of men's underpants
vest ....undershirt	
	Z
W	
	Z (zed) ....Z (zee)
waistcoat ....vest	zebra crossing...........................pedestrian crossing
washing......................................laundry	zip fastener ....zipper

American to British

American ....British

A

accommodations ....accommodation
acetaminophen ....paracetamol
affordable ....value for money
after-dinner drink or liquer ....liqueur
aluminum ....aluminium
amusement park ....funfair
annex ....annexe
antenna ....aerial
apartment ....flat
appetizer ....starter
area code ....dialling code
ATM (Automated Teller Machine) ..cash dispenser
attorney...solicitor, lawyer

B

baby carriage ....pram
backpack ....rucksack
baggage cart ....luggage trolley
baggage cart ....trolley
baggage claim ....baggage reclaim
baggage room, storage ....left-luggage office
bakery, pastry shop ....cake shop
band-aid ....elastoplast, sticking plaster
bar...pub
bathrobe ....dressing gown
bathroom, toilet, rest rooms ....lavatory, toilet, WC
bathtub, tub ....bath
beet ....beetroot
bell-boy, bell hop............................page (in hotel)
bell-captain ....head porter
beltway ....ring road, orbital road
bid (for a contract)..tender
bill ($10 bill) ....banknote
billboard (advertising)..............................hoarding
block (city block) ....area bounded by streets on four sides, distance between two streets
blowout ....puncture
boondocks, boonies ....remote location, backwoods
boxcar ....railway goods wagon

American ....British

broiled (meat) ....grilled
brownie.......................small rich chocolate biscuit
bus ....coach
busy (phone) ....engaged

C

cabbage and potato ....bubble and squeak
caboose ....last wagon on goods train, guard's van
call (on the phone)...ring
call collect................................reverse the charges
candy ....sweets, confectionery
canned ....tinned
car (railroad) ....coach (railway)
carbonated ....fizzy
carry-on bags ....hand luggage
carryout, take-out (meal) ....take-away
check (banking) ....cheque
check (in restaurant) ....bill
check room ....cloakroom
checking account..........................current account
circle (verb) ....encircle
clippings (newspaper) ....cuttings
closet...cupboard
coffee with milk, or cream ....white coffee
collect call ....reverse charge telephone call
comforter ....duvet, eiderdown
conductor (on a vehicle) ....guard
continue, drive on ....carry on
cookie ....biscuit (sweet)
corn ....corn on the cob, maize
cotton candy ....candy floss
counter clockwise ....anticlockwise
cracker ....biscuit (savoury)
crazy bone ....funny bone
crib ....cot
curb ....kerb
czar ....tsar

D

dead end ....cul-de-sac
deck of cards ....pack of cards

American ....British

deck shoe ....plimsoll
defroster..demister
dessert....................................afters, sweet, pudding
detour ....diversion, bypass
dial tone ....dialling tone
diaper ....nappy
dirt road ....unmade, unsurfaced road
dishtowel ....tea towel
divided highway ....dual carriageway
divider (of a highway) ....central reservation
draft (wind under a door)............................draught
dresser ....chest of drawers
driver's license ....driving licence
drugstore ....chemist's shop, pharmacy
duplex ....semi-detached

E

efficiency ....self-catering apartment,
room with kitchenette
eggplant..aubergine
electric heater..electric fire
elevator..................................lift (for people)
emergency room ....casualty unit
engineer ....train driver
English muffin ....muffin
enter ....join (a highway)
entrée ....main course
eraser ....rubber (pencil)
excuse me? pardon me?............................pardon?
expressway ....dual-carriageway,
generally in and around cities

F

fall ....autumn
fanny pack ....bumbag
faucet..tap
fender (car) ....wing
field hockey ....hockey
fire (dismiss from a job) ....sack
fire department ....fire brigade
firehouse ....fire station
first floor ....ground floor
fishstore..fishmonger
flashlight ....torch
flat (tire) ....puncture
flight attendant (female) ....stewardess, air hostess
flight attendant (male) ....steward

American ....British

football ....American football
for sale ....on offer
formula ....liquid baby-food
four lane road ....dual carriageway
fourteen pounds (weight) ....one stone
(only for weights of people)
freeway ....dual-carriageway,
generally in and around cities
French fries ....chips
front desk ....reception

G

garbage can ....rubbish bin
garden..flower garden
garters ....suspenders
gas heater ....gas fire
gas station..................filling station, petrol station
gas, gasoline ....petrol
gearshift ....gear stick, gear lever
grade crossing ....level crossing
granola ....muesli
ground meat, ground beef............................mince
gumboots ....wellingtons

H

half-and-half ....half cream/half milk
mixture for coffee
ham, hamsteak ....gammon
high beams, brights ....full headlights
high rise ....tower block
highway construction..............................roadworks
highway..road, carriageway
hockey ....ice hockey
hood (car) ....bonnet
horseback riding................................horse riding
huddle ....planning or tactics
meeting or conference

I

incorporated (company) ....limited
insure..ensure
intersection..crossroads
interstate highway ....motorway

J

jam ....jam (with fruit)

American ....British

janitor ....caretaker
jello ....jelly
jelly ....jam (clear)
john (the john) ....toilet, lavatory
juice concentrate ....squash

K

kerosene ....paraffin, aviation fuel
knickers ....plus-fours

L

laundromat ....laundrette
laundry ....washing
layover ....stopover
legumes ....pulses
license plate ....number plate
light coffee ....white coffee
line (of people) ....queue
liquor store ....off-licence
liquor ....alcoholic spirits
lobby ....foyer
longshoreman...................................dock worker
low beams ....dipped headlights
lox...smoked salmon

M

mail ....post
mailbox....................letterbox, pillar box, post box
mailman...postman
main street....................................high street
median strip (of a highway) ......central reservation
men's room ....gents, gent's toilet
meter (electricity meter) ....meter
meter (unit of measurement) ....metre
minibus...van
minivan...minibus
mobile home ....motorhome, trailer, caravan
motorhome, trailer.................................caravan
movie theater...cinema
muffin ....American muffin
muffler (car) ....silencer

N

nature preserve ....nature reserve
night crawler ....worm used by fishermen
nipple (on a baby's bottle)................................teat

American ....British

O

oatmeal..porridge
odometer ....milometer
off-hours ....out-of-hours
on display ....on show
one-way ticket ....single ticket
open house...open day
orchestra seats...front stalls
outlet (electrical)...socket
outlet (factory)..................................discount store
outlet ....electrical socket
oven ....cooker
overpass ....flyover

P

pacifier ....baby's dummy
paddy wagon ....Black Maria
pantiehose...tights
pants ....trousers
parka ....anorak
parking lot ....car park
passing ....overtaking
paved (road)..metalled
pavement....................................tarmaced road
pay-phone ....phone box
Ped Xing ....pedestrian crossing, zebra crossing
period (punctuation)..full stop
pharmacy ....chemist's shop
pickup (car rental) ....collection
pocket book...handbag
pop ....soft drink
popsicle..ice lolly
potato chips ....crisps
power train......................................transmission
practice (verb)..practise
practise (noun) ....practice
prenatal..antenatal
preserves ....conserves, jams
prime rib ....roast beef, entrecôte steak
principal (school)...............................head teacher
private (bathroom)..en suite
private school ....public school
program ....programme
prom ....a school/university formal ball or dance
provide, arrange ....lay on
public address system...................................tannoy
pullman ....sleeping car

American ....British

American	British
pull-off	lay-by
purse	handbag

R

American	British
railroad tie	sleeper
railroad	railway
raincheck	postponement
raise (in salary)	rise
rate-sheet	tariff
real estate	land, or the property on it
realtor	estate agent
reflectors (embedded in road)	cat's eyes
regular coffee	coffee with milk and sugar
relish	pickle
rent	hire
reservation	booking
rest stop	lay-by
restrooms	toilets
roller coaster	big dipper
roundtrip ticket	return ticket
rubber	condom
RV (recreational vehicle)	motor home, caravan

S

American	British
savings account	deposit account
scallion	spring onion
scotch tape	sellotape
second floor	first floor
sedan	saloon car
semester (academic year)	term
shade (on a window)	blind
shellac	high-gloss varnish
short pants	shorts
shorts (underwear)	pants
shrimp	prawn
side wheeler	paddle-steamer
sidewalk	pavement
sled	sledge
sleeper	sleeping car
sneakers	trainers
snow pea	mange-tout
soccer	football
soda	soft drink
specialty	speciality
speed bump	sleeping policeman
sports utility vehicle (SUV)	people carrier, generally with off-road capability

American ....British

American	British
squash (vegetable)	a sort of marrow
stand in line	queue
standard or regular	proper (of coffee, white)
sternwheeler	paddle-steamer with rear propulsion
stick shift (car)	manual transmission
stop lights	traffic lights
storm windows	double glazing
street musician	busker
subway (train)	underground railway
superintendent, super	porter (in a building)
suspenders	braces

T

American	British
tail lights	rear lights
taxi stand	taxi rank
tear down (demolish)	pull down
tenement	housing estate
thumbtack	drawing pin
tire (on a car)	tyre
tire (to exhaust)	tire
title	entitle
tow truck	recovery vehicle
tractor-trailer	articulated lorry
traffic circle	roundabout
traffic jam	hold up, backup
train crossing	level crossing
transmission	gearbox
transportation	transport
trash bag	bin liner
trashcan	dustbin
trial lawyer, attorney	barrister
truck (road)	lorry
trunk	boot (car)
turn signals	indicators
turnpike	toll road
tuxedo	dinner jacket

U

American	British
underpants (men's)	pants
underpants (women's)	knickers
underpass	subway
undershirt	vest
unpaved road	dirt road

V

American	British
vacation	holiday

American ....British

vacationer ....holidaymaker
van ....van (if carrying goods),
minibus or people carrier
(if carrying people)
vanilla pudding ....blancmange
vest ....waistcoat
vet...ex-serviceman, veteran

W

wax paper ....greaseproof paper
whole wheat ....wholemeal
windshield...windscreen

wrench...spanner

American ....British

Y

yard..............any piece of land around a property,
regardless of whether or not it is cultivated

Z

Z (zee) ....Z (zed)
zip code ....postcode
zipper..zip fastener, zip
zucchini ....courgette

Appendix 6

Phonetic Alphabets

Although English is effectively the international language of travel, and although many communications within the industry are in writing and so can, if necessary, be translated at leisure, there are times when phone conversations need to take place with someone who does not speak English. This section has been designed to enable names, dates and the like to be spelled out in French, German, Spanish and Italian, using one of two methods: the Alpha-Bravo-Charlie-style phonetic alphabet; and a pronunciation guide to the A-B-C and the numbers from 0 to 9.

For the English Alpha-Bravo-Charlie-style phonetic alphabet, please see under phonetic alphabet in the main listing.

Many languages have more than one phonetic alphabet and there is no one 'official' one for all purposes. Some languages have separate phonetic terms for certain diagraphs (such as sch in German and ch in Spanish) and for accented letters (such as ü in German), but for reasons of simplicity these have not been included here.

The pronunciation guides are approximate, as in some cases there is no exact sound in English that corresponds with that used to pronounce certain letters in other languages. It must be stressed that these only represent how the letters are pronounced in a recital of each language's alphabet, and not how they are pronounced when forming words. Where the guide consists of a single letter in capitals, the pronunciation of that letter is similar to how a British person would pronounce that letter in English: the few occasions where an example word has been used also assumes the British pronunciation. It can be seen that many letters, including most of the vowels, are often pronounced in quite different ways from one language to another. In some languages, certain diagraphs (such as ch in Spanish) and accented letters (such as é in French) are, in a recital of the alphabet, sometimes regarded as if they were letters in their own right. As these will only very rarely affect the sense of what is being communicated, they have not been included here.

The pronunciation guides for the numbers generally bear little similarity to how they are actually spelled. Numbers from 10 and above can either be concocted from these basic integers, or learned in the appropriate language, or spoken in English; space does not permit listing them here.

Any suggestions as to how this section can be updated, refined or expanded for future editions will be gratefully received.

French

A	Anatole	a (as in bat)
B	Berthe	bay
C	Célestin	say
D	Désiré	day
E	Eugène	uh
F	François	F
G	Gaston	gea (as in orangeade)
H	Henri	arsh
I	Irma	ee
J	Joseph	gee (as in orangey)
K	Kléber	car
L	Louis	L
M	Marcel	M
N	Nicolas	N
O	Oscar	o (as in dot)
P	Pierre	pay
Q	Quintal	coo
R	Raoul	air
S	Suzanne	S
T	Thérèse	tay
U	Ursule	oo
V	Victor	vay
W	William	doob-ler-vay
X	Xavier	eeks
Y	Yvonne	ee-grek
Z	Zoé	Z
0		zair-oh
1		urn
2		dur
3		twah
4		katre
5		sank
6		cease
7		set
8		wheat
9		nurf

German

A	Anton	a (as in bat)
B	Berta	bay
C	Cäsar	tzee
D	Dora	day
E	Emil	ay
F	Friedrich	F
G	Gustav	geh (as in get)
H	Heinrich	ha
I	Ida	ee
J	Julius	yott
K	Kaufmann	car
L	Ludwig	L
M	Martha	M
N	Nordpol	N
O	Otto	O
P	Paula	pay
Q	Quelle	coo
R	Richard	air
S	Samuel	S
T	Theodor	te
U	Ulrich	uh
V	Viktor	fowe
W	Wilhelm	vee
X	Xanthippe	eeks
Y	Ypsilon	ip-seelon
Z	Zeppelin	tsett
0		null
1		einz
2		svy
3		dry
4		fear
5		funf
6		zex
7		zeeben
8		acht
9		noin